MAXON CINEMA 4D R20 Studio for Digital Artists

Sham Tickoo
Professor
Purdue University Northwest
Hammond, Indiana, USA

Contributing Authors
Arti Deshpande
Tickoo Institute of Emerging Technologies(TIET)

Tickoo Institute of Emerging Technologies (TIET)
Gurugram, India

CADCIM Technologies
Indiana, USA

BPB PUBLICATIONS

ISBN: 978-93-89423-17-4
(For distribution in Saarc countries only)

Distributors

COMPUTER BOOK CENTRE
12, Shrungar Shopping Centre
M.G. Road
BENGALURU–560001
Ph: 25587923/25584641

DECCAN AGENCIES
4-3-329, Bank Street
HYDERABAD-500195
Ph: 24756967/24756400

MICRO MEDIA
Shop No. 5, Mahendra Chambers
150 DN Rd. Next to Capital Cinema
V.T (C.S.T.) Station
MUMBAI-400001

BPB BOOK CENTRE
376 Old Lajpat Rai Market
DELHI-110006
Ph: 23861747

INFOTECH
G-2, Sidhartha Building, 96 Nehru Place
NEW DELHI-110019
Ph: 26438245

BPB PUBLICATIONS
20, Ansari Road, Darya Ganj
New Delhi-110002
Ph: 23254990/23254991

Published by Manish Jain for BPB Publications, 20 Ansari Road, Darya Ganj
New Delhi-110002 and Printed by Repro India Pvt. Ltd., Mumbai

DEDICATION

To teachers, who make it possible to disseminate knowledge to enlighten the young and curious minds of our future generations

To students, who are dedicated to learning new technologies and making the world a better place to live in

THANKS

To employees of CADCIM Technologies and Tickoo Institute of Emerging Technologies (TIET) for their valuable help

Online Training Program Offered by CADCIM Technologies

CADCIM Technologies provides effective and affordable virtual online training on various software packages including Computer Aided Design, Manufacturing and Engineering (CAD/CAM/CAE), computer programming languages, animation, architecture, and GIS. The training is delivered 'live' via Internet at any time, any place, and at any pace to individuals as well as the students of colleges, universities, and CAD/CAM/CAE training centers. The main features of this program are:

Training for Students and Companies in a Classroom Setting

Highly experienced instructors and qualified engineers at CADCIM Technologies conduct the classes under the guidance of Prof. Sham Tickoo of Purdue University Northwest, USA. This team has authored several textbooks that are rated "one of the best" in their categories and are used in various colleges, universities, and training centers in North America, Europe, and in other parts of the world.

Training for Individuals

CADCIM Technologies with its cost effective and time saving initiative strives to deliver the training in the comfort of your home or work place, thereby relieving you from the hassles of traveling to training centers.

Training Offered on Software Packages

CADCIM provides basic and advanced training on the following software packages:

***CAD/CAM/CAE**: CATIA, Pro/ENGINEER Wildfire, Creo Parametric, Creo Direct, SOLIDWORKS, Autodesk Inventor, Solid Edge, NX, AutoCAD, AutoCAD LT, AutoCAD Plant 3D, Customizing AutoCAD, EdgeCAM, and ANSYS*

***Architecture and GIS**: Autodesk Revit (Architecture, Structure, MEP), AutoCAD Civil 3D, AutoCAD Map 3D, Navisworks, Oracle Primavera, and Bentley STAAD Pro*

***Animation and Styling**: Autodesk 3ds Max, Autodesk Maya, Autodesk Alias, Foundry NukeX, and MAXON CINEMA 4D*

***Computer Programming**: C++, VB.NET, Oracle, AJAX, and Java*

For more information, please visit the following link: ***http://www.cadcim.com***

Table of Contents

Preface

MAXON CINEMA 4D R20 Studio

MAXON CINEMA 4D R20 Studio is a 3D software application developed by MAXON Computer. This application is mainly used by professional 3D artists to create impressive 3D scenes, VFX, and broadcast artwork. CINEMA 4D comes in four versions: Prime, Visualize, Broadcast, and Studio. CINEMA 4D Prime is used to create stunning 3D graphics. CINEMA 4D Visualize provides fast and easy solution to architects, designers, and photographers to create realistic animations and is used for product visualization. It also has the ability to import models from all major 2D and 3D file formats. CINEMA 4D Broadcast is a perfect solution for creating high quality broadcast graphics. CINEMA 4D Studio contains all features of CINEMA 4D Prime, CINEMA 4D Visualize, and CINEMA 4D Broadcast. Moreover, it includes character animation tools that makes it easier to create rigs and character animations. It is a user-friendly application which includes features such as sculpting, advance particle system, hair system, and MoGraph.

MAXON CINEMA 4D R20 Studio for Digital Artists is a tutorial-based textbook and aims at harnessing the power of MAXON CINEMA 4D R20 Studio for modelers, animators, and designers. The textbook caters to the needs of both the novice and the advance users of MAXON CINEMA 4D R20 Studio. Keeping in view the varied requirements of users, the textbook first introduces the basic features of CINEMA 4D R20 Studio and then progresses to cover the advanced techniques. In this textbook, two projects based on the tools and concepts covered in the book have been added to enhance the knowledge of users.

This textbook will help you unleash your creativity and transform your imagination into reality with ease.

The main features of this textbook are as follows:

- **Tutorial Approach**
  The author has adopted the tutorial point-of-view and the learn-by-doing theme throughout the textbook.

- **Tips and Notes**
  Additional information related to various topics is provided to the users in the form of tips and notes.

- **Learning Objectives**
  The first page of every chapter summarizes the topics that will be covered in that chapter. This will help the users to easily refer to a topic.

- **Self-Evaluation Test, Review Questions, and Exercises**
  Every chapter ends with Self-Evaluation Test so that the users can assess their knowledge of the chapter. The answers to Self-Evaluation Test are given at the end of the chapter. Also, Review Questions and Exercises are given at the end of the chapters and they can be used by the Instructors as test questions and exercises.

Conventions Used in this Textbook

Tip

Special information and techniques are provided in the form of tips that help in increasing the efficiency of the users.

Note

The author has provided additional information to the users about the topic being discussed in the form of notes.

This symbol indicates that the command or tool being discussed is new.

This symbol indicates that the command or tool being discussed is enhanced in the current release.

Formatting Conventions Used in the Textbook

Refer to the following list for the formatting conventions used in this textbook.

• Names of tools, buttons, options, and menus are written in boldface.	Example: The **Move** tool, **Basic** button, **Multiply** option, **Create** menu, and so on.
• Names of dialog boxes, drop-down lists, windows, text boxes, spinners, areas, and check boxes are written in boldface.	Example: The **Save** dialog box, the **Mode** drop-down list, the **Timeline** window, the **Object** text box, the **Size . X** spinner, the **Object Properties** area, the **Fillet** check box, and so on.
• Values entered in spinners are written in boldface.	Example: Enter **0.2** in the **Size . X** spinner.

- The path for choosing a tool from the main menu. — Example: Choose **Create > Object > Cube** from the main menu.
- Names of the files are italicized — Example: *c05_tut2_start.c4d*

Naming Conventions Used in the Textbook

The naming conventions used in this textbook are as follows:

Tool

If on clicking an item in the Command Palette or Modes Palette, a command is invoked to create/edit an object or perform some action, then that item is termed as **Tool**. For example: **Live Selection** tool, **Move** tool, **Edit Render Settings** tool, **Freehand** tool, **Points** tool, and **Polygons** tool.

Flyout

If on choosing a tool, a menu containing tools having similar type of function is displayed then that menu is called a flyout. Figure 1 shows the flyout which is displayed on choosing the **Cube** tool from the Command Palette.

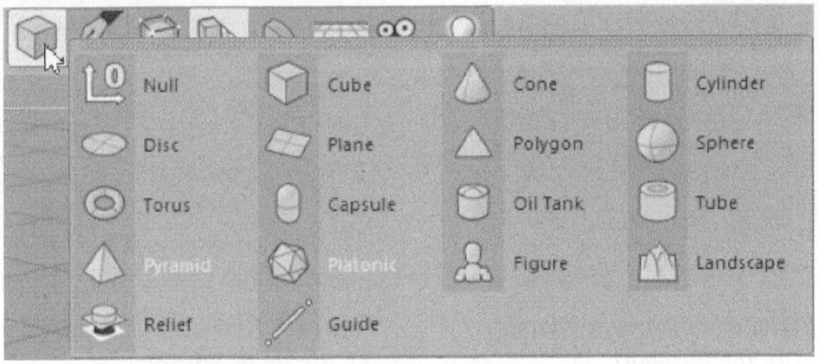

***Figure 1** Flyout displayed on choosing the **Cube** tool*

Shortcut Menu

In CINEMA 4D, the shortcut menus provide quick access to the commonly used commands that are related to the current selection of an object. A shortcut menu is displayed on right-clicking on an object, a viewport, and so on, refer to Figure 2. Some of the options in the shortcut menus have an arrow on their right side. If you move the cursor on such options, a cascading menu will be displayed showing some more options related to the selected option, refer to Figure 2.

Button

The item in a dialog box and Attribute Manager that has a rectangular shape is termed as **Button**. For example, **OK** button, **Cancel** button, **Save** button, **Basic** button, **Coord** button, and so on, refer to Figure 3.

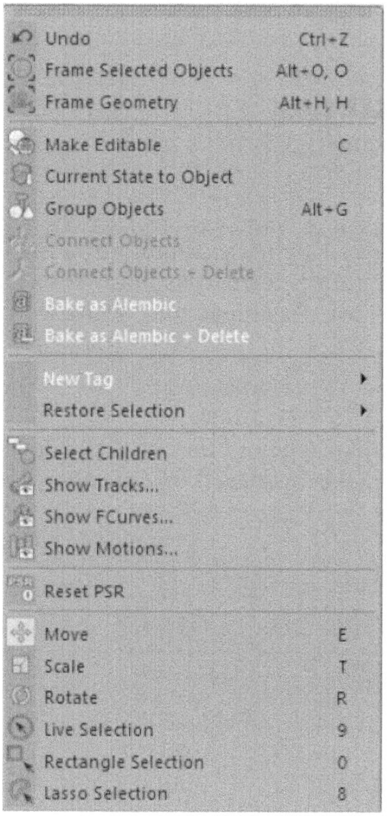

Figure 2 Shortcut menu displayed on right-clicking in the viewport

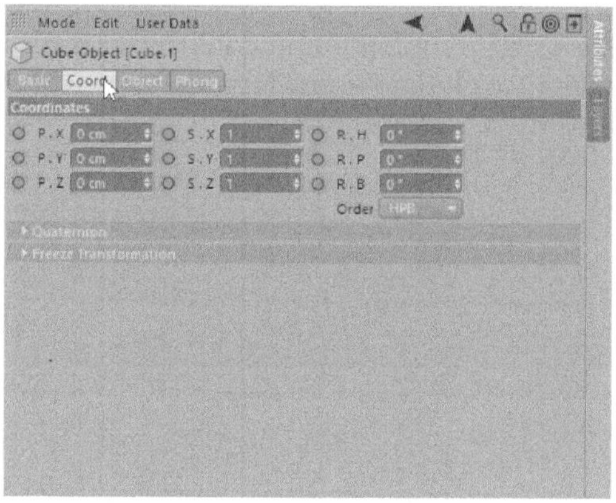

*Figure 3 Choosing the **Coord** button from the Attribute Manager*

Dialog Box

In this textbook, different terms are used for referring to the components of a dialog box. Refer to Figure 4 for the terminology used.

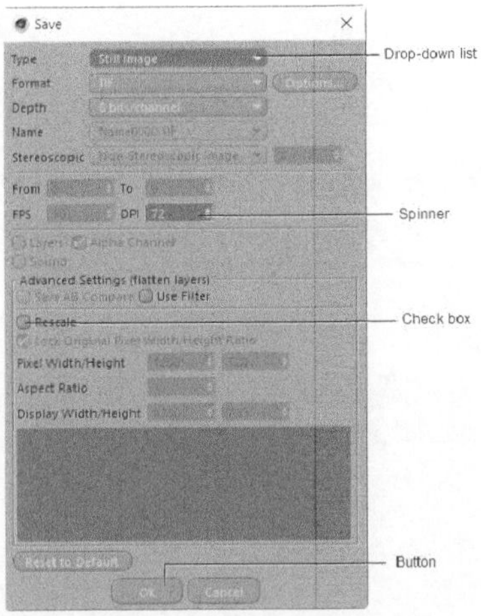

Figure 4 Terminologies used in a dialog box

Drop-down List

A drop-down list is the one in which a set of options are grouped together. You can set various parameters using these options. You can identify a drop-down list with a down arrow on it. For example, **Mode** drop-down list, **Type** drop-down list, and so on, refer to Figure 5.

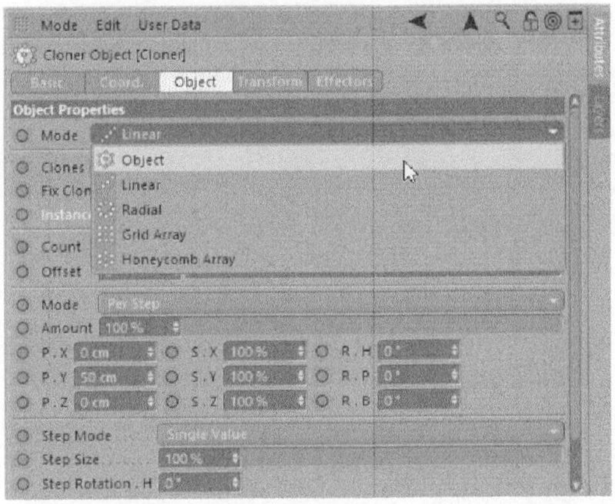

*Figure 5 The **Mode** drop-down list*

Options

Options are the items that are available in shortcut menus, drop-down lists, dialog boxes, and so on, refer to Figure 6.

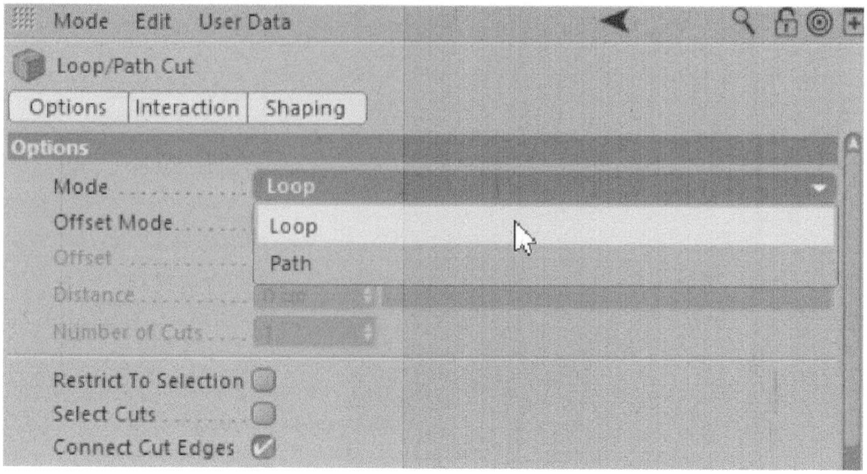

***Figure 6** Selecting the **Loop** option from the **Mode** drop-down list*

Window

A window consists of various components such as tools, buttons, main menu, and so on. Different types of windows available in CINEMA 4D are **XPresso Editor**, **Timeline**, **Render Settings**, and so on. The components of a window differ depending on the type of window, refer to Figure 7.

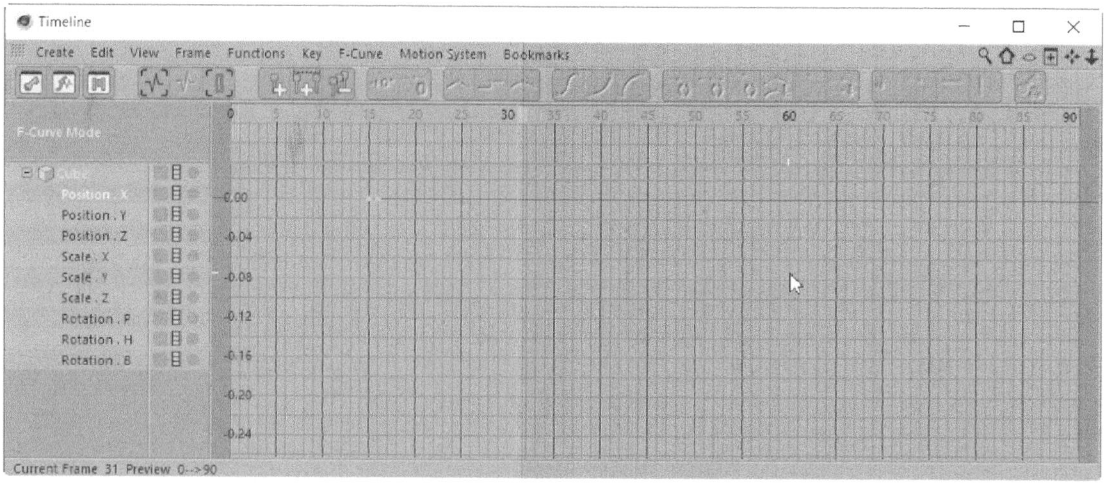

***Figure 7** The **Timeline** window*

Free Companion CD

It has been our constant endeavor to provide you the best textbooks and services at affordable price. In this endeavor, we have come up with a Free Companion CD that will facilitate the process of teaching and learning of MAXON CINEMA 4D R20 Studio. If you purchase this textbook, you will get access to the files on the companion CD.

The resources like Tutorial files, Part files, Exercise files, Render files, Instructor guide etc. are available in the Free Companion CD.

If you face any problem in accessing these files, please contact us at ***sales@cadcim.com*** or the author at ***stickoo@pnw.edu*** or ***tickoo525@gmail.com***.

Stay Connected

You can now stay connected with us through Facebook and Twitter to get the latest information about our textbooks, videos, and teaching/learning resources. To stay informed of such updates, follow us on Facebook ***(www.facebook.com/cadcim)*** and Twitter (@cadcimtech). You can also subscribe to our YouTube channel ***(www.youtube.com/cadcimtech)*** to get the information about our latest video tutorials.

Chapter 1

Exploring CINEMA 4D R20 Studio Interface

Learning Objectives

After completing this chapter, you will be able to:

- *Work with Viewport Navigation Tools in CINEMA 4D*
- *Understand various terms related to CINEMA 4D interface*
- *Work with tools in CINEMA 4D*

INTRODUCTION

MAXON CINEMA 4D R20 Studio is a high-end 3D application developed by MAXON Computer. This application is used by professional 3D artists to create impressive 3D scenes, VFX, and broadcast artwork. CINEMA 4D comes in four versions: Prime, Visualize, Broadcast, and Studio. CINEMA 4D Prime is used to create stunning 3D graphics. CINEMA 4D Visualize provides fast and easy solution to architects, designers, and photographers for creating realistic animations and better product visualization. It also has the ability to import models from all major 2D and 3D file formats. CINEMA 4D Broadcast is a perfect solution for creating high quality broadcast graphics. CINEMA 4D Studio contains all the features of CINEMA 4D Prime, CINEMA 4D Visualize, and CINEMA 4D Broadcast. Moreover, it includes character animation tools that makes it easier for its users to create rigs and character animations.

MAXON CINEMA 4D is a user-friendly application which is used for sculpting, creating particles using advance particle system, hair system, and for creating motion graphics using MoGraph. In this chapter, you will be introduced to MAXON CINEMA 4D Studio R20 interface elements.

STARTING MAXON CINEMA 4D R20 Studio

To start MAXON CINEMA 4D R20 Studio, click on the icon of this software available on the desktop of your PC; the default interface of MAXON CINEMA 4D R20 Studio will be displayed, as shown in Figure 1-1.

EXPLORING MAXON CINEMA 4D R20 Studio INTERFACE

CINEMA 4D interface consists of various components such as title bar, Viewport, Command Palette, Modes Palette, main menu, and so on, as shown in Figure 1-2. All these components are discussed next.

Viewport

Viewport is a part of the work area where you can create a 3D scene. Every viewport has a grid placed at the center. A grid is a framework of intersecting lines placed perpendicularly in the X-Z plane. At the center point (origin), the X, Y, and Z coordinates will be 0, 0, and 0, respectively.

Note

In CINEMA 4D, the X, Y, and Z axes are displayed in red, green, and blue colors, respectively, refer to Figure 1-2.

When you start CINEMA 4D, the Perspective viewport is displayed by default, refer to Figure 1-2. This viewport displays objects from a perspective camera. You can also display other viewports such as Top, Right, Bottom, and Front in the work area. These viewports display objects from orthographic camera view and do not display the perspective view. To switch to the 4-view viewport arrangement, hover the cursor over the Perspective viewport and then press the middle-mouse button once. If you need to maximize any of the four viewports, hover the cursor over the required viewport and then press the middle-mouse button once.

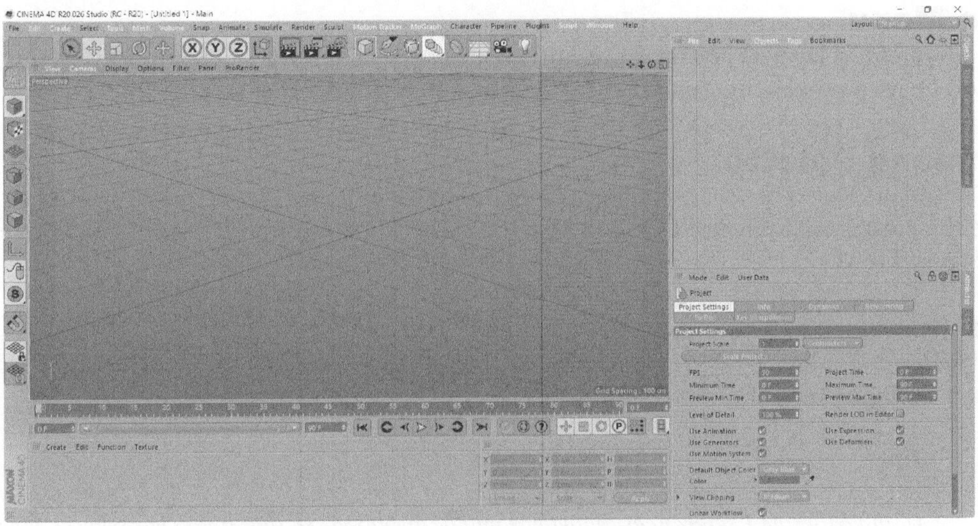

Figure 1-1 The default interface of CINEMA 4D R20 Studio

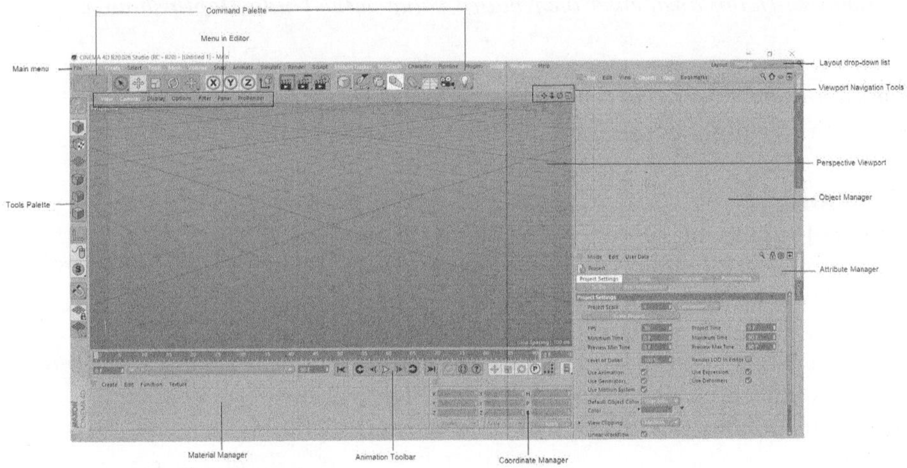

Figure 1-2 Various components of CINEMA 4D R20 Studio interface

Title Bar

The title bar, located at the top of the interface, displays the name and version of the software, and the name of the opened file. A CINEMA 4D file is saved with the *.c4d* extension.

> **Tip**
> *You can display different viewports by using the functional keys: F1 (Perspective), F2 (Top), F3 (Right), F4 (Front), and the F5 key (for all viewports).*

Main Menu

The main menu is located just below the title bar, refer to Figure 1-2. The options in this menu are used to access tools, functions, or commands in CINEMA 4D.

Command Palette

The Command Palette is located below the main menu, refer to Figure 1-2. It is used to invoke the most commonly used tools in CINEMA 4D. The tools in the Command Palette are discussed next.

Undo

The **Undo** tool is used to revert the last action performed in the scene. By default, the user can undo maximum of 30 changes.

Tip

*You can increase or decrease the undo limit. To do so, choose **Edit > Preferences** from the main menu; the **Preferences** dialog box will be displayed. In this dialog box, choose **Memory** from the list of options on the left of the **Preferences** dialog box; the **Memory** area will be displayed. In this area, enter the required value in the **Undo Depth** spinner.*

Redo

The **Redo** tool is used to revert the last action performed by the **Undo** tool. The number of redo actions cannot exceed the number of times a change is made.

Live Selection

The **Live Selection** tool is used to select objects in the scene. You can also select elements (points, edges, and polygons) using this tool. It works like a paint brush where the user paints over points, edges, and polygons to be selected. When you press and hold the left mouse button on the **Live Selection** tool, a flyout will be displayed, as shown in Figure 1-3. The various types of selection tools in this flyout will be discussed in the later chapters.

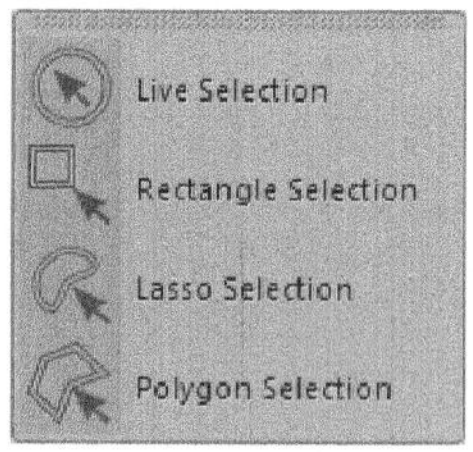

***Figure 1-3** The flyout displayed*

Tip

*You can interactively change the size of the **Live Selection** tool's brush by pressing and holding the middle mouse button and then dragging the cursor to the left or right. You can also use the { and } keys to increase and decrease the size of the **Live Selection** tool's brush.*

Move

This tool is used to move an object in the viewport provided the axes are not locked. Moreover, this tool is used to select points, polygons, and edges by clicking on them. You can increase the selection by pressing and holding SHIFT and then clicking on the elements. You can also remove elements from the selection by pressing and holding CTRL and then clicking on the elements.

Scale

This tool is used to scale an object in the viewport.

Rotate

This tool is used to rotate an object in the viewport.

Active Tool

This tool displays the icon of the last used tool.

X-Axis/Heading

This tool is used to lock or unlock the transformation along the X axis. If this tool is chosen, the object will not move, scale, or rotate along the X axis. The shortcut key for invoking this tool is X.

Y-Axis/Pitch

This tool is used to lock or unlock the transformation along the Y axis. If this tool is chosen, the object will not move, scale, or rotate along the Y axis. The shortcut key for invoking this tool is Y.

Z-Axis/Bank

This tool is used to lock or unlock the transformation along the Z axis. If this tool is chosen, the object will not move, scale, or rotate along the Z axis. The shortcut key for invoking this tool is Z.

Coordinate System

This is a toggle tool and is used to switch between Object and World coordinate systems for the movement, scaling, or rotation of an object. By default, Object coordinate system is activated in CINEMA 4D. It operates using the HPB system (Heading, Pitch, and Banking). The shortcut for invoking this tool is W.

Render View

This tool is used to render the currently active view. On choosing this tool, the rendered output will be displayed in the active view. If you click in the rendered output, the active view will be displayed in the viewport. You can also choose this tool by pressing CTRL+R.

Render to Picture Viewer

This tool is used to render the scene in the **Picture Viewer** window. On choosing this tool, the **Picture Viewer** window will be displayed. The progress of the render and the frame number being rendered will be displayed in the status bar of the **Picture Viewer** window. In CINEMA 4D, you can also render a region, make previews of the animations, and add scene to the render queue. To access these rendering options, press and hold the left mouse button on the **Render to Picture Viewer** tool; a flyout with various rendering options will be displayed, as shown in Figure 1-4. Next, choose the desired option from the flyout.

Edit Render Settings

This tool is used to invoke the **Render Settings** window. The options in this window are used to specify various settings to control the rendering process. In this window, you can set the size, quality, and so on of the scene that has to be rendered.

Figure 1-4 The rendering options displayed in the flyout

Cube

This tool is used to create a cube in the viewport. When you press and hold the left mouse button on the **Cube** tool, a flyout with various tools will be displayed, as shown in Figure 1-5. These tools are used to create the parametric objects in the scene.

Pen

The **Pen** tool also referred to as the Spline Pen tool replaces the previous versions of the **Bezier**, **B-Spline**, **Linear**, and **Akima Spline** tools and is equipped with new functions and used to draw spline curves in the viewport. When you press and hold the left mouse button on the **Pen** tool, a flyout with various spline modeling tools will be displayed, as shown in Figure 1-6.

Subdivision Surface

This tool is used to interactively subdivide and smoothen the objects. This feature is very useful in organic modeling. When you press and hold the left mouse button on the **Subdivision Surface** tool, a flyout with various generators will be displayed, as shown in Figure 1-7.

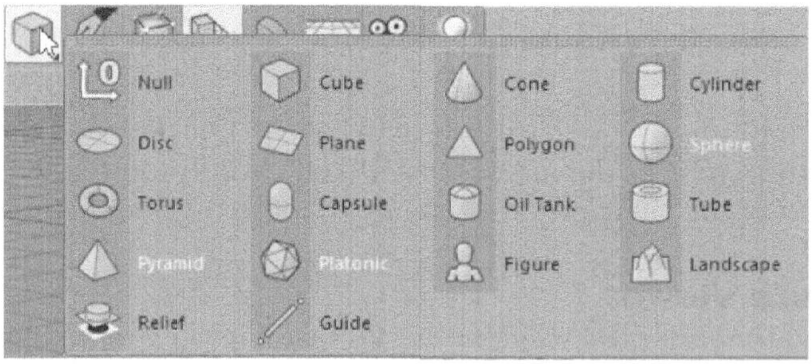

***Figure 1-5** The tools to create the parametric objects displayed in the flyout*

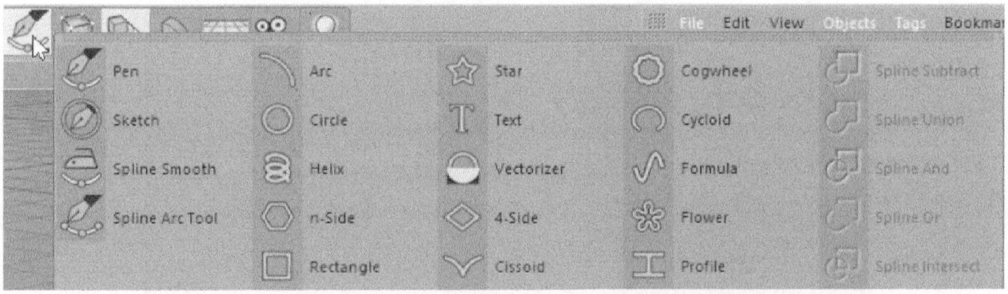

Figure 1-6 *The spline modeling tools displayed in the flyout*

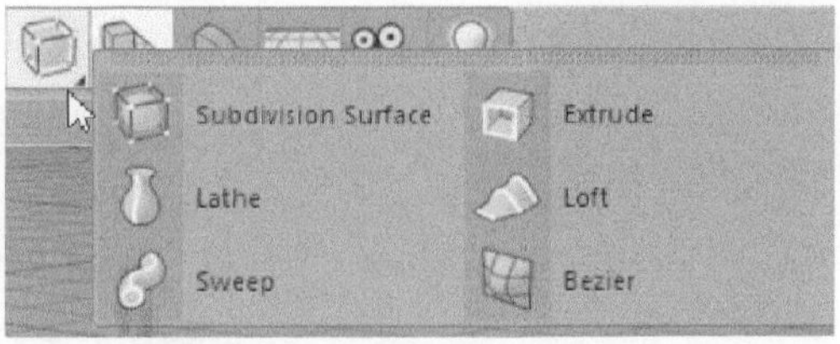

Figure 1-7 *The generators displayed in the flyout*

Instance

This tool is used to create an instance of the selected object. When you press and hold the left mouse button on the **Instance** tool, a flyout with special modeling tools will be displayed, as shown in Figure 1-8. These tools will be discussed in the later chapters.

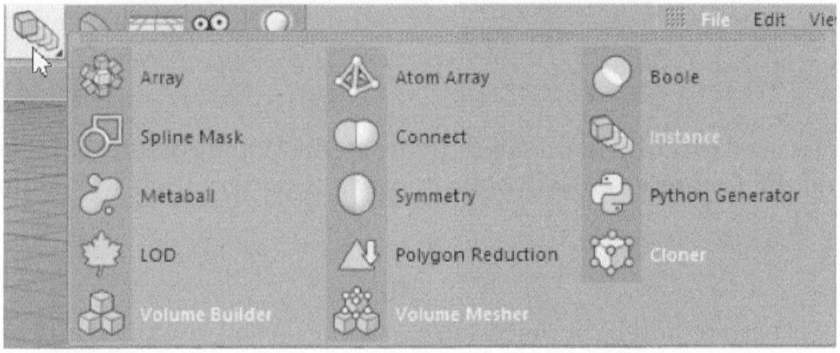

Figure 1-8 *The special modeling tools displayed in the flyout*

Bend

This tool is used to bend a selected object in the specified direction. When you press and hold the left mouse button on the **Bend** tool, a flyout with various deforming tools will be displayed, as shown in Figure 1-9.

Floor

This tool is used to create a floor object in the viewport. When you press and hold the left mouse button on the **Floor** tool, a flyout with various tools will be displayed, as shown in Figure 1-10.

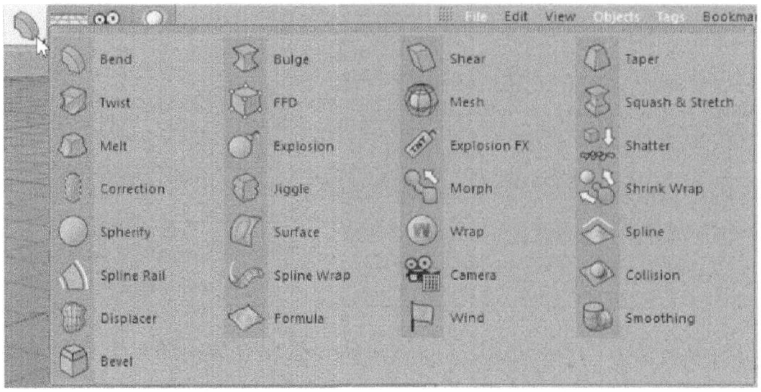

Figure 1-9 *Various deforming tools displayed in the flyout*

Figure 1-10 *Various tools displayed in the flyout*

Camera

This tool is used to add camera object to the scene. When you press and hold the left mouse button on the **Camera** tool, a flyout with various camera tools will be displayed, as shown in Figure 1-11.

Light

This tool is used to add light objects to the scene. When you press and hold the left mouse button on the **Light** tool, a flyout with various light tools will be displayed, as shown in Figure 1-12.

Tools Palette

The Tools Palette is located on the extreme left of the interface, refer to Figure 1-2. It consists of various tools. These tools are discussed next.

Make Editable

This tool is used to convert primitive objects into polygon objects. By default, all the primitive objects and splines are parametric. The shortcut key for this tool is C.

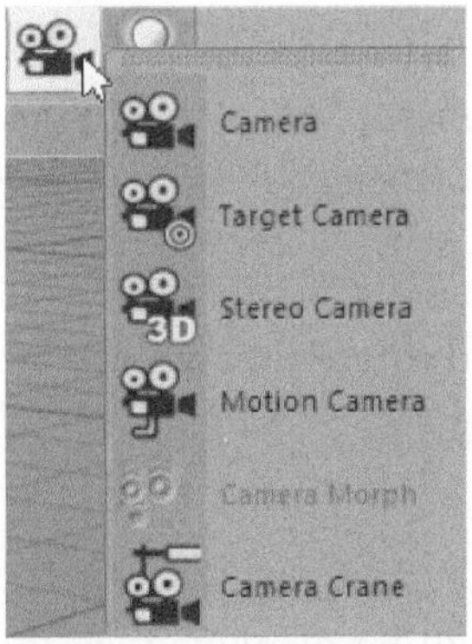

Figure 1-11 Various camera tools displayed in the flyout

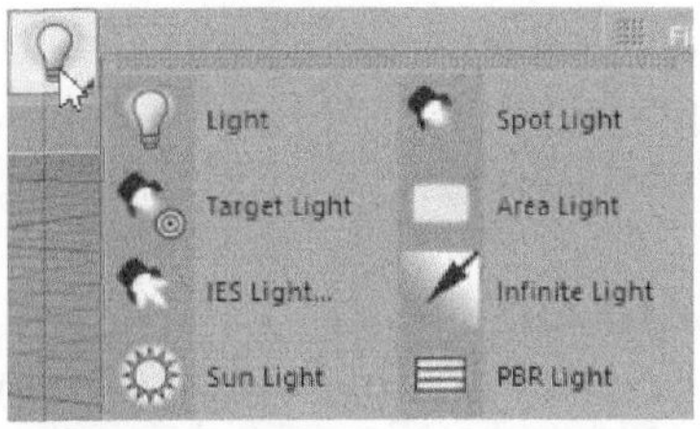

Figure 1-12 Various light tools displayed in the flyout

Model

The **Model** tool is used to activate the Model mode. In this mode, you can move, scale, and rotate an object. When you press and hold the left mouse button on this tool, a flyout will be displayed. Choose the **Object** tool from the flyout to activate the Object mode. In this mode, you can move, scale, or rotate the axes of the object. The Object Mode is used when the animations are created. You can use the **Animation** mode to transform entire animation path of an object.

Texture

This tool is used to edit the active texture. When this tool is chosen, the projection type is also considered. The grid lines are drawn in the viewport according to the projection type. The texture can be moved, scaled, or rotated by using the **Move**, **Scale**, and **Rotate** tools.

Workplane

This tool is used to modify the workplane manually by using the **Move**, **Rotate**, and **Scale** tools. A workplane in CINEMA 4D is a plane that can be positioned and rotated for arranging newly created objects, snapping spline points, and so on.

Points

This tool is used to display an object in the Point mode. In this mode, you can select and edit the points of an object. On choosing this tool, the points of the object are displayed. This tool can be used only when an object is converted into a polygonal object.

Edges

This tool is used to display an object in the Edge mode. In this mode, you can select and edit the edges of an object. This tool can be used only when an object is converted into a polygonal object.

Polygons

This tool is used to display an object in the Polygon mode. In this mode, you can select and edit the polygons of the selected object. This tool can be used only when an object is converted into a polygonal object.

Tip

To select one or more points, edges, or polygons, press and hold SHIFT and then click on them. To deselect one or more points, edges, or polygons, press and hold CTRL and then click on them.

Enable Axis

The **Enable Axis** tool is used to move, scale, and rotate the axis of an object. The shortcut key for this tool is L.

Viewport Solo Off

This tool is used for hiding or displaying the selected objects in complex scenes. On choosing this tool, a flyout with various tools will be displayed, as shown in Figure 1-13. By default, the **Viewport Solo mode off** tool is chosen. As a result, all the objects in the scene are visible.

Enable Snap

On choosing this tool, a flyout with various snapping tools will be displayed. You can snap objects, edges, points, and polygons.

Figure 1-13 Various options displayed in the flyout

Locked Workplane

The **Locked Workplane** tool is used to disable any defined automatic workplane modes. When you press and hold the left mouse button on this tool, a flyout will be displayed, as shown in Figure 1-14. You can use the tools in this flyout to align the workplane on different axes.

Planar Workplane

The **Planar Workplane** tool is used to display one of the world coordinate planes as the workplane, depending on the angle of the view of the camera. When you press and hold the left mouse button on this tool, a flyout with various planar workplane tools will be displayed, as shown in Figure 1-15.

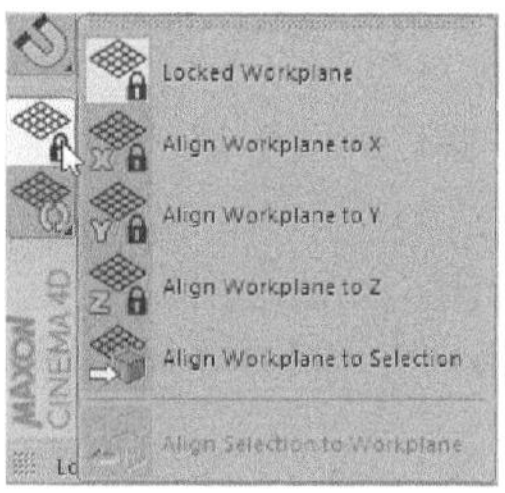

*Figure 1-14 Flyout displayed on choosing the **Locked Workplane** tool*

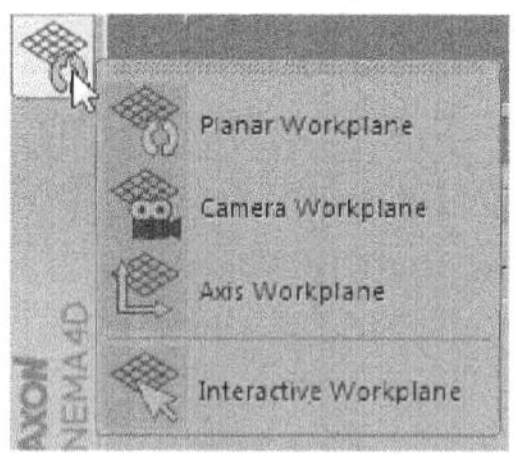

*Figure 1-15 Flyout displayed on choosing the **Planar Workplane** tool*

Animation Toolbar

The Animation toolbar is located below the viewport area. It consists of all the animation controls that are used to control animation in a scene, refer to Figure 1-16. These controls are discussed next.

Timeline Ruler

The Timeline Ruler is located at the top of the Animation toolbar. You can move the timeslider on the Timeline Ruler to view the animation at a particular frame in the viewport.

Start Frame

The **Start Frame** spinner is used to set the first frame of the animation displayed in the Timeline Ruler.

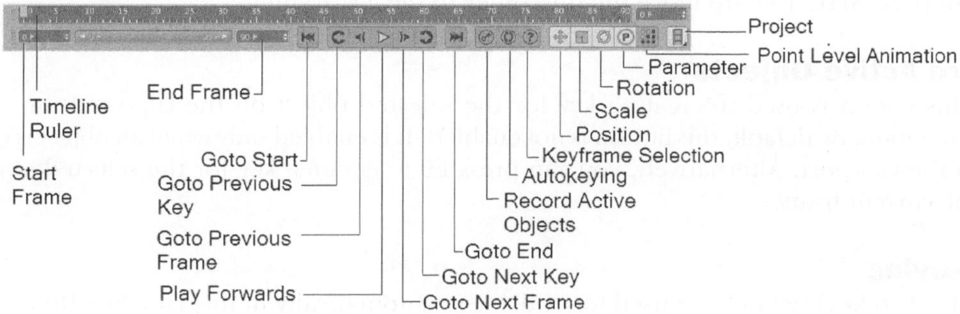

Figure 1-16 The Animation toolbar

End Frame

The **End Frame** spinner is used to set the last frame of the animation displayed in the Timeline Ruler.

Go to Start

The **Go to Start** button is used to move the timeslider to the start frame of the animation in the Timeline Ruler. Alternatively, you can press SHIFT+F to move the timeslider to the start frame.

Go to Previous Key

The **Go to Previous Key** button is used to move the timeslider backward by one keyframe from the current keyframe in the Timeline Ruler. Alternatively, you can use CTRL+F to move to the previous key.

Go to Previous Frame

The **Go to Previous Frame** button is used to move the timeslider backward by one frame from the current frame in the Timeline Ruler. Alternatively, press F.

Play Forwards

The **Play Forwards** button is used to play the animation in the forward direction. Alternatively, you can press F8 to play the animation in the forward direction.

Go to Next Frame

The **Go to Next Frame** button is used to move the timeslider to the next frame in the Timeline Ruler. Alternatively, you can press G to move the timeslider to the next frame.

Go to Next Key

The **Go to Next Key** button is used to move the timeslider to the next keyframe in the Timeline Ruler. Alternatively, you can press CTRL+G to move the timeslider to the next keyframe.

Go to End

The **Go to End** button is used to move the timeslider to the last frame. Alternatively, you can press SHIFT+G to move the timeslider to the last frame.

Record Active Objects

This button is used to create a key for the selected object on the current frame in the animation. By default, this button is not enabled. It is enabled only when an object is created in the viewport. Alternatively, you can press F9 to create a key for the selected object on the current frame.

Autokeying

The **Autokeying** button is used to set the keys automatically in the Timeline Ruler for the changes made in the animation. It saves the time of the user as the user need not manually choose the **Record Active Objects** button repeatedly to save the animation. Alternatively, you can press CTRL+F9 to set the keys automatically.

Keyframe Selection

On choosing this tool, a flyout will be displayed with the tools that restrict the setting of keys to selected objects only

Position

This button is used to record the position of the object on the current frame.

Scale

This button is used to record the scaling of the object on the current frame.

Rotation

This button is used to record the rotation of the object on the current frame.

Parameter

This button is chosen to ensure that only the selected parameters are applied while recording keyframes. It works in both **Automatic Keyframing** and **Record Active Objects** modes.

Point Level Animation

This button is used to record the position of the points in the object. This mode only works with the polygonal objects.

Project

This button is used to set the playback rate to the value that is specified in the project settings. This button is enabled by default. When you press and hold the left mouse button on this button, a flyout will be displayed, as shown in Figure 1-17. This flyout consists of options to determine the playback speed of the animation.

Material Manager

The Material Manager is located at the bottom left corner of the interface, as shown in Figure 1-18. It is used to create materials and shaders used in the scene. In Cinema 4D R20 version, uber material, node material, and some in-built node based materials are added to create complex materials.

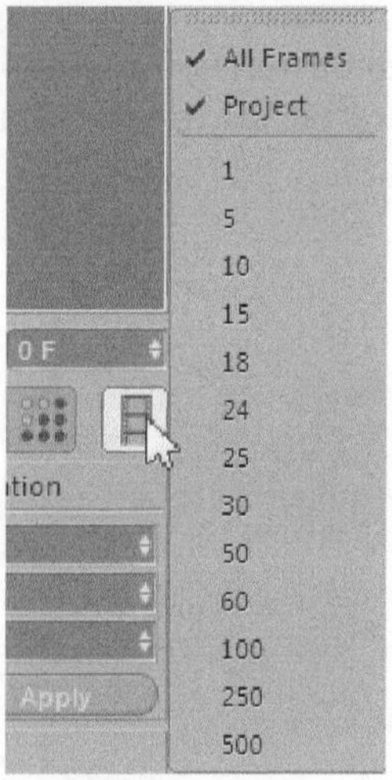

*Figure 1-17 The flyout displayed on choosing the **Project** button*

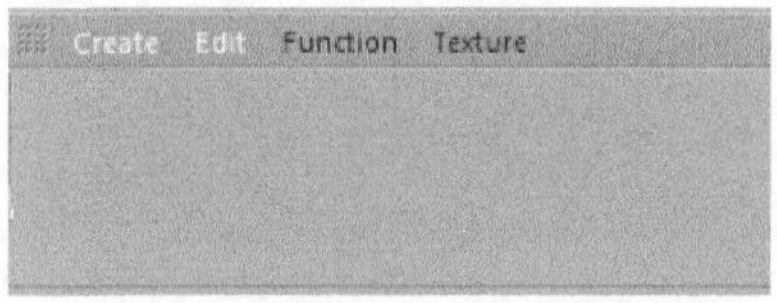

Figure 1-18 The Material Manager

Coordinate Manager

The Coordinate Manager is located at the right of the Material Manager, refer to Figure 1-19. It is used to position, rotate, and scale the objects created in the scene. You need to choose the **Apply** button to apply the values in the spinners of the Coordinate Manager.

Object Manager

The Object Manager is located at the upper right corner of the interface, as shown in Figure 1-20. It consists of a list of objects used in the scene. You can specify tags for objects, rename the objects, and select the objects in the Object Manager. Therefore, it is defined as the control center of the objects created in the scene.

Attribute Manager

The Attribute Manager is used to display the attributes of a selected tool or object in the scene. You can also modify the attributes of the objects and materials in it. Moreover, you can set keys for animation to the attributes that have a circle next to their name. By default, it displays the project settings, as shown in Figure 1-21.

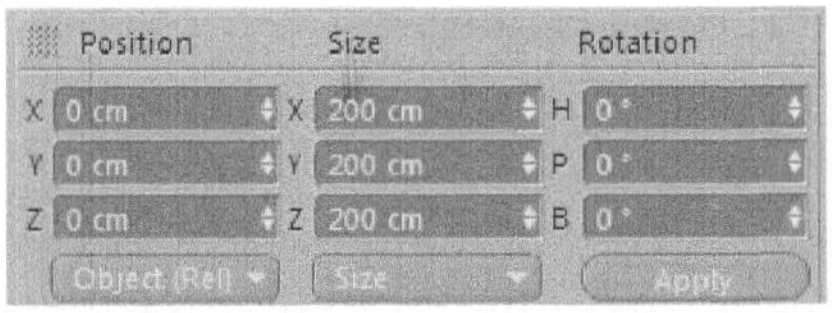

Figure 1-19 The Coordinate Manager

Figure 1-20 The Object Manager

Layers Manager

The Layers Manager is used to manage the objects in layers when you need to work in complex scenes. To invoke the Layers Manager, choose the **Layers** tab in the Attribute Manager. The Layer Manager will be displayed, as shown in Figure 1-22.

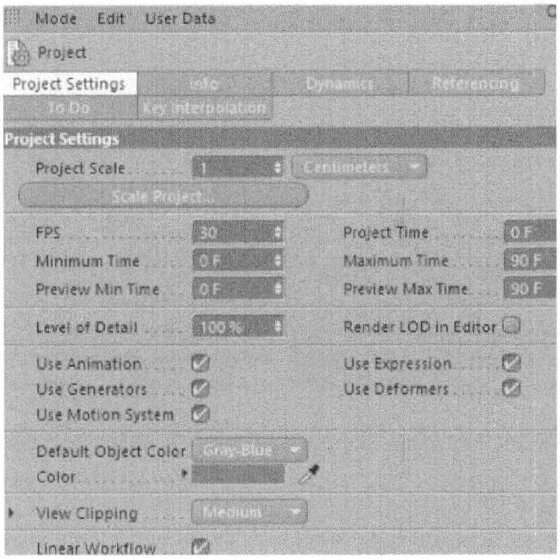

Figure 1-21 The Attribute Manager

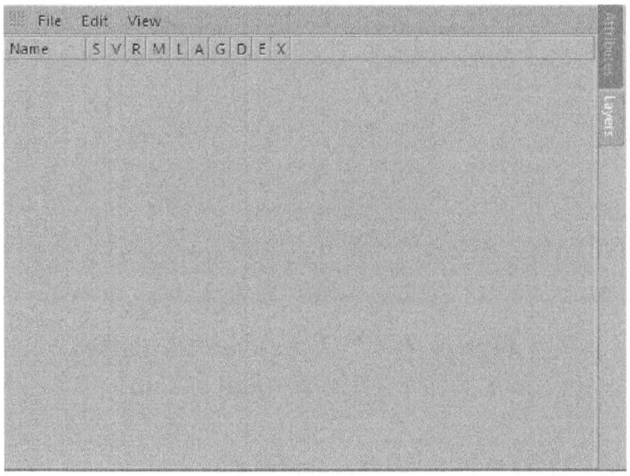

Figure 1-22 The Layers Manager

Viewport Navigation Tools

The Viewport Navigation Tools are located on the top right corner of each viewport, refer to Figure 1-2. These tools are used to pan, zoom, and rotate the camera in the viewport.

Pan Tool

The **Pan** tool is used to move the camera in X and Y directions in a scene. You can also pan the camera by pressing 1 along with the left mouse button or by pressing ALT along with the middle mouse button.

Zoom In/Out Tool

The **Zoom In/Out** tool is used to move the camera in the Z direction only. You can also zoom the camera by pressing 2 along with the left mouse button or by pressing ALT along with the right mouse button.

Orbit Tool

The **Orbit** tool is used to rotate the camera in all directions. You can also rotate the camera by pressing 3 along with the left mouse button or ALT along with the left mouse button.

Viewport Tool

The **Viewport** tool is used to toggle between four viewport and single viewport display.

Note

You can maximize a viewport by pressing the middle mouse button inside that viewport.

Menu in editor view

The Menu in editor view is available in every viewport and is used to perform various tasks. It consists of **View**, **Cameras**, **Display**, **Options**, **Filter**, and **Panel** menus, refer to Figure 1-2. These menus are discussed next.

View Menu

On choosing the **View** menu, a flyout will be displayed, as shown in Figure 1-23. The options in this flyout are discussed next.

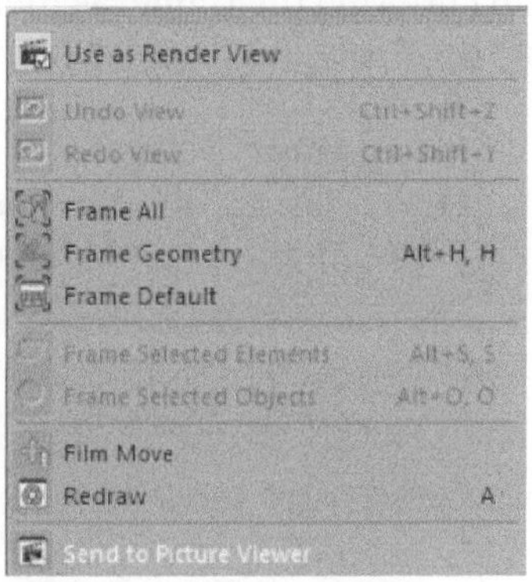

***Figure 1-23** The flyout displayed on choosing the **View** menu*

Use as Render View

The **Use as Render View** option is used to set the active viewport for rendering in the **Picture Viewer** window.

Undo View

The **Undo View** option is used to undo the last change made to the view angle in the viewport.

Redo View

The **Redo View** option is used to redo the last change made to the view angle in the viewport.

Frame All

The **Frame All** option is used to position the camera such that all the objects including the lights and cameras fill the active viewport and are centered in it.

Frame Geometry

The **Frame Geometry** option is used to position the camera such that objects (excluding the lights and camera) are at the center of the viewport.

Frame Default

The **Frame Default** option is used to reset the viewport to its default value.

Frame Selected Elements

The **Frame Selected Elements** option is used to move the camera such that the selected objects and polygons are at the center of the viewport.

Frame Selected Objects

The **Frame Selected Objects** option is used to position the camera such that the active objects are at the center of the viewport.

Film Move

The **Film Move** option is used to move the camera in the viewport.

Redraw

Usually CINEMA 4D updates the viewport automatically. However, sometimes it is not possible. In such a case, the **Redraw** tool is used to redraw the scene.

Send to Picture Viewer

The **Send to Picture Viewer** option is used to quickly view the rendered output in the **Picture Viewer** window to visualize the effects of modifications done in the active view.

Cameras Menu

On choosing the **Cameras** menu, a flyout will be displayed, as shown in Figure 1-24. The options in this flyout are discussed next.

Navigation

On choosing the **Navigation** option, a cascading menu will be displayed, as shown in Figure 1-25. It displays various modes of the camera which are discussed next.

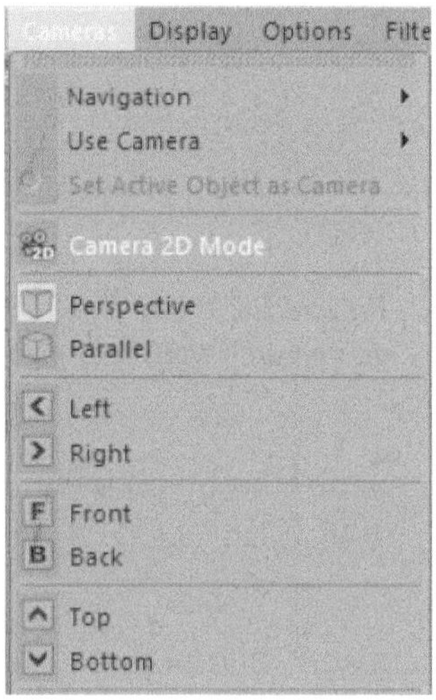

*Figure 1-24 The flyout displayed on choosing the **Cameras** menu*

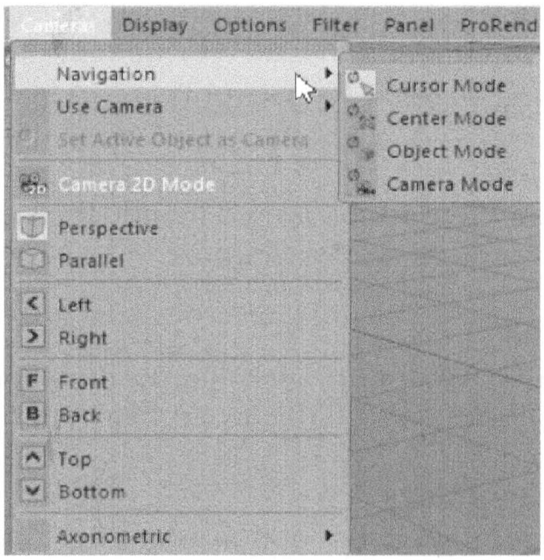

*Figure 1-25 The cascading menu displayed on choosing the **Navigation** option from the **Cameras** menu*

Cursor Mode: On choosing the **Cursor Mode** option, the camera will rotate around the selected point of the object.

Center Mode: On choosing the **Center Mode** option, the camera will rotate around the screen center only.

Object Mode: On choosing the **Object Mode** option, the camera will rotate around the center of the selected objects or elements in the viewport.

Camera Mode: On choosing the **Camera Mode** option, the camera will rotate around its own axis only.

Use Camera

The **Use Camera** option is used to set the camera present in the scene to view the scene through this camera. On placing the cursor on the **Use Camera** option in the **Cameras** menu, a cascading menu will be displayed, as shown in Figure 1-26.

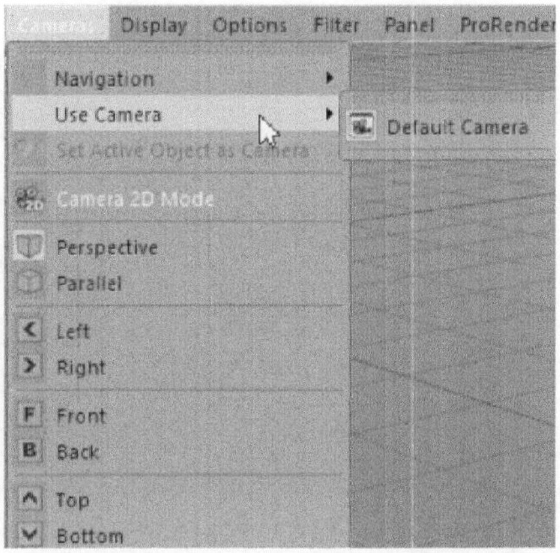

*Figure 1-26 The cascading menu displayed on choosing the **Use Camera** option*

The **Default Camera** option is used to set the viewport back to the default camera settings.

Set Active Object as Camera

The **Set Active Object as Camera** option is used to orient the view of the scene along the z-axis of the active object.

Camera 2D Mode

The **Camera 2D Mode** option displays 3D object as 2D object. In this mode, position of the camera does not change when you navigate, move, and zoom-in and zoom-out in the view.

Perspective

The **Perspective** option is used to view the scene using the default perspective projection mode, as shown in Figure 1-27. The Perspective viewport shows a horizon line which represents the horizon at infinity.

Parallel

The **Parallel** option is used to view the scene using the parallel camera projection mode, as shown in Figure 1-28. In this type of camera projection, the projection lines are parallel to each other with an infinite focal length.

Left

The **Left** option is used to display the YZ view, as shown in Figure 1-29.

Right

The **Right** option is used to display the ZY view, as shown in Figure 1-30.

Figure 1-27 *The perspective camera projection mode*

Figure 1-28 *The parallel camera projection mode*

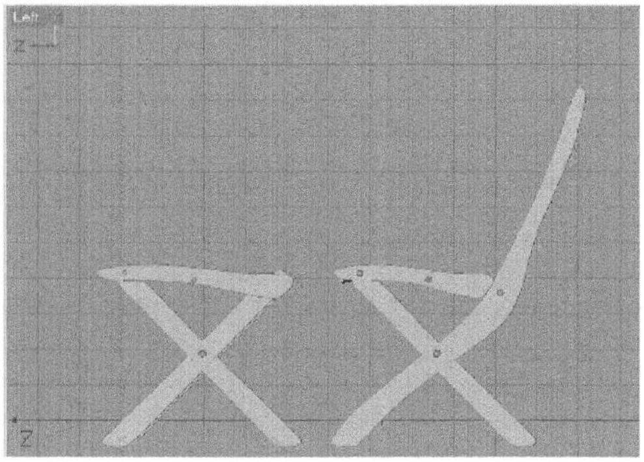

Figure 1-29 *The left camera projection*

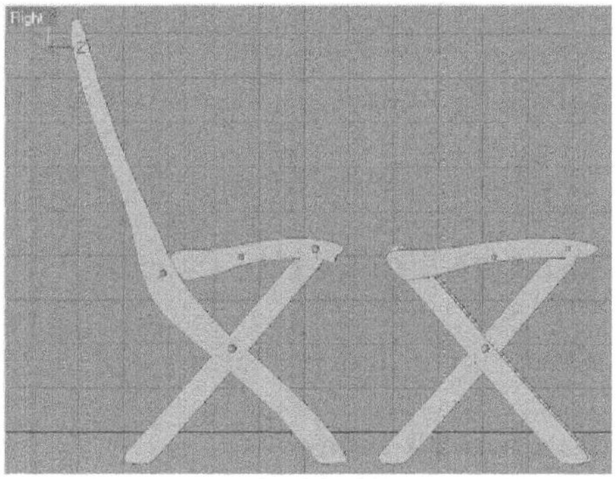

Figure 1-30 *The right camera projection*

Front

The **Front** option is used to display the XY view, as shown in Figure 1-31.

Back

The **Back** option is used to display the YZ view, as shown in Figure 1-32.

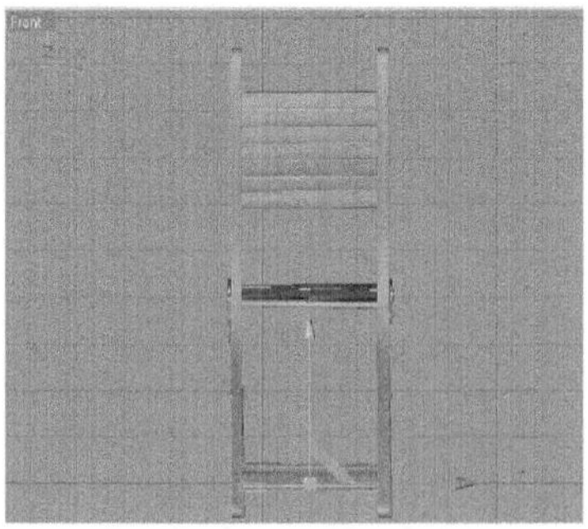

Figure 1-31 *The front camera projection*

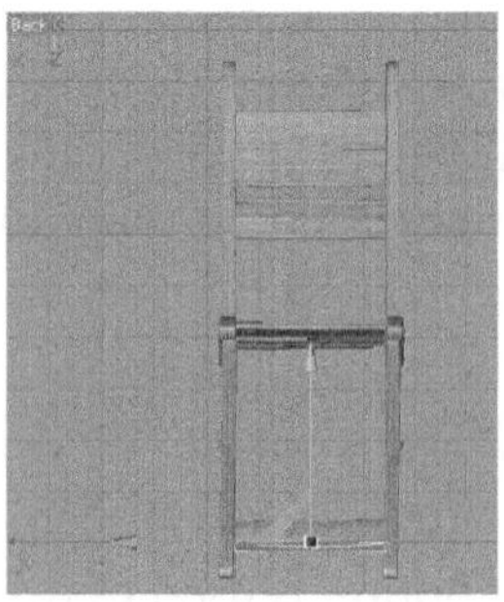

Figure 1-32 *The back camera projection*

Top

The **Top** option is used to display the XZ view, as shown in Figure 1-33.

Bottom

The **Bottom** option is used to display the ZX view, as shown in Figure 1-34.

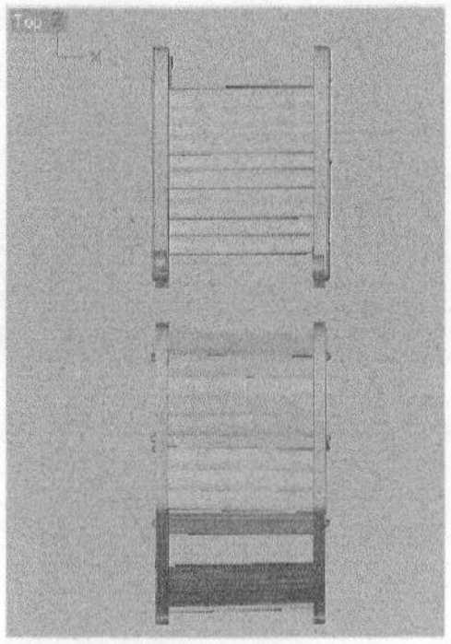

Figure 1-33 *The top camera projection*

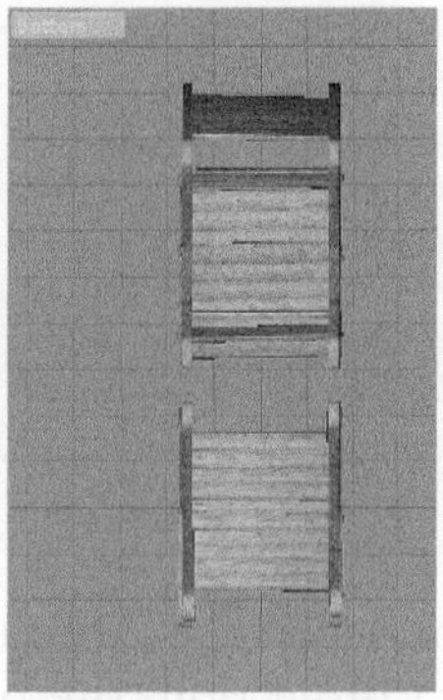

Figure 1-34 *The bottom camera projection*

Axonometric

The **Axonometric** option is used to display the scene using the advanced views other than the Perspective, Top, Left, and Right views. On placing the cursor on this option, a cascading menu will be displayed, as shown in Figure 1-35. The options in the cascading menu are discussed next.

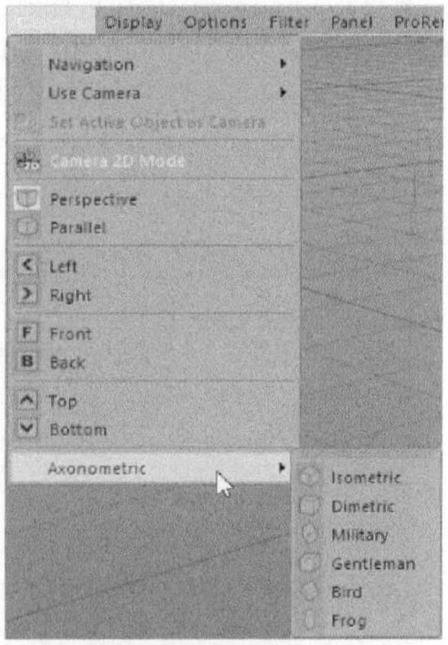

Figure 1-35 *The cascading menu displayed on choosing the* ***Axonometric*** *option from the* ***Cameras*** *menu*

Isometric: The **Isometric** option is used to view the scene using the isometric camera projection, as shown in Figure 1-36. In this type of camera projection, the projection lines are in exact proportion. This projection is mostly used for technical objects.

Dimetric: The **Dimetric** option is used to view the scene using the dimetric camera projection, as shown in Figure 1-37.

Military: The **Military** option is used to view the scene using the military camera projection, as shown in Figure 1-38. The proportion of XYZ in this case is 1:1:1.

Gentleman: The **Gentleman** option is used to view the scene using the gentleman camera projection, as shown in Figure 1-39. This type of projection is suitable for architecture. The proportion of XYZ in this case is 1:1:0.5.

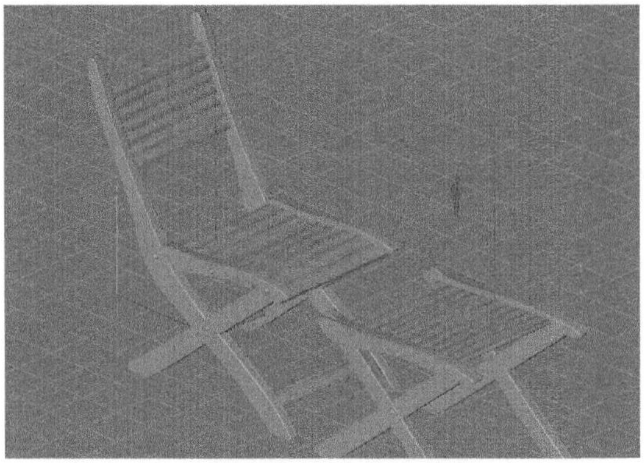

Figure 1-36 The isometric camera projection

Figure 1-37 The dimetric camera projection

Bird: The **Bird** option is used to view the scene using the bird camera projection, as shown in Figure 1-40. In this type of camera projection, the projection lines will have no perspective distortion and the objects are not scaled. The proportion of XYZ in this case is 1:0.5:1.

Frog: The **Frog** option is used to view the scene using the frog camera projection, as shown in Figure 1-41. In this type of camera projection, the projection lines are not parallel to each other. The proportion of XYZ in this case is 1:2:1.

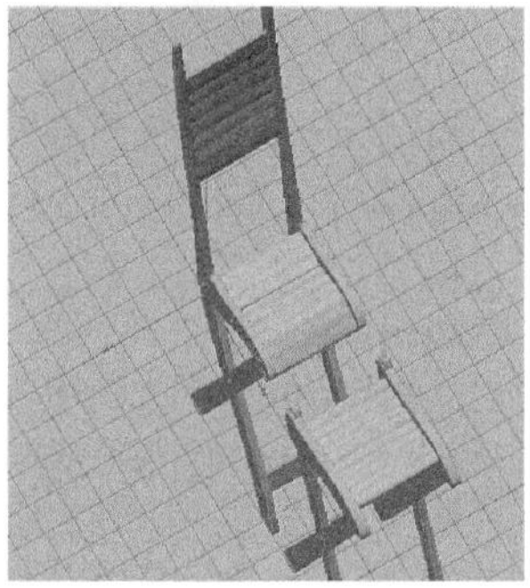

Figure 1-38 The military camera projection

Figure 1-39 The gentleman camera projection

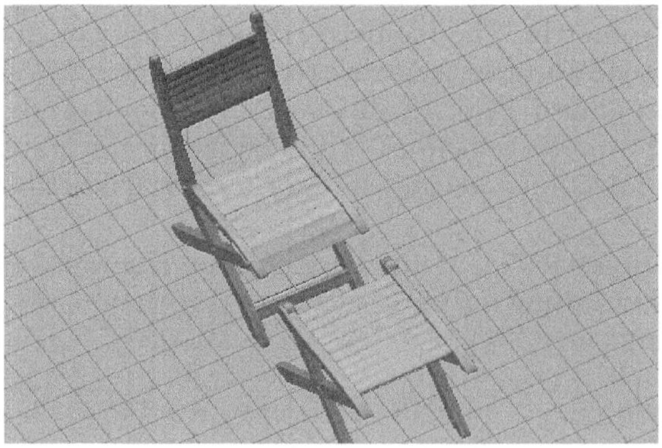

Figure 1-40 The bird camera projection

Display Menu

On choosing the **Display** menu, a flyout will be displayed, as shown in Figure 1-42. It consists of various options that are used to manipulate the preview of the model in the viewport. These options are discussed next.

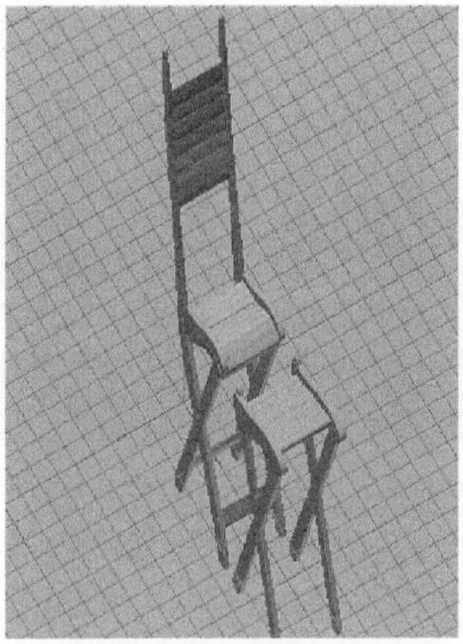

Figure 1-41 The frog camera projection

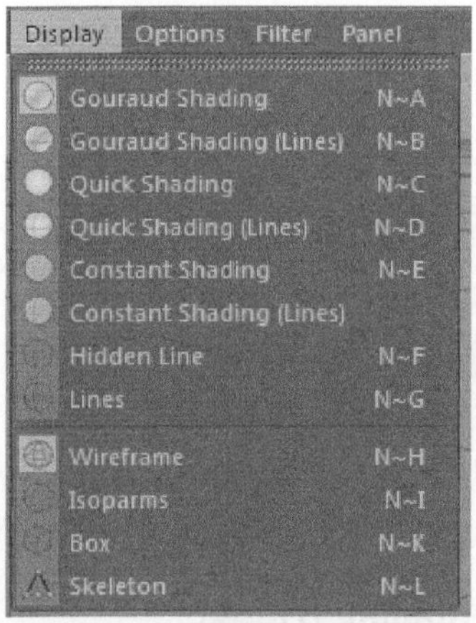

***Figure 1-42** The flyout displayed on choosing the **Display** menu*

Gouraud Shading

The **Gouraud Shading** option is used to display the object in best quality possible. On choosing this option, the object in the viewport will be displayed with smooth shading and lights, as shown in Figure 1-43.

Gouraud Shading (Lines)

The **Gouraud Shading (Lines)** option is used to display the object with smooth shading and with wireframes or isoparms, as shown in Figure 1-44.

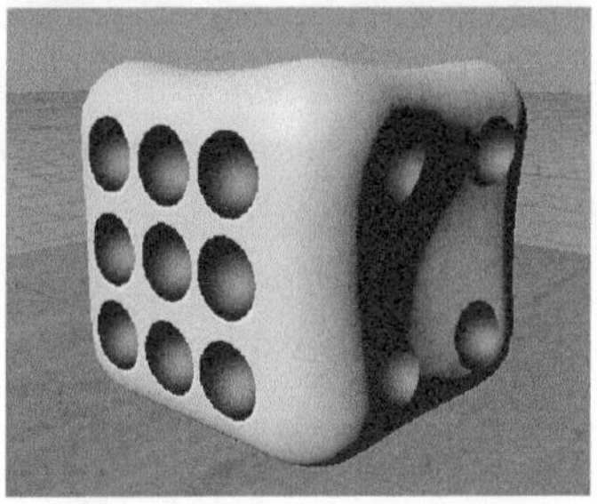

***Figure 1-43** The object displayed in the viewport on choosing the **Gouraud Shading** option*

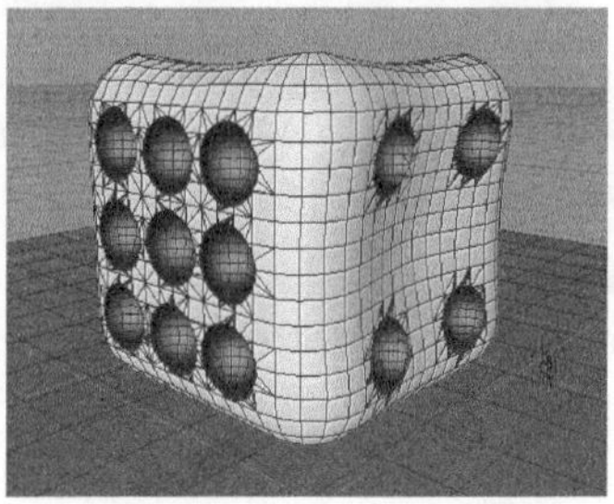

***Figure 1-44** The object displayed in the viewport on choosing the **Gouraud Shading (Lines)** option*

Quick Shading

The **Quick Shading** option is used to display the object with smooth shading and default lights instead of the scene lights in the viewport, as shown in Figure 1-45.

Quick Shading (Lines)

The **Quick Shading (Lines)** option is used to display the object with smooth shading, wireframes or isoparms, and default lights instead of the scene lights, as shown in Figure 1-46.

Constant Shading

The **Constant Shading** option is used to illuminate an object with flat shades, as shown in Figure 1-47.

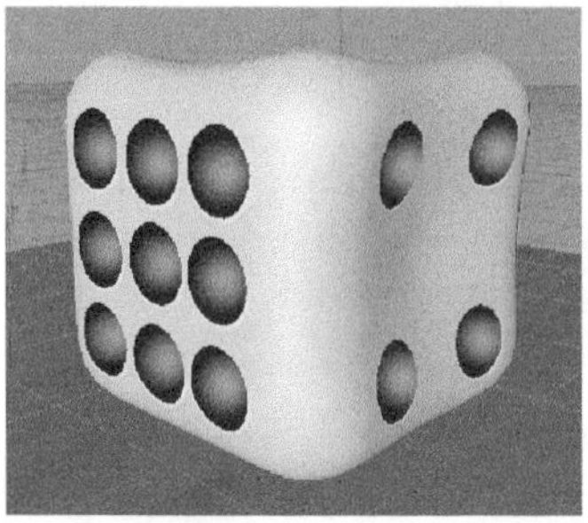

Figure 1-45 *The object displayed in the viewport on choosing the* ***Quick Shading*** *option*

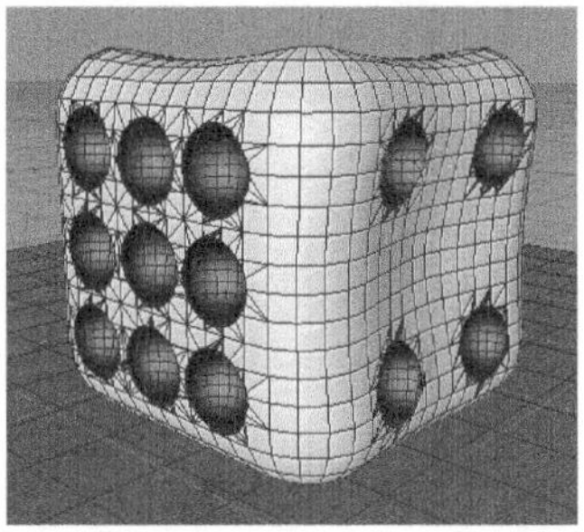

Figure 1-46 *The object displayed in the viewport on choosing the* ***Quick Shading (Lines)*** *option*

Constant Shading (Lines)

The **Constant Shading (Lines)** option is used to display the object with flat shades along with the wireframes added to it, as shown in Figure 1-48.

Figure 1-47 *The object displayed in the viewport on choosing the* ***Constant Shading*** *option*

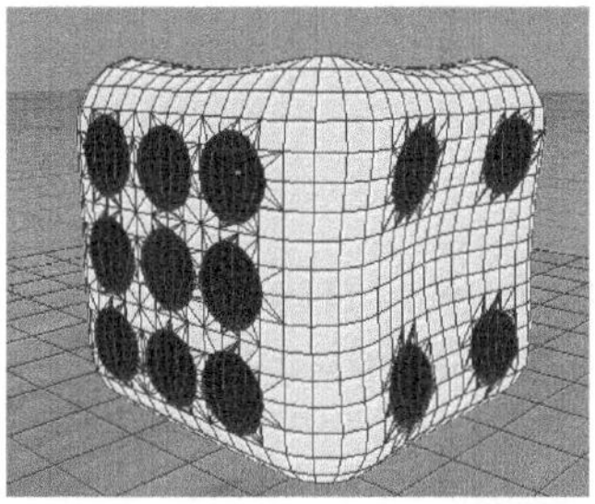

Figure 1-48 *The object displayed in the viewport on choosing the* ***Constant Shading (Lines)*** *option*

Hidden Line

The **Hidden Line** option is used to display the polygon mesh excluding the hidden lines of the object, as shown in Figure 1-49.

Lines

The **Lines** option is used to display the polygon mesh in the wireframe mode, including the hidden lines of the object, as shown in Figure 1-50.

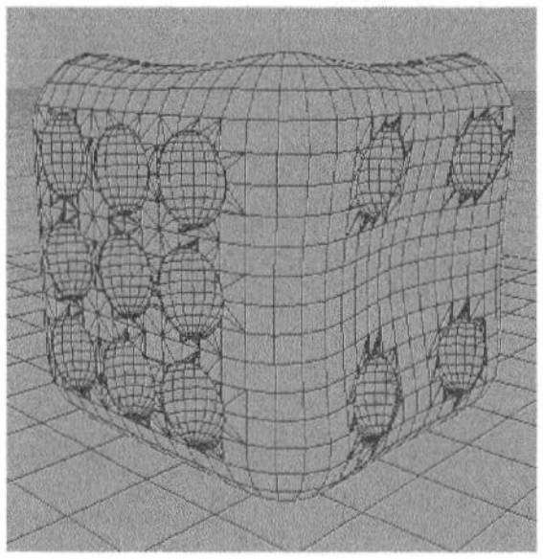

Figure 1-49 *The object displayed in the viewport on choosing the* ***Hidden Line*** *option*

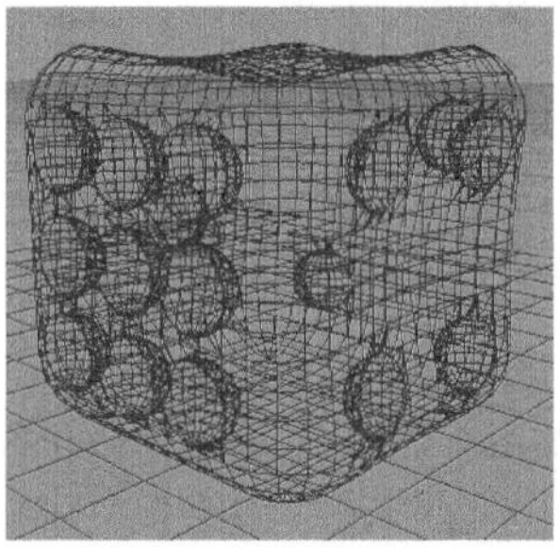

Figure 1-50 *The object displayed in the viewport on choosing the* ***Lines*** *option*

Wireframe

The **Wireframe** option is used to display the polygon mesh along with the lines so that the object is displayed with the combination of other shading modes. To activate this option, you need to choose any of the display options along with it. Figure 1-51 displays the object in the **Quick Shading (Lines)** and **Wireframe** shading modes.

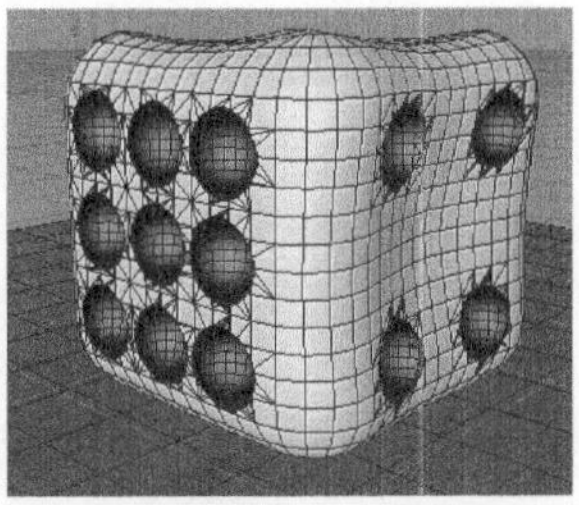

Figure 1-51 *The object displayed in the **Wireframe** and **Quick Shading (Lines)** shading modes*

Isoparms

The **Isoparms** option is used to display the isoparms lines on the objects. These isoparms are useful when you use generators on the objects.

Box

The **Box** option is used to display each object in a box shape having same dimensions as that of the object.

Skeleton

The **Skeleton** option is used to display the objects in the form of dots. This option is the fastest display mode and is used to display the hierarchical structure. This mode is used in character animation.

Options Menu

On choosing the **Options** menu, a flyout will be displayed, as shown in Figure 1-52. It consists of various options that are used to display the detail view of a model. These options are discussed next.

Level of Detail

The **Level of Detail** option is used to affect the display quality of the object in the viewport. On placing the cursor on the **Level of Detail** option, a cascading menu will be displayed, as shown in Figure 1-53. The options in this cascading menu are discussed next.

Low: This option is used to display the objects with low details, upto 25% maximum. When you choose this option, the object takes very less time in getting displayed in the viewport.

Medium: This option is used to display the objects with medium detail, upto 50% maximum.

High: This option is used to display the objects with highest details upto 100 %. When you choose this option, the object takes more time in getting displayed in the viewport.

Use Render LOD for Editor Rendering: This option is used to render the object in the viewport with the same level of detailing as specified in the **Level of Detail** option for that viewport.

Stereoscopic

The **Stereoscopic** option is used to enable stereoscopic display for viewport. This option is activated only in the Perspective and Parallel viewports.

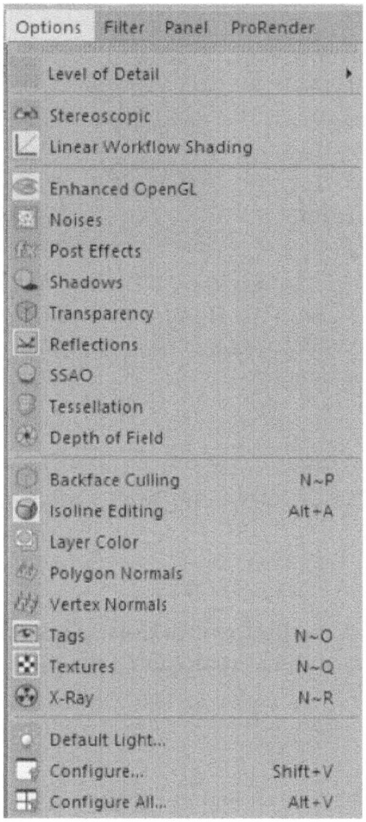

*Figure 1-52 The partial view of the flyout displayed on choosing the **Options** menu*

*Figure 1-53 The cascading menu displayed on placing the cursor on the **Level of Detail** option*

Linear Workflow Shading

The **Linear Workflow Shading** option is used to control the display of colors and shaders in the viewport while following the linear workflow.

Enhanced OpenGL

This option is used to display objects in the scene with Enhanced OpenGL quality. This option is dependent on the type of graphics card and drivers installed in the system. There are five OpenGL display modes available in the viewport in CINEMA 4D.

Noises

The **Noises** option is used to display the Noise shader when the **Enhanced OpenGL** option is enabled.

Post Effects

The **Post Effects** option is used to display post effects when the **Enhanced OpenGL** option is enabled.

Shadows

The **Shadows** option is used to display the shadow when the **Enhanced OpenGL** option is enabled.

Transparency
The **Transparency** option is used to display the transparency in high quality when **Enhanced OpenGL** option is enabled.

Reflections
The **Reflections** option is used to display sky reflections when the **Enhanced OpenGL** option is enabled.

Tessellation
The **Tessellation** option is used to display the tessellation on an object when the **Enhanced OpenGL** option is enabled.

SSAO
The **SSAO** option is used to display ambient occlusion approximation when the **Enhanced OpenGL** option is enabled.

Backface Culling
The **Backface Culling** option is used to toggle the backface culling on or off in the lines mode. It makes the editing of the objects easier. Figure 1-54 displays the object with **Backface Culling** on and off.

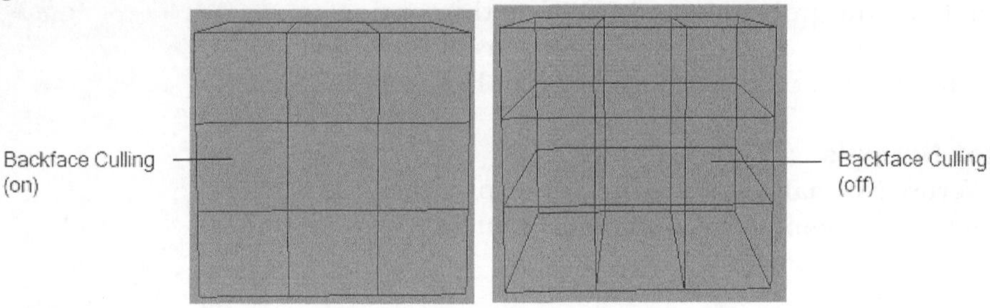

*Figure 1-54 The object displayed with the **Backface Culling** option on and off*

Isoline Editing
The **Isoline Editing** option is used to project all subdivision surface cage objects onto the smooth subdivision surface object such that these elements can be selected directly on the smoothened object. Figure 1-55 displays the object with the **Isoline Editing** option on and off.

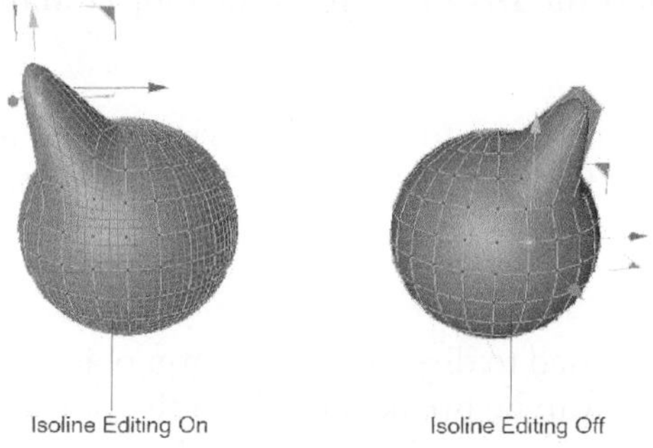

*Figure 1-55 The object displayed with the **Isoline Editing** option on and off*

Layer Color

The **Layer Color** option makes the color of the object in the viewport same as the color of the layer to which it belongs. For example, if the color of the layer is green, then the object belonging to that layer will be displayed in green color, refer to Figure 1-56. This makes the selection of the objects easier.

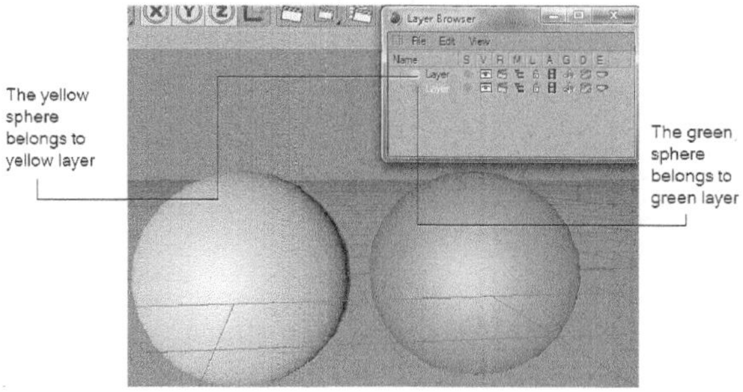

*Figure 1-56 The color of the objects displayed same as the color of layers on choosing the **Layer Color** option*

Polygon Normals

The **Polygon Normals** option is used to toggle the display of normals in the polygon mode. When this option is activated, normals of the selected polygons of the object are displayed in the viewport, as shown in Figure 1-57.

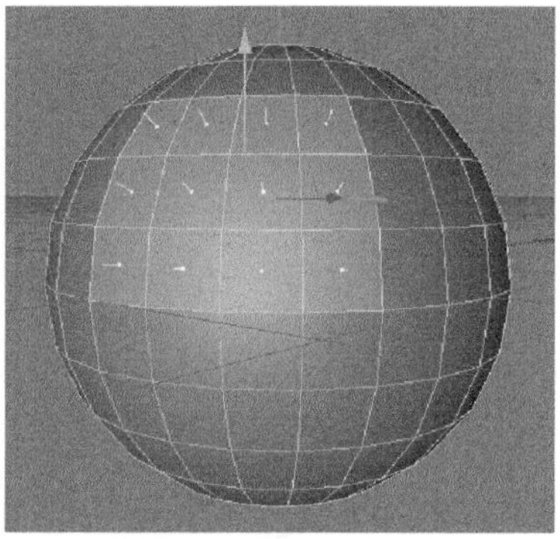

Figure 1-57 Displaying the normals of the selected polygons

Vertex Normals

The **Vertex Normals** option is used to display the vertex normals in the point, edge, and polygon modes.

Tags

The **Tags** option is used to display the selected object in the display mode defined in their display tag. On choosing this option, you can edit the display settings of a selected object individually in the Attribute Manager. To add a tag to the Object Manager, right-click on the object; a shortcut menu will be displayed. From the shortcut menu, choose **CINEMA 4D Tags > Display**; a display tag will be added to the Object Manager. Now, select the **Display Tag** in the Object Manager to edit the display settings.

Textures

The **Textures** option is used to toggle the view of the textures in the viewport. Realtime Texture Mapping (RTTM) allows the viewing of the texture applied to the object in the viewport.

X-Ray

The **X-Ray** option is used to display the polygon objects in a semi-transparent color so that the points and edges can be tweaked easily in the polygon based modeling.

Default Light
The **Default Light** option is used to illuminate the object easily from any angle. Each viewport has its own independent default lighting system. On choosing this option, the **Default Light** window will be displayed, as shown in Figure 1-58. Click and drag the sphere in the **Default Light** window to adjust the light in the viewport. When you choose this option, the display mode automatically changes to **Quick Shading**.

***Figure 1-58** The **Default Light** window*

Configure
The **Configure** option is used to edit or control the parameters of a particular viewport in the Attribute Manager.

Configure All
The **Configure All** option is used to edit or control the parameters of all viewports in the Attribute Manager.

Filter Menu
On choosing the **Filter** menu, a flyout will be displayed. The options in this flyout are used to select the objects to be displayed in the respective viewports.

Panel Menu
On choosing the **Panel** menu, a flyout will be displayed, as shown in Figure 1-59. The options in this flyout are used to choose between single or multiple views of viewports. By default, the Perspective viewport will be displayed.

ProRender Menu
On choosing the **ProRender** menu, a flyout will be displayed. You can use the options in this flyout to set a view for the ProRender to use as an interactive preview renderer. This helps you to avoid the use of the **Picture Viewer** window constantly for previewing the renderers.

Layout
The **Layout** drop-down list is located on the top right corner of the interface, as shown in Figure 1-60. The options in this drop-down list are used to switch between various layouts available in CINEMA 4D. You can select the required layout from this drop-down list.

Content Browser
The Content Browser is an integral part of CINEMA 4D. It is used to manage scenes, images, materials, shaders, and presets. The Content Browser is docked with the Object Manager in CINEMA 4D interface.

Structure Manager
The Structure Manager is a type of spreadsheet that is used to calculate the data. It displays the data of the polygon objects only. On converting the parametric object into a polygon object,

the data of the points, polygons, UVW coordinates, and so on will be displayed in the rows and columns of the Structure Manager. The Structure Manager is docked with the Object Manager and Content Browser in CINEMA 4D interface.

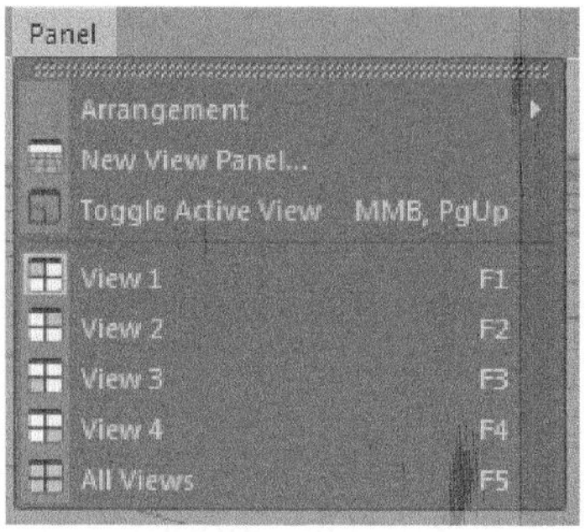

*Figure 1-59 The flyout displayed on choosing the **Panel** menu*

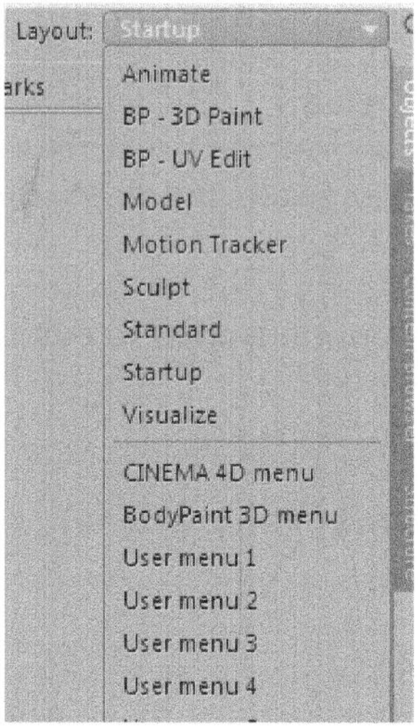

*Figure 1-60 The **Layout** drop-down list*

CREATING PROJECT FOLDER WITH ASSETS

When you transfer the scene in Cinema 4D to another computer, make sure texture files are also transferred with the scene in a single project folder. To create this project folder, choose **Save Project with Assets** from the **File** menu; the **Save File** dialog box will be displayed. In this dialog box, navigate to the desired location and enter the name of the folder in the **File name** text box. Next, choose the **Save** button; the project folder will be created at the specified location. This project folder contains a cinema 4D file and a folder named **tex** that contains texture files used in the scene.

HOT KEYS

Table 1-1 displays the hot keys of tools used in CINEMA 4D.

***Table 1-1** The tools and their hot keys*

Tool	Hot keys
Undo	CTRL+Z
Redo	CTRL+Y
Move	E
Scale	T
Rotate	R
X-Axis / Heading	X
Y-Axis / Pitch	Y
Z-Axis / Bank	Z

Tool	Hot keys
Coordinate System	W
Render View	CTRL+R
Render to Picture Viewer	SHIFT+R
Edit Render Settings	CTRL+B
Make Editable	C
Undo View	CTRL+SHIFT+Z
Redo View	CTRL+SHIFT+Y

Tip
If you want to view the documentation of a tool or option in CINEMA 4D, place the cursor over that tool or option and then press CTRL+F1; the ***Help*** *window will be displayed with the documentation.*

Self-Evaluation Test

Answer the following questions and then compare them to those given at the end of this chapter:

1. Which of the following options is used to display the polygon objects in a semi-transparent mode?

    (a) **Display Tags** (b) **Textures**
    (c) **X-Ray** (d) **Default Light**

2. Which of the following shortcut keys is used to convert the primitive objects into editable objects?

    (a) A (b) C
    (c) B (d) D

3. Which of the following combinations of shortcut keys is used to render the current view?

    (a) CTRL+W (b) CTRL+D
    (c) CTRL+R (d) CTRL+ J

4. The __________ tool is used to add light objects to a scene.

5. The __________ tool is used to select sub-objects of an editable object like a paint brush in the viewport.

6. The __________ button is used to move the timeslider to the start of the animation.

7. The shortcut key for the **Autokeying** button is __________ .

8. The shortcut key for the **Redo** tool is CTRL+Z. (T/F)

9. The **Bend** tool is used to create an array of objects in spherical or wave form. (T/F)

10. The Object Manager is defined as the control center of the objects created in the scene. (T/F)

Review Questions

Answer the following questions:

1. Which of the following tools from the Tools Palette is used to edit the polygons of the selected object?

    (a) **Points** (b) **Edges**
    (c) **Polygons** (d) **Model**

2. Which of the following keys is the shortcut for the **Rotate** tool?

    (a) E (b) R
    (c) T (d) W

3. Which of the following options in the **Options** menu is used to edit or control the parameters of all viewports in the Attribute Manager?

    (a) **Configure All** (b) **Normals**
    (c) **Backface Culling** (d) **Configure**

4. The __________ option in the **Options** menu is used to enable the stereoscopic display in the viewport individually.

5. The __________ tool is used to move the camera horizontally.

6. The Attribute Manager is used to control the attributes of a selected tool or object in the scene. (T/F)

7. Snapping cannot be performed on objects, edges, points, polygons, and model. (T/F)

8. You can use the **Frog** camera projection in the **Cameras** menu to view the parallel camera projection in a scene. (T/F)

9. The shortcut key to invoke the **Render Settings** window is CTRL+B. (T/F)

Answers to Self-Evaluation Test

1. c, **2.** b, **3.** c, **4. Light**, **5. Live Selection**, **6. Go to Start**, **7.** CTRL+F9, **8.** F, **9.** F, **10.** T

Chapter 2

Working with Splines

Learning Objectives

After completing this chapter, you will be able to:

- *Work with spline primitives*
- *Understand spline modeling techniques*
- *Create geometries using Generators*

INTRODUCTION

In computer graphics, a spline is a line formed by connecting a sequence of vertices lying in 3D space. Although, it is formed in 3D space, it has no depth. A spline is not visible on rendering. You can create complete parametric spline primitives (with pre-defined shapes) as well as empty splines whose shapes can be defined interactively in the viewport. You can use splines to create complex geometries using Generator objects in CINEMA 4D. Generators are CINEMA 4D's most powerful modeling tools.

TUTORIALS

Before you start tutorials of this chapter, you need to download the *c02_cinema4d_r20_tut.zip* file from *www.cadcim.com*. The path of the file is as follows: *Textbooks > Animation and Visual Effects > MAXON CINEMA 4D > MAXON CINEMA 4D R20 Studio: A Tutorial Approach*

Next, you need to extract the contents of the zip file. To do so, navigate to the *Documents* folder and create a new folder in it with the name *c4dr20*. Next, you need to browse to *\Documents\c4dr20* and create a new folder in it with the name *c02*. Then, extract the contents of the zip file in this folder.

Tutorial 1

In this tutorial, you will create 3D model of a door lock system with the help of splines and Generators. The final output of the model is shown in Figure 2-1.

(Expected time: 35 min)

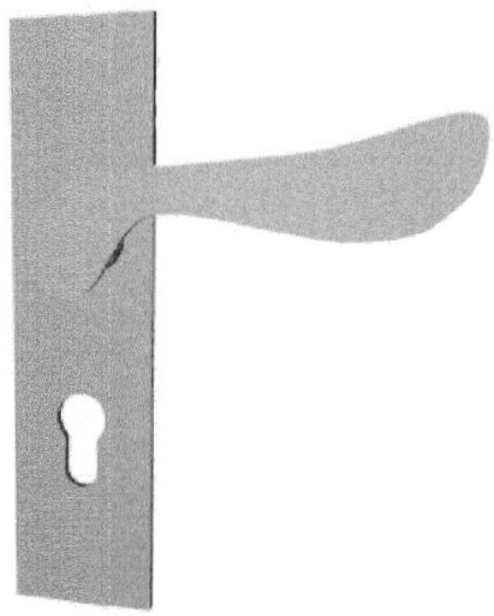

Figure 2-1 *The model of door lock system*

The following steps are required to complete this tutorial:

a. Set the viewport background.
b. Create the base of the door lock system.
c. Create the key hole.
d. Create the handle.
e. Change the background color of the scene.
f. Save and render the scene.

Setting the Viewport Background

In this section, you will set the background image in the Front viewport.

1. Choose **File > New** from the main menu; a new scene is displayed.

2. Press the middle mouse button in the Perspective viewport; all viewports are displayed. Next, hover the cursor over the Front viewport and then press MMB to maximize it. Alternatively, choose **Cameras > Front** from the Menu in editor view, as shown in Figure 2-2; the Front viewport is maximized.

3. Choose **Options > Configure** from the Menu in editor view, as shown in Figure 2-3; the **Viewport [Front]** settings are displayed in the Attribute Manager. In the Attribute Manager, choose the **Back** button; the **Back** area is displayed. In this area, choose the browse button next to the **Image** text box, as shown in Figure 2-4; the **Open File** dialog box is displayed. Browse to *\Documents\c4dr20\c02\keyhole.jpg*. Next, choose the **Open** button; the *keyhole.jpg* is opened as the background image in the Front viewport.

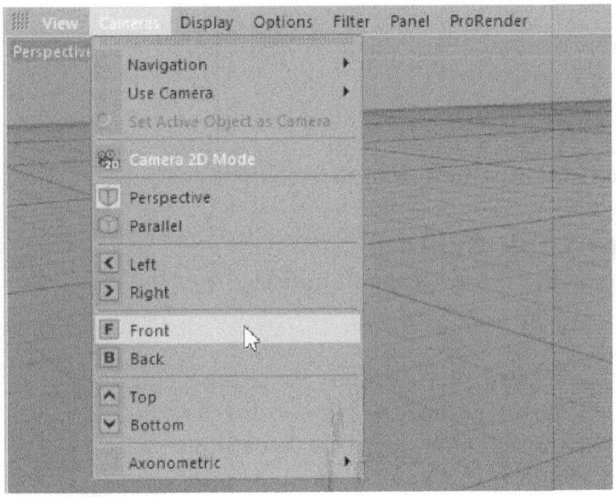

***Figure 2-2** Choosing the **Front** option from the Menu in editor view*

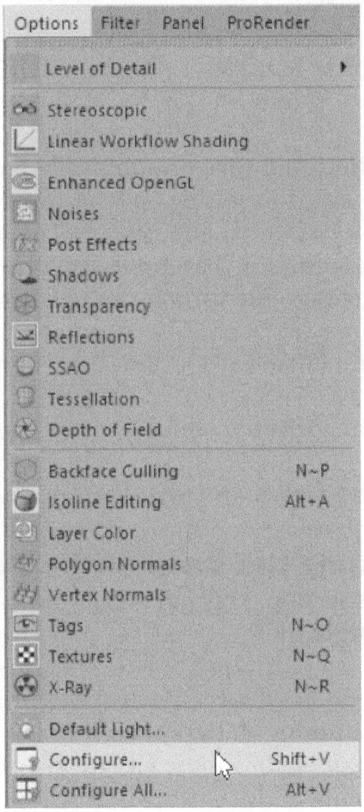

***Figure 2-3** Choosing the **Configure** option from the Menu in editor view*

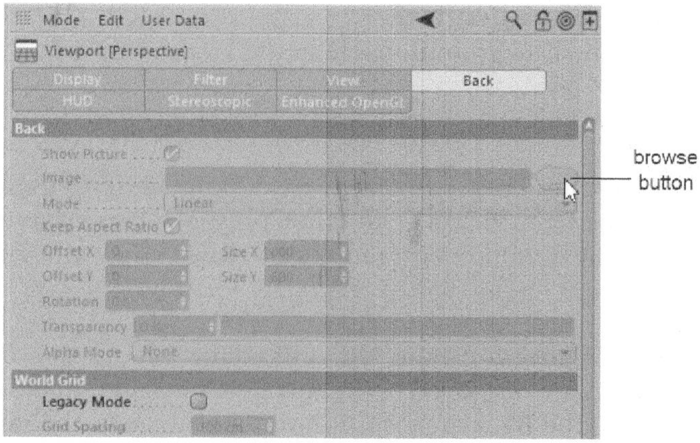

Figure 2-4 *Choosing the browse button next to the* ***Image*** *text box*

4. In the **Back** area, clear the **Keep Aspect Ratio** check box and then set the parameters as follows:

   Offset X: **122** Offset Y: **2** Size X: **445**
   Size Y: **500**

   The **Configure** option available in the **Options** menu of the Menu in editor view is used to edit the settings of the respective viewport. It applies to all viewports. The options in the **Back** area are used to place the reference image at the desired location as the viewport background. The **Image** text box displays the location of the loaded file. Any image with a recognizable format can be loaded in CINEMA 4D.

   The **Offset X** option is used to move the reference image horizontally.

   The **Offset Y** option is used to move the reference image vertically.

   The **Size X** and **Size Y** options are used to scale the reference image.

Creating the Base of the Door Lock System

In this section, you will create the base of the door lock system using the **Rectangle** tool.

1. Press F1; the Perspective viewport is maximized. Alternatively, choose **Cameras > Perspective** from the Menu in editor view, refer to Figure 2-2. Choose **Create > Spline** from the main menu; a cascading menu is displayed. Next, choose **Rectangle** from it, as shown in Figure 2-5; a rectangle is created in the Perspective viewport. Also, *Rectangle* is added to the Object Manager.

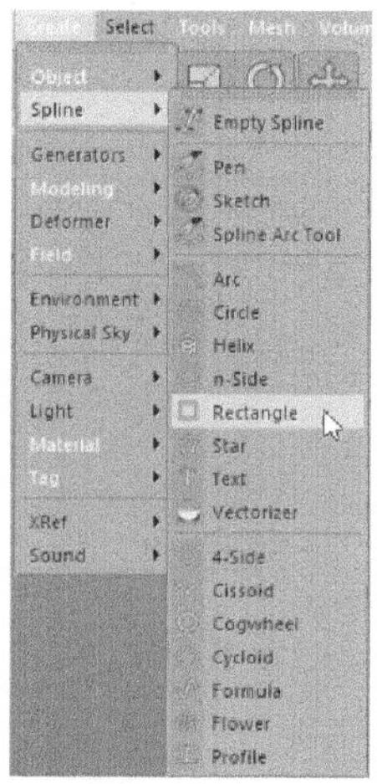

Figure 2-5 *Choosing* ***Rectangle*** *from the* ***Create*** *menu*

Note

The spline primitives are parametric in nature as their attributes such as height, radius, and so on can be altered in the Attribute Manager.

2. Make sure that *Rectangle* is selected in the Object Manager. In the Attribute Manager, make sure the **Object** button is chosen and then enter **121** and **465** in the **Width** and **Height** spinners, respectively, of the **Object Properties** area, refer to Figure 2-6.

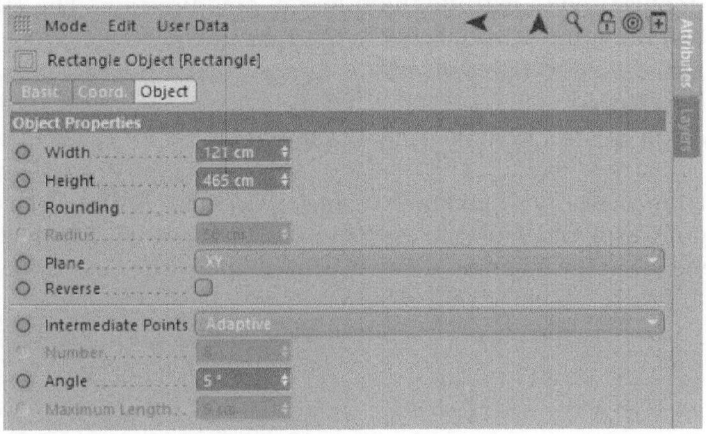

Figure 2-6 Setting the width and height of the rectangle

By default, the value of these parameters is set to 400. As a result, a square is displayed in the viewport.

Next, you will extrude the rectangle.

Note

*You can change the units of parametric objects. To do so, choose **Mode > Project** in the Attribute Manager; the **Project** area is displayed in the Attribute Manager. Make sure the **Project Settings** button is chosen in this area. In the **Project Settings** area, by default **Centimeters** is selected in the drop-down list located next to the **Project Scale** spinner. You can select any other unit from the drop-down list as per your requirement.*

3. Press and hold the left mouse button on the **Subdivision Surface** tool in the Command Palette; a flyout is displayed. Next, choose the **Extrude** tool from it, as shown in Figure 2-7; *Extrude* is added to the Object Manager, refer to Figure 2-8.

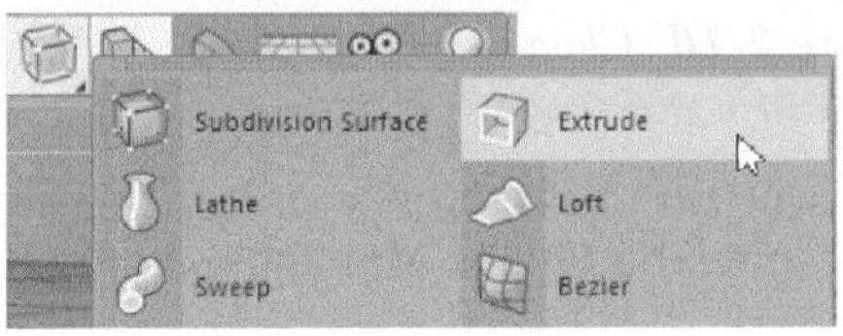

*Figure 2-7 Choosing **Extrude** from the flyout*

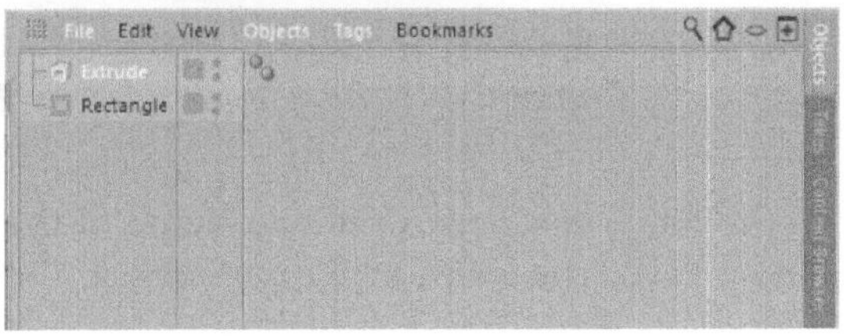

Figure 2-8 Extrude added to the Object Manager

4. Select *Rectangle* in the Object Manager. Press and hold the left mouse button on *Rectangle* and drag the cursor to *Extrude* in the Object Manager; *Rectangle* is connected to *Extrude* in the Object Manager. Also, *Rectangle* is extruded in the Perspective viewport, as shown in Figure 2-9.

On pressing and holding the left mouse button on **Subdivision Surface**, a flyout is displayed with various tools. You can use these tools to create complex models with relatively less number of control points. Models created using these tools can be converted into polygons. The **Extrude** tool is used to extrude the spline in any direction. The effect of this tool is only visible when the spline is connected to the Extrude object.

Creating the Keyhole

In this section, you will create a keyhole using the **Pen** tool.

1. Press F4; the Front viewport is maximized. Choose **Create > Spline** from the main menu; a cascading menu is displayed. Now, choose **Pen** from it, as shown in Figure 2-10. Alternatively, choose the **Pen** tool in the Command Palette; the shape of the cursor changes, as shown in Figure 2-11.

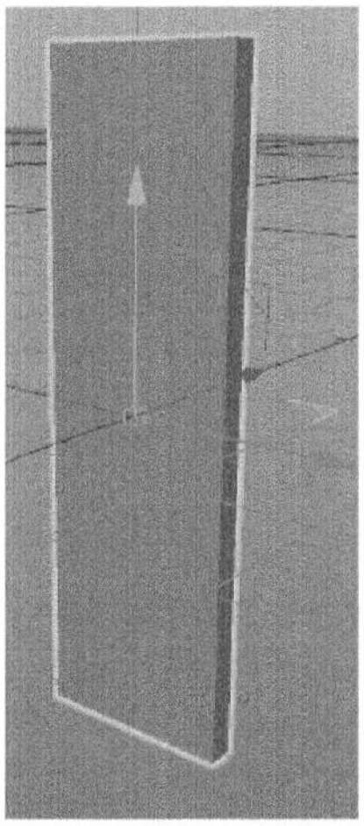

Figure 2-9 Rectangle extruded in the Perspective viewport

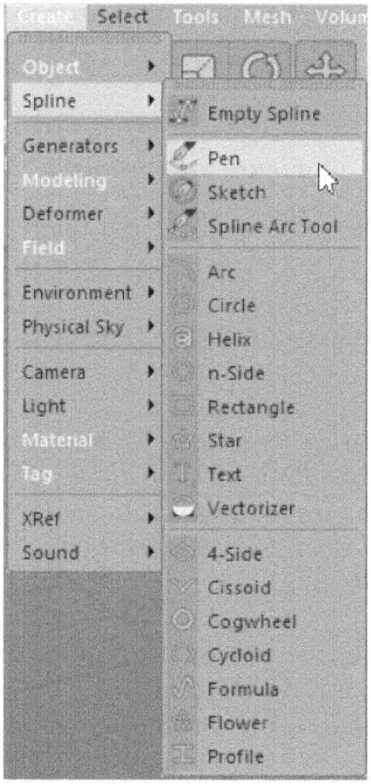

*Figure 2-10 Choosing **Pen** from the main menu*

2. In the Front viewport, draw the shape of the keyhole on the reference image, as shown in Figure 2-12. You will notice that *Spline* is also added to the Object Manager.

3. Invoke the **Move** tool from the Command Palette and select the points of *Spline*. Next, edit the shape of *Spline* to give it the shape of a keyhole, as shown in the reference image, refer to Figure 2-12. You can also use the **Pen** tool to move and edit points on the line.

4. Select the *Spline* in the Object Manager. In the Attribute Manager, make sure that the **Object** button is chosen. In the **Object Properties** area, make sure the **Close Spline** check box is selected. Next, choose the **Basic** button; the **Basic Properties** area is displayed. In this area,

enter **keyhole** in the **Name** text box; *Spline* is renamed as *keyhole* in the Object Manager, as shown in Figure 2-13.

Note

The spline also closes if you click on the first point of the spline.

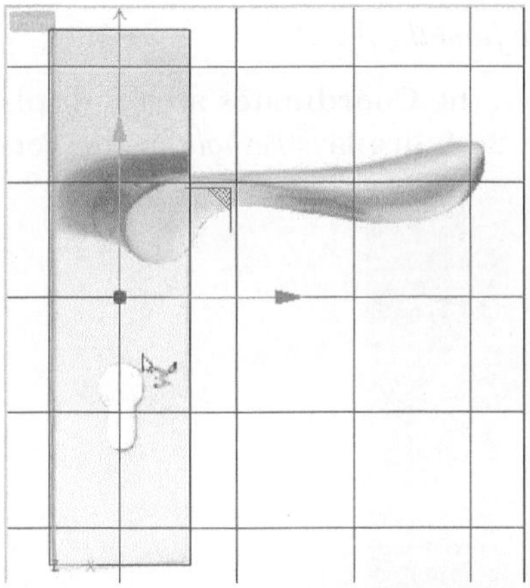

Figure 2-11 *The changed shape of the cursor*

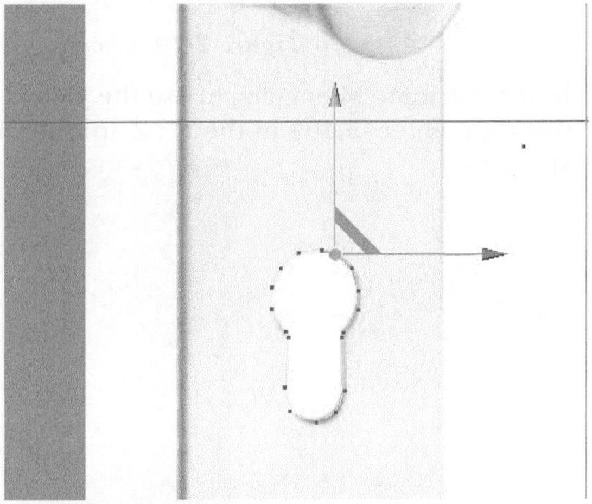

Figure 2-12 *Shape of the keyhole*

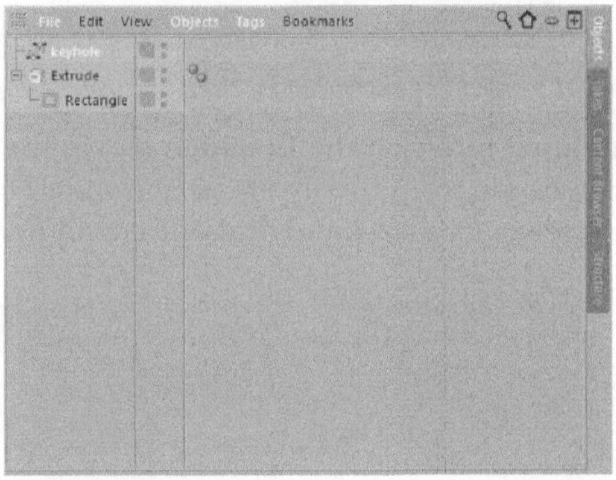

Figure 2-13 *Spline renamed as keyhole*

5. Press F1; the Perspective viewport is maximized. Press and hold the left mouse button on the **Subdivision Surface** tool in the Command Palette; a flyout is displayed. Next, choose **Extrude** from it, as shown in Figure 2-14; *Extrude.1* is added to the Object Manager. Next, drag *keyhole* on *Extrude.1* in the Object Manager; *keyhole* is connected to *Extrude.1*.

6. Select *Extrude.1* in the Object Manager. Next, choose the **Object** button in the Attribute Manager, if it is not already chosen; the **Object Properties** area is displayed. In this area, enter **40** in the Z spinner of the **Movement** parameter; the *keyhole* is extruded.

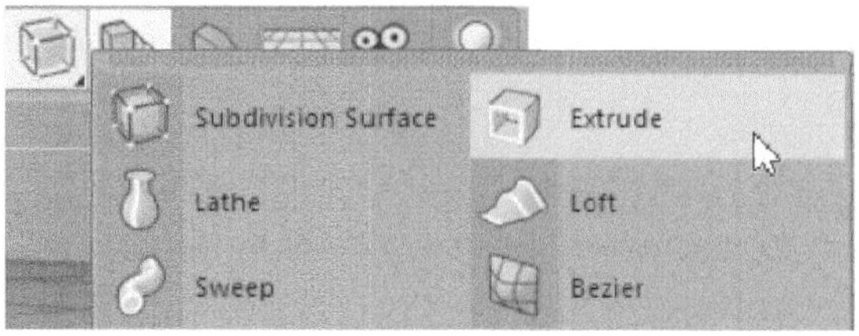

Figure 2-14 Choosing ***Extrude*** *from the flyout*

7. In the Attribute Manager, choose the **Coord** button; the **Coordinates** area is displayed. In this area, enter **-5.409** in the **P . Z** spinner. Figure 2-15 displays *keyhole* in the Perspective viewport.

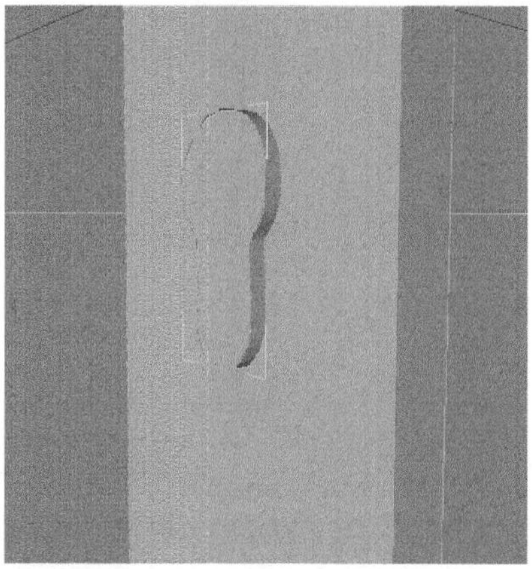

Figure 2-15 keyhole extruded in the Perspective viewport

8. Press and hold the left mouse button on the **Instance** tool in the Command Palette; a flyout is displayed. Next, choose **Boole** from the flyout, as shown in Figure 2-16; *Boole* is added to the Object Manager. Now, select *Extrude.1* and drag the cursor to *Boole*; *Extrude.1* is connected to *Boole*.

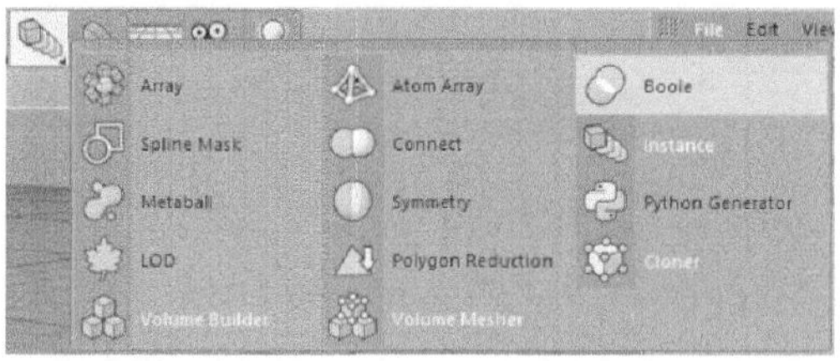

Figure 2-16 Choosing ***Boole*** *from the flyout*

9. In the Object Manager, select *Extrude* and press and hold the left mouse button; the shape of the cursor is changed. Next, drag *Extrude* to *Boole*; *Extrude* is connected to *Boole*, as shown in Figure 2-17. Also, *keyhole* is subtracted from *Extrude* and a hole is created in the Perspective viewport, as shown in Figure 2-18.

   The **Boole** tool is used to subtract two or more objects to create a hole in the object. Mostly, this tool is used to perform operations on splines and polygon primitives.

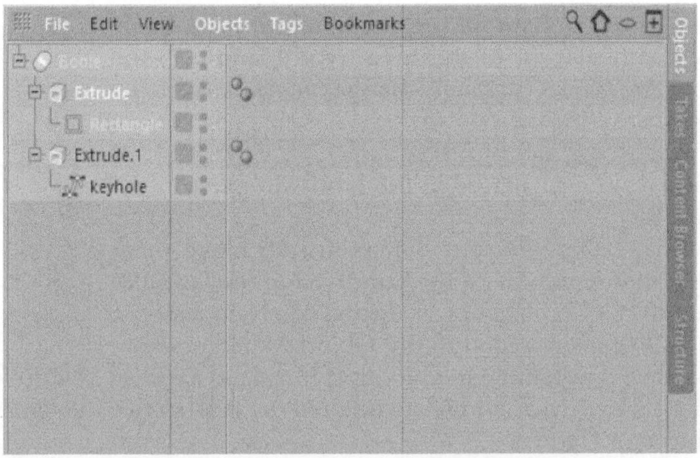

Figure 2-17 *Extrude connected to Boole*

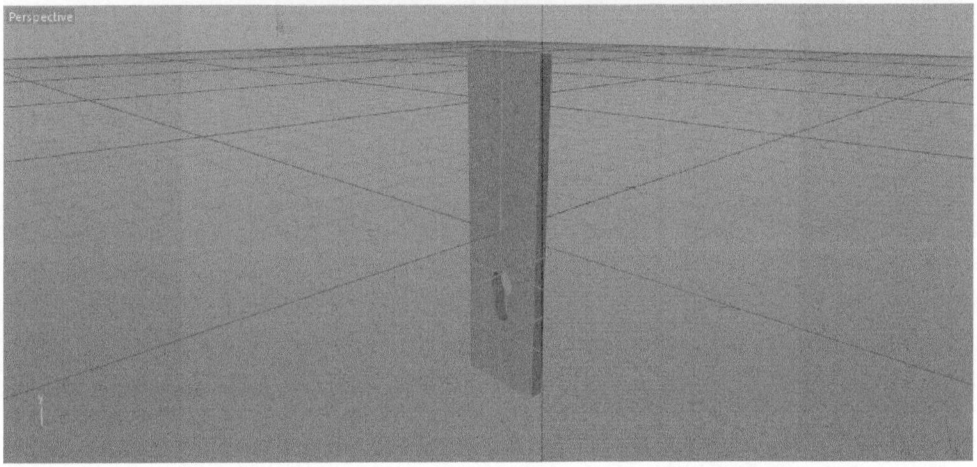

Figure 2-18 *The hole created in the Perspective viewport*

Creating the Handle

In this section, you will create the handle of the door using the **Pen** tool.

1. Press F4; the Front viewport is maximized. Choose **Create > Spline** from the main menu; a cascading menu is displayed. Choose **Pen** from it; the shape of the cursor is changed. Alternatively, choose the **Pen** tool from the Command Palette.

2. In the Front viewport, draw the shape of the door handle on the reference image, refer to Figure 2-19. You will notice that *Spline* is added to the Object Manager. Make sure that the **Close Spline** check box is selected in the **Object Properties** area in the Attribute Manager.

3. In the Attribute Manager, choose the **Basic** button; the **Basic Properties** area is displayed. In this area, type **Handle** in the **Name** text box; the name of *Spline* changes to *Handle* in the Object Manager.

   Figure 2-19 displays *Handle* placed in the Front viewport.

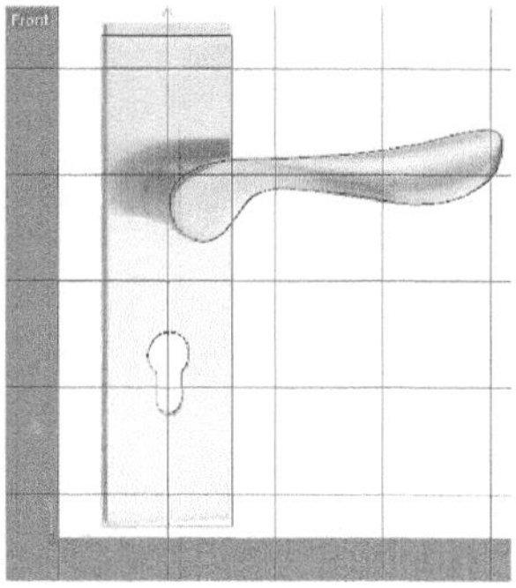

Figure 2-19 *Handle placed in the front viewport*

4. Press F1; the Perspective viewport is maximized. Next, press and hold the left mouse button on the **Subdivision Surface** tool in the Command Palette; a flyout is displayed. Next, choose **Extrude** from it; *Extrude* is added to the Object Manager. Now, select *Handle* in the Object Manager and drag *Handle* to *Extrude*; *Handle* is connected to *Extrude* and is extruded in the Perspective viewport, as shown in Figure 2-20.

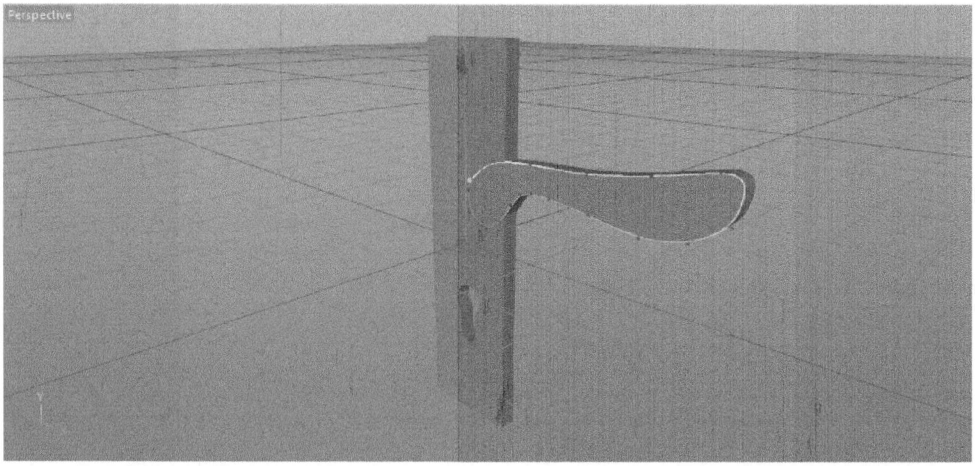

Figure 2-20 *Handle extruded in the Perspective viewport*

5. In the Attribute Manager, choose the **Coord** button; the **Coordinates** area is displayed. In this area, set the parameters as follows:

   P . X: **-30.7** P . Y: **18.1** P . Z: **-45**

   P . X, **P . Y**, and **P . Z** parameters are used to specify the position values of X, Y, and Z axes. The **S . X**, **S . Y**, and **S . Z** parameters are used to specify the scale values of X, Y, and Z axes. Similarly, the **R . X**, **R . Y**, and **R . Z** parameters are used to specify the rotational values of X, Y, and Z axes.

   Next, you will create the joint behind the handle and the base of the door.

6. Press F2; the Top viewport is maximized. Next, choose **Create > Spline** from the main menu; a cascading menu is displayed. Choose **Circle** from it, as shown in Figure 2-21; a circle is created in the Top viewport and *Circle* is added to the Object Manager.

7. Make sure that *Circle* is selected in the Object Manager. Next, in the Attribute Manager, choose the **Basic** button. In the **Basic Properties** area, type **Joint** in the **Name** text box; *Circle* is renamed as *Joint* in the Attribute Manager. Next, choose the **Coord** button; the **Coordinates** area is displayed. In this area, set the parameters as follows:

   P . Y: **81.591** R . P: **90**

8. Choose the **Object** button in the Attribute Manager; the **Object Properties** area is displayed. In this area, enter **20** in the **Radius** spinner.

9. Press F1; the Perspective viewport is maximized. Make sure that *Joint* is selected in the Object Manager. Now, create a copy of *Joint* by pressing both the CTRL key and the left mouse button. Now, drag the cursor and release the left mouse button; a copy of *Joint* is created in the Object Manager with the name *Joint.1*. You can also create a copy in the viewport by CTRL dragging.

10. Make sure that *Joint.1* is selected in the Object Manager. In the Attribute Manager, make sure that the **Coordinates** area is displayed and enter **-24.05** in the **P . Z** spinner. Figure 2-22 shows the position of *Joint* and *Joint.1* in the Perspective viewport.

Figure 2-21 *Choosing* ***Circle*** *from the main menu*

Next, you will create the surface of the joints.

11. Press and hold the left mouse button on the **Subdivision Surface** tool in the Command Palette; a flyout is displayed. Next, choose the **Loft** tool from it; *Loft* is added to the Object Manager.

12. Press F5; all viewports are displayed. Select *Joint* and *Joint.1* in the Object Manager by using the SHIFT key and then press and hold the left mouse button and drag the cursor on *Loft*; the *Joint* and *Joint.1* are connected to the *Loft* in the Object Manager. Also, a surface is created. Figure 2-23 displays the surface in all viewports.

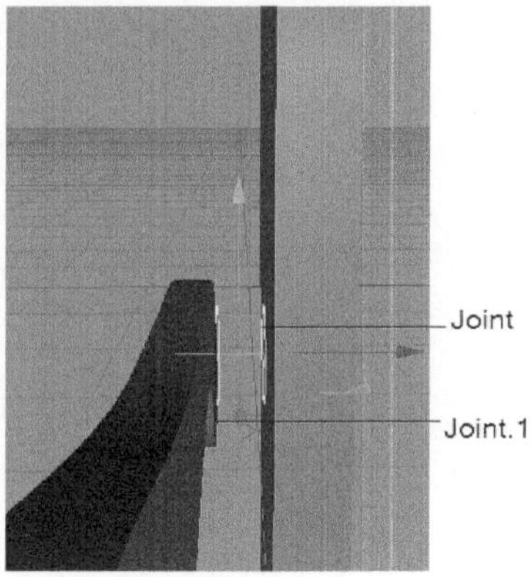

Figure 2-22 *The position of Joint and Joint.1 displayed in the Perspective viewport*

Next, you will group the surfaces together.

13. In the Object Manager, select *Boole*, *Extrude*, and *Loft* by using the CTRL key. Next, choose **Group Objects** from the **Objects** menu in the Object Manager, refer to Figure 2-24; all selected objects are grouped and *Null* is added to the Object Manager. Rename *Null* as **Door Lock** by double-clicking its label in the Object Manager.

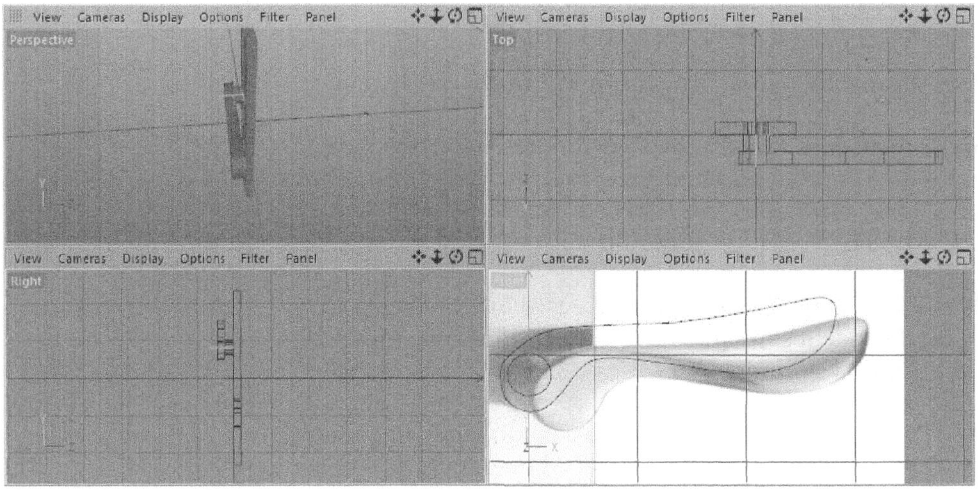

Figure 2-23 Joint and Joint.1 lofted to create a surface

Changing the Background Color of the Scene

In this section, you will change the background color of the scene.

1. Choose **Create > Environment** from the main menu; a cascading menu is displayed. Choose the **Background** option from it, as shown in Figure 2-25; *Background* is added to the Object Manager.

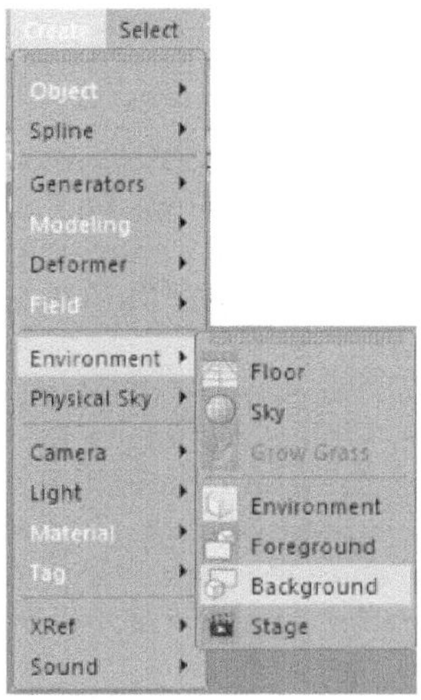

***Figure 2-24** Choosing **Group Objects** from the **Objects** menu*

***Figure 2-25** Choosing the **Background** option from the main menu*

The **Background** option is used to change the background with the color or image which is only visible in the render view.

Next, you will change the background color to white.

2. Make sure *Background* is selected in the Object Manager, as shown in Figure 2-26. In the Attribute Manager, choose the **Basic** button; the **Basic Properties** area is displayed. In this area, select **On** from the **Use Color** drop-down list. On doing so, the **Display Color** parameter is activated, as shown in Figure 2-27. By default, the white color is selected in this spinner. As a result, the background color changes to white.

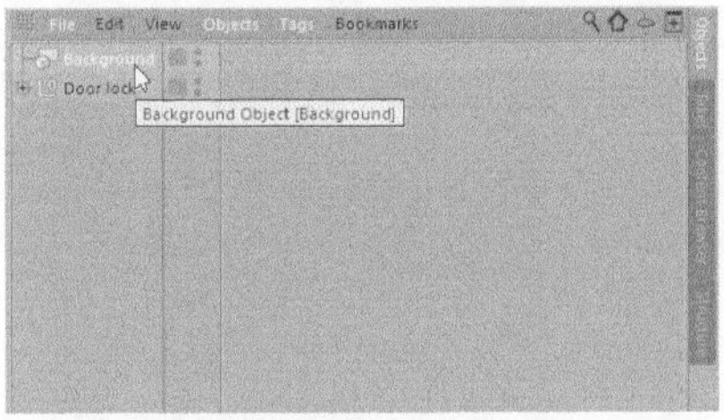

Figure 2-26 The ***Background*** *Object selected in the Object Manager*

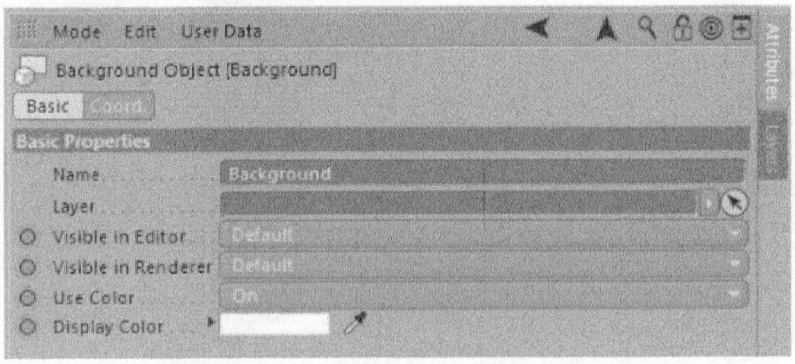

Figure 2-27 The ***Display Color*** *parameter activated*

The options in the **Use Color** drop-down list are used to determine whether the selected objects in the viewport use the color assigned to them or not. You need to select the **On** option from the **Use Color** drop-down list to ensure that the display color is used even if the materials are applied to it.

Saving and Rendering the Scene

In this section, you will save and render the scene. You can also view the final render of the scene by downloading the file *c02_cinema4d_r20_rndr.zip* from *www.cadcim.com*. The path of the file is mentioned at the beginning of the chapter.

1. Choose **File > Save** from the main menu; the **Save File** dialog box is displayed. In this dialog box, browse to the location *\Documents\c4dr20\c02*.

2. Enter **c02tut1** in the **File name** text box and then choose the **Save** button.

3. In the Perspective viewport, set the camera angle using the Viewport Navigation Tools located at the top right of the Perspective viewport. Next, choose the **Render to Picture Viewer** tool from the Command Palette. Alternatively, press SHIFT+R; the **Picture Viewer** window is displayed, as shown in Figure 2-28.

   The **Render to Picture Viewer** tool is used to render the scene in the **Picture Viewer** window. The **Picture Viewer** window is also known as the output window in CINEMA 4D. It is used to view the output of the scene as well as to save it.

   Next, you will save the rendered image.

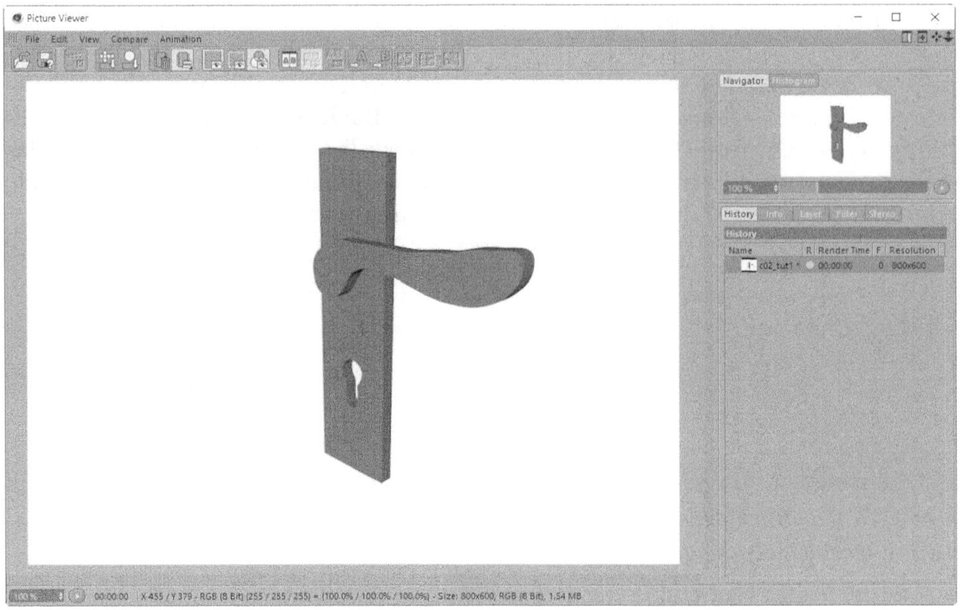

*Figure 2-28 The **Picture Viewer** window*

4. In the **Picture Viewer** window, choose **File > Save as**, as shown in Figure 2-29; the **Save** dialog box is displayed, as shown in Figure 2-30.

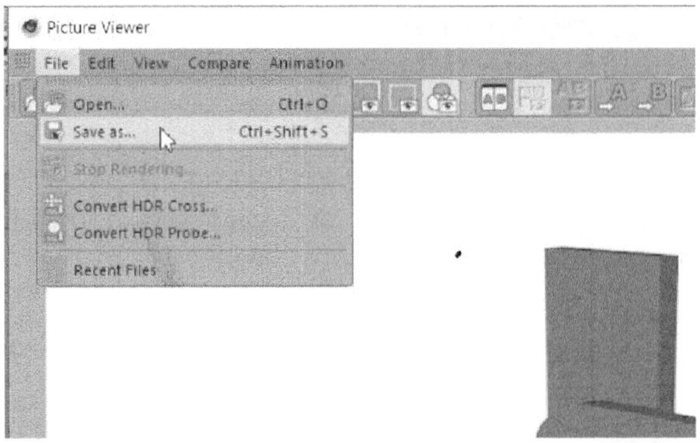

*Figure 2-29 Choosing the **Save as** option from the **File** menu*

The **Save as** option is used to save a scene or an image sequence in the format based on your requirement. The **Save** dialog box is displayed with specific parameters which helps you in saving the still image or image sequence in an uncompressed format.

5. In the **Save** dialog box, select **JPEG** from the **Format** drop-down list and then choose the **OK** button; the **Save Dialog** dialog box is displayed. Next, browse to *\Documents\c4dr20\c02*. In the **File Name** text box, type **c02_tut1_rndr**. Next, choose the **Save** button; the rendered image is saved at the desired location.

The output of the model is shown in Figure 2-1.

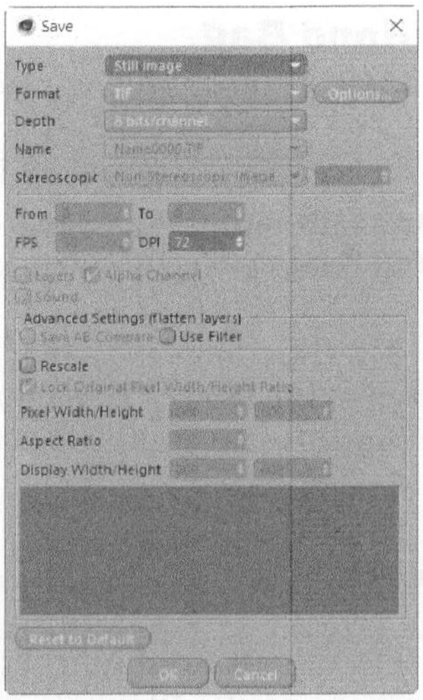

*Figure 2-30 The **Save** dialog box*

Tutorial 2

In this tutorial, you will create a hand bag with the help of splines and generators. The final output of the model is shown in Figure 2-31. **(Expected time: 25 min)**

***Figure 2-31** The model of a hand bag*

The following steps are required to complete this tutorial:

a. Create the shape of the hand bag.
b. Create the handles of the hand bag.
c. Create text on the hand bag.
d. Change the background color of the scene.
e. Save and render the scene.

Creating the Shape of the Hand Bag

In this section, you will create the shape of the hand bag using the **Spline** tool.

1. Choose **File > New** from the menu bar; a new scene is started. Next, choose **Create > Spline** from the main menu; a cascading menu is displayed. Choose **Rectangle** from the menu; a rectangle is created in the Perspective viewport and *Rectangle* is added to the Object Manager.

2. Make sure that *Rectangle* is selected in the Object Manager. In the Attribute Manager, choose the **Object** button; the **Object Properties** area is displayed. In this area, set the values of the parameters as follows:

   Width: **980** Height: **340**

3. In the **Object Properties** area, select the **Rounding** check box and enter **55** in the **Radius** spinner. Next, select the **XZ** option from the **Plane** drop-down list.

4. In the Attribute Manager, choose the **Coord** button; the **Coordinates** area is displayed. In this area, set the parameters as follows:

   P . X: **1.6** P . Z: **-4**

   After entering the values, *Rectangle* is placed in the Perspective viewport, as shown in Figure 2-32.

5. Make sure that *Rectangle* is selected in the Object Manager. Press and hold the left mouse button and the CTRL key and then drag and drop the cursor in the empty space above it; the copy of *Rectangle* is created in the Perspective viewport and added to the Object Manager with the name *Rectangle.1*, as shown in Figure 2-33.

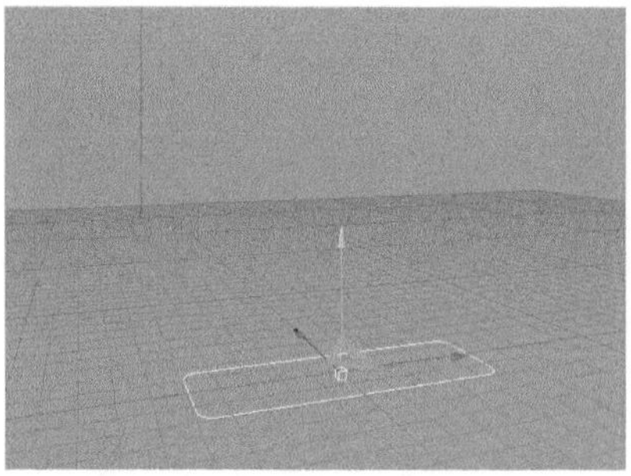

***Figure 2-32** Rectangle placed in the Perspective viewport*

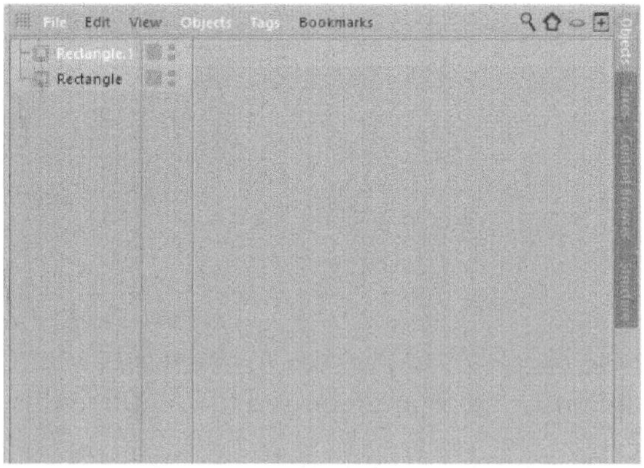

***Figure 2-33** Rectangle.1 added to the Object Manager*

6. Make sure that *Rectangle.1* is selected in the Object Manager. In the Attribute Manager, make sure that the **Object** button is chosen. In the **Object Properties** area, set the parameters as follows:

   Width: **730** Height: **129**

7. In the Attribute Manager, choose the **Coord** button; the **Coordinates** area is displayed. In this area, enter **286.8** in the **P . Y** spinner.

   After entering the values, *Rectangle.1* is placed in the Perspective viewport, as shown in Figure 2-34.

8. Make sure that *Rectangle.1* is selected in the Object Manager. Press and hold the left mouse button and the CTRL key and then drag and drop the cursor in the empty space; a copy of the *Rectangle.1* is created and added to the Object Manager with the name *Rectangle.2*, as shown in Figure 2-35.

9. Make sure that *Rectangle.2* is selected in the Object Manager. In the Attribute Manager, make sure that the **Object** button is chosen. In the **Object Properties** area, set the parameters as follows:

   Width: **815** Height: **165**

   Make sure that the **Rounding** check box is selected and enter **82.5** in the **Radius** spinner.

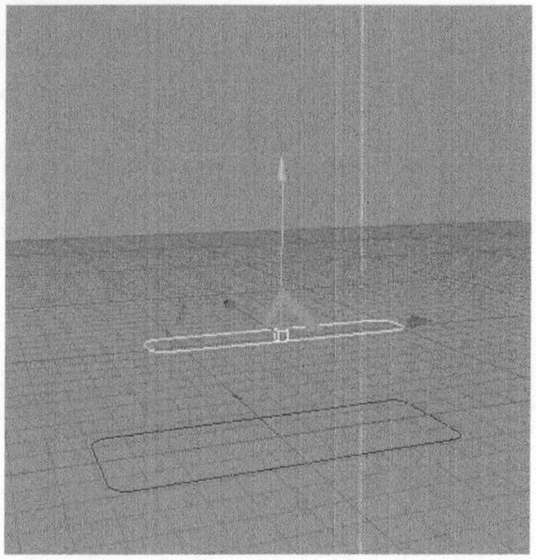

Figure 2-34 *Rectangle.1 placed in the Perspective viewport*

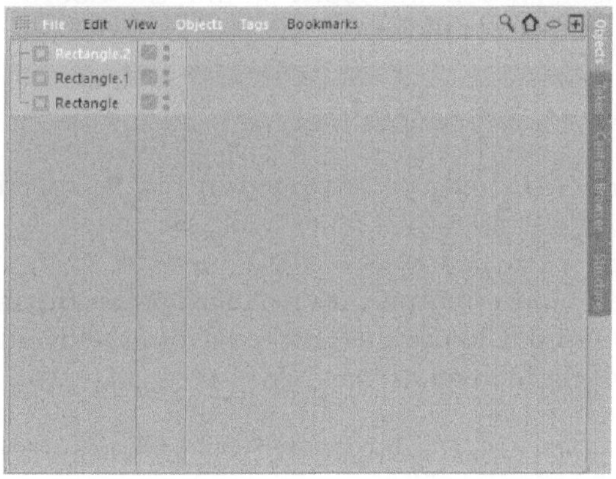

Figure 2-35 *Rectangle.2 added to the Object Manager*

10. In the Attribute Manager, choose the **Coord** button; the **Coordinates** area is displayed. In this area, enter **-3.66** in the **P . Y** spinner. After entering the values, *Rectangle.2* is placed in the Perspective viewport, as shown in Figure 2-36.

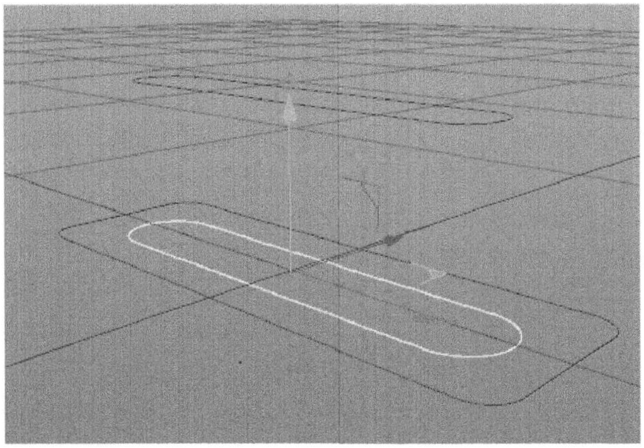

Figure 2-36 *Rectangle.2 placed in the Perspective viewport*

11. Make sure that *Rectangle.2* is selected in the Object Manager. Next, press and hold the left mouse button and the CTRL key and then drag and drop the cursor in the empty space; a copy of *Rectangle.2* is created and added to the Object Manager with the name *Rectangle.3*, as shown in Figure 2-37.

12. Make sure that *Rectangle.3* is selected in the Object Manager. In the Attribute Manager, make sure that the **Object** button is chosen. In the **Object Properties** area, set the parameters as follows:

    Width: **527** Height: **55**

    Clear the **Rounding** check box.

13. In the Attribute Manager, choose the **Coord** button; the **Coordinates** area is displayed. In this area, set the parameters as follows:

    P . X: **-1.9** P . Y: **647.4**

    After entering the values, *Rectangle.3* is placed in the Perspective viewport, as shown in Figure 2-38.

14. Press and hold the left mouse button on the **Subdivision Surface** tool in the Command Palette; a flyout is displayed. Choose the **Loft** tool from the flyout, as shown in Figure 2-39; *Loft* is added to the Object Manager.

15. In the Object Manager, select *Rectangle*.2. Next, drag and drop *Rectangle.2* on *Loft*; *Rectangle.2* is connected to *Loft*, as shown in Figure 2-40. Also, *Rectangle*.2 is lofted with a surface in the Perspective viewport.

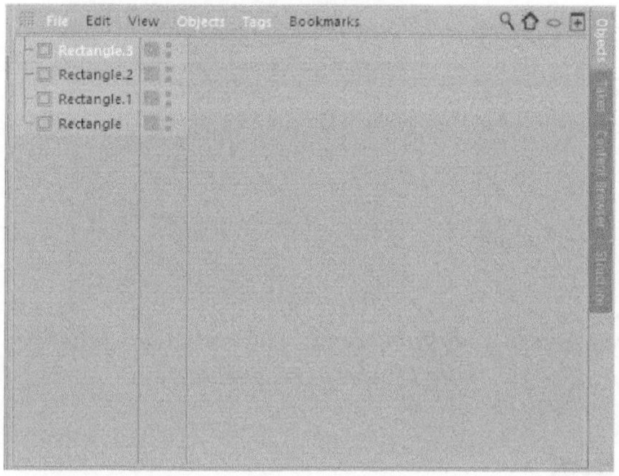

***Figure 2-37** Rectangle.3 added to the Object Manager*

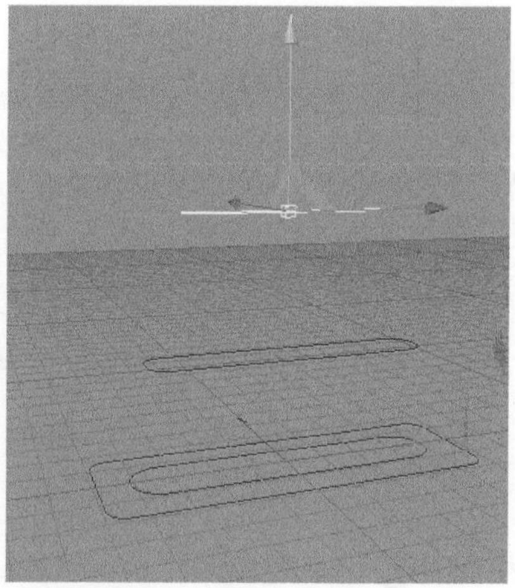

***Figure 2-38** Rectangle.3 placed in the Perspective viewport*

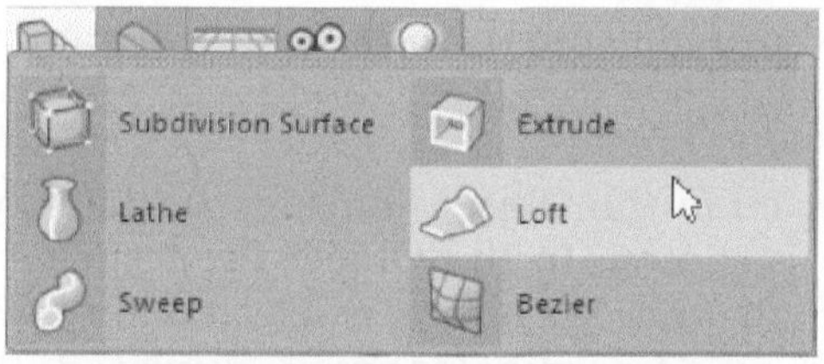

***Figure 2-39** Choosing **Loft** from the flyout*

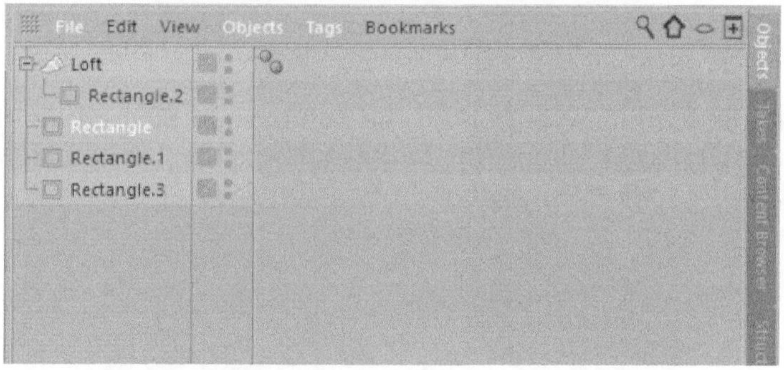

***Figure 2-40** Rectangle.2 connected to Loft in the Object Manager*

16. Connect *Rectangle.1*, *Rectangle.3*, and *Rectangle* to *Loft* in the Object Manager in the order as shown in Figure 2-41; a lofted surface resembling the shape of a hand bag is created in the Perspective viewport, as shown in Figure 2-42.

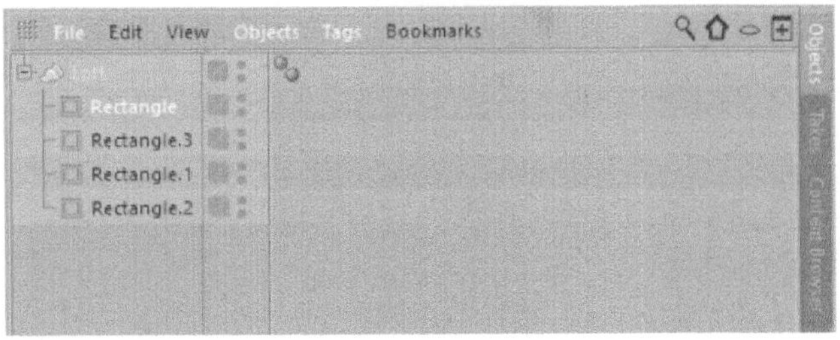

Figure 2-41 Rectangle, Rectangle.1, and Rectangle.3 connected to Loft

Figure 2-42 All rectangles lofted in the Perspective viewport

Creating the Handles of the Hand Bag

In this section, you will create the handles of the bag using the **Lathe** tool.

1. Choose **Create > Spline** from the main menu; a cascading menu is displayed. Choose **Circle** from it; a circle is created in the Perspective viewport and *Circle* is added to the Object Manager.

2. Make sure *Circle* is selected in the Object Manager. In the Attribute Manager, make sure that the **Object** button is chosen. In the **Object Properties** area, enter **8** in the **Radius** spinner. Also, make sure that the **XY** option is selected in the **Plane** drop-down list. Next, choose the **Coord** button; the **Coordinates** area is displayed. In the **Coordinates** area, set the parameters as follows:

   P . X: **242.63** P . Y: **293.5** P . Z: **-110.8**

3. Press and hold the left mouse button on the **Subdivision Surface** tool in the Command Palette; a flyout is displayed. Choose the **Lathe** tool from the flyout, as shown in Figure 2-43; *Lathe* is added to the Object Manager, refer to Figure 2-44.

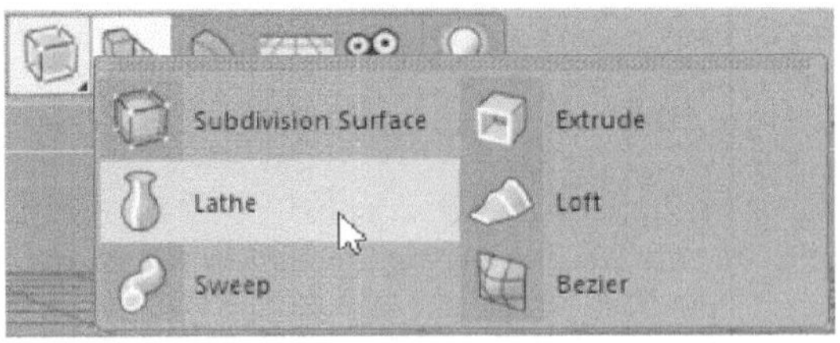

Figure 2-43 Choosing ***Lathe*** *from the flyout*

4. In the Object Manager, drag *Circle* and drop it on *Lathe*; *Circle* is connected to *Lathe*, as shown in Figure 2-44.

   The **Lathe** tool is used to rotate the profile curve on the Y-axis of the local axis system of the shape. It is used to generate a revolved surface.

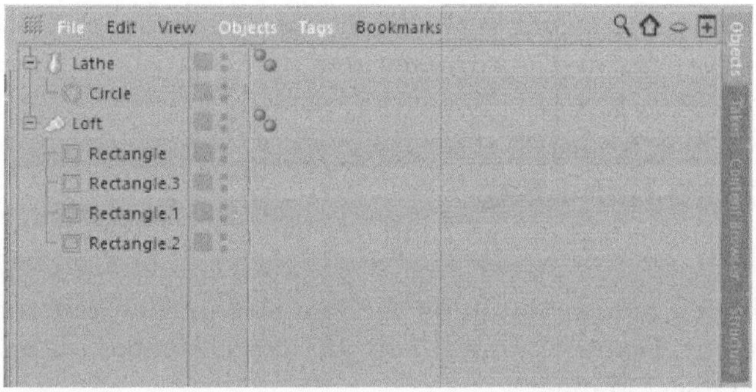

Figure 2-44 *Circle connected to Lathe in the Object Manager*

5. Select *Lathe* in the Object Manager. In the Attribute Manager, choose the **Object** button; the **Object Properties** area is displayed. In this area, enter **75** in the **Subdivision** spinner and **227** in the **Angle** spinner.

6. Choose the **Coord** button; the **Coordinates** area is displayed. In this area, set the parameters as follows:

P . X: **5.715**	P . Y: **634.142**	P . Z: **291.176**
S . X: **0.87**	S . Z: **1.62**	R . H: **90**
R . P: **90**	R . B: **-90**	

Figure 2-45 displays the hand bag with its handle. Next, you will create a copy of the handle.

7. Select *Lathe* in the Object Manager. Press and hold the left mouse button along with the CTRL key; the shape of the cursor is changed, as shown in Figure 2-46. Next, drag *Lathe* in the empty space above it and then release the left mouse button; a copy of *Lathe* is added with the name *Lathe.1* to the Object Manager.

Figure 2-45 *The handle of the hand bag created*

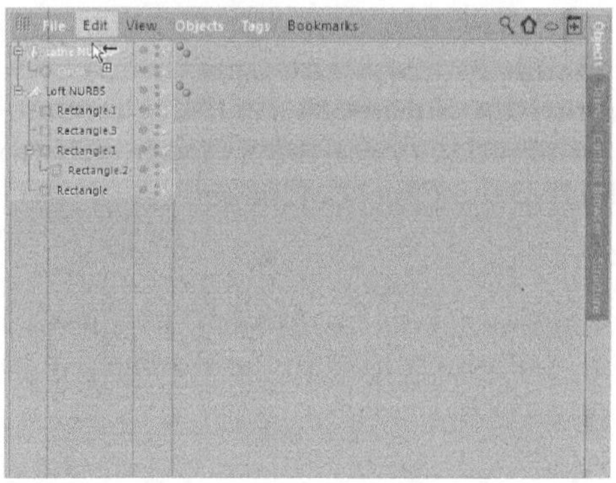

Figure 2-46 *The changed shape of the cursor in the Object Manager*

8. Make sure that *Lathe.1* is selected in the Object Manager and the **Coord** button is chosen in the Object Manager. In the **Coordinates** area of the Attribute Manager, enter **282.25** in the **P . Z** spinner.

Creating Text on the Hand Bag

In this section, you will create text on the hand bag using the **Extrude** tool.

1. Press and hold the left mouse button on the **Pen** tool in the Command Palette; a flyout is displayed. Choose the **Text** tool from the flyout; *Text* is created in the Perspective viewport and added to the Object Manager.

2. Make sure that *Text* is selected in the Object Manager. In the Attribute Manager, choose the **Object** button. In the **Object Properties** area, set the parameters as follows:

   Text: **S&S** Height: **274** Horizontal Spacing: **5**
   Vertical Spacing: **11**

   The **Text** edit box in the **Object Properties** area is used to write the text in the viewport. You can also type multiple lines. The **Height** parameter is used to determine the height of the text displayed in the viewport. The **Horizontal Spacing** parameter is used to determine the horizontal spaces or gaps between the characters. The **Vertical Spacing** parameter is used to determine the vertical spaces or gaps between the characters.

3. In the Attribute Manager, choose the **Coord** button; the **Coordinates** area is displayed. In this area, set the parameters as given next:

   P . X: **-249.402** P . Y: **354.604**
   P . Z: **-109.475** R . P: **-12**

   The text is placed in the Perspective viewport, as shown in Figure 2-47. Next, you will extrude the text.

***Figure 2-47** The text placed in the Perspective viewport*

4. Press and hold the left mouse button on the **Subdivision Surface** tool in the Command Palette; a flyout is displayed. Choose the **Extrude** tool from it; *Extrude* is added to the Object Manager.

5. In the Object Manager, drag *Text* and drop it on *Extrude*; *Text* is connected to *Extrude*, as shown in Figure 2-48. Also, *Text* is extruded in the Perspective viewport, refer to Figure 2-49.

Changing the Background Color of the Scene

To change the background color of the scene to white in the final output, follow the steps given in Tutorial 1 of Chapter 2.

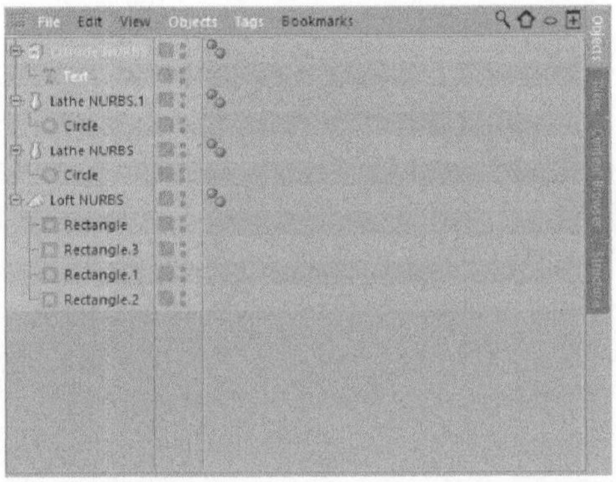

Figure 2-48 *Text connected to Extrude in the Object Manager*

Figure 2-49 *The extruded text on the hand bag*

Saving and Rendering the Scene

In this section, you will save and render the scene. You can also view the final render of the scene by downloading the file *c02_cinema4d_r20_rndr.zip* from *www.cadcim.com*. The path of the file is mentioned at the beginning of the chapter.

1. Choose **File > Save** from the main menu; the **Save File** dialog box is displayed. In this dialog box, browse to the location *\Documents\c4dr20\c02*.

2. Enter **c02tut2** in the **File name** text box and then choose the **Save** button.

3. In the Perspective viewport, set the camera angle using the Viewport Navigation Tools located on the extreme top right of the Perspective viewport. Next, you need to render the scene. For rendering, refer to Tutorial 1.

   Figure 2-31 displays the final output.

Tutorial 3

In this tutorial, you will create a cigar pipe with the help of splines and the **Loft** generator. The final output of the model is shown in Figure 2-50. **(Expected time: 25 min)**

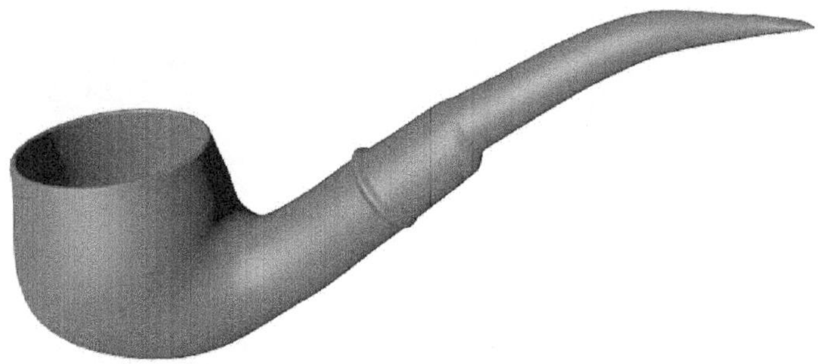

Figure 2-50 *The model of the cigar pipe*

The following steps are required to complete this tutorial:

a. Set the viewport background.
b. Define the shape of the pipe.
c. Create geometry of the pipe.
d. Change the background color of the scene.
e. Save and render the scene.

Setting the Viewport Background

In this section, you will set a background image in the Front viewport.

1. Choose **File > New** from the main menu, a new scene is displayed. Press F4; the Front viewport is maximized.

2. In the Front viewport, choose **Options > Configure** from the Menu in editor view; the **Viewport [Front]** settings are displayed in the Attribute Manager. In the Attribute Manager, choose the **Back** button, if it is not already chosen; the **Back** area is displayed. In this area, choose the browse button next to the **Image** text box; the **Open File** dialog box is displayed. Browse to *\Documents\c4dr20\c02\pipe.jpg*. Next, choose the **Open** button; the *pipe.jpg* is placed as the background image in the Front viewport.

3. Enter **75** in the **Transparency** spinner.

Defining the Shape of the Pipe

In this section, you will define the shape of the pipe using the **Circle** spline.

1. Choose **Create > Spline > Circle** from the main menu bar; *Circle* is displayed in the Front viewport.

2. Make sure *Circle* is selected in the Object Manager and the **Object** button is chosen in the Attribute Manager. In the **Object Properties** area of the Attribute Manager, select **XZ** from the **Plane** drop-down list.

3. In the Attribute Manager, select the **Ellipse** check box and then enter **7** and **27.846** in the **Radius** and **Radius Y** spinners, respectively.

4. Choose the **Coord** button and then specify the values for the following parameters:

   P . X: **375.332** P . Y: **168.154** R . B: **89.613**

   After entering the values *Circle* is placed at the end of the pipe, as shown in Figure 2-51.

5. Double click on *Circle* in the Object Manager and rename the object as *Ellipse*.

6. In the Object Manager, create a copy of *Ellipse* using CTRL; a duplicate copy of *Ellipse* is created with the name *Ellipse.1*.

7. Make sure *Ellipse.1* is selected in the Object Manger. In the Attribute Manager, choose the **Object** button and then enter **8** and **24.818** in the **Radius** and **Radius Y** spinners, respectively.

8. In the Attribute Manager, choose the **Coord** button and then specify the following values for the following parameters:

   P . X: **344.115** P . Y: **167.142** R . B: **89.613**

   After entering the values *Ellipse.1* is next to the *Ellipse*, as shown in Figure 2-52.

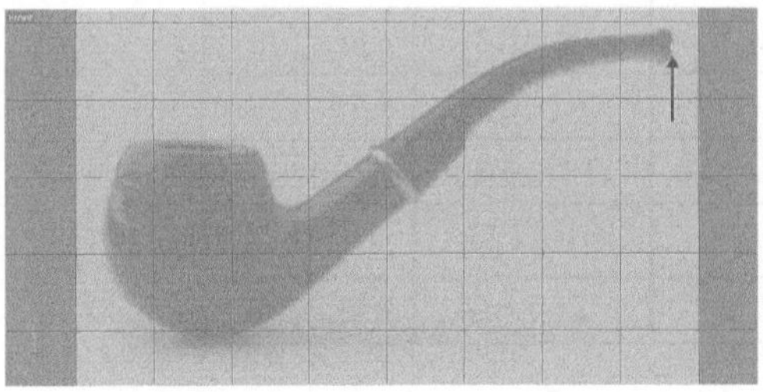

Figure 2-51 *Ellipse displayed in the Front viewport*

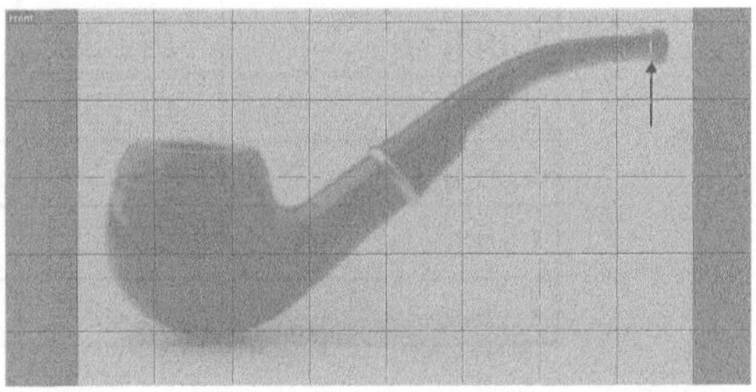

Figure 2-52 *Ellipse.1 displayed in the Front viewport*

9. Create a **Circle** spline as done in steps 1 through 2. In the Attribute Manager, make sure the **Object** button is chosen and then enter **18.477** in the **Radius** spinner. Choose the **Coord** button and then specify the values for the following parameters:

   P . X: **313.585** P . Y: **165.525** R . B: **89.613**

   After entering the values, *Circle* is displayed in the Front viewport, as shown in Figure 2-53.

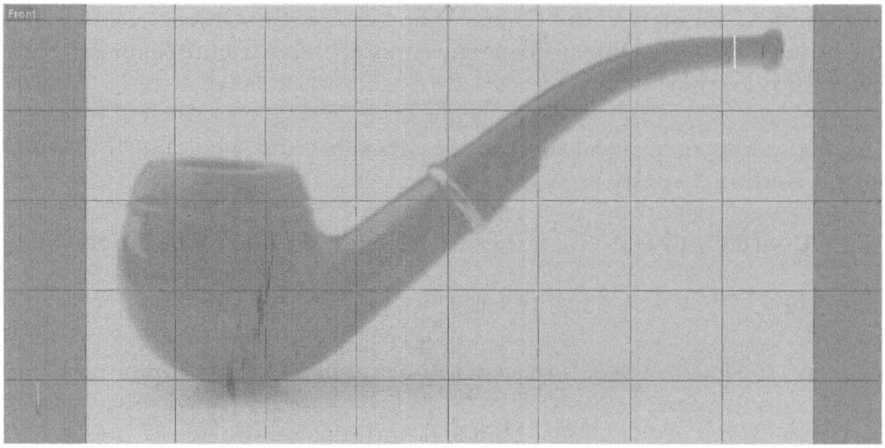

Figure 2-53 Circle displayed in the Front viewport

10. Create more copies of *Circle* and then use the values given in Table 2-1 to create the profile of the pipe:

Table 2-1 Values used for creating the profile of the pipe

Spline	Radius	P . X	P . Y	R . B
Circle.1	20.934	220.543	152.49	70.072
Circle.2	28.328	87.649	73.091	55.525
Circle.3	32.124	83.145	66.897	55.525
Circle.4	36.397	78.077	59.577	55.525
Circle.5	41.459	17.261	8.334	50.255
Circle.6	46.102	9.377	3.829	50.255
Circle.7	42.322	4.309	-2.365	50.255
Circle.8	49.721	-95.667	-82.505	57.328
Circle.9	86.573	-179.395	-115.462	111.91
Circle.10	117.524	-254.216	-66.472	149.363
Circle.11	90.684	-253.325	41.306	180.75

After entering the values the profile of the pipe is completed, as shown in Figure 2-54.

Creating Geometry of the Pipe

In this section, you will create the shape of the pipe using the **Loft** generator.

1. Choose **Create > Generators > Loft** from the menu bar; *Loft* is displayed in the Object Manager.

2. Select *Ellipse* in the Object Manager and then press and hold down SHIFT. Next, click on *Circle.11* to select all splines and then release SHIFT.

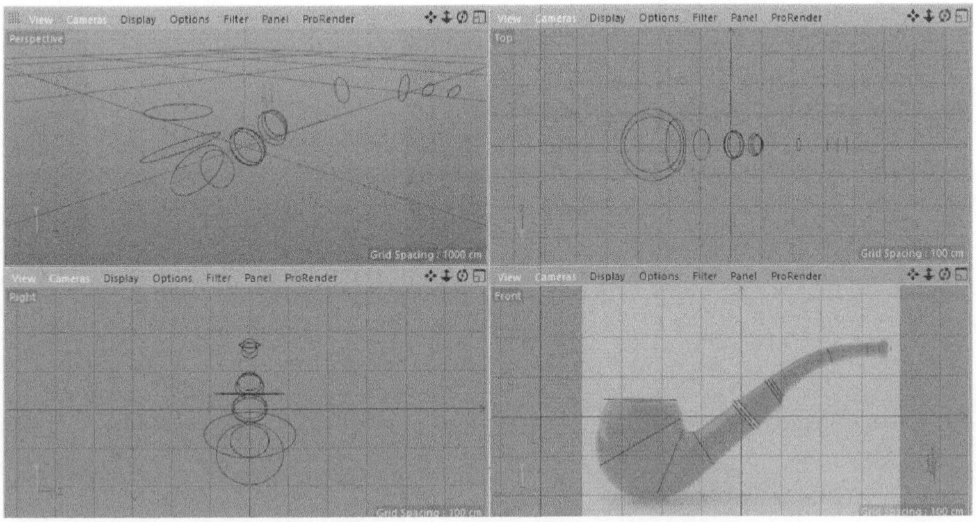

Figure 2-54 The profile of the pipe displayed

3. Press and hold the left mouse button and then drag the splines to *Loft*; all splines are connected to *Loft*, refer to Figure 2-55. Also, shape of the pipe is displayed in the scene, as shown in Figure 2-56.

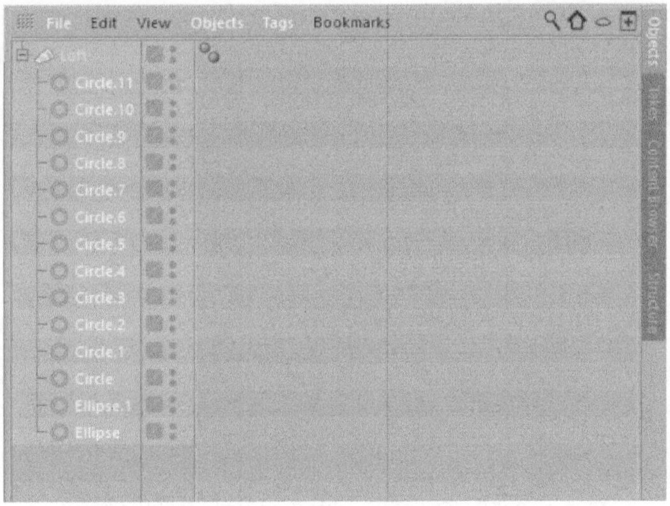

Figure 2-55 The splines connected with Loft

4. Press F1 to activate the Perspective viewport.

5. Make sure *Loft* is selected in the Object Manager and then choose the **Caps** button in the Attribute Manager; the **Caps and Rounding** area is displayed.

6. In this area, select **Fillet** from the **Start** and **End** drop-down lists. Next, select the **Constrain** check box. Select **Half Circle** from the **Fillet Type** drop-down list.

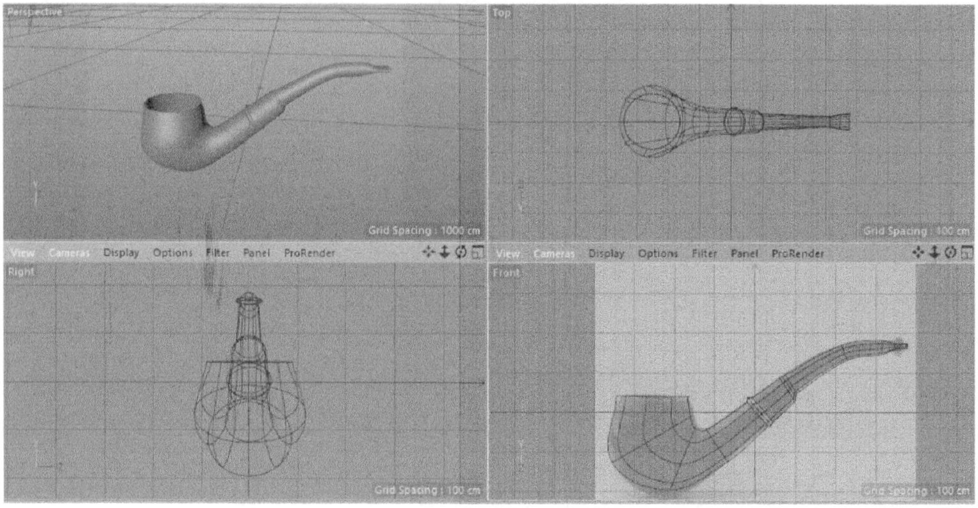

***Figure 2-56** The shape of the pipe displayed*

7. Enter **10** and **1** in the **Steps** and **Radius** spinners, respectively, corresponding to the **Start** drop-down list. Similarly, enter **10** and **6** in the **Steps** and **Radius** spinners, respectively, corresponding to the **End** drop-down list. After entering the values, the cigar pipe is displayed with the fillet caps, as shown in Figure 2-57.

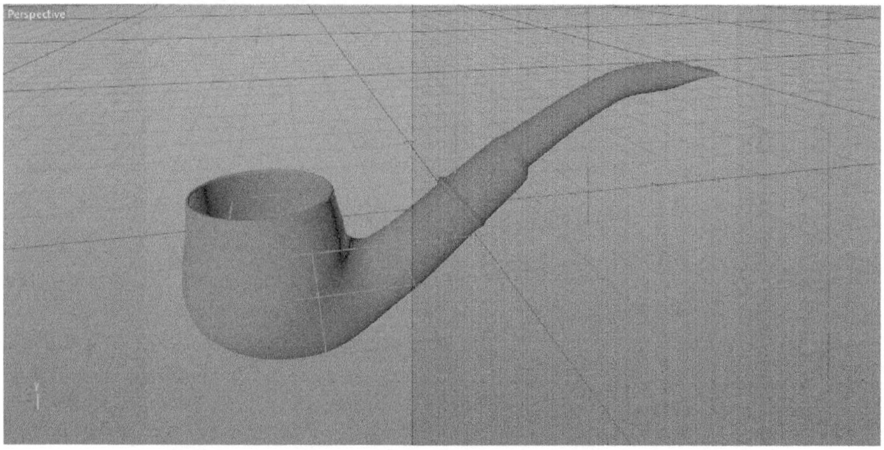

***Figure 2-57** The pipe with the fillet caps displayed*

Next, you will modify the end part of the pipe to maintain the flow of the geometry.

8. Select *Circle* in the Object Manager and then make sure the **Object** button is chosen in the Attribute Manager. Set the value **9.652** for the **Radius** parameter.

9. Select *Ellipse* in the Object Manager and make sure the **Object** button is chosen in the Attribute Manager. Next, set the values **1.757** and **12.231** for the **Radius** and **Radius Y** spinners, respectively. Similarly, set the values **4.178** and **12.962** for the **Radius** and **Radius Y** spinners, respectively, for *Ellipse.1*. After entering the values, the modified shape of the pipe is displayed, refer Figure 2-50.

Changing the Background Color of the Scene

To change the background color of the scene to white in the final output, follow the steps given in Tutorial 1.

Saving and Rendering the Scene

In this section, you will save and render the scene. You can also view the final render of the scene by downloading the file *c02_cinema4d_r20_rndr.zip* from *www.cadcim.com*. The path of the file is mentioned at the beginning of the chapter.

1. Choose **File > Save** from the main menu; the **Save File** dialog box is displayed. In this dialog box, browse to the location *\Documents\c4dr20\c02*.

2. Enter **c02tut3** in the **File name** text box and then choose the **Save** button.

3. In the Perspective viewport, set the camera angle using the Viewport Navigation Tools located on the extreme top right of the Perspective viewport. Next, you need to render the scene. For rendering, refer to Tutorial 1.

   Figure 2-50 displays the final output.

Self-Evaluation Test

Answer the following questions and then compare them to those given at the end of this chapter:

1. Which of the following tools is used to create complex models using relatively less number of control points?

   (a) **Pen** (b) **Subdivision Surface**
   (c) **Move** (d) None of these

2. Which of the following tools is used to extrude a spline object or a curve?

   (a) **Pen** (b) **Loft**
   (c) **Extrude** (d) All of these

3. Which of the following combinations of shortcut keys is used to render a scene?

   (a) ALT+Q (b) CTRL+D
   (c) SHIFT+R (d) None of these

4. The __________ tool in the Command Palette is used to subtract two or more objects from an object to create a hole in that object.

5. The __________ option in the **Options** menu is used to edit the settings of the respective viewport.

6. The **Angle** parameter in the __________ area of the Attribute Manager is used to define the angle of rotation of the spline.

7. The Viewport Navigation Tools are located at the top right corner of the viewport. (T/F)

8. The three spinners corresponding to the **Movement** parameter are used to specify the extrusion taking place along the **X**, **Y**, or **Z** axis. (T/F)

9. The **Background** tool is used to change the foreground with the color or the image which is visible only in the render view. (T/F)

10. The **R . P** parameter in the Attribute Manager is used to determine the rotational values of the X axis. (T/F)

Review Questions

Answer the following questions:

1. Which of the following tools is used to revolve a profile curve about the Y axis of the local axis system of the spline shape?

   (a) **Lathe** (b) **Subdivision Surface**
   (c) **Pen** (d) None of these

2. Which of the following tools is used to create text in the viewport in CINEMA 4D?

   (a) **Lathe** (b) **Text**
   (c) **Pen** (d) **Render to Picture Viewer**

3. The __________ parameter of the **Background** object is used to select the background color of the scene for the rendering purpose.

4. By default, the height of a rectangle spline primitive is set to __________ .

5. The __________ dialog box consists of specific parameters which help you in saving a still image or image sequence in an uncompressed format.

6. CINEMA 4D consists of default predefined curves known as spline primitives. (T/F)

7. The **Render to Picture Viewer** tool is used to render a scene or model in a separate window. (T/F)

8. The **Picture Viewer** window is also known as the output window in CINEMA 4D. (T/F)

9. The default units of measurement in CINEMA 4D can be changed from the drop-down list located next to the **Project Scale** spinner in the **Project Settings** area. (T/F)

10. The ALT+G key combination is used to group objects in the Object Manager. (T/F)

EXERCISES

The rendered output of the model used in the following exercises can be accessed by downloading the *c02_cinema4d_r20_exr.zip* file from *www.cadcim.com*. The path of the file is as follows: *Textbooks > Animation and Visual Effects > MAXON CINEMA 4D > MAXON CINEMA 4D R20 Studio: A Tutorial Approach*

Exercise 1

Using various Generators and spline modeling tools, create the model of a chair, as shown in Figure 2-58. **(Expected time: 25 min)**

Exercise 2

Using various Generators and spline modeling tools, create the model of a table clock, as shown in Figure 2-59. **(Expected time: 45 min)**

Figure 2-58 *The model of a chair*

Figure 2-59 *The model of a table clock*

Answers to Self-Evaluation Test

1. b, **2.** c, **3.** c, **4. Boole**, **5. Configure**, **6. Object Properties**, **7.** T, **8.** T, **9.** F, **10.** F

Chapter 3

Introduction to Polygon Modeling

Learning Objectives

After completing this chapter, you will be able to:

- *Create polygon primitives*
- *Work with various polygon modeling tools*

INTRODUCTION

In the previous chapters, you learned to create 3D objects and shapes using the spline modeling techniques. In CINEMA 4D, you can modify the objects at an advanced level by converting them into editable polygons. The converted objects consist of sub-objects that can be modified using the **Move**, **Rotate**, and **Scale** tools. The sub-objects are points, edges, and polygons. In this chapter, you will learn to modify the objects at an advanced level by converting them into polygons.

TUTORIALS

Before you start the tutorials of this chapter, you need to download the *c03_cinema4d_r20_tut.zip* file from *www.cadcim.com*. The path of the file is as follows: *Textbooks > Animation and Visual Effects > MAXON CINEMA 4D > MAXON CINEMA 4D R20 Studio: A Tutorial Approach*

Next, you need to browse to *\Documents\c4dR20* and create a new folder in it with the name *c03*. Next, extract the contents of the zip file in this folder.

Tutorial 1

In this tutorial, you will create 3D model of a computer mouse, as shown in Figure 3-1, using the polygon modeling techniques. **(Expected time: 35 min)**

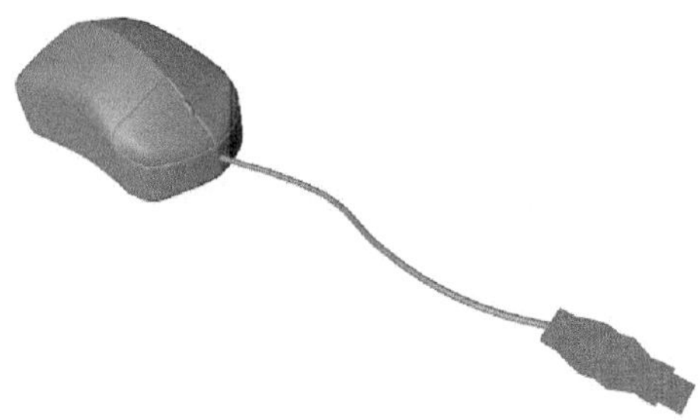

Figure 3-1 *The model of a computer mouse*

The following steps are required to complete this tutorial:

a. Create the body of the computer mouse.
b. Create the left-click and right-click buttons of the mouse.
c. Create the scroll wheel of the mouse.
d. Create the bottom of the mouse.
e. Create the USB cable of the mouse.
f. Change the background color of the scene.
g. Save and render the scene.

Creating the Body of the Computer Mouse

In this section, you will create the body of the computer mouse using the **Cube** tool.

1. Choose **Create > Object** from the main menu; a cascading menu is displayed. Next, choose **Cube** from it; a cube is created in the Perspective viewport, as shown in Figure 3-2, and *Cube* is added to the Object Manager.

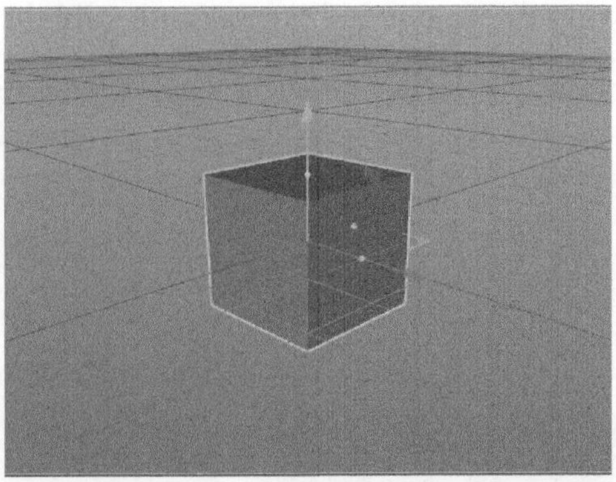

Figure 3-2 Cube created in the Perspective viewport

2. In the Attribute Manager, make sure the **Object** button is chosen. In the **Object Properties** area, set the parameters as follows:

   Size . X: **91** Size . Y: **37** Size . Z: **137**
   Segments X: **6** Segments Y: **4** Segments Z: **6**

   The **Size . X**, **Size . Y**, and **Size . Z** parameters in the **Object Properties** area are used to set width, height, and depth, respectively of the cube.

3. In the Attribute Manager, choose the **Basic** button; the **Basic Properties** area is displayed. In this area, enter **Computer mouse** in the **Name** text box; *Cube* is renamed as *Computer mouse* in the Object Manager.

4. Make sure *Computer mouse* is selected in the Object Manager and choose the **Make Editable** tool from the Modes Palette; *Computer mouse* is converted into a polygon object. 

Note

*After converting Computer mouse into a polygon object, you will notice that when you hover the cursor over it, the name of the Computer mouse changes to **Polygon Object [Computer mouse]** on hovering the cursor on it. Also, the icon of the Cube object changes into a triangle.*

5. Press F2; the Top viewport is maximized. Choose the **Points** tool from the Modes Palette; the *Computer mouse* is displayed in the points mode.

6. Invoke the **Live Selection** tool from the Command Palette. The shape of the cursor changes. To increase or decrease the size of the cursor, press the } or { key, respectively. In the Attribute Manager, make sure the **Options** button is chosen. In the **Options** area, clear the **Only Select Visible Elements** check box, if not already cleared.

   The **Only Select Visible Elements** check box is cleared to select the polygons that are behind the visible sub-objects.

7. Using the **Live Selection** tool and the SHIFT key, select the corner points of *Computer mouse*, as shown in Figure 3-3.

8. Invoke the **Scale** tool from the Command Palette and scale the selected points uniformly in the Top viewport, as shown in Figure 3-4.

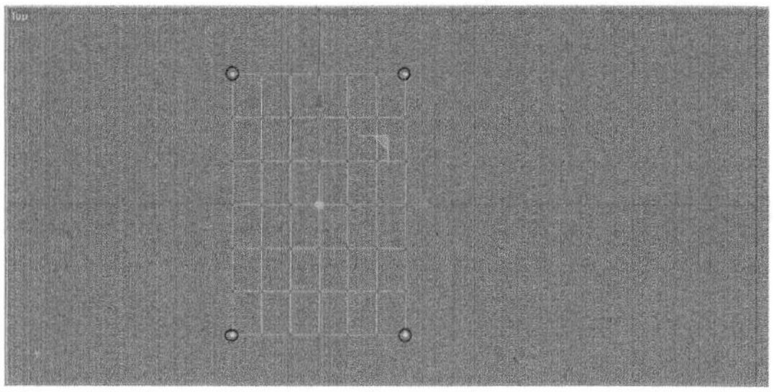

Figure 3-3 *The corner points of Computer mouse to be selected*

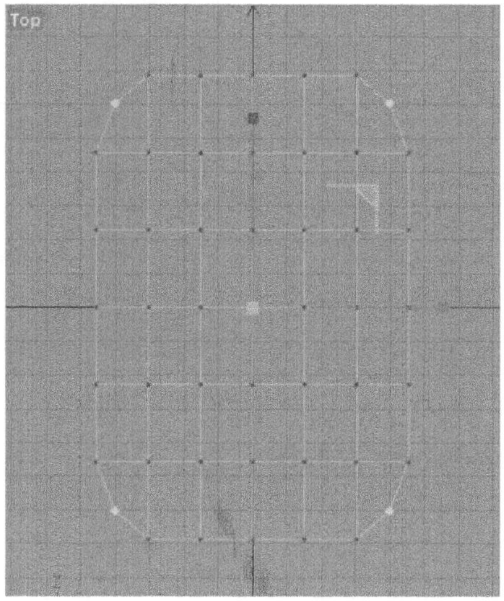

Figure 3-4 *Scaling the selected points of Computer mouse*

9. Deselect the corner points of *Computer mouse* by clicking on the empty area of the viewport. Invoke the **Live Selection** tool from the Command Palette and select the center points of *Computer mouse* in the Top viewport by dragging the cursor on them, as shown in Figure 3-5.

10. Invoke the **Scale** tool from the Command Palette and scale the selected points in the Top viewport, as shown in Figure 3-6.

11. Press and hold the 9 key on the main keyboard to temporarily invoke the **Live Selection** tool and then select the center points of *Computer mouse* in the Top viewport, as shown in Figure 3-7. Now, release the 9 key.

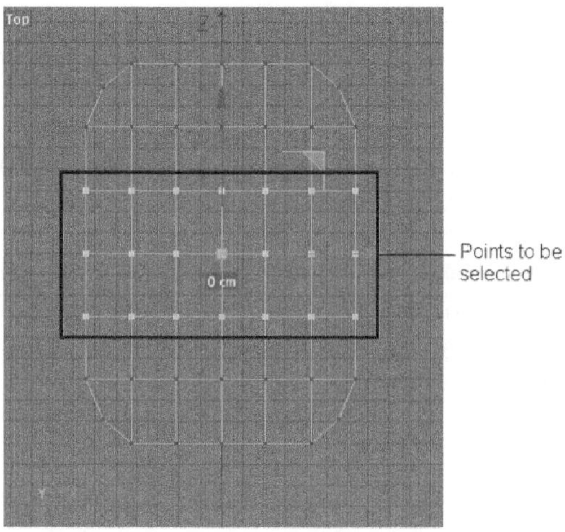

Figure 3-5 *The points to be selected*

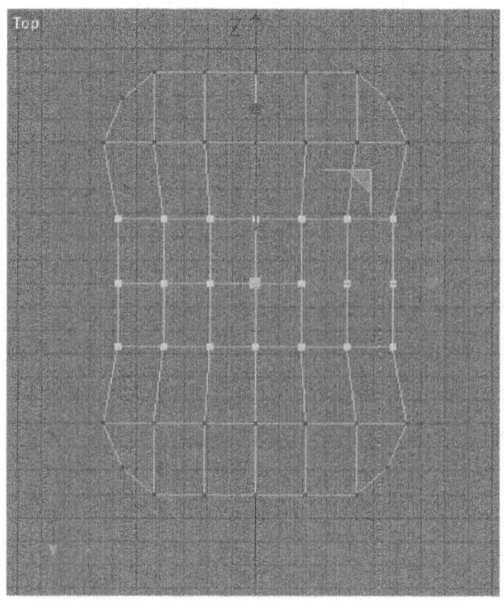

Figure 3-6 *Scaling the selected points of Computer mouse*

On releasing the 9 key, the **Scale** tool is activated which is the last used tool.

12. Scale the selected points inward in the Top viewport, as shown in Figure 3-8.

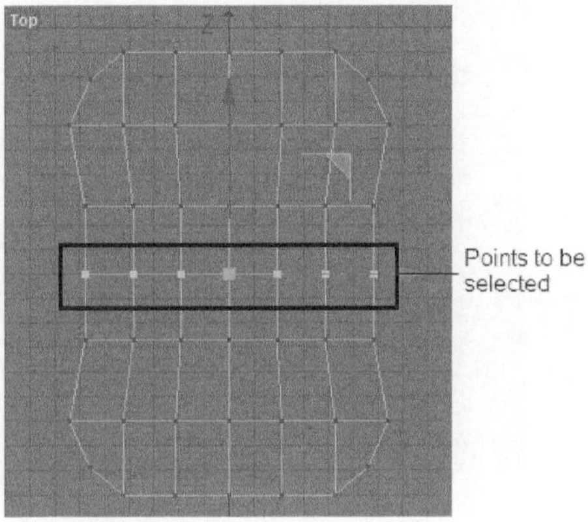

Figure 3-7 *The center points to be selected*

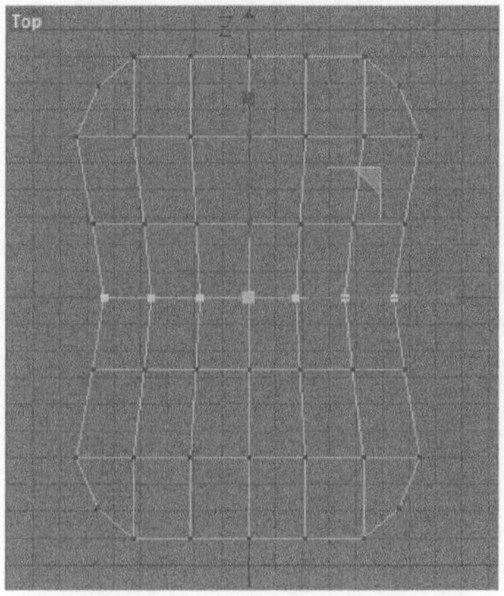

Figure 3-8 *Scaling the selected points of Computer mouse*

13. Press and hold the 9 key and select the top and bottom points of *Computer mouse* by using the SHIFT key, as shown in Figure 3-9. Next, release the 9 and SHIFT keys. Now, scale the selected points along the Z-axis, as shown in Figure 3-10.

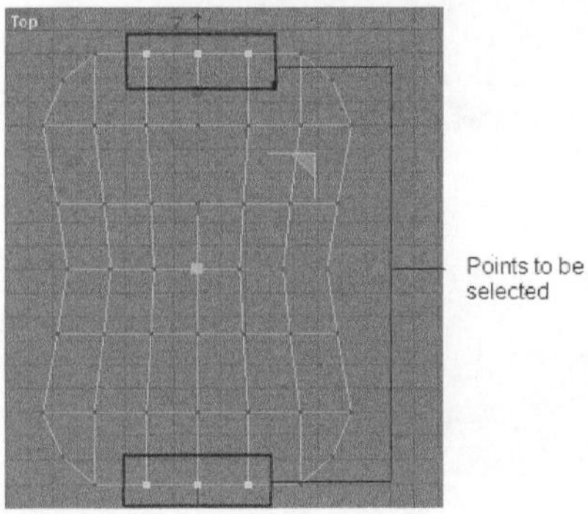

Figure 3-9 *The selected points of Computer mouse*

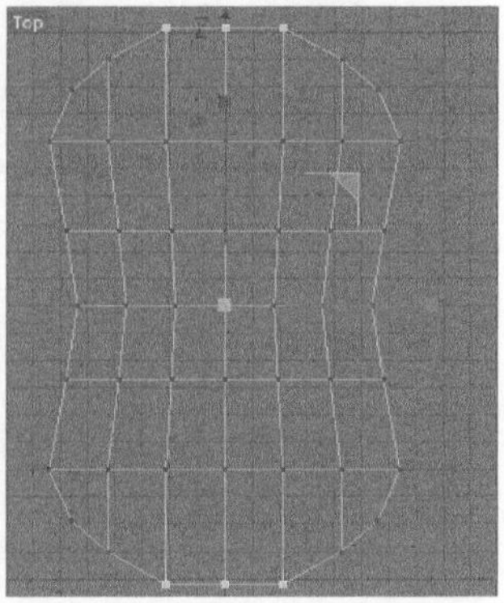

Figure 3-10 *Scaling the selected points of Computer mouse*

14. Press and hold the 9 key and select the top and bottom center points of *Computer mouse* using the SHIFT key, as shown in Figure 3-11.

15. Scale the selected points along the Z-axis in the Top viewport, as shown in Figure 3-12.

16. Press F3; the Right viewport is maximized. Invoke the **Live Selection** tool from the Command Palette. In the Attribute Manager, make sure the **Options** button is chosen. In the **Options** area, make sure that the **Only Select Visible Elements** check box is cleared.

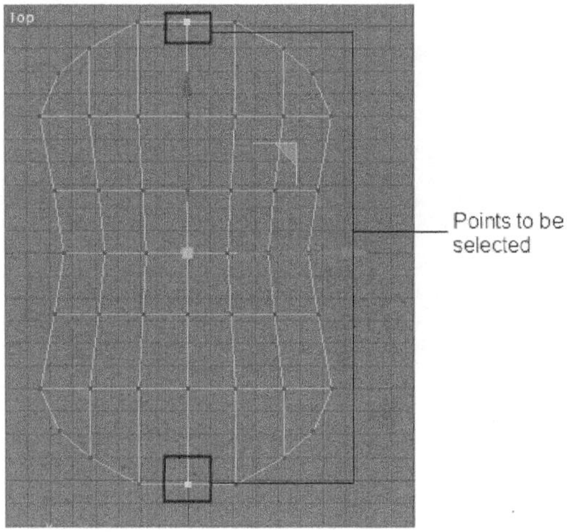

***Figure 3-11** The top and bottom center points of Computer mouse selected*

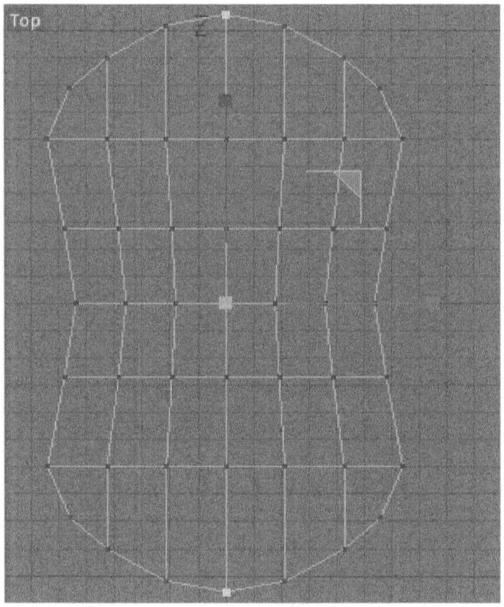

***Figure 3-12** Scaling the selected points of Computer mouse*

17. Using the **Live Selection** tool, select the center points of *Computer mouse* in the Right viewport, as shown in Figure 3-13. Next, move the selected points upward in the Right viewport, as shown in Figure 3-14.

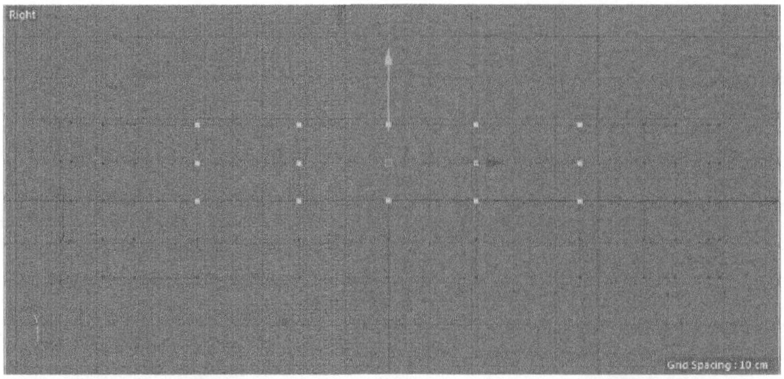

***Figure 3-13** The points to be selected*

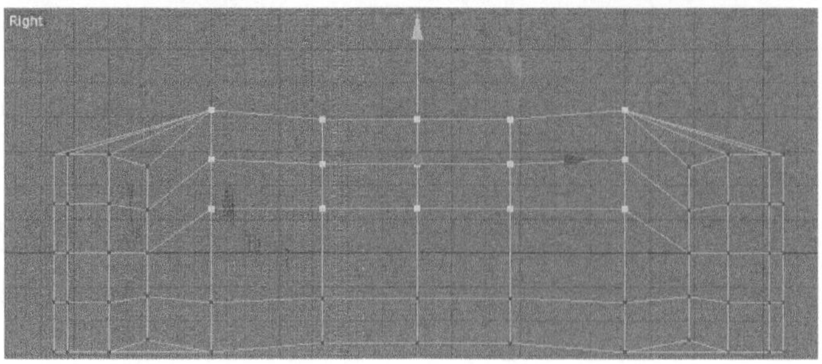

***Figure 3-14** Moving the selected points of Computer mouse*

18. Select the top points of *Computer mouse* in the Right viewport, as shown in Figure 3-15. Next, move the selected points upward in the Right viewport, as shown in Figure 3-16.

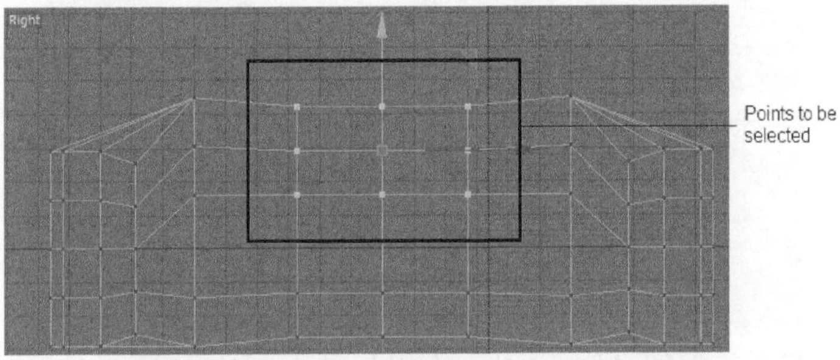

Figure 3-15 *The selected points of Computer mouse*

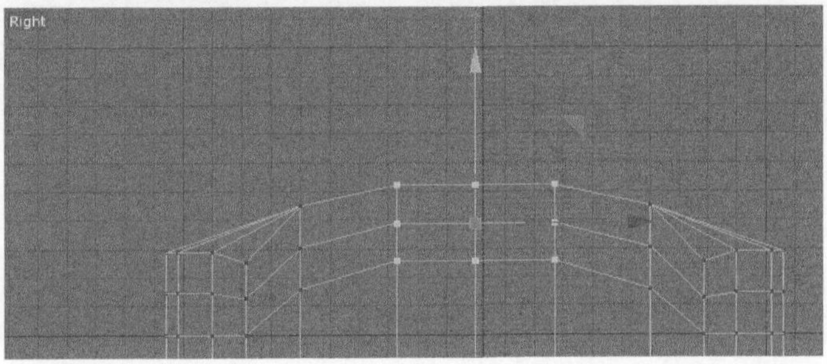

Figure 3-16 *Moving the selected points of Computer mouse*

19. Select the top center points of *Computer mouse*, as shown in Figure 3-17. Move the selected points upward in the Right viewport, as shown in Figure 3-18.

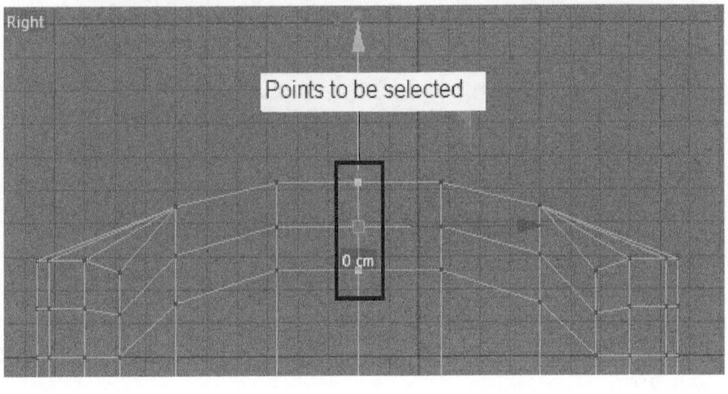

Figure 3-17 *The top center points of Computer mouse selected*

20. Select the points of *Computer mouse* in the Right viewport, as shown in Figure 3-19.

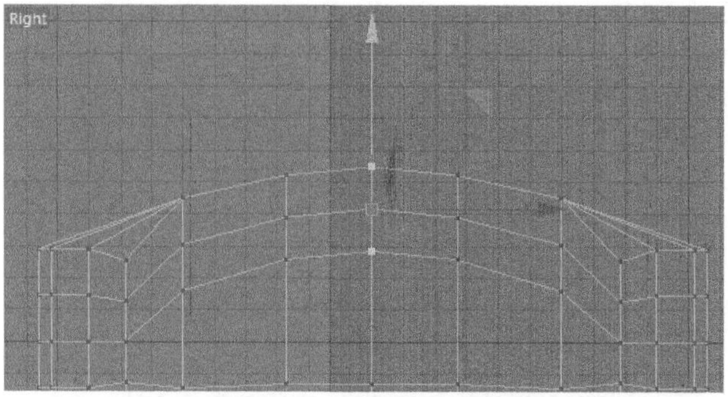

Figure 3-18 Moving the selected points of Computer mouse

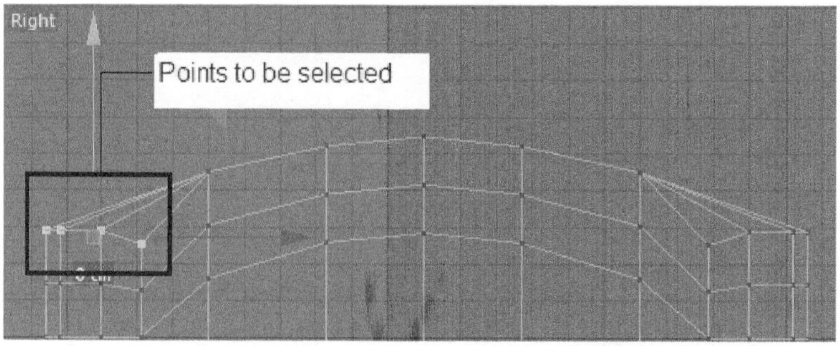

Figure 3-19 The points to be selected

21. Invoke the **Rotate** tool from the Command Palette and rotate the selected points along the YZ axis in the Right viewport, as shown in Figure 3-20.

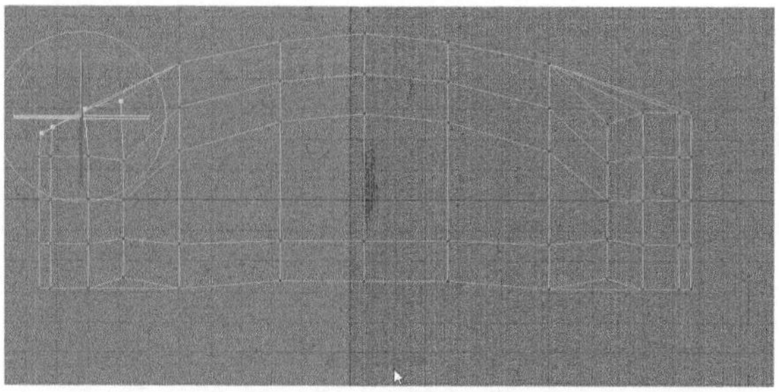

Figure 3-20 Rotating the selected points of Computer mouse

22. Select the points of *Computer mouse* in the Right viewport using the 9 key, as shown in Figure 3-21. Next, rotate the selected points along the YZ axis in the Right viewport, as shown in Figure 3-22.

23. Press F4; the Front viewport is maximized. Invoke the **Live Selection** tool from the Command Palette. In the Attribute Manager, make sure the **Options** button is chosen. In the **Options** area, make sure that the **Only Select Visible Elements** check box is cleared.

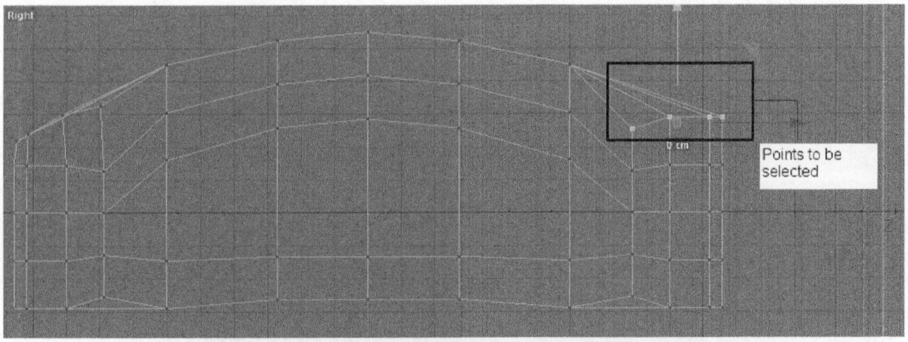

Figure 3-21 The points to be selected

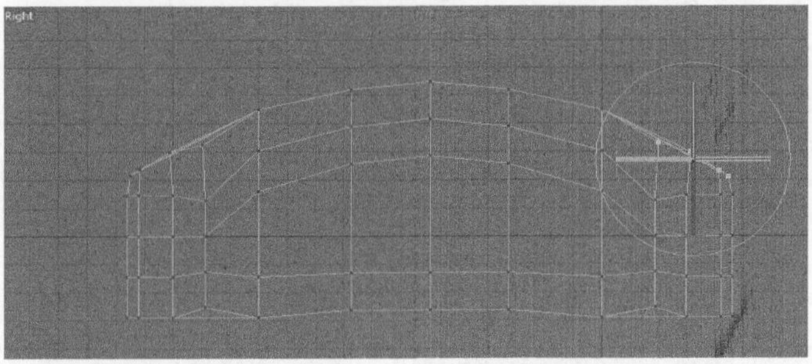

Figure 3-22 Rotating the selected points of Computer mouse

24. Select the center points of *Computer mouse* in the Front viewport, as shown in Figure 3-23. Next, move the selected points upward in the Front viewport, as shown in Figure 3-24.

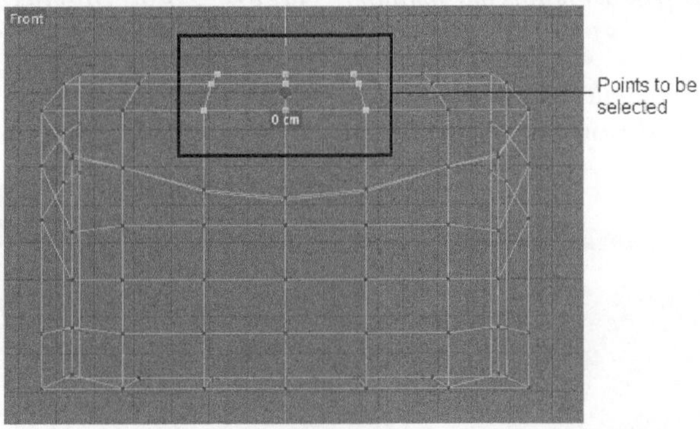

Figure 3-23 The points to be selected

25. Select the points of *Computer mouse* using the 9 key, as shown in Figure 3-25. Next, move the selected points upward in the Front viewport, as shown in Figure 3-26.

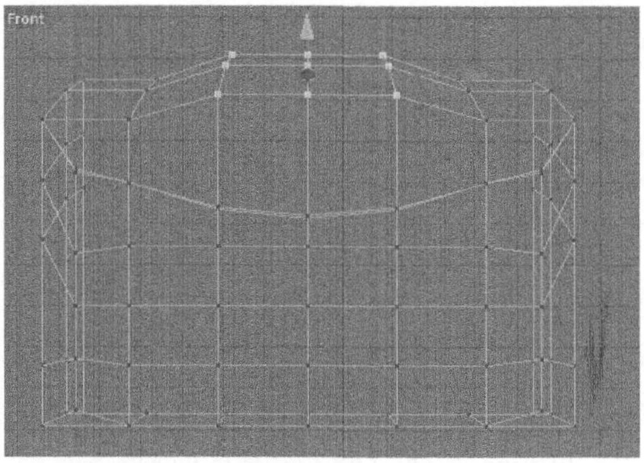

Figure 3-24 *Moving the selected points upward*

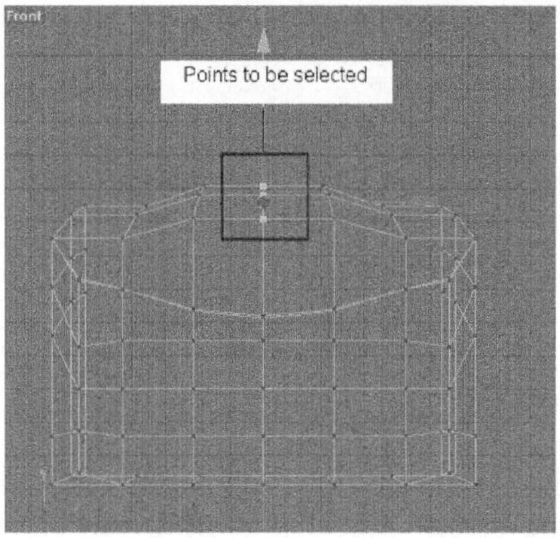

Figure 3-25 *The selected points of Computer mouse*

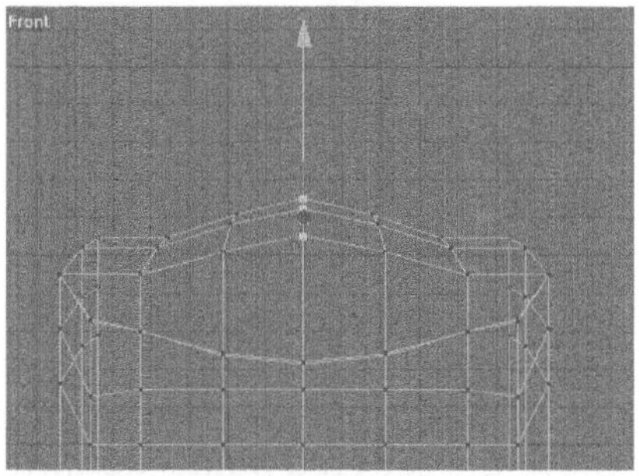

Figure 3-26 *Moving the selected points of Computer mouse*

26. Select the points of *Computer mouse* using the 9 and SHIFT keys, as shown in Figure 3-27. Next, move the selected points upward in the Front viewport, as shown in Figure 3-28.

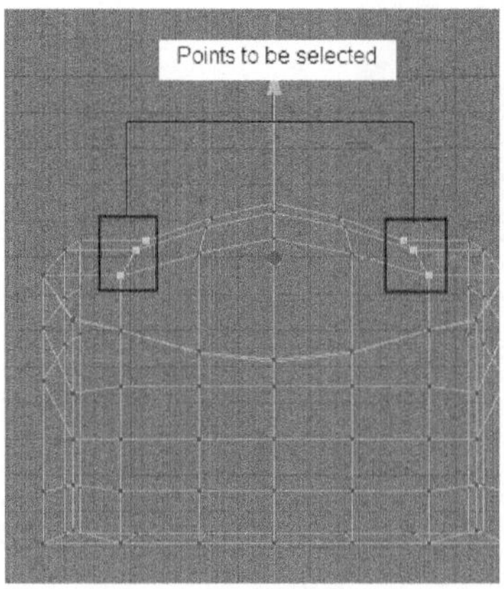

Figure 3-27 *The points to be selected*

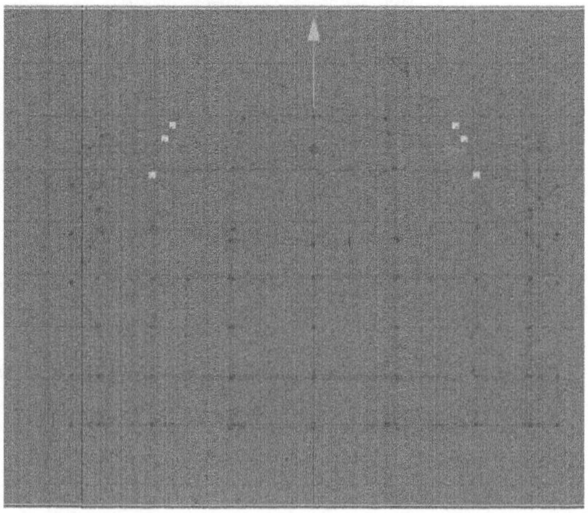

Figure 3-28 *Moving the selected points of Computer mouse*

27. Press F1; the Perspective viewport is maximized. Choose the **Edges** tool from the Modes Palette; *Computer mouse* is displayed in the edge mode.

28. Select the edges of *Computer mouse* in the Top viewport using the 9 and SHIFT keys, as shown in Figure 3-29.

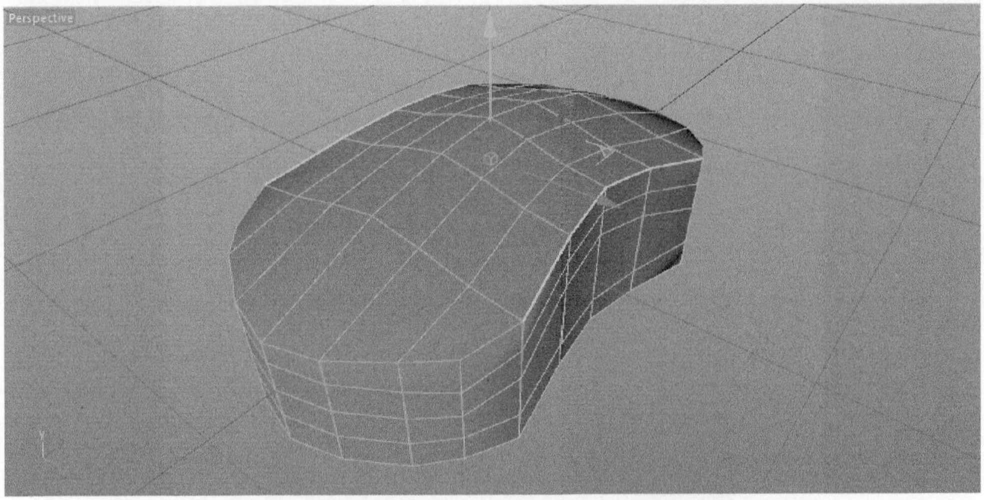

Figure 3-29 *The selected edges in the Perspective viewport*

29. Invoke the **Scale** tool from the Command Palette and scale down the selected edges to 95 percent along the x-axis, as shown in Figure 3-30.

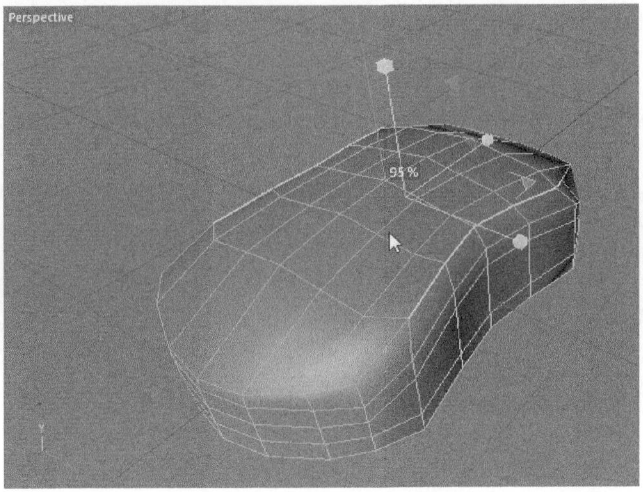

Figure 3-30 *Scaling down the edges of Computer mouse in the Perspective viewport*

30. Press F3; the Right viewport is maximized. Choose the **Points** tool from the Modes Palette; the *Computer mouse* is displayed in the points mode.

31. Select the points of *Computer mouse* in the Right viewport using the 9 key, as shown in Figure 3-31.

32. Invoke the **Move** tool from the Command Palette and move the selected points upward in the Right viewport, as shown in Figure 3-32.

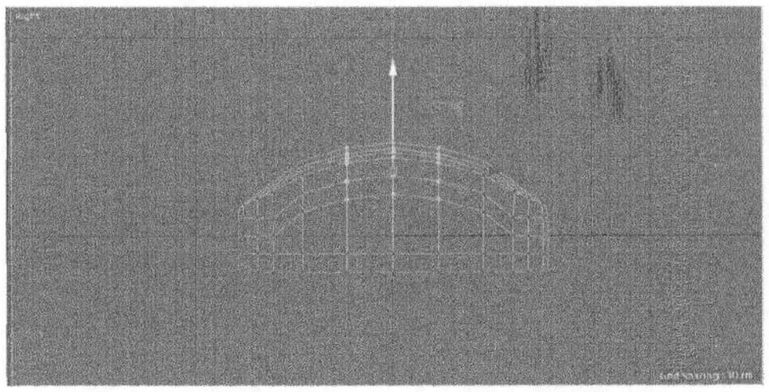

Figure 3-31 *The points to be selected*

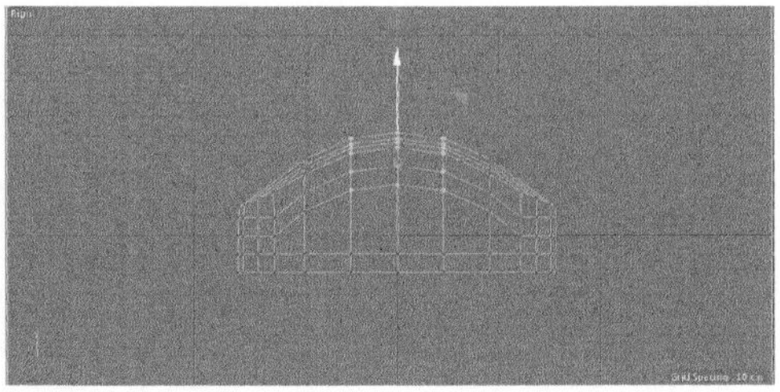

Figure 3-32 *Moving the selected points of Computer mouse*

33. Select the center points of *Computer mouse* using the 9 key, as shown in Figure 3-33.

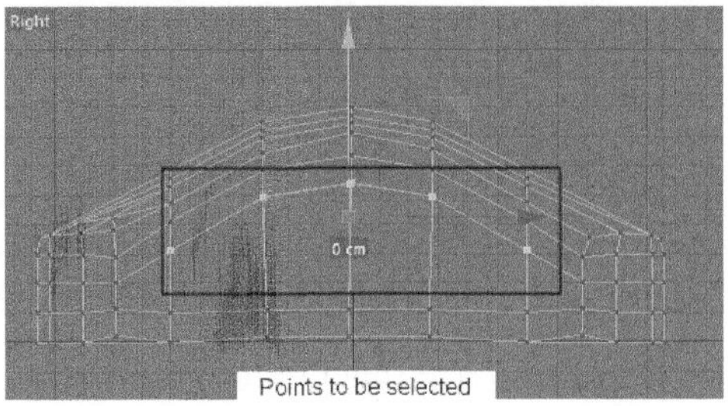

Figure 3-33 *The points to be selected*

34. Invoke the **Scale** tool from the Command Palette. Scale the selected points downward along the Y-axis and then move them downwards to get a straight line in the Right viewport, as shown in Figure 3-34.

35. Select the points of *Computer mouse* using the 9 key, as shown in Figure 3-35. Next, scale the selected points along the Y axis to 87.2 percent in the Right viewport, as shown in Figure 3-36.

Figure 3-34 *Scaling and moving the points of Computer mouse*

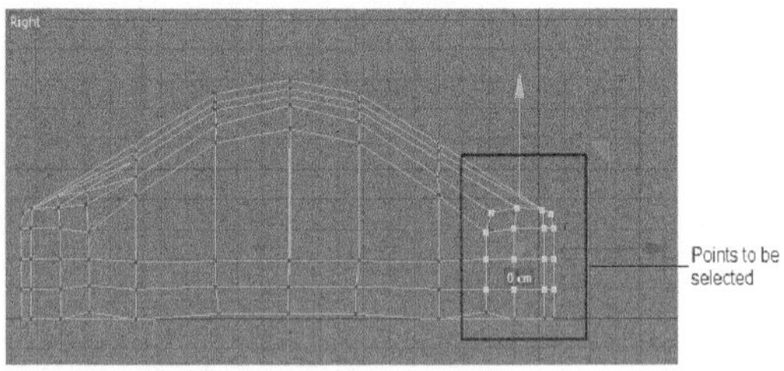

Figure 3-35 *The points of Computer mouse to be selected*

36. Invoke the **Move** tool from the Command Palette and move the selected points downward in the Right viewport, as shown in Figure 3-37.

Figure 3-36 *Scaling the points of Computer mouse*

Figure 3-37 *Moving the selected points in the Right viewport*

37. Select the bottom points of *Computer mouse* using the 9 key, refer to Figure 3-38. Next, invoke the **Scale** tool and scale the selected points to get a straight line in the Right viewport, if they are not straight, as shown in Figure 3-38.

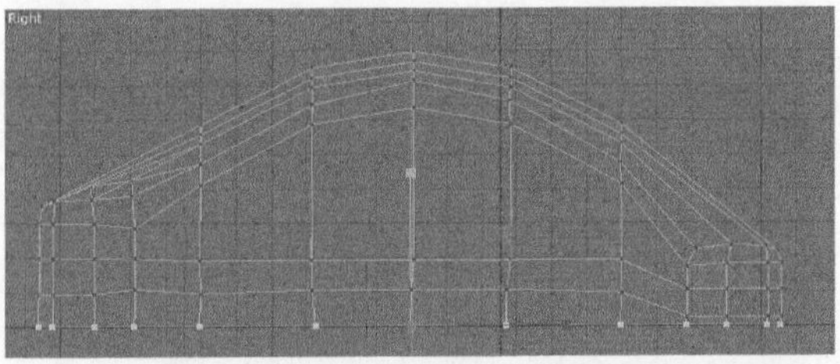

Figure 3-38 *Scaling the points of Computer mouse*

Creating the Left-Click and Right-Click Buttons of the Mouse

In this section, you will create the left-click and the right-click buttons of *Computer mouse*.

1. Press F1; the Perspective viewport is maximized. Choose the **Edges** tool from the Modes Palette; the *Computer mouse* is displayed in the edge mode.
2. Right-click in the empty area of the Perspective viewport; a shortcut menu is displayed. Choose **Loop/Path Cut** from the shortcut menu; the **Loop/Path Cut** tool settings are displayed in the Attribute Manager. In the **Options** area, make sure **Loop** is selected in the **Mode** drop-down list.

3. Make sure the **Enable Snap** tool is deactivated in the Modes Palette. In the **Options** area, make sure the **Restrict to Selection** check box is cleared and then click on the right of the middle edge loop of the *Computer mouse* in the Perspective viewport, as shown in Figure 3-39; a new edge is created next to it, as shown in Figure 3-40.

   When you create an edge loop using the **Loop/Path Cut** tool, you can interactively slide the edge loop using the slider that appears at the top of the viewport, as shown in Figure 3-41.

4. Again, create three new edge loops using the **Loop/Path Cut** tool, refer to Figures 3-42 and 3-43.

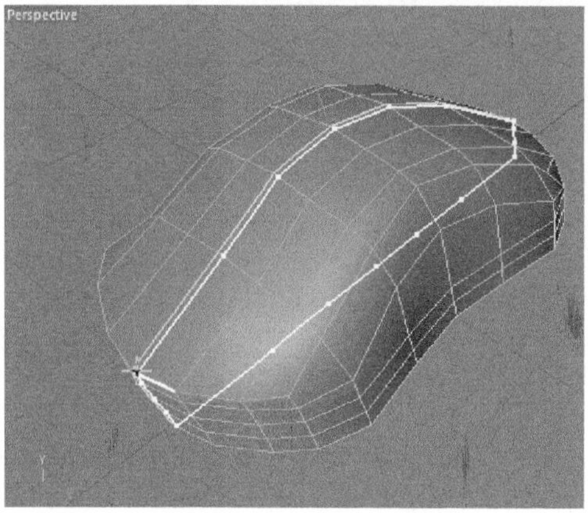

Figure 3-39 *Clicking on the right of the middle edge loop*

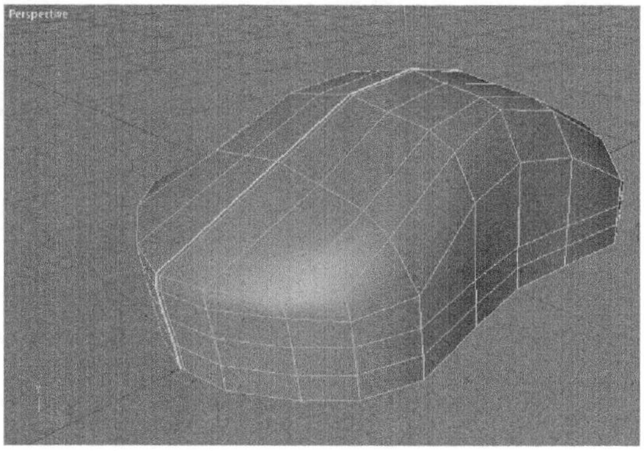

Figure 3-40 *A new edge loop added to the Computer mouse*

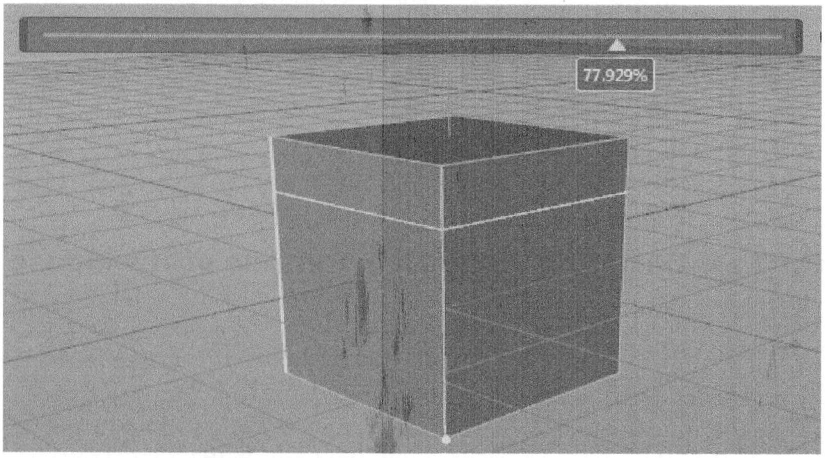

Figure 3-41 *The slider displayed at the top of the viewport*

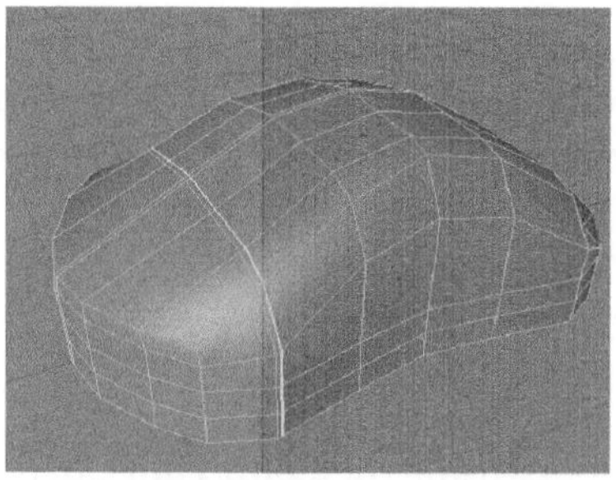

Figure 3-42 *A new edge added to Computer mouse*

5. Choose the **Live Selection** tool from the Command Palette and then choose the **Polygons** tool from the Modes Palette; the *Computer mouse* is displayed in the polygon mode. In the

Attribute Manager, choose the **Options** button; the **Options** area is displayed. In this area, select the **Only Select Visible Elements** check box, if not already selected. Next, using the **Live Selection** tool, select the polygons of *Computer mouse* in the Perspective viewport, as shown in Figure 3-44. If required, decrease the size of the selection cursor.

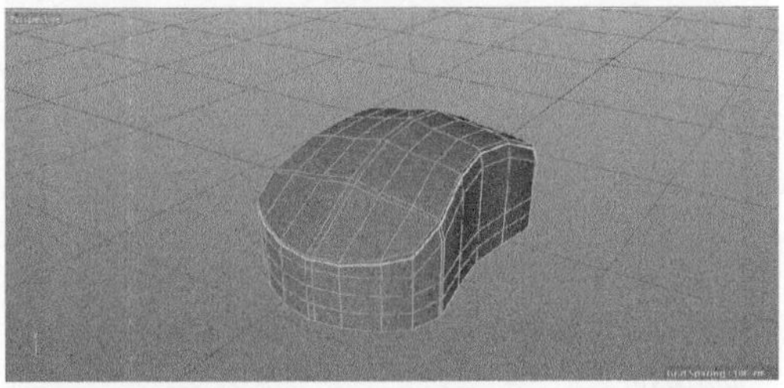

Figure 3-43 *A new edge added to Computer mouse*

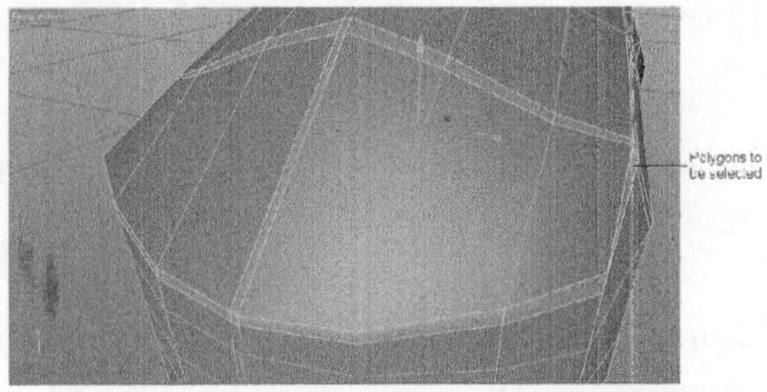

Figure 3-44 *The polygons selected*

6. In the Perspective viewport, right-click on the selected polygons of *Computer mouse*; a shortcut menu is displayed. Choose **Extrude** from the shortcut menu; the **Extrude** tool settings are displayed in the Attribute Manager. Choose the **Options** button; the **Options** area is displayed. Specify the value **-1** in the **Offset** spinner and then press ENTER; the selected polygons of *Computer mouse* are extruded, as shown in Figure 3-45.

7. Right-click on the empty area of the Perspective viewport; a shortcut menu is displayed. Choose **Loop/Path Cut** from the shortcut menu; the **Loop/ Path Cut** tool settings are displayed in the Attribute Manager. In the **Options** area, make sure that **Loop** is selected in the **Mode** drop-down list.

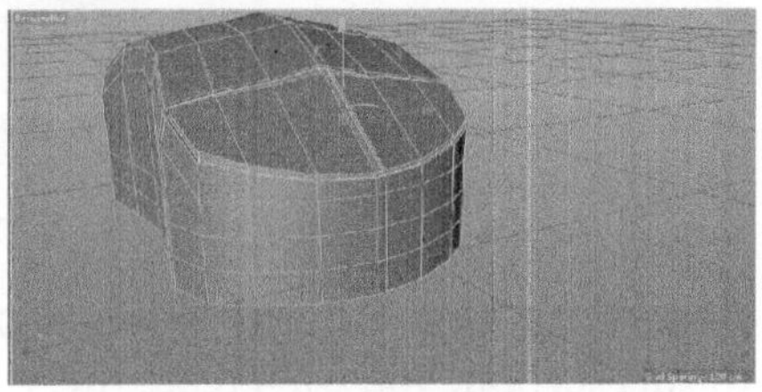

Figure 3-45 *The extruded polygons of Computer mouse*

8. Using the **Loop/Path Cut** tool, create an edge, refer to Figure 3-46.

9. Add two more edges, refer to Figures 3-47 and 3-48. Figure 3-49 shows the edges.

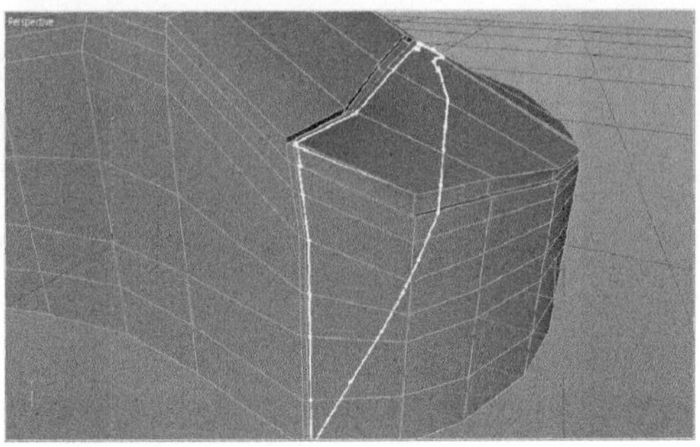

Figure 3-46 *An edge loop added to Computer mouse*

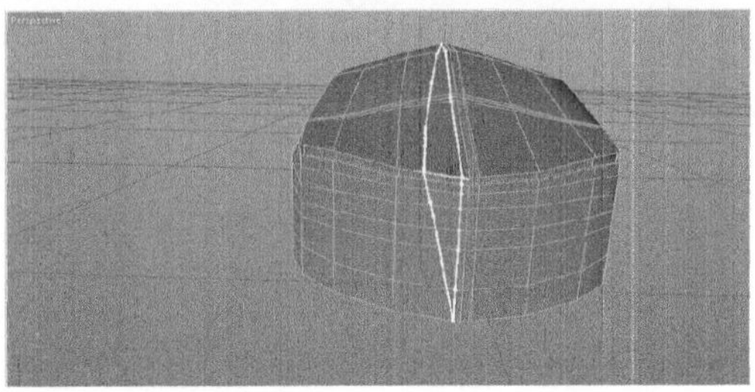

Figure 3-47 *An edge loop added to Computer mouse*

10. To smoothen the surface of the Computer mouse, choose the **Subdivision Surface** tool from the Command Palette; **Subdivision Surface** is added to the Object Manager. Next, select *Computer mouse* in the Object Manager and press and hold the left mouse button and then

drag it on the **Subdivision Surface**; the *Computer mouse* is connected to the **Subdivision Surface** and the smoothened result is displayed, as shown in Figure 3-50.

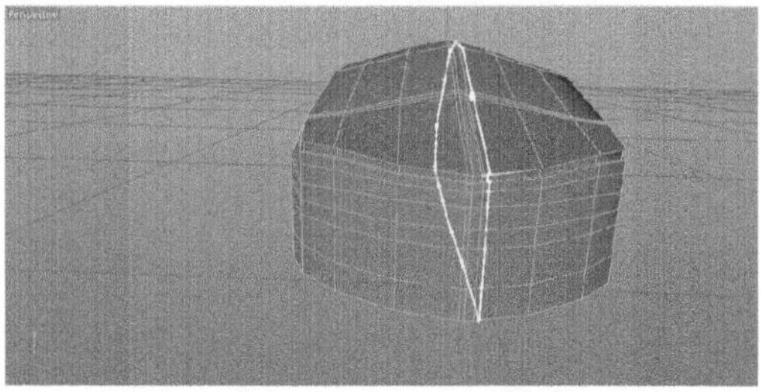

Figure 3-48 *An edge loop added to Computer mouse*

Figure 3-49 *The edges added to Computer mouse*

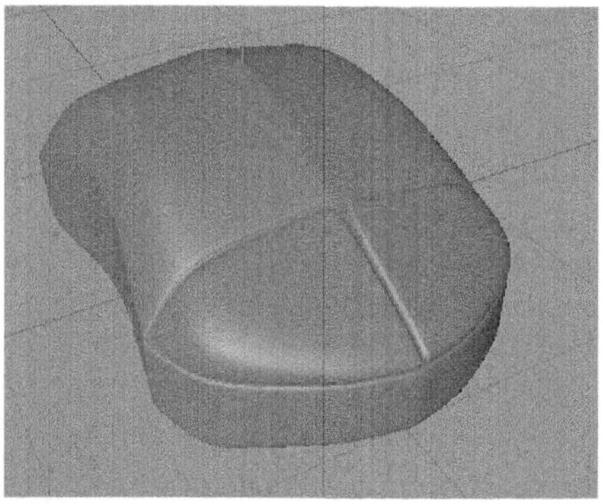

Figure 3-50 *The smoothened Computer mouse*

Creating the Scroll Wheel of the Mouse

In this section, you will create the scroll wheel of the *Computer mouse*.

1. Choose **Create > Object** from the main menu; a cascading menu is displayed. Next, choose **Torus** from it; a torus is created in the Perspective viewport and *Torus* is added to the Object Manager.

2. In the Attribute Manager, choose the **Basic** button; the **Basic Properties** area is displayed. In this area, enter **Scroll wheel** in the **Name** text box; *Torus* is renamed as *Scroll wheel* in the Object Manager.

3. In the Attribute Manager, choose the **Object** button; the **Object Properties** area is displayed. In this area, set the parameters as follows:

   Ring Radius: **6** Pipe Radius: **2** Pipe Segments: **7**
   Orientation: **-X**

4. Make sure that *Scroll wheel* is selected in the Object Manager. Invoke the **Move** tool from the Command Palette and place *Scroll wheel* on *Computer mouse*, as shown in Figure 3-51.

Creating the Bottom of the Mouse

In this section, you will create the bottom of *Computer mouse*.

1. Choose **Cameras** in Menu in editor view in the Perspective viewport; a flyout is displayed. Choose **Bottom** from the flyout; the Bottom viewport is displayed.

2. Select the *Computer mouse* in the Object Manager. Make sure the **Polygons** tool is chosen from the Modes Palette; the *Computer mouse* is displayed in the polygon mode. Make sure the **Live Selection** tool is chosen from the Standard palette. In the Attribute Manager, choose the **Options** button; the **Options** area is displayed. In this area, make sure the **Only Select Visible Elements** check box is selected. Select the polygons of *Computer mouse*, as shown in Figure 3-52.

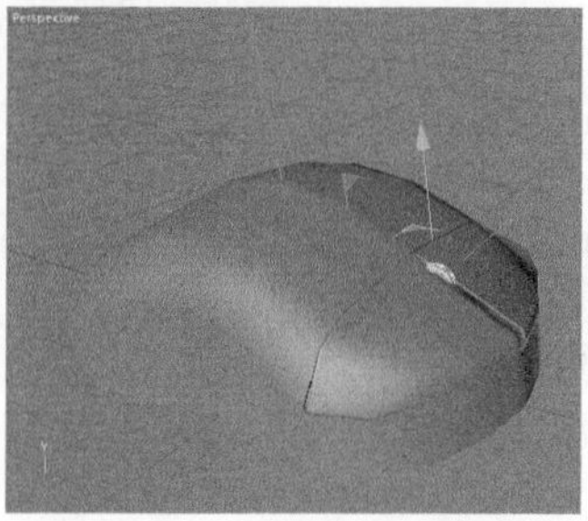

Figure 3-51 *The Scroll wheel placed on Computer mouse*

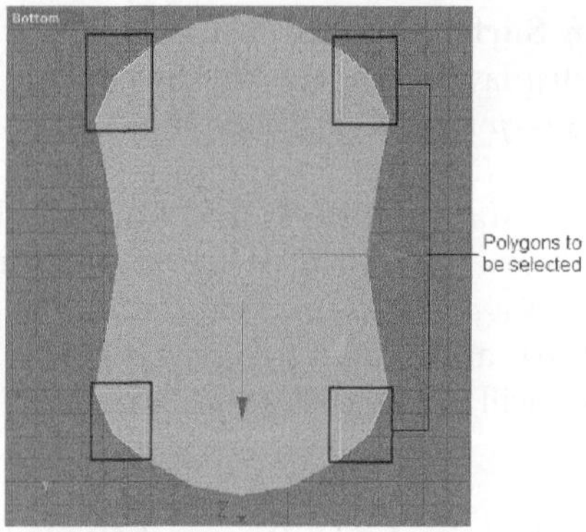

Figure 3-52 *The selected polygons of Computer mouse*

3. In the Bottom viewport, right-click on the selected polygons of *Computer mouse*; a shortcut menu is displayed. Choose **Extrude Inner** from the shortcut menu; the **Extrude Inner** tool settings are displayed in the Attribute Manager. Choose the **Options** button; the **Options** area is displayed. Specify the value **3** in the **Offset** spinner and then press ENTER; the selected polygons of the *Computer mouse* are extruded.

4. In the Perspective viewport, right-click on the selected polygons of *Computer mouse*; a shortcut menu is displayed. Choose **Extrude** from the shortcut menu; the **Extrude** tool settings are displayed in the Attribute Manager. Choose the **Options** button; the **Options** area is displayed. Specify the value **1.5** in the **Offset** spinner and then press ENTER; the selected polygons of the *Computer mouse* are extruded.

5. Choose **Cameras** from the Menu in editor view; a flyout is displayed. Choose **Perspective** from the flyout; the Perspective viewport is maximized.

Creating the USB Cable of the Mouse

In this section, you will create the USB cable of *Computer mouse* using the **Sweep NURBS** tool.

1. Choose **Create > Spline** from the main menu; a cascading menu is displayed. Next, choose **Circle** from it; a circle is created in the Perspective viewport and *Circle* is added to the Object Manager.

2. Make sure that *Circle* is selected in the Object Manager. In the Attribute Manager, make sure the **Object** button is chosen. In the **Object Properties** area, enter **2** in the **Radius** spinner.

3. In the Attribute Manager, choose the **Coord** button; the **Coord** area is displayed. In this area, enter **-80** in the **P . Z** spinner; the *Circle* is positioned in the Perspective viewport.

4. Press F2; the Top viewport is maximized. Choose **Create > Spline** from the main menu; a cascading menu is displayed. Choose **Pen** from it. Next, create a curve in the Top viewport, as shown in Figure 3-53. Press ESC to exit the **Pen** tool.

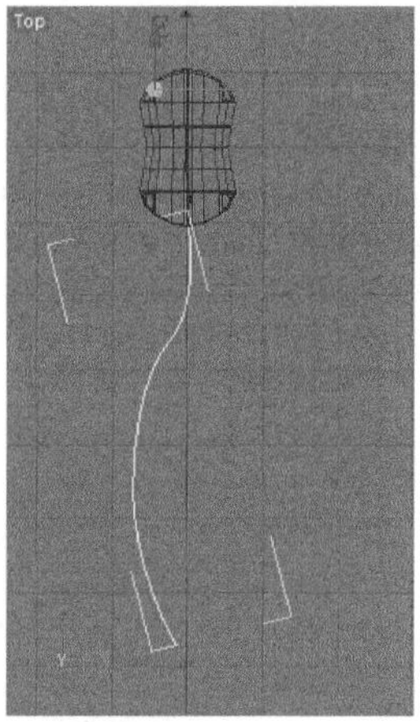

Figure 3-53 *Spline created in the Top viewport*

5. Press and hold the left mouse button on the **Subdivision Surface** tool from the Command Palette; a flyout is displayed. Choose the **Sweep** tool from the flyout; the *Sweep* is added to the Object Manager.

6. In the Object Manager, press and hold the left mouse button on *Spline* and drag it to *Sweep*; the *Spline* is connected to *Sweep*. Next, press and hold the left mouse button on *Circle* and drag it to *Sweep*; *Circle* is connected to *Sweep*. You will notice that a wire is created in the Top viewport.

   Next, you will create the USB port of *Computer mouse*.

7. Choose **Create > Object** from the main menu; a cascading menu is displayed. Next, choose **Cube** from it; a cube is created in the Top viewport and a *Cube* is added to the Object Manager.

8. Make sure that *Cube* is selected in the Object Manager. In the Attribute Manager, choose the **Object** button; the **Object Properties** area is displayed. In this area, set the parameters as follows:

   Size . X: **28**   Size . Y: **8**   Size . Z: **62**
   Segments X: **10**   Segments Y: **10**   Segments Z: **10**

9. Invoke the **Move** tool from the Command Palette and move *Cube* in the Top viewport to place it, as shown in Figure 3-54.

10. Make sure *Cube* is selected in the Object Manager. Next, choose the **Make Editable** tool from the Modes Palette; the *Cube* is converted into a polygonal object.

11. Choose the **Edges** tool from the Modes Palette; the *Cube* is displayed in the edge mode. Choose the **Live Selection** tool from the Command Palette. In the Attribute Manager, make sure the **Only Select Visible Elements** check box is cleared in the **Options** area. Next, select the edges of *Cube* in the Top viewport, as shown in Figure 3-55.

12. Invoke the **Scale** tool from the Command Palette and scale down the selected edges to 70 percent uniformly.

13. Choose the **Points** tool from the Modes Palette; *Cube* is displayed in the points mode. Select the points of *Cube* using the 9 and SHIFT keys, as shown in Figure 3-56.

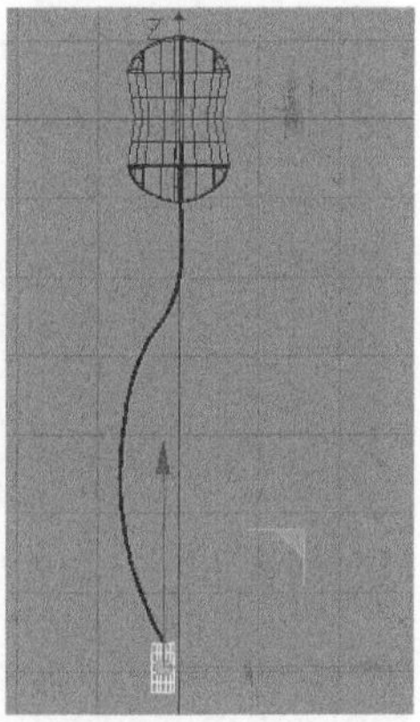

Figure 3-54 *Cube placed in the Top viewport*

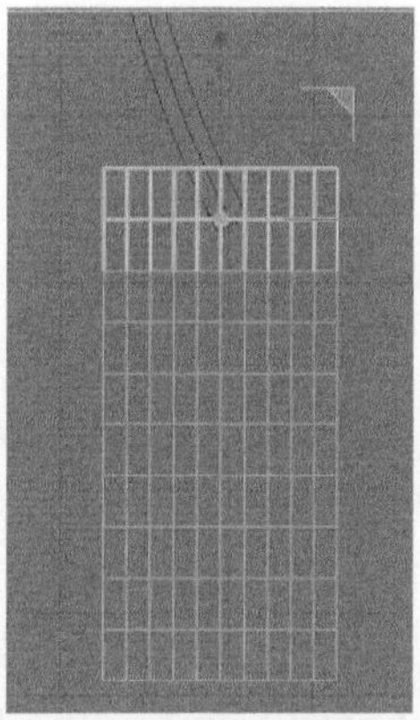

Figure 3-55 *The edges to be selected in the Top viewport*

14. Scale down the selected points along the X axis to get the shape, as shown in Figure 3-57.

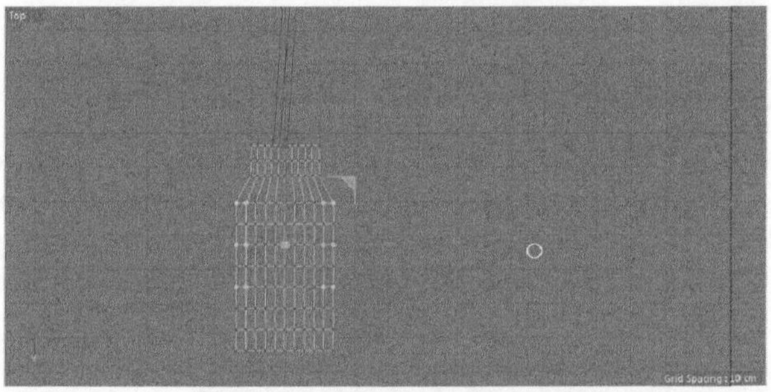

Figure 3-56 *The points to be selected*

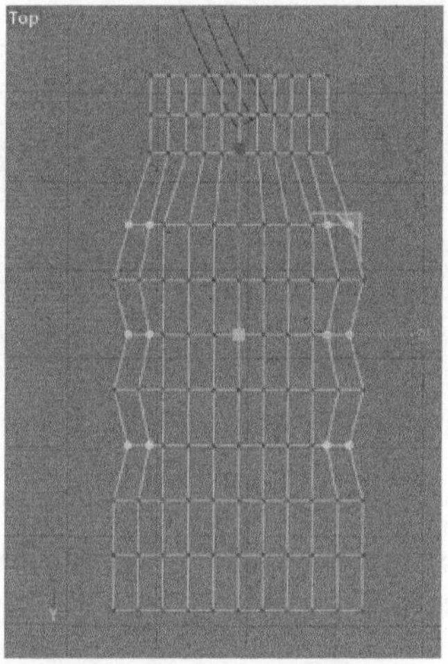

Figure 3-57 *Scaling the selected points*

15. Choose the **Edges** tool from the Modes Palette; *Cube* is displayed in the edge mode. Choose the **Live Selection** tool from the Command Palette. In the Attribute Manager, select the **Only Select Visible Elements** check box in the **Options** area. Select the edges of *Cube* in the Top viewport, as shown in Figure 3-58.

16. Scale down the selected edges along the X and Y axis to get the shape, as shown in Figure 3-59.

17. Press F1; the Perspective viewport is maximized. Choose the **Polygons** tool from the Modes Palette; *Cube* is displayed in the polygon mode. Select the polygons of *Cube* using the 9 key, as shown in Figure 3-60. Make sure the **Only Selected Visible Elements** check box is cleared.

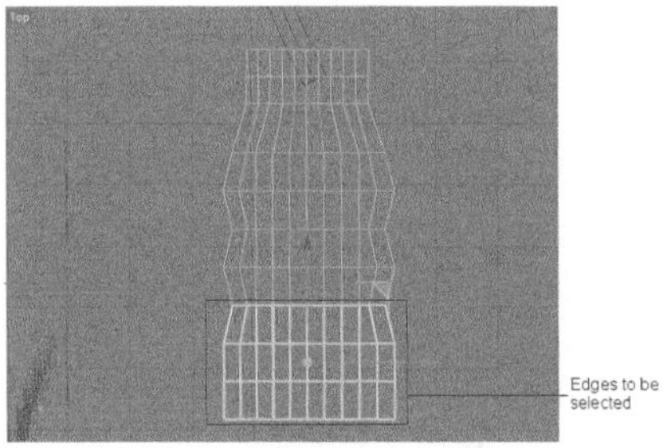

Figure 3-58 *The edges selected*

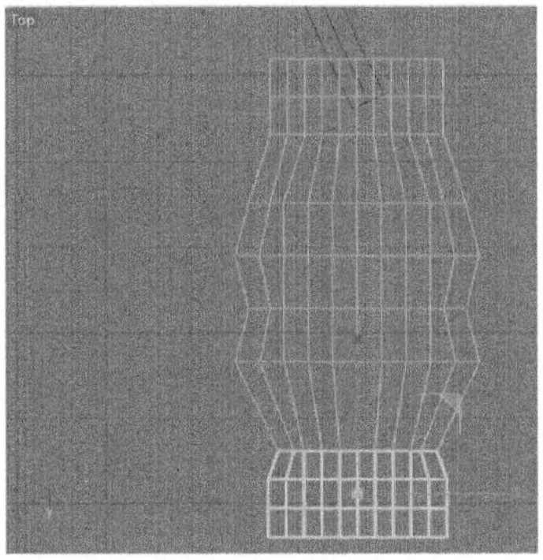

Figure 3-59 *Scaling the selected edges*

18. Right-click on the selected polygons of *Computer mouse*; a shortcut menu is displayed. Choose **Extrude** from the shortcut menu; the **Extrude** tool settings are displayed in the Attribute Manager. In the **Extrude** tool settings area, specify the value **10** in the **Offset** spinner and then press ENTER; the selected polygons of *Computer mouse* are extruded, as shown in Figure 3-61.

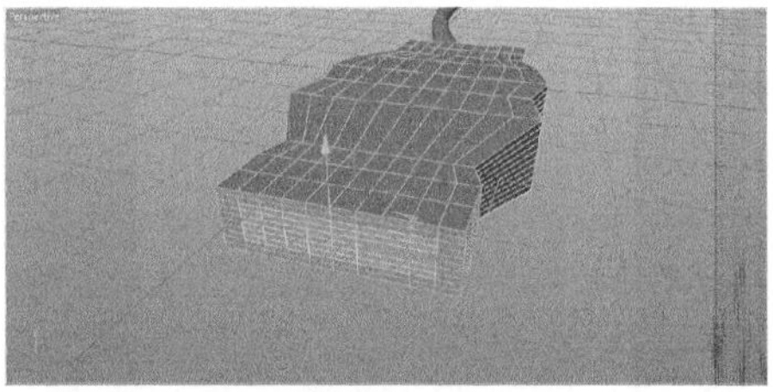

Figure 3-60 *The polygons to be selected*

Figure 3-61 *The extruded edge loop*

19. Choose the **Polygons** tool from the Modes Palette. Right-click on the Perspective viewport; a shortcut menu is displayed. Choose **Loop/Path Cut** from the shortcut menu; the **Loop/Path Cut** tool settings are displayed in the Attribute Manager. In the Attribute Manager, make sure **Loop** is selected in the **Mode** drop-down list. Next, add two edges, as shown in Figure 3-62.

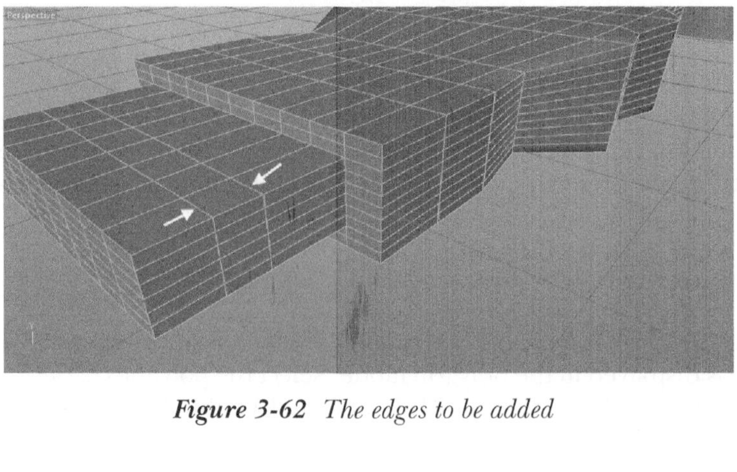

Figure 3-62 *The edges to be added*

20. Choose the **Polygons** tool from the Modes Palette; *Cube* is displayed in the polygon mode. Select the polygons of *Cube* using the **Live Selection** tool, as shown in Figure 3-63. Next, delete the selected polygons of *Cube*, refer to Figure 3-64.

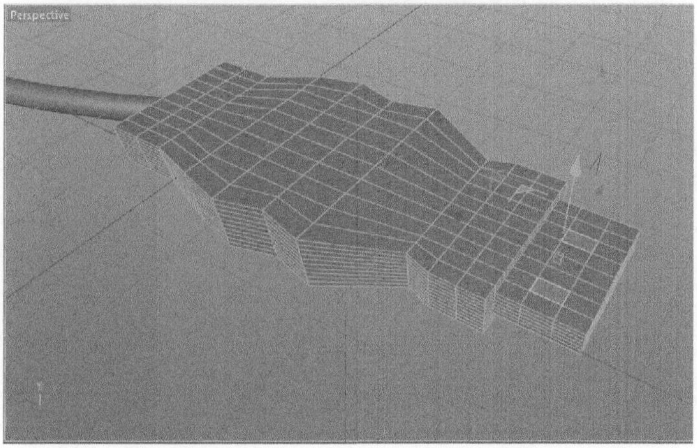

Figure 3-63 *The polygons to be selected*

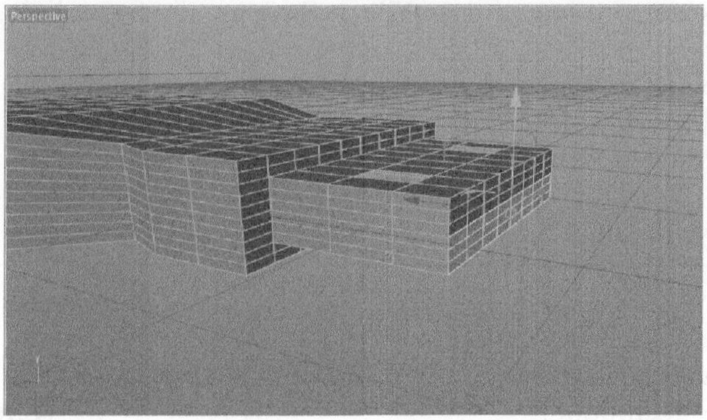

Figure 3-64 *The selected polygons*

21. Again, select the polygons of *Cube* using the **Live Selection tool**, refer to Figure 3-64. Next, delete the selected polygons of *Cube*, refer to Figure 3-65.

Changing the Background Color of the Scene

To change the background color of the scene to white in the final output, follow the steps given in Tutorial 1 of Chapter 2.

Saving and Rendering the Scene

In this section, you will save and render the scene. You can also view the final render of the scene by downloading the file *c03_cinema4d_R20_rndr.zip* from *www.cadcim.com*. The path of the file is mentioned at the beginning of the chapter.

1. Choose **File > Save** from the main menu; the **Save File** dialog box is displayed. In this dialog box, browse to the location *\Documents\c4dR20\c03*.

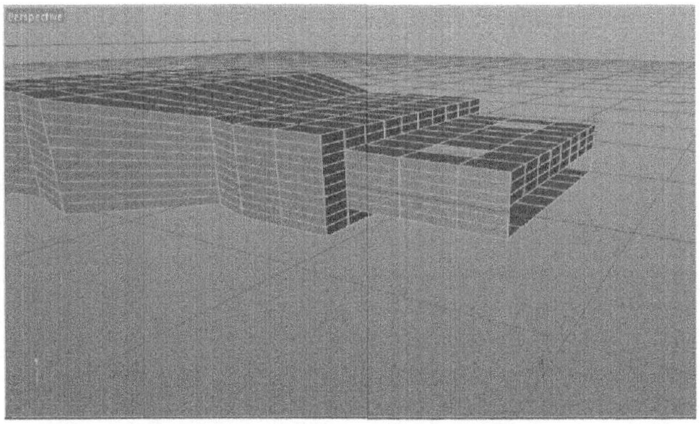

Figure 3-65 The deleted polygons

2. Enter **c03tut1** in the **File name** text box and then choose the **Save** button.

3. In the Perspective viewport, set the camera angle using the Viewport Navigation Tools. Next, choose the **Render to Picture Viewer** tool from the Command Palette. Alternatively, press SHIFT+R; the **Picture Viewer** window is displayed.

4. In the **Picture Viewer** window, choose **File > Save as**; the **Save** dialog box is displayed.

5. In the **Save** dialog box, choose the **OK** button; the **Save Dialog** dialog box is displayed. Next, browse to *\Documents\c4dR20\c03*. In the **File Name** text box, type **c03_tut1_rndr**. Next, choose the **Save** button; the file is saved at the desired location.

   Figure 3-1 displays the final output.

Tutorial 2

In this tutorial, you will create the model of a computer table, as shown in Figure 3-66, using the polygon modeling technique. **(Expected time: 35 min)**

Figure 3-66 The model of computer table

The following steps are required to complete this tutorial:

a. Create the base of the computer table.
b. Create the support for the CPU.
c. Create the support for the keyboard.
d. Create the base for the monitor.
e. Create the top shelves of the computer table.
f. Create the bottom shelf of the computer table.
g. Create the magazine stand.
h. Change the background color of the scene.
i. Save and render the scene.

Creating the Base of the Computer Table

In this section, you will create the base of the computer table.

1. Press F2; the Top viewport is maximized. Choose **Create > Object** from the main menu; a cascading menu is displayed. Next, choose **Cube** from it; a cube is created in the Top viewport and *Cube* is added to the Object Manager.

2. In the Attribute Manager, choose the **Basic** button; the **Basic Properties** area is displayed. In this area, enter **Computer table** in the **Name** text box; *Cube* is renamed as *Computer table* in the Object Manager.

3. Make sure *Computer table* is selected in the Object Manager. In the Attribute Manager, choose the **Object** button; the **Object Properties** area is displayed. In the **Object Properties** area, set the parameters as follows:

Size . X: **743**	Size . Y: **18**	Size . Z: **295**
Segments X: **6**	Segments Y: **6**	Segments Z: **6**

   Select the **Fillet** check box and enter **3** in the **Fillet Radius** spinner.

4. Press F1; the Perspective area is maximized. Choose the **Make Editable** tool from the Modes Palette; *Computer table* is converted into a polygonal object.

   Figure 3-67 displays *Computer table* in the Perspective viewport.

5. Choose the **Edges** tool from the Modes Palette; the *Computer table* is displayed in the edge mode. Choose **Select > Loop Selection** from the main menu and then right-click in the Perspective viewport; a shortcut menu is displayed. Choose **Loop/Path Cut** from the shortcut menu; the **Loop/Path Cut** tool settings are displayed in the Attribute Manager.

6. Choose the **Enable Snap** tool from the Modes Palette. Next, click on *Computer mouse*, refer to Figure 3-68; an edge loop is added to *Computer table*. Again, create two new edge loops using the **Loop/Path Cut** tool, as shown in Figure 3-69.

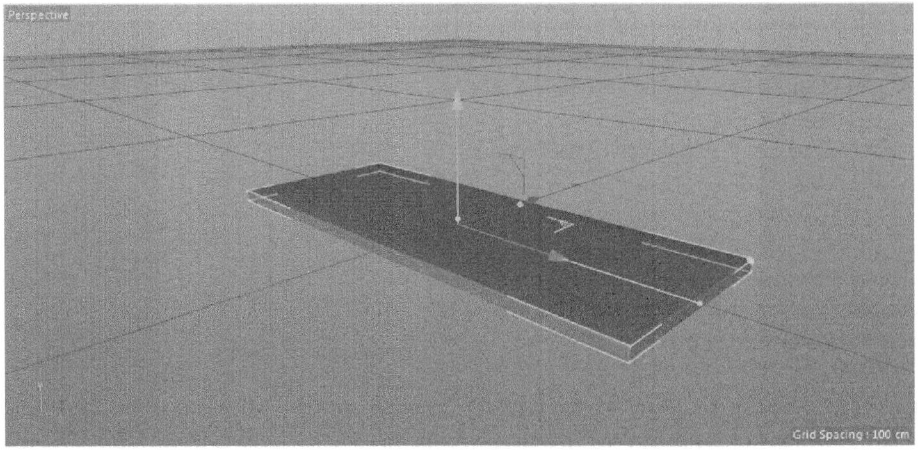

Figure 3-67 *The Computer table in the Perspective viewport*

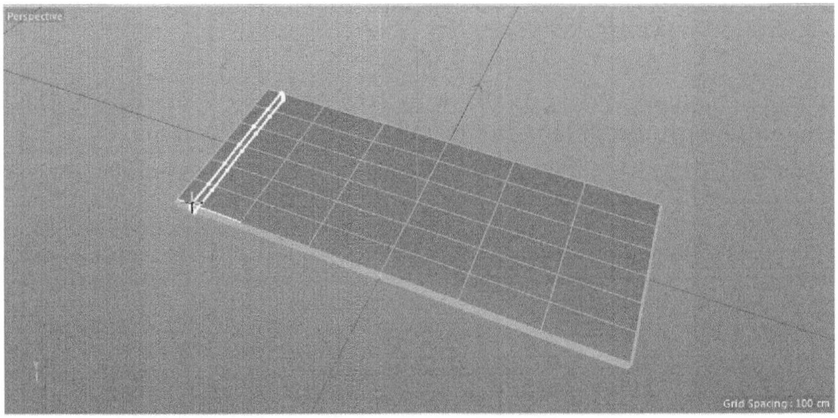

Figure 3-68 *Adding an edge loop*

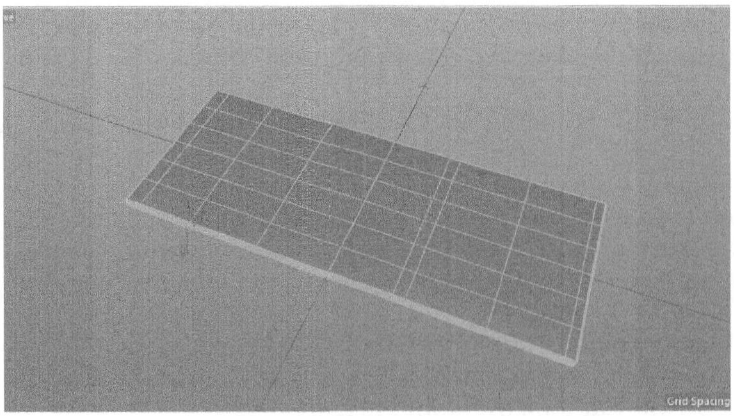

Figure 3-69 *The edge loops added*

Next, you will create the supports for *Computer table*.

7. Choose the **Polygons** tool from the Modes Palette; the *Computer table* is displayed in the polygon mode. Choose **Cameras > Bottom** from the Menu in editor view; the Bottom viewport is maximized. Choose the **Live Selection** tool from the Command Palette and make sure that the **Only Select Visible Elements** check box is selected. Next, enter **1** in the **Radius** spinner. Now, select the polygons of *Computer table*, as shown in Figure 3-70, using the **Live Selection** tool and the SHIFT key.

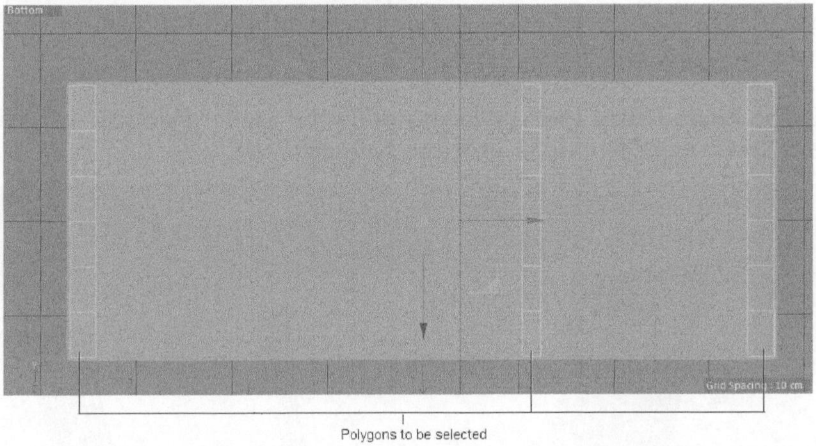

***Figure 3-70** The selected polygons of Computer table*

8. Choose **Cameras > Perspective** from the Menu in editor view; the Perspective viewport is maximized. Right-click in the Perspective viewport; a shortcut menu is displayed. Choose **Extrude** from the shortcut menu; the **Extrude** tool settings are displayed in the Attribute Manager. In the **Extrude** tool settings area, set the value **400** in the **Offset** spinner and then press the ENTER key. Set the value **4** in the **Subdivision** spinner and then press the ENTER key.

   After entering the value, the selected polygons are extruded in the Perspective viewport, as shown in Figure 3-71.

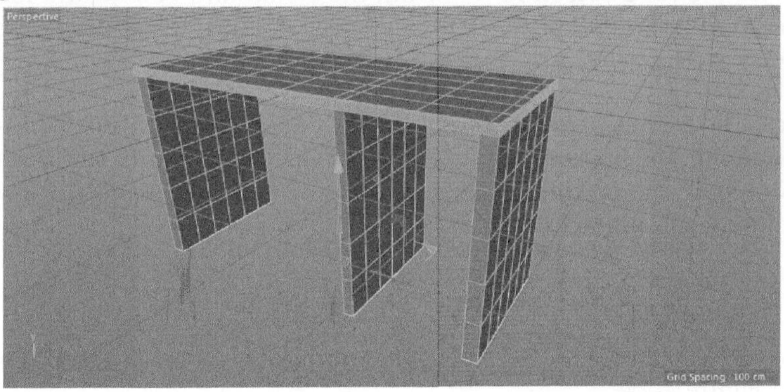

***Figure 3-71** The selected polygons extruded in the Perspective viewport*

Creating the Support for the CPU

In this section, you will create the support for the CPU.

1. Choose the **Edges** tool from the Modes Palette; *Computer table* is displayed in the edge mode. Right-click in the Perspective viewport; a shortcut menu is displayed. Choose **Loop/Path Cut** from the shortcut menu; the **Loop/Path Cut** tool settings are displayed in the Attribute Manager. Make sure **Loop** is selected in the **Mode** drop-down list and the **Restrict to Selection** check box is cleared.

2. Make sure the **Enable Snap** tool is deactivated in the Modes Palette. Next, click, as shown in Figure 3-72; a new edge loop is added to *Computer table.*

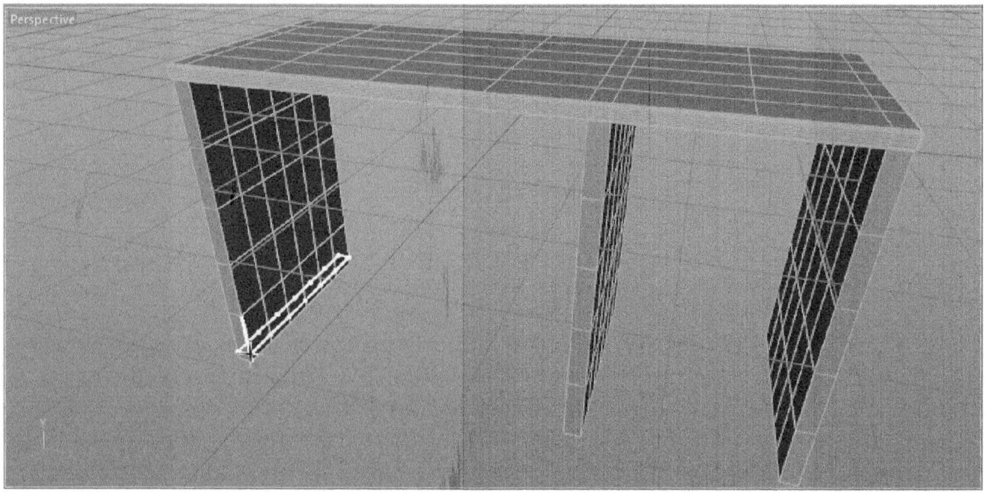

Figure 3-72 *Clicking on edge to create a new edge loop*

3. Choose the **Polygons** tool from the Modes Palette; *Computer table* is displayed in the polygon mode. Choose the **Live Selection** tool from the Command Palette and make sure that the **Only Select Visible Elements** check box is selected. Now, select the polygons of *Computer table*, as shown in Figure 3-73.

4. Right-click in the Perspective viewport; a shortcut menu is displayed. Choose **Extrude** from the shortcut menu; the **Extrude** tool settings are displayed in the Attribute Manager. In the Attribute Manager, choose the **Options** button; the **Options** area is displayed. In this area, set the parameters as follows:

   Offset: **200** Subdivision: **6**

   After entering the values, the selected polygons are extruded in the Perspective viewport, as shown in Figure 3-74.

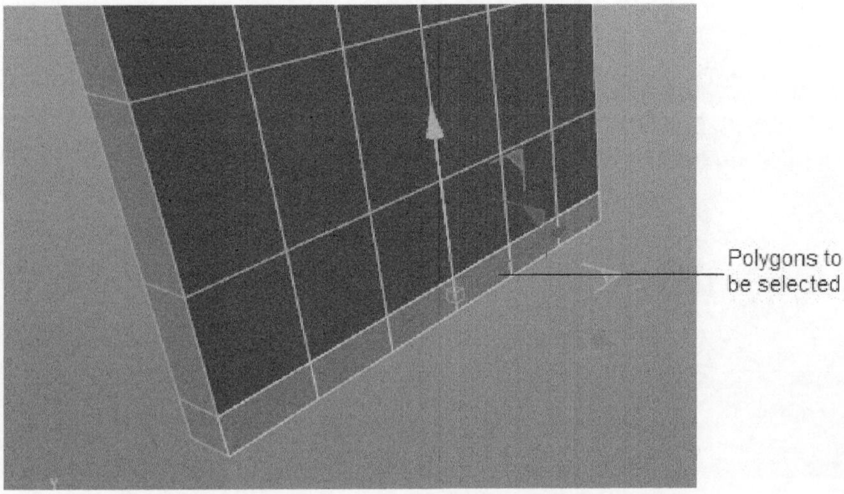

Figure 3-73 *The selected polygons of Computer table*

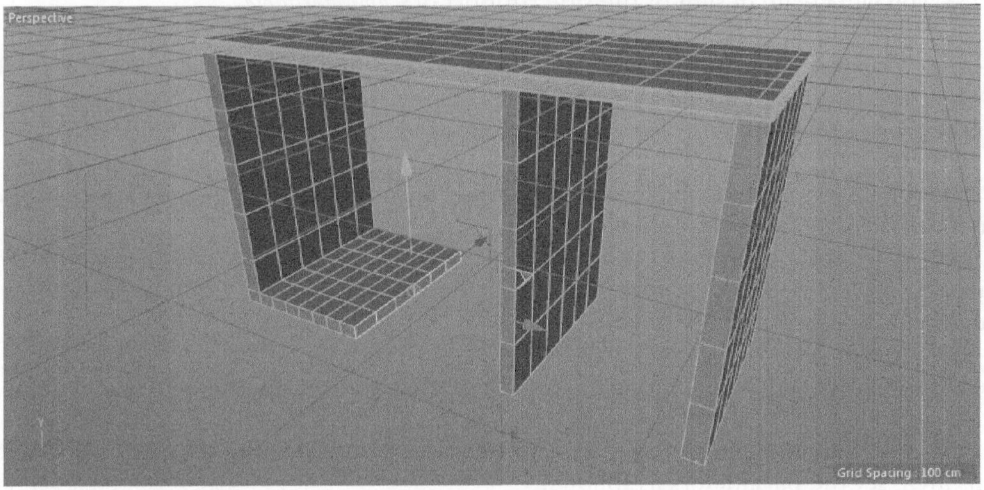

Figure 3-74 *The selected polygons extruded in the Perspective viewport*

5. Choose **Create > Object** from the main menu; a cascading menu is displayed. Next, choose **Cube** from it; the *Cube* object is added to the Object Manager.

6. In the Attribute Manager, choose the **Object** button; the **Object Properties** area is displayed. In this area, set the parameters as follows:

   Size . X: **10** Size . Y: **118** Size . Z: **291**
   Segments X: **4** Segments Y: **3** Segments Z: **3**

7. Align *Cube* in the Perspective viewport, as shown in Figure 3-75.

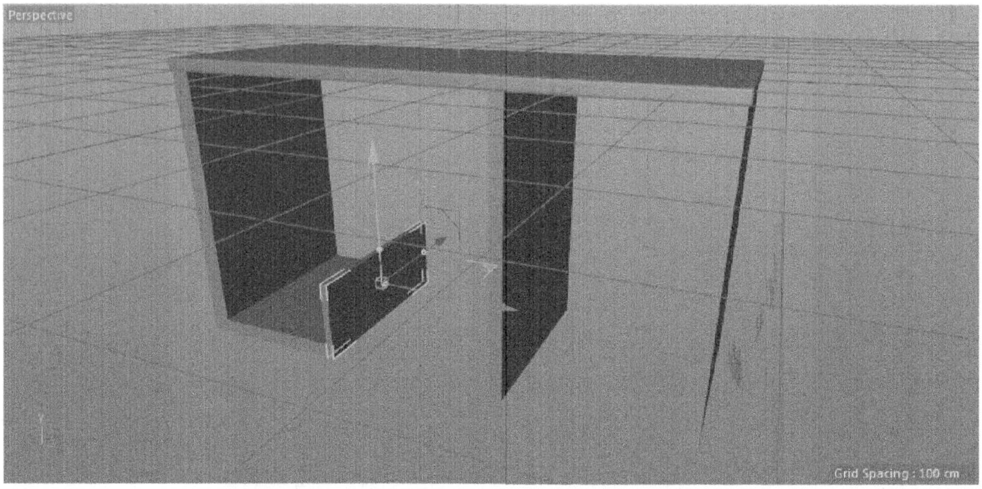

Figure 3-75 *Cube aligned in the Perspective viewport*

Next, you will create design of the side support of *Computer table*.

8. Choose **Create > Object** from the main menu; a cascading menu is displayed. Next, choose **Cube** from it; a cube is created in the Perspective viewport and the *Cube.1* object is added to the Object Manager.

9. In the Attribute Manager, make sure the **Object** button is chosen. In the **Object Properties** area, set the parameters as follows:

   Size . X: **53** Size . Y: **37**
   Segments X: 5 Segments Y: 3 Segments Z: 3

   Select the **Fillet** check box and enter **5** in the **Fillet Radius** spinner.

10. In the Attribute Manager, choose the **Coord** button; the **Coordinates** area is displayed. In this area, set the parameters as follows:

    P . X: **-345.355** P . Y: **-89.77**

    Figure 3-76 displays *Cube.1* positioned in the Perspective viewport.

    Next, you will create a copy of *Cube.1*.

11. Make sure the *Cube.1* object is selected in the Object Manager. Press and hold the left mouse button and the CTRL key and then drag the cursor above *Cube.1* in the Object Manager. Next, release the left mouse button; the *Cube.2* object is added to the Object Manager.

12. Make sure *Cube.2* is selected in the Object Manager. In the Attribute Manager, make sure the **Coord** button is chosen. In the **Coordinates** area, enter **-168.162** in the **P . Y** spinner; the *Cube.2* object is positioned in the Perspective viewport.

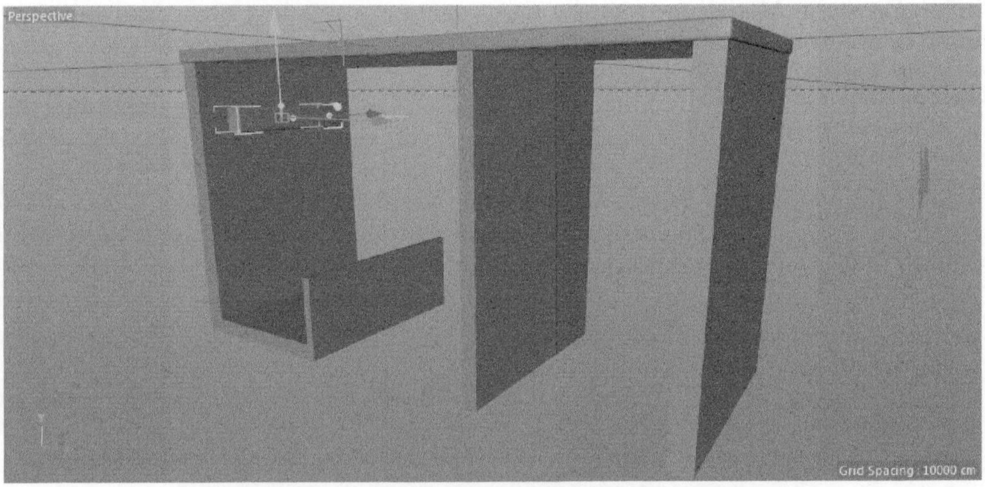

***Figure 3-76** Cube.1 positioned in the Perspective viewport*

13. Make sure the *Cube.2* is selected in the Object Manager. Press and hold the left mouse button and the CTRL key and then drag the cursor above *Cube.2* in the Object Manager. Next, release the left mouse button; the *Cube.3* is added in the Object Manager.

14. Make sure *Cube.3* is selected in the Object Manager. In the Attribute Manager, make sure the **Coord** button is chosen. In the **Coordinates** area, enter **-255.253** in the **P . Y** spinner; the *Cube.3* object is positioned in the Perspective viewport.

15. Select *Cube.1*, *Cube.2,* and *Cube.3* using the CTRL key in the Object Manager. Next, press ALT+G; the *Null* object is added to the Object Manager. Rename it as **left side**. Figure 3-77 displays *left side* positioned in the Perspective viewport.

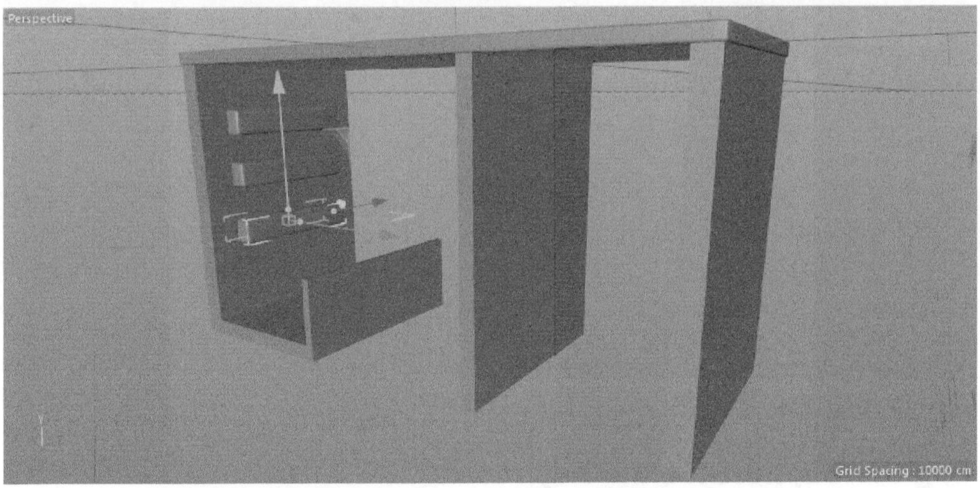

***Figure 3-77** Left side positioned in the Perspective viewport*

16. Choose **Create > Modeling** from the main menu; a cascading menu is displayed. Next, choose **Boole** from it; the *Boole* object is added to the Object Manager.

17. In the Object Manager, press and hold the left mouse button on *left side* and drag it on *Boole*. Now, release the left mouse button; the *left side* is connected to *Boole* in the Object Manager.

18. In the Object Manager, press and hold the left mouse button on *Computer table* and drag it on *Boole*; the *Computer table* is connected to *Boole* in the Object Manager, as shown in Figure 3-78 and holes are created in *Computer table*, as shown in Figure 3-79.

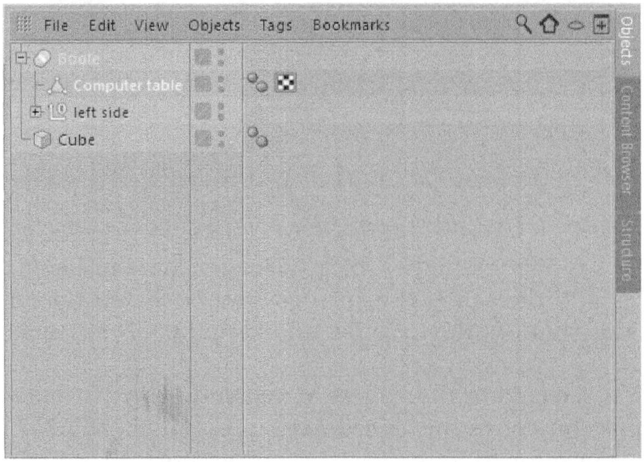

Figure 3-78 *Boole connected to Computer table*

Figure 3-79 *The holes created in the side support of the Computer table*

Creating the Support for the Keyboard

In this section, you will create support for the keyboard.

1. Press F4; the Front viewport is maximized. Choose the **Edges** tool from the Modes Palette; *Computer table* is displayed in the edges mode.

2. Right-click in the Front viewport; a shortcut menu is displayed. Choose **Plane Cut** from the shortcut menu; the **Plane Cut** tool settings are displayed in the Attribute Manager. In the Front viewport, drag the cursor to create a cut, refer to Figure 3-80.

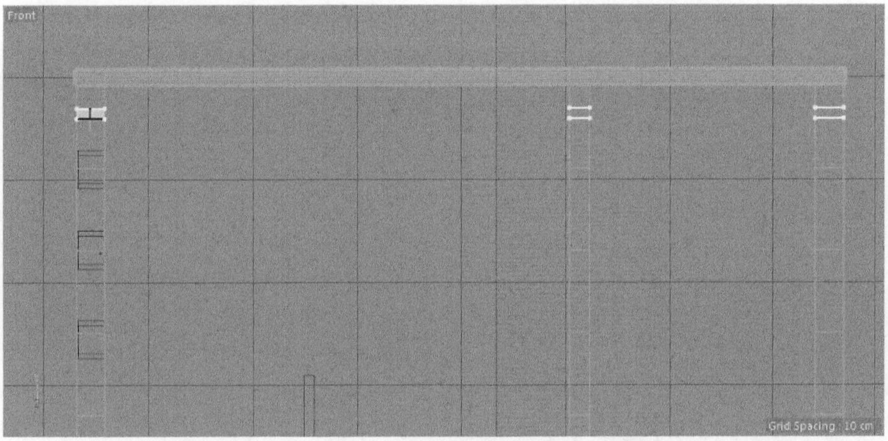

Figure 3-80 *Creating an edge using the* ***Plane Cut*** *tool*

3. Click and drag again to create second cut below the first cut that you created earlier, refer to Figure 3-80; two new edge loops are added to *Computer table*. Similarly, create two more cuts using the **Plane Cut** tool. Figure 3-81 displays four new edge loops added to the *Computer table*.

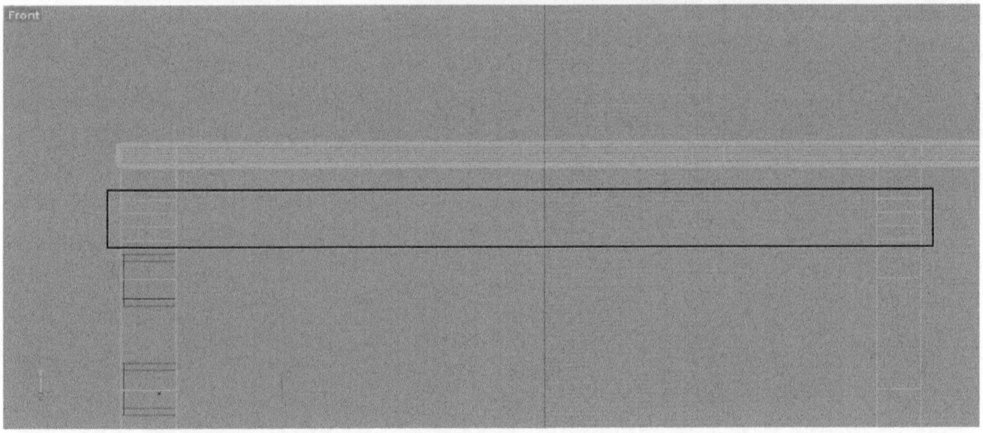

Figure 3-81 *Four new edge loops added to the Computer table*

4. Press F1; the Perspective viewport is maximized. Choose the **Polygons** tool from the Modes Palette; *Computer table* is displayed in the polygon mode. Choose the **Live Selection** tool from the Command Palette and make sure that the **Only Select Visible Elements** check box is selected. Now, select the polygons of both sides of *Computer table*, as shown in Figure 3-82.

5. Right-click in the Perspective viewport; a shortcut menu is displayed. Choose **Extrude** from the shortcut menu; the **Extrude** tool settings are displayed in the Attribute Manager. In the

Attribute Manager, choose the **Options** button; the **Options** area is displayed. In this area, set the value **30** in the **Offset** slider and then press the ENTER key.

Figure 3-83 displays the selected polygons extruded in the Perspective viewport.

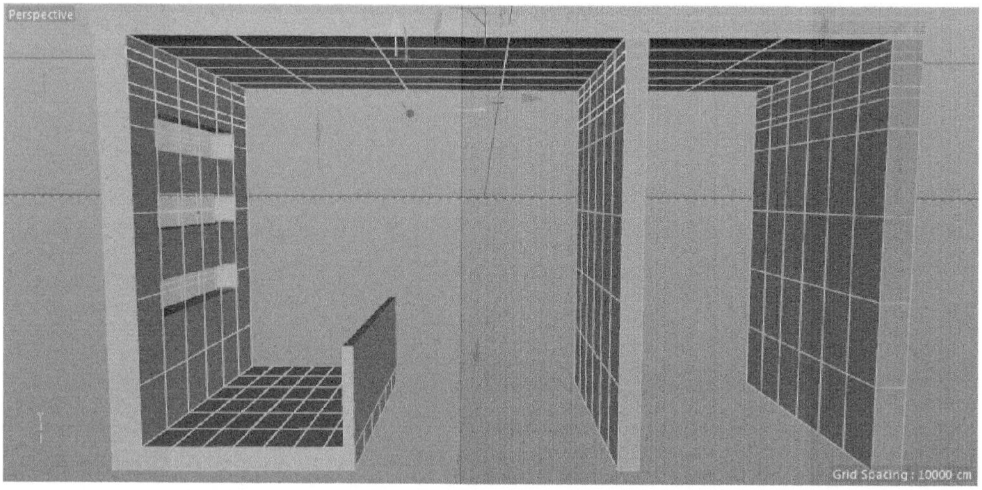

Figure 3-82 *The selected polygons of Computer table*

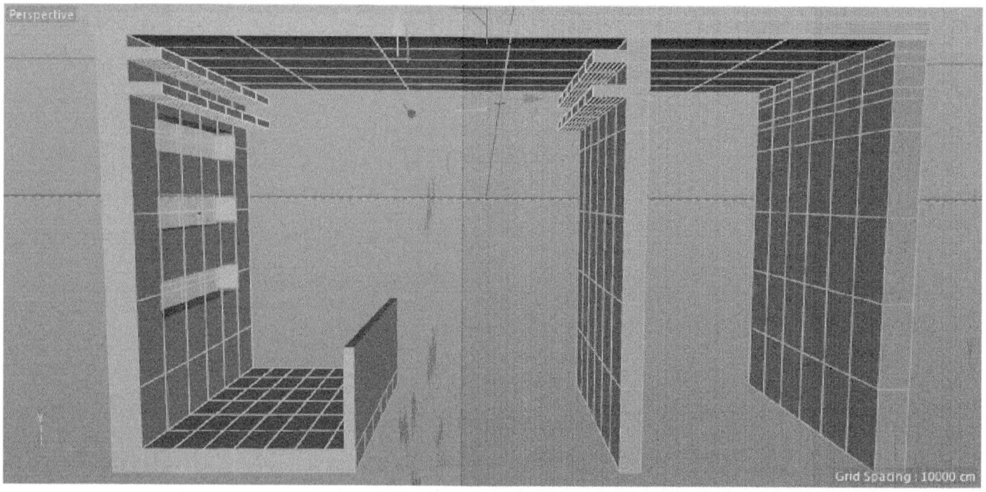

Figure 3-83 *The selected polygons extruded in the Perspective viewport*

6. Press F2; the Top viewport is maximized. Choose **Create > Object** from the main menu; a cascading menu is displayed. Next, choose **Cube** from it; a cube is created in the Top viewport and the *Cube.1* object is added to the Object Manager.

7. In the Attribute Manager, choose the **Basic** button; the **Basic Properties** area is displayed. In this area, enter **Keyboard support** in the **Name** text box; *Cube* is renamed as *Keyboard support* in the Object Manager.

8. Make sure *Keyboard support* is selected in the Object Manager. In the Attribute Manager, choose the **Object** button; the **Object Properties** area is displayed. In the **Object Properties** area, set the parameters as follows:

   Size . X: **429.61** Size . Y: **10** Size . Z: **284**
   Segments X: **6** Segments Y: **2** Segments Z: **6**

   Select the **Fillet** check box and enter **3** in the **Fillet Radius** spinner.

9. In the Attribute Manager, choose the **Coord** button; the **Coordinates** area is displayed. In this area, set the parameters as follows:

   P . X: **-123.684** P . Y: **-44.68** P . Z: **0**

   Press F1; the Perspective viewport is maximized. Figure 3-84 displays *Keyboard support* in the Perspective viewport.

Figure 3-84 *The Keyboard support of Computer table*

Creating the Base for the Monitor

In this section, you will create the base for the monitor.

1. Make sure *Computer table* is selected in the Object Manager. Choose the **Edges** tool from the Modes Palette; the *Computer table* is displayed in the edges mode.

2. Right-click in the Perspective viewport; a shortcut menu is displayed. Choose **Loop/Path Cut** from the shortcut menu; the **Loop/Path Cut** tool settings are displayed in the Attribute Manager.

3. Make sure the **Enable Snap** tool is not chosen in the Modes Palette. Next, click to create a new edge loop, refer to Figure 3-85. Again, create one more edge loop using the **Loop/Path Cut** tool, as shown in Figure 3-86.

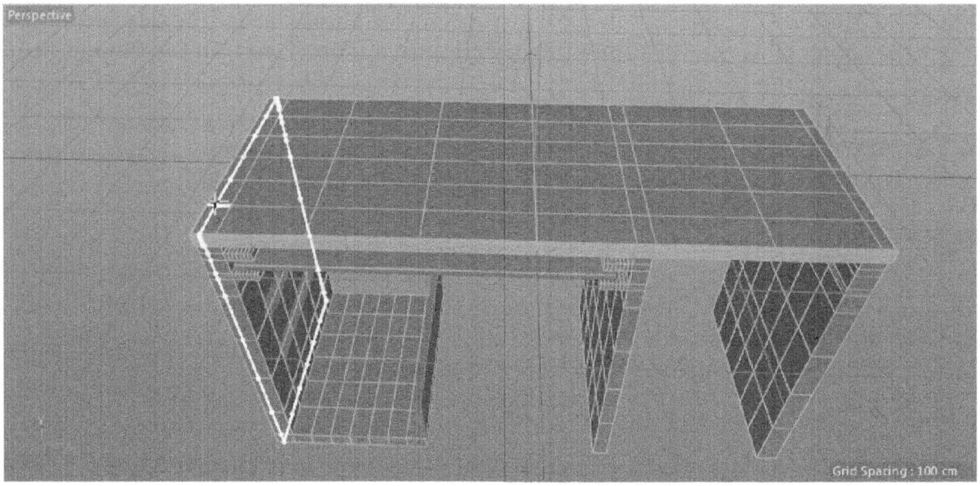

Figure 3-85 New edge loop created

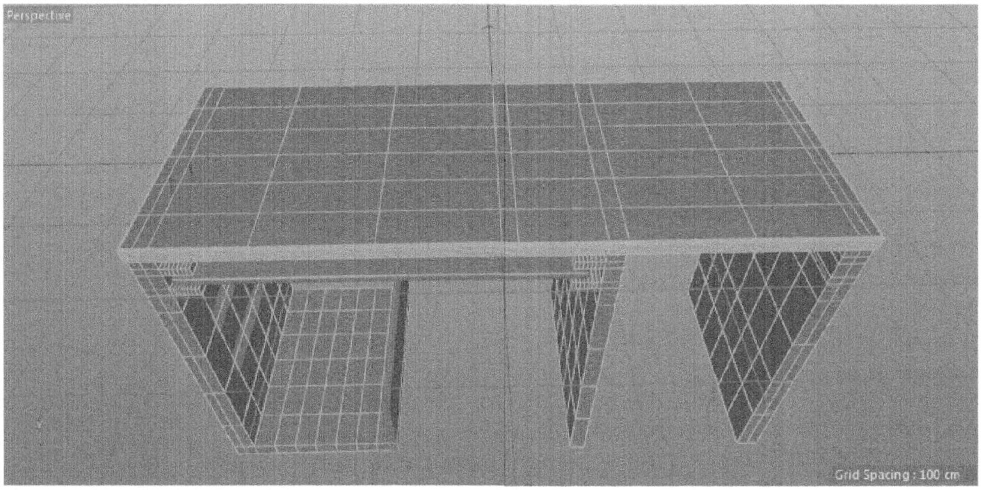

Figure 3-86 Another edge loop added to Computer table

4. Choose the **Polygons** tool from the Modes Palette; the *Computer table* is displayed in the polygon mode. Choose the **Live Selection** tool from the Command Palette and make sure that the **Only Select Visible Elements** check box is selected. Now, select the polygons of *Computer table*, as shown in Figure 3-87.

5. Right-click in the Perspective viewport; a shortcut menu is displayed. Choose **Extrude** from the shortcut menu; the **Extrude** tool settings are displayed in the Attribute Manager. In the Attribute Manager, make sure the **Options** button is chosen. In the **Options** area, set the parameters as follows:

   Offset: **40** Subdivision: **4**

   Figure 3-88 displays the selected polygons extruded in the Perspective viewport.

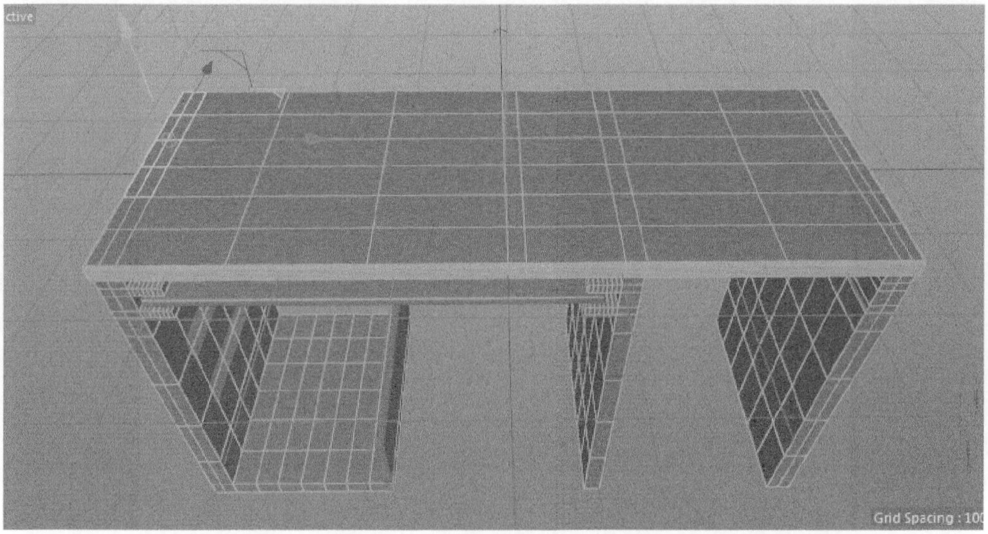

Figure 3-87 The selected polygons of Computer table

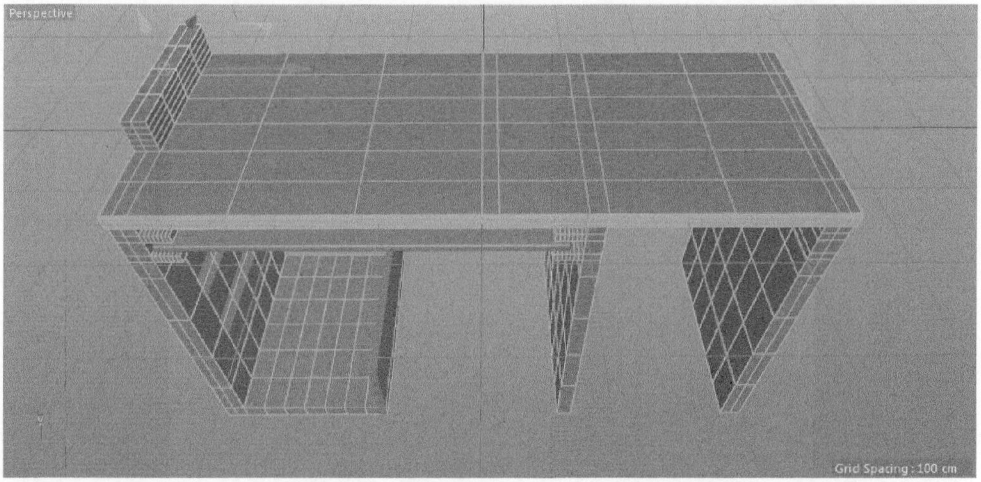

Figure 3-88 The selected polygons extruded in the Perspective viewport

6. Choose the **Live Selection** tool from the Command Palette and make sure that the **Only Select Visible Elements** check box is selected. Now, select the polygons of *Computer table*, as shown in Figure 3-89.

7. Right-click in the Perspective viewport; a shortcut menu is displayed. Choose **Extrude** from the shortcut menu; the **Extrude** tool settings are displayed in the Attribute Manager. In the Attribute Manager, choose the **Options** button; the **Options** area is displayed. In this area, set the parameters as follows:

   Offset: **345** Subdivision: **8**

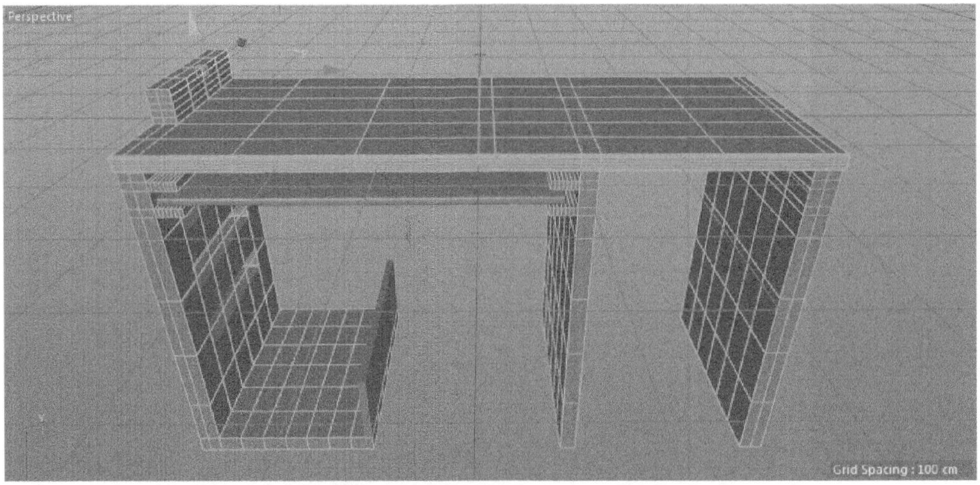

Figure 3-89 The selected polygons of Computer table

Figure 3-90 displays the selected polygons extruded in the Perspective viewport.

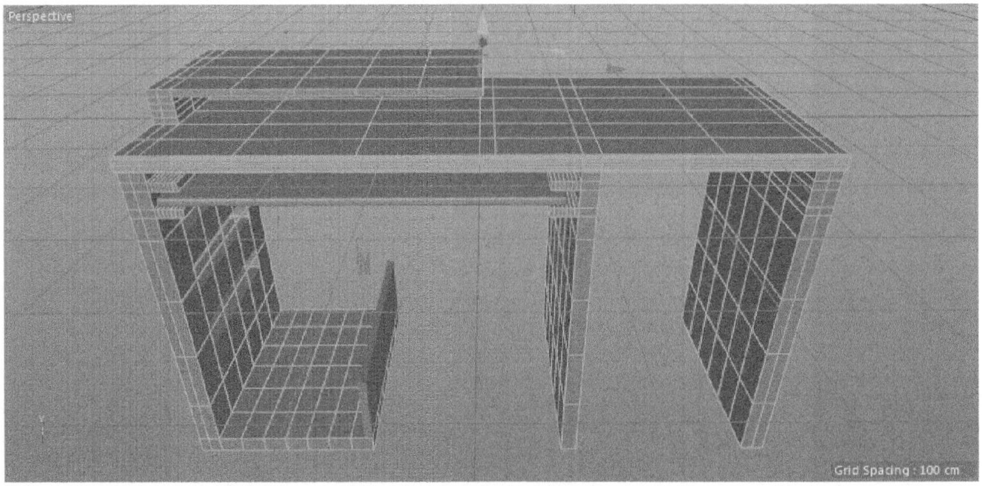

Figure 3-90 The selected polygons extruded in the Perspective viewport

Creating the Top Shelves of the Computer Table

In this section, you will create the top shelves of the computer table.

1. Make sure the polygon mode is activated. Choose the **Live Selection** tool from the Command Palette and make sure that the **Only Select Visible Elements** check box is selected. Now, select the polygons of *Computer table*, as shown in Figure 3-91.

2. Right-click in the Perspective viewport; a shortcut menu is displayed. Choose **Extrude** from the shortcut menu; the **Extrude** tool settings are displayed in the Attribute Manager. In the Attribute Manager, make sure the **Options** button is chosen. In the **Options** area, enter the value **160** in the **Offset** spinner and then press ENTER.

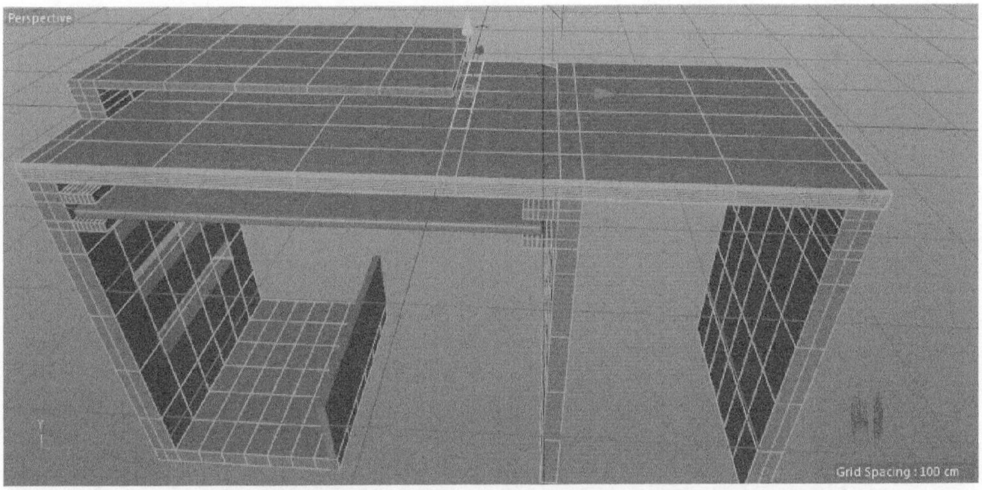

Figure 3-91 *The selected polygons of Computer table*

Figure 3-92 displays the selected polygons extruded in the Perspective viewport.

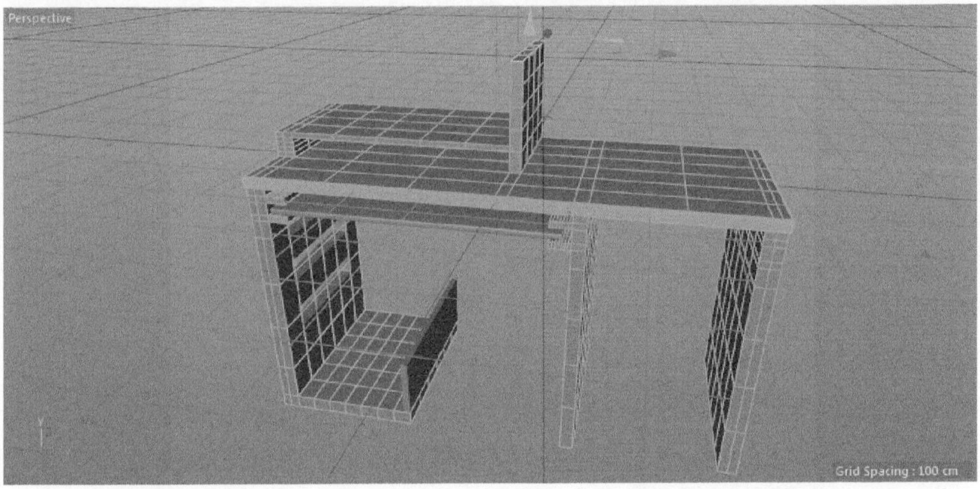

Figure 3-92 *The selected polygons extruded in the Perspective viewport*

3. Choose the **Edges** tool from the Modes Palette; *Computer table* is displayed in the edges mode.

4. Right-click in the Perspective viewport; a shortcut menu is displayed. Choose **Loop/Path Cut** from the shortcut menu; the **Loop/Path Cut** tool settings are displayed in the Attribute Manager.

5. Make sure the **Enable Snap** tool is deactivated in the Modes Palette. Next, click on the edge, refer to Figure 3-93; a new edge loop is added to *Computer table.* Again, create an edge loop using the **Loop/Path Cut** tool, refer to Figure 3-94.

Figure 3-93 Clicking on edge to create a new edge loop

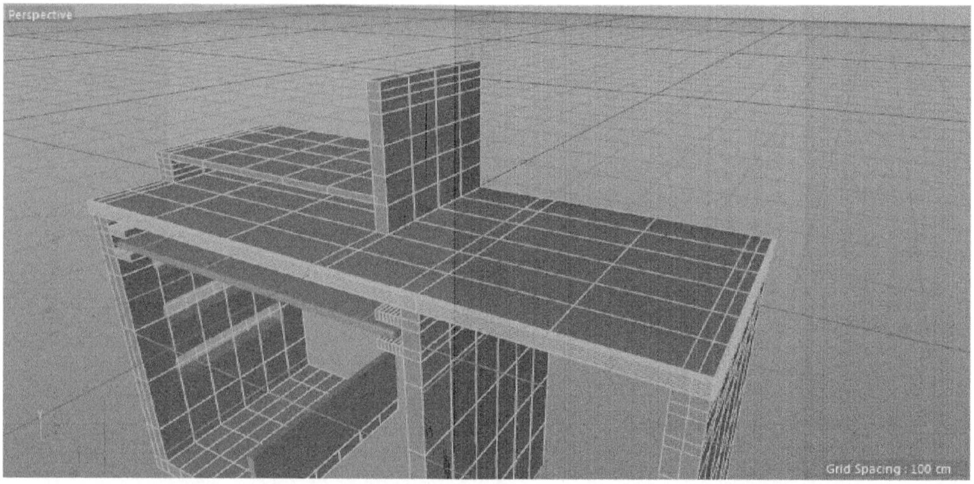

Figure 3-94 Two new edge loops added to the Computer table

6. Choose the **Polygons** tool from the Modes Palette; the Computer table is displayed in the polygon mode. Choose the **Live Selection** tool from the Command Palette and make sure that the **Only Select Visible Elements** check box is selected. Now, select the polygons of Computer table, as shown in Figure 3-95.

7. Right-click in the Perspective viewport; a shortcut menu is displayed. Choose **Extrude** from the shortcut menu; the **Extrude** tool settings are displayed in the Attribute Manager. Make sure the **Options** button is chosen in this manager. In the **Options** area, set the parameters as follows:

   Offset: **335** Subdivision: **12**

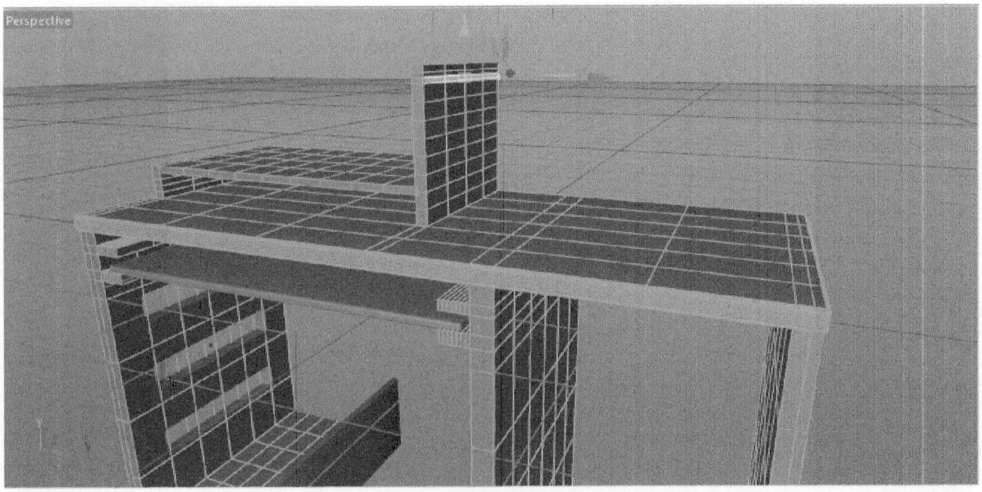

Figure 3-95 *The selected polygons of Computer table*

Figure 3-96 displays the selected polygons extruded in the Perspective viewport.

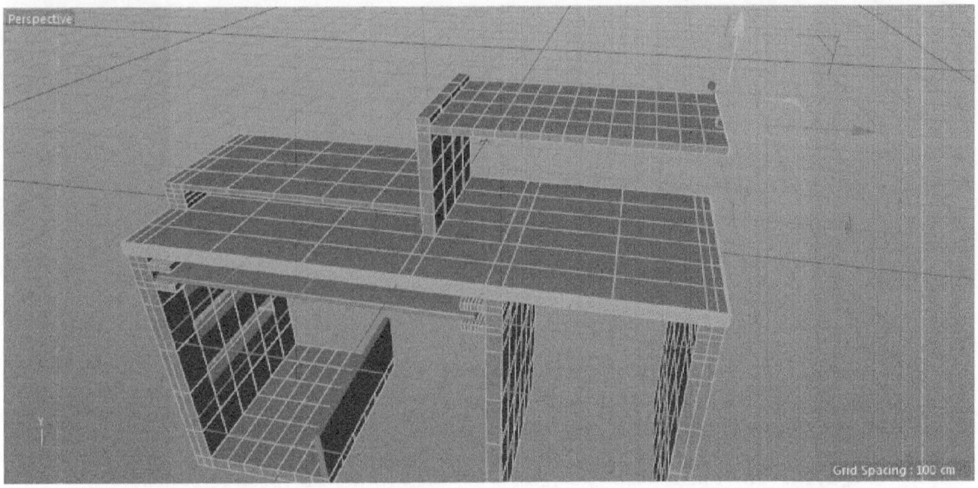

Figure 3-96 *The selected polygons extruded in the Perspective viewport*

8. Make sure the polygon mode is activated. Choose the **Live Selection** tool from the Command Palette and make sure that the **Only Select Visible Elements** check box is selected. Now, select the four polygons of *Computer table*, as shown in Figure 3-97.

9. Right-click in the Perspective viewport; a shortcut menu is displayed. Choose **Extrude** from the shortcut menu; the **Extrude** tool settings are displayed in the Attribute Manager. Choose the **Options** button in this manager; the **Options** area is displayed. In this area, enter **160** in the **Offset** spinner.

Figure 3-98 displays the selected polygons extruded in the Perspective viewport.

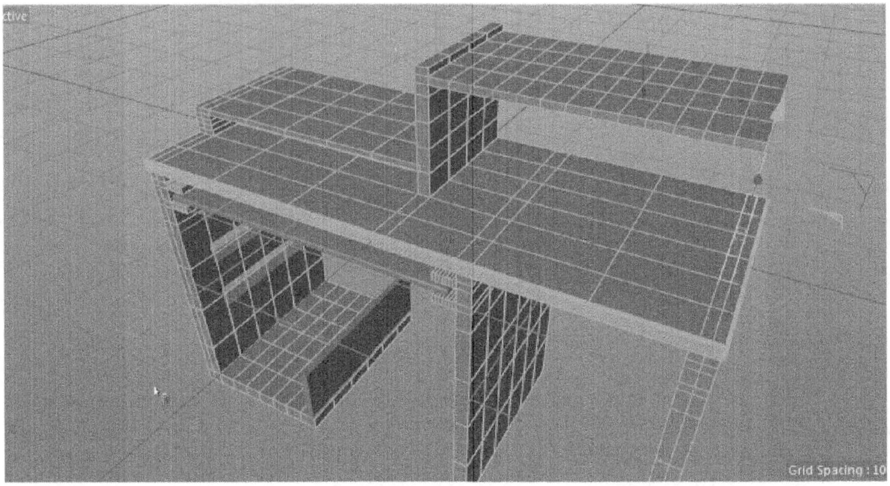

Figure 3-97 The selected polygons of Computer table

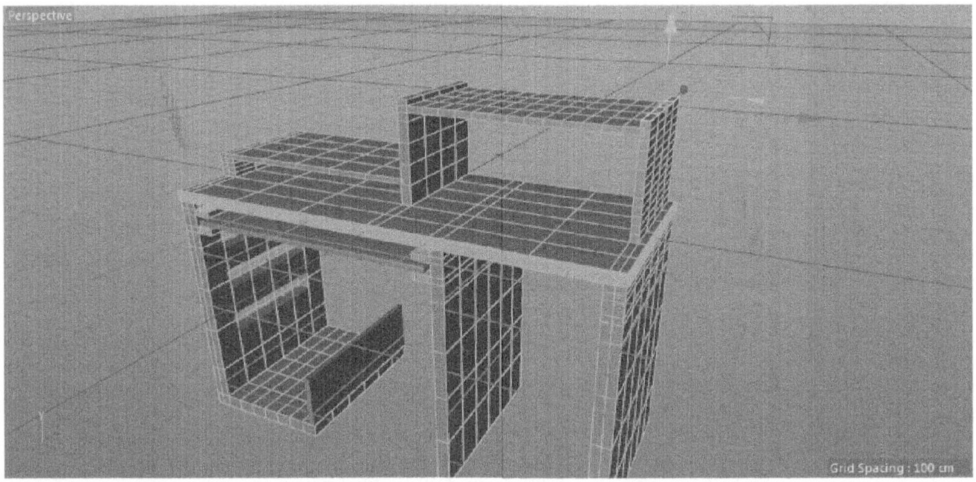

Figure 3-98 The selected polygons extruded in the Perspective viewport

10. Choose the **Edges** tool from the Modes Palette; the *Computer table* is displayed in the edges mode.

11. Right-click in the Perspective viewport; a shortcut menu is displayed. Choose **Loop/Path Cut** from the shortcut menu; the **Loop/Path Cut** tool settings are displayed in the Attribute Manager. Make sure **Loop** is selected in the **Mode** drop-down list and then clear the **Restrict to Selection** check box.

12. Make sure the **Enable Snap** tool is deactivated in the Modes Palette. Next, click to create an edge loop, refer to Figure 3-99; a new edge loop is added to *Computer table.* Again, create an edge loop using the **Loop/Path Cut** tool, refer to Figure 3-100.

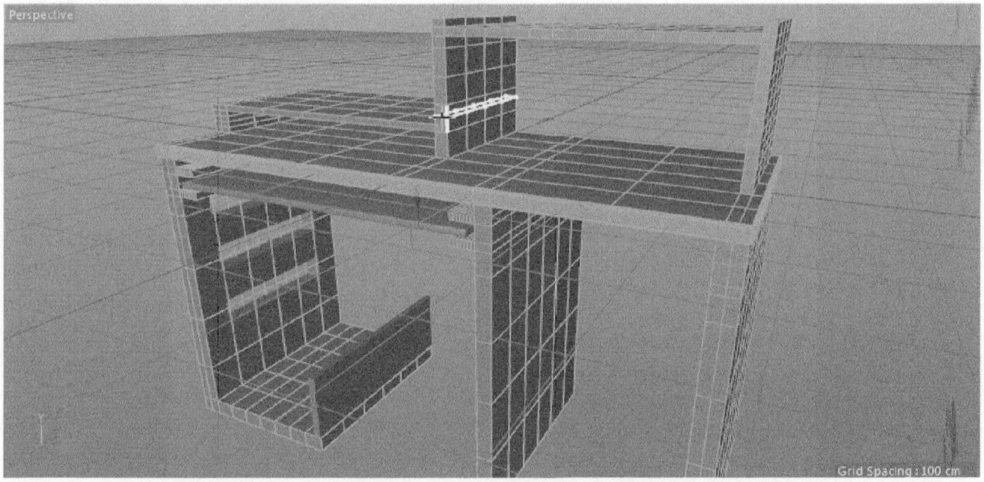

Figure 3-99 *Clicking on edge to create a new edge loop*

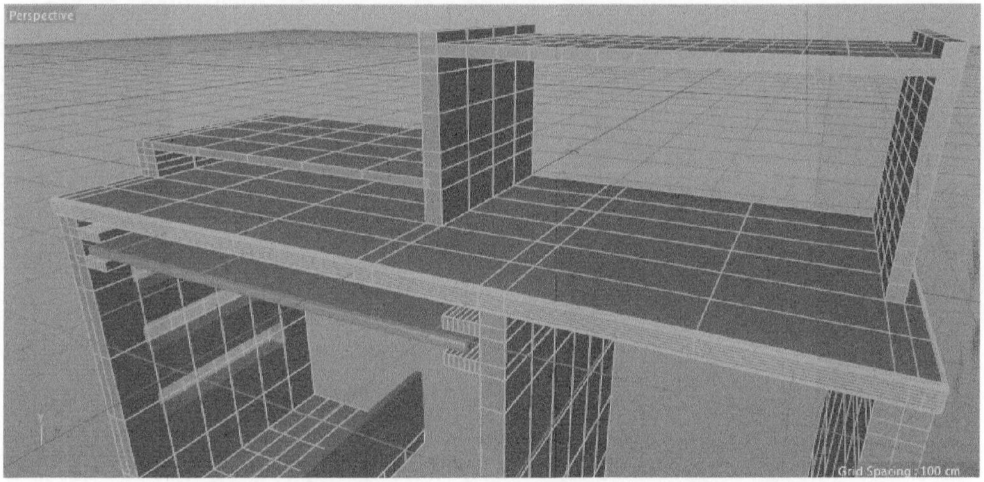

Figure 3-100 *The new edge loop added to the Computer table*

13. Make sure the polygon mode is activated. Choose the **Live Selection** tool from the Command Palette and make sure that the **Only Select Visible Elements** check box is selected. Now, select the polygons of *Computer table*, as shown in Figure 3-101.

14. Right-click in the Perspective viewport; a shortcut menu is displayed. Choose **Extrude** from the shortcut menu; the **Extrude** tool settings are displayed in the Attribute Manager. Choose the **Options** button in this manager; the **Options** area is displayed. In this area, enter **335** in the **Offset** spinner.

    Figure 3-102 displays the selected polygons extruded in the Perspective viewport.

Figure 3-101 The selected polygons of Computer table

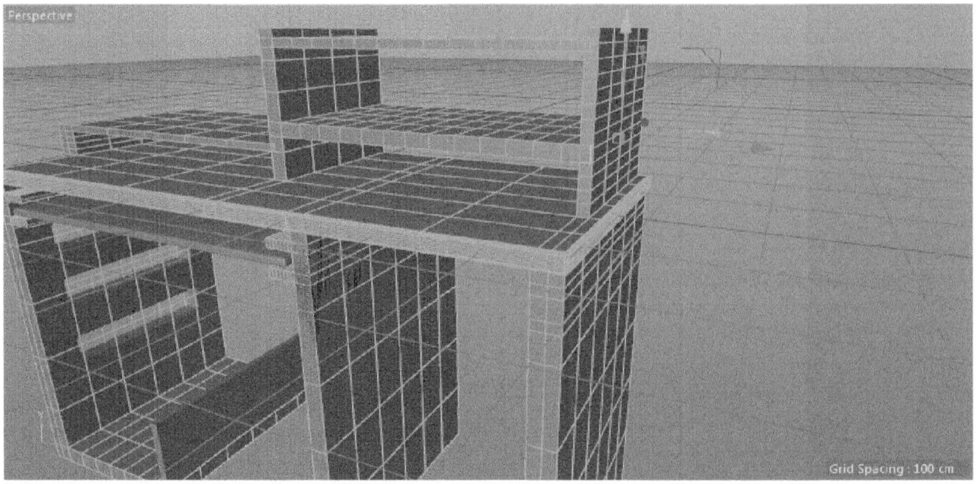

Figure 3-102 The selected polygons extruded in the Perspective viewport

Creating the Bottom Shelf of the Computer Table

In this section, you will create the bottom shelf of *Computer table*.

1. Choose **Create > Object** from the main menu; a cascading menu is displayed. Next, choose **Cube** from it; a cube is created in the Perspective viewport and *Cube* is added to the Object Manager.

2. In the Attribute Manager, choose the **Basic** button; the **Basic Properties** area is displayed. In this area, enter **Shelf1** in the **Name** text box; *Cube* is renamed as *Shelf1* in the Object Manager.

3. In the Attribute Manager, choose the **Object** button; the **Object Properties** area is displayed. In this area, set the parameters as follows:

   Size . X: **254.61** Size . Y: **15** Size . Z: **280**
   Segments X: **6** Segments Y: **4** Segments Z: **6**

   Select the **Fillet** check box and enter **3** in the **Fillet Radius** spinner.

4. In the Attribute Manager, choose the **Coord** button; the **Coordinates** area is displayed. In this area, set the parameters as follows:

   P . X: **234.854** P . Y: **-119.37** P . Z: **0**

   Figure 3-103 displays *Shelf1* positioned in the Perspective viewport.

Figure 3-103 *Shelf1 positioned in the Perspective viewport*

5. Make sure the *Shelf1* is selected in the Object Manager. Press and hold the left mouse button and the CTRL key and then drag the cursor above *Shelf1* in the Object Manager. Next, release the left mouse button; the *Shelf1.1* object is added in the Object Manager.

6. Make sure the *Shelf1.1* object is selected in the Object Manager. In the Attribute Manager, make sure the **Coord** button is chosen. In the **Coordinates** area, enter **-291.892** in the **P . Y** spinner; the *Shelf1.1* object is positioned in the Perspective viewport, as shown in Figure 3-104.

Creating the Magazine Stand

In this section, you will create the magazine stand of Computer table by using the **Polygon Pen** tool.

1. Select the **Model** option from the **Layout** drop-down list located at the upper right corner of the interface; the Modeling Tool Palette is displayed at the lower portion of the interface, refer to Figure 3-105.

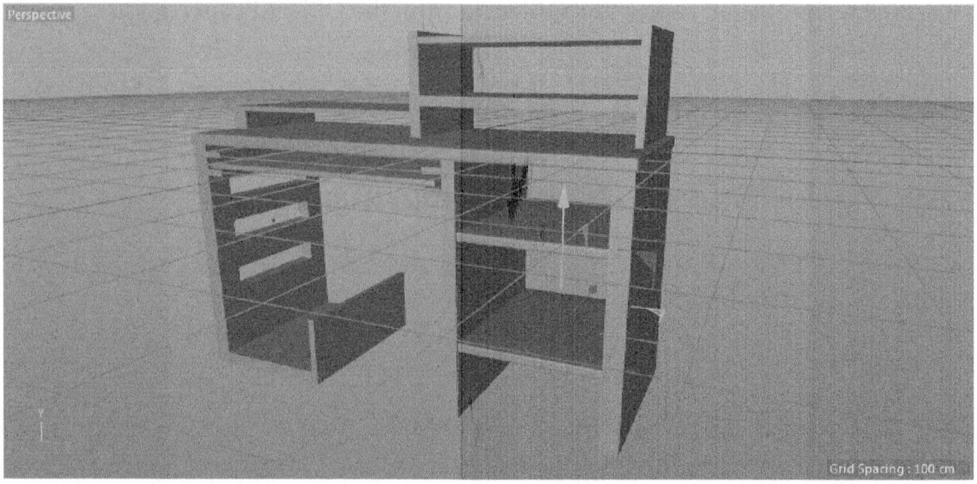

Figure 3-104 *Shelf1.1 positioned in the Perspective viewport*

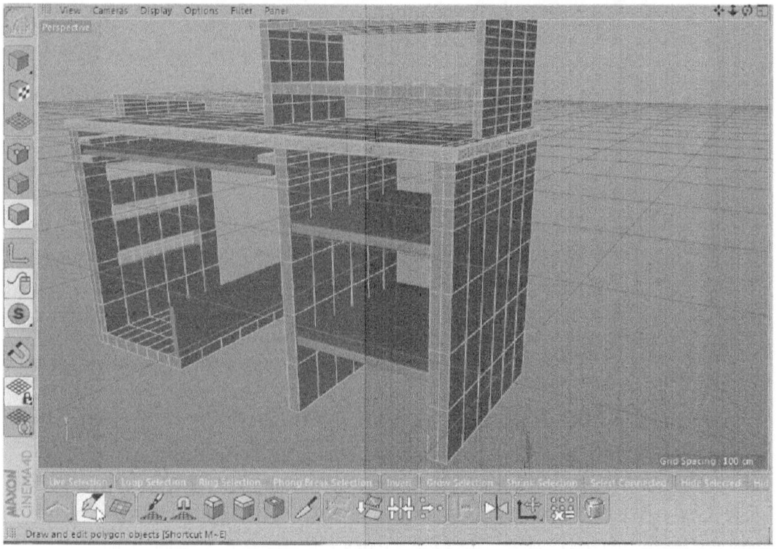

Figure 3-105 *Choosing the* ***Polygon Pen*** *tool from the Modeling Tool Palette*

2. Choose the **Polygon Pen** tool from the Modeling Tool Palette and then hover the cursor on the polygon of the *Computer table*, as shown in Figure 3-106; the highlighted polygon is displayed in the Perspective viewport.

3. Hold the CTRL key and drag the highlighted polygon, as shown in Figure 3-107.

Figure 3-106 The highlighted polygon

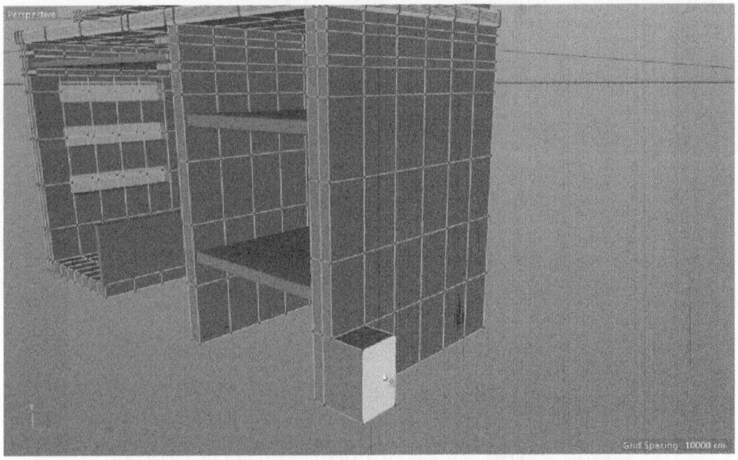

Figure 3-107 Dragging the highlighted polygon

4. Hover the cursor on the top polygon; the polygon is highlighted, as shown in Figure 3-108. Next, hold the CTRL key and drag the highlighted polygon, as shown in Figure 3-109.

5. Rotate the viewport using the ALT key and then hover the cursor on the polygon; the polygon is highlighted, as shown in Figure 3-110. Next, hold the CTRL key and drag the highlighted polygon, as shown in Figure 3-111.

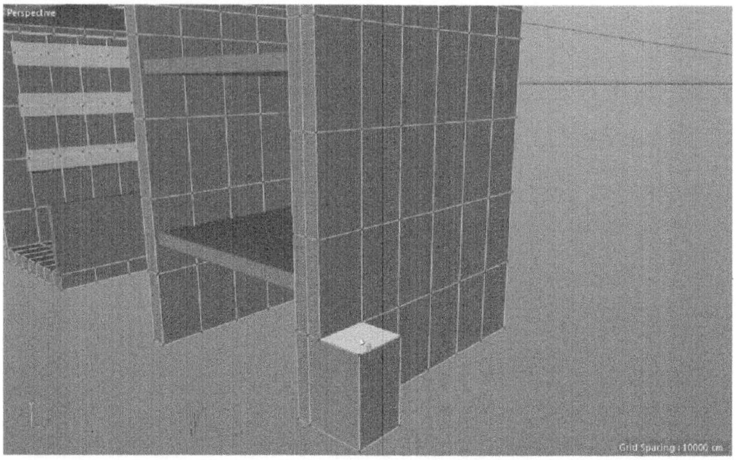

Figure 3-108 The highlighted polygon of magazine stand

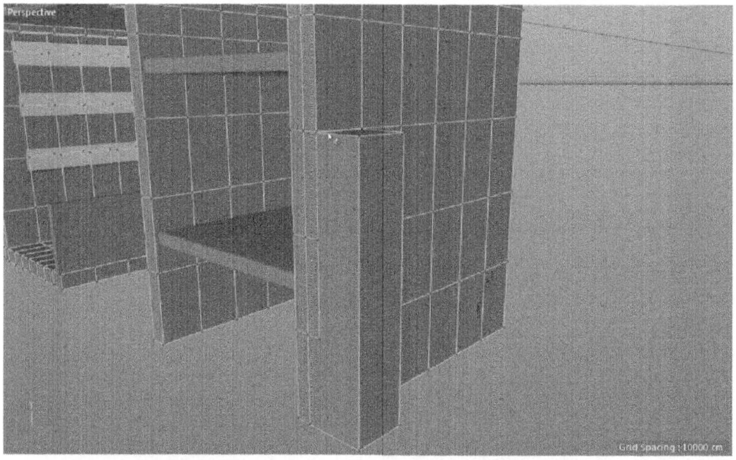

Figure 3-109 Dragging the highlighted polygon

Figure 3-110 Highlighted polygon

Figure 3-111 *Dragging the highlighted polygon*

Next, you will create the edges on the magazine stand surface.

6. Choose the **Edges** tool in the Mode palette and make sure the **Polygon Pen** tool is chosen in the Modeling Tool Palette. Next, click on an edge, as shown in Figure 3-112 and then click again on another edge; a new edge is created, as shown in Figure 3-113. Similarly, create two more edges, refer to Figure 3-114.

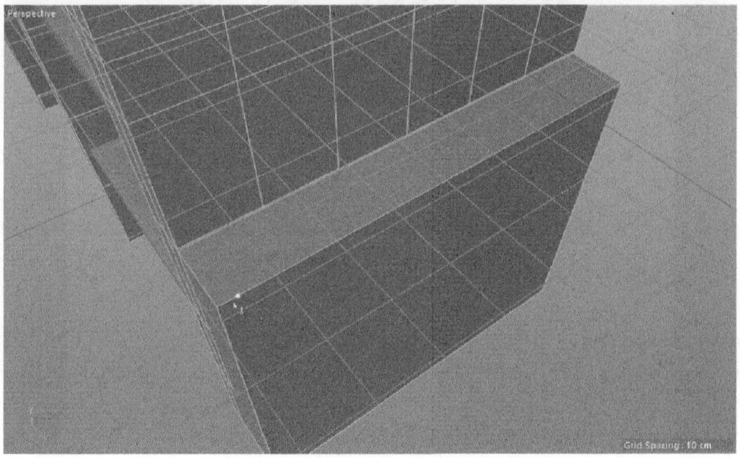

Figure 3-112 *Clicking on an edge*

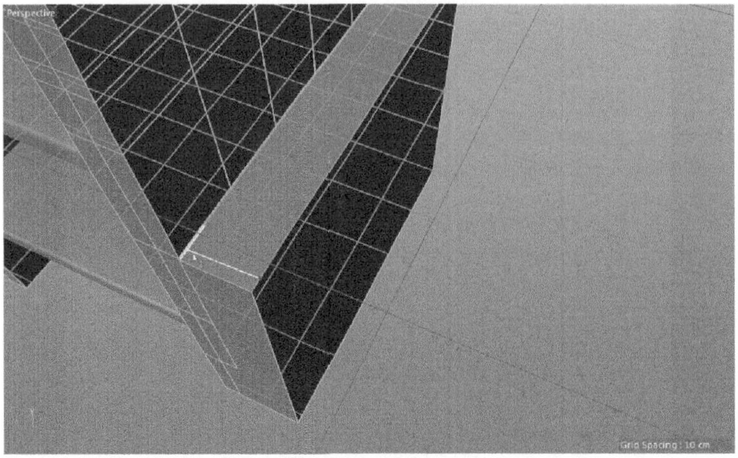

Figure 3-113 Clicking on second edge to create a new edge

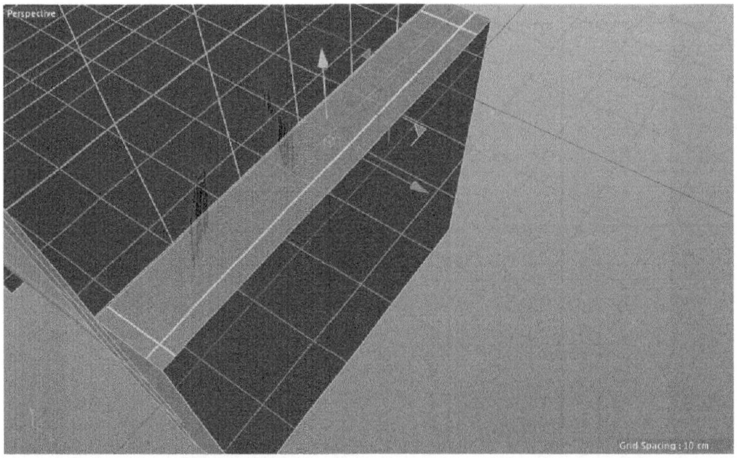

Figure 3-114 Three new edges added to the magazine stand

7. Hover the cursor on the polygon; the polygon is highlighted, as shown in Figure 3-115. Next, hold the CTRL key and drag the highlighted polygon downward, as shown in Figure 3-116.

   Next, you will create a design on the magazine support.

8. Choose the **Edges** tool in the Mode palette. Make sure the **Polygon Pen** tool is chosen in the Modeling Tool Palette. Next, click on the bottom-left point, as shown in Figure 3-117 and then click on the top-right corner point; a new edge is created, as shown in Figure 3-118.

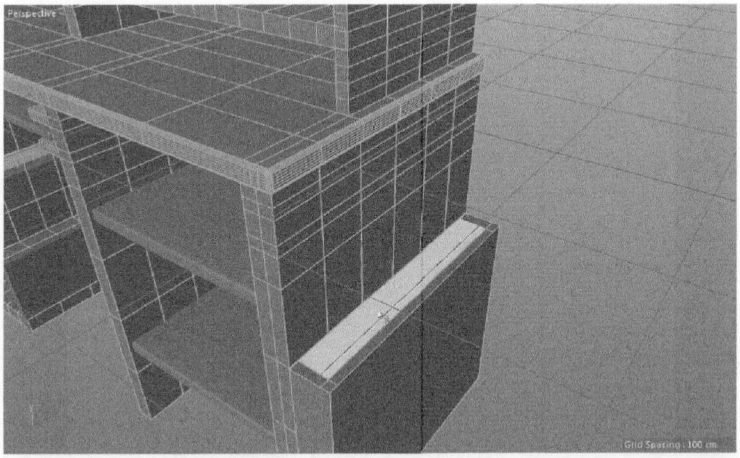

Figure 3-115 *Highlighted polygon*

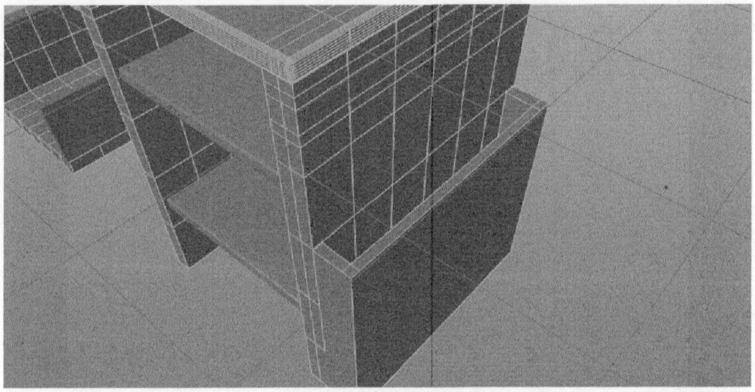

Figure 3-116 *Dragging the highlighted polygon downward*

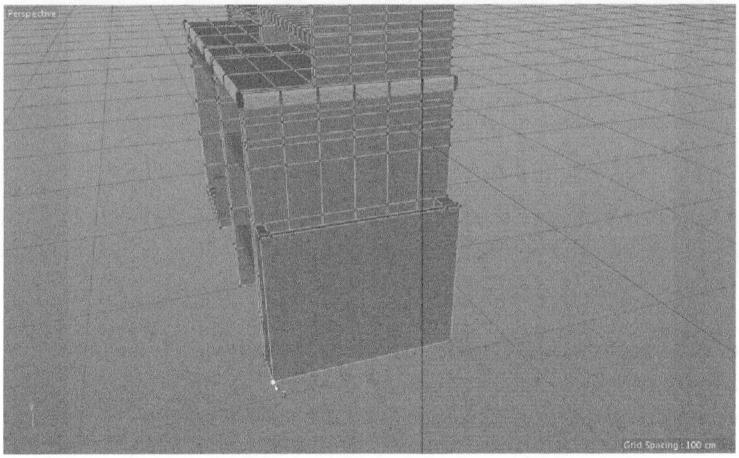

Figure 3-117 *Clicking on the corner point*

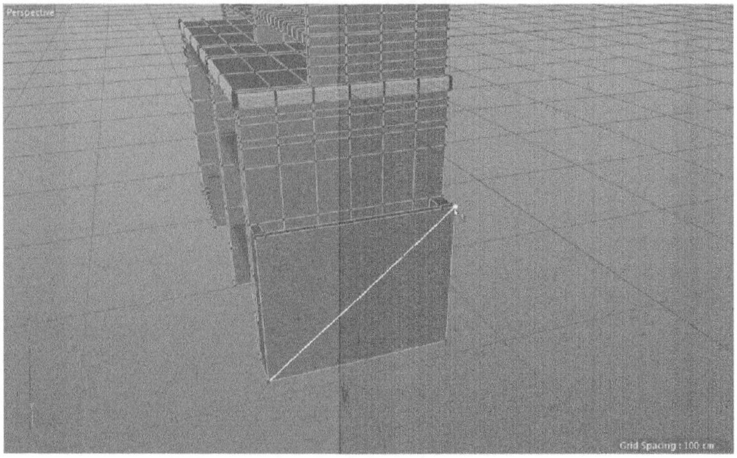

Figure 3-118 The new edge created

9. Hover the cursor over the created edge. Press and hold the CTRL+SHIFT keys and then drag (do not click, just drag); the shape of the edge is changed to an arc shape, refer to Figure 3-119.

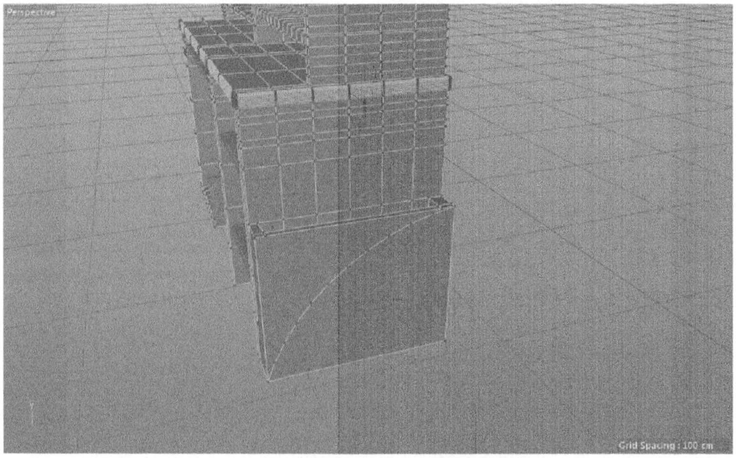

Figure 3-119 The edge converted to an arc shape

10. Hover the cursor on the polygon; the polygon is highlighted, as shown in Figure 3-120. Next, hold the CTRL key and drag the highlighted polygon; the selected polygon is extruded, as shown in Figure 3-121.

Changing the Background Color of the Scene

To change the background color of the scene to white in the final output, follow the steps given in Tutorial 1 of Chapter 2.

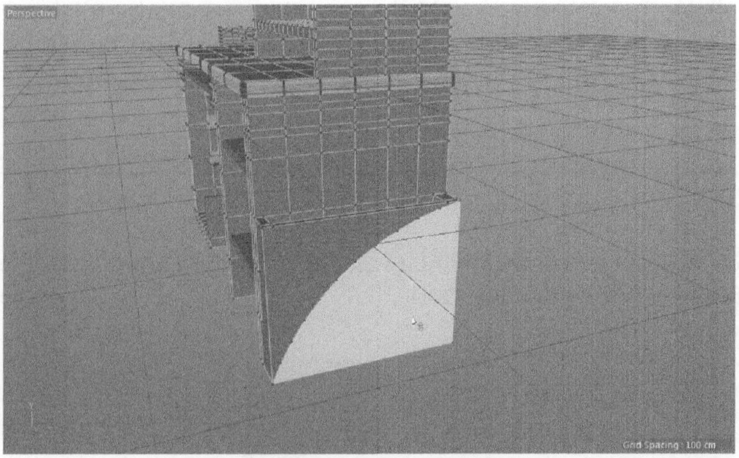

Figure 3-120 Highlighted polygon

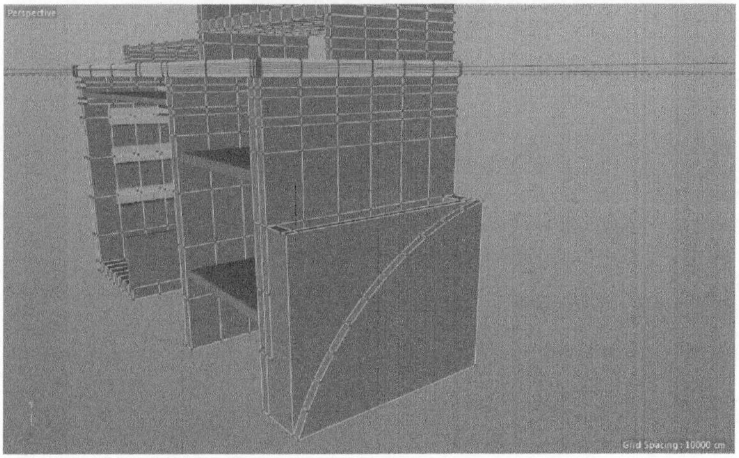

Figure 3-121 The extruded polygon

Saving and Rendering the Scene

In this section, you will save and render the scene. You can also view the final render of the model by downloading the file *c03_cinema4d_r20_rndr.zip* from *www.cadcim.com*. The path of the file is mentioned at the beginning of the chapter.

1. Choose **File > Save** from the main menu; the **Save File** dialog box is displayed. In this dialog box, browse to the location *\Documents\c4dR20\c03*.

2. Enter **c03tut2** in the **File name** text box and then choose the **Save** button.

3. In the Perspective viewport, set the camera angle using the Viewport Navigation Tools located at the extreme top right of the Perspective viewport. Next, choose the **Render to Picture Viewer** tool from the Command Palette. Alternatively, press SHIFT+R; the **Picture Viewer** window is displayed.

4. In the **Picture Viewer** window, choose **File > Save as**; the **Save** dialog box is displayed.

5. In the **Save** dialog box, choose the **OK** button; the **Save Dialog** dialog box is displayed. Next, browse to *\Documents\c4dR20\c03*. In the **File Name** text box, type **c03_tut2_rndr**. Next, choose the **Save** button; the file is saved at the desired location.

   Figure 3-66 displays the final output.

Tutorial 3

In this tutorial, you will create the model of a vase, as shown in Figure 3-122, using the **Cloner**, **Volume Builder**, and **Volume Mesher** tools. **(Expected time: 20 min)**

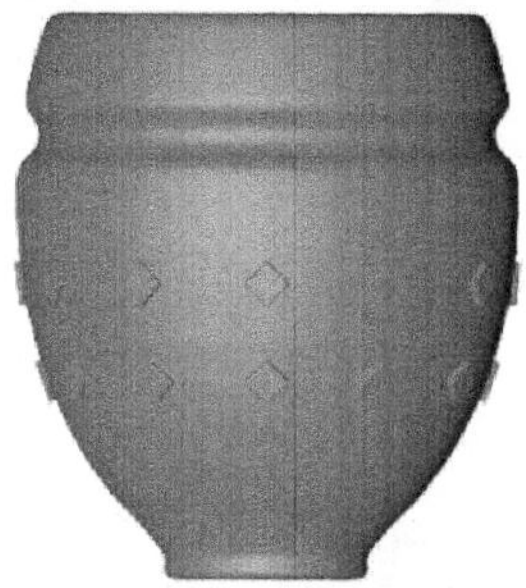

Figure 3-122 *Model of a vase*

The following steps are required to complete this tutorial:

a. Create the vase.
b. Create groove on the vase.
c. Create design on the vase.
c. Change the background color of the scene.
d. Save and render the scene.

Creating the Vase

In this section, you will create vase using the **Sphere** tool.

1. Press F4; the Front viewport is activated. Choose **Create > Object** from the main menu; a cascading menu is displayed. Next, choose **Sphere** from it; a sphere is created in the Front viewport and *Sphere* is added to the Object Manager. Choose **Display > Gouraud Shading** from the Menu in editor view; *Sphere* is displayed in the shading mode.

2. In the Attribute Manager, choose the **Basic** button; the **Basic Properties** area is displayed. In this area, enter **vase** in the **Name** text box; *Sphere* is renamed as *vase* in the Object Manager.

3. Make sure *vase* is selected in the Object Manager. In the Attribute Manager, choose the **Object** button; the **Object Properties** area is displayed. In the **Object Properties** area, set the parameters as follows:

   Radius: **200** Segments: **48**

4. Choose the **Coord.** button and enter **1.5** in the **S.Y** spinner; *vase* is displayed as shown in Figure 3-123.

5. Make sure *vase* is selected in the Front viewport. Now, choose the **Make Editable** tool from the Modes Palette; *vase* is converted into a polygonal object.

6. Choose the **Live Selection** tool from the Command Palette and then choose the **Polygons** tool from the Modes Palette; *vase* is displayed in the polygon mode. In the Attribute Manager, make sure the **Options** button is chosen. In the **Options** area, clear the **Only Select Visible Elements** check box. Next, choose the **Live Selection** tool and select the polygons of *vase* in the Front viewport, as shown in Figure 3-124. If required, decrease the size of the cursor for selection.

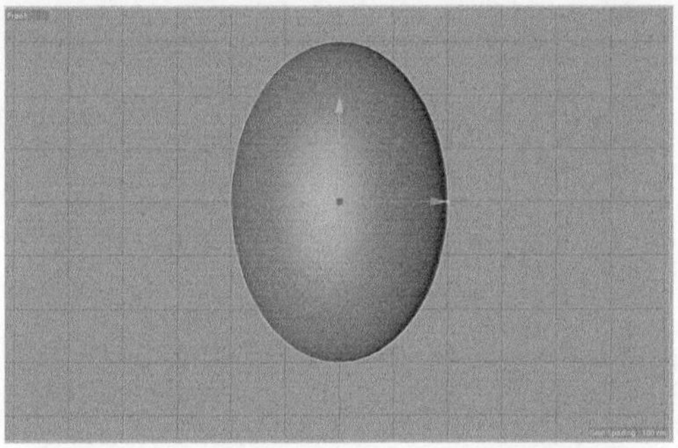

Figure 3-123 *vase displayed in the Front viewport*

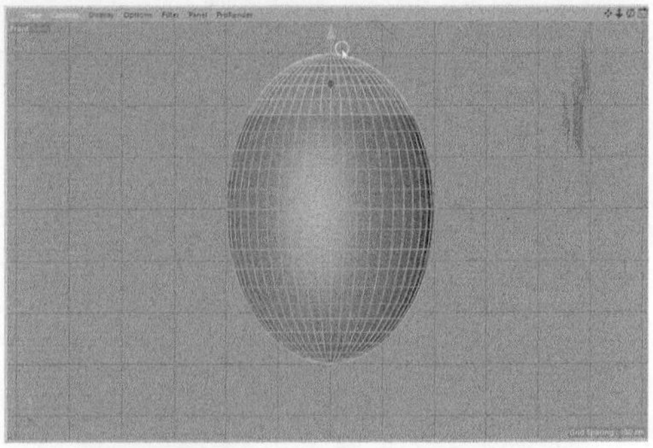

Figure 3-124 *Selected Polygons*

7. Scale down the selected polygons uniformly, refer to Figure 3-125. Next scale the polygons only in Y-axis to set them on the upper edge of *vase*, refer to Figure 3-126.

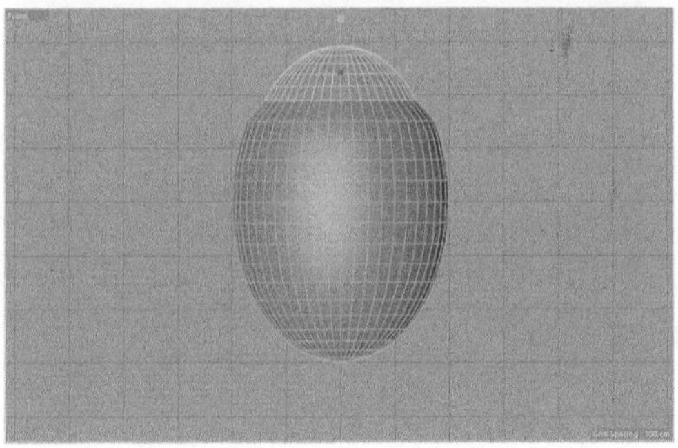

Figure 3-125 *Selected polygons scaled uniformly*

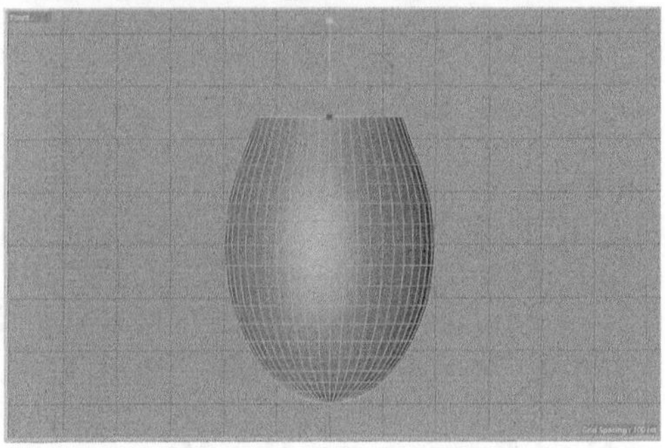

Figure 3-126 *Selected Polygons scaled in Y-axis*

8. Choose the **Move** tool from the Command Palette and move the selected polygons downword, as shown in Figure 3-127.

9. Right-click in the Front viewport; a shortcut menu is displayed. Choose **Extrude** from the shortcut menu; the **Extrude** tool settings are displayed in the Attribute Manager. In the **Extrude** tool settings area, make sure the **Options** button is chosen. In the **Options** area, set **-230** as the value in the **Offset** spinner and then press the ENTER key; the selected polygons are extruded in the Perspective viewport, as shown in Figure 3-128.

10. Choose the **Live Selection** tool and select the bottommost polygons of *vase,* as shown in Figure 3-129. Next, activate the **Scale** tool and scale these polygons in Y-axis as shown in Figure 3-130.

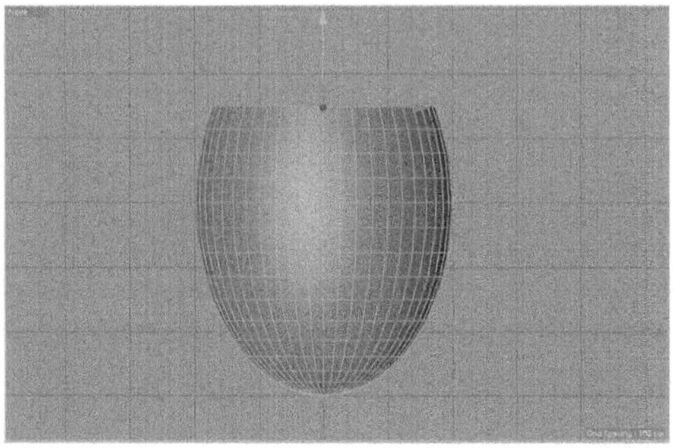

Figure 3-127 *Selected polygons moved downword*

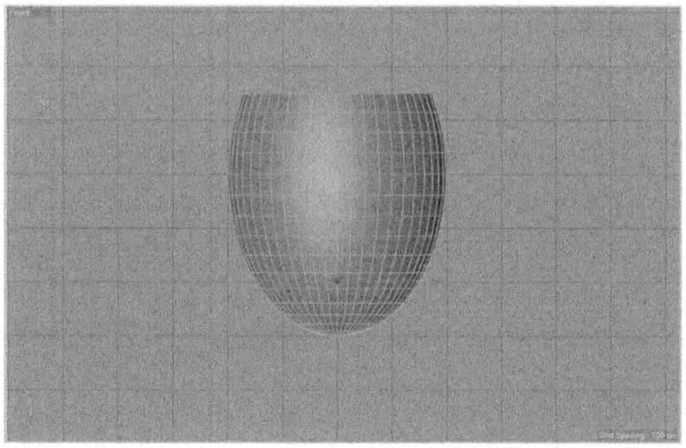

Figure 3-128 *Selected Polygons Extruded*

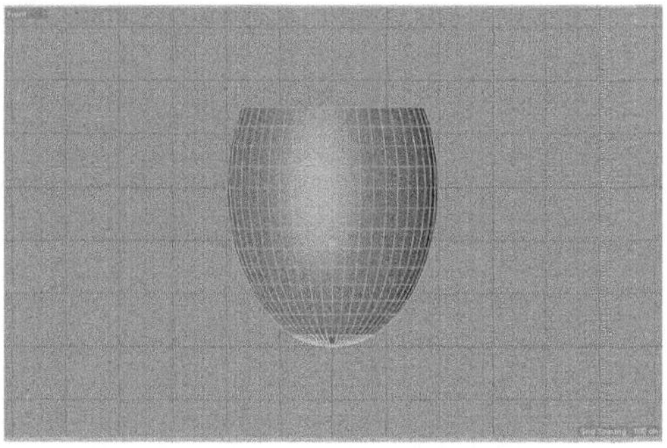

Figure 3-129 *Bottommost polygons selected*

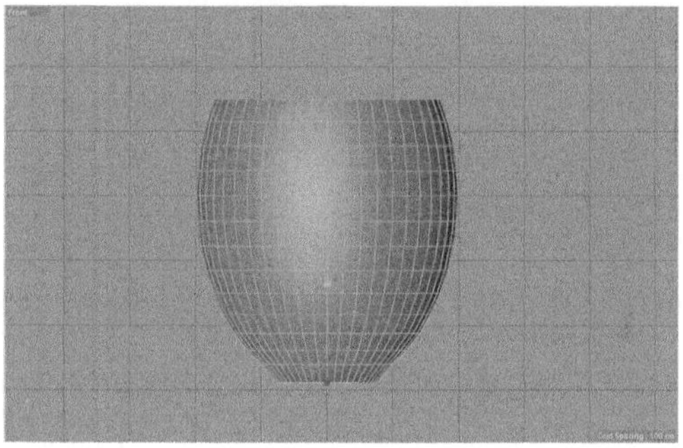

Figure 3-130 *Selected polygons scaled in y-axis*

11. Make sure the scaled polygons are selected. Next, right-click in the Front viewport; a shortcut menu is displayed. Choose **Bevel** from the shortcut menu; the **Bevel** tool settings are displayed in the Attribute Manager. In the **Bevel** tool settings area, make sure the **Tool Option** button is chosen. Next, set **-40** in the **Offset** spinner and **4** in the **Subdivision** spinner and then press the ENTER key; the selected polygons are beveled in the Perspective viewport, as shown in Figure 3-131.

Creating Groove on the Vase

In this section, you will create groove on vase using the **Torus**, **Volume Builder**, and **Volume Mesher** tools.

1. Choose **Create > Object** from the main menu; a cascading menu is displayed. Next, choose **Torus** from it; a torus is created in the Front viewport and *Torus* is added to the Object Manager.

2. Double-click on *Torus* in the Object Manager; a text box is displayed. Enter **ring** in the text box; *Torus* is renamed as *ring*.

3. Make sure *ring* is selected in the Object Manager. In the Attribute Manager, choose the **Object** button; the **Object Properties** area is displayed. In the **Object Properties** area, enter **20** in the **Pipe Radius** spinner.

4. Choose the **Coord.** button and enter **51** in the **P.Y** spinner; *Torus* is moved upwards, as shown in Figure 3-132.

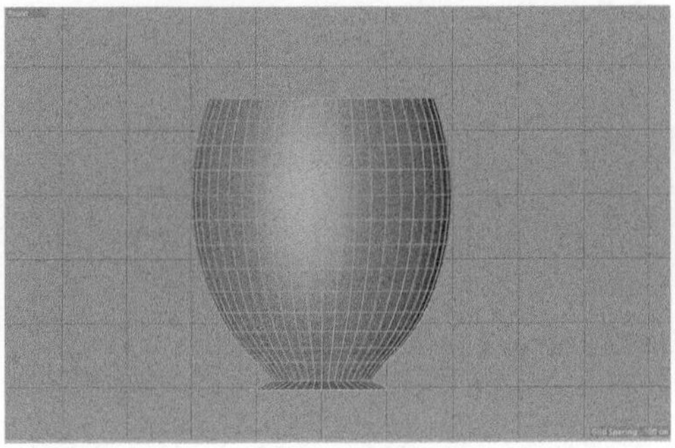

Figure 3-131 *Selected polygons beveled*

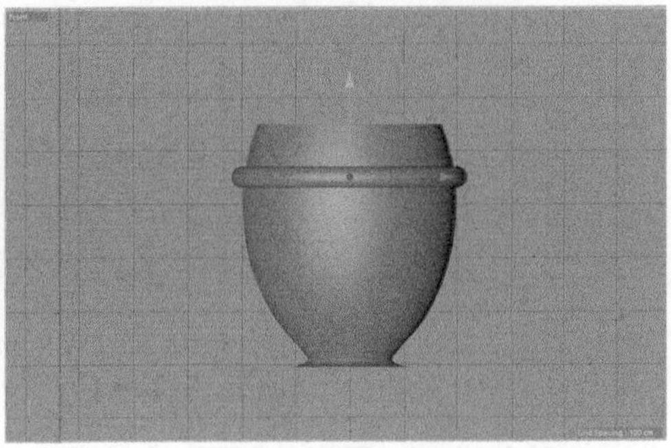

Figure 3-132 *Torus moved upwards*

5. Choose **Volume > Volume Builder** from the main menu, as shown in Figure 3-133; *Volume Builder* is added to the Object Manager.

6. Select *vase* in the Object Manager. Next, press and hold the left mouse button and then drag it on *Volume Builder*; *vase* is connected to *Volume Builder*. Next, select *ring* in the Object Manager and press and hold the left mouse button and then drag it on *Volume Builder; ring* is also connected to *Volume Builder.* Notice that *vase* and *ring* turns white and both objects are converted into voxel objects, refer to Figure 3-134.

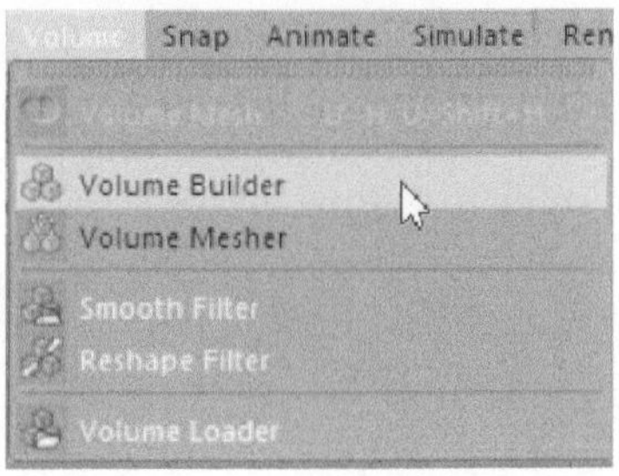

Figure 3-133 *Choosing* ***Volume Builder*** *from the* ***Volume*** *menu*

7. Select *Volume Builder* in the Object Manager. In the Attribute Manager, make sure the **Object** button is chosen. In the **Object Properties** area, enter **1** in the **Voxel Size** spinner; *vase* and *ring* are smoothened comparatively, refer to Figure 3-135.

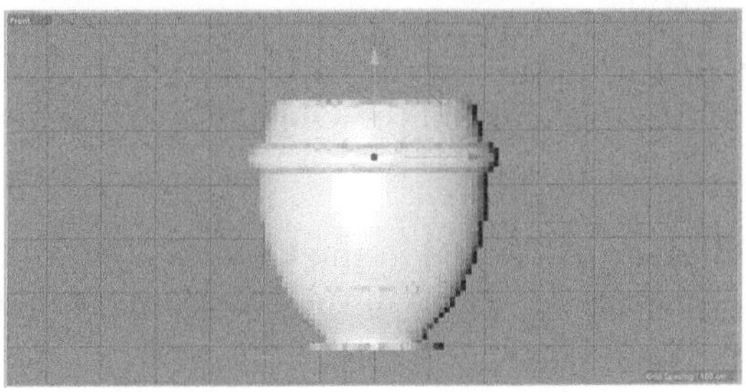

Figure 3-134 *Voxel objects displayed*

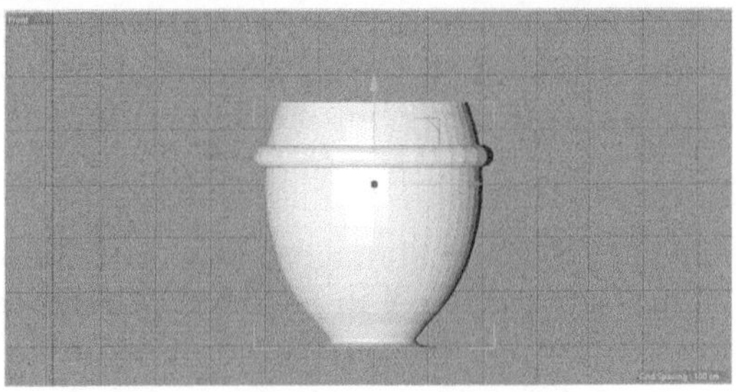

Figure 3-135 *Voxel objects smoothened*

8. Select **Subtract** from the **Mode** drop-down list located next to *ring*, as shown in Figure 3-136; groove is created on *vase*, as shown in Figure 3-137.

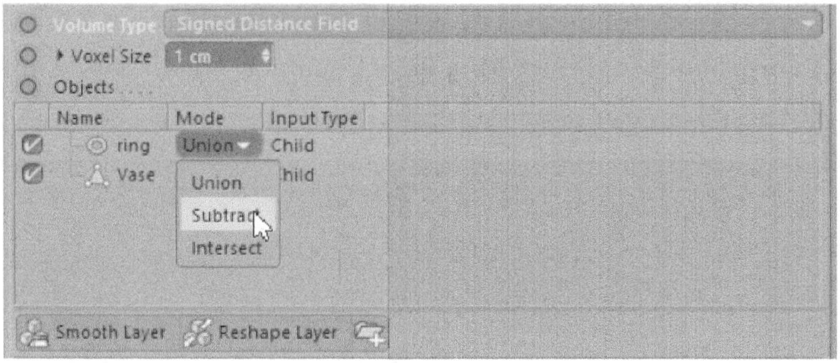

Figure 3-136 *Choosing* ***Subtract*** *from the* ***Mode*** *drop-down list*

9. Choose **Volume > Volume Mesher** from the main menu; *Volume Mesher* is added to the Object Manager.

10. Select *Volume Builder* in the Object Manager. Next, press and hold the left mouse button and then drag *Volume Builder* on *Volume Mesher*; *Volume Builder* is connected to *Volume Mesher* and *vase* is converted into polygon object. Also, notice that the color of *vase* turns dark grey, refer to Figure 3-138.

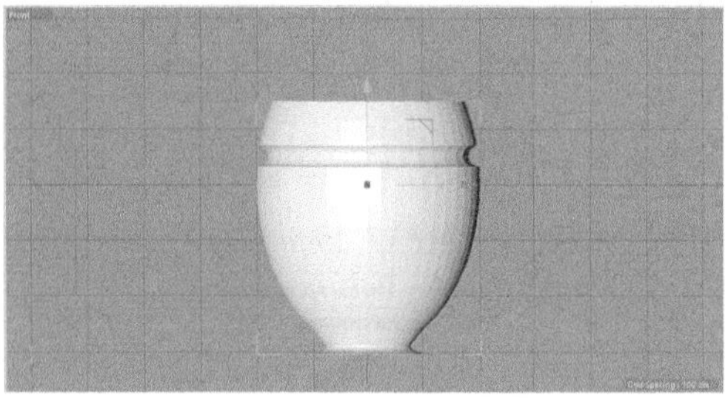

Figure 3-137 *Groove created on vase*

Figure 3-138 *vase turns dark grey*

Next, you will smoothen *vase*.

11. Select *Volume Builder* in the Object Manager. In the Attribute Manager, make sure the **Object** button is chosen. In the **Objects** area, select **ring** from the list displayed and then choose the **Smooth Layer** button; **Smooth Layer** is added to the list in the **Objects** area, as shown in Figure 3-139.

12. In the Attribute Manager, make sure **Smooth Layer** is selected in the **Objects** area. In the **Filter** area, enter **4** in the **Voxel Distance** spinner and enter **2** in the **Iterations** spinner; *vase* is smoothened, as shown in Figure 3-140.

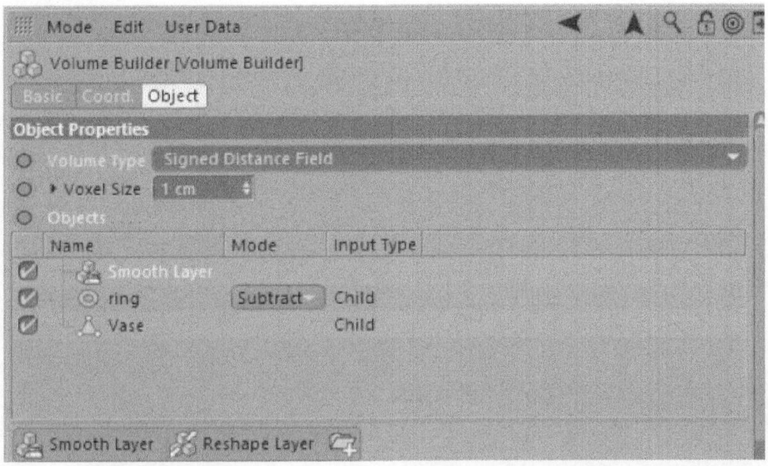

*Figure 3-139 **Smooth Layer** added to the **Objects** area*

Creating Design on the Vase

In this section, you will create design on vase using the **Cloner** and **Volume Builder** tools.

1. Choose **Create > Object** from the main menu; a cascading menu is displayed. Next, choose **Cube** from the cascading menu; a cube is created in the Front viewport and *Cube* is added to the Object Manager.

2. Make sure *Cube* is selected in the Object Manager. In the **Object Properties** area of the Attribute Manager, enter **25** in the **Size.X**, **Size.Y** spinners, and **10** in the **Size.Z** spinner.

3. Choose **MoGraph > Cloner** from the main menu, as shown in Figure 3-141; *Cloner* is added to the Object Manager.

4. Select *Cube* in the Object Manager. Next, press and hold the left mouse button and then drag it on *Cloner*; *Cube* is connected to *Cloner*.

5. Select *Cloner* in the Object Manager. In the Attribute Manager, make sure the **Object** button is chosen. In the **Object Properties** area, select **Radial** from the **Mode** drop-down list and **XZ** from the **Plane** drop-down list. Also, enter **12** and **194** in the **Count** and **Radius** spinners, respectively.

6. In the Attribute Manager, choose the **Transform** button and enter **-67** in the **P.Y** spinner in the **Transform** area. Next, enter **-6** and **-45** in the **R.P** and **R.B** spinners, respectively. *Cloner* is placed on *vase* as shown in Figure 3-142.

7. Make sure that *Cloner* is selected in the Object Manager. Now, create a copy of *Cloner* by pressing both the CTRL key and the left mouse button. Now, drag the cursor and release the left mouse button; a copy of *Cloner* is created in the Object Manager with the name *Cloner.1*.

Figure 3-140 vase smoothened

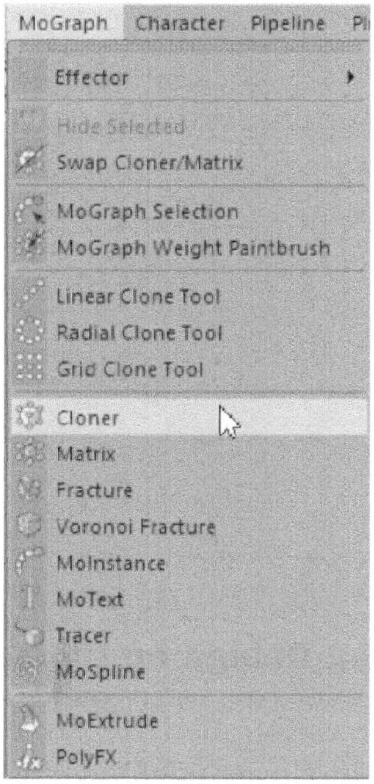

Figure 3-141 *Choosing* ***Cloner*** *from the* ***MoGraph*** *menu*

8. Make sure *Cloner.1* is selected in the Object Manager. In the Attribute Manager, choose the **Object** button. Next, enter **174** in the **Radius** spinner.

9. Choose the **Transform** button and enter **-145** in the **P.Y** spinner. Also, enter **-20** in the **R. P** spinner; *Cloner.1* is placed on *vase* as shown in Figure 3-143.

Figure 3-142 *Cloner placed on vase*

Figure 3-143 *Cloner.1 placed on vase*

10. Select *Cloner* in the Object Manager. Next, press and hold the left mouse button and then drag it on *Volume Builder*; *Cloner* is connected to *Volume Builder*. Next, select *Cloner.1* in the Object Manager and press and hold the left mouse button and then drag it on *Volume Builder; Cloner.1* is also connected to *Volume Builder.* Figure 3-144 shows vase displayed in the viewport and Figure 3-145 shows list of all the objects in the Object Manager.

Changing the Background Color of the Scene

To change the background color of the scene to white in the final output, follow the steps given in Tutorial 1 of Chapter 2.

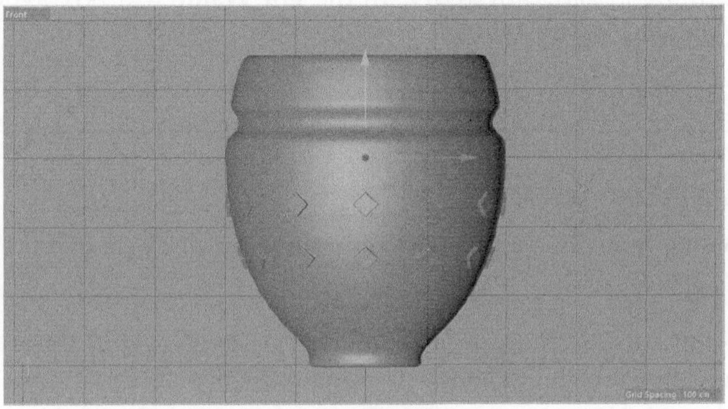

Figure 3-144 vase displayed in the viewport

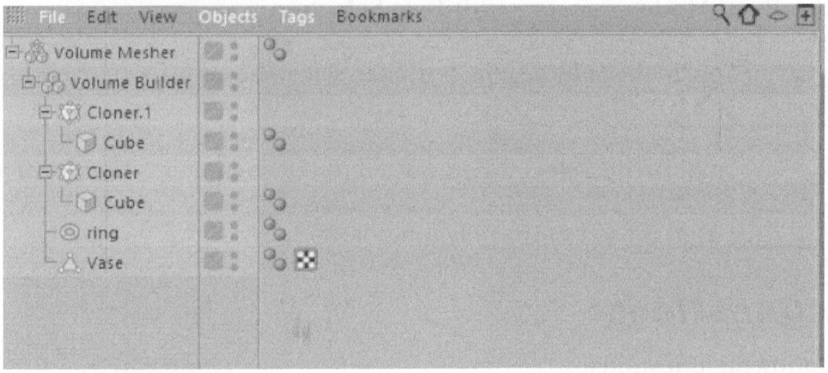

Figure 3-145 List of all the objects in the Object Manager

Saving and Rendering the Scene

In this section, you will save and render the scene. You can also view the final render of the model by downloading the file *c03_cinema4d_r20_rndr.zip* from *www.cadcim.com*. The path of the file is mentioned at the beginning of the chapter.

1. Choose **File > Save** from the main menu; the **Save File** dialog box is displayed. In this dialog box, browse to the location *\Documents\c4dR20\c03*.

2. Enter **c03tut3** in the **File name** text box and then choose the **Save** button.

3. In the Perspective viewport, set the camera angle using the Viewport Navigation Tools located at the extreme top right of the Perspective viewport. Next, choose the **Render to Picture Viewer** tool from the Command Palette. Alternatively, press SHIFT+R; the **Picture Viewer** window is displayed.

4. In the **Picture Viewer** window, choose **File > Save as**; the **Save** dialog box is displayed.

5. In the **Save** dialog box, choose the **OK** button; the **Save Dialog** dialog box is displayed. Next, browse to *\Documents\c4dR20\c03*. In the **File Name** text box, type **c03_tut3_rndr**. Next, choose the **Save** button; the file is saved at the desired location.

   Figure 3-122 displays the final output.

Self-Evaluation Test

Answer the following questions and then compare them to those given at the end of this chapter:

1. Which of the following tools in the Command Palette is used to select points, edges, or polygons by creating a rectangular frame around the object?

   (a) **Move** (b) **Rectangle Selection**
   (c) **Use Point Mode** (d) **Live Selection**

2. The __________ tool in the **Select** menu is used to select the edge loop to modify a polygonal object.

3. The __________ tool in the **Select** menu is used to select elements that form a ring shape.

4. The ___________ tool is used to cut polygon objects.

Review Questions

Answer the following questions:

1. Which of the following combinations of shortcut keys is used to display the **Picture Viewer** window?

   (a) CTRL+B (b) SHIFT+ R
   (c) CTRL+C (d) CTRL+V

2. Which of the following functional keys is used to maximize the Perspective viewport?

   (a) F1 (b) F5
   (c) F4 (d) F6

3. The **Loop** option in the **Mode** drop-down list located in the **Loop/Path Cut** tool settings is used to create edge loops in a polygonal object. (T/F)

EXERCISE

The rendered output of the model used in the exercise can be accessed by downloading the *c03_cinema4d_R20_exr.zip* file from *www.cadcim.com*. The path of the file is as follows: *Textbooks > Animation and Visual Effects > MAXON CINEMA 4D > MAXON CINEMA 4D R20 Studio: A Tutorial Approach*

Exercise 1

Using the polygon modeling tools, create the model of the chair, as shown in Figure 3-146.

(Expected time: 30 min)

Figure 3-146 *The model of a chair*

Answers to Self-Evaluation Test

1. b, 2. Loop Selection, 3. Ring Selection, 4. Loop/Path Cut

Chapter 4

Sculpting

Learning Objectives

After completing this chapter, you will be able to:

- *Use various sculpting tools and brushes*
- *Sculpt polygon objects*

INTRODUCTION

Sculpting is a traditional modeling method which is entirely different from the NURBS and polygon modeling. It is very much similar to clay modeling and has tools that are used in other conventional modeling methods. In this chapter, you will learn the techniques to create models using the sculpting brushes.

TUTORIALS

Before you start the tutorials of this chapter, you need to download the *c04_cinema4d_r20_tut.zip* file from *www.cadcim.com*. The path of the file is as follows: *Textbooks > Animation and Visual Effects > MAXON CINEMA 4D > MAXON CINEMA 4D R20 Studio: A Tutorial Approach*

Next, you need to browse to *\Documents\c4dr20* and create a new folder in it with the name *c04*. Next, extract the contents of the zip file in this folder.

Tutorial 1

In this tutorial, you will create the model of a candle, as shown in Figure 4-1.

(Expected time: 30 min)

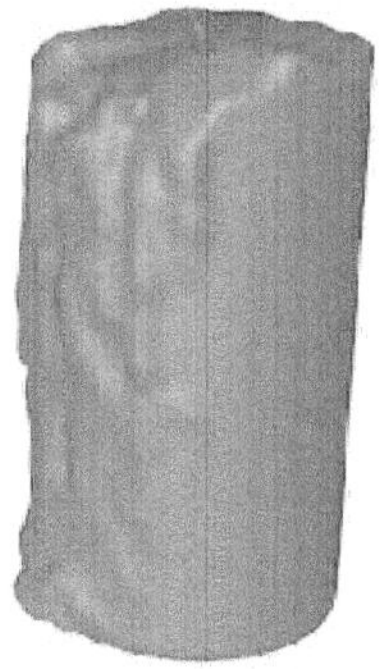

Figure 4-1 *The model of a candle*

The following steps are required to complete this tutorial:

a. Create the base of the candle.
b. Sculpt the candle.
c. Create the wick of the candle.
d. Change the background color of the scene.
e. Save and render the scene.

Creating the Base of the Candle

In this section, you will create the base of the candle using the **Cylinder** tool.

1. Choose **Create > Object** from the main menu; a cascading menu is displayed. Choose **Cylinder** from it; a cylinder is created in the Perspective viewport and the *Cylinder* object is added to the Object Manager.

2. Press SHIFT+V; the **Viewport [Perspective]** area is displayed in the Attribute Manager. Make sure the **Sel.: Bounding Box** check box is selected from the **Active Object** area.

The **Sel.: Bounding Box** check box is used to toggle the display of the selection outline in the viewport.

3. Make sure *Cylinder* is selected in the Object Manager. In the Attribute Manager, make sure the **Object** button is chosen. In the **Object Properties** area, set the parameters as follows:

   Radius:**100** Height: **366** Height Segments: **100**
   Rotation Segments:**100**

   The **Rotation Segments** option is used to determine the number of subdivisions of cylinder along its circumference. More the number of subdivisions, smoother will be the cylinder.

4. In the Attribute Manager, choose the **Caps** button; the **Caps** area is displayed. In this area, make sure the **Caps** check box is selected. Next, enter **36** in the **Segments** spinner.

   The **Segments** spinner located below the **Caps** check box is used to determine the number of subdivisions vertically.

5. In the **Caps** area, select the **Fillet** check box and then set the parameters as follows:

   Segments: **36** Radius: **7**

6. In the Attribute Manager, choose the **Basic** button; the **Basic Properties** area is displayed. In this area, enter **Candle** in the **Name** text box; the cylinder is renamed as *Candle* in the Object Manager.

7. Make sure *Candle* is selected in the Object Manager and choose the **Make Editable** tool from the Modes Palette; the *Candle* is converted into a polygonal object.

8. Choose the **Polygons** tool from the Modes Palette; the *Candle* is displayed in the polygon mode in the viewport.

9. Press F2; the Top viewport is maximized. Invoke the **Live Selection** tool from the Command Palette. In the Attribute Manager, choose the **Options** button if it is not chosen; the **Options** area is displayed. In this area, make sure the **Only Select Visible Elements** check box is selected.

10. Select the polygons in the Top viewport, as shown in Figure 4-2.

11. Press F1; the Perspective viewport is maximized. Make sure the polygons of *Candle* are selected in the Perspective viewport. Next, move the selected polygons of *Candle* downward, as shown in Figure 4-3.

12. Invoke the **Scale** tool from the Command Palette and uniformly scale down the selected polygons of *Candle*, as shown in Figure 4-4.

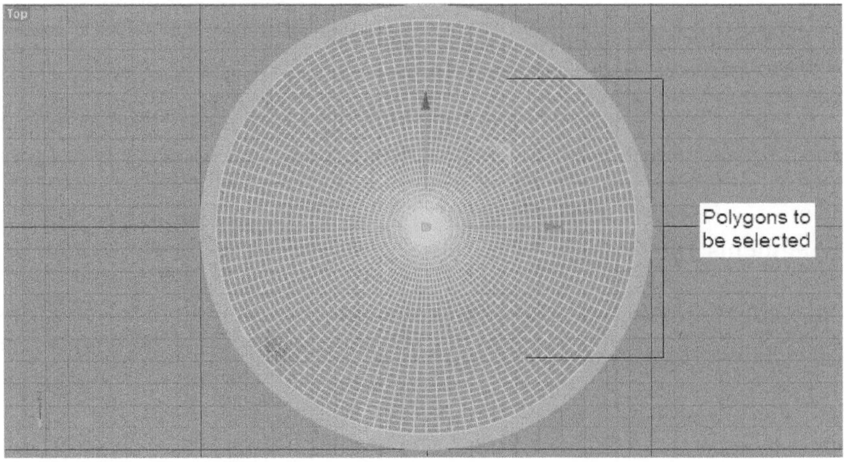

Figure 4-2 *The polygons to be selected*

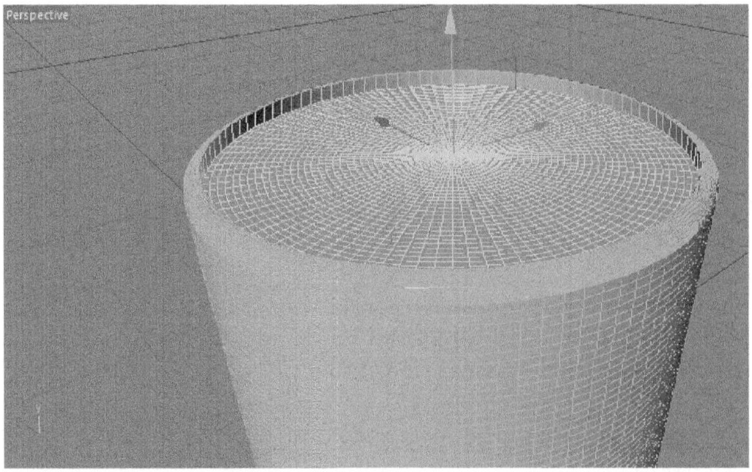

Figure 4-3 *Moving the polygons of the Candle downward*

Figure 4-4 *Scaling down the polygons of Candle*

Sculpting the Candle

In this section, you will sculpt *Candle* using the sculpting brushes.

1. Select **Sculpt** from the **Layout** drop-down list located in the extreme right corner of the interface, as shown in Figure 4-5; the **Sculpt** layout is displayed with the **Sculpting** menu on the right of the viewport, refer to Figure 4-6.

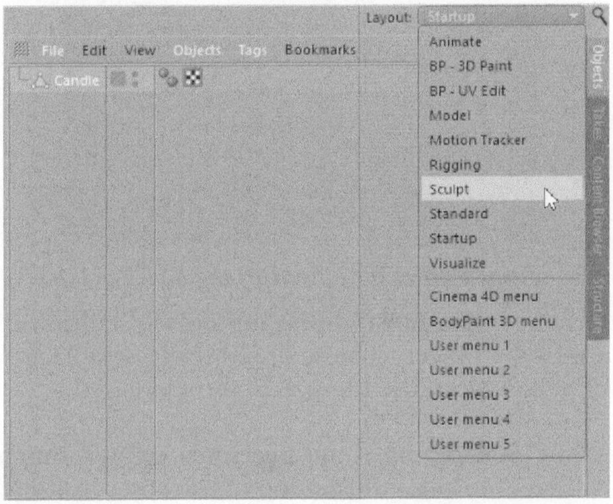

Figure 4-5 *Selecting* ***Sculpt*** *from the* ***Layout*** *drop-down list*

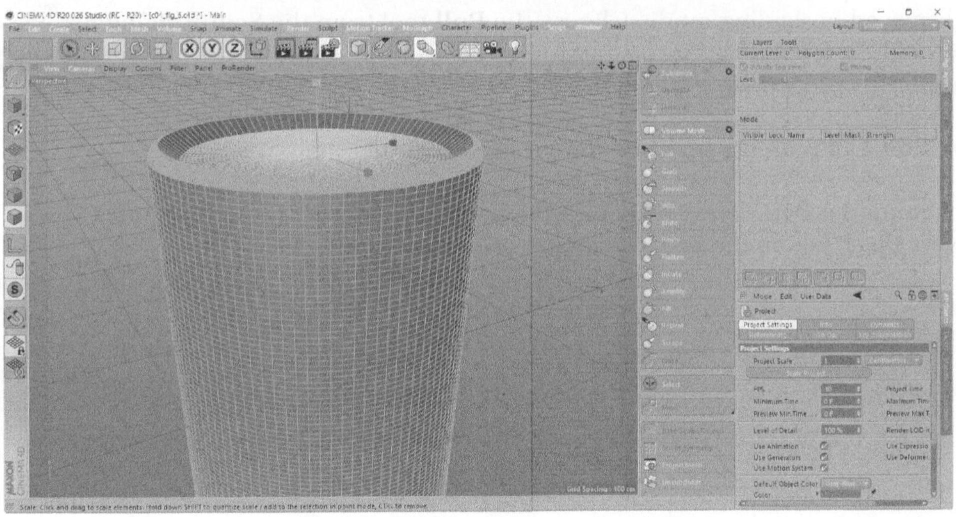

Figure 4-6 *The* ***Sculpt*** *layout*

2. Choose the **Model** tool from the Modes Palette. Next, choose the **Subdivide** tool from the **Sculpting** menu; the *Candle* is subdivided. Next, choose the **Objects** tab to display the Object Manager. In the Object Manager, you will notice that the **Sculpt Expression [Sculpt]** tag is added, as shown in Figure 4-7.

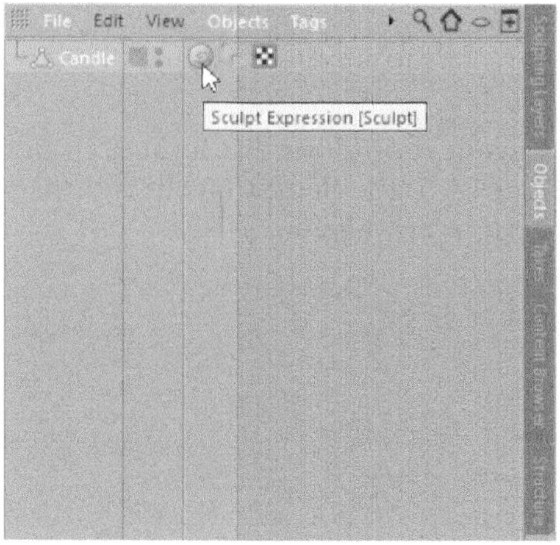

***Figure 4-7** The **Sculpt Expression [Sculpt]** tag added to the Object Manager*

The **Subdivide** tool is one of the most important tools in sculpting. It is used to create the points on the surface of the object to be sculpted using sculpting brushes. On increasing the subdivision level of an object, the file size is also increased.

The **Sculpt Expression [Sculpt]** tag is automatically created on choosing the **Subdivide** tool. It consists of all the sculpting information of the object to which it is assigned.

3. Choose **Display > Gouraud** from the Menu in editor view, if not already chosen; *Candle* is displayed in shading mode. Choose the **Pull** tool from the **Sculpting** menu. Next, press and hold the left mouse button and move the brush downward on *Candle* in the Perspective viewport to add strokes to the *Candle*, refer to Figure 4-8.

   The **Pull** tool is used to extrude the mesh toward the camera.

4. Make sure the **Pull** tool is chosen in the **Sculpting** menu. In the **Attributes** tab, select the **Invert** check box in the **Settings** area, as shown in Figure 4-9.

***Figure 4-8** The strokes added*

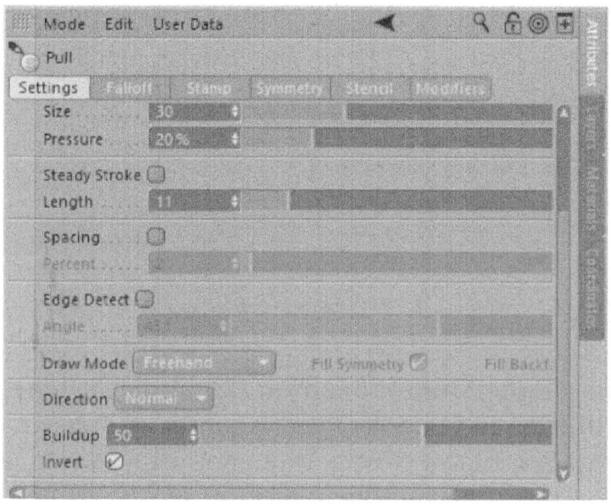

***Figure 4-9** The **Invert** check box selected in the **Settings** area in the Attribute Manager*

The **Invert** check box is used to reverse the effect of the brush. It pushes down the points of the surface.

5. Again, press and hold the left mouse button and move the brush downward on *Candle* in the Perspective viewport, refer to Figure 4-10.

6. Choose the **Wax** tool from the **Sculpting** menu. Next, press and hold the left mouse button and add strokes on the top of *Candle*, as shown in Figure 4-11.

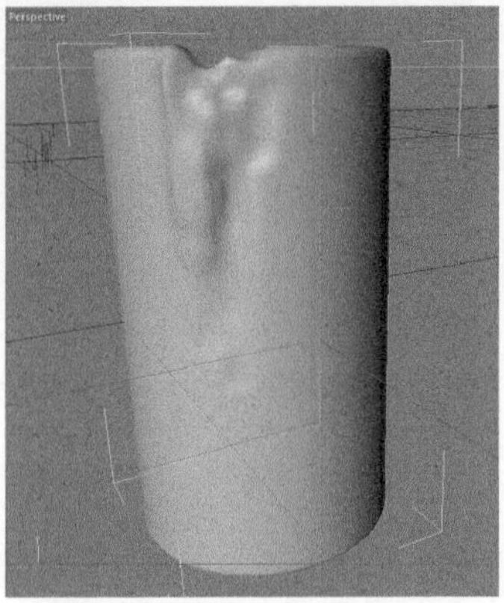

Figure 4-10 *Strokes added to the Candle*

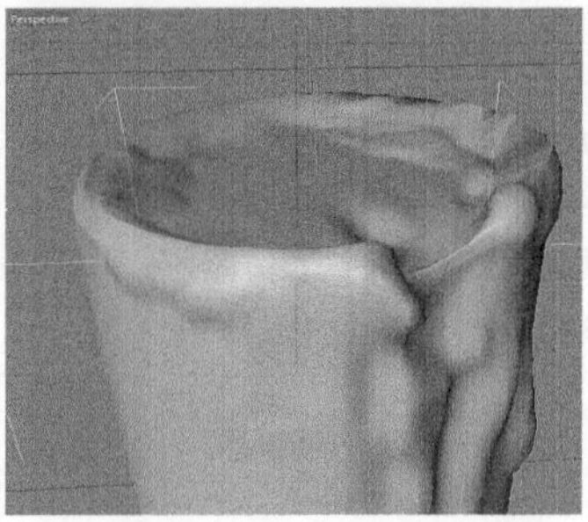

Figure 4-11 *Strokes added on the top of Candle*

The **Wax** tool is used to apply or remove the effect of material from the surface of the object. It can be compared to applying or removing clay or wax on a real-world object.

7. Choose the **Inflate** tool from the **Sculpting** menu. In the **Attributes** tab, select the **Steady Stroke** check box in the **Settings** area and enter **7** in the **Length** spinner. Next, press and hold the left mouse button and add strokes to the bottom of *Candle* in the Perspective viewport, refer to Figure 4-12.

   The **Inflate** tool is used to move the vertices of the surface along the direction of normals to create bumps on the surface. The **Steady Stroke** check box is used to attach a string that helps in making the brush straight. The **Length** spinner is used to define the length of the string.

8. Make sure the **Inflate** tool is chosen in the **Sculpting** menu. In the **Attributes** tab, set the parameters as follows:

   Size: **24** Pressure: **26.2**

   Next, press and hold the left mouse button and add strokes to the bottom of *Candle*, refer to Figure 4-13.

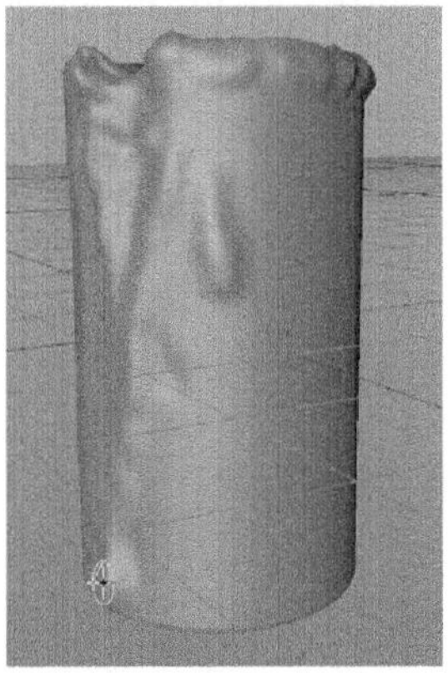

Figure 4-12 *Adding strokes to the bottom of the Candle*

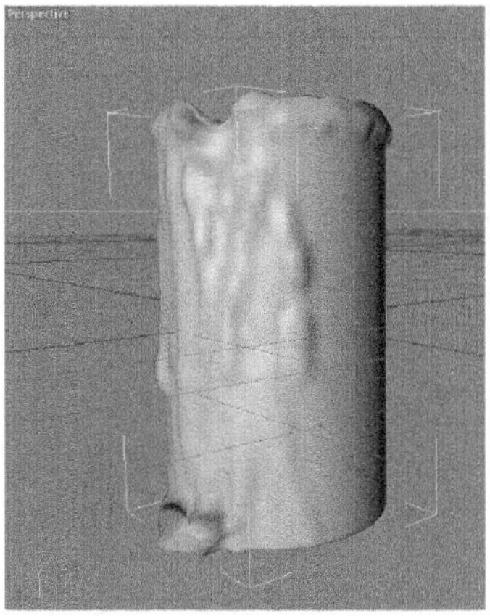

Figure 4-13 *More strokes added to the bottom of the Candle*

9. Choose the **Pull** tool from the **Sculpting** menu. In the **Attributes** tab, set the parameters as follows:

   Size: **25** Pressure: **30**

10. Press and hold the left mouse button and add strokes to the top of *Candle* in the Perspective viewport, as shown in Figure 4-14.

11. Choose the **Smooth** tool from the **Sculpting** menu. In the **Attributes** tab, set the parameters as follows:

    Size: **10** Pressure: **12**

12. Press and hold the left mouse button and add strokes to the top of *Candle* in the Perspective viewport to smoothen it, refer to Figure 4-15. Press SPACEBAR to deactivate the current tool.

    The **Smooth** tool is used to smoothen the surface of the object while sculpting.

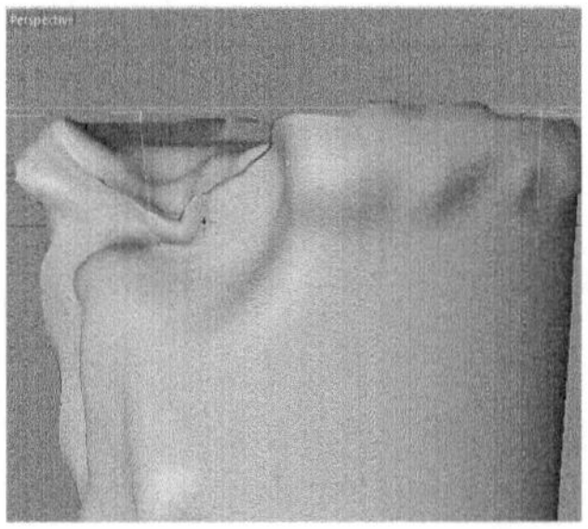

Figure 4-14 *Adding strokes to the top of Candle*

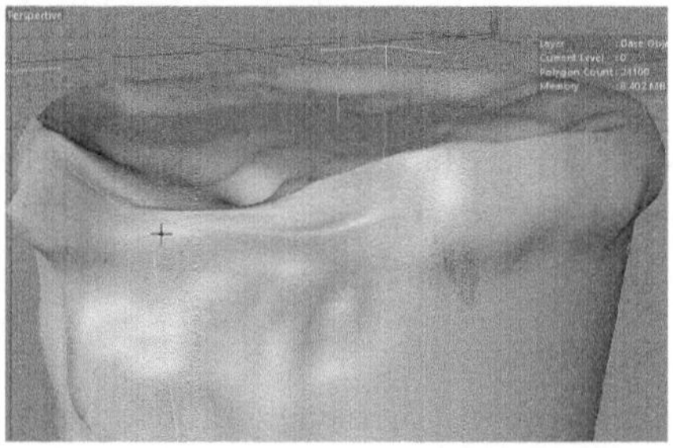

Figure 4-15 *The smoothened surface of Candle*

Creating the Wick of the Candle

In this section, you will create the wick of *Candle* using the **Cylinder** tool.

1. Select **Standard** from the **Layout** drop-down list located in the extreme right corner of the interface; the **Standard** layout is displayed. Choose **Create > Object** from the main menu; a cascading menu is displayed. Choose **Cylinder** from it; a cylinder is created in the Perspective viewport and the *Cylinder* object is added to the Object Manager.

2. Make sure *Cylinder* is selected in the Object Manager. In the Attribute Manager, choose the **Object** button; the **Object Properties** area is displayed. In this area, set the parameters as follows:

   Radius: **1** Height: **59** Height Segments: **25**

3. Choose the **Coord** button; the **Coordinates** area is displayed. In this area, enter **174.8** in the **P . Y** spinner.

4. In the Attribute Manager, choose the **Basic** button; the **Basic Properties** area is displayed. In this area, enter **Wick** in the **Name** text box; the cylinder is renamed as *Wick* in the Object Manager.

5. Make sure *Wick* is selected in the Object Manager and then choose the **Make Editable** tool from the Modes Palette; *Wick* is converted into a polygonal object.

6. Choose the **Bend** tool from the Command Palette; the *Bend* object is added to the Object Manager.

7. Make sure *Bend* is selected in the Object Manager. Press and hold the left mouse button on *Bend* and drag it to *Wick* in the Object Manager; the *Bend* object is connected to *Wick* in the Object Manager.

8. Make sure *Bend* object is selected in the Object Manager. In the Attribute Manager, choose the **Object** button; the **Object Properties** area is displayed. In this area, choose the **Fit to Parent** button and then set the other parameters as follows:

   Strength: **51** Angle: **-16**

   Figure 4-16 displays the *Bend* object applied to *Wick* in the Perspective viewport.

Changing the Background Color of the Scene

To change the background color of the scene to white in the final output, follow the steps given in Tutorial 1 of Chapter 2.

Saving and Rendering the Scene

In this section, you will save and render the scene. You can also view the final render of the scene by downloading the file *c04_cinema4d_r20_rndr.zip* from *www.cadcim.com*. The path of the file is mentioned at the beginning of the chapter.

1. Choose **File > Save** from the main menu; the **Save File** dialog box is displayed. In this dialog box, browse to the location *\Documents\c4dr20\c04*.

2. Enter **c04tut1** in the **File name** text box and then choose the **Save** button.

3. Choose the **Render to Picture Viewer** tool from the Command Palette; the **Picture Viewer** window is displayed.

4. In the **Picture Viewer** window, choose **File > Save as**; the **Save** dialog box is displayed.

Figure 4-16 *The Wick of the Candle*

5. In the **Save** dialog box, select **JPEG** from the **Format** drop-down list and then choose the **OK** button; the **Save Dialog** dialog box is displayed. Next, browse to *\Documents\c4dr20\c04*. In the **File name** text box, enter **c04_tut1_rndr**. Next, choose the **Save** button; the rendered image is saved at the specified location.

   Figure 4-1 displays the final output.

Tutorial 2

In this tutorial, you will sculpt an ice cream cone, as shown in Figure 4-17.

(Expected time: 30 min)

Figure 4-17 *The ice cream cone*

The following steps are required to complete this tutorial:

a. Create the base model of the ice cream cone.
b. Sculpt the ice cream cone.
c. Create the scoop of the ice cream.
d. Sculpt the scoop of the ice cream.
e. Change the background color of the scene.
f. Save and render the scene.

Creating the Base Model of the Ice Cream Cone

In this section, you will create the base model of an ice cream cone using the **Cone** tool.

1. Press SHIFT+V and then make sure the **Sel.: Bounding Box** check box is selected in the **Viewport [Perspective]** area. Choose **Create > Object** from the main menu; a cascading menu is displayed. Choose **Cone** from it; a cone is created in the Perspective viewport and the *Cone* object is added to the Object Manager.

2. Choose the **Object** button from the Object Manage; the **Object Properties** area is displayed. In this area, set the parameters as follows:

   Top Radius: **94** Bottom Radius: **0** Height: **457**
   Height Segments: **72** Rotation Segments: **72**

3. Choose the **Caps** button; the **Caps** area is displayed. In this area, clear the **Caps** check box.

   Figure 4-18 displays *Cone* in the Perspective viewport.

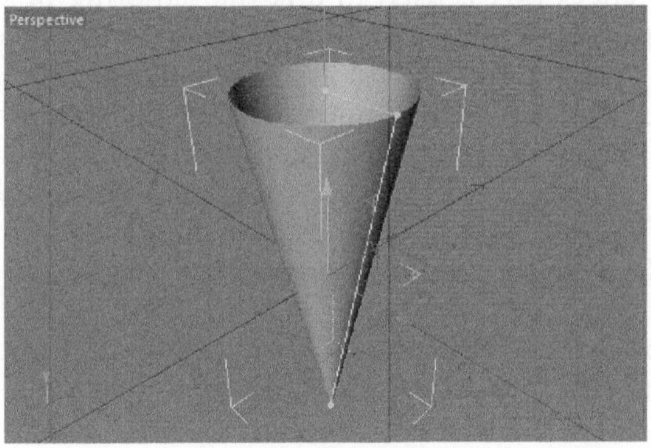

Figure 4-18 *The Cone displayed in the Perspective viewport*

4. Make sure *Cone* is selected in the Object Manager and choose the **Make Editable** tool from the Modes Palette; the *Cone* is converted into a polygonal object.

Sculpting the Ice Cream Cone

In this section, you will sculpt *Cone* using the sculpting brushes.

1. Select **Sculpt** from the **Layout** drop-down list; the **Sculpt** layout is displayed with the **Sculpting** menu on the right of the viewport.

2. Make sure that *Cone* is selected in the Perspective viewport. Next, choose the **Subdivide** tool from the **Sculpting** menu, refer to Figure 4-19; the *Cone* is subdivided and the **Sculpt Expression [Sculpt]** tag is added to *Cone* in the **Objects** tab.

Figure 4-19 *Choosing the* ***Subdivide*** *tool from the* ***Sculpting*** *menu*

3. Choose the **Pull** tool from the **Sculpting** menu. In the **Attributes** tab, set the parameters in the **Settings** area as follows:

   Size: **10** Pressure: **9.4**

4. Select the **Link Symmetry** check box and then select the **Steady Stroke** check box.

   The **Link Symmetry** check box is used to link the sculpting in such a way that when it is done on one side of the object, the other side of the object is automatically sculpted.

5. In the **Attributes** tab, choose the **Symmetry** button; the **Symmetry** area is displayed. In this area, select the **Z (XY)** check box. Next, select the **Radial** check box; the radial settings below the **Radial** check box are activated. Select the **ZX** radio button corresponding to the **Radial Symmetry Mode** parameter and then enter **5** and **3** in the **Number of Radial Strokes** and **Radial Gap Angle** spinners, respectively.

   The **Z (XY)** check box is used to determine the axis on which the object mirror plane will be placed. The **Radial** check box is used to draw the radial strokes on the object.

6. Using the **Pull** tool, press and hold the left mouse button and apply strokes to the top of the *Cone* in the Perspective viewport, refer to Figure 4-20.

7. Press and hold the left mouse button and apply strokes on *Cone*, refer to Figure 4-21.

8. Choose the **Smooth** tool from the **Sculpting** menu. In the **Attributes** tab, choose the **Settings** button. Next, set the value of **Size** and **Pressure** to **2.5** and **4**, respectively in the **Settings** area. Make sure the **Link Symmetry** check box is selected.

Figure 4-20 *Applying strokes on the top of the Cone*

Figure 4-21 *The strokes added*

9. Press and hold the left mouse button and smoothen the surface of *Cone*, refer to Figure 4-22.

   Next, you will draw a pattern on *Cone*.

10. Choose the **Inflate** tool from the **Sculpting** menu. In the **Attributes** tab, set the following parameters in the **Settings** area:

    Size: **11** Pressure: **48**

11. In the **Attributes** tab, make sure that the **Link Symmetry** check box is selected. Also, choose the **Symmetry** button; the **Symmetry** area is displayed. In this area, make sure that the **X (YZ)** and **Z (XY)** check boxes are selected. Next, enter **3** and **0** in the **Number of Radial Strokes** and **Radial Gap Angle** spinners, respectively.

12. Press and hold the left mouse button and add strokes on *Cone* in the Perspective viewport to create a pattern, refer to Figure 4-23.

13. Choose the **Settings** button; the **Settings** area is displayed. In this area, enter **90** in the **Pressure** spinner. Press and hold the left mouse button and add strokes to create a pattern on *Cone*, refer to Figure 4-24.

14. Repeat the procedure explained in step 13 and add strokes on *Cone* to get the pattern, refer to Figure 4-25.

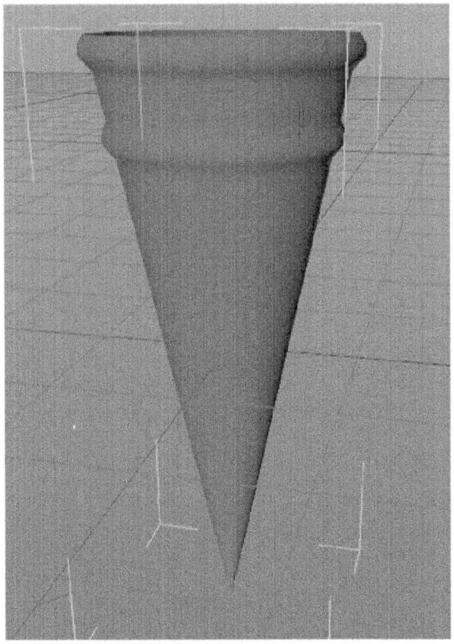

*Figure 4-22 Cone smoothened using the **Smooth** tool*

Figure 4-23 Creating a pattern on Cone in the Perspective viewport

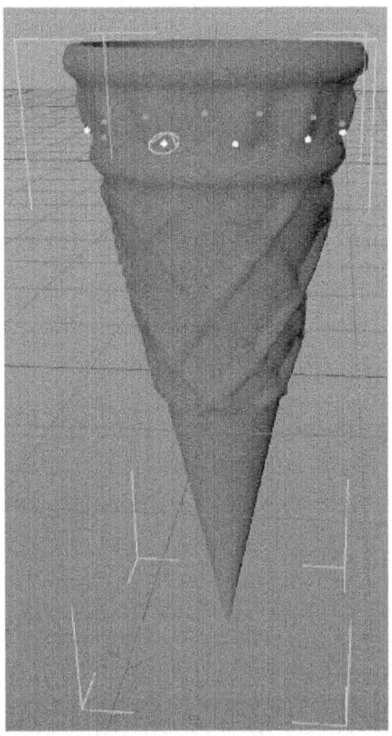

*Figure 4-24 Creating a pattern on Cone using the **Inflate** tool*

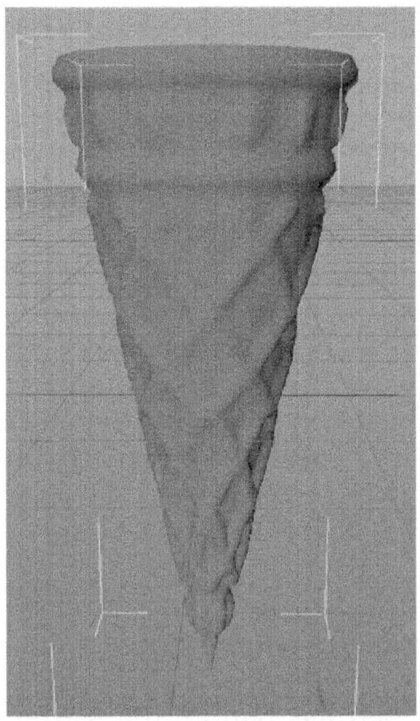

Figure 4-25 The pattern displayed on Cone

15. Choose the **Smooth** tool from the **Sculpting** menu. In the **Attributes** tab, choose the **Settings** button; the **Settings** area is displayed. In this area, enter **54** in the **Size** spinner. Make sure that the **Link Symmetry** check box is selected in this tab.

16. In the **Attributes** tab, choose the **Symmetry** button; the **Symmetry** area is displayed. In this area, make sure the **X (YZ)** and **Z (XY)** check boxes are selected. Next, press and hold the left mouse button and smoothen the surface of *Cone* in the Perspective viewport, as shown in Figure 4-26.

Creating the Scoop of the Ice Cream

In this section, you will create the scoop of the ice cream using the **Sphere** tool.

1. Choose **Create > Object** from the main menu; a cascading menu is displayed. Choose **Sphere** from it; a sphere is created in the Perspective viewport.

2. Choose the **Objects** tab; the **Object Properties** area is displayed in the Attribute Manager. In this area, enter **72** in the **Segments** spinner.

3. Choose the **Coord** button; the **Coordinates** area is displayed. In this area, enter **260** in the **P . Y** spinner.

4. Choose the **Basic** button; the **Basic Properties** area is displayed. In this area, enter **Scoop** in the **Name** text box; the sphere is renamed as *Scoop* in the Object Manager. Figure 4-27 displays *Scoop* in the Perspective viewport.

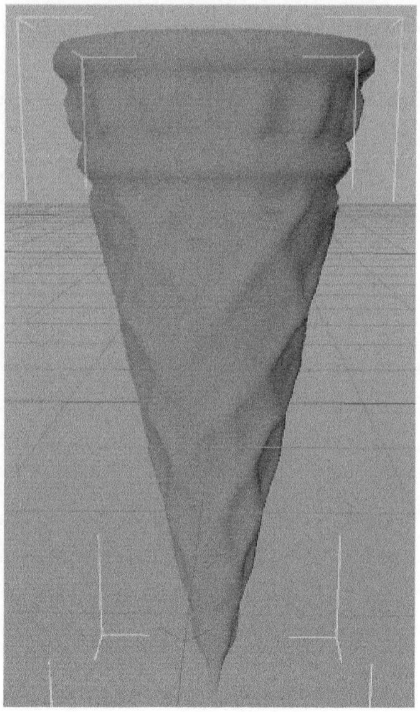

***Figure 4-26** Smoothening the surface of Cone using the **Smooth** tool*

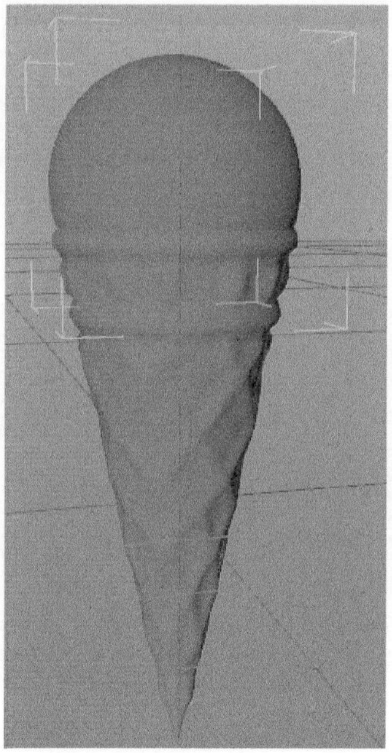

***Figure 4-27** The Scoop displayed in the Perspective viewport*

5. Choose the **Make Editable** tool from the Modes Palette; the *Scoop* is converted into a polygonal object.

Sculpting the Scoop of the Ice Cream

In this section, you will sculpt *Scoop* using the sculpting brushes.

1. Make sure that *Scoop* is selected in the Perspective viewport. Next, invoke the **Subdivide** tool; the *Scoop* is subdivided and the **Sculpt Expression [Sculpt]** tag is added in the Object Manager.

2. Choose the **Pull** tool from the **Sculpting** menu. In the **Attributes** tab, choose the **Settings** button; the **Settings** area is displayed. In this area, set the parameters as follows:

   Size: **50** Pressure: **100**

   In the **Settings** area, make sure that the **Link Symmetry** check box is selected.

3. Choose the **Symmetry** button; the **Symmetry** area is displayed. In this area, make sure that the **Local** is selected in the **Axis** drop-down list. Next, clear the **Z (XY)** and **Radial** check boxes and select the **X (YZ)** check box if it is not selected.

4. Press and hold the left mouse button and add strokes diagonally on *Scoop* in the Perspective viewport, refer to Figure 4-28.

5. Repeat step 4 and paint on *Scoop* using the **Pull** tool to create a stroke in the Perspective viewport, refer to Figure 4-29.

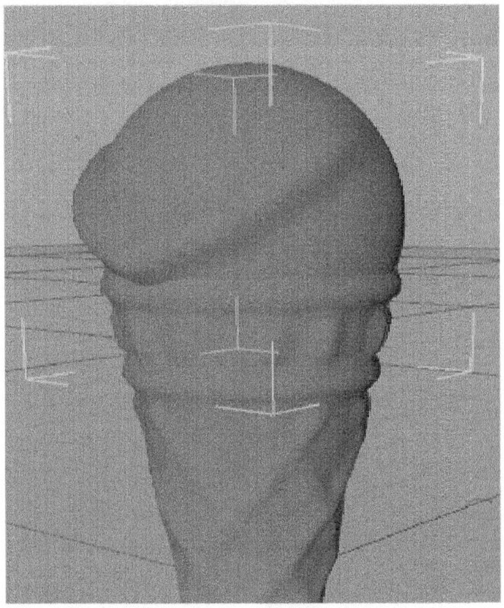

Figure 4-28 *Adding strokes on the Scoop in the Perspective viewport*

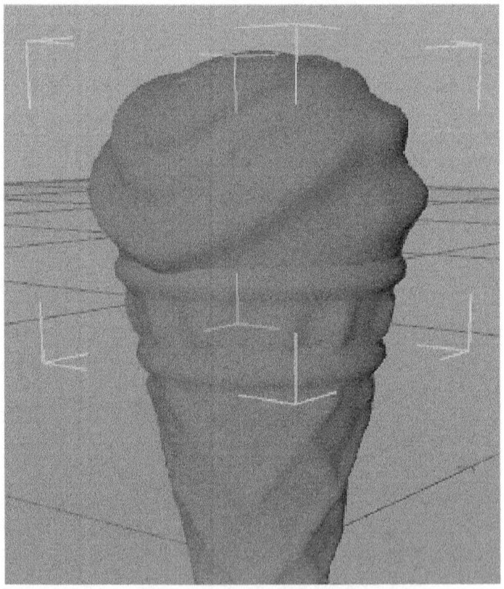

Figure 4-29 *Adding stroke on Scoop using the **Pull** tool*

6. Again, add strokes on *Scoop* using the **Pull** tool to create a pattern on the front and back of *Scoop* in the Perspective viewport, refer to Figure 4-30.

   Next, you will create the peak of *Scoop*.

7. Choose the **Grab** tool from the **Sculpting** menu. In the **Attributes** tab, choose the **Settings** button; the **Settings** area is displayed. In this area, enter **80** in the **Size** spinner and clear the **Link Symmetry** check box.

8. Choose the **Symmetry** button; the **Symmetry** area is displayed. In this area, clear the **X (YZ)** check box.

   The **Grab** tool is used to grab a particular part of the mesh and pull it in the desired direction.

9. Press and hold the left mouse button and add strokes upward on *Scoop* to create the peak of *Scoop* in the Perspective viewport, as shown in Figure 4-31.

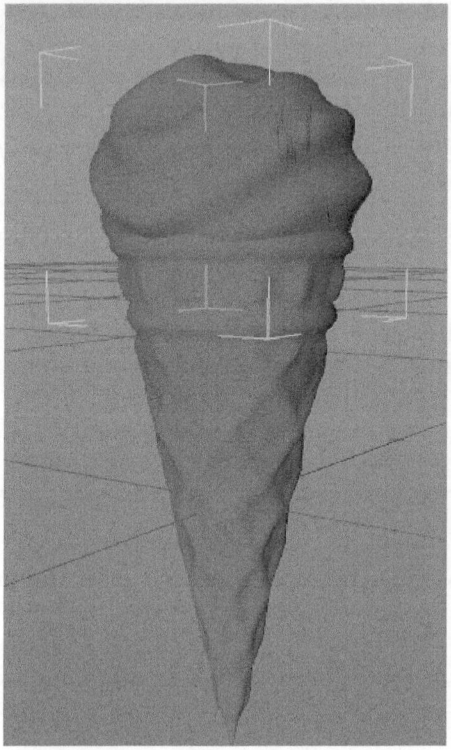

Figure 4-30 *Creating the pattern on Scoop in the Perspective viewport*

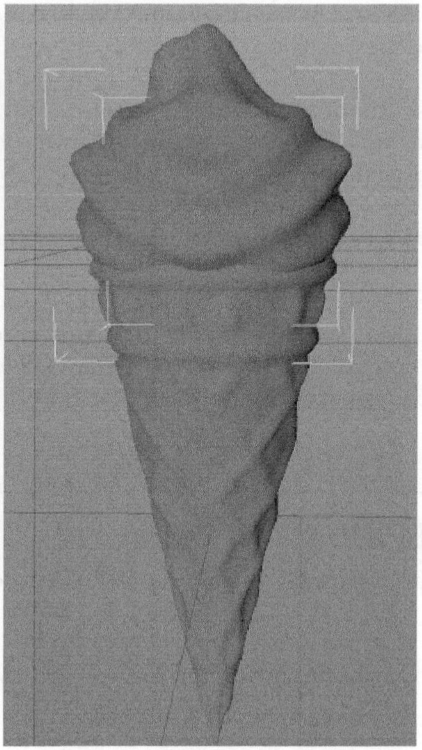

Figure 4-31 *The peak of Scoop created*

10. Choose the **Smooth** tool from the **Sculpting** menu. In the **Attributes** tab, choose the **Settings** button. In the **Settings** area, enter **10** and **2.5** in the **Size** and **Pressure** spinners, respectively.

11. Using the **Smooth** tool, press and hold the left mouse button and add strokes on the top of *Scoop* to smoothen the scoop in the Perspective viewport, refer to Figure 4-32.

Changing the Background Color of the Scene

To change the background color of the scene to white in the final output, follow the steps given in Tutorial 1 of Chapter 2.

Saving and Rendering the Scene

In this section, you will save and render the scene. You can also view the final render of the scene by downloading the file *c04_cinema4d_r20_rndr.zip* from *www.cadcim.com*. The path of the file is mentioned at the beginning of the chapter.

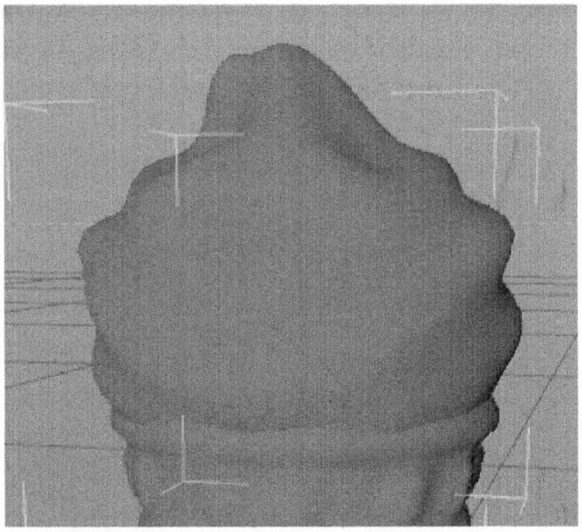

Figure 4-32 The smooth peak of the Scoop in the Perspective viewport

1. Choose **File > Save** from the main menu; the **Save File** dialog box is displayed. In this dialog box, browse to the location *\Documents\c4dr20\c04*.

2. Enter **c04tut2** in the **File name** edit box and then choose the **Save** button.

3. Choose **Render to Picture Viewer** tool from the Command Palette; the **Picture Viewer** window is displayed.

4. In the **Picture Viewer** window, choose **File > Save as**; the **Save** dialog box is displayed.

5. In the **Save** dialog box, select **JPEG** from the **Format** drop-down list and then choose the **OK** button; the **Save Dialog** dialog box is displayed. Next, browse to *\Documents\c4dr20\c04*. In the **File name** text box, type **c04_tut2_rndr**. Next, choose the **Save** button; the rendered image is saved at the desired location.

   Figure 4-17 displays the final output.

Self-Evaluation Test

Answer the following questions and then compare them to those given at the end of this chapter:

1. Which of the following layouts in CINEMA 4D is considered to be the default layout for sculpting?

   (a) **BP UV Edit** (b) **BP 3D Paint**
   (c) **Sculpt** (d) **Startup**

2. Which of the following tools in the **Sculpting** menu is most commonly used for sculpting?

   (a) **Subdivide** (b) **Sculpting**
   (c) **Segments** (d) None of the above

3. The __________ tag is automatically created on choosing the **Subdivide** tool from the **Sculpting** menu.

4. The __________ tool in the **Sculpting** menu is used to pull the vertices of the normals of the surface.

5. The __________ check box in the **Symmetry** area of the **Attributes** tab is used to draw radial brush strokes.

6. The __________ spinner in the **Settings** area is used to define the length of the stroke.

Review Questions

Answer the following questions:

1. Which of the following tools in the **Sculpting** menu is used to grab a particular part of the mesh and pull it in the desired direction?

   (a) **Grab** (b) **Pull**
   (c) **Subdivision** (d) **Push**

2. The __________ tool in the **Sculpting** menu of the **Sculpting** layout is used to move the vertex points to create bumps on the surface.

3. The __________ check box in the **Settings** area is selected to attach a string which helps in making the brush straight.

4. On increasing the subdivision level of an object, the file size also increases. (T/F)

EXERCISE

The rendered output of the model used in the exercise can be accessed by downloading the *c04_cinema4d_r20_exr.zip* file from *www.cadcim.com*. The path of the file is as follows: *Textbooks > Animation and Visual Effects > MAXON CINEMA 4D > MAXON CINEMA 4D R20 Studio: A Tutorial Approach*

Exercise 1

Using various sculpting tools, sculpt a barrel with cracks, as shown in Figure 4-33.

(Expected time: 10 min)

Figure 4-33 A barrel with cracks

Answers to Self-Evaluation Test

1. c, **2.** a, **3. Sculpt Expression [Sculpt]**, **4. Pull**, **5. Radial**, **6. Length**

Chapter 5

Texturing

Learning Objectives

After completing this chapter, you will be able to:

- *Work with the Material Manager*
- *Use shaders*
- *Apply textures and colors to the objects*

INTRODUCTION

The appearance of the surface of an object in CINEMA 4D is defined by the material applied to it. The material describes how an object reflects or transmits light. When light hits an object, some of it gets absorbed and some is reflected. The smoother the surface, the shiner it will be. In this chapter, you will learn to assign various materials and textures to the objects in the scene to make them more realistic.

NODE BASED MATERIALS

In CINEMA 4D R20, uber, node, and some in-built node based materials are introduced, which can be used to create complex materials.

To create a uber material, choose **Create > New Uber Material** from the Material Manager; a material with the name **Uber** will be created in the Material Manager. Uber material is a generic material which is simple and very easy to use. You can edit this material in the Attribute Manager and in the **Material Editor** window. To edit node flow of this material, right-click on the material in the Material Manager and choose **Node Editor** from the shortcut menu displayed; the **Node Editor** window will be displayed with the **Uber Material.1** node. Right-click on this node and choose **Edit Asset** from the shortcut menu displayed; a node flow will be displayed in the **Node Editor** window. You can now edit this node flow as per the requirement.

To create a node material, choose **Create > New Node Material** from the Material Manager; a material with the name **Node** will be created and displayed in the Material Manager. Double-click on this material in the Material Manager; the **Node Editor** window will be displayed with default connected nodes, **Diffuse.1** and **Material.1**. In the **Node Editor** window, the **Assets** area contains variety of nodes under various categories to modify the node material. You can also add number of inputs to theses nodes, replace nodes, organize nodes, create asset, and so on in the **Node Editor** window. Besides, you can edit this node material in the Attribute Manager and in the **Material Editor** window also.

To use in-built node based materials such as car paint, ceramic, concrete, marble, and so on, choose **Create > Node Materials** from the Material Manager; a cascading menu will be displayed. Choose desired material from the cascading menu; the corresponding node material will be displayed in the Material Manager. This material can be modified in the Attribute Manager, in the **Node Editor** window, and in the **Material Editor** window.

TUTORIALS

Before you start the tutorials of this chapter, you need to download the *c05_cinema4d_r20_tut.zip* file from *www.cadcim.com*. The path of the file is as follows: *Textbooks > Animation and Visual Effects > MAXON CINEMA 4D > MAXON CINEMA 4D R20 Studio: A Tutorial Approach*

Next, you need to browse to *\Documents\c4dr20* and create a new folder in it with the name *c05*. Next, extract the contents of the zip file in this folder.

Tutorial 1

In this tutorial, you will apply texture to the model of a dice. The final output of the textured model is shown in Figure 5-1. **(Expected time: 25 min)**

Figure 5-1 The textured model of a dice

The following steps are required to complete this tutorial:

a. Open the file.
b. Apply shader to the dice model.
c. Apply shader to the floor.
d. Change the background color of the scene.
e. Save and render the scene.

Opening the File

In this section, you will open the dice file.

1. Choose **File > Open** from the main menu; the **Open File** dialog box is displayed.

2. In the **Open File** dialog box, browse to *\Documents\c4dr20\c05\c05_tut1_start* and then choose the **Open** button; the *c05_tut1_start.c4d* file is displayed in the Perspective viewport, as shown in Figure 5-2.

Applying Shader to the Dice Model

In this section, you will apply shader to the dice model using the Material Manager.

1. Choose **Create > New Material** from the Material Manager menu, as shown in Figure 5-3; a new material slot is created in the Material Manager, refer to Figure 5-4. Alternatively, double-click in the empty area of the Material Manager; a new material with the name **Mat** is created in the Material Manager.

   The **New Material** option in the **Create** menu is used to create a new material. By default, the new material created is white in color and has specularity.

2. Make sure that the new material is selected in the Material Manager and then choose the **Basic** button from the Attribute Manager; the **Basic Properties** area is displayed. Enter **matDice** in the **Name** text box in the **Basic Properties** area; the new material is renamed as *matDice*.

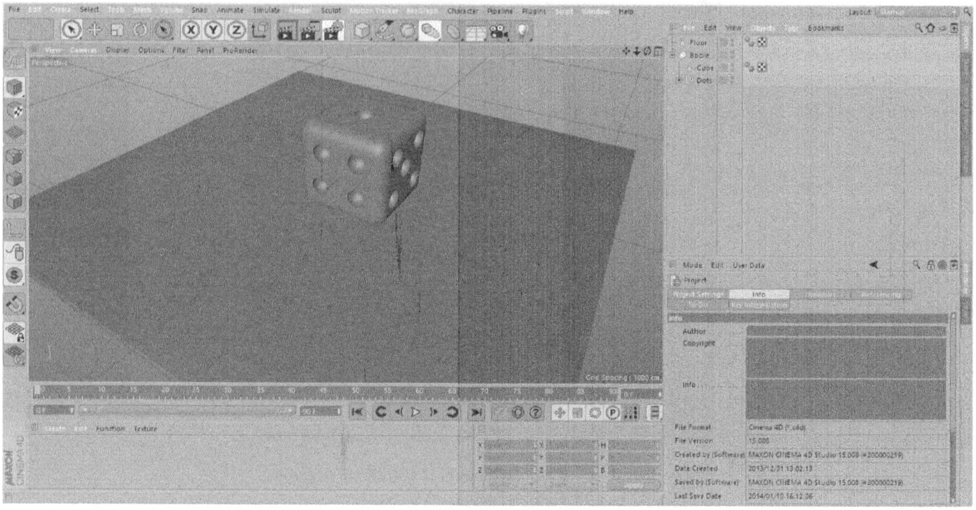

Figure 5-2 *The c05_tut1_start.c4d file*

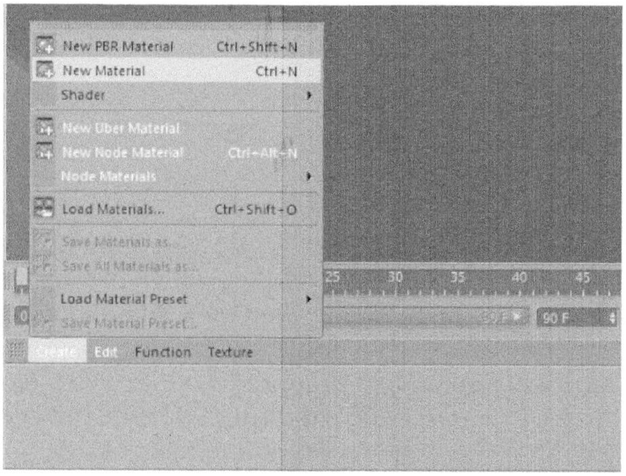

Figure 5-3 *Choosing **New Material** from the Material Manager menu*

Figure 5-4 *Displaying the material slot in the Material Manager*

Note

*You can rename the material by right-clicking on the material slot; a shortcut menu is displayed. Choose **Rename** from the shortcut menu; the **Name** dialog box is displayed. Enter a new name in the **Name** text box of this dialog box and choose the **OK** button. Alternatively, double-click on the material name in the Material Manager and enter a new name for it.*

3. In the **Basic Properties** area, make sure the **Reflectance** check box is selected; refer to Figure 5-5.

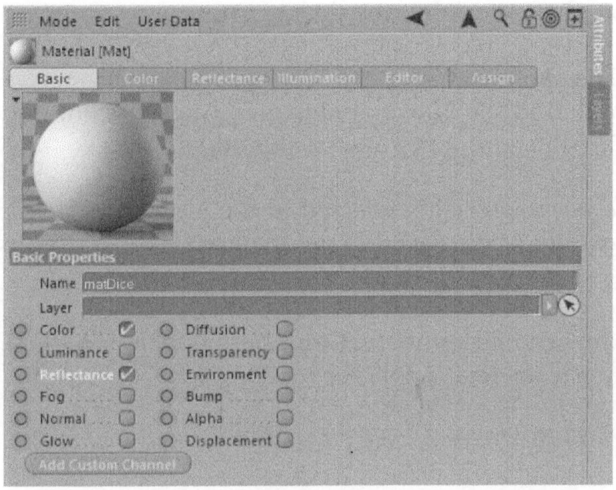

*Figure 5-5 The **Reflectance** check box selected*

4. In the Attribute Manager, choose the **Reflectance** button; the **Reflectance** area is displayed. In this area, choose the **Add** button; a flyout is displayed. Now, choose **Phong** from the flyout; a reflectance layer with the name **Layer 1** is added.

5. In the **Reflectance > Layer Color** area, click on the **Color** swatch to open the **Color Picker** dialog box. In this dialog box, choose the **RGB** button and then set the parameters as given below. Next, choose the **OK** button.

   R: **197** G: **145** B: **145**

   Enter **50** in the **Brightness** spinner.

   The **Color** option in the **Reflectance > Layer Color** area is used to set the color of the reflection. The **Brightness** option is used to adjust the brightness of the color reflected by the material.

6. Make sure *matDice* is selected in the Material Manager. In the Attribute Manager, choose the **Color** button; the **Color** area is displayed. In the **Color** area, choose the **RGB** button and then set the parameters as follows:

   R: **163** G: **216** B: **246**

   The color of *matDice* changes to light blue.

   The **Color** area is used to choose a color using the R, G, and B values.

7. Press and hold the left mouse button on *matDice* in the Material Manager and drag the cursor on *Cube* in the Object Manager; the *matDice* is applied to *Cube* in the Perspective viewport, refer to Figure 5-6.

***Figure 5-6** The matDice material applied to Cube*

Next, you will apply the material to the dots of *Cube*.

8. Choose **Create > New Material** from the Material Manager menu; a new material slot with the name **Mat** is added to the Material Manager. Alternatively, double-click in the empty area of the Material Manager; a new material is added to it.

9. Make sure that the new material is selected in the Material Manager and double-click on the name **Mat**; a text box is displayed in the material slot. In this text box, enter **matDots**; the new material is renamed as *matDots*.

10. In the Attribute Manager, make sure the **Color** button is chosen; the **Color** area is displayed. In this area, set the parameters as follows:

    R: **0** G: **0** B: **0**

11. In the Attribute Manager, choose the **Reflectance** button; the **Reflectance** area is displayed. In this area, choose the **Add** button; a flyout is displayed. Now, choose **Phong** from the flyout; a reflectance layer with the name **Layer 1** is added.

12. In the **Layer Color** area, click on the **Color** swatch to open the **Color Picker** dialog box. In this dialog box, choose the **RGB** button and then set the parameters as given below. Next, choose the **OK** button:

    R: **68** G: **62** B: **62**

    Enter **34** in the **Brightness** spinner.

13. Press and hold the left mouse button on *matDots* in the Material Manager and drag the cursor on *Dots* in the Object Manager; the *matDots* is applied to all the dots in the Perspective viewport, as shown in Figure 5-7.

Applying Shader to the Floor

In this section, you will apply shader to the floor.

1. Double-click in the empty area of the Material Manager; a new material slot is created in the Material Manager.

2. Make sure that the new material is selected in the Material Manager and double-click on the name **Mat**; a text box is displayed. In this text box, enter **matFloor**; the new material is renamed as *matFloor*.

3. In the Attribute Manager, make sure the **Reflectance** button is chosen; the **Reflectance** area is displayed. In this area, choose the **Add** button; a flyout is displayed. Now, choose **Phong** from the flyout; a reflectance layer with the name **Layer 1** is added.

4. In the Attribute Manager, choose the **Color** button; the **Color** area is displayed. In this area, choose the browse button located next to the **Texture** parameter, as shown in Figure 5-8; the **Open File** dialog box is displayed.

Figure 5-7 The Dot material applied to dots of the Cube

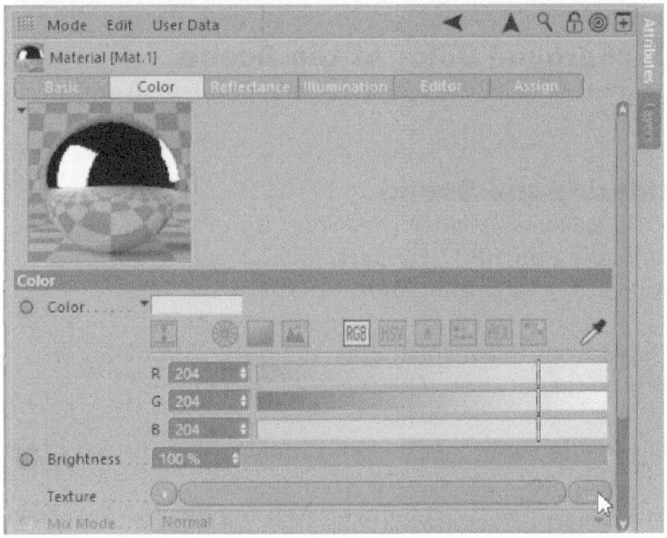

Figure 5-8 Choosing the browse button

5. In this dialog box, browse to *\Documents\c4dr20\c05\Wood_Texture.jpg*. Next, choose the **Open** button; the texture is applied to the material slot in the **Color** area of the Attribute Manager.

6. In the Attribute Manager, choose the **Reflectance** button; the **Reflection** area is displayed. In the **Layer Color** area, enter **10** in the **Brightness** spinner.

7. Press and hold the left mouse button on *matFloor* in the Material Manager and drag the cursor to *Floor* in the Object Manager; the *matFloor* is applied to *Floor* in the Perspective viewport, as shown in Figure 5-9.

Figure 5-9 *The matFloor applied to Floor*

Changing the Background Color of the Scene

To change the background color of the scene to white in the final output, follow the steps given in Tutorial 1 of Chapter 2.

Saving and Rendering the Scene

In this section, you will save and render the scene. You can also view the final render of the composition by downloading the file *c05_cinema4d_r20_rndr.zip* from *www.cadcim.com*. The path of the file is mentioned at the beginning of the chapter.

1. Choose **File > Save** from the main menu; the **Save File** dialog box is displayed. In this dialog box, browse to the location *\Documents\c4dr20\c05*.

2. Enter **c05tut1** in the **File name** text box and then choose the **Save** button.

3. In the Perspective viewport, set the camera angle using the Viewport Navigation Tools located at the top right of the Perspective viewport. Next, choose the **Render to Picture Viewer** tool from the Command Palette. Alternatively, press SHIFT+R; the **Picture Viewer** window is displayed.

4. In the **Picture Viewer** window, choose **File > Save as**; the **Save** dialog box is displayed.

5. In the **Save** dialog box, select **JPEG** from the **Format** drop-down list and then choose the **OK** button; the **Save Dialog** dialog box is displayed. Next, browse to *\Documents\c4dr20\c05*.

In the **File name** text box, type **c05_tut1_rndr**. Next, choose the **Save** button; the rendered image is saved at the desired location.

Figure 5-1 displays the final output.

Tutorial 2

In this tutorial, you will apply texture to a dining table set. The final output of the textured dining table set is shown in Figure 5-10. **(Expected time: 40 min)**

Figure 5-10 *The textured dining table set*

The following steps are required to complete this tutorial:

a. Open the file.
b. Apply texture to the chairs and the table.
c. Apply texture to the floor.
d. Apply the glass shader to wine glasses.
e. Apply texture to the table cover and table mats.
f. Apply texture to the wine bottle.
g. Apply texture to the plates.
h. Add physical sky.
i. Save and render the scene.

Opening the File

In this section, you will open the file of the dining table set.

1. Choose **File > Open** from the main menu; the **Open File** dialog box is displayed.

2. In the **Open File** dialog box, browse to *\Documents\c4dr20\c05\c05_tut2_start* and then choose the **Open** button; the models are displayed in the Perspective viewport, as shown in Figure 5-11.

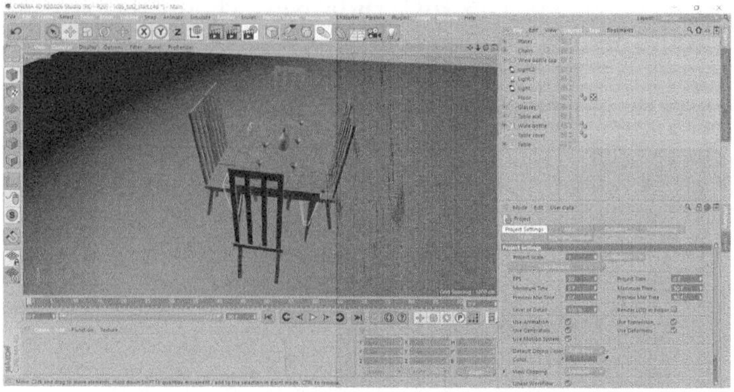

Figure 5-11 The c05_tut2_start.c4d file

Applying Texture to the Chairs and Table

In this section, you will apply the wooden texture to the chairs and table.

1. Double-click in the empty area of the Material Manager; a new material is created.

2. Double-click on the name **Mat**; a text box is displayed. In this text box, enter **matChair**; the new material is renamed as *matChair*.

3. In the Attribute Manager, choose the **Color** button; the **Color** area is displayed. In this area, choose the browse button located next to the **Texture** parameter; the **Open File** dialog box is displayed.

4. In this dialog box, browse to *\Documents\c4dr20\c05\Wood_Texture.jpg*. Next, choose the **Open** button; the texture is applied to the new material slot and *Wood_Texture.jpg* is added to the **Color** area of Attribute Manager, as shown in Figure 5-12.

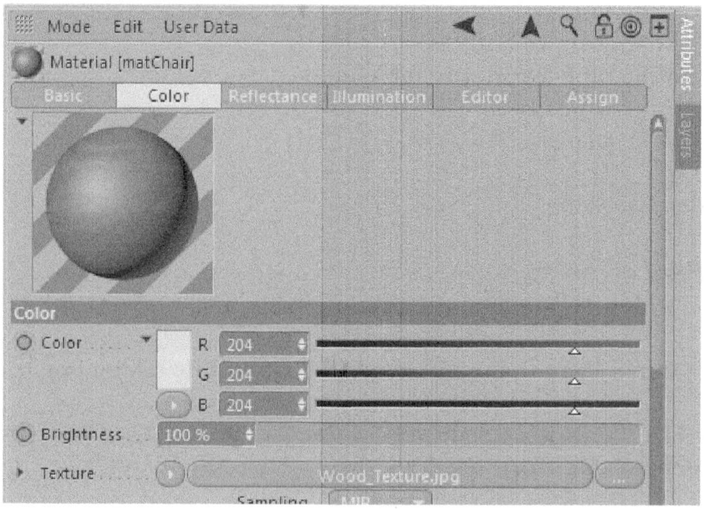

Figure 5-12 The Wood_Texture.jpg added to the ***Color*** *area of Attribute Manager*

5. Press and hold the left mouse button on *matChair* in the Material Manager and drag the cursor to the *Chairs* group in the Object Manager; the *matChair* material is applied to the chairs, as shown in Figure 5-13.

Figure 5-13 *The matChair applied to the chairs*

Next, you will apply texture to the table.

6. Press and hold the CTRL key along with the left mouse button on the **Texture Tag "matChair"** texture tag from the Object Manager and then drag the cursor to the *Table* group in the Object Manager, refer to Figure 5-14; a copy of the **matChair** texture tag is created and the *matChair* material is applied to the *Table* group.

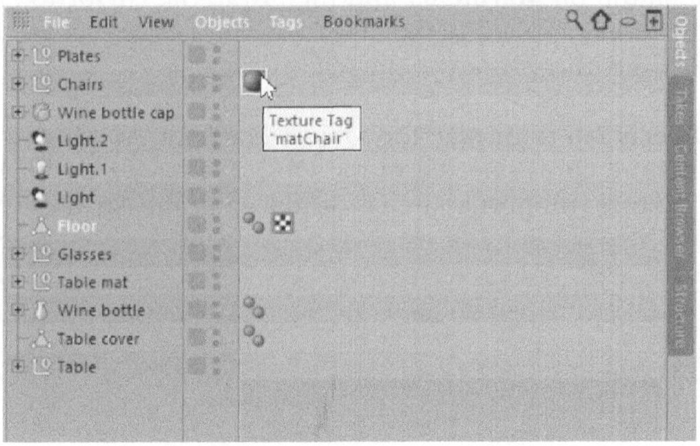

Figure 5-14 *The **Texture Tag "matChair"** in the Object Manager*

Applying Texture to the Floor

In this section, you will apply texture to the floor using the Content Browser.

1. Choose the **Content Browser** tab next to the **Takes** tab in the Object Manager; the Content Browser with various options is displayed. In the Content Browser, double-click on **Presets**;

various other options are displayed. Next, double-click on **Visualize**, refer to Figure 5-15; more options are displayed in the Content Browser.

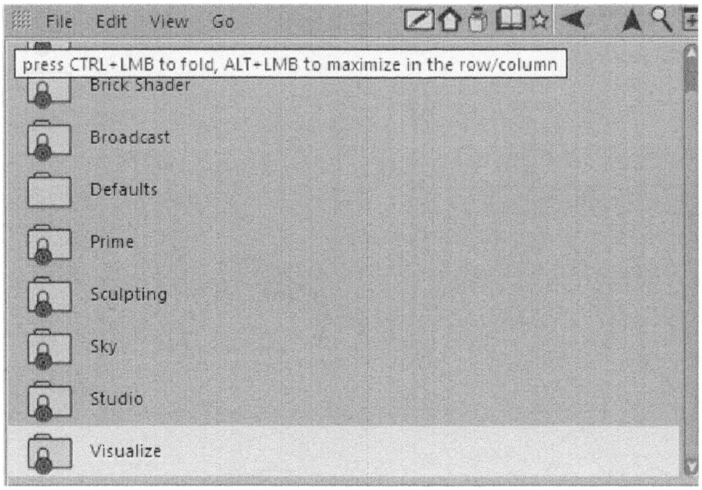

Figure 5-15 *Choosing the **Visualize** folder in the Content Browser*

The **Presets** option in the Content Browser is used to display the presets from other software packages developed by MAXON. For example, **Visualize** is a software package developed by MAXON, so you can display its presets in the Content Browser.

2. Choose **Materials > Stone > Marble 03** from the Content Browser. Next, press and hold the left mouse button on **Marble 03** and then drag the cursor to *Floor* in the Perspective viewport; the texture is applied to the *Floor*. You will notice that the texture is stretched. Next, you will modify the settings of the texture tag.

3. Choose the **Objects** tab to display the Object Manager. Make sure that the **Texture Tag "Marble 03"** texture tag is selected in the Object Manager, as shown in Figure 5-16; the **Texture Tag [Texture]** properties area is displayed in the Attribute Manager.

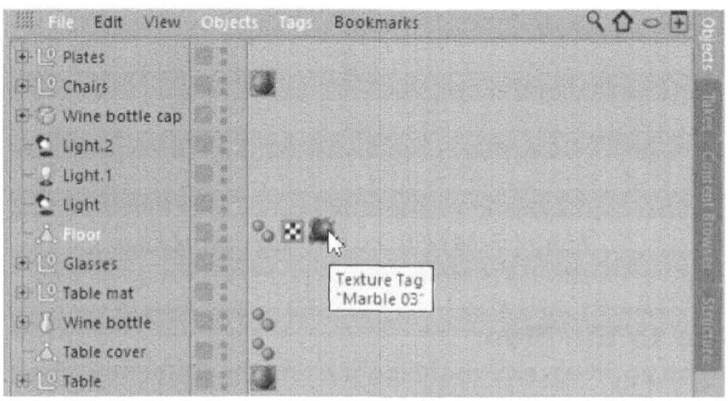

Figure 5-16 *The **Texture Tag "Marble 03"** selected in the Object Manager*

A **Texture Tag** is created automatically after texture is applied to an object. The parameters in the **Texture Tag [Texture]** area are used to define the mapping of a texture on a 3D surface. Multiple texture tags can be assigned to an object.

4. In the Attribute Manager, make sure the **Tag** button is chosen if not already chosen. In the **Tag Properties** area, select the **Cubic** option from the **Projection** drop-down list and set the parameters as given next:

   Offset U: **1** Offset V: **1**
   Length U: **170** Length V: **170**

   After entering these values, the texture is projected uniformly on *Floor*, as shown in Figure 5-17.

Figure 5-17 *The Marble 03 texture uniformly projected on the Floor*

The **Cubic** projection type is used to map texture on an object in a cube pattern. The **Offset U** spinner is used to set the position of texture in the U direction. The **Offset V** spinner is used to set the position of texture in the V direction. The **Length U** spinner is used to set the length of the texture in the U direction. The **Length V** spinner is used to set the length of the texture in the V direction.

Applying the Glass Shader to Wine Glasses

In this section, you will apply the glass shader to wine glasses.

1. Double-click in the empty area of the Material Manager; a new material is created in the Material Manager.

2. Double-click on the name **Mat** in the Material Manager; a text box is displayed. In this text box, enter **matGlass**; the new material is renamed as *matGlass*.

3. In the Attribute Manager, choose the **Basic** button; the **Basic Properties** area is displayed. In this area, select the **Transparency** check box.

4. Choose the **Transparency** button in the Attribute Manager; the **Transparency** area is displayed. In this area, set **92** in the **Brightness** spinner and **1.5** in the **Refraction** spinner.

   The **Brightness** spinner in the **Transparency** area is used to specify the transparency of a 3D surface. Lesser the value of brightness, more will be the transparency of the object. The **Refraction** parameter is used to control the refractive index of the surface.

5. In the Attribute Manager, choose the **Reflectance** button; the **Reflectance** area is displayed. In this area, choose the **Add** button; a flyout is displayed. Now, choose **Phong** from the flyout; a reflectance layer with the name **Layer 1** is added.

6. In the **Reflectance > Layer Color** area, enter **5** in the **Brightness** spinner. Choose the **Default Specular** button in the **Reflectance** area; the **Default Specular** area is displayed. In this area, enter **52** in the **Width** spinner and **15** in the **Falloff** spinner.

7. Press and hold the left mouse button on *matGlass* and then drag the cursor on the *Glasses* group in the Object Manager; the *matGlass* is applied to *Glasses* in the Perspective viewport, as shown in Figure 5-18.

Figure 5-18 *The matGlass material applied to the Glasses*

Applying Texture to the Table Cover and Table Mats

In this section, you will apply texture to the table cover and table mats.

1. Double-click in the empty area of the Material Manager; a new material is created in the Material Manager.

2. Double-click on the name **Mat** in the Material Manager; a text box is displayed. In this text box, enter **matCover**; the material is renamed as *matCover*.

3. In the Attribute Manager, choose the **Color** button; the **Color** area is displayed. In this area, choose the browse button located next to the **Texture** parameter; the **Open File** dialog box is displayed.

4. In this dialog box, browse to *\Documents\c4dr20\c05\Table cloth.jpg*. Next, choose the **Open** button; the texture is applied to the material slot, as shown in Figure 5-19.

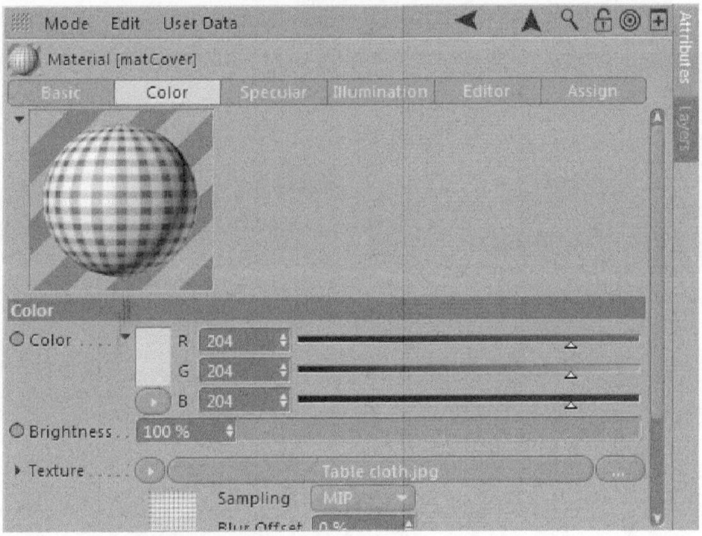

Figure 5-19 *The matCover material applied to the material slot*

5. Press and hold the left mouse button on the *matCover* material in the Material Manager and drag the cursor to *Table cover* in the Object Manager; the *matCover* material is applied to *Table cover* in the Perspective viewport. You will notice that the texture is not projected properly.

6. Make sure the **Texture Tag "matCover"** tag is selected in the Object Manager, as shown in Figure 5-20; the **Texture Tag [Texture]** area is displayed in the Attribute Manager.

7. In the **Tag Properties** area, select the **Cubic** option from the **Projection** drop-down list; the texture is projected uniformly on *Table cover* in the Perspective viewport, as shown in Figure 5-21.

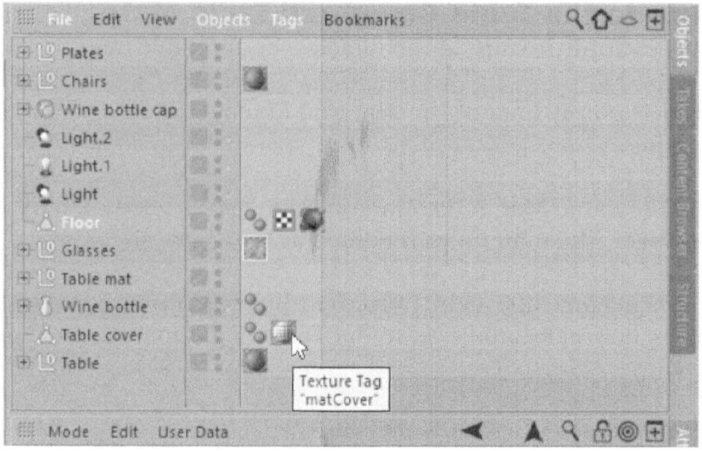

*Figure 5-20 The **Texture Tag "matCover"** selected in the Object Manager*

Figure 5-21 The matCover material applied to Table cover

Next, you will apply the texture to the Table mats.

8. Double-click in the empty area of the Material Manager; a new material is created in the Material Manager.

9. Make sure that the new material is selected in the Material Manager and double-click on the name **Mat** in the Material Manager; a text box is displayed. In this text box, enter **matTableMats**; the new material is renamed as *matTableMats*.

10. In the Attribute Manager, choose the **Basic** button; the **Basic Properties** area is displayed. In this area, make sure that the **Color** check box is selected. Next, select the **Bump** check box.

The **Bump** check box is used to apply or edit the bump created on the surface.

11. Choose the **Color** button; the **Color** area is displayed. In this area, choose the browse button located next to the **Texture** parameter; the **Open File** dialog box is displayed.

12. In the **Open File** dialog box, browse to *\Documents\c4dr20\c05\Table mat.jpg*. Next, choose the **Open** button; the texture is displayed in the material slot.

13. Press and hold the left mouse button on the *matTableMats* material in the Material Manager and drag the cursor to the *Table mat* group; the *matTableMats* material is applied to the table mats in the Perspective viewport.

14. Select the *matTableMats* material in the Material Manager and choose the **Bump** button in the Attribute Manager; the **Bump** area is displayed. In this area, choose the browse button located next to the **Texture** parameter; the **Open File** dialog box is displayed.

15. In the **Open File** dialog box, browse to *\Documents\c4dr20\c05\Table mat.jpg*. Next, choose the **Open** button; the texture is displayed in the **Bump** area. Figure 5-22 displays the *matTableMats* material applied to the *Table mat* group.

***Figure 5-22** The matTableMats material applied to the Table mat group*

Applying Texture to the Wine Bottle

In this section, you will apply texture to the wine bottle.

1. Double-click in the empty area of the Material Manager; a new material is created in the Material Manager.

2. Make sure that the new material is selected in the Material Manager and double-click on the name **Mat** in the Material Manager; a text box is displayed. In this text box, enter **matWine**; the new material is renamed as *matWine*.

3. In the Attribute Manager, choose the **Basic** button; the **Basic Properties** area is displayed. In this area, select the **Transparency** check box.

4. In the Attribute Manager, choose the **Color** button; the **Color** area is displayed. In this area, set the parameters as follows:

   R: **80** G: **19** B: **17**

   Enter **12** in the **Brightness** spinner.

5. Choose the triangle button located next to the **Texture** parameter; a flyout is displayed, refer to Figure 5-23. Choose the **Gradient** option from the flyout.

   The **Gradient** option is used to create gradient textures.

6. Choose the **Gradient** button in the **Color** area; the **Shader Properties** area is displayed in the Attribute Manager, as shown in Figure 5-24.

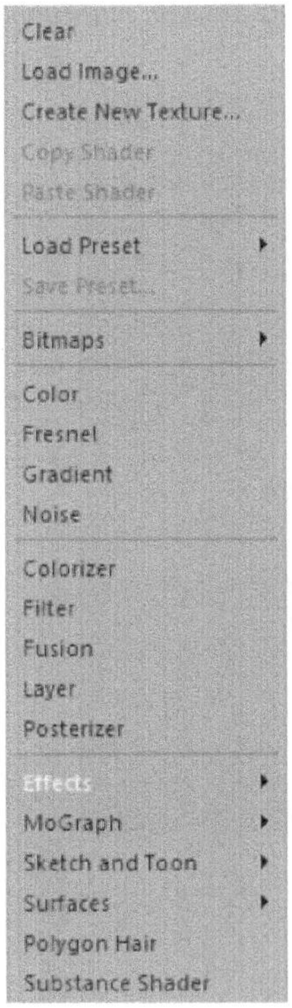

*Figure 5-23 The flyout displayed on choosing the triangle button next to the **Texture** parameter*

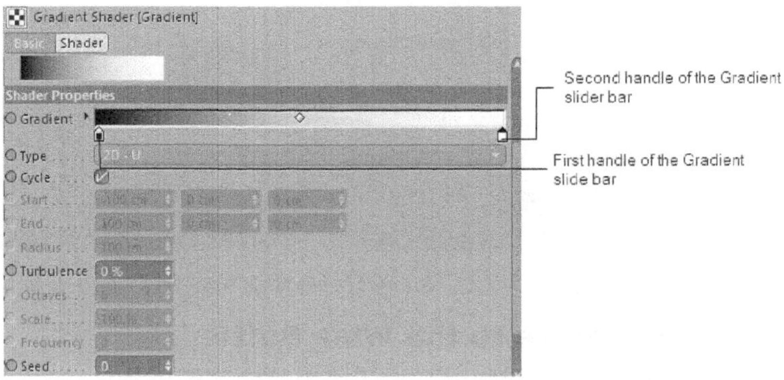

*Figure 5-24 The **Shader Properties** area of **Gradient** in the Attribute Manager*

7. In this area, double-click on the first handle of the **Gradient** slide bar; the **Color Picker** dialog box is displayed, refer to Figure 5-25.

The handles of the **Gradient** slide bar are used to set the color of gradient.

8. In the **Color Picker** dialog box, choose the RGB button and then set the parameters as follows:

   R: **70** G: **7** B: **7**

   In the **Color Picker** dialog box, choose the **OK** button; the color is set to brown.

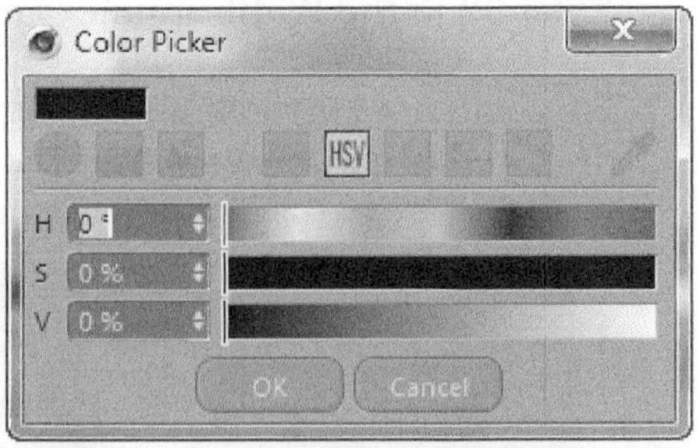

Figure 5-25 *The* ***Color Picker*** *dialog box*

9. Double-click on the second handle of **Gradient**; the **Color Picker** dialog box is displayed, refer to Figure 5-25.

10. In the **Color Picker** dialog box, choose the **RGB** button and then set the parameters as follows:

    R: **15** G: **1** B: **1**

    Choose the **OK** button in the **Color Picker** dialog box; the color is set to dark brown.

11. Select the *matWine* material in the Material Manager. Next, choose the **Color** button in the Attribute Manager; the **Color** area is displayed. In this area, select **Subtract** from the **Mix Mode** drop-down list and then enter **51** in the **Mix Strength** spinner.

    The options in the **Mix Mode** drop-down list are used to combine the color and the texture channel shaders using one of the four modes in the **Mode** drop-down list. By default, the **Mix Mode** is set to **Normal**.

    The **Subtract** mode subtracts the color's RGB values from the texture's RGB value. The **Mix Strength** spinner is used to define the mixing proportion between the color values in the **Color** area with the texture's color value. The value of **Mix Strength** is dependent on the mode from the **Mix Mode** drop-down list.

12. In the Attribute Manager, choose the **Transparency** button; the **Transparency** area is displayed. In this area, choose the **RGB** button and then set the parameters as follows:

    R: **65** G: **21** B: **21**

    Enter **56** in the **Brightness** spinner.

13. In the Attribute Manager, choose the **Reflectance** button; the **Reflectance** area is displayed. In this area, choose the **Add** button; a flyout is displayed. Now, choose **Phong** from the flyout; a reflectance layer with the name **Layer 1** is added.

14. In the **Reflectance > Layer Color** area, enter **16** in the **Brightness** spinner.

15. Choose the **Default Specular** button in the **Reflectance** area; the **Default Specular** area is displayed. In this area, select **Specular - Phong (Legacy)** from the **Type** drop-down list. Enter **32** in the **Width** spinner and **48** in the **Specular Strength** spinner.

16. Press and hold the left mouse button on the *matWine* material in the Material Manager and drag the cursor on *Wine bottle* group in the Object Manager; the *matWine* material is applied to *Wine bottle* in the Perspective viewport, as shown in Figure 5-26.

Figure 5-26 *The matWine material applied to Wine bottle*

Next, you will add label to *Wine bottle*.

17. Double-click in the empty area of the Material Manager; a new material is created in the Material Manager.

18. Make sure that the new material is selected in the Material Manager and double-click on the name **Mat** in the Material Manager; a text box is displayed. In this text box, enter **matLabel**; the new material is renamed as *matLabel*.

19. In the Attribute Manager, choose the **Color** button; the **Color** area is displayed. In the **Color** area, choose the browse button located next to the **Texture** parameter; the **Open File** dialog box is displayed.

20. In this dialog box, browse to *\Documents\c4dr20\c05\Label.png*. Next, choose the **Open** button; a texture is displayed in the **Color** area, as shown in Figure 5-27.

21. Press and hold the left mouse button on the *matLabel* material in the Material Manager and drag the cursor to *Wine bottle* in the Object Manager; the *matLabel* material is applied to *Wine bottle* in the Perspective viewport, as shown in Figure 5-28. You will notice that the texture is stretched.

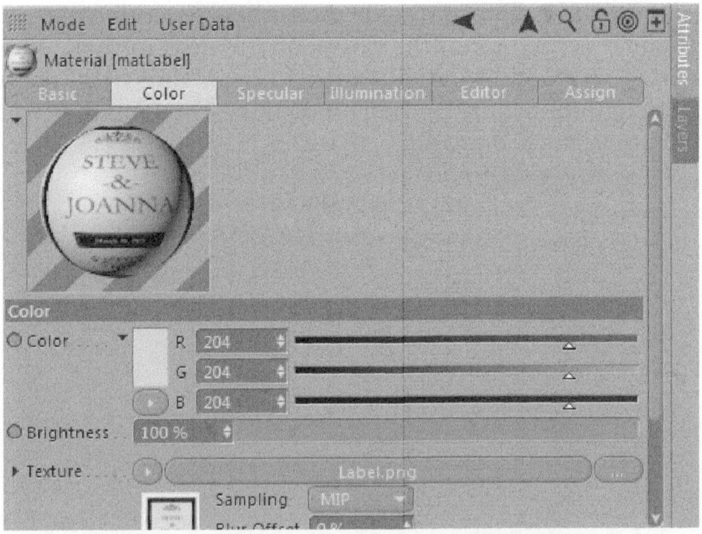

*Figure 5-27 The matLabel texture displayed in the **Color** area of Material Manager*

Figure 5-28 The matLabel texture applied to Wine bottle

22. Select the **Texture Tag "matLabel"** texture tag in the Object Manager, as shown in Figure 5-29. Make sure that the **Tag** button is chosen in the Attribute Manager. Also, make sure that the **Tile** check box is cleared

23. In the **Tag Properties** area, select **Cylindrical** from the **Projection** drop-down list. Next, clear the **Tile** check box and set the parameters as follows:

    Offset U: **-29** Offset V: **-5** Length U: **24**
    Length V: **50**

    The **Cylindrical** option in the **Projection** drop-down list is used to set texture on cylindrical shaped objects. It is the most preferred type of projection on cylindrical objects.

The **Tile** option is used to enable or disable the endless repetition of texture on the surface. The **Offset U** spinner is used to set the position of texture in the U direction. The **Offset V** spinner is used to set the position of texture in the V direction. The **Length U** spinner is used to set the length of texture in the U direction. The **Length V** spinner is used to set the length of texture in the V direction.

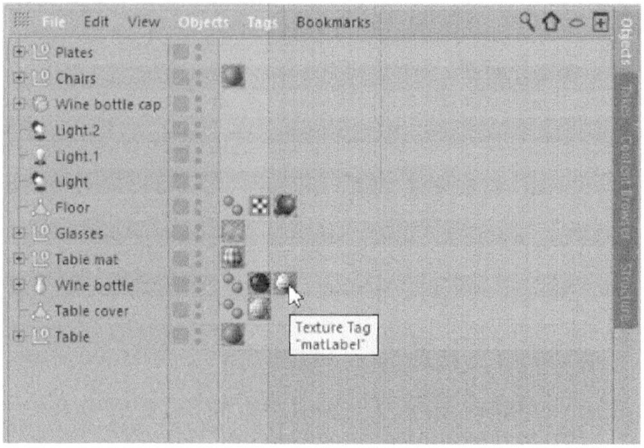

***Figure 5-29** Selecting the **Texture Tag "matLabel"** in the Object Manager*

24. In the Attribute Manager, choose the **Coordinates** button; the **Coordinates** area is displayed. In this area, set the parameters as follows:

    P . X: **-1**　　　　P . Y: **628**

    After entering these values, the mat*Label* material is projected properly on *Wine bottle*, as shown in Figure 5-30.

    Next, you will apply the texture to the cap of *Wine bottle*.

25. Create a new material by double-clicking in the empty space of the Material Manager.

26. Make sure that the new material is selected in the Material Manager and double-click on the name **Mat**; a text box is displayed. In this text box, enter **matCap**; the new material is renamed as *matCap*.

27. Make sure the **Color** button is chosen in the Attribute Manager; the **Color** area is displayed. In this area, choose the **Color** swatch; the **Color Picker** dialog box is displayed. In the **Color Picker** dialog box, choose the black color and then choose the **OK** button; the black color is displayed in the material slot.

28. Choose the **Reflectance** button; the **Reflectance** area is displayed. In this area, choose the **Default Specular** button; the **Default Specular** area is displayed. In this area, make sure **Specular - Blinn (Legacy)** is selected in the **Type** drop-down list. Next, set the parameters as follows:

    Width: **24**　　　　Specular Strength: **44**　　　　Falloff: **-6**

29. Press and hold the left mouse button on the *mapCap* material in the Material Manager and drag the cursor to *Wine bottle cap* in the Object Manager; the *matCap* material is applied to *Wine bottle cap* in the Perspective viewport, as shown in Figure 5-31.

Figure 5-30 *The matLabel material projected properly on the wine bottle in the Perspective viewport*

Figure 5-31 *The matCap material applied to the Wine bottle cap*

Applying Texture to the Plates

In this section, you will apply texture to the plates using node material.

1. Choose **Create > Node Materials** from the Material Manager menu; a cascading menu is displayed. Choose **Ceramic** from the cascading menu; a node material with the name **Ceramic** is created in the Material Manager.

2. Double-click on the name **Ceramic** in the Material Manager; a text box is displayed. In this text box, enter **matplate**; the new material is renamed as *matplate*.

3. Press and hold the left mouse button on the *matplate* material in the Material Manager and drag the cursor to *plate1* in the Object Manager; the *matplate* material is applied to *plate1* in the Perspective viewport.

4. Make sure the *matplate* material is selected in the Material Manager and the **Base** button is chosen in the Attribute Manager. In the **Base** area, choose the **RGB** button and then set the parameters as follows:

   R: **45** G: **49** B:**251**

5. Make sure that the **Texture Tag "matPlates"** texture tag is selected in the Object Manager. Next, choose the **Tag** button; the **Tag Properties** area is displayed. In this area, select **Cubic** from the **Projection** drop-down list. Make sure that the **Tile** check box is selected.

6. Press the CTRL key and then drag the **Texture Tag "matPlates"** in the Object Manager to *Plate.2*, *Plate.3*, *Plate.4*, *Plate.5*, and *Plate.6* one by one; the plates get textured.

7. Choose the **Render to Picture Viewer** tool from the Command Palette. Alternatively, press SHIFT+R; the **Picture Viewer** window is displayed that shows *matplate* material, refer to Figure 5-32.

Figure 5-32 *The matplate material applied to the plates*

Adding Physical Sky

In this section, you will add **Physical Sky** to the scene.

1. Choose **Create > Physical Sky > Physical Sky** from the main menu; physical sky is created in the viewport and the *Physical Sky* object is added to the Object Manager.

Saving and Rendering the Scene

In this section, you will save and render the scene. You can also view the final render of the scene by downloading the file *c05_cinema4d_r20_rndr.zip* from *www.cadcim.com*. The path of the file is mentioned at the beginning of the chapter.

1. Choose **File > Save** from the main menu; the **Save File** dialog box is displayed. In this dialog box, browse to the location *\Documents\c4dr20\c05*.

2. Enter **c05tut2** in the **File name** text box and then choose the **Save** button.

3. In the Perspective viewport, set the camera angle using the Viewport Navigation Tools located at the top right of the Perspective viewport. Next, you will render the scene. For rendering, refer to Tutorial 1.

   Figure 5-10 displays the final output.

Tutorial 3

In this tutorial, you will apply material to the exterior scene that you downloaded earlier using Node Editor. The final output of the scene with the materials applied is shown in Figure 5-33.

(Expected time: 25 min)

The following steps are required to complete this tutorial:

a. Open the file.
b. Create and apply material to floor.
c. Create and apply material to wall.

d. Modify and apply material to table.
e. Modify and apply material to cup.
f. Modify and apply material to glass.
g. Save and render the scene.

Figure 5-33 *The exterior scene with the materials applied*

Opening the File

In this section, you will open the scene.

1. Choose **File > Open** from the main menu; the **Open File** dialog box is displayed.

2. In the **Open File** dialog box, browse to *\Documents\c4dr20\c05\c05_tut3_start* and then choose the **Open** button; the *c05_tut3_start.c4d* file is displayed in the Perspective viewport, as shown in Figure 5-34.

Creating and Applying Material to Floor

In this section, you will create and apply new node material to floor using Node Editor.

1. Choose **Create > New Node Material** from the Material Manager menu, as shown in Figure 5-35. Alternatively, press CTRL+ALT+N in the empty area of the Material Manager; a new node material with the name **Node** is created in the Material Manager, refer to Figure 5-36.

2. Double-click on the name **Node** in the Material Manager; a text box is displayed. In this text box, enter **matfloor**; the new material is renamed as *matfloor*.

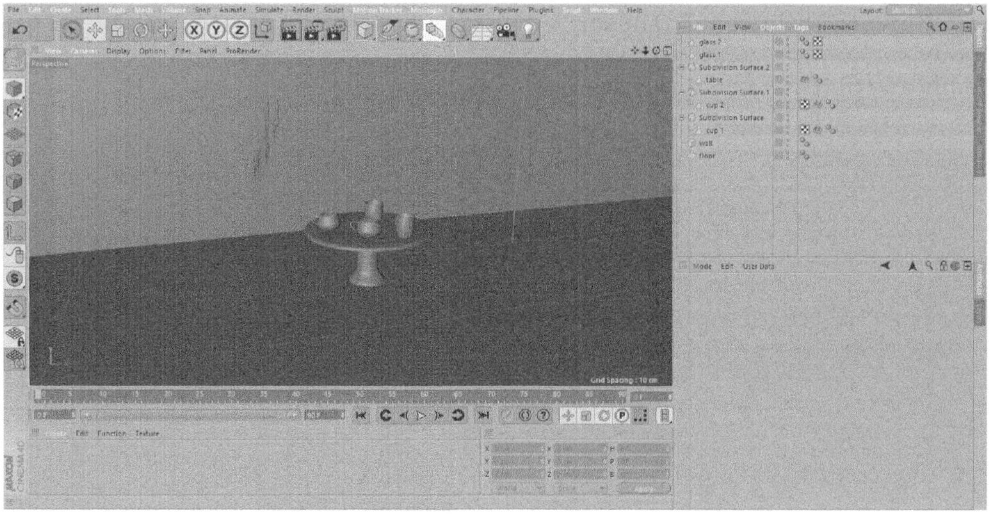

***Figure 5-34** The c05_tut3_start.c4d file*

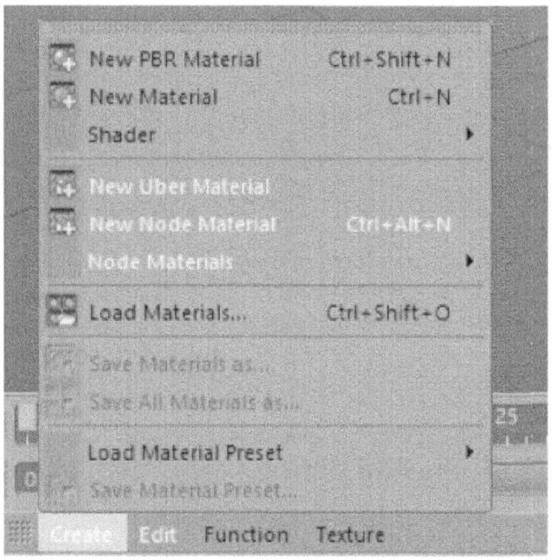

***Figure 5-35** Choosing **New Node Material** from the **Create** menu*

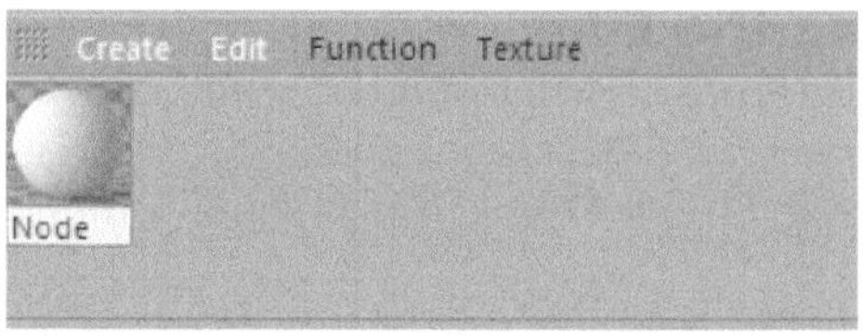

***Figure 5-36** New node material created in the Material Manager*

3. Double click on *matfloor* in the Material Manager; the **Node Editor (1) [matfloor]** window is displayed, as shown in Figure 5-37.

   You will notice that two nodes, **Diffuse.1** and **Material.1** are available in the **Node Editor (1) [matfloor]** window.

4. Right-click on the **Color** input of the **Diffuse.1** node; a shortcut menu is displayed. Choose **Load Texture** from the shortcut menu, as shown in Figure 5-38; the **Choose an image to load** dialog box is displayed.

5. In this dialog box, browse to *\Documents\c4dr20\c05\floor texture.jpg*. Next, choose the **Open** button; the **floor texture.jpg** node is added to the **Color** input of the **Diffuse.1** node, as shown in Figure 5-39.

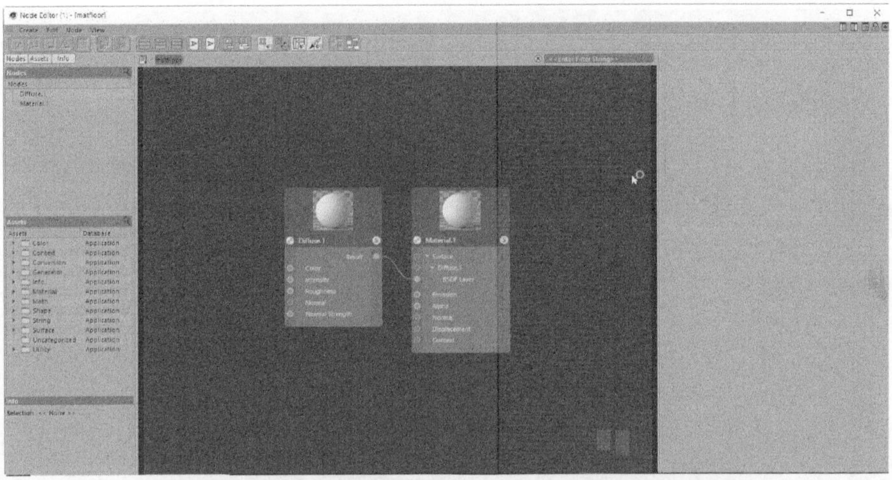

*Figure 5-37 The **Node Editor (1) [matfloor]** window*

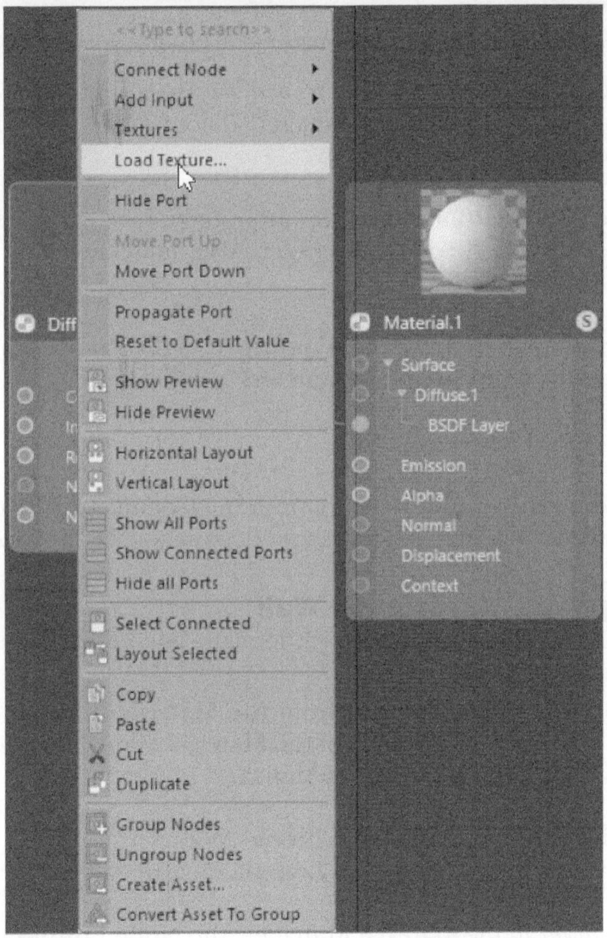

*Figure 5-38 Choosing **Load Texture** from the shortcut menu*

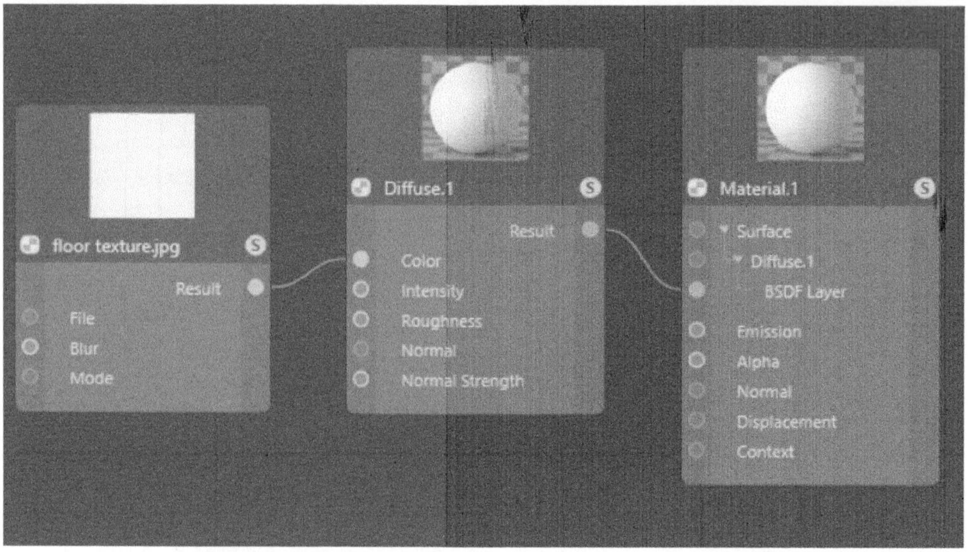

*Figure 5-39 The **floor texture.jpg** node added to the **Color** input of the **Diffuse.1** node*

6. Press and hold the left mouse button on the *matfloor* material in the Material Manager and drag the cursor to *floor* in the Object Manager; the *matfloor* material is applied to *floor* in the Perspective viewport.

7. Select the **Texture Tag "matfloor"** texture tag in the Object Manager. Make sure that the **Tag** button is chosen in the Attribute Manager. Also, make sure that the **Tile** check box is selected.

8. In the **Tag Properties** area, select **UVW mapping** from the **Projection** drop-down list. Next, select the **Tile** check box and set the parameters as follows:

   Tiles U: **8** Tiles V: **8**

9. Choose the **Render to Picture Viewer** tool from the Command Palette. Alternatively, press SHIFT+R; the **Picture Viewer** window that shows floor material is displayed, refer to Figure 5-40.

Creating and Applying Material to Wall

In this section, you will create and apply new node material to wall using Node Editor.

1. Choose **Create > New Node Material** from the Material Manager menu. Alternatively, press CTRL+ALT+N in the empty area of the Material Manager; a new node material with the name **Node** is created in the Material Manager.

2. Double-click on the name **Node** in the Material Manager; a text box is displayed. In this text box, enter **matwall** in the **Name** text box; the new material is renamed as *matwall*.

3. Double click on *matwall* in the Material Manager; the **Node Editor (1) [matwall]** window is displayed.

Figure 5-40 *The floor material displayed*

4. Right-click on the **Color** input of the **Diffuse.1** node; a shortcut menu is displayed. Choose **Load Texture** from the shortcut menu, as shown in Figure 5-38; the **Choose an image to load** dialog box is displayed.

5. In this dialog box, browse to *\Documents\c4dr20\c05\wall texture.jpg*. Next, choose the **Open** button; the **wall texture.jpg** node is added to the **Color** input of the **Diffuse.1** node. Close the **Node Editor (1) [matwall]** window.

6. Press and hold the left mouse button on the *matwall* material in the Material Manager and drag the cursor to *wall* in the Object Manager; the *matfloor* material is applied to *wall* in the Perspective viewport.

7. Select the **Texture Tag "matwall"** texture tag in the Object Manager. Make sure that the **Tag** button is chosen in the Attribute Manager. Also, make sure that the **Tile** check box is selected.

8. In the **Tag Properties** area, select **Cubic** from the **Projection** drop-down list and set the parameters as follows:

   Tiles U: **24** Tiles V: **24**

9. Choose the **Render to Picture Viewer** tool from the Command Palette. Alternatively, press SHIFT+R; the **Picture Viewer** window is displayed that shows the render view of wall material, refer to Figure 5-41. Close the **Picture Viewer** window.

Figure 5-41 *The wall material displayed*

Modifying and Applying Material to Table

In this section, you will modify the existing wood node material.

1. Choose **Create > Node Materials** from the Material Manager menu; a cascading menu is displayed, as shown in Figure 5-42. Choose **Wood** from the cascading menu; a node material with the name **Wood** is created in the Material Manager.

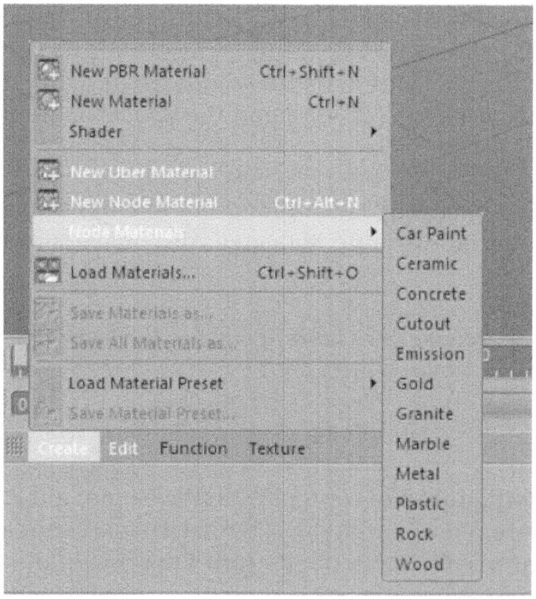

Figure 5-42 *The cascading menu displayed*

2. Double-click on the name **Wood** in the Material Manager; a text box is displayed. In this text box, enter **mattable** in the **Name** text box; the new material is renamed as *mattable*.

3. Press and hold the left mouse button on the *mattable* material in the Material Manager and drag the cursor to *table* in the Object Manager; the *mattable* material is applied to *table* in the Perspective viewport.

4. Make sure that the *mattable* material is selected in the Material Manager and then choose the **Base** button from the Attribute Manager; the **Base** area is displayed. Enter **33** in the **Grains** edit box.

5. Choose the **Veins Deformation** button from the Attribute Manager; the **Veins Deformation** area is displayed. Enter **60** in the **Deformation** edit box.

6. Choose the **Render to Picture Viewer** tool from the Command Palette. Alternatively, press SHIFT+R; the **Picture Viewer** window is displayed that shows table material, refer to Figure 5-43. Close the **Picture Viewer** window.

Figure 5-43 *The mattable material displayed*

Modifying and Applying Material to Cup

In this section, you will modify the existing ceramic node material.

1. Choose **Create > Node Materials** from the Material Manager menu; a cascading menu is displayed, refer to Figure 5-42. Choose **Ceramic** from the cascading menu; a node material with the name **Ceramic** is created in the Material Manager.

2. Double-click on the name **Ceramic** in the Material Manager; a text box is displayed. In this text box, enter **matcup**; the new material is renamed as *matcup*.

3. Press and hold the left mouse button on the *matcup* material in the Material Manager and drag the cursor to *cup1* and *cup2* in the Object Manager; the *matcup* material is applied to cups in the Perspective viewport.

4. Double-click on the **matcup** material in the Material Manager; the **Material Editor** window is displayed. Choose the **Node Editor** button from this window; the **Node Editor (1) - matcup** window is displayed.

5. Right-click on the **Color** input of the **Ceramic Material** node; a shortcut menu is displayed. Choose **Load Texture** from the shortcut menu; the **Choose an image to load** dialog box is displayed.

6. In this dialog box, browse to *\Documents\c4dr20\c05\ceramic texture.jpg*. Next, choose the **Open** button; the **ceramic texture.jpg** node is added to the **Color** input of the **Ceramic Material** node. Next, close the **Node Editor (1) - matcup** and **Material Editor** windows.

7. Select the **Texture Tag "matcup"** texture tag corresponding to *cup1* in the Object Manager. Make sure that the **Tag** button is chosen in the Attribute Manager.

8. Make sure that the **Tile** check box is selected. Also, select the **Seamless** check box; the **matcup** material is displayed properly on *cup1*.

9. Select the **Texture Tag "matcup"** texture tag corresponding to *cup2* in the Object Manager. Make sure that the **Tag** button is chosen in the Attribute Manager.

10. Make sure that the **Tile** check box is selected. Also, select the **Seamless** check box; the **matcup** material is displayed properly on *cup2*, refer to Figure 5-44.

Figure 5-44 *The matcup material displayed*

Modifying and Applying Material to Glass

In this section, you will modify the existing plastic node material.

1. Choose **Create > Node Materials** from the Material Manager menu; a cascading menu is displayed. Choose **Plastic** from the cascading menu; a node material with the name **Plastic** is created in the Material Manager.

2. Double-click on the name **Plastic** in the Material Manager; a text box is displayed. In this text box, enter **matglass**; the new material is renamed as *matglass*.

3. Press and hold the left mouse button on the *matglass* material in the Material Manager and drag the cursor to *glass1* and *glass2* in the Object Manager; the *matglass* material is applied to glasses in the Perspective viewport.

4. Make sure the **matglass** material is selected in the Material Manager. Also, make sure that the **Base** button is chosen in the Attribute Manager.

5. In the **Base** area, choose the **RGB** button and then set the parameters as follows:

   R: **140** G: **12** B: **54**

   Figure 5-45 shows *matglass* material applied to glasses.

***Figure 5-45** The matglass material displayed*

Saving and Rendering the Scene

In this section, you will save and render the scene. You can also view the final render of the scene by downloading the file *c05_cinema4d_r20_rndr.zip* from *www.cadcim.com*. The path of the file is mentioned at the beginning of the chapter.

1. Choose **File > Save** from the main menu; the **Save File** dialog box is displayed. In this dialog box, browse to the location *\Documents\c4dr20\c05*.

2. Enter **c05tut3** in the **File name** text box and then choose the **Save** button.

3. In the Perspective viewport, set the camera angle using the Viewport Navigation Tools located at the top right of the Perspective viewport. Next, you will render the scene. For rendering, refer to Tutorial 1.

   Figure 5-33 displays the final output.

Self-Evaluation Test

Answer the following questions and then compare them to those given at the end of this chapter:

1. Which of the following options in the **Create** menu of the Material Manager is used to create a new material in the Material Manager?

   (a) **New Material** (b) **Basic**
   (c) **Specular** (d) **Color**

2. Which of the following areas is displayed on choosing the **Basic** button in the Attribute Manager?

   (a) **Color** (b) **Coordinates**
   (c) **Basic Properties** (d) **Tag Properties**

3. Which of the following options is available in the **Projection** drop-down list in the **Tag Properties** area?

   (a) **Spherical** (b) **Cylindrical**
   (c) **UVW Mapping** (d) All of these

4. The __________ option in the **Content Browser** tab is used to open the presets from other software packages developed by MAXON.

5. The __________ parameter in the **Transparency** area is used to specify the transparency of a 3D surface.

6. The __________ type of projection in the **Tag Properties** area is preferred the most to project the texture on all sides of a cube.

7. The __________ icon is created automatically after assigning texture to an object.

8. The __________ texture is used to create gradients.

9. Multiple texture tags can be assigned to an object. (T/F)

10. The **Reflection** check box in the **Basic Properties** area is used to make the object reflective. (T/F)

Review Questions

Answer the following questions:

1. Which of the following areas is displayed on choosing the **Tag** button in the Attribute Manager?

   (a) **Object Properties** (b) **Coordinates**
   (c) **Basic Properties** (d) **Tag Properties**

2. The __________ spinner in the **Transparency** area is used to control the refractive index of the surface.

3. In the **Basic Properties** area, the __________ and __________ check boxes are selected by default.

4. The __________ check box in the **Basic Properties** area in the Attribute Manager is selected to edit or control the bump created on the surface.

5. The options in the __________ area are used to define the mapping of texture on a 3D surface.

6. The __________ check box in the **Tag Properties** area is selected to duplicate the texture in such a way that it is able to hide the visible seams of texture.

7. The options in the __________ drop-down list are used to combine the color and texture channel shaders using the four modes.

8. The __________ option in the **Tag Properties** area is used to enable or disable the endless repetition of texture on the surface.

9. The **Offset V** spinner in the **Tag Properties** area is used to set the position and size of the texture in the U direction. (T/F)

EXERCISE

The rendered output of the model used in the exercise can be accessed by downloading the *c05_cinema4d_r20_exr.zip* file from *www.cadcim.com*. The path of the file is as follows: *Textbooks > Animation and Visual Effects > MAXON CINEMA 4D > MAXON CINEMA 4D R20 Studio: A Tutorial Approach*

Exercise 1

Download the file *c05_cinema4d_r20_exr.zip* containing the camera model shown in Figure 5-46 from *www.cadcim.com*. Next, extract the contents of the file and then texture the camera model using various textures and shaders. Render the scene to get the final output, as shown in Figure 5-47. **(Expected time: 30 min)**

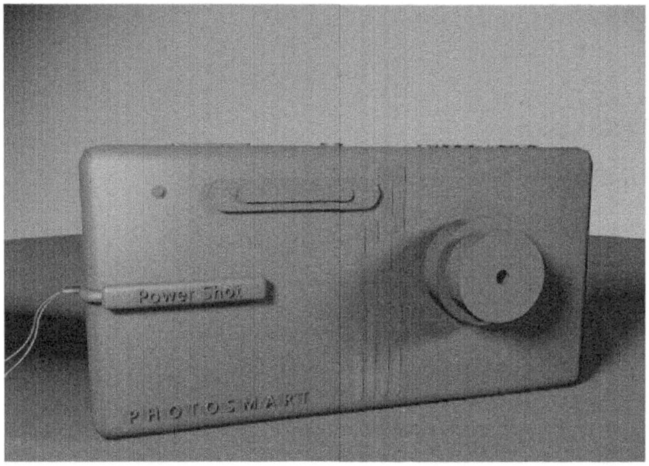

Figure 5-46 The camera model

Figure 5-47 The final output

Answers to Self-Evaluation Test

1. a, **2.** c, **3.** d, **4. Presets**, **5. Brightness**, **6. Cubic**, **7. Texture Tag**, **8. Gradient**, **9.** T, **10.** T

Chapter 6

Lighting

Learning Objectives

After completing this chapter, you will be able to:

- *Add lights to a scene*
- *Illuminate a scene*
- *Add Physical Sky to a scene*

INTRODUCTION

In computer graphics, lighting plays a vital role in defining the look of a scene. Lighting is primarily used to produce the effect of light and shadows. Also, you can add depth to the scene by using advanced lighting techniques. There are seven types of lights available in CINEMA 4D. All the lights are treated as objects, and can be transformed, deleted, and duplicated.

TUTORIALS

Before you start the tutorials of this chapter, you need to download the *c06_cinema4d_r20_tut.zip* file from *www.cadcim.com*. The path of the file is as follows: *Textbooks > Animation and Visual Effects > MAXON CINEMA 4D > MAXON CINEMA 4D R20 Studio: A Tutorial Approach*

Next, you need to browse to *\Documents\c4dr20* and create a new folder in it with the name *c06*. Next, extract the contents of the zip file in this folder.

Tutorial 1

In this tutorial, you will illuminate a scene using the torch light, as shown in Figure 6-1.

(Expected time: 15 min)

Figure 6-1 *The torch light*

The following steps are required to complete this tutorial:

a. Open the file.
b. Add lights to the scene.
c. Save and render the scene.

Opening the File

In this section, you will open the file.

1. Choose **File > Open** from the main menu; the **Open File** dialog box is displayed.

2. In the **Open File** dialog box, browse to *\Documents\c4dr20\c06\c06_tut1_start.c4d* and then choose the **Open** button; the *c06_tut1_start.c4d* file is opened, as shown in Figure 6-2.

Figure 6-2 *The c06_tut1_start.c4d file*

Adding Lights to the Scene

In this section, you will add lights to the scene.

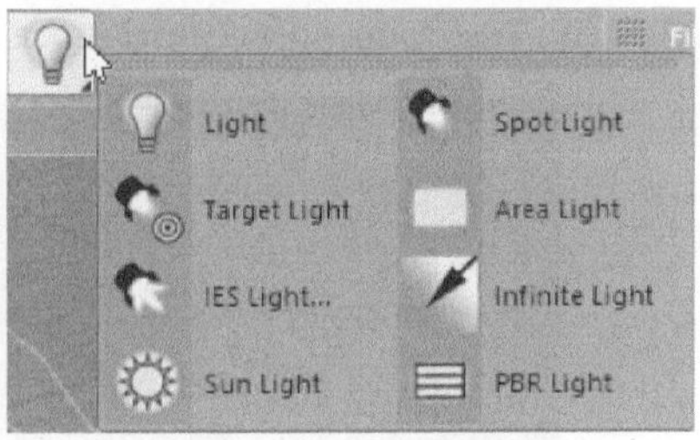

Figure 6-3 *The flyout displayed with various tools*

1. Press and hold the left mouse button on the **Light** tool in the Command Palette; a flyout with various tools is displayed, as shown in Figure 6-3. Choose the **Spot Light** tool from it; the *Light* object is added to the Object Manager.

   The **Spot Light** tool is used to cast a beam of light in a conical shape.

2. In the Attribute Manager, choose the **Coord** button; the **Coordinates** area is displayed. In this area, set the parameters as follows:

   P . X: **53** P . Y: **6** R . H: **90**

3. Choose the **Details** button; the **Details** area is displayed. In this area, make sure the **Aspect Ratio** is set to 1 and then set the parameters as follows:

   Inner Angle: **12** Outer Angle:**16** Contrast: **31**

4. In the Attribute Manager, choose the **General** button; the **General** area is displayed. In this area, enter **180** in the **Intensity** spinner and select the **Shadow Maps (Soft)** option from the **Shadow** drop-down list. Next, select **Inverse Volumetric** from the **Visible Light** drop-down list.

The value in the **Intensity** spinner is used to set the brightness of the light. More the value of intensity, brighter will be the light.

The options in the **Shadow** drop-down list are used to enable shadows in the scene. The **Shadows Maps (Soft)** option in the drop-down list is used to enable a smooth transition from lighting to shadow effect in the scene.

The **Inner Angle** spinner is used to adjust the inner angle of the standard spotlight. The **Outer Angle** spinner is used to adjust the illumination of the light in total. The **Aspect Ratio** spinner is used to adjust the shape of the cone of the spot light. The **Contrast** spinner is used to adjust the transition between the softness and the hardness of the lit surface.

5. Choose the **Visibility** button; the **Visibility** area is displayed. In this area, set the parameters as follows:

   Edge Falloff: **60** Inner Distance: **227** Outer Distance: **538**
   Sample Distance: **65**

   The value of the **Edge Falloff** spinner specifies the speed at which the density of light decreases when it moves toward the cone of the spotlight.

   After entering these values, you need to render the scene in the Perspective viewport to get the result, as shown in Figure 6-4.

***Figure 6-4** The rendered view of the Perspective viewport*

Next, you will illuminate the scene.

6. Press and hold the left mouse button on the **Light** tool in the Command Palette; a flyout with various tools is displayed, refer to Figure 6-3. Choose the **Light** tool from it; the *Light.1* object is added to the Object Manager.

7. Make sure *Light.1* is selected in the Object Manager. In the Attribute Manager, choose the **General** button; the **General** area is displayed. In this area, enter **50** in the **Intensity** spinner and select **Square Spot** from the **Type** drop-down list. Next, select **Shadow Maps (Soft)** from the **Shadow** drop-down list.

   The options in the **Type** drop-down list are used to define the types of lights to be used in a scene. The **Square Spot** option is best suited to cast a square-shaped light ray on the surface.

8. In the Attribute Manager, choose the **Coord** button; the **Coordinates** area is displayed. In this area, set the parameters as follows:

   P . X: **-500** P . Y: **500** P . Z: **-500**
   R . H: **-45** R . P: **-35**

9. Choose the **Details** button; the **Details** area is displayed. In this area, enter **105** in the **Outer Angle** spinner.

   Figure 6-5 displays *Light.1* in the Perspective viewport.

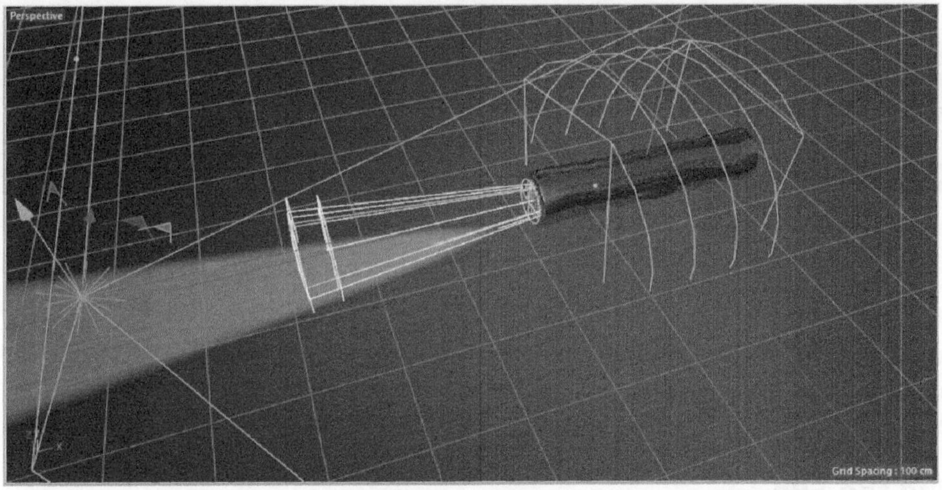

Figure 6-5 *Light.1 displayed in the Perspective viewport*

Saving and Rendering the Scene

In this section, you will save and render the file. You can also view the final render of the scene by downloading the file *c06_cinema4d_r20_rndr.zip* from *www.cadcim.com*. The path of the file is mentioned at the beginning of the chapter.

1. Choose **File > Save** from the main menu; the **Save File** dialog box is displayed. In this dialog box, browse to the location *\Documents\c4dr20\c06*.

2. Enter **c06tut1** in the **File name** text box and then choose the **Save** button.

3. In the Perspective viewport, set the camera angle using the Viewport Navigation Tools located at the top right of the Perspective viewport. Next, you will render the scene. For rendering, refer to Tutorial 1 of Chapter 2.

   The output of the scene is shown in Figure 6-1.

Tutorial 2

In this section, you will illuminate a night scene, as shown in Figure 6-6.

(Expected time: 25 min)

Figure 6-6 *The illuminated night scene*

The following steps are required to complete this tutorial:

a. Open the file.
b. Illuminate the street lights.
c. Save and render the scene.

Opening the File

In this section, you will open the file.

1. Choose **File > Open** from the main menu; the **Open File** dialog box is displayed. In the **Open File** dialog box, browse to *\Documents\c4dr20\c06\c06_tut2_start.c4d* and then choose the **Open** button; the *c06_tut2_start* file is opened, as shown in Figure 6-7.

Illuminating the Street Lights

In this section, you will illuminate the street lights using the **Spot Light** tool.

1. Press and hold the left mouse button on the **Light** tool in the Command Palette; a flyout is displayed. Choose the **Spot Light** tool from the flyout; *Light* is added to the Object Manager.

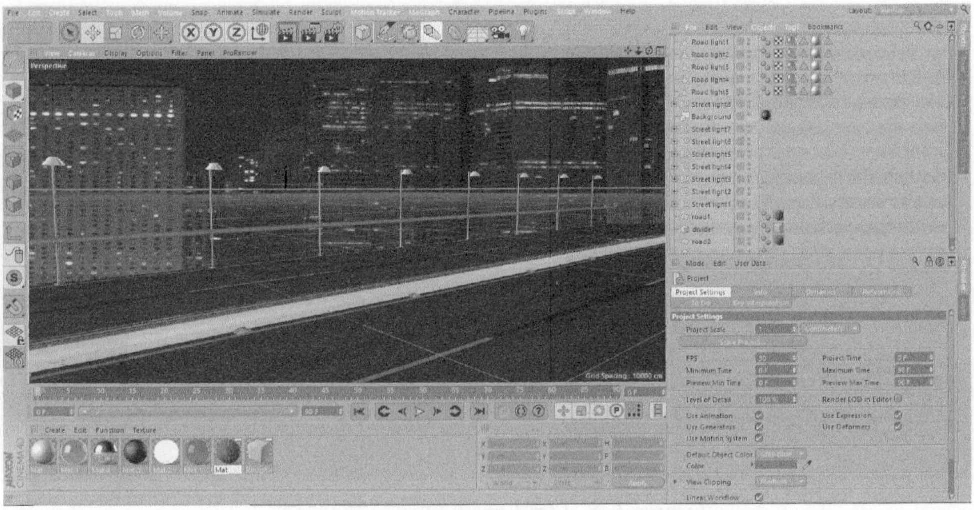

Figure 6-7 The c06_tut2_start.c4d file

2. In the Attribute Manager, choose the **General** button; the **General** area is displayed. In this area, select **Shadow Maps (Soft)** from the **Shadow** drop-down list and **Volumetric** from the **Visible Light** drop-down list. Also, choose the **RGB** button and then set the parameters corresponding to the **Color** option as follows:

   R: **252** G: **222** B: **204**

   The options in the **Visible Light** drop-down list are used to define the volumetric effects of the light. The **Visible Light** drop-down list is available only when the **Omni** and **Spot** lights are used. Selecting **Volumetric** from the **Visible Light** drop-down list ensures that the light emitted from the object will cast shadow. However, on selecting this option, rendering time will increase.

3. In the Attribute Manager, choose the **Coord** button; the **Coordinates** area is displayed. In this area, set the parameters as follows:

   P . X: **-25160.40** P . Y: **10997** P . Z: **-34089.09**
   R . P: **-90**

4. Choose the **Details** button; the **Details** area is displayed. In this area, enter **65** in the **Outer Angle** spinner.

5. In the Attribute Manager, choose the **Visibility** button; the **Visibility** area is displayed. In this area, enter **15000** in the **Outer Distance** spinner.

   After entering the values, the spot light is positioned in the scene in the Perspective viewport, as shown in Figure 6-8.

Figure 6-8 *Light positioned in the scene*

6. Select *Light* in the Object Manager and create a copy of *Light* using the CTRL key; a copy of *Light* is created with the name *Light.1*.

7. Make sure *Light.1* is selected in the Object Manager. In the Attribute Manager, choose the **Coord** button; the **Coordinates** area is displayed. In this area, enter **-20323.77** in the **P . Z** spinner.

   After entering the values, *Light.1* is positioned in the scene in the Perspective viewport, as shown in Figure 6-9.

8. Create 6 more copies of *Light.1* and enter corresponding value in the **P . Z** spinner for the copied lights, as shown in Table 6-1.

Table 6-1 *Values to be entered in the* ***P . Z*** *spinner*

Light to be selected	Value to be entered in the P . Z spinner
Light.2	-6768.247
Light.3	6827.229
Light.4	21833.845
Light.5	35865.109
Light.6	49681.329
Light.7	64076.595

Figure 6-9 *Light.1 positioned in the scene*

After entering the values, all the lights are positioned in the Perspective viewport, as shown in Figure 6-10.

Figure 6-10 *Lights positioned in the Perspective viewport*

Next, you will create a light to illuminate the other side of the road.

9. Press F2; the Top viewport is activated. In the Top viewport, press and hold the left mouse button on the **Light** tool in the Command Palette; a flyout is displayed. Choose the **Light** tool from the flyout; *Light.8* is created in the Top viewport and added to the Object Manager, as shown in Figure 6-11.

10. Make sure *Light.8* is selected in the Object Manager. In the Attribute Manager, choose the **General** button; the **General** area is displayed. In this area, set the value of the **Intensity** spinner to **45**. Next, select the **Raytraced (Hard)** option from the **Shadow** drop-down list and the **Inverse Volumetric** option from the **Visible Light** drop-down list.

The Raytraced (Hard) option in the **Shadow** drop-down list is used to cast hard shadows for any type of light settings.

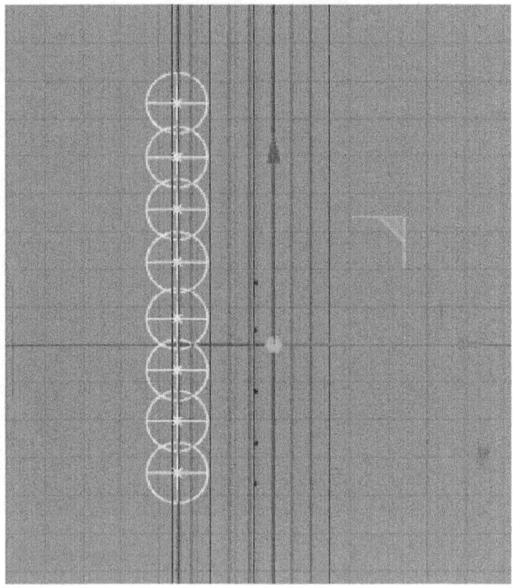

Figure 6-11 Light.8 created in the Top viewport

11. Choose the **Coord** button; the **Coordinates** area is displayed. In this area, set the parameters as follows:

    P . X: **13044** P . Y: **15504**

12. Choose the **Visibility** button; the **Visibility** area is displayed. In this area, enter **12416** in the **Outer Distance** spinner.

    Press F1; the Perspective viewport is maximized. After entering the values, *Light.8* is positioned in the scene, as shown in Figure 6-12.

Figure 6-12 *Light.8 positioned in the scene*

Saving and Rendering the Scene

In this section, you will save the scene. You can also view the final rendered scene by downloading the file *c06_cinema4d_r20_rndr.zip* from *www.cadcim.com*. The path of the file is mentioned at the beginning of the chapter.

1. Choose **File > Save** from the main menu; the **Save File** dialog box is displayed. In this dialog box, browse to the following location *\Documents\c4dr20\c06*. Enter **c06tut2** in the **File name** text box and then choose the **Save** button.

2. In the Perspective viewport, set the camera angle using the Viewport Navigation Tools located on the top right of the Perspective viewport. Next, you need to render the scene. For rendering, refer to Tutorial 1 of Chapter 2.

Tutorial 3

In this tutorial, you will illuminate the scene using lights in the light house, as shown in Figure 6-13. **(Expected time: 20 min)**

Figure 6-13 *The light house*

The following steps are required to complete this tutorial:

a. Open the file.
b. Add lights to the scene.
c. Add Physical Sky.
d. Save and render the scene.

Opening the File

In this section, you will open the file of the lighthouse scene.

1. Choose **File > Open** from the main menu; the **Open File** dialog box is displayed.

2. In the **Open File** dialog box, browse to *\Documents\c4dr20\c06\c06_tut3_start.c4d* and then choose the **Open** button; the *c06_tut3_start.c4d file* is opened, as shown in Figure 6-14.

Adding Lights to the Scene

In this section, you will add lights to the scene.

1. Press and hold the left mouse button on the **Light** tool in the Command Palette; a flyout is displayed. Choose the **Spot Light** tool from the flyout; *Light* is added to the Object Manager.

2. In the Attribute Manager, choose the **Coord** button; the **Coordinates** area is displayed. In this area, set the parameters as follows:

   P . X: **-272** P . Y: **1508** P . Z: **742**
   R . H: **-180** R . P: **-9**

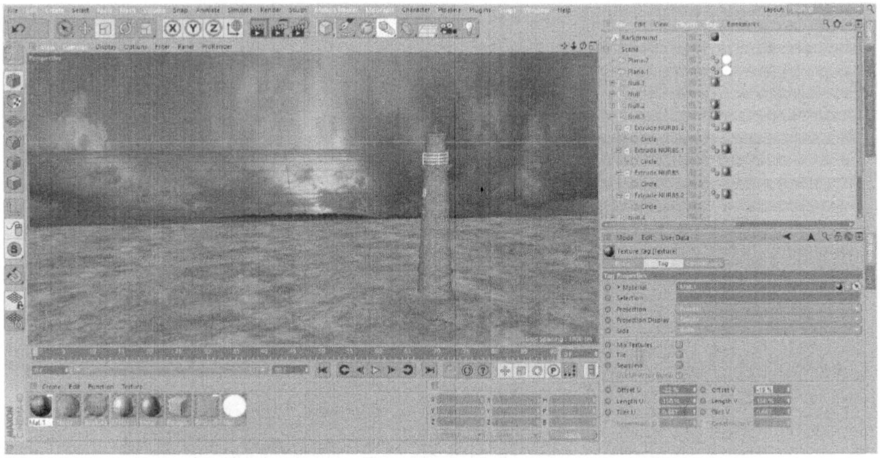

Figure 6-14 The c06_tut3_start.c4d file

3. Choose the **General** button; the **General** area is displayed. In this area, enter **16** in the **Intensity** spinner. Next, click on the Color swatch next to the **Color** parameter; the **Color Picker** dialog box is displayed. In this dialog box, choose the **RGB** button and set the parameters as follows:

   R: **255** G: **251** B: **184**

4. Make sure **Spot** is selected in the **Type** drop-down list and select **Shadow Maps (Soft)** from the **Shadow** drop-down list. Next, select **Inverse Volumetric** from the **Visible Light** drop-down list.

5. Choose the **Details** button; the **Details** area is displayed. In this area, make sure that the **Use Inner** check box is selected. Next, set the parameters as follows:

   Inner Angle: **3.3** Contrast: **27**

6. In the **Details** area, select **Inverse Square (Physically Accurate)** from the **Falloff** drop-down list. Next, enter **10000** in the **Radius/Decay** spinner.

   The value in the **Radius/Decay** spinner is used to determine the range of the scene that will be illuminated.

7. Choose the **Visibility** button; the **Visibility** area is displayed. In this area, make sure that the **Use Falloff** and **Use Edge Falloff** check boxes are selected. Next, set the parameters as follows:

   Edge Falloff: **66** Inner Distance: **67** Outer Distance: **7000**
   Dust: **22**

   The value in the **Dust** spinner is used to darken the light cone by reducing the intensity of the light cone. On increasing the value of this parameter, the brightness of light is reduced. After entering the values, the spot light is positioned in the Perspective viewport, as shown in Figure 6-15.

Figure 6-15 *The spot light positioned in the Perspective viewport*

Next, you will add lights to the windows of the lighthouse.

8. Press and hold the left mouse button on the **Light** tool in the Command Palette; a flyout is displayed. Choose the **Area Light** tool from the flyout; *Light.1* is added to the Object Manager.

   The **Area light** tool is used to spread light rays from the surface into all directions.

9. In the Attribute Manager, choose the **Coord** button; the **Coordinates** area is displayed. In this area, set the parameters as follows:

   P . X: **-250** P . Y: **1253** P . Z: **682**

10. Choose the **General** button; the **General** area is displayed. In this area, enter **30** in the **Intensity** spinner. Next, select **Shadow Maps (Soft)** from the **Shadow** drop-down list.

11. Choose the **Details** button; the **Details** area is displayed. Next, set the parameters as follows:

    Outer Radius: **8** Size X: **20** Size Y: **32**

    The **Size X** spinner is used to set the width of the Area light. The **Size Y** spinner is used to set the height of the Area light.

    Next, you will create a copy of *Light.1* for the second window of the light house.

12. In the Object Manager, select *Light.1*. Press and hold the left mouse button along with the CTRL key and then drag the cursor above *Light.1* in the Object Manager. Next, release the left mouse button; a copy of *Light.1* is created with the name *Light.2*.

13. In the Attribute Manager, choose the **Coord** button; the **Coordinates** area is displayed. In this area, set the parameters as follows:

    P . X: **-246** P . Y: **1133**

    After entering the values, the area lights are positioned in the Perspective viewport, as shown in Figure 6-16.

Figure 6-16 *The Area lights positioned in the Perspective viewport*

Adding Physical Sky

In this section, you will add physical sky to the scene.

1. Choose **Create > Physical Sky > Physical Sky** from the main menu, as shown in Figure 6-17; a physical sky is created in the Perspective viewport and *Physical Sky* is added to the Object Manager, as shown in Figure 6-18.

2. Make sure *Physical Sky* is selected in the Object Manager. In the Attribute Manager, choose the **Time and Location** button; the **Time and Location** area is displayed. In this area, enter **19:30:00** in the **Time** spinner, as shown in Figure 6-19.

    The **Time** spinner is used to adjust the current time of the scene. The light of sun is dependent on the value entered in the **Time** spinner and it changes with the time set in the spinner.

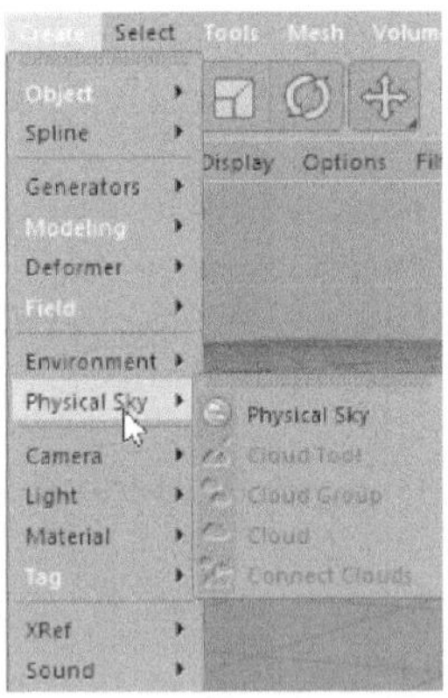

Figure 6-17 *Choosing* ***Physical Sky*** *from the main menu*

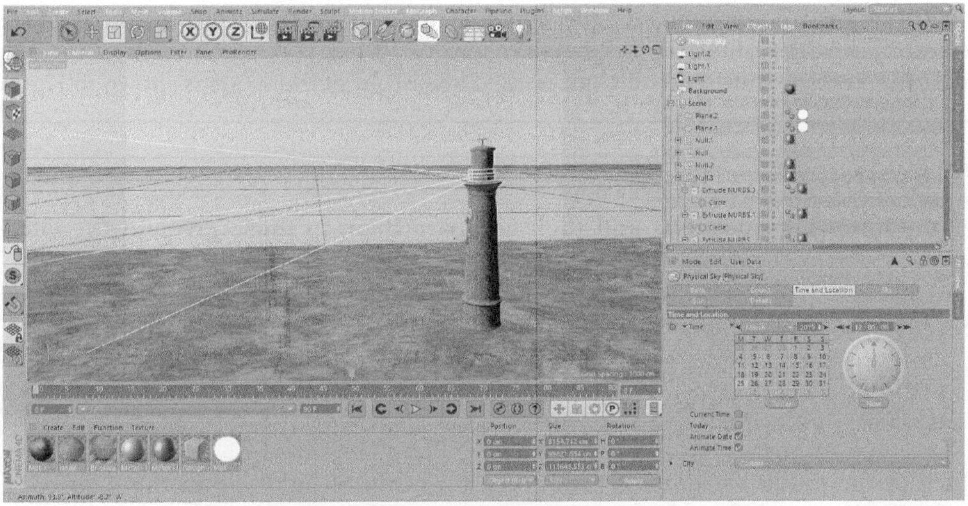

Figure 6-18 Physical Sky added to the Object Manager

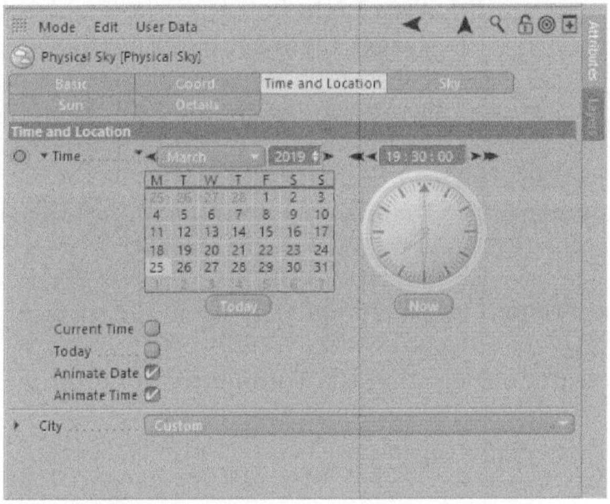

*Figure 6-19 The **Time and Location** area*

Saving and Rendering the Scene

In this section, you will save the scene. You can also view the final render of the scene by downloading the file *c06_cinema4d_r20_rndr.zip* from *www.cadcim.com*. The path of the file is mentioned at the beginning of the chapter.

1. Choose **File > Save** from the main menu; the **Save File** dialog box is displayed. In this dialog box, browse to the location *\Documents\c4dr20\c06*. Next, enter **c06tut3** in the **File name** text box and then choose the **Save** button.

2. In the Perspective viewport, set the camera angle using the Viewport Navigation Tools located on the top right of the Perspective viewport. Next, you need to render the scene. For rendering, refer to Tutorial 1 of Chapter 2. The output of the scene is shown in Figure 6-13.

Self-Evaluation Test

Answer the following questions and then compare them to those given at the end of this chapter:

1. How many types of lights are available in CINEMA 4D?

   (a) Ten (b) Six
   (c) Four (d) Seven

2. Which of the following lights is used to cast a beam of light within the narrow range of directions that are defined by a cone?

   (a) **Spot Light** (b) **Area Light**
   (c) **Omni Light** (d) **Target Light**

3. The options in the __________ drop-down list are used to define the type of lights used in a scene.

4. The ___________ spinner in the **Details** area is used to adjust the shape of the cone of the spot light.

5. The ___________ tool is used to spread light rays from the surface to all the directions.

6. Rendering time increases on selecting the **Volumetric** option from the **Visible** drop-down list. (T/F)

Review Questions

Answer the following questions:

1. Which of the following options in the **General** area in the Attribute Manager is used to set the brightness of the light?

   (a) **Intensity** (b) **Visibilty**
   (c) **Edge Falloff** (d) **Falloff**

2. The __________ spinner in the **Details** area of the Attribute Manger is used to adjust the inner angle of the standard spotlight.

3. The __________ option from the **Type** drop-down list is best suited to cast a square-shaped light ray on the wall or the floor.

4. The __________ spinner in the **Details** area is used to edit the width of the area light.

5. The light of sun is dependent on the value entered in the **Time** spinner. (T/F)

EXERCISE

The rendered output of the model used in the following exercise can be accessed by downloading the *c06_cinema4d_r20_exr.zip* file from *www.cadcim.com*. The path of the file is as follows: *Textbooks > Animation and Visual Effects > MAXON CINEMA 4D > MAXON CINEMA 4D R20Studio: A Tutorial Approach*

Exercise 1

Extract the contents of the *c06_cinema4d_r20_exr.zip* file and then open *c06_exr01_start.c4d*, as shown in Figure 6-20. Add lights to the scene to get the output shown in Figure 6-21.

(Expected time: 30 min)

Figure 6-20 *The living room scene*

Figure 6-21 *The scene after adding lights to it*

Answers to Self-Evaluation Test

1. d, **2.** a, **3. Type**, **4. Aspect Ratio**, **5. Area Light**, **6.** T

Chapter 7

Rigging

Learning Objectives

After completing this chapter, you will be able to:

- *Understand the concept of rigging*
- *Apply constraints*

INTRODUCTION

Rigging is the process of preparing an object or a character for animation. To rig an object, you need to add bones and controls to it. In this chapter, you will learn to create a functional rig for a human hand and a table lamp by adding bones to it and later skinning it. You will also learn the concept of forward and inverse kinematics and apply constraints.

TUTORIALS

Before you start the tutorials of this chapter, you need to download the *c07_cinema4d_r20_tut.zip* file from *www.cadcim.com*. The path of the file is as follows: *Textbooks > Animation and Visual Effects > MAXON CINEMA 4D > MAXON CINEMA 4D Studio R20: A Tutorial Approach*

Next, you need to browse to *\Documents\c4dr20* and create a new folder in it with the name *c07*. Next, extract the contents of the zip file in this folder.

Tutorial 1

In this tutorial, you will rig a hand, as shown in Figure 7-1. **(Expected time: 25 min)**

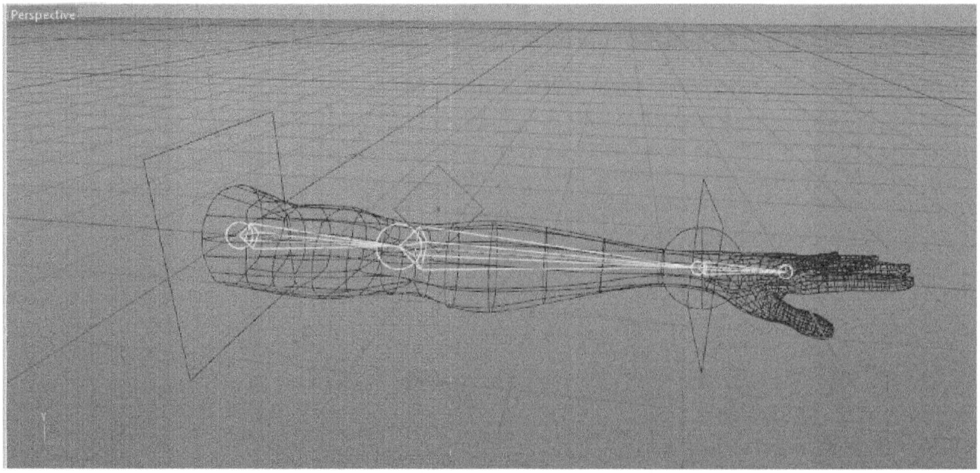

Figure 7-1 *The rig of the hand*

The following steps are required to complete this tutorial:

a. Open the file.
b. Create bone structure for the hand.
c. Create IK chain of the bone structure.
d. Create controllers for the hand.
e. Add constraint to the bones and controllers.
f. Bind the rig.
g. Save the scene.

Opening the File

In this section, you will open the file.

1. Choose **File > Open** from the main menu; the **Open File** dialog box is displayed.

2. In the **Open File** dialog box, browse to *\Documents\c4dr20\c07\c07_tut1_start.c4d* and then choose the **Open** button; the *c07_tut1_start* file is opened, as shown in Figure 7-2.

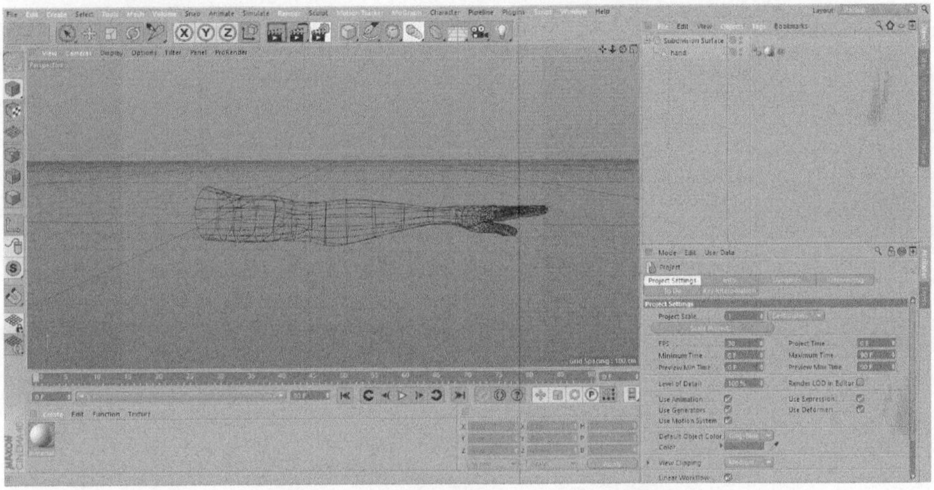

***Figure 7-2** The c07_tut1_start file*

Creating Bone Structure for Hand

In this section, you will create bone structure for hand using **Joint Tool**.

1. Press F2; the Top viewport is activated. Choose **Character > Joint Tool** from the main menu.

   The **Joint Tool** is used to create bones in the mesh of the object or character.

2. Select *hand* in the Object Manager. In the Top viewport, press and hold the CTRL key and click on the shoulder joint of the hand, as shown in Figure 7-3. Next, click on the elbow part, on the wrist part, and then on the palm; a bone structure is created in the viewport, as shown in Figure 7-4.

3. In the Object Manager, expand *hand*. You will notice that hierarchy of joints is also created in the Object Manager.

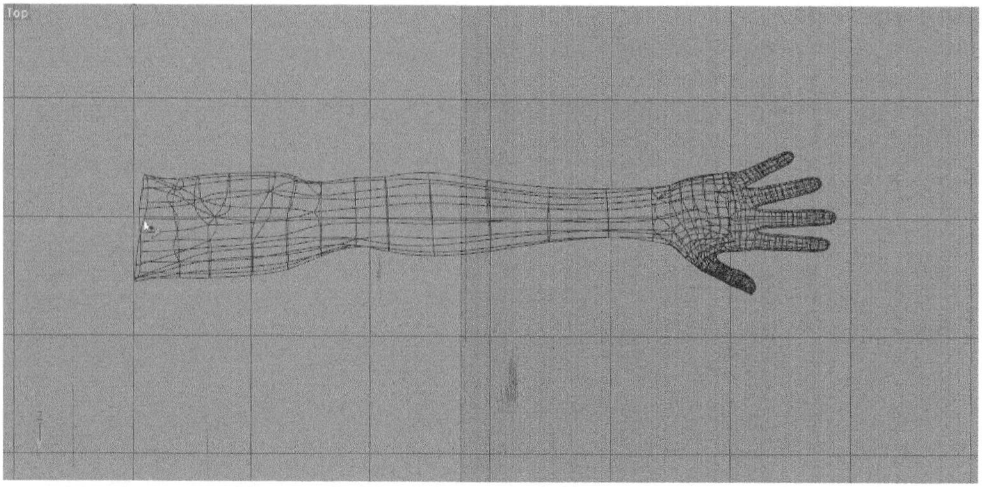

Figure 7-3 *Clicking on the shoulder joint of the hand*

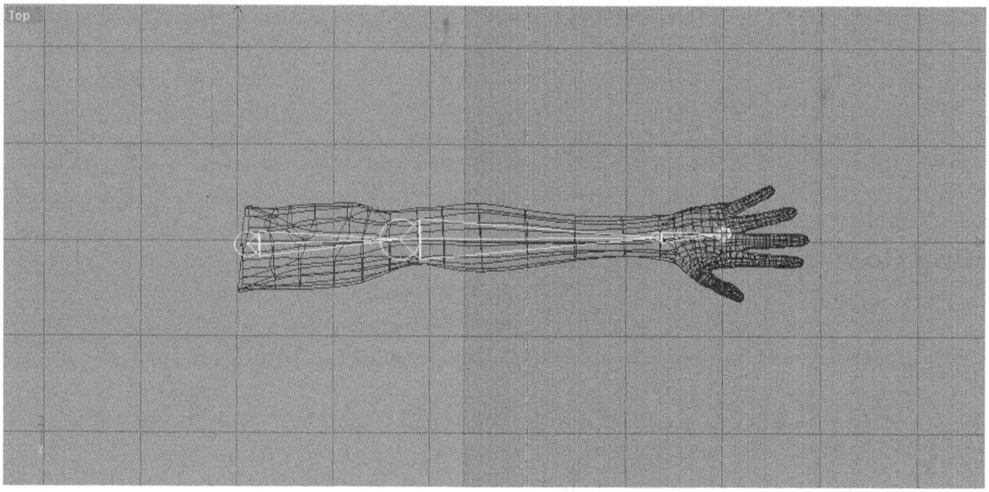

Figure 7-4 *Bone structure created*

4. Press F4 to maximize the Front viewport. Next, align the joints in the Front viewport, as shown in Figure 7-5.

5. In the Object Manager, rename *Joint.1* as *shoulder_joint*, *Joint.2* as *elbow_joint*, *Joint.3* as *wrist_joint*, and *Joint.4* as *end_joint*.

Creating IK Chain of the Bone Structure

In this section, you will create IK chain of the bone structure.

1. Select *shoulder_joint* and *wrist_joint* using the CTRL key in the Object Manager. Next, choose **Character > Commands > Create IK Chain** from the main menu, as shown in Figure 7-6; an IK Chain is created and *wrist_joint.Goal* is added to the Object Manager. Press F1; the

Perspective viewport is maximized. Figure 7-7 shows the IK chain created in the Perspective viewport.

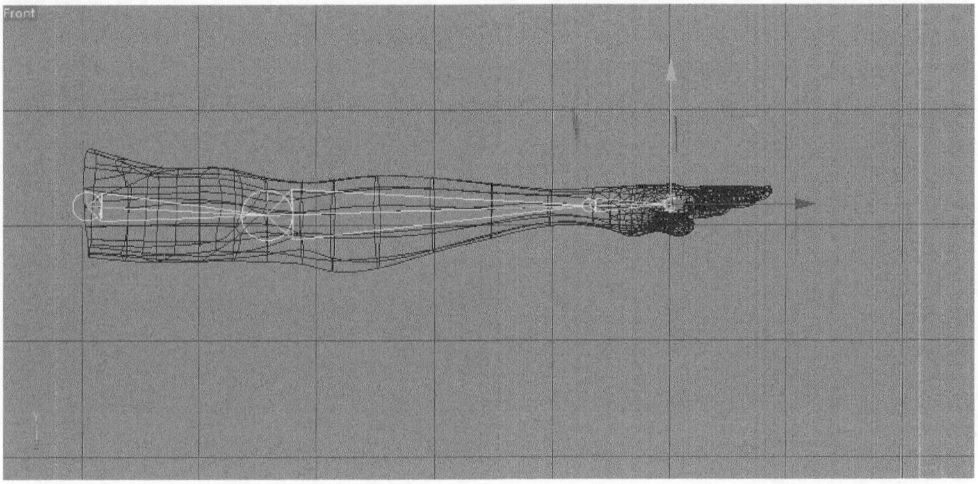

Figure 7-5 *All joints aligned in the Front viewport*

The **Create IK Chain** tool is used to create a complete IK chain for the selected joint objects in a hierarchy.

Next, you will change the icon of *wrist_joint.Goal* to make it clearly visible. You can use the O key to zoom.

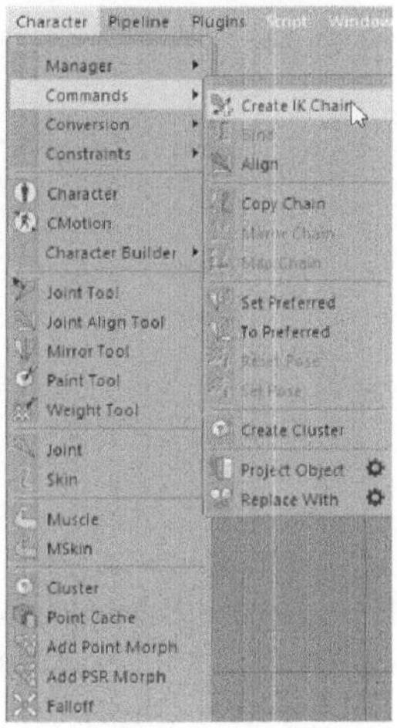

Figure 7-6 *Choosing the* ***Create IK Chain*** *from the main menu*

2. Make sure *wrist_joint.Goal* is selected in the Object Manager. In the Attribute Manager, choose the **Object** button; the **Object Properties** area is displayed. In this area, select **Sphere** from the **Display** drop-down list; the icon of *wrist_joint.Goal* gets modified. Next, enter **40** in the **Radius** spinner. Figure 7-8 shows the changed icon of *wrist_joint.Goal*.

Creating Controllers for the Hand

In this section, you will create controllers for the hand using splines.

1. Press F3; the Right viewport is maximized. Choose **Create > Spline > Rectangle** from the main menu; a rectangle is created in the Right viewport and is added to the Object Manager.

2. Make sure that *Rectangle* is selected in the Object Manager and the **Object** button is chosen in the Attribute Manager. In the **Object Properties** area, enter **200** in both the **Width** and **Height** spinners.

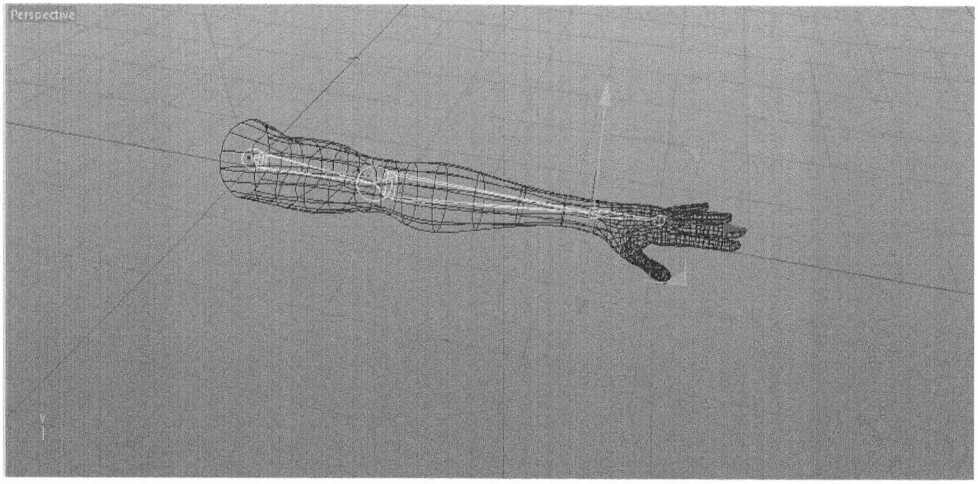

Figure 7-7 The IK chain created in the Perspective viewport

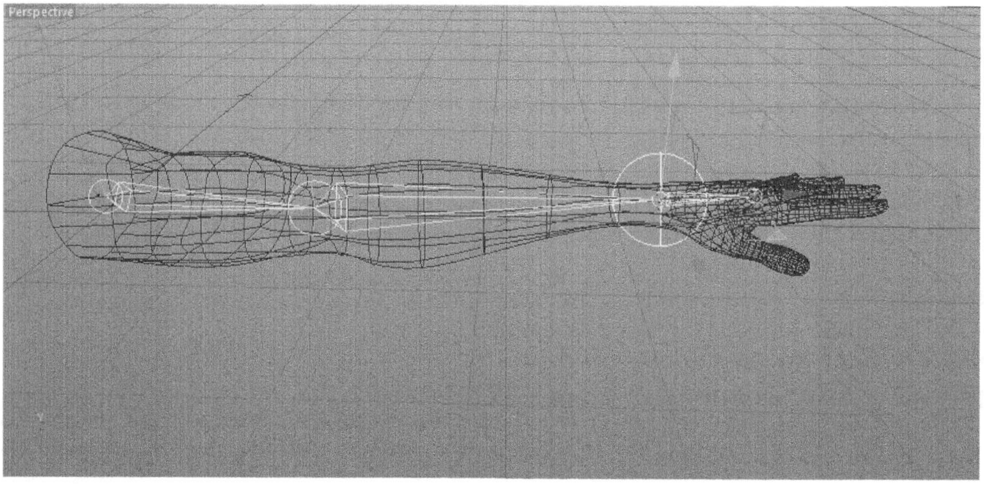

Figure 7-8 The changed icon of wrist_joint.Goal

3. Choose the **Basic** button; the **Basic Properties** area is displayed. In this area, enter **shoulder control** in the **Name** text box; *Rectangle* is renamed as *shoulder control*. Next, press F1; the Perspective viewport is maximized. Figure 7-9 shows *shoulder control* in the Perspective viewport.

   Next, you will create a wrist control.

4. In the Object Manager, make sure *shoulder control* is selected. Next, press and hold the left mouse button along with the CTRL key and drag the cursor above *shoulder control*. Next, release the left mouse button and the CTRL key; a copy of *shoulder control* is created with the name *shoulder control.1*. Rename it as *wrist control*.

5. In the Attribute Manager, choose the **Object** button; the **Object Properties** area is displayed.

In this area, enter **125** in both the **Width** and **Height** spinners.

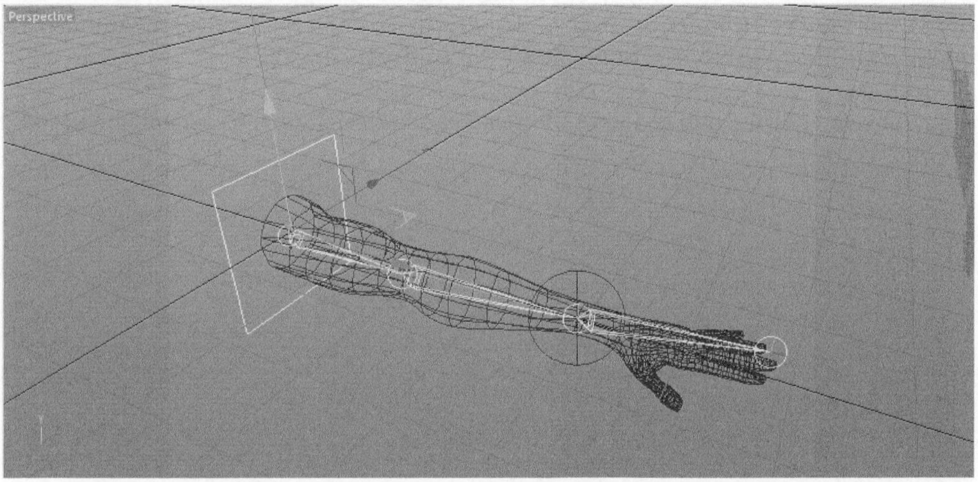

Figure 7-9 *The shoulder control in the Perspective viewport*

6. Choose the **Coord** button in the Attribute Manager; the **Coordinates** area is displayed. In this area, enter **431.053** in the **P . X** spinner; *wrist control* is aligned with the wrist.

   Figure 7-10 displays *wrist control* in the Perspective viewport.

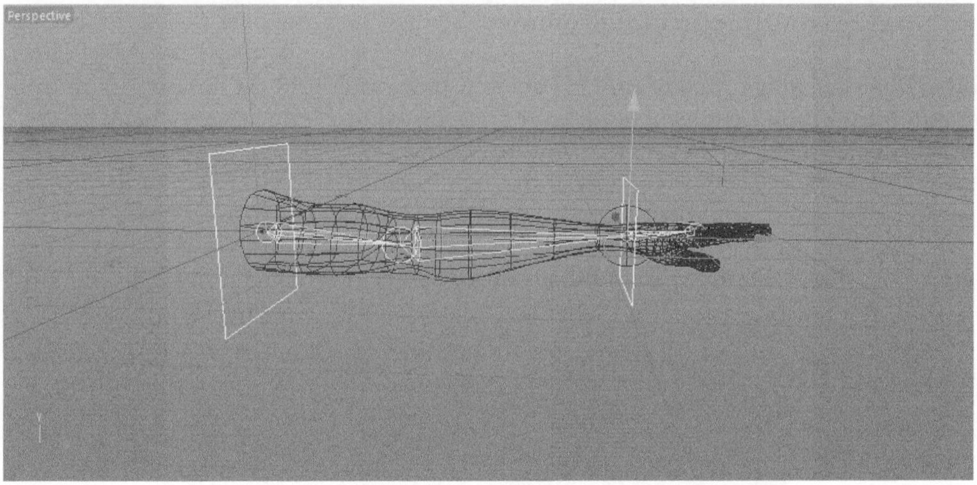

Figure 7-10 *Displaying the controllers of hand*

Next, you will create pole control for rotational movement of hand.

7. In the Object Manager, select **IK Expression (IK)** tag of *shoulder_joint*. 
8. In the Attribute Manager, make sure the **Tag** button is chosen. In the **Pole Vector** area, choose the **Add Pole** button; *shoulder_joint.Pole* is displayed in the **Object** edit box located on the left of the **Add Pole** button and *shoulder_joint.Pole* is added to the Object Manager.

9. Select *shoulder_joint.Pole* in the Object Manager. In the Attribute Manager, choose the **Object** button; the **Object Properties** area is displayed. In this area, select **Diamond** from the **Display** drop-down list. Next, enter **50** in the **Radius** spinner.

   Figure 7-11 shows the changed icon of *shoulder_joint.Pole* in the Perspective viewport.

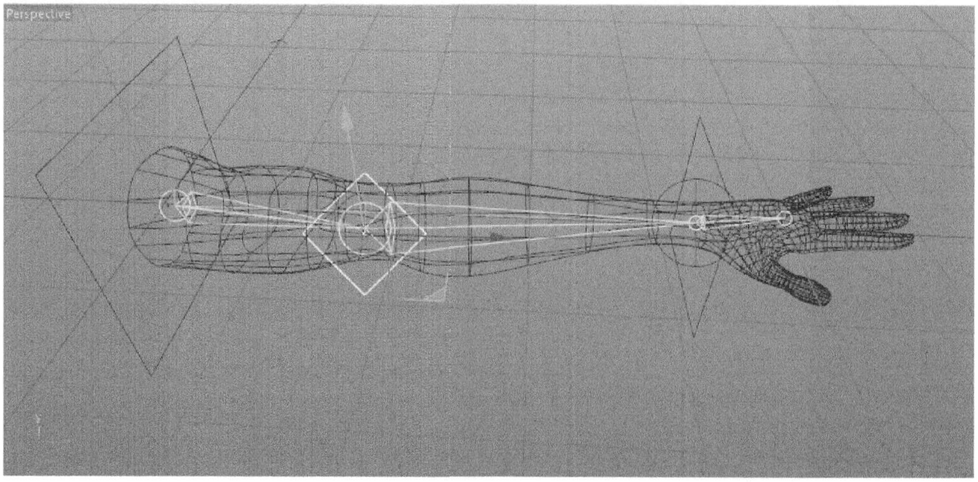

Figure 7-11 *The changed icon of shoulder_joint.Pole*

Next, you will create hierarchy for controls.

10. In the Object Manager, select *wrist control* and press and hold the left mouse button. Next, drag and drop it on *wrist_joint.Goal*; *wrist control* is connected with *wrist_joint.Goal.*

11. Select *wrist_joint.Goal* and press and hold the left mouse button. Next, drag and drop it on *shoulder control*; *wrist_joint.Goal* is connected with *shoulder control.*

    Figure 7-12 shows hierarchy for controls in the Object Manager.

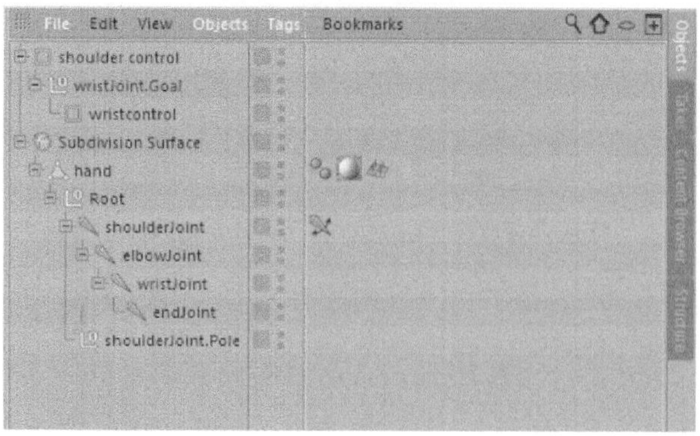

Figure 7-12 *Hierarchy for controls in the Object Manager*

Adding Constraints to the Bones and Controllers

In this section, you will add constraints to the joints.

1. In the Object Manager, select *Root* and right-click on it; a shortcut menu is displayed. In this shortcut menu, choose **Character Tags > Constraint**, refer to Figure 7-13. The constraint is applied to *Root* and the **Constraint Expression [Constraint]** tag is added to the Object Manager.

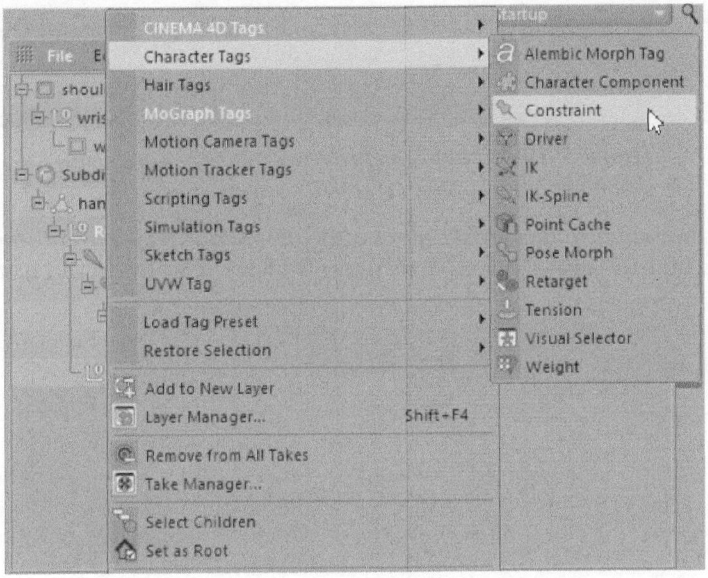

*Figure 7-13 Choosing **Constraint** from the shortcut menu*

2. In the **Constraints** area, select the **PSR** check box from the Attribute Manager. Next, choose the **PSR** button; the **PSR** area is displayed. In the **PSR** area, choose the arrow button on the right of the **Target** edit box and select *shoulder control* in the Object Manager; *shoulder control* is displayed in the **Target** edit box.

   The PSR constraint is used to move, rotate, and scale an object along with the target object.

3. In the Object Manager, select *shoulder control* and rotate it; all joints and controls also rotate along with *shoulder control*, refer to Figure 7-14. Next, press CTRL+ Z to undo the rotation.

4. In the Object Manager, select *wrist_joint* and right-click on it; a shortcut menu is displayed. In this shortcut menu, choose **Character Tags > Constraint**. The constraint is applied to *wrist_joint* and added to the Object Manager.

5. In the **Constraints** area, select the **Parent** check box from the Attribute Manager. Next, choose the **Parent** button; the **Parent** area is displayed. In the **Parent** area, choose the arrow button on the right of the **Target** edit box and select *wrist control* in the Object Manager; *wrist control* is displayed in the **Target** edit box.

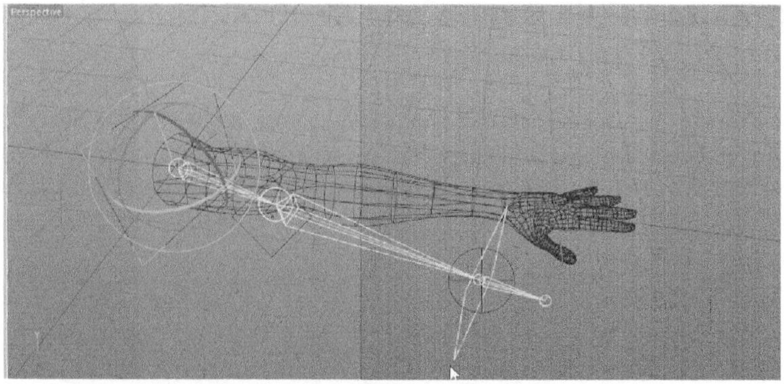

***Figure 7-14** All joints and controls rotating along with shoulder control in the Perspective viewport*

6. In the Object Manager, select *wrist control* and rotate it; *wrist_joint* and *end_joint* also rotate along with it, refer to Figure 7-15. Next, press CTRL+ Z to undo the rotation.

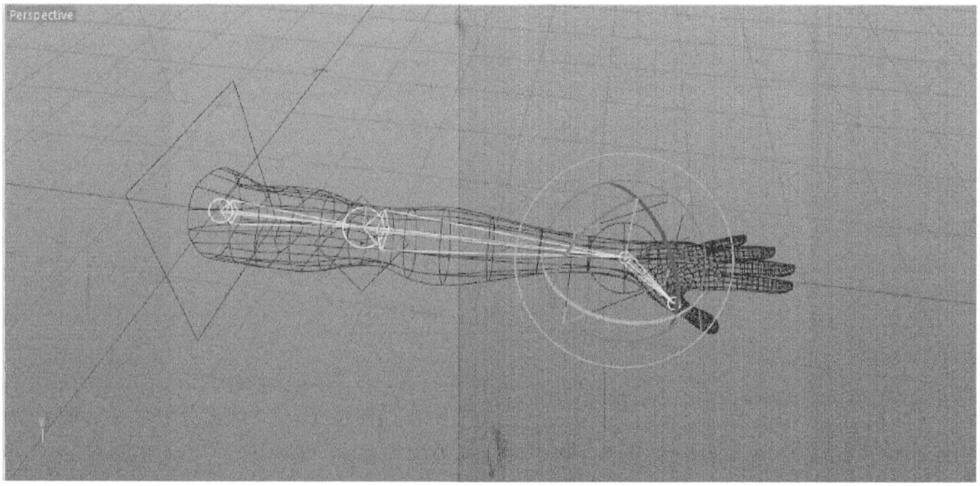

***Figure 7-15** The wrist_joint and end_joint rotating along with wrist control*

7. In the Object Manager, select *shoulder_joint.Pole* and move it in the Perspective viewport to change its position, as shown in Figure 7-16.

8. In the Object Manager, select *wrist_joint.Goal* and move it in the Perspective viewport, as shown in Figure 7-17. You will notice that elbow movement is controlled by *wrist_joint.Goal,* refer to Figure 7-17. Next, press CTRL+ Z to undo the rotation.

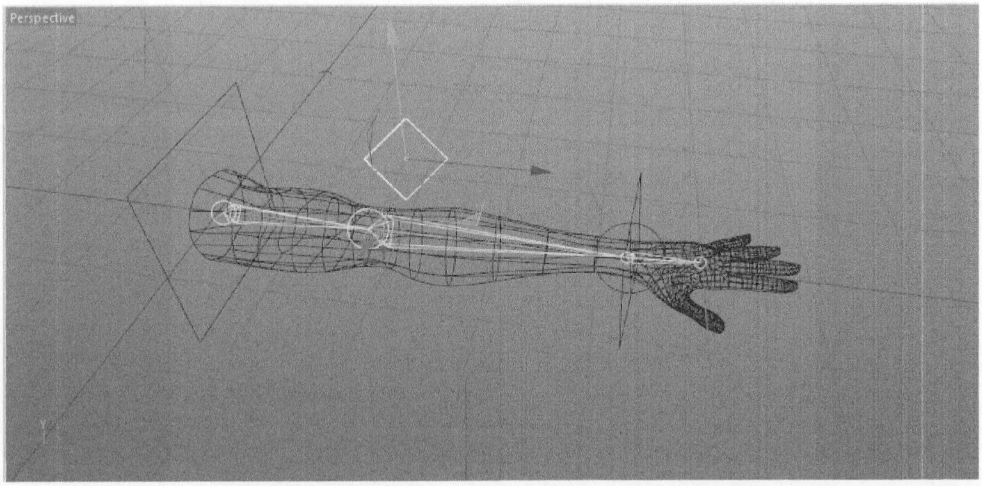

Figure 7-16 *Position of shoulder_joint.Pole changed*

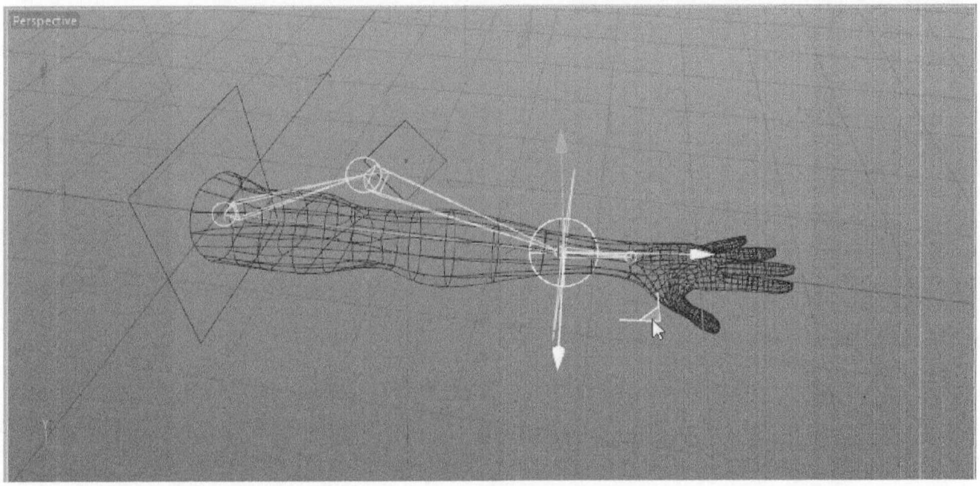

Figure 7-17 *Elbow movement controlled by wrist_joint.Goal*

9. In the Object Manager, select *shoulder_joint.Pole* and move it in the Perspective viewport, refer to Figure 7-18. You will notice that elbow rotation is controlled with *shoulder_joint.Pole*. Next, press CTRL+ Z to undo the rotation.

Binding the Rig

In this section, you will bind the rig using the **Bind** tool.

1. Select *hand, Root, shoulder_joint, elbow_joint, wrist_joint,* and *end_joint* in the Object Manager using the CTRL key.

2. Choose **Character > Commands > Bind** from the main menu; *Skin* is added to the Object Manager, as shown in Figure 7-19.

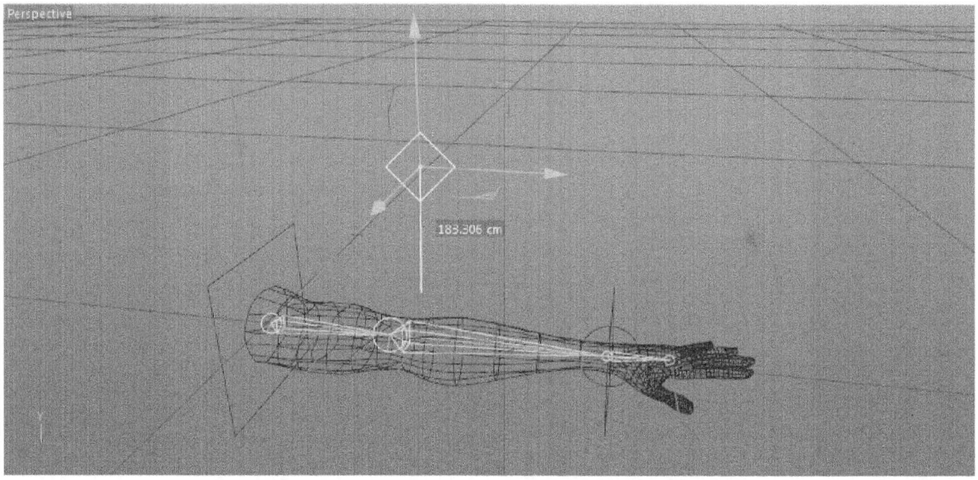

Figure 7-18 *Elbow rotation controlled by shoulder_joint.Pole*

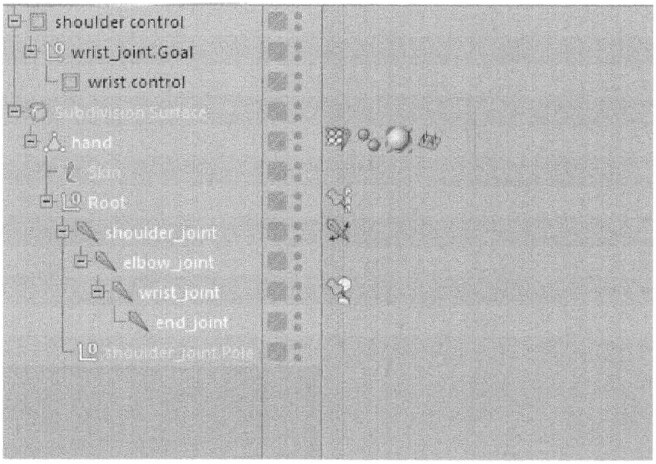

Figure 7-19 *Skin added to the Object Manager*

Now, rotate *shoulder control*; full arm rotates along with it. Also, move *wrist_joint.Goal*; the elbow moves along with it. Similarly, rotate *wrist control* to rotate wrist. Finally move *shoulder_joint. pole* to rotate the arm.

Saving the Scene

After completing the tutorial, you will save the file using the steps given next.

1. Choose **File > Save As** from the main menu; the **Save File** dialog box is displayed. In this dialog box, browse to the location *\Documents\c4dr20\c07*.

2. Enter **c07tut1** in the **File name** edit box and then choose the **Save** button.

Tutorial 2

In this tutorial, you will create rig for a table lamp, as shown in Figure 7-20.

(Expected time: 25 min)

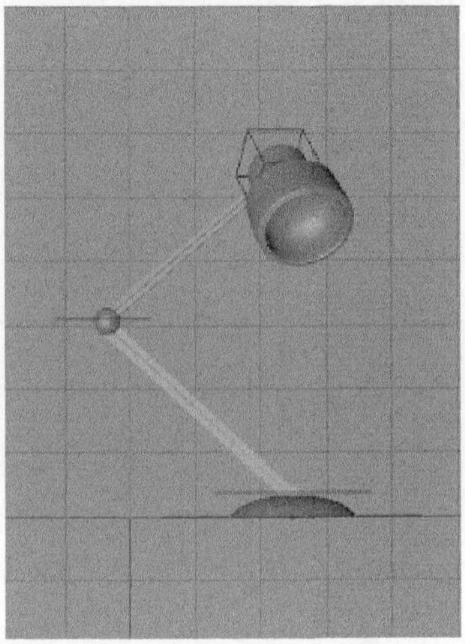

Figure 7-20 *Rig for a table lamp*

The following steps are required to complete this tutorial:

a. Open the file.
b. Create controllers.
c. Add constraints.
d. Save the scene.

Opening the File

In this section, you will open the file of the electric lamp.

1. Choose **File > Open** from the main menu; the **Open File** dialog box is displayed.

2. In the **Open File** dialog box, browse to *\Documents\c4dr20\c07\c07_tut2_start.c4d* and then choose the **Open** button; the *c07_tut2_start* file is opened, refer to Figure 7-21.

Creating Controllers

In this section, you will create controllers for the table lamp.

1. Press F2; the Top viewport is maximized. Choose **Create > Spline > Circle** from the main menu; a circle is created in the Top viewport and *Circle* is added to the Object Manager. Double-click on *Circle* in the Object Manager and enter **main control**; *Circle* is renamed as *main control*. Figure 7-22 displays the *main control* in the Top viewport.

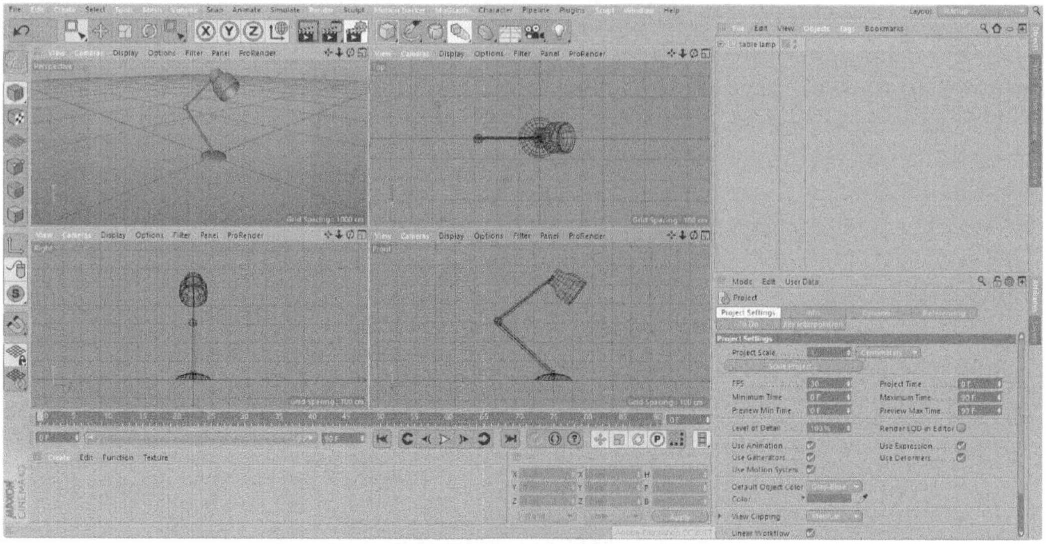

Figure 7-21 The c07_tut2_start file

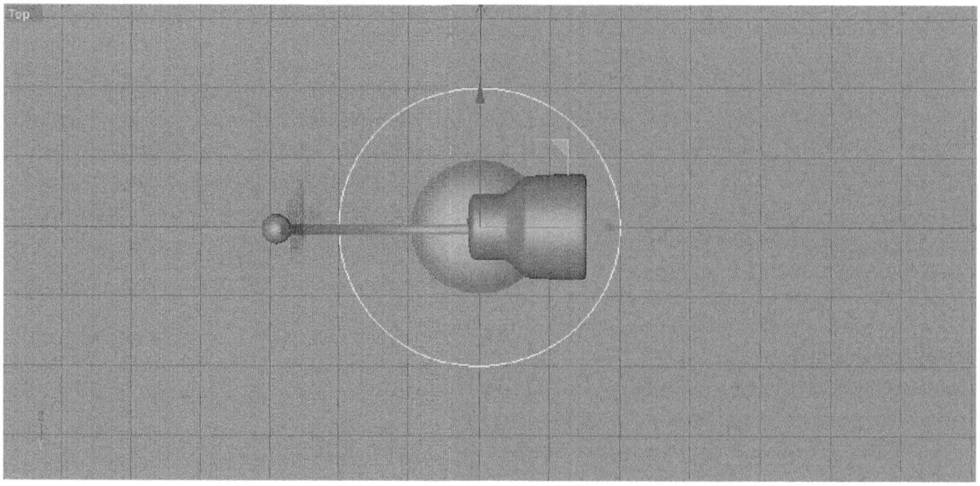

Figure 7-22 The main control in the Top viewport

2. Make sure *main control* is selected in the Object Manager. Next, press and hold the CTRL key and drag it above *main control;* a copy of *main control* is created with the name *main control.1*. Rename it as *support control*.

3. Make sure *support control* is selected in the Object Manager. In the Attribute Manager, make sure the **Object** button is chosen; the **Object Properties** area is displayed. In this area, enter **120** in the **Radius** spinner.

4. In the Attribute Manager, choose the **Coord** button; the **Coordinates** area is displayed. In this area, enter **37.948** in the **P . Y** spinner. Next, press F1 to maximize the Perspective viewport. Figure 7-23 shows *support control* in the Perspective viewport.

5. Make sure *support control* is selected in the Object Manager. Next, press and hold the CTRL key and drag it above *support control;* a copy of *support control* is created with the name *support control.1*. Rename it as *center control*.

6. Make sure *center control* is selected in the Object Manager. In the Attribute Manager, choose the **Object** button; the **Object Properties** area is displayed. In this area, enter **75** in the **Radius** spinner.

7. In the Attribute Manager, choose the **Coord** button; the **Coordinates** area is displayed. In this area, set the parameters as follows:

   P . X: **-292.049** P . Y: **310.303** P . Z: **-2.876**

   Figure 7-24 shows *center control* in the Perspective viewport.

***Figure 7-23** The support control in the Perspective viewport*

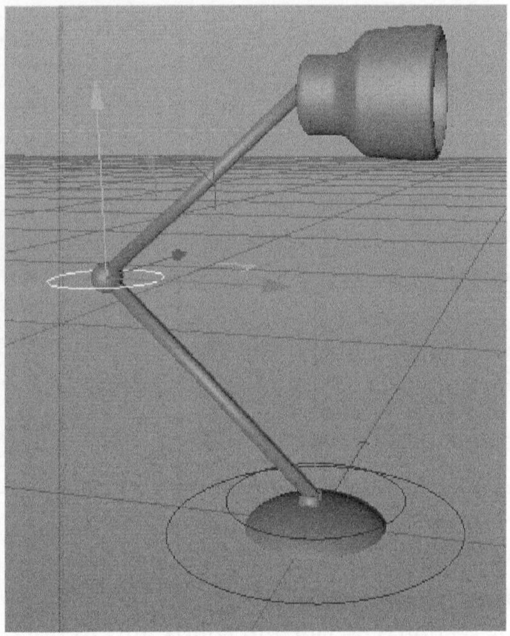

***Figure 7-24** The center control in the Perspective viewport*

8. Choose **Create > Object > Null** from the main menu; null is created in the Perspective viewport and *Null* is added to the Object Manager. Rename it as *lamp control*.

9. In the Attribute Manager, choose the **Object** button; the **Object Properties** area is displayed. In this area, select **Cube** from the **Display** drop-down list. Next, enter **45** in the **Radius** spinner and select **XY** from the **Orientation** drop-down list.

10. Choose the **Coord** button; the **Coordinates** area is displayed. In this area, enter **543.236** in the **P . Y** spinner.

    Figure 7-25 shows *lamp control* in the Perspective viewport.

Next, you will connect all controls with each other.

11. In the Object Manager, press and hold the left mouse button on *lamp control* and then drag and drop it on *center control*; *lamp control* is connected with *center control.*

12. Press and hold the left mouse button on *center control* and then drag and drop it on *support control*; *center control* is connected with *support control.*

13. Press and hold the left mouse button on *support control* and then drag and drop it on *main control*; *support control* is connected with *main control.*

Figure 7-26 shows all controls connected in the Object Manager.

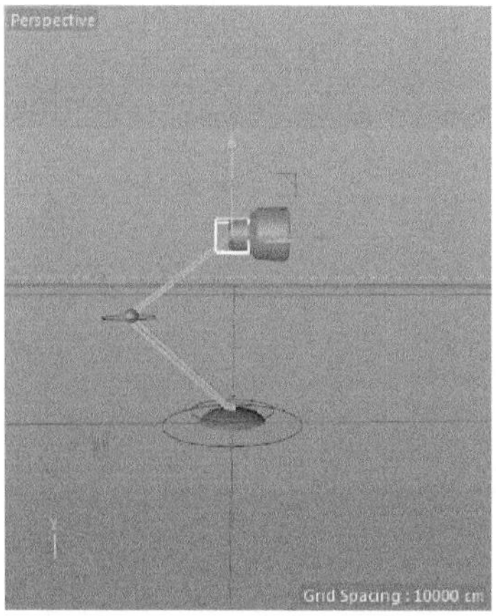

Figure 7-25 *The lamp control in the Perspective viewport*

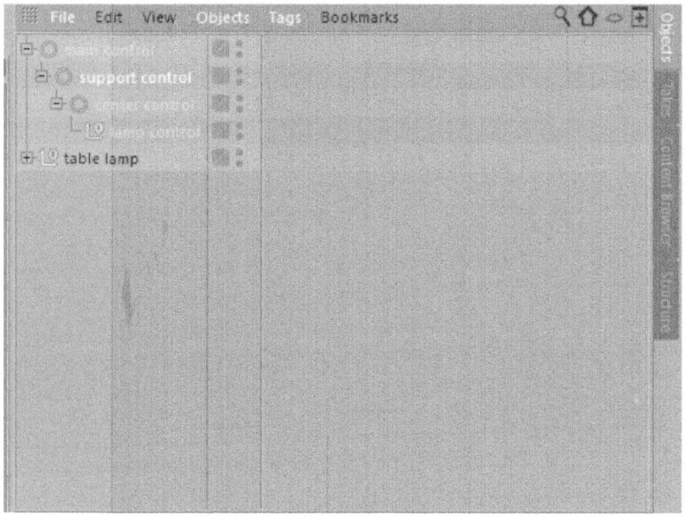

Figure 7-26 *All controls connected in the Object Manager*

Adding Constraints

In this section, you will add constraints to the controllers.

1. Select *table lamp* in the Object Manager and right-click on it; a shortcut menu is displayed. Choose **Character Tags > Constraint** from the shortcut menu; the **Constraint Expression [Constraint]** tag is added to the Object Manager and the **Constraint [Constraint]** area is displayed in the Attribute Manager.

2. In the **Constraints** area, select the **Parent** check box and choose the **Parent** button; the **Parent** area is displayed. Next, choose the arrow button next to the **Target** edit box in the **Targets** area; the shape of the cursor changes. Next, select *main control* in the Object Manager; *main control* is constrained with *table lamp*. Now if you move *main control*, *table lamp* will move along with it, refer to Figure 7-27.

The Parent constraint is used to create a parent-child relationship between two or more objects. The object selected in the **Target** edit box acts as the parent of the object to which the constraint is applied.

3. Select *support1* in the Object Manager and right-click on it; a shortcut menu is displayed. Choose **Character Tags > Constraint** from the shortcut menu; the **Constraint Expression [Constraint]** tag is added to the Object Manager and the **Constraint [Constraint]** area is displayed in the Attribute Manager.

4. In the **Constraints** area, select the **Parent** check box and make sure the **Parent** button is chosen. In the **Parent** area, choose the arrow button next to the **Target** edit box in the **Targets** area; the shape of the cursor changes. Now, select *support control* in the Object Manager; *support control* is constrained with *support1*. Now, if you rotate *support control*, supports and *lamp shade* will rotate along with it, refer to Figure 7-28.

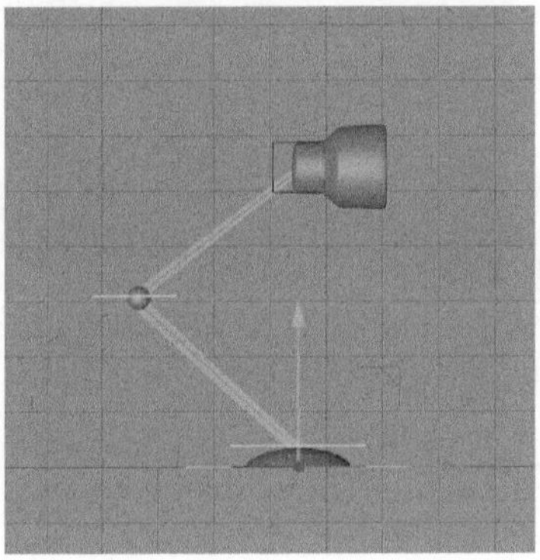

Figure 7-27 *The table lamp moving along with main control*

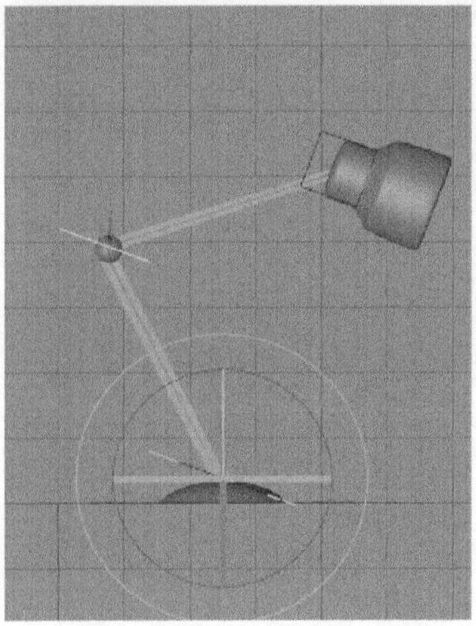

Figure 7-28 *Supports and lamp shade rotating along with support control*

5. Select *support2* in the Object Manager and right-click on it; a shortcut menu is displayed. Choose **Character Tags > Constraint** from the shortcut menu; the **Constraint Expression [Constraint]** tag is added to the Object Manager and the **Constraint [Constraint]** area is displayed in the Attribute Manager.

6. Make sure the **Constraint Expression [Constraint]** tag is selected in the Object Manager. Next, in the Attribute Manager, select the **Parent** check box in the **Constraints** area and then choose the **Parent** button if not already chosen. In the **Parent** area, choose the arrow button next to the **Target** edit box in the **Targets** area; the shape of the cursor changes. Now, select *center control* in the Object Manager; *center control* is constrained with *support2*. Now, if you rotate *center control* and *support2, lamp shade* will rotate along with it, refer to Figure 7-29.

7. Select *lamp shade* in the Object Manager and right-click on it; a shortcut menu is displayed. Choose **Character Tags > Constraint** from the shortcut menu; the **Constraint Expression [Constraint]** tag is added to the Object Manager and the **Constraint [Constraint] Settings** area is displayed in the Attribute Manager.

8. Make sure the **Constraint Expression [Constraint]** tag is selected in the Object Manager Next, in the Attribute Manager, select the **Parent** check box in the **Constraints** area and then choose the **Parent** button if not already chosen; the **Parent** area is displayed.

9. In this area, choose the arrow button next to the **Target** edit box in the **Targets** area; the shape of the cursor changes. Now, select *lamp control* in the Object Manager; *lamp control* is constrained with *lamp shade*. Now, if you rotate *lamp control, lamp shade* will rotate along with it, refer to Figure 7-30.

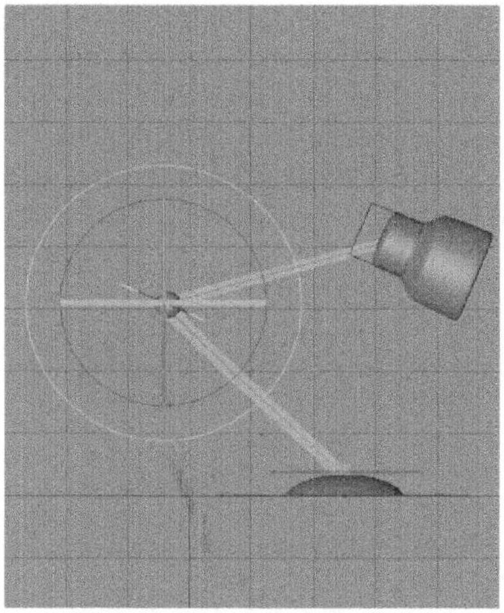

Figure 7-29 *The support2 and lamp shade rotating along with center control*

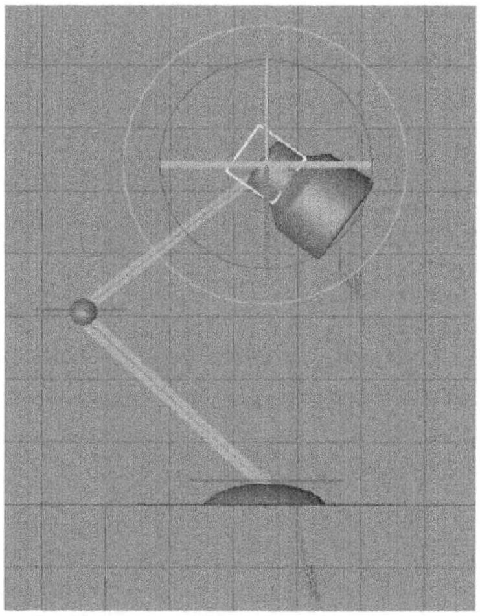

Figure 7-30 *The lamp shade rotating along with lamp control*

Saving the Scene

After completing the tutorial, you need to save the file using the steps given next.

1. Choose **File > Save As** from the main menu; the **Save File** dialog box is displayed. In this dialog box, browse to the location *\Documents\c4dr20\c07*.

2. Enter **c07tut2** in the **File name** edit box and then choose the **Save** button.

Self-Evaluation Test

Answer the following questions and then compare them to those given at the end of this chapter:

1. Which of the following tools in the main menu is used to create bones in the mesh of the object or character?

   (a) **Joint Tool** (b) **Move**
   (c) **Bind** (d) **Create IK Chain**

2. Which of the following commands is used to create a complete IK chain?

   (a) **Create IK Chain** (b) **Constraints**
   (c) **Skin** (d) None of these

3. __________ is the process of preparing an object or a character for animation.

4. The __________ are used to restrict the changes in position, orientation, or scaling of an object by specifying its limits.

5. The __________ constraint is used to create a parent-child relationship between two or more than two objects.

Review Questions

Answer the following questions:

1. Which of the following areas in the Attribute Manager is used to add or delete objects that would act as parents?

   (a) **Offset** (b) **Parent**
   (c) **Targets** (d) None of these

2. In the rigging process, you need to add _________ and _________ to the object to be rigged.

3. The _________ check box in the **Constraints** area is used to constrain the position, rotation, and scaling of an object to another object.

4. The **Joint Tool** is used to create a complete IK chain for the selected joint objects in a hierarchy from the start to the end of the joints. (T/F)

EXERCISE

The rendered output of the model used in the following exercise can be accessed by downloading the *c07_cinema4d_r20_exr.zip* from *www.cadcim.com*. The path of the file is as follows: *Textbooks > Animation and Visual Effects > MAXON CINEMA 4D > MAXON CINEMA 4D R20 Studio: A Tutorial Approach*

Exercise 1

Extract the contents of the *c07_cinema4d_r20_exr.zip* file of a human leg from *www.cadcim.com* and then create a rig for the leg, as shown in Figure 7-31. **(Expected time: 30 min)**

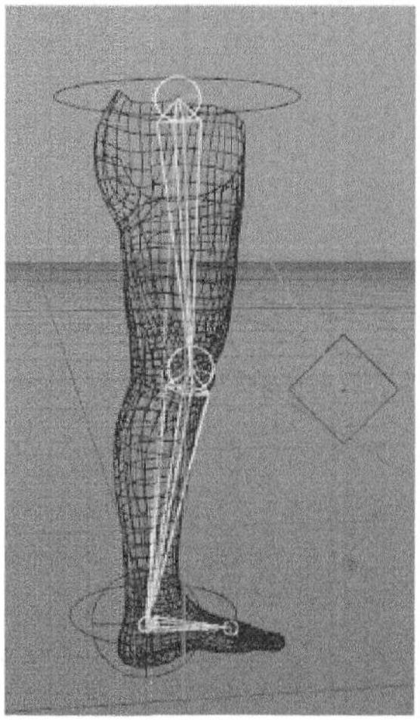

Figure 7-31 *Rig for a human leg*

Answers to Self-Evaluation Test

1. a, **2.** a, **3.** Rigging, **4.** constraints, **5.** Parent

Chapter 8

Animation

Learning Objectives

After completing this chapter, you will be able to:

- *Create key animation*
- *Create path animation*
- *Work with the Timeline panel*

INTRODUCTION

Animation is an act of giving life to a 3D object or character. To animate an object, you need to define different positions, rotations, and scaling of an object at different frames in the time slider. On playing an animation, all frames are displayed one after the other in quick succession to create an illusion of movement. In this chapter, you will learn about the playback control buttons available in the Animation toolbar. You will also learn to use the Timeline panel.

TUTORIALS

Before you start the tutorials of this chapter, you need to download the *c08_cinema4d_r20_tut.zip* file from *www.cadcim.com*. The path of the file is as follows: *Textbooks > Animation and Visual Effects > MAXON CINEMA 4D > MAXON CINEMA 4D R20 Studio: A Tutorial Approach*

Next, you need to browse to *\Documents\c4dr20* and create a new folder in it with the name *c08*. Next, extract the contents of the zip file in this folder.

Tutorial 1

In this tutorial, you will create an animated logo, refer to Figure 8-1.

(Expected time: 25 min)

Figure 8-1 *The animated logo at frame 65*

The following steps are required to complete this tutorial:

a. Open the file.
b. Add keyframes to the text.
c. Fine-tune the animation.
d. Save and render the animation.

Opening the File

In this section, you will open the file.

1. Choose **File > Open** from the main menu; the **Open File** dialog box is displayed.

2. In the **Open File** dialog box, browse to *\Documents\c4dr20\c08\c08_tut1_start.c4d* and then choose the **Open** button; the *c08_tut1_start.c4d* file is opened, as shown in Figure 8-2.

Figure 8-2 The c08_tut1_start.c4d file

Adding Keyframes to the Text

In this section, you will add keyframes to the text.

1. In the Animation toolbar, choose the **Autokeying** button and make sure that the time slider is set to frame 0.

   The **Autokeying** button is used to set the keys automatically. On choosing this button, the boundary of the viewport turns red.

> **Tip**
> *The automatic keyframing should be used carefully as it may lead to addition of keys on those frames as well in which they are not required.*

2. Select *CADCIM* in the Object Manager; the **Text Object [CADCIM]** settings are displayed in the Attribute Manager.

3. Make sure that the **Object** button is chosen in the Attribute Manager. In the **Object Properties** area, right-click on the **Horizontal Spacing** option; a shortcut menu is displayed. Choose **Animation > Add Keyframe** from the shortcut menu, as shown in Figure 8-3; a keyframe is added and the circle located at the left of the **Horizontal Spacing** option turns red.

   The **Add Keyframe** option is used to add a keyframe to the selected frame.

4. In the Animation toolbar, move the timeslider to frame 20. Alternatively, enter **20** in the **Current Time** spinner; the timeslider is set to frame 20, refer to Figure 8-4.

> **Tip**
> *You can also add a keyframe by pressing and holding the CTRL key and then clicking on the circle located on the left of the* ***Horizontal Spacing*** *option in the Attribute Manager.*

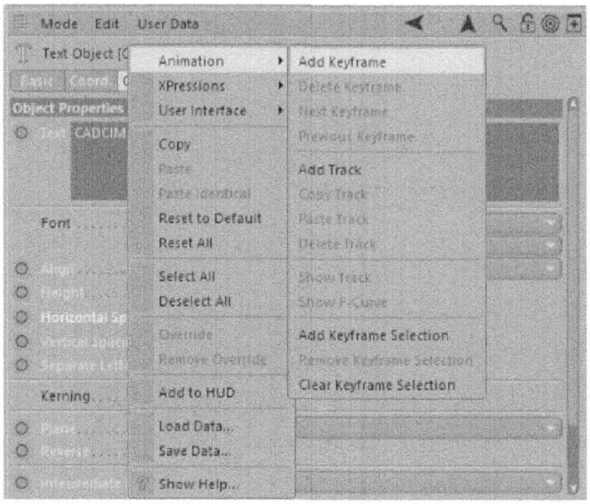

Figure 8-3 *Choosing the **Add Keyframe** option from the shortcut menu*

Figure 8-4 *Timeslider set to frame 20*

Next, you will animate the text.

5. Make sure that *CADCIM* is selected in the Object Manager. In the **Object Properties** area, enter **274** in the **Horizontal Spacing** spinner; the horizontal space between the text increases in the Perspective viewport, as shown in Figure 8-5.

   The **Horizontal Spacing** spinner is used to increase or decrease space between the characters.

6. In the Animation toolbar, move the timeslider to frame 40. Alternatively, enter **40** in the **Current Time** spinner; the timeslider is set to frame 40.

Figure 8-5 The space added between the text

7. Make sure that *CADCIM* is selected in the Object Manager. In the **Object Properties** area, enter **0** in the **Horizontal Spacing** spinner; the horizontal space between the text decreases in the Perspective viewport.

8. In the Animation toolbar, move the timeslider to frame 45.

9. Make sure that *CADCIM* is selected in the Object Manager. In the **Object Properties** area, enter **8** in the **Horizontal Spacing** spinner; the horizontal space between the text increases slightly in the Perspective viewport.

10. In the Animation toolbar, move the timeslider to frame 48.

11. Make sure that *CADCIM* is selected in the Object Manager. In the **Object Properties** area, enter **0** in the **Horizontal Spacing** spinner; the horizontal space between the text increases in the Perspective viewport.

    Next, you will animate the height of the text, *CADCIM*.

12. Make sure that *CADCIM* is selected in the Object Manager. In the **Object Properties** area, right-click on the **Height** option; a shortcut menu is displayed. From this shortcut menu, choose **Animation > Add Keyframe**, refer to Figure 8-3; a keyframe is added and the circle located at the left of the **Height** option turns red.

    The **Height** spinner is used to modify the height of the text.

13. In the Animation toolbar, move the timeslider to frame 65. Make sure that *CADCIM* is selected in the Object Manager. In the **Object Properties** area, enter **345** in the **Height** spinner; the height of the text increases in the Perspective viewport, refer to Figure 8-6.

14. In the Animation toolbar, move the timeslider to frame 75. Make sure that *CADCIM* is selected in the Object Manager. In the **Object Properties** area, enter **166** in the **Height** spinner; the height of the text decreases in the Perspective viewport, as shown in Figure 8-7.

Figure 8-6 The CADCIM text at frame 65

Figure 8-7 The CADCIM text at frame 75

15. In the Animation toolbar, move the timeslider to frame 83. Make sure that *CADCIM* is selected in the Object Manager. In the **Object Properties** area, enter **226** in the **Height** spinner; the height of the text increases in the Perspective viewport.

16. In the Animation toolbar, move the timeslider to frame 90. Make sure that *CADCIM* is selected in the Object Manager. In the **Object Properties** area, enter **187** in the **Height** spinner; the height of the text decreases.

    Next, you will animate the text, *Technologies*.

17. Select *Technologies* in the Object Manager; the **Text Object [Technologies]** settings are displayed in the Attribute Manager.

18. In the Animation toolbar, move the timeslider to frame 100. In the **Object Properties** area, enter **0** in the **Height** spinner and then right-click on the **Height** option; a shortcut menu is displayed. Choose **Animation > Add Keyframe** from the shortcut menu.

19. In the Animation toolbar, move the timeslider to frame 120. Make sure that *Technologies* is selected in the Object Manager. In the **Object Properties** area, enter **200** in the **Height** spinner; the height of the text increases in the Perspective viewport.

    Next, you will animate the rotation of the text, *Technologies.*

20. Choose the **Coord** button in the Attribute Manager; the **Coordinates** area is displayed. In the **Coordinates** area, right-click on the **R . H** option; a shortcut menu is displayed. Choose **Animation > Add Keyframe** from the shortcut menu; a keyframe is added to the timeslider and the circle on the left of the **R . H** option turns red.

21. In the Animation toolbar, move the timeslider to frame 200. Make sure that *Technologies* is selected in the Object Manager. In the **Coordinates** area, enter **360** in the **R . H** spinner; a keyframe is added at frame 200.

Fine-Tuning the Animation

In this section, you will fine-tune the animation in the **Timeline** window.

1. Select *CADCIM* in the Object Manager and right-click on it; a shortcut menu is displayed. Choose **Show FCurves** from the shortcut menu, as shown in Figure 8-8; the **Timeline** window is displayed, as shown in Figure 8-9.

    The **Show FCurves** option is used to display the **Timeline** window with the **F-Curve Mode** activated.

    The **Timeline** window is the most essential part of animation in CINEMA 4D. It is used to control and edit the animation. The **Timeline** window has three modes: **Key Mode**, **F-Curve Mode**, and **Motion Mode**.

2. In the **Timeline** window, make sure that the **F-Curve Mode** button is chosen. Next, press CTRL+A to select all the keys in the **Timeline** window, as shown in Figure 8-10.

    The **F-Curve Mode** is used to modify the interpolation of the keyframes.

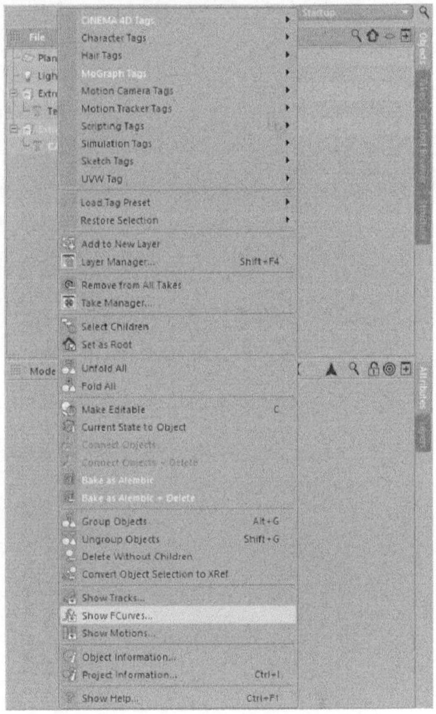

*Figure 8-8 Choosing **Show FCurves** from the shortcut menu*

3. In the **Timeline** window, choose the **Linear** button; all the curves are set to linear, as shown in Figure 8-11. Now, close the **Timeline** window. 

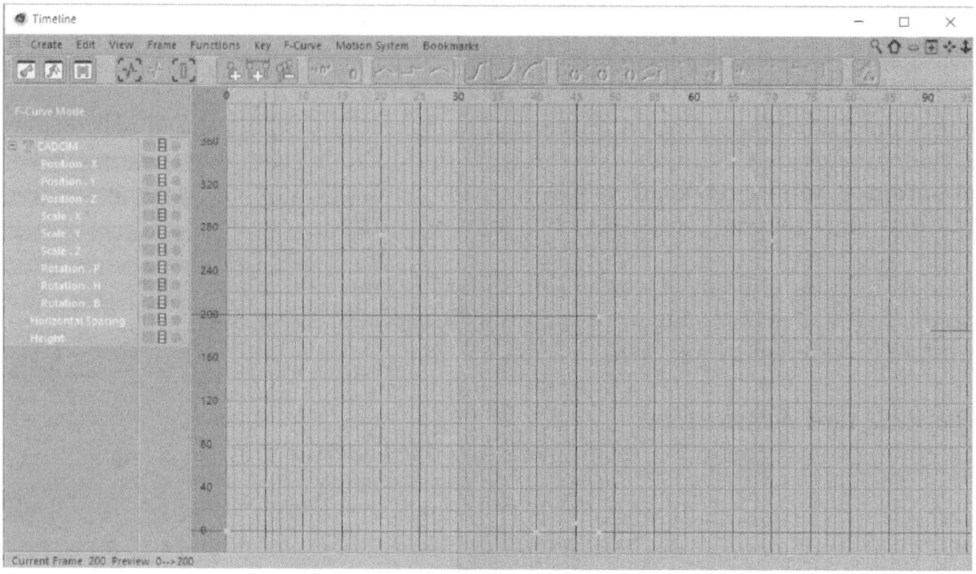

Figure 8-9 *The* ***Timeline*** *window*

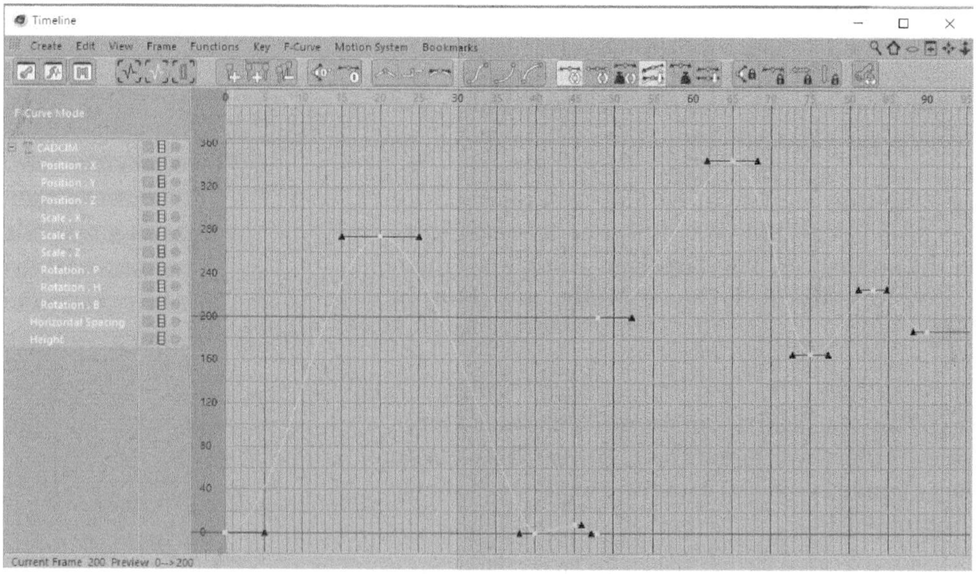

Figure 8-10 *Selecting all the keys in the* ***Timeline*** *window*

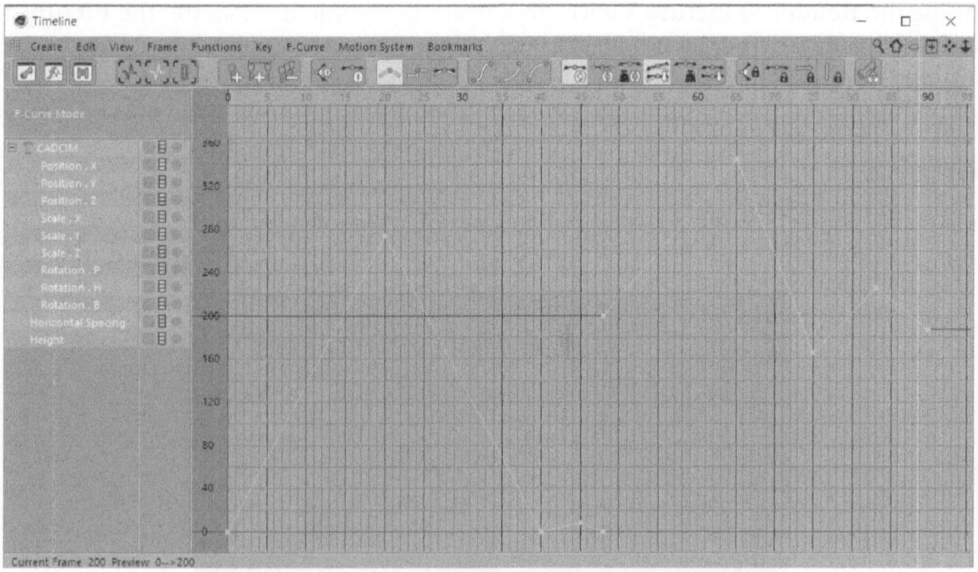

***Figure 8-11** Displaying the linear shape of curves*

The **Linear** button is used to set a linear interpolation between the selected keyframes.

Saving and Rendering the Animation

In this section, you will save and render the animation. You can also view the final render sequence by downloading the file *c08_cinema4d_r20_rndr.zip* from *www.cadcim.com*. The path of the file is mentioned at the beginning of the chapter.

1. Choose the **Edit Render Settings** tool from the Command Palette; the **Render Settings** window is displayed. In this window, make sure that the **Output** option is selected in the list displayed at the left side of the window. In the **Output** area, make sure that the **To** spinner is set to **200**.

2. Select the **Save** option from the list displayed on the left in the **Render Settings** window; the **Regular Image** area is displayed. In this area, make sure that the **Save** check box is selected. Next, choose the browse button located next to the **File** spinner; the **Save File** dialog box is displayed.

   The **Save** check box is selected by default. It is used to render the image or sequence automatically on choosing the **Render to Picture Viewer** tool.

3. In the **Save File** dialog box, browse to *\Documents\c4dr20\c08* and enter **c08tut1** in the **File name** text box. Next, choose the **Save** button.

4. Make sure that the **AVI Movie** option is selected in the **Format** drop-down list. Next, close the **Render Settings** window.

5. Choose the **Render to Picture Viewer** tool from the Command Palette; the **Picture Viewer** window is displayed and the rendering begins. The file is automatically saved at the specified location.

Tutorial 2

In this tutorial, you will create a basket ball animation, as shown in Figure 8-12.

(Expected time: 35 min)

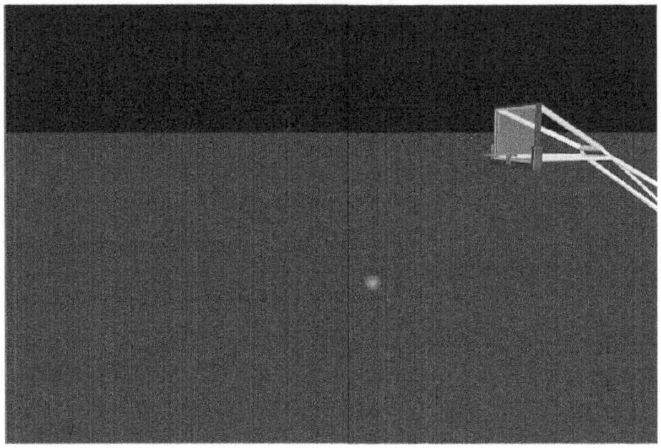

Figure 8-12 The basket ball at frame 66

The following steps are required to complete this tutorial:

a. Open the file.
b. Animate the basketball.
c. Fine-tune the animation.
d. Save and render the animation.

Opening the File

In this section, you will open the file.

1. Choose **File > Open** from the main menu; the **Open File** dialog box is displayed.

2. In the **Open File** dialog box, browse to *\Documents\c4dr20\c08\c08_tut2_start.c4d* and then choose the **Open** button; the *c08_tut2_start.c4d* file is opened, as shown in Figure 8-13.

Animating the Basketball

In this section, you will animate the *basketball* by adding the keyframes.

1. Press F3; the Right viewport is maximized. In the Animation toolbar, choose the **Autokeying** button and make sure that the timeslider is set to frame 0.

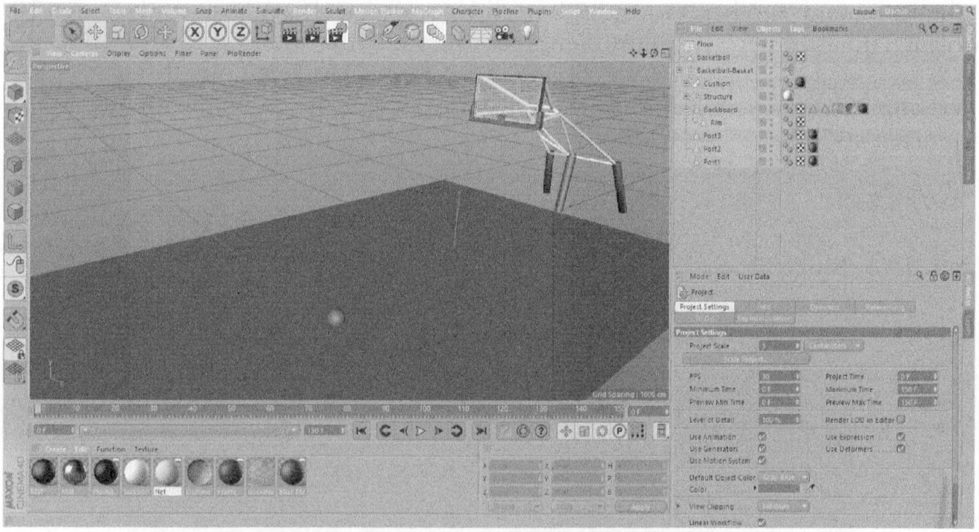

Figure 8-13 The c08_tut2_start.c4d file

2. Select *basketball* in the Object Manager and then choose the **Coord** button in the Attribute Manager, if not already chosen; the **Coordinates** area is displayed. In the **Coordinates** area, right-click on the circle located on the left of the **P . X** spinner; a shortcut menu is displayed. Choose **Animation > Add Keyframe** from the shortcut menu; the circle located on the left of **P . X**, **P . Y**, and **P . Z** turns red.

3. In the **Coordinates** area, set the parameters as follows:

   P . X: **-40.84** P . Y: **464.471** P . Z: **-815.996**

   Figure 8-14 displays *basketball* at frame 0.

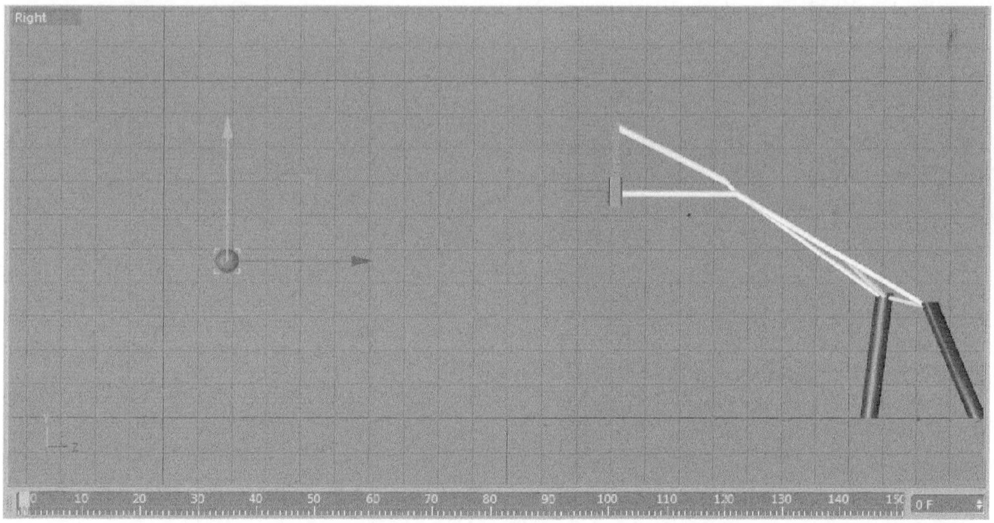

Figure 8-14 The basketball at frame 0

4. In the Animation toolbar, move the timeslider to frame 10. Alternatively, enter **10** in the **Current Time** spinner; the timeslider is set to frame 10.

5. Make sure *basketball* is selected in the Object Manager. In the **Coordinates** area, set the parameters as follows:

   P . Y: **796.753** P . Z: **-455.277**

   Figure 8-15 displays *basketball* at frame 10.

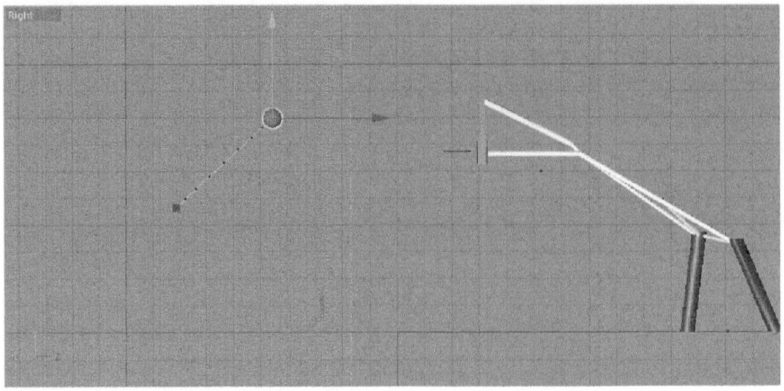

Figure 8-15 *The basketball at frame 10*

6. In the Animation toolbar, move the timeslider to frame 20.

7. Make sure *basketball* is selected in the Object Manager. In the **Coordinates** area, set the parameters as follows:

   P . Y: **954.44** P . Z: **28.102**

   Figure 8-16 displays *basketball* at frame 20.

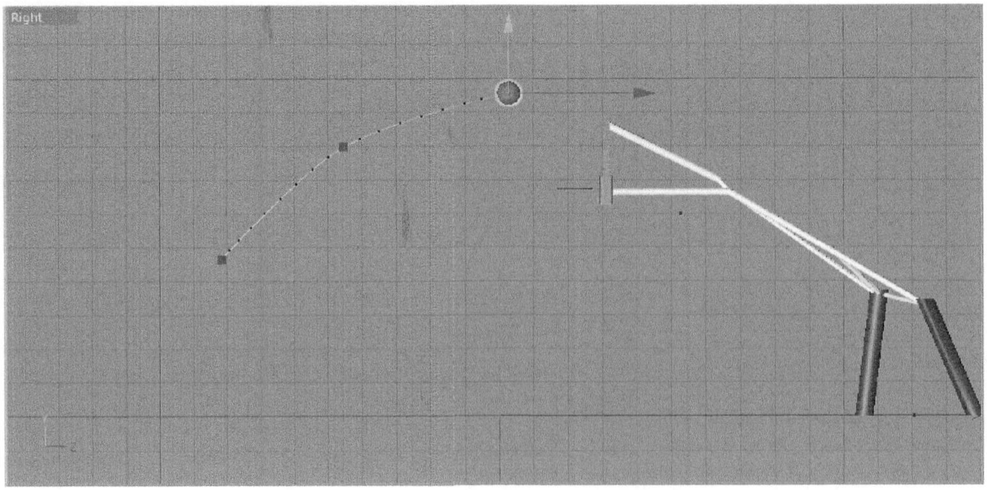

Figure 8-16 *The basketball at frame 20*

8. In the Animation toolbar, move the timeslider to frame 30.

9. Make sure *basketball* is selected in the Object Manager. In the **Coordinates** area, set the parameters as follows:

   P . Y: **739.71** P . Z: **248.523**

Figure 8-17 displays *basketball* at frame 30.

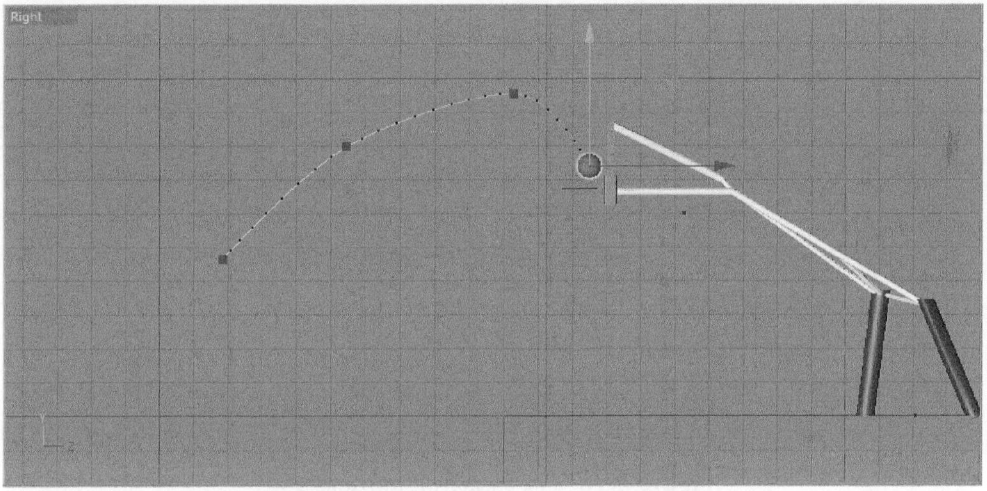

Figure 8-17 *The basketball at frame 30*

10. In the Animation toolbar, move the timeslider to frame 34.

11. Make sure *basketball* is selected in the Object Manager. In the **Coordinates** area, set the parameters as follows:

    P . Y: **567.025** P . Z: **235.442**

    Figure 8-18 displays *basketball* at frame 34.

12. Similarly, move the timeslider to frames and set the values in the Attribute Manager as given in Table 8-1.

Table 8-1 *The transformation values of basketball*

Frame to be selected	P . Y	P . Z
40	29.429	18.251
50	332.391	-95.207
64	30.581	-229.294

73	227.576	-322.123
84	31.041	-435.581
91	141.612	-507.782
100	32.92	-609.611
150	32.92	-1061.761

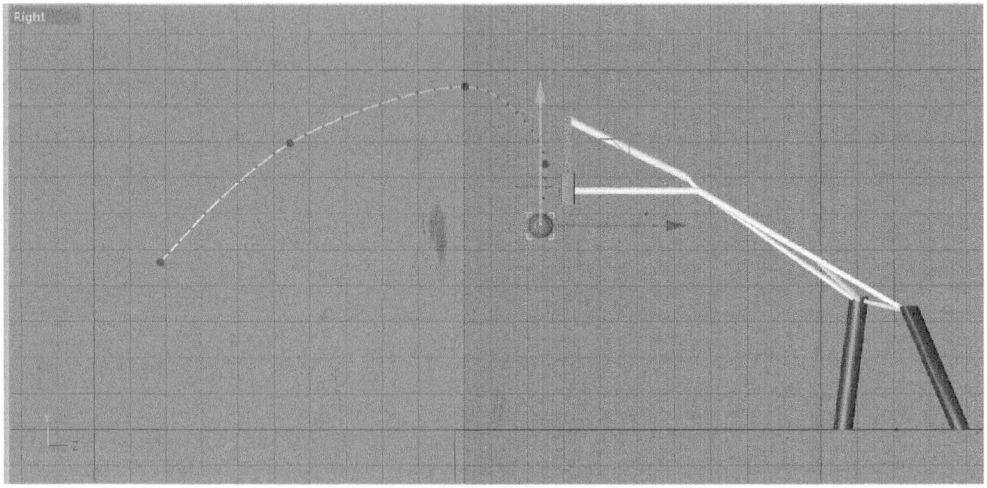

Figure 8-18 *The basketball at frame 34*

Figure 8-19 displays *basketball* at frame 150.

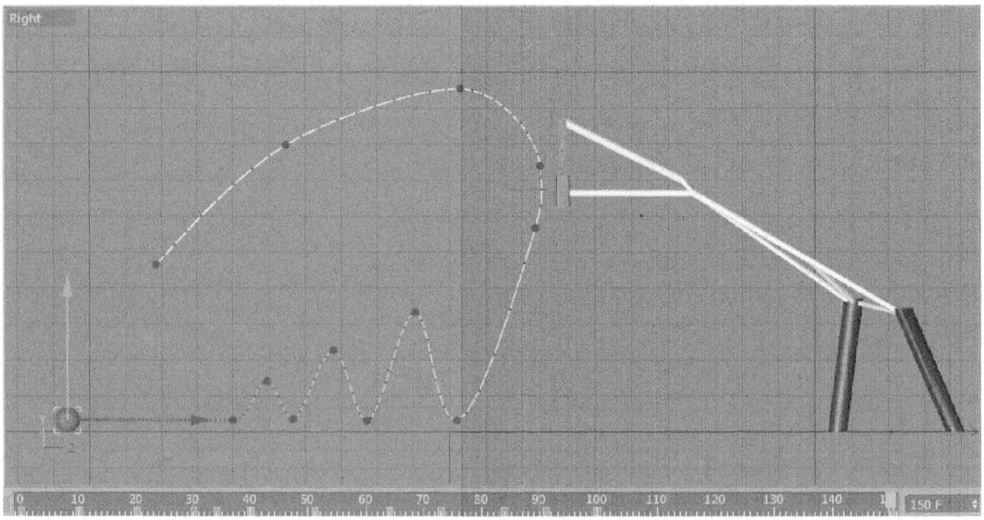

Figure 8-19 *The basketball at frame 150*

13. Choose the **Play Forwards** button from the Animation toolbar to view the animation of *basketball*.

    Next, you will rotate *basketball.*

14. Make sure *basketball* is selected in the Object Manager. Next, move the timeslider to frame 0. In the **Coordinates** area, right-click on the circle located on the left of the **R . H** spinner; a shortcut menu is displayed. From this shortcut menu, choose **Animation > Add Keyframe**; the circle located at the left of the **R . H**, **R . P**, and **R . B** spinners turn red.

15. Move the timeslider to frames and set the values in the Attribute Manager as given in Table 8-2.

Table 8-2 *The rotation values of basketball*

Frame to be selected	R . P
40	90
64	180
84	270
100	360
150	520

Next, you will create the squash and stretch effect on *basketball* when it touches *Floor*.

16. Move the timeslider to frame 39. In the **Coordinates** area, right-click on the circle located on the left of the **S . X** spinner; a shortcut menu is displayed. From this shortcut menu, choose **Animation > Add Keyframe**; the circle located at the left of the **S . X**, **S . Y**, and **S . Z** spinners turns red.

    Next, you need to copy the keyframe created at frame 39 to other frames.

17. Make sure *basketball* is selected in the Object Manager and right-click on it; a shortcut menu is displayed. Choose **Show FCurves** from the shortcut menu, refer to Figure 8-8; the **Timeline** window is displayed.

18. Select **Scale . X**, **Scale . Y**, and **Scale . Z**, from the list displayed on the left pane of the **Timeline** window. Next, select the keyframe at frame 39 by using the rectangular marquee selection, as shown in Figure 8-20. Next, press CTRL+C. Now, move the timeslider to frame 43 and press CTRL+V; the selected keyframe is copied to frame 43.

Note

Choose ***F-Curve > Show All Tracks*** *from the* ***Timeline*** *window menu bar to display only the selected curves in the window.*

19. Similarly copy the selected keyframe at frames 67 and 87. Next, minimize the **Timeline** window.

20. Move the timeslider to frame 40. Select *basketball* in the Object Manager again. In the **Coordinates** area, enter the value **0.87** in the **S . Z** spinner; *basketball* is squashed and a keyframe is created at this frame, refer to Figure 8-21.

Figure 8-20 *Selecting the keyframe from the* ***Timeline*** *window*

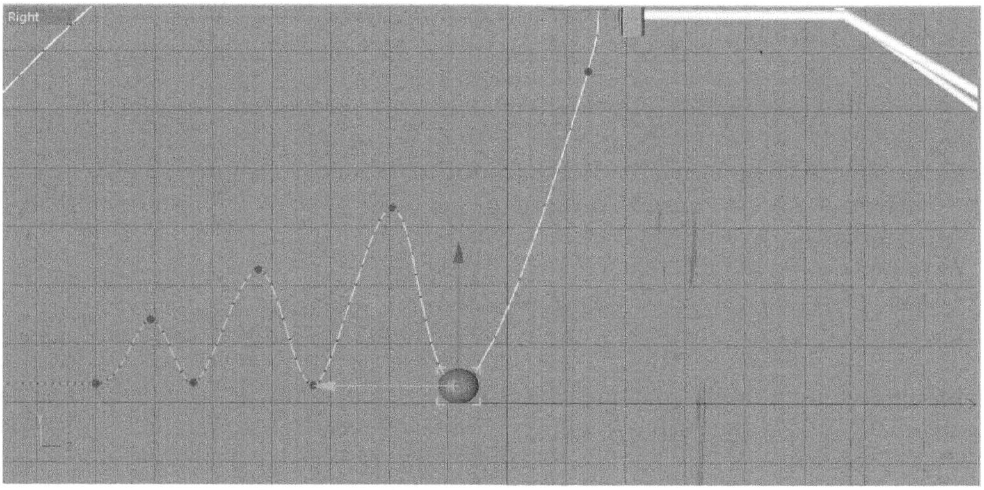

Figure 8-21 *Squashed basketball at frame 40*

21. Move the timeslider to frame 64. In the **Coordinates** area, enter the value **0.87** in the **S . Y** spinner; basketball is squashed and a keyframe is created at this frame.

22. Move the timeslider to frame 84. In the **Coordinates** area, enter the value **0.87** in the **S . X** spinner; basketball is squashed and a keyframe is created at this frame.

23. Choose the **Play Forwards** button from the Animation toolbar to view the animation of *basketball*.

Fine-Tuning the Animation

In this section, you will fine-tune the animation using the **Timeline** window.

1. In the Animation toolbar, move the timeslider to frame 40. Next, maximize the **Timeline** window. Select **Position Y** from the list displayed on the left pane of the **Timeline** window. Select the keyframe at frame 40 by using the rectangular marquee selection, refer to Figure 8-22.

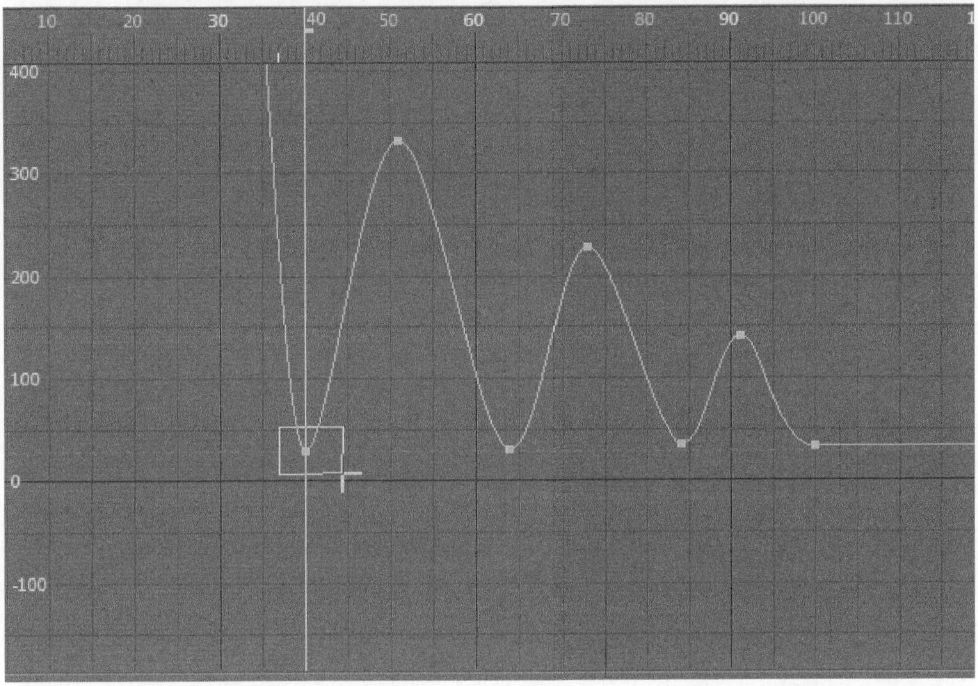

Figure 8-22 Selecting the keyframe from the ***Timeline*** *window*

2. Choose the **Break Tangents** button from the **Timeline** window and then move the tangents using the **Move** tool to add weight to *basketball* when it touches *Floor*, refer to Figure 8-23.

3. Similarly, select the keyframes at frame 64, 84, and 100, one by one, by using the rectangular marquee selection and then move their tangents, as shown in Figure 8-24 as done in previous steps.

4. Select the keyframes at frames 50, 73, and 91 one by one from the **Timeline** window and then choose the **Ease Ease** button.

5. Choose the **Play Forwards** button from the Animation toolbar to view the animation of *basketball*.

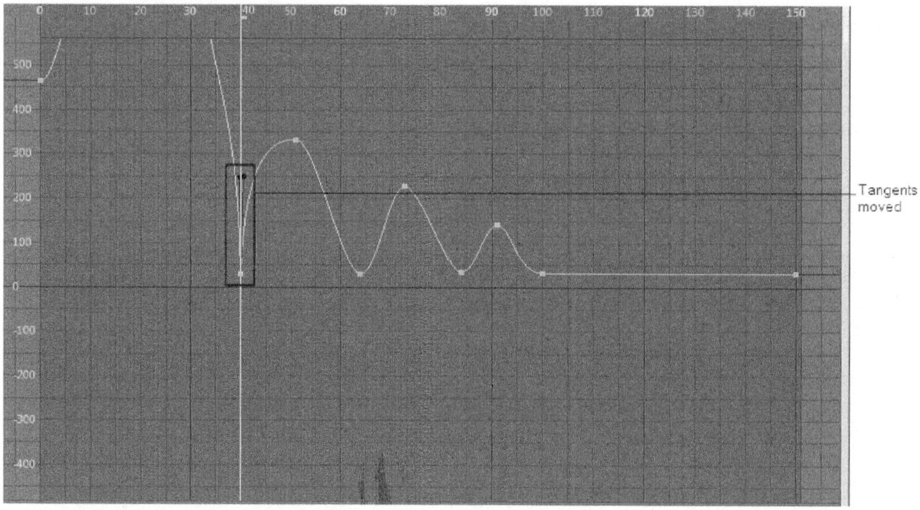

Figure 8-23 Moving the tangents in the ***Timeline*** *window*

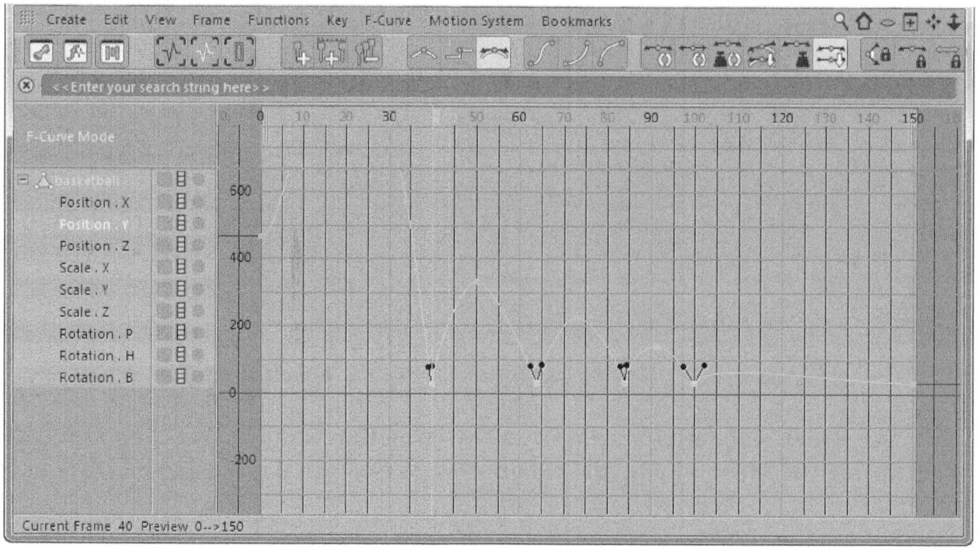

Figure 8-24 Moving the tangents at other frames

Saving and Rendering the Animation

In this section, you will save and render the animation. You can also view the final render sequence by downloading the file *c08_cinema4d_r20_rndr.zip* from *www.cadcim.com*. The path of the file is mentioned at the beginning of the chapter.

1. Choose the **Edit Render Settings** tool from the Command Palette; the **Render Settings** window is displayed. In this window, choose the **Output** button; the **Output** area is displayed. In this area, enter **150** in the **To** spinner; the **Frames** option gets updated to **151** (from 0 to 150).

2. Choose the **Save** button from the list displayed on the left in the **Render Settings** window; the **Regular Image** area is displayed. In this area, make sure that the **Save** check box is selected. Next, choose the browse button located next to the **File** text box; the **Save File** dialog box is displayed.

3. In the **Save File** dialog box, browse to the location *\Documents\c4dr20\c08* and enter **c08tut2** in the **File name** text box. Next, choose the **Save** button.

4. Select the **AVI Movie** option from the **Format** drop-down list. Next, close the **Render Settings** window.

5. Choose the **Render to Picture Viewer** tool from the Command Palette; the **Picture Viewer** window is displayed and the rendering begins. The file is automatically saved at the specified location.

Tutorial 3

In this tutorial, you will animate the cart using the path animation and key animation, refer to Figure 8-25. **(Expected time: 25 min)**

The following steps are required to complete this tutorial:

a. Open the file.
b. Align the cart along a spline path.
c. Move the cart.
d. Rotate the wheels of the cart.
e. Save and render the scene.

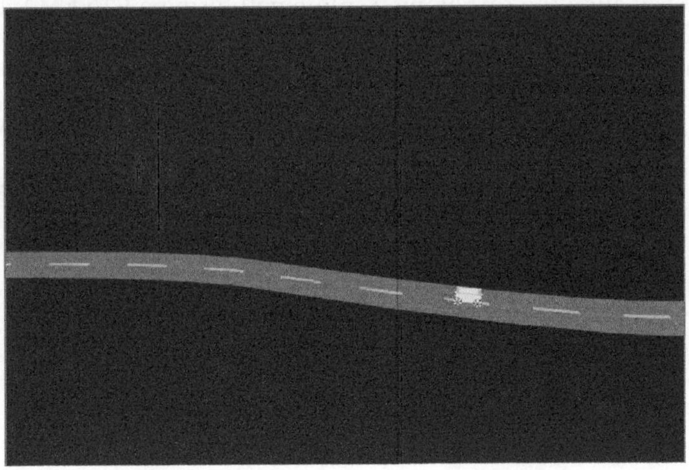

Figure 8-25 *Moving cart at frame 45*

Opening the File

In this section, you will open the file.

1. Choose **File > Open** from the main menu; the **Open File** dialog box is displayed.

2. In the **Open File** dialog box, browse to *\Documents\ c4dr20\c08\c08_tut3_start.c4d* and then choose the **Open** button; the *c08_tut3_start* file is opened, as shown in Figure 8-26.

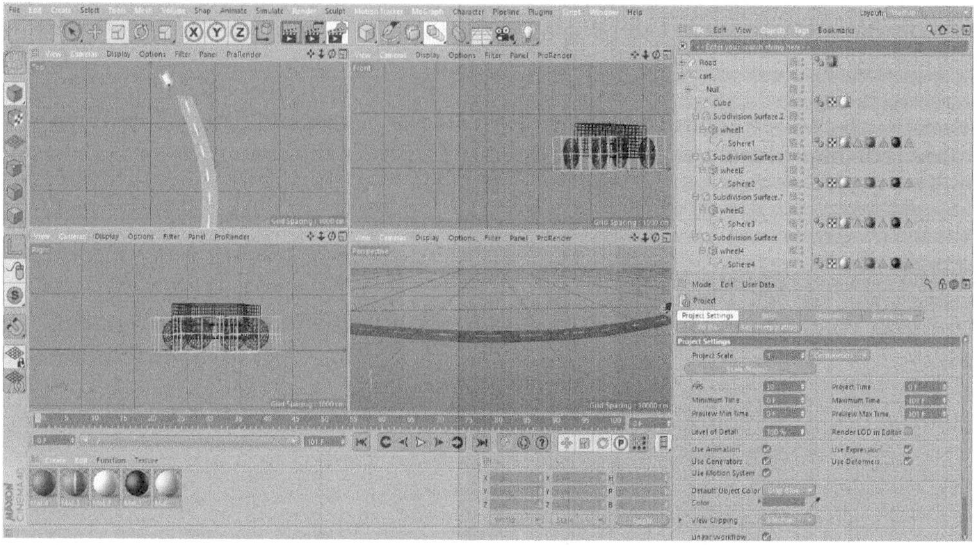

Figure 8-26 The c08_tut3_start file

Aligning the Cart along a Spline Path

In this section, you will align the cart along a spline path using a CINEMA 4D tag.

1. Select *cart* in the Object Manager. Next, right-click on it; a shortcut menu is displayed. Choose **CINEMA 4D Tags > Align to Spline** from the shortcut menu, as shown in Figure 8-27; the **Align to Spline Expression [Align to Spline]** tag is added to the Object Manager, as shown in Figure 8-28.

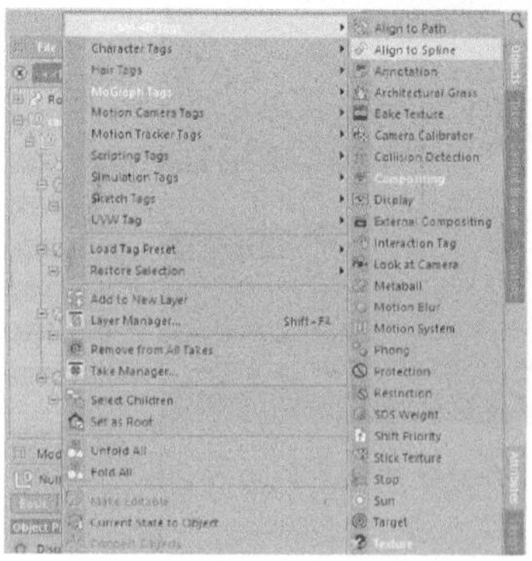

Figure 8-27 *Choosing* ***Align to Spline*** *from the shortcut menu*

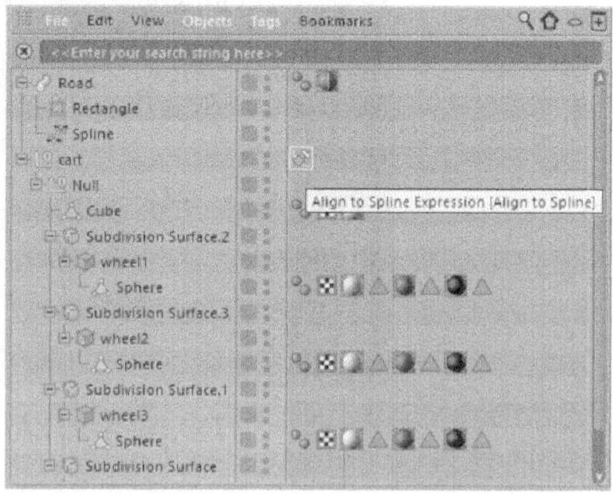

Figure 8-28 *The* ***Align to Spline Expression [Align to Spline]*** *tag in the Object Manager*

2. Expand *Road* in the Object Manager. Also, make sure the **Align to Spline Expression [Align to Spline]** tag is selected in the Object Manager.

3. In the Attribute Manager, make sure the **Tag** button is chosen. Next, choose the Arrow button located next to the **Spline Path** option in the **Tag Properties** area; the shape of the cursor is changed. Next, select *Spline* from the Object Manager; *Spline* is displayed in the **Spline Path** edit box in the Attribute Manager, refer to Figure 8-29. Maximize the Perspective viewport. You will notice that *cart* is aligned with *Road* in the Perspective viewport, as shown in Figure 8-30.

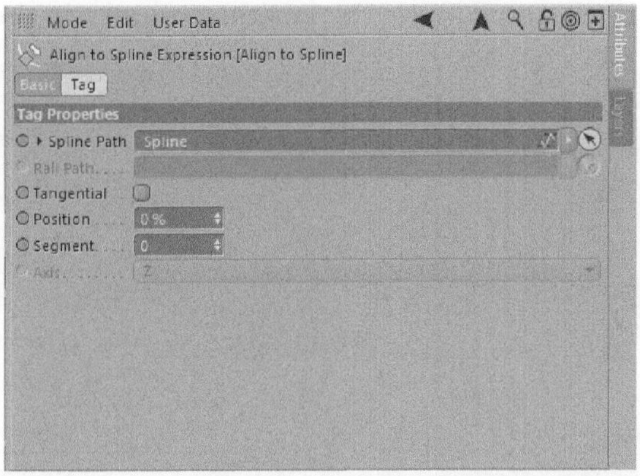

Figure 8-29 *Spline displayed in the **Spline Path** edit box*

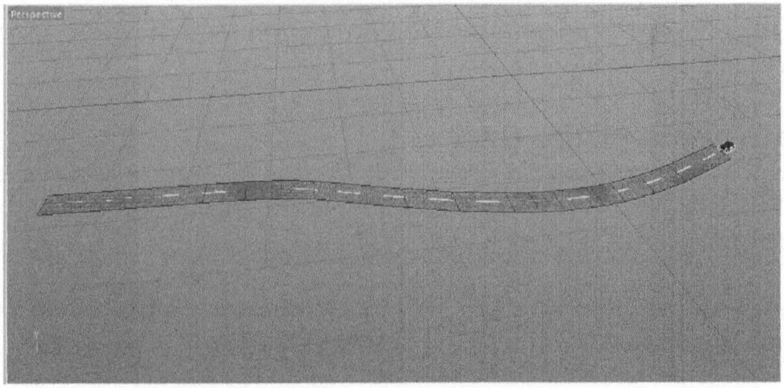

Figure 8-30 *cart aligned with Road*

Moving the Cart

In this section, you will move *cart* by setting the keyframe for the **Position** spinner of the **Align to Spline Expression [Align to Spline]** tag.

1. Make sure the timeslider is at frame 0. In the Attribute Manager, right-click on the circle located at the left of the **Position** spinner in the **Tag Properties** area; a shortcut menu is displayed. Choose **Animation > Add Keyframe** from it; the circle turns red and a keyframe is added at frame 0.

2. Move the time slider to frame 101. Next, in the Attribute Manager, enter **100** in the **Position** spinner.

3. Right-click on the circle located at the left of the **Position** spinner; a shortcut menu is displayed. Choose **Animation > Add Keyframe** from it; the circle turns red and a keyframe is added at frame 101. Also, *cart* is moved to the end of *Road*.

4. Choose the **Play Forwards** button from the Animation toolbar. You will notice that *cart* is not moving exactly along *Road* on its curved stretch, refer to Figure 8-31. To overcome it, select the **Tangential** check box located above the **Position** spinner in the Attribute Manager.

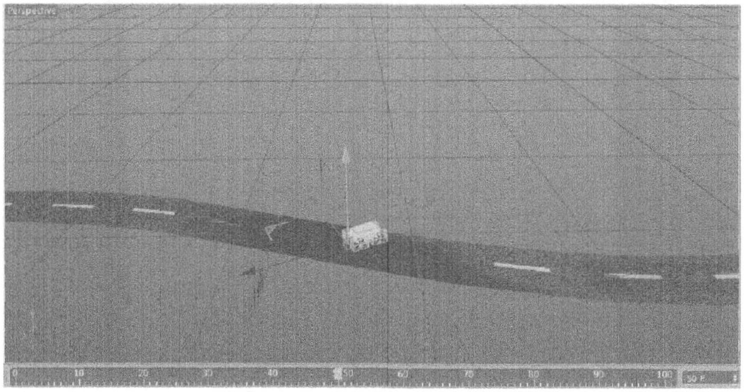

Figure 8-31 *cart at frame 50*

5. Choose the **Play Forwards** button from the Animation toolbar again. Now, you will notice that *cart* is moving exactly along *Road*.

Rotating the Wheels of the Cart

In this section, you will rotate the wheels of *cart* by setting keyframes at different frames to get a realistic look. You will also use the Timeline panel in the **Animation** layout to copy and paste the repetitive keyframes.

1. In the Object Manager, select *Sphere1*. In the Animation toolbar, choose the **Autokeying** button and make sure that the timeslider is set to frame 0.

2. In the Attribute Manager, choose the **Coord** button; the **Coordinates** area is displayed. Next, right-click on the circle located at the left of the **R . H** spinner and choose **Animation > Add Keyframe** from the shortcut menu displayed; a keyframe is added for *Sphere1* at frame 0.

3. Similarly, move the timeslider to the frames mentioned in Table 8-3 and add keyframes by setting the rotation values in the Attribute Manager as given in Table 8-3.

Table 8-3 Rotation values for Sphere1

Frame to be selected	R . H
5	-90
10	-180
15	-270
20	-360
21	0

You will notice that one round of rotation of *wheel1* is completed by setting the keyframes mentioned above.

Next, you need to copy these keyframes to repeat the rotation of *wheel1*. To copy the keyframes, you will use the Timeline panel in the **Animate** layout.

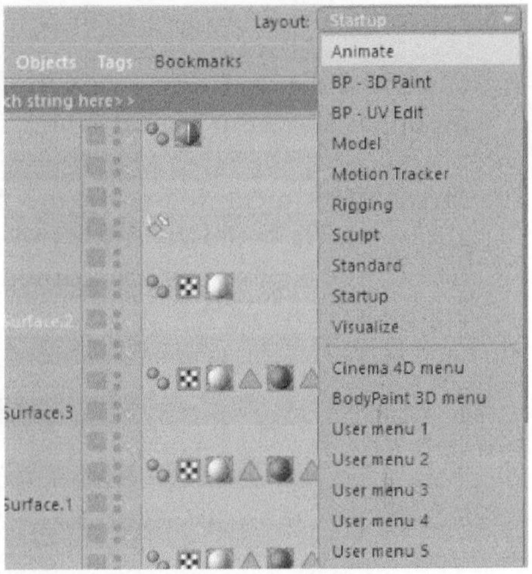

Figure 8-32 Selecting ***Animate*** *from the* ***Layout*** *drop-down list*

4. Select **Animate** from the **Layout** drop-down list located at the top right corner of the interface, as shown in Figure 8-32; the Animation layout is displayed, as shown in Figure 8-33.

5. In the **Animate** layout, enlarge the Timeline panel and zoom in the newly keyframes created using the navigation tools in it, refer to Figure 8-34. Figure 8-34 shows the modified size of the Timeline panel.

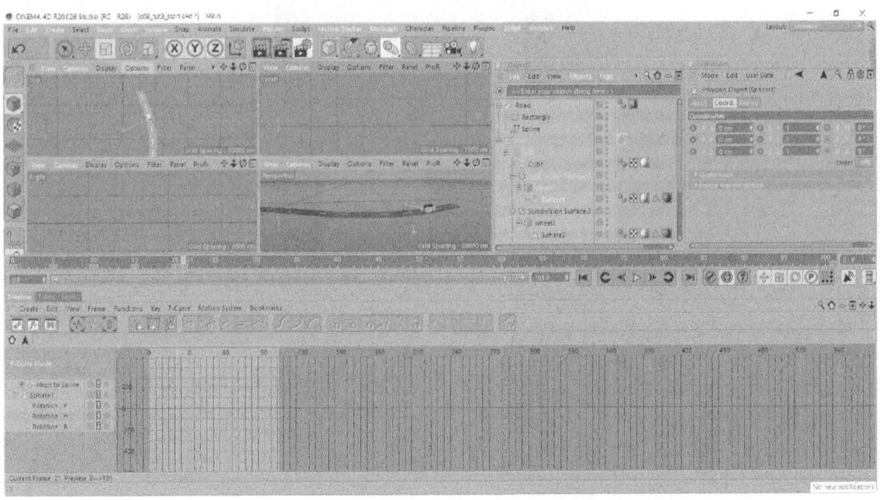

Figure 8-33 The ***Animate*** *layout displayed*

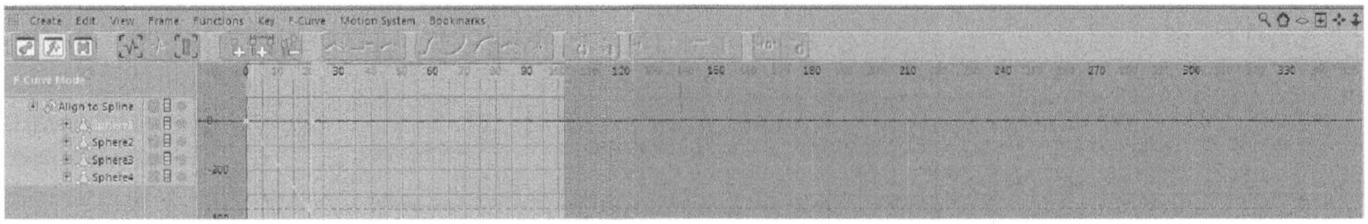

Figure 8-34 The modified size of the Timeline panel

6. Select five keyframes (excluding the keyframe at frame 0) in the Timeline panel by using the rectangular marquee selection, as shown in Figure 8-35.

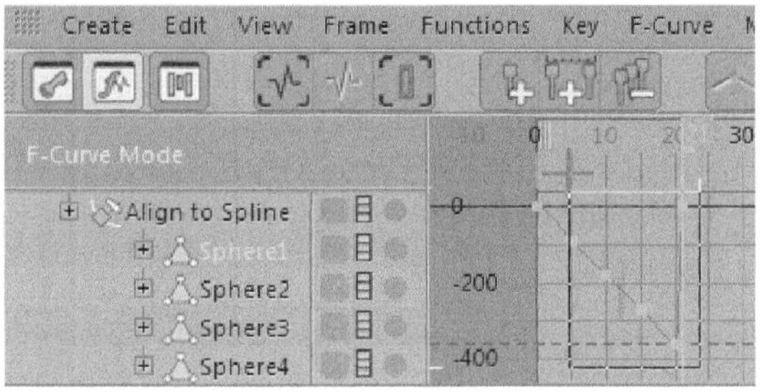

Figure 8-35 Selecting all keyframes

7. Choose **Edit > Copy** from the Timeline menu, as shown in Figure 8-36.

8. Move the timeslider to frame 25. Next, choose **Edit > Paste** from the Timeline menu; the keyframes are copied, refer to Figure 8-37.

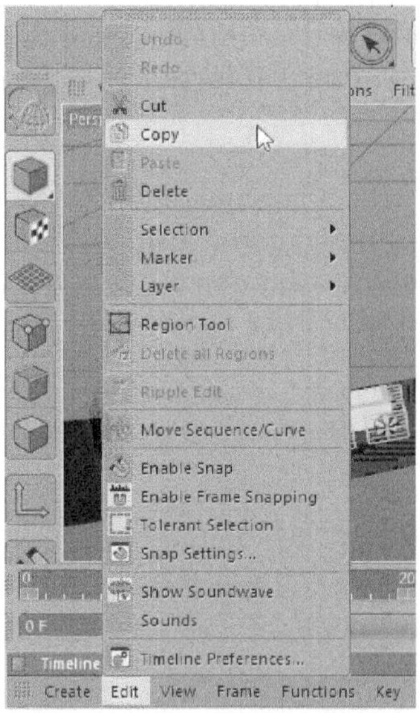

*Figure 8-36 Choosing **Copy** from the **Edit** menu*

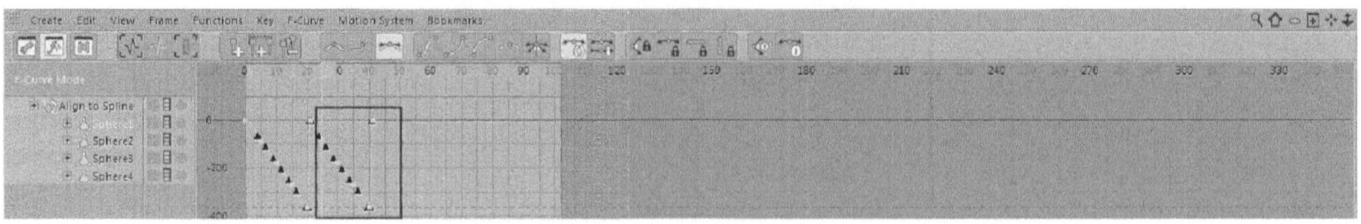

Figure 8-37 Copied keyframes

9. Move the timeslider to frame 45. Next, choose **Edit > Paste** from the Timeline menu; the keyframes are copied.

10. Move the timeslider to frame 65. Next, choose **Edit > Paste** from the Timeline menu; the keyframes are copied.

11. Move the timeslider to frame 85. Next, choose **Edit > Paste** from the Timeline menu; the keyframes are copied. Figure 8-38 shows all keyframes for *Sphere1*.

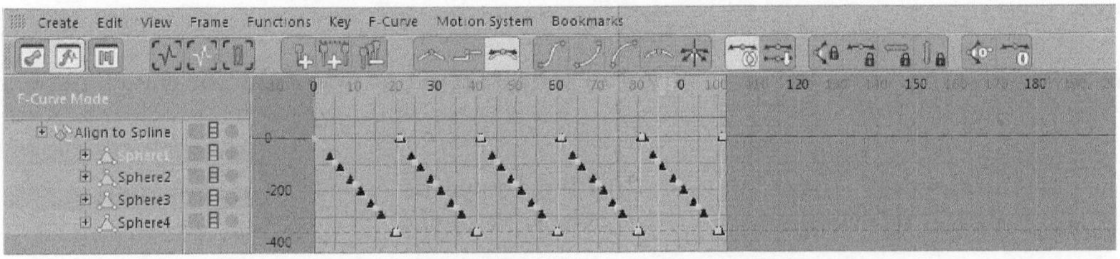

***Figure 8-38** All keyframes for Sphere1*

12. Move the timeslider to frame 0. In the Object Manager, select *Sphere2*.

13. In the Attribute Manager, choose the **Coord** button; the **Coordinates** area is displayed. Next, right-click on the circle located at the left of the **R . H** spinner and choose **Animation > Add Keyframe** from the shortcut menu displayed; a keyframe is added for *Sphere2* at frame 0.

14. Choose the **Dope Sheet** button and then select *Sphere1*. Next, select all keyframes from the Timeline panel using the rectangular marquee selection.

15. Choose **Edit > Copy** from the Timeline menu. Next, select *Sphere2* and make sure the timeslider is at frame 0. Now, choose **Edit > Paste** from the Timeline menu; all keyframes of *Sphere1* are copied to *Sphere2*.

16. Repeat the steps 13 through 15 for *Sphere3* and *Sphere4* in the Object Manager to set keyframes for them.

Saving and Rendering the Animation

In this section, you will save and render the animation. You can also view the final render sequence by downloading the file *c08_cinema4d_r20rndr.zip* from *www.cadcim.com*. The path of the file is mentioned at the beginning of the chapter.

1. Choose the **Edit Render Settings** tool from the Command Palette; the **Render Settings** window is displayed. In this window, choose the **Output** button; the **Output** area is displayed. In this area, enter **101** in the **To** spinner; the **Frames** option gets updated to **102** (from 0 to 101).

2. Choose the **Save** button from the list displayed on the left in the **Render Settings** window; the **Regular Image** area is displayed. In this area, make sure that the **Save** check box is selected. Next, choose the browse button located next to the **File** text box; the **Save File** dialog box is displayed.

3. In the **Save File** dialog box, browse to the location *\Documents\c4dr20\c08* and enter **c08tut3** in the **File name** text box. Next, choose the **Save** button. Select the **AVI Movie** option from the **Format** drop-down list. Next, close the **Render Settings** window.

Self-Evaluation Test

Answer the following questions and then compare them to those given at the end of this chapter:

1. Which of the following buttons is used to set the keys automatically for the changes made in the animation?

(a) **Autokeying** (b) **Play Forwards**
(c) **Edit Render Settings** (d) **Show FCurves**

2. Which of the following options is used to add a keyframe to a selected frame?

(a) **Render to Picture Viewer** (b) **Create Preview**
(c) **Add Keyframe** (d) None of these

3. Which of the following combination of shortcut keys is used to add a keyframe?

(a) SHIFT+LMB (b) CTRL+LMB
(c) CTRL+Click (d) SHIFT+Click

4. __________ is an act of giving life to a 3D object or character.

5. The __________ check box in the Attribute Manager is used to move an object exactly along the path.

Review Questions

Answer the following questions:

1. Which of the following buttons in Animation toolbar is used to play an animation?

(a) **Play Forwards** (b) **Autokeying**
(c) **Keyframe Selection** (d) None of these

2. The __________ panel in the Animation layout is used to copy and paste repetitive keyframes.

3. The __________ button in the **Timeline** window is used to set linear interpolation between the selected keyframes.

4. The __________ spinner is used to manually enter the starting frame of the animation to be rendered.

EXERCISE

The rendered video sequence of the animation in the exercise can be accessed by downloading the *c08_cinema4d_r20_exr.zip* file from *www.cadcim.com*. The path of the file is as follows: *Textbooks > Animation and Visual Effects > MAXON CINEMA 4D > MAXON CINEMA 4D R20 Studio: A Tutorial Approach*

Exercise 1

Open the model shown in Figure 8-39 and then animate the keys falling from the table. Also, fine-tune the animation. **(Expected time: 35 min)**

Figure 8-39 *The c08_exr01_start file*

Answers to Self-Evaluation Test

1. a, **2.** c, **3.** c, **4.** Animation, **5. Tangential**

Chapter 9

Introduction to UV Mapping

Learning Objectives

After completing this chapter, you will be able to:

- *Work in different UV layouts*
- *Unwrap 3D models*
- *Paint texture on 3D models*

INTRODUCTION

UV mapping is a process to project texture maps onto a 3D object. UVs are two dimensional texture coordinates that define a two dimensional coordinate system called UV texture space. The letters U and V in UV indicate the axes in the coordinate space. You can use the UV texture space to place image maps on a 3D surface in CINEMA 4D. UV mapping is a method used to provide a connection between a 3D model and the image or the texture map to be mapped on it. In CINEMA 4D, you need to UV map the model to apply a texture on it.

The BodyPaint 3D layout in CINEMA 4D is used to create and edit UV maps. In this chapter, you will learn to UV map the models and project textures on them. Also, you will learn to paint textures on the models using the Body Paint 3D.

TUTORIAL

Before you start the tutorials of this chapter, you need to download the *c09_cinema4d_r20_tut.zip* file from *www.cadcim.com*. The path of the file is as follows: *Textbooks > Animation and Visual Effects > MAXON CINEMA 4D > MAXON CINEMA 4D R20 Studio: A Tutorial Approach*

Next, you need to browse to *\Documents\c4dr20* and create a new folder in it with the name *c09*. Next, extract the contents of the zip file in this folder.

Tutorial 1

In this tutorial, you will texture a 3D model of pencil and eraser. The final output is shown in Figure 9-1. **(Expected time: 60 min)**

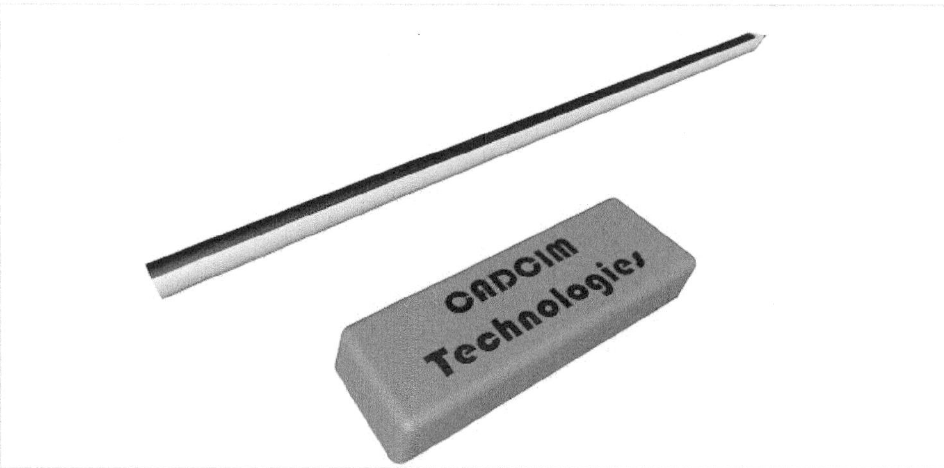

Figure 9-1 *The final output*

The following steps are required to complete this tutorial:

a. Open the file.
b. Assign materials to the pencil and eraser.
c. Unwrap the pencil.
d. Create the texture of the pencil in Adobe Photoshop.

e. Unwrap the eraser.
f. Create texture of the eraser in Adobe Photoshop.
g. Save and render the scene.

Opening the File

In this section, you will open the file.

1. Choose **File > Open** from the main menu; the **Open File** dialog box is displayed.

2. In the **Open File** dialog box, browse to *\Documents\c4dr20\c09\c09_tut1_start* and then choose the **Open** button; the *c09_tut1_start.c4d* file is opened, as shown in Figure 9-2.

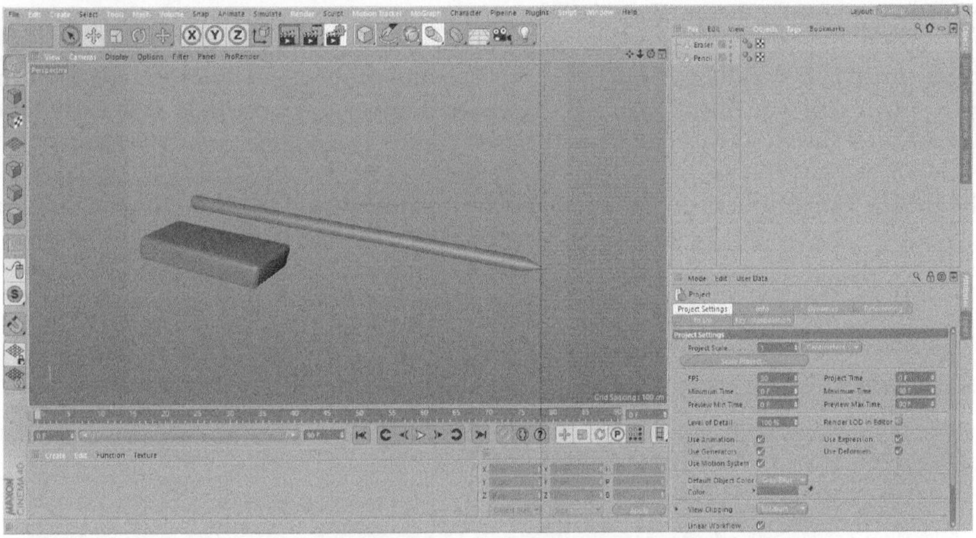

Figure 9-2 *The c09_tut1_start.c4d file*

Assigning Materials to the Pencil and Eraser

In this section, you will assign materials to pencil and eraser.

1. Double-click in the empty area of the Material Manager; a new material is created in the Material Manager.

2. Make sure that the new material is selected in the Material Manager. In the Attribute Manager, choose the **Basic** button; the **Basic Properties** area is displayed. In the **Basic Properties** area, enter **matPencil** in the **Name** text box; the new material is renamed as *matPencil* in the Material Manager.

3. Press and hold the left mouse button and drag the *matPencil* material from the Material Manager and drop it on *Pencil* in the Object Manager; the material is applied to *Pencil* in the Perspective viewport, as shown in Figure 9-3.

   Next, you will assign material to *Eraser*.

4. Double-click in the empty area of the Material Manager; a new material is created in the Material Manager.

5. Make sure that the new material is selected in the Material Manager. In the Attribute Manager, make sure that the **Basic** button is chosen. In the **Basic Properties** area, enter **matEraser** in the **Name** text box; the new material is renamed as *matEraser*.

6. Press and hold the left mouse button and drag the *matEraser* material from the Material Manager and drop it on *Eraser* in the Object Manager; the material is assigned to *Eraser*.

Unwrapping the Pencil

In this section, you will unwrap *Pencil*.

1. Select the **BP UV Edit** option from the **Layout** drop-down list located at the upper right corner of the interface, as shown in Figure 9-4; the **BP UV Edit** layout is displayed, as shown in Figure 9-5.

   The **BP UV Edit** layout is considered to be the default layout for UV editing in CINEMA 4D.

Figure 9-3 The material applied to Pencil

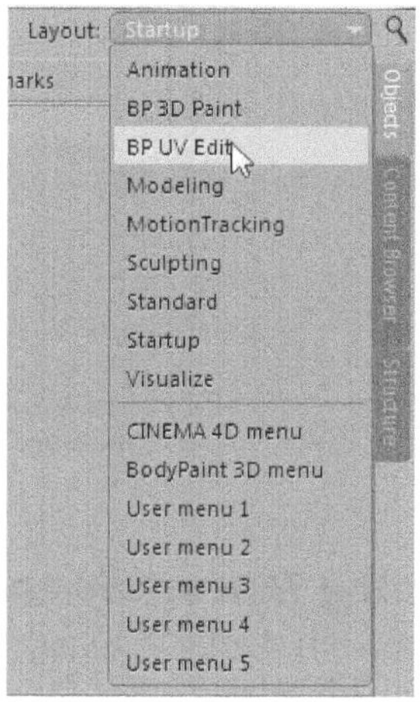

*Figure 9-4 The **Layout** drop-down list*

2. Select *Pencil* from the **Objects** tab and then choose the **Paint Setup Wizard** tool from the Command Palette, as shown in Figure 9-6; the **BodyPaint 3D Setup Wizard** dialog box is displayed, as shown in Figure 9-7.

   The **Paint Setup Wizard** tool is used to prepare the model for painting textures on it. It is the initial step in the process of UV editing. It also helps in adding missing materials and textures.

   The options in the **Select Objects** area of the **BodyPaint 3D Setup Wizard** dialog box are used to select all those objects or materials that are to be modified using the **Paint Setup Wizard** tool.

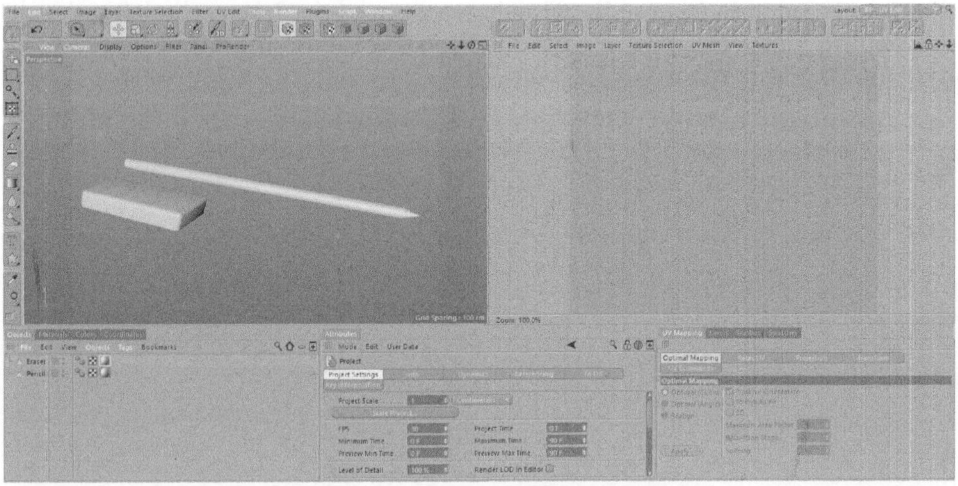

***Figure 9-5** The **BP UV Edit** layout*

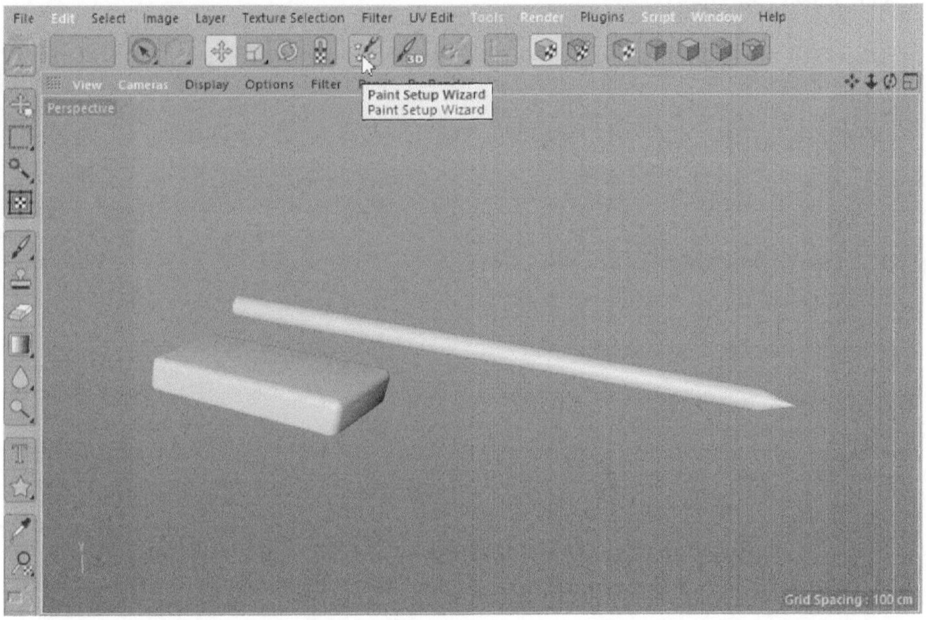

***Figure 9-6** Choosing the **Paint Setup Wizard** tool from the Command Palette*

3. In the **BodyPaint 3D Setup Wizard** dialog box, make sure that the **Objects** radio button is selected. Next, click on the green tick corresponding to the **Eraser** option. Now, choose the **Next >>** button; the **STEP 2: UV Setup** area is displayed in the **BodyPaint 3D Setup Wizard** dialog box, as shown in Figure 9-8.

   The options in the **UV Setup** area are used to calculate the UV mesh.

4. Clear the **Single Material Mode** check box from the **BodyPaint 3D Setup Wizard** dialog box. Now, choose the **Next >>** button; the **STEP 3: Material Options** area is displayed,

as shown in Figure 9-9. Choose the **Finish >>** button; the UV mesh of *Pencil* is displayed in the Texture View, as shown in Figure 9-10. Now, choose the **Close** button to close the **BodyPaint 3D Setup Wizard** dialog box.

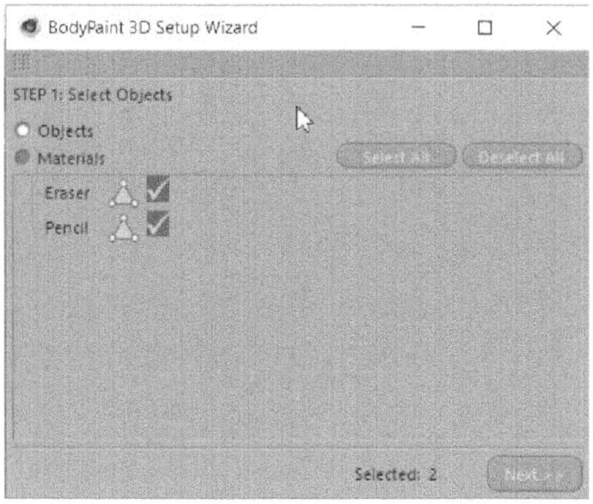

*Figure 9-7 The **BodyPaint 3D Setup Wizard** dialog box*

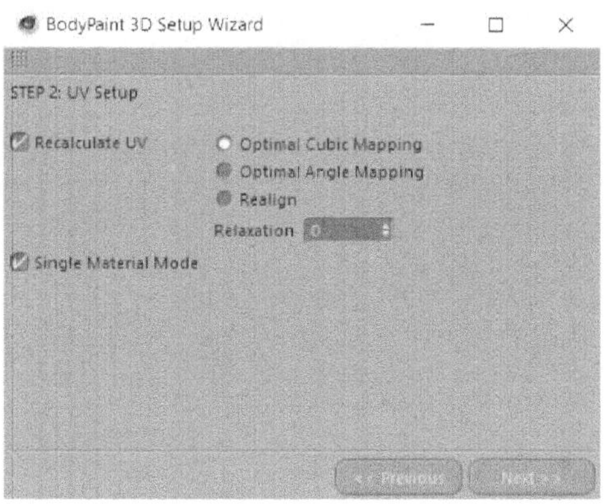

*Figure 9-8 The **STEP 2: UV Setup** area*

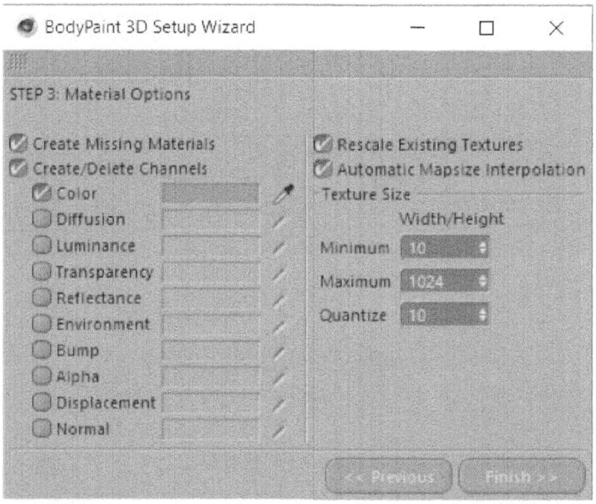

*Figure 9-9 The **Material Options** area in the **BodyPaint 3D Setup Wizard** dialog box*

The **Single Material Mode** check box is selected to ensure that the selected object will have a single material. The options in the **STEP 3: Material Options** area are used to choose the channels to be painted along with their fill colors. Also, they are used to choose the textures to be scaled if any.

Note

*If the UV mesh is not displayed in the Texture View, choose **UV Mesh > Show UV Mesh** from the Texture View menu; the UV mesh of the model is displayed in the Texture View.*

5. Make sure that *matPencil_Color.tif* is chosen in the **Textures** menu of the Texture View menu, refer to Figure 9-11. Make sure the **UV Polygons** tool is chosen in the Command Palette.

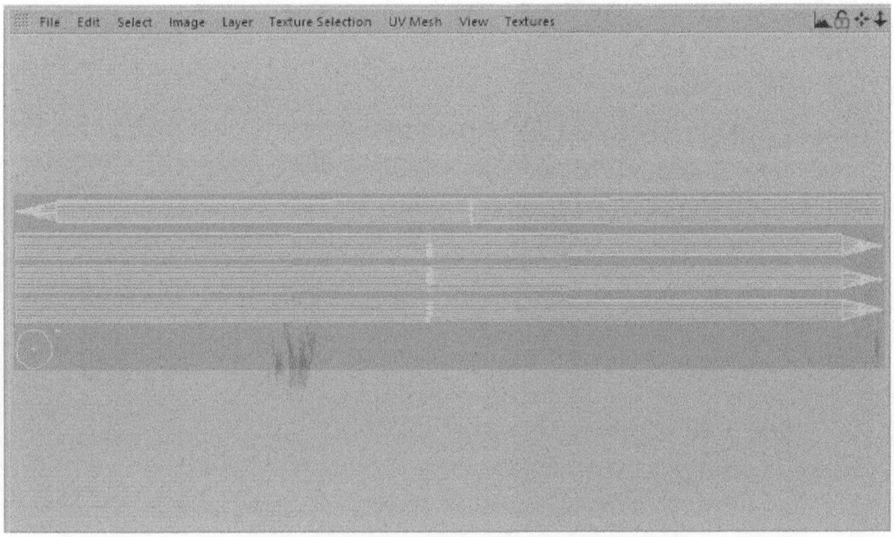

Figure 9-10 The UV Mesh of Pencil

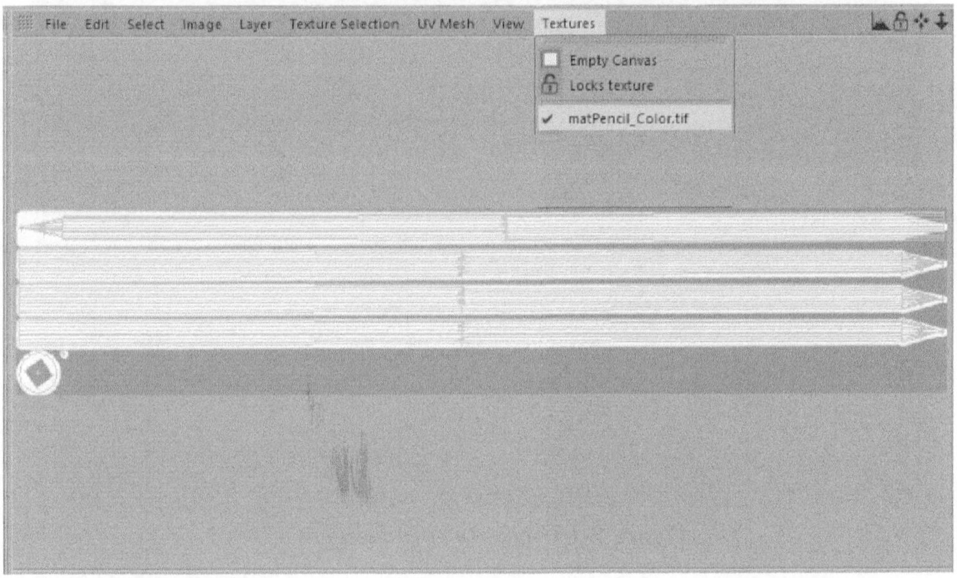

Figure 9-11 *The matPencil_Color.tif option chosen from the **Textures** menu*

6. Choose the **Live Selection** tool from the Command Palette and select the polygons of the UV mesh of *Pencil* in the Texture View, as shown in Figure 9-12. Next, choose the **Mirror U** tool from the Texture View Command Palette to flip the selected UVs, refer to Figure 9-13. 

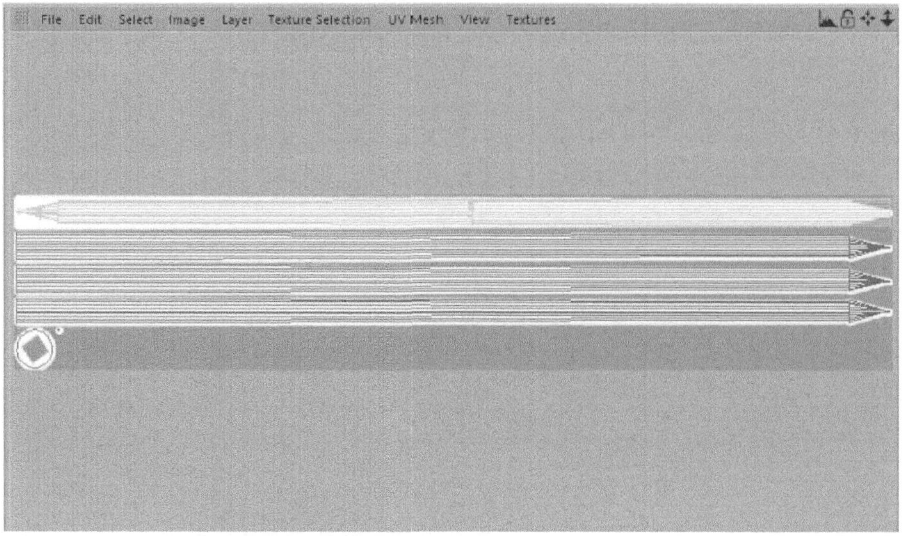

Figure 9-12 The selected polygons of Pencil

Figure 9-13 The mirrored polygons

7. Press CTRL+A to select all the UV polygons of *Pencil*.

8. Choose **Layer > Outline Polygons** from the Texture View menu; the polygons are outlined, as shown in Figure 9-14.

   The **Outline Polygons** option is used to add a stroke to the selected UV polygons with a color.

9. Make sure that the polygons are selected in the Texture View and choose **File > Save Texture as** from the Texture View menu; the **Please choose the file format** dialog box is displayed.

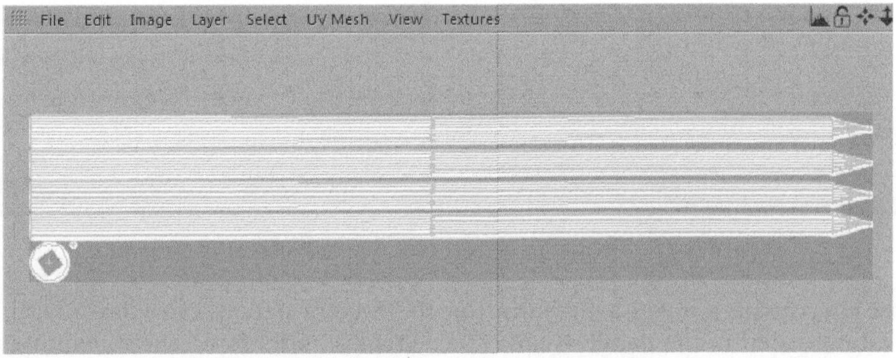

Figure 9-14 The outlined polygons

10. Select the **Photoshop (PSD) (*.psd)** option from the **Save File as** drop-down list in the **Please choose the file format** dialog box. Next, choose the **OK** button; the **Save Channel as *.psd** dialog box is displayed. In the **Save Channel as *.psd** dialog box, enter **texturePencil** in the **File name** text box. Next, browse to the location *\Documents\c4dr20\c09* and choose the **Save** button; the file is saved at the specified location.

Note
In this tutorial, Adobe Photoshop CC is used , wherever required, for working on Photoshop files.

Creating the Texture of the Pencil in Adobe Photoshop

In this section, you will create texture for pencil using Adobe Photoshop.

1. Open the *texturePencil.psd* file in Adobe Photoshop. The file opens in the canvas area and a layer with the name **Background** is displayed in the **Layers** panel. Double-click on the **Background** layer in the **Layers** panel; the **New Layer** dialog box is displayed. In this dialog box, choose the **OK** button; the **Background** layer is unlocked and replaced with **Layer 0** in the **Layers** panel.

2. Choose the **Create a new layer** button from the **Layers** panel; a new layer with the name **Layer 1** is created in the **Layers** panel.

3. Select **Layer 0** from the **Layers** panel. Choose **Magic Wand Tool** from the Tool Box and then click on the first white strip in the canvas to make a selection. Next, press and hold SHIFT and then click on the third strip to add it to the selection. Now, select **Layer 1** layer from the **Layers** panel.

4. Select yellow color for the **Set Foreground Color** swatch in the Tool Box and then press ALT+BACKSPACE; the selection is filled with yellow color, as shown in Figure 9-15. Next, press CTRL+D to clear the selection.

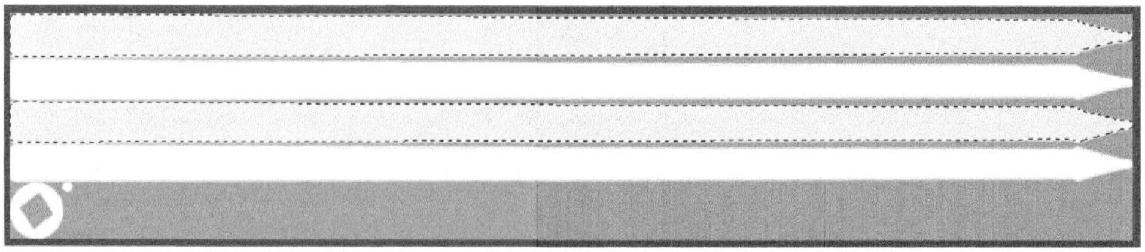

Figure 9-15 The yellow color in the selected area of the canvas

5. Choose the **Create a new Layer** button in the **Layers** panel; a new layer with the name **Layer 2** is created in the panel. Next, repeat steps 3 and 4 to fill the remaining two strips with the black color, refer to Figure 9-16. Similarly, fill the remaining white areas with the black color.

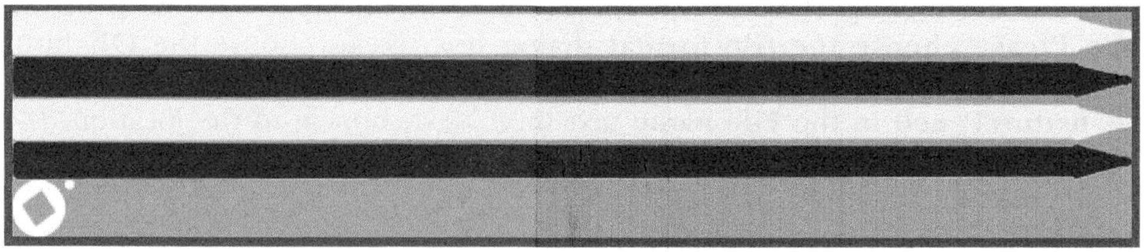

Figure 9-16 The black color in the selected area of the canvas

Next, you will color the tip of the pencil.

6. Create a new layer and invoke **Brush Tool** in the Tool Box. Next, paint colors in the tip area of the pencil, as shown in Figure 9-17.

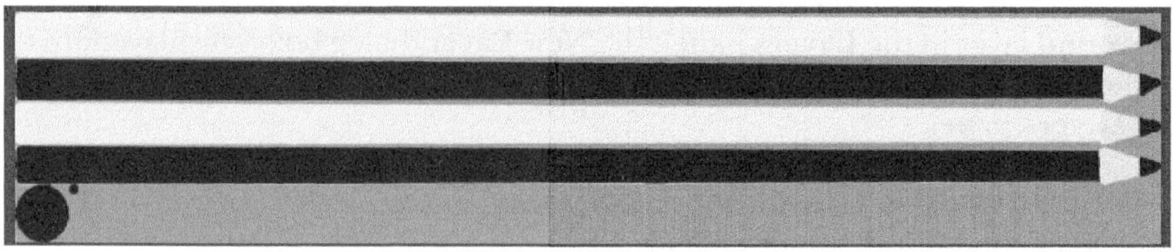

Figure 9-17 Color filled in the remaining parts of pencil

7. Choose **File > Save As** from the main menu; the **Save As** dialog box is displayed. In this dialog box, enter *texturePencilColor* in the **File Name** text box and make sure that **Photoshop (*.PSD;*.PDD)** is selected in the **Save as type** drop-down list. Next, browse to *\Documents\c4dr20\c09* and choose the **Save** button; the file is saved at the specified location.

   Next, you will switch back to CINEMA 4D and apply the texture created in Photoshop to *Pencil*.

8. Double-click on **Texture Tag "matPencil"** in the Object Manager; the **Material [matPencil]** settings area is displayed in the Attribute Manager. In this area, choose the **Color** button, refer to Figure 9-18. In the **Color** area, choose the browse button located next to the **Texture** option; the **Open File** dialog box is displayed.

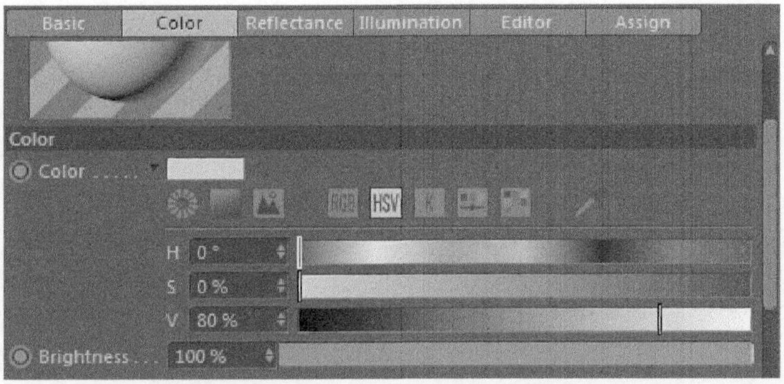

Figure 9-18 *Choosing the browse button in the Attribute Manager*

9. Browse to *\Documents\c4dr20\c09\texturePencilColor.psd*; the texture is applied to *Pencil* in the Perspective viewport; as shown in Figure 9-19. You need to deselect polygons to properly view the texture in the Perspective viewport. Next, choose **Textures > texturePencilColor.psd** from the Texture View menu; the texture becomes visible in the Texture View.

Figure 9-19 *The texture applied to Pencil*

Unwrapping the Eraser

In this section, you will unwrap *Eraser*.

1. Make sure that the **BP UV Edit** option is selected from the **Layout** drop-down list. Next, select *Eraser* in the **Objects** tab.

2. Make sure the **UV Polygons** tool is chosen from the Command Palette and then select the top polygon of *Eraser*, as shown in Figure 9-20.

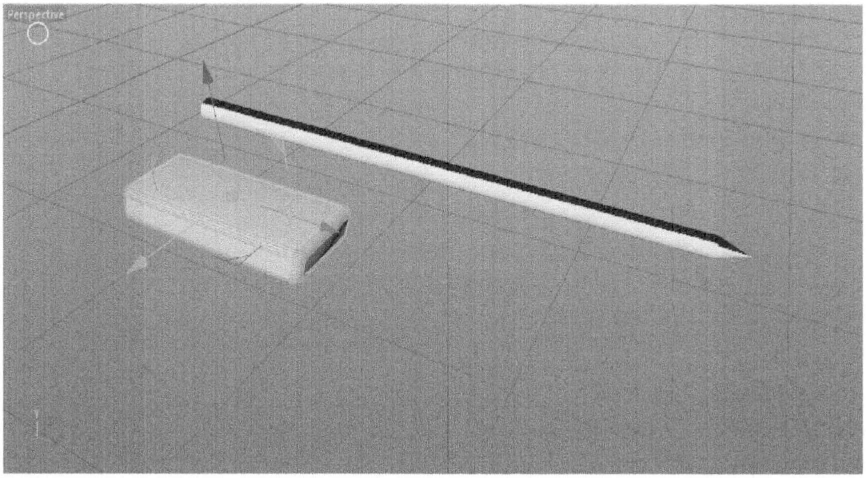

Figure 9-20 The top polygon of the Eraser selected

3. Maximize the Top viewport. Make sure the cursor is on the Top viewport and then press O to frame *Eraser*.

4. Choose **File > New Texture** from the Texture View menu; the **New Texture** dialog box is displayed. In this dialog box, enter **r** in the **Name** field and then choose the **OK** button to close the dialog box.

5. In the **UV Mapping** tab, choose the **Projection** button and then choose the **Frontal** button.

   The **Frontal** button is used to project the texture from the camera position.

6. Make sure the **UV Polygons** tool is chosen from the Command Palette and make sure that the polygon is selected in the Texture View. Next, align the UV polygon in the Texture View using the **Scale** and **Move** tools, refer to Figure 9-21.

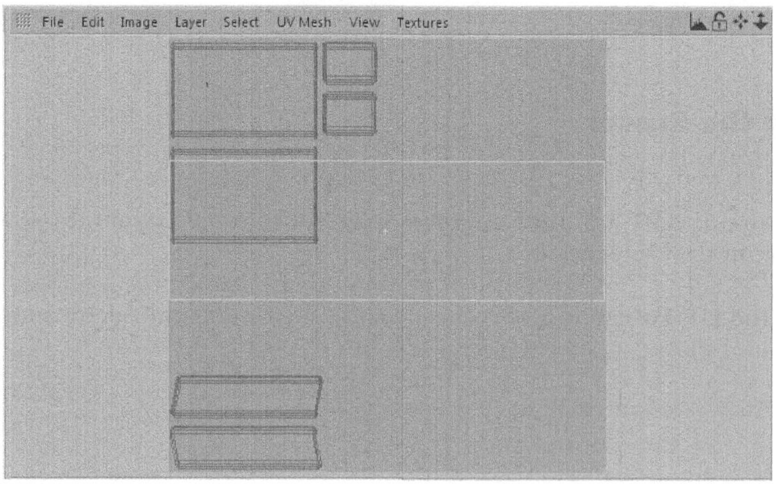

Figure 9-21 The top polygon aligned in the Texture View

7. Choose **Layer > New Layer** from the Texture View menu to create a new layer.

   The **New Layer** option creates a new layer in the **Layers** tab. You can use this layer to outline the polygons. When you will export this layer to Photoshop, the polygon outlines will be created in a new Photoshop layer.

8. Choose **Layer > Outline Polygons** from the Texture View menu; the polygon is outlined.

9. Choose **File > Save Texture as** from the Texture View menu; the **Please choose the file format** dialog box is displayed.

10. Select the **Photoshop (PSD) (*.psd)** option from the **Save File as** drop-down list in the **Please choose the file format** dialog box. Next, choose the **OK** button; the **Save Channel as *.psd** dialog box is displayed. In the **Save Channel as *.psd** dialog box, enter **textureEraser** in the **File name** text box. Next, browse to the location *\Documents\c4dr20\c09* and choose the **Save** button; the file is saved at the specified location.

Creating the Texture of Eraser in Adobe Photoshop

In this section, you need to create a texture for *Eraser* using Adobe Photoshop.

1. Open the *textureEraser.psd* file in Adobe Photoshop. The file opens in the canvas area and two layers with the name **Background** and **Layer** are displayed in the **Layers** panel. Double-click on the **Background** layer in the **Layers** panel; the **New Layer** dialog box is displayed. In this dialog box, choose the **OK** button; the **Background** layer is unlocked and replaced with **Layer 0** in the **Layers** panel.

2. Make sure **Layer 0** is selected in the **Layers** panel and then set the following values in the **Set Foreground Color** swatch in the Tool Box:

   R: **126** G: **131** B:**137**

3. Press ALT+BACKSPACE; the Layer 0 is filled with the specified color.

4. Choose the **Horizontal Type Tool** from the Tool Box and then type the words **CADCIM Technologies**. Use font type and font size of your choice. Use black color for the font color. Make sure that the text should be placed inside the white outline only, as shown in Figure 9-22.

***Figure 9-22** The text placed inside the white outline*

5. Click on the eye icon of the **Layer** layer in the **Layers** panel to turn off its visibility.

6. Choose **File > Save As** from the main menu; the **Save As** dialog box is displayed. In this dialog box, enter **textureEraserColor** in the **File Name** text box. Next, select **Photoshop (*.PSD; *.PDD)** from the **Save as type** drop-down list. Next, browse to *\Documents\c4dr20\c09* and choose the **Save** button; the file is saved at the specified location.

   Next, you will switch back to CINEMA 4D and apply the texture created in Photoshop to *Eraser*.

7. Choose **File > Open Texture** from the Texture View menu; the **Open File** dialog box is displayed. In this dialog box, browse to *\Documents\c4dr20\c09\textureEraserColor.psd* and then choose the **Open** button; the texture is displayed in the Texture View.

8. Maximize the Perspective viewport. Hover the cursor over the Perspective viewport and then press O to frame the eraser in the scene. Double-click on **Texture Tag "matEraser"** in the Object Manager; the **Color** area is displayed in the Attribute Manager. In the **Color** area, choose the browse button located next to the **Texture** option; the **Open File** dialog box is displayed.

9. Browse to *\Documents\c4dr20\c09\textureEraserColor.psd*; the texture is applied on *Eraser* in the Perspective viewport, as shown in Figure 9-23.

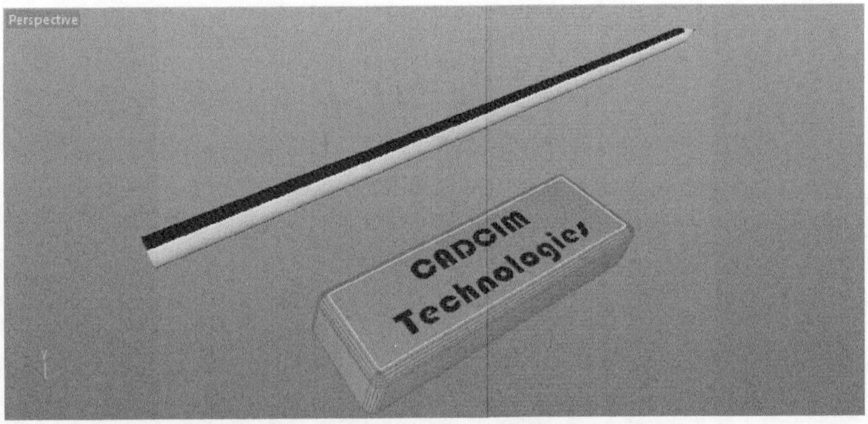

Figure 9-23 The texture applied to Eraser

Saving and Rendering the Scene

In this section, you will save and render the scene. You can also view the final render of the composition by downloading the file *c09_cinema4d_r20_rndr.zip* from *www.cadcim.com*. The path of the file is mentioned at the beginning of the chapter.

1. Change the background color of the scene to white, as discussed in earlier chapters.

2. Choose **File > Save As** from the main menu; the **Save File** dialog box is displayed. In this dialog box, browse to the location *\Documents\c4dr20\c09*.

3. Enter **c09tut1** in the **File name** text box and then choose the **Save** button.

4. In the Perspective viewport, set the camera angle using the Viewport Navigation Tools located on the top right of the Perspective viewport. Next, you need to render the scene. For rendering, refer to Tutorial 1 of Chapter 2.

   The output of the model is shown in Figure 9-1.

Tutorial 2

In this tutorial, you will paint texture on a 3D model using the **BodyPaint 3D** tool. The final output is shown in Figure 9-24. **(Expected time: 30 min)**

The following steps are required to complete this tutorial:

a. Open the file.
b. Unwrap the body of the model.
c. Paint the body of the model.
d. Paint clothes of the model.
e. Save and render the scene.

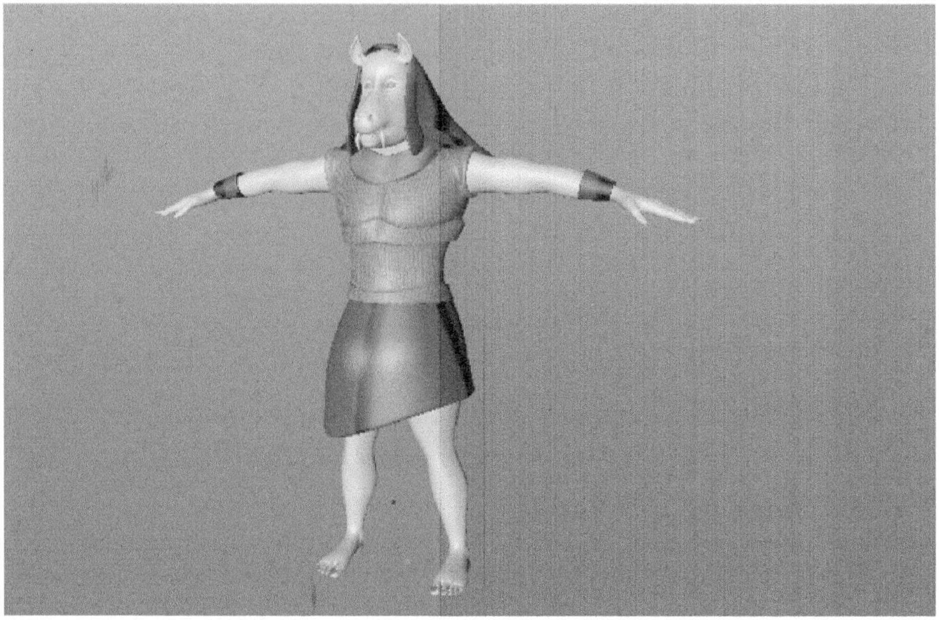

Figure 9-24 The 3D model after applying body paint

Opening the File

In this section, you will open the file.

1. Choose **File > Open** from the main menu; the **Open File** dialog box is displayed.

2. In the **Open File** dialog box, browse to *\Documents\c4dr20\c09\c09_tut2_start* and then choose the **Open** button; the *c09_tut2_start.c4d* file is opened, as shown in Figure 9-25.

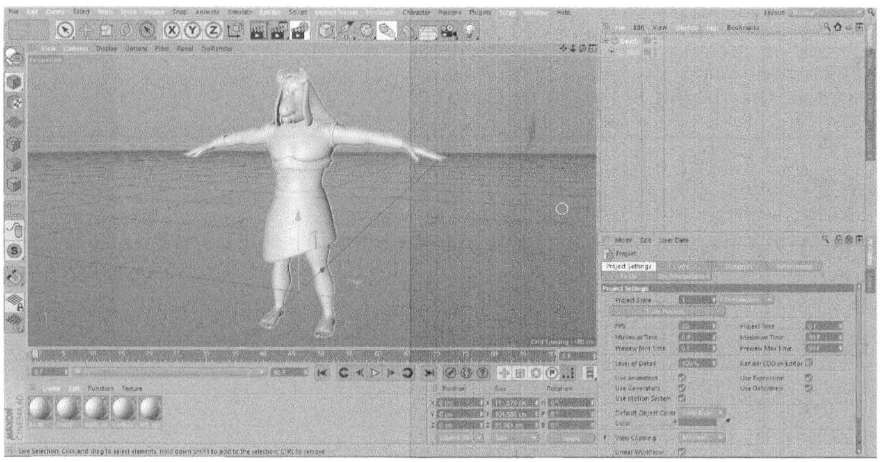

Figure 9-25 The c09_tut2_start.c4d file

Unwrapping the Body of the Model

In this section, you will unwrap the body of the model.

1. Make sure that the **BP UV Edit** option is selected from the **Layout** drop-down list.

2. Make sure *beast* is selected in the Object Manager and choose the **Paint Setup Wizard** tool from the Command Palette; the **BodyPaint 3D Setup Wizard** dialog box is displayed.

3. In the **BodyPaint 3D Setup Wizard** dialog box, make sure that the **Objects** radio button is selected. Next, choose the **Next>>** button; the **UV Setup** area is displayed in the **BodyPaint 3D Setup Wizard** dialog box, refer to Figure 9-8.

4. In the **BodyPaint 3D Setup Wizard** dialog box, choose the **Next>>** button; the **Material Options** area is displayed. Now, choose the **Finish >>** button and the **Close** button to close the dialog box.

Painting the Body of the Model

In this section, you will paint the body of the model.

1. Make sure that the **BP UV Edit** option is selected from the **Layout** drop-down list.

2. In the Object Manager, expand *Beast* and then expand *Null*. Now, select *Body* from the list of objects displayed.

3. Choose the **Colors** tab; the **Color** area is displayed, refer to Figure 9-26. Also, choose the **RGB** button. In the **Color** area, set the parameters as follows:

   R: **239** G: **200** B: **159**

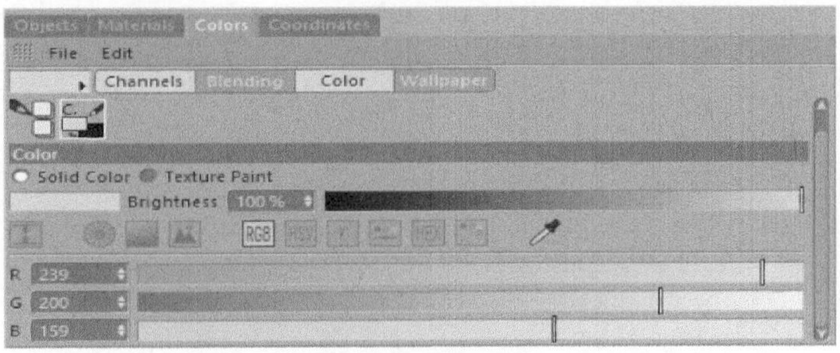

Figure 9-26 The ***Color*** *area displayed*

4. Choose **Tools > Paint Tools > Fill Bitmap** from the main menu, as shown in Figure 9-27.

   The **Fill Bitmap** tool is used to fill the adjoining pixels with the selected color on a single click.

5. Using the **Fill Bitmap** tool, click on *Body* of the model in the Perspective viewport; *Body* is filled with the selected color, as shown in Figure 9-28.

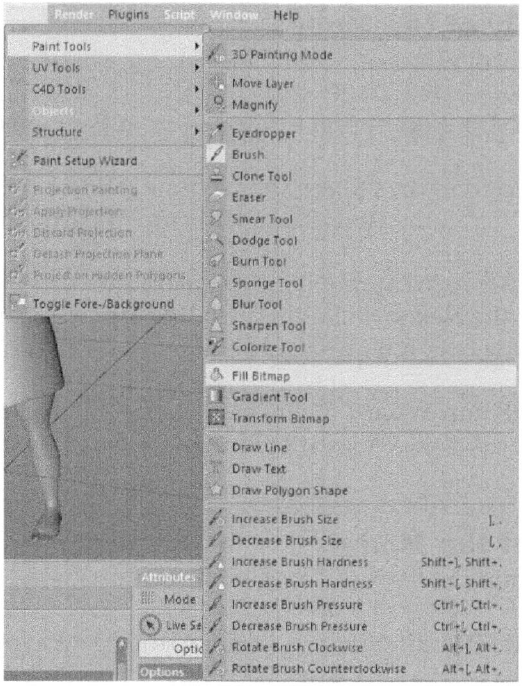

*Figure 9-27 Choosing **Paint Tools > Fill Bitmap** tool from the **Tools** menu*

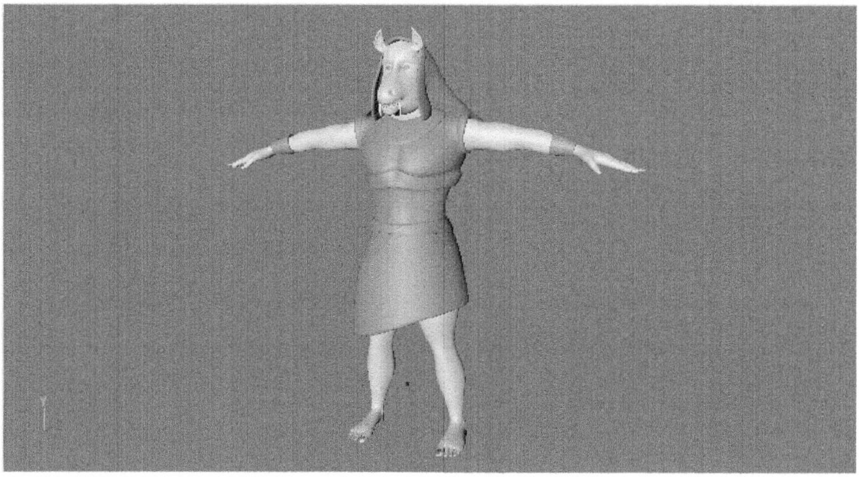

Figure 9-28 The model filled with the selected color in the Perspective viewport

Next, you will paint *chest* of the model.

6. In the **BP UV Edit** layout, choose the **Objects** tab; the Object Manager is displayed.

7. Select *chest* from the Object Manager. Now, choose the **Colors** tab; the **Color** area is displayed. In this area, select the **Texture Paint** radio button.

8. Choose the arrow button located below the **Texture Paint** radio button; a flyout is displayed. Choose the **Load from Disc** option from the flyout; the **Select a Pattern** dialogue box is displayed. Now, select the **Armour.jpg** file from the list.

9. Move the cursor on *chest* and click; the texture gets applied on *chest*, as shown in Figure 9-29.

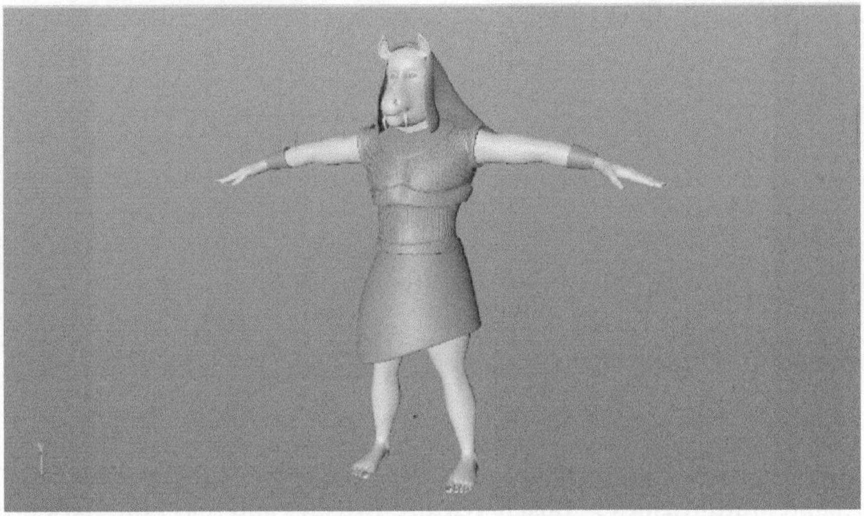

Figure 9-29 *The color filled on chest*

Painting the Clothes of the Model

In this section, you will paint the clothes of the model.

1. Make sure that the **BP UV Edit** option is selected from the **Layout** drop-down list.

2. Choose the **Objects** tab; the Object Manager is displayed. Select *Clothes* from the Object Manager.

3. Choose the **Colors** tab; the **Color** area is displayed. In this area, select the **Solid Color** radio button. Next, choose the **RGB** button and set the values for the parameters as follows:

   R: **106** G: **68** B: **29**

4. Choose **Tools > Paint Tools > Fill Bitmap** from the main menu. Next, click on *Clothes*; *Clothes* is filled with the selected color.

5. Choose the **Colors** tab; the **Color** area is displayed. In this area, enter **3** in the **Brightness** spinner.

6. Choose the **Brushes** tab from the bottom right side of the **BP UV Edit** layout. Next, expand **Default Presets> BodyPaint Presets> Brushes**: the list of brushes is displayed.

7. Expand the **Standard Tools** group of brushes by clicking on the triangle located on the left side. Next, select the **Airbrush** brush.

8. Choose the **Brush** tool from the Modes Palette and paint the clothes of the model, refer to Figure 9-30.

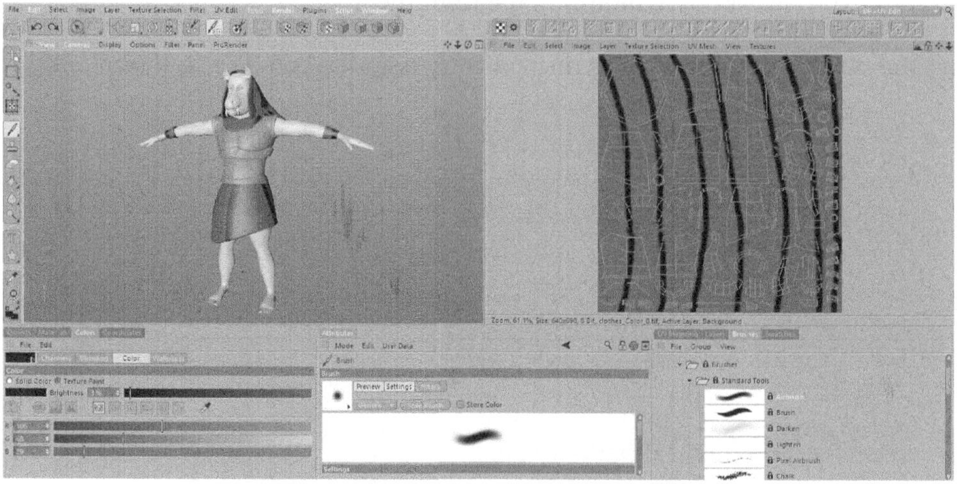

Figure 9-30 *The clothes painted using the **Brush** tool*

9. Make sure the **Brushes** tab is chosen on the bottom right side of the **BP UV Edit** layout. Next, expand **Multibrushes > Dosch Texture Brushes** and select the **Bark** brush.

10. Choose the **Settings** button in the **Attributes** tab; the **Settings** area is displayed. In this area, enter **2** in the **Hardness** spinner.

11. Choose the **Brush** tool from the Modes Palett and paint on the clothes of the model, as shown in Figure 9-31.

Saving and Rendering the Scene

In this section, you will save and render the scene. You can also view the final render of the model by downloading the file *c09_cinema4d_r20_rndr.zip* from *www.cadcim.com*. The path of the file is mentioned at the beginning of the chapter.

1. Choose **File > Save As** from the main menu; the **Save File** dialog box is displayed. In this dialog box, browse to the location *\Documents\c4dr20\c09.*

2. Enter **c09tut2** in the **File name** text box and then choose the **Save** button.

3. In the Perspective viewport, set the camera angle using the Viewport Navigation Tools located on the top right of the Perspective viewport. Next, you need to render the scene. For rendering, refer to Tutorial 1 of Chapter 2.

   The output of the model is shown in Figure 9-31.

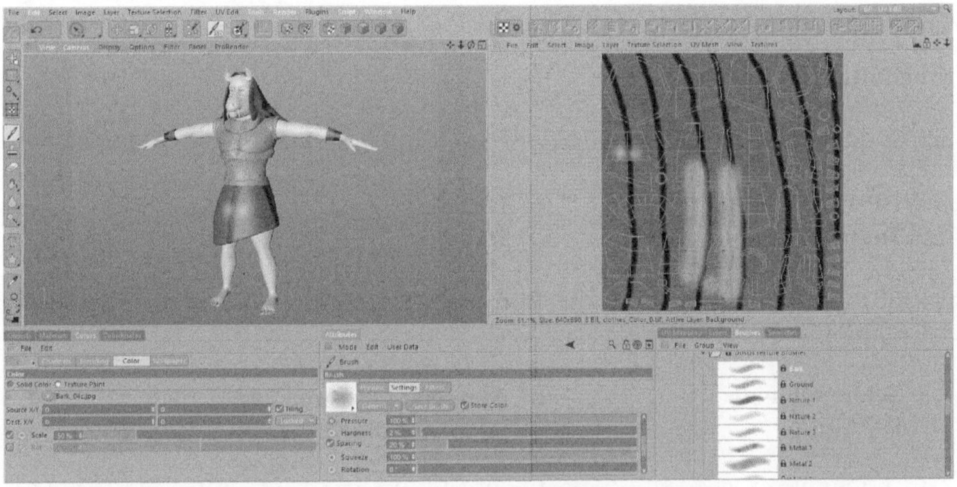

*Figure 9-31 The clothes painted using the **Brush** tool in the Texture View*

Self-Evaluation Test

Answer the following questions and then compare them to those given at the end of this chapter:

1. Which of the following layouts is used for UV editing in CINEMA 4D?

   (a) **BP UV Edit** (b) **BP 3D Paint**
   (c) **Texture View window** (d) **Standard**

2. Which of the following options is used to add a stroke to the selected UV polygons with a color?

   (a) **Empty Canvas** (b) **Show UV Mesh**
   (c) **Outline Polygons** (d) None of the above

3. The __________ tool in the Modes Palette is used to paint textures on the model.

4. The __________ tool in the **Tools** menu of the main menu is used to fill the adjacent pixels with a color on a single click.

5. The __________ area in the **BodyPaint 3D Setup Wizard** dialog box is used to select all those objects or materials that are to be modified.

Review Questions

Answer the following questions:

1. Which of the following layouts is used for painting on models in CINEMA 4D?

   (a) **BP UV Edit** (b) **3D Paint**
   (c) **Texture View window** (d) **Standard**

2. Which of the following areas in the **BodyPaint 3D Setup Wizard** dialog box is used to calculate the UV mesh?

   (a) **Select Objects** (b) **Material Options**
   (c) **UV Setup** (d) All of the above

3. Which of the following options is used to display the UV mesh of the selected object in the Texture View of the **BP UV Edit** layout?

   (a) **Show UV Mesh** (b) **Layout**
   (c) **Size** (d) **UV Mesh**

4. The **Single Material Mode** check box is used to ensure that the selected object will have a single material. (T/F)

EXERCISE

The rendered output of the model used in the exercise can be accessed by downloading the *c09_cinema4d_r20_exr.zip* from *www.cadcim.com*. The path of the file is as follows: *Textbooks > Animation and Visual Effects > MAXON CINEMA 4D > MAXON CINEMA 4D R20 Studio: A Tutorial Approach*

Exercise 1

Extract the contents of the *c09_cinema4d_r20_exr.zip* file. Open the model of a T-shirt and then paint it using the paint tools available in the **BP 3D Paint** layout, refer to Figure 9-32. **(Expected time: 30 min)**

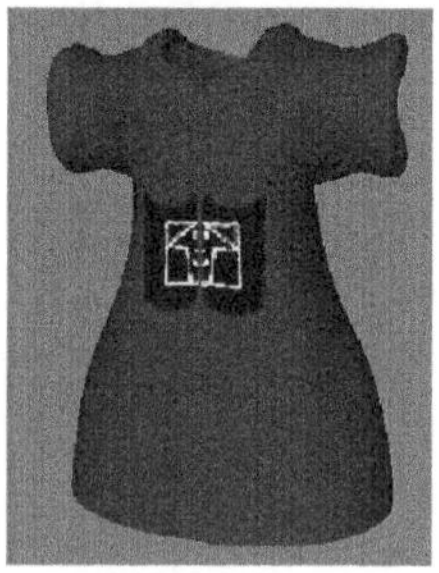

Figure 9-32 *The final output*

Answers to Self-Evaluation Test

1. a, **2.** c, **3. Brush**, **4. Fill Bitmap**, **5. Select Objects**

Chapter 10

Compositing 3D Objects

Learning Objectives

After completing this chapter, you will be able to:

- *Composite objects in a scene*
- *Work with the Camera Calibrator tag*

INTRODUCTION

In computer graphics, camera is considered an essential aspect of a 3D application. The **Camera** object in CINEMA 4D controls how the audience will see and interpret the image. The cameras are used to display a viewport scene. Every viewport has a default camera whose settings can be modified. In addition to the default camera, the users can create as many cameras as they want to view and render the scene from different angles.

Compositing is defined as as a process of merging different visual elements of a scene or an image to make them look as if they are all part of the same scene or image. When you composite rendered images into a real world image or image sequences, one problem you might face is the unknown camera angle and focal length. In order to convincingly composite real world objects with 3D elements, you will have to define a **Camera** object in CINEMA 4D that reflects the settings of the real world camera. You can use the **Camera Calibrator** tag in CINEMA 4D to reconstruct the real world camera. To reconstruct a camera, you need two vanishing points and two vertically stacked planes. To create a vanishing point, parallel lines must be drawn on the image. These parallel lines form a vanishing point that you can view in the Perspective view.

In this chapter, you will learn to add camera and composite 3D elements in a scene using the **Camera Calibrator** tag in such a way that they appear the part of a scene.

TUTORIAL

Before you start the tutorial of this chapter, you need to download the *c10_cinema4d_r20_tut.zip* file from *www.cadcim.com*. The path of the file is as follows: *Textbooks > Animation and Visual Effects > MAXON CINEMA 4D > MAXON CINEMA 4D R20 Studio: A Tutorial Approach*

Next, you need to browse to *\Documents\c4dr20* and create a new folder there with the name *c10*. Next, extract the contents of the zip file in this folder.

Tutorial 1

In this tutorial, you will composite 3D objects in a 2D image using the **Camera Calibrator** tag. The final composition is shown in Figure 10-1. **(Expected time: 45 min)**

The following steps are required to complete this tutorial:

a. Set the camera in the scene.
b. Composite 3D objects in the scene.
c. Add light to the scene.
d. Save and render the scene.

Setting the Camera in the Scene

In this section, you will set the camera in the scene.

1. Choose **File > New** from the main menu; a new scene is displayed.

2. Choose **Create > Camera** from the main menu; a cascading menu is displayed. Now, choose **Camera** from it; the *Camera* object is added to the Object Manager.

Figure 10-1 *The final composition*

3. Make sure that the *Camera* is selected in the Object Manager and then right-click on it; a shortcut menu is displayed. In this shortcut menu, choose **CINEMA 4D Tags > Camera Calibrator**, as shown in Figure 10-2; the **Camera Calibrator Expression Camera Calibrator]** tag is added to the Object Manager, as shown in Figure 10-3.

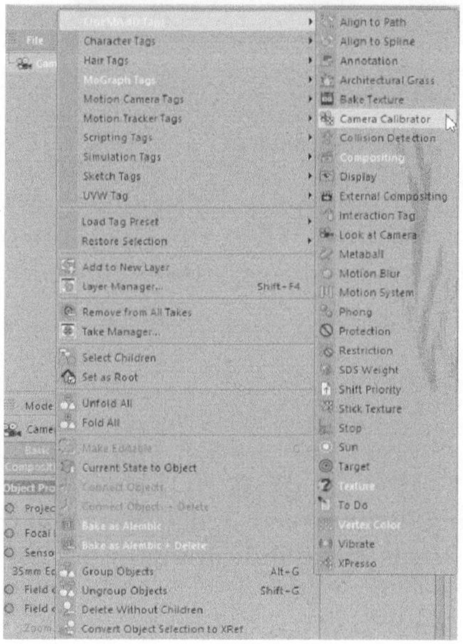

Figure 10-2 *Choosing* ***Camera Calibrator*** *from the shortcut menu*

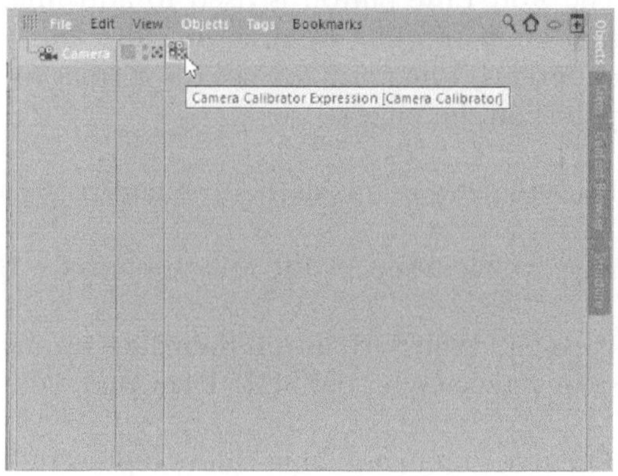

Figure 10-3 *The* ***Camera Calibrator*** *tag added to the Object Manager*

4. Select the **Camera Calibrator Expression [Camera Calibrator]** tag in the Object Manager. In the Attribute Manager, choose the **Image** button; the **Image** area is displayed. In this area, choose the browse button located next to the **Image** text box; the **Open File** dialog box is displayed.

5. In this dialog box, browse to *\Documents\c4dr20\c10\room.jpg*. Next, choose the **Open** button; the *room.jpg* is displayed in the Perspective viewport.

6. In the **Image** area, enter **1.77** in the **Film Aspect** spinner.

7. In the Attribute Manager, choose the **Calibrate** button; the **Calibrate** area is displayed. From this area, choose the **Add Line** button; first line is created in the Perspective viewport, as shown in Figure 10-4.

Figure 10-4 *The line created in the Perspective viewport*

The **Add Line** button is used to add lines whose end points can be modified. You can reposition the line by dragging the end points of the line. When you drag any of the endpoints, a magnifying area is displayed. It helps you in precisely positioning the end points on the image.

8. Place the end points of the first line, as shown in Figure 10-5.

Next, you will specify the relevant axis for the first line.

9. Press and hold SHIFT and then click on the first line; the line turns red. Click again on the same line keeping the SHIFT key pressed; the line turns green indicating the Y-axis.

The red, green, and blue colors represent the X, Y, and Z axes, respectively.

Figure 10-5 *The position of first line in the Perspective viewport*

Next, you will create the second line representing the Y-axis.

10. Create a duplicate of the first line using the CTRL key and then place the line in the scene, as shown in Figure 10-6.

Figure 10-6 *The position of second line in the Perspective viewport*

As soon as you place the second line, you will notice that **Y Vanishing Point** has been solved in the Attribute Manager. Next, you will solve the **X Vanishing Point** by creating two more lines. On solving the **X Vanishing Point**, the **Z Vanishing Point** will be calculated automatically.

Note

To calibrate the camera with accuracy, at least two vanishing points must be solved.

11. Choose the **Add Line** button from the Attribute Manager; the third line is created in the Perspective viewport. Next, place the line in the scene, refer to Figure 10-7.

12. Press and hold SHIFT and then click on the line; the line turns red which represents the X-axis.

13. Choose the **Add Line** button from the Attribute Manager; the fourth line is created in the Perspective viewport. Next, place the line in the scene, refer to Figure 10-7.

Figure 10-7 *The two red lines representing the X-axis*

14. Press and hold SHIFT and then click on the line; the line turns red.

    Notice in the Attribute Manager, the focal length of the camera has been solved now, refer to Figure 10-8.

15. In the Attribute Manager, choose the **Create Camera Mapping Tag** button; a texture tag with the name **room** is added to the *Camera* object in the Object Manager.

16. Choose the **Create Background Object** button from the Attribute Manager; the *Background* object is added to the Object Manager and the texture tag **room** is applied to the *Background* object.

    Next, you will create a pin.

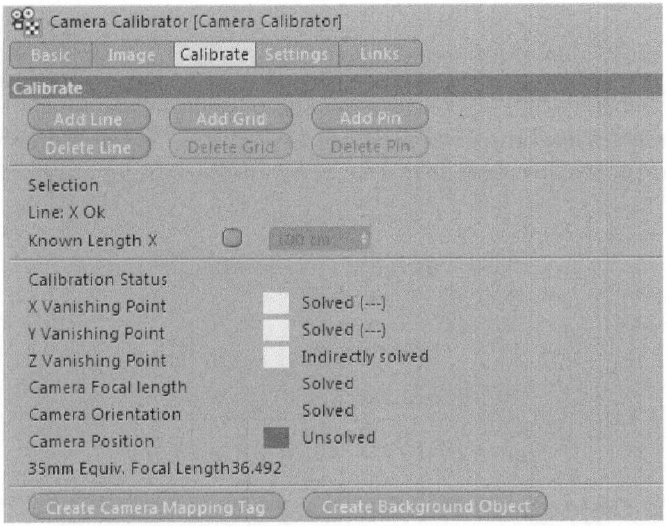

***Figure 10-8** The focal length of the camera solved*

17. Choose the **Add Pin** button from the Attribute Manager; a pin in the form of a small orange circle is displayed in the scene. Next, using the left mouse button, snap it with the starting point of the forth line representing X-axis, refer to Figure 10-9.

***Figure 10-9** The pin snapped to the fourth line in the scene*

In CINEMA 4D, pins can be used to define the exact position of the camera. With pins, you can precisely place and render a 3D object on the image such that it looks a part of the image. Notice that, in the Attribute Manager, the **Camera Position** has been solved.

Tip
When you move a pin, it gets locked with the lines. To release the pin, press and hold SHIFT and then click on the pin.

18. Choose the Camera View button located on the right of *Camera* in the Object Manager, as shown in Figure 10-10; the scene is displayed from the camera angle of view.

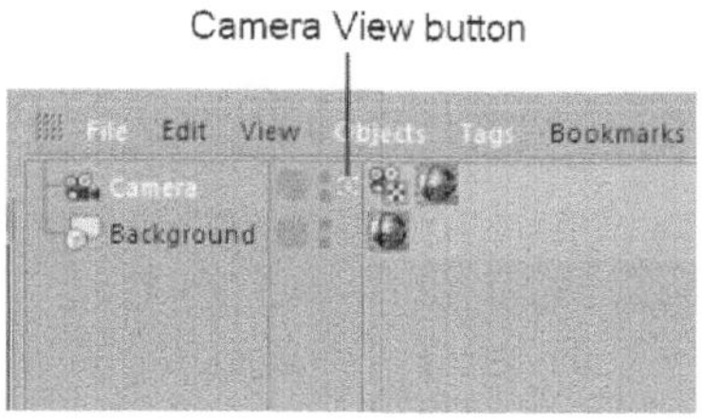

Figure 10-10 *The Camera View button*

Compositing 3D Objects in the Scene

In this section, you will composite 3D objects in the scene.

1. Choose **Create > Object > Plane** from the main menu; the *Plane* object is created in the Object Manager. Notice that the pin that you had created earlier is now acting as the origin of the scene.

2. Scale and align the plane with the sides of the tables, as shown in Figure 10-11.

Figure 10-11 *The plane positioned in the scene*

Note
To properly align objects with the pin, you can switch to the Perspective viewport by using the Camera View button, refer to Figure 10-10.

3. Choose **MoGraph > MoText** from the main menu; the *MoText* object is added to the Object Manager.

4. Choose the **Object** button from the Attribute Manager; the **Object Properties** area is displayed. In this area, enter **CADCIM** in the **Text** text box. Next, enter a value in the **Height** spinner as required.

5. Align the text with the plane, as shown in Figure 10-12.

Figure 10-12 The MoText displayed in the scene

6. In the Object Manager, press the CTRL key and then drag the texture tag **room** of *Background* to *Plane*; the image is now projected on the *Plane* in the scene.

7. Press CTRL+R to preview the render, refer to Figure 10-13.

Figure 10-13 The rendered scene

Adding Light in the Scene

In this section, you will add an area light to the scene.

1. Choose **Create > Light > Area Light** from the main menu; the *Light* object is created in the Object Manager.

2. In the Attribute Manager, make sure the **General** button is chosen. In the **General** area, select **Shadow Maps (Soft)** from the **Shadow** drop-down list. Next, enter **120** in the **Intensity** spinner.

3. Choose the **Coord** button; the **Coordinates** area is displayed. In this area, set the parameters as follows:

   P . X: **163.248** P . Y: **77.88** P . Z: **-158.125**
   R . P: **-30.043**

4. In the Attribute Manager, choose the **Shadow** button; the **Shadow** area is displayed. In this area, select **Shadow Maps (Soft)** from the **Shadow** drop-down list and enter **49** in the **Density** spinner.

5. Choose the **Edit Render Settings** tool from the Command Palette; the **Render Settings** window is displayed. In this window, choose the **Effect** button; a flyout is displayed.

6. Choose **Ambient Occlusion** from this flyout; the **Ambient Occlusion** effect is enabled. Next, close the **Render Settings** window.

7. Double-click on the Material Manager; a material with the name **Mat** is created in the Material Manager. Next, double-click on the **Mat** material; the **Material Editor** window is displayed.

8. In this window, clear the **Color** check box and then select the **Luminance** check box; the **Luminance** area is displayed. In this area, choose the **RGB** button and then enter **0** in the **R**, **G**, and **B** spinners associated with the **Color** parameter. Next, close the **Material Editor** window.

9. Drag the *Mat* material from Material Manager to the *MoText* object in the Object Manager; the material is applied to *MoText*.

10. Press CTRL+R to preview the render, refer to Figure 10-1. Figure 10-14 shows all objects in the Perspective viewport. Figure 10-15 shows all objects in the Object Manager.

Saving and Rendering the Scene

In this section, you will save and render the scene. You can also view the final render of the composition by downloading the file *c10_cinema4d_r20_rndr.zip* from *www.cadcim.com*. The path of the file is mentioned at the beginning of the chapter.

1. Choose **File > Save As** from the main menu; the **Save File** dialog box is displayed. In this dialog box, browse to the location *\Documents\c4dr20\c10*.

Figure 10-14 All objects in the Perspective viewport

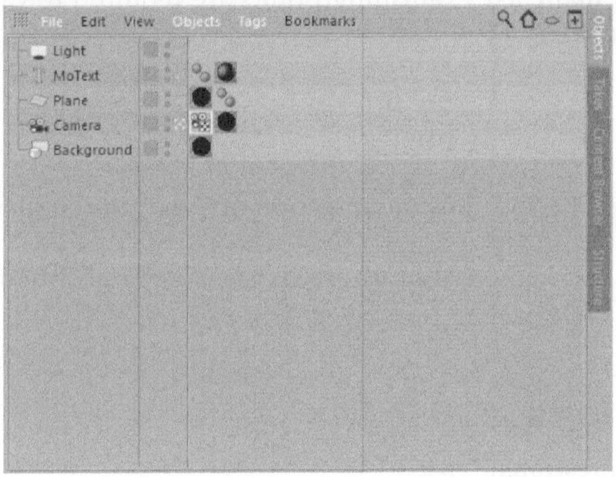

Figure 10-15 All objects in the Object Manager

2. Enter **c10tut1** in the **File name** text box and then choose the **Save** button.

3. Choose the **Render to Picture Viewer** tool from the Command Palette; the **Picture Viewer** window is displayed.

4. In this window, choose **File > Save as**; the **Save** dialog box is displayed.

5. In the **Save** dialog box, choose the **OK** button; the **Save Dialog** dialog box is displayed. Next, browse to *\Documents\c4dr20\c10*. In the **File Name** text box, type **c10_tut1_rndr**. Next, choose the **Save** button; the rendered composition is saved at the desired location.

   Figure 10-1 displays the final output

Self-Evaluation Test

Answer the following questions and then compare them to those given at the end of this chapter:

1. Which of the following tags is used to match a 3D camera to an existing image so that you can composite 3D elements into a real image?

   (a) **Protection** (b) **Cinema 4D tag**
   (c) **Camera Calibrator** (d) **Camera**

2. Which of the following buttons in the **Calibrate** area is used to add lines whose end points can be altered?

   (a) **Add Line** (b) **Create Preview**
   (c) **Add Grid** (d) **Add Pin**

3. A minimum of how many axes vanishing points are required to calibrate the camera with high degree of accuracy?

   (a) four (b) two
   (c) six (d) five

4. The red color of the line specifies the direction of Y axis in the image. (T/F)

5. The camera orientation in the **Calibrate** area is calculated only when all the vanishing points have been solved. (T/F)

Review Questions

Answer the following questions:

1. Which of the following options in the **Calibrate** area is used to generate a background object with the reference image projected on it?

   (a) **Calibrate** (b) **Known Length Y**
   (c) **Add Pin** (d) **Create Background Object**

2. Two __________ and two vertically stacked planes are required to reconstruct the camera.

3. A pin in CINEMA 4D is used to define the actual position of the camera. (T/F)

EXERCISE

The rendered output of the model used in the exercise can be accessed by downloading the *c10_cinema4d_r20_exr.zip* file from *www.cadcim.com*. The path of the file is as follows: *Textbooks > Animation and Visual Effects > MAXON CINEMA 4D > MAXON CINEMA 4D R20 Studio: A Tutorial Approach*

Exercise 1

Extract the contents of the *c10_cinema4d_r20_exr.zip* file. Create a new scene in CINEMA 4D and then solve the camera using the *Background.jpg* image, refer to Figure 10-16 and Figure 10-17. The lines and pin are indicated by arrows in Figure 10-16. **(Expected time: 15 min)**

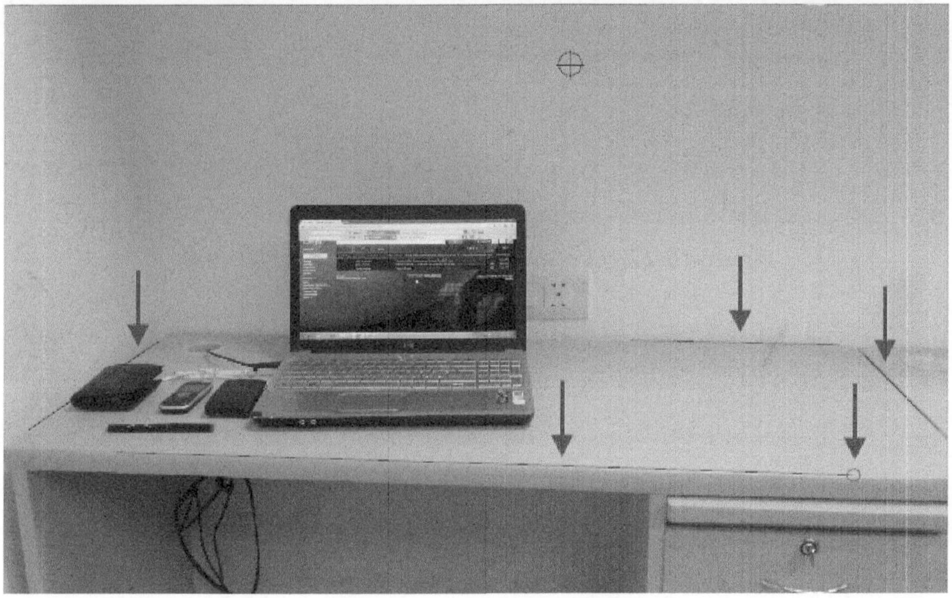

Figure 10-16 *The lines and pin in the scene*

Figure 10-17 The 3D elements composited in the scene

Answers to Self-Evaluation Test

1. c, **2.** a, **3.** b, **4.** F, **5.** T

Chapter 11

Rendering

Learning Objectives

After completing this chapter, you will be able to:

- *Understand Global Illumination*
- *Create render passes*
- *Create the caustic patterns*

INTRODUCTION

The term render is derived from a French word which means to give back or yield. The process of rendering translates the created scene into a finalized 2D image. In this process, all textures and lighting in the scene are combined together to create a single flat image.

TUTORIALS

Before you start the tutorials of this chapter, you need to download the *c11_cinema4d_r20_tut.zip* file from *www.cadcim.com*. The path of the file is as follows: *Textbooks > Animation and Visual Effects > MAXON CINEMA 4D > MAXON CINEMA 4D R20 Studio: A Tutorial Approach*

Next, you need to browse to *\Documents\c4dr20* and create a new folder in it with the name *c11*. Next, extract the contents of the zip file in this folder.

Tutorial 1

In this tutorial, you will render a table clock, as shown in Figure 11-1, and create render passes. **(Expected time: 25 min)**

Figure 11-1 *The final rendered table clock*

The following steps are required to complete this tutorial:

a. Open the file.
b. Set lights in the scene.
c. Set global illumination and ambient occlusion attributes.
d. Create render passes.
e. Save and render the scene.

Opening the File

In this section, you will open the file.

1. Choose **File > Open** from the main menu; the **Open File** dialog box is displayed.

2. In the **Open File** dialog box, browse to *\Documents\c4dr20\c11\c11_tut1_start* and then choose the **Open** button; the *c11_tut1_start.c4d* file is opened, as shown in Figure 11-2.

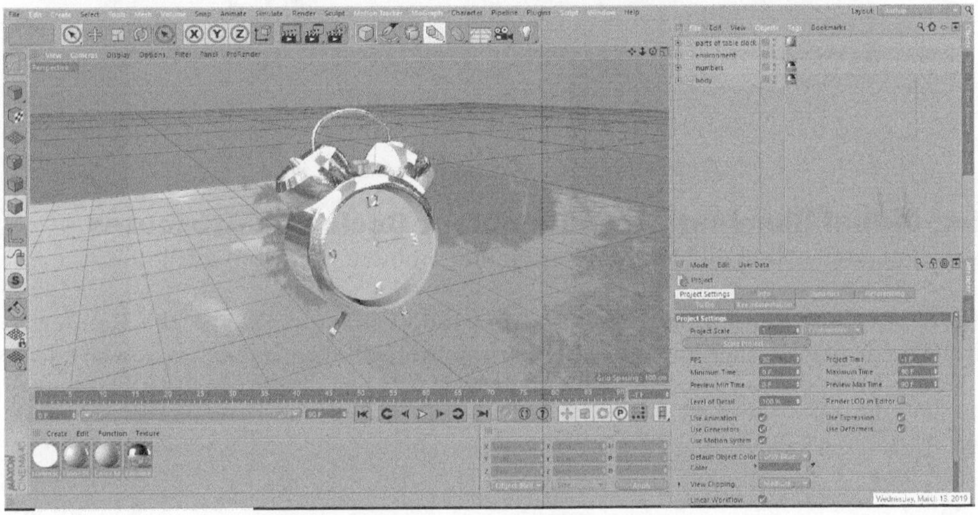

Figure 11-2 *The c11_tut1_start.c4d file*

Setting Lights in the Scene

In this section, you will illuminate the scene using the Light object.

1. Choose the **Light** tool from the Command Palette; the *Light* object is added to the Object Manager.

2. In the Attribute Manager, make sure the **General** button is chosen. In the **General** area, select **Shadow Maps (Soft)** from the **Shadow** drop-down list.

3. Choose the **Coord.** button; the **Coordinates** area is displayed. In this area, set the parameters as follows:

   P . X: **298.829** P . Y: **361.2** P . Z: **124.33**

4. Choose the **Shadow** button in the Attribute Manager; the **Shadow** area is displayed. In this area, enter **72** in the **Density** spinner.

   After entering these values, press CTRL+R; the rendered output is displayed in the viewport, as shown in Figure 11-3.

Figure 11-3 Displaying the rendered view

Setting Global Illumination and Ambient Occlusion Attributes

In this section, you will set global illumination and ambient occlusion attributes.

1. Choose the **Edit Render Settings** tool from the Command Palette; the **Render Settings** window is displayed. In this window, choose the **Effect** button; a flyout is displayed, as shown in Figure 11-4.

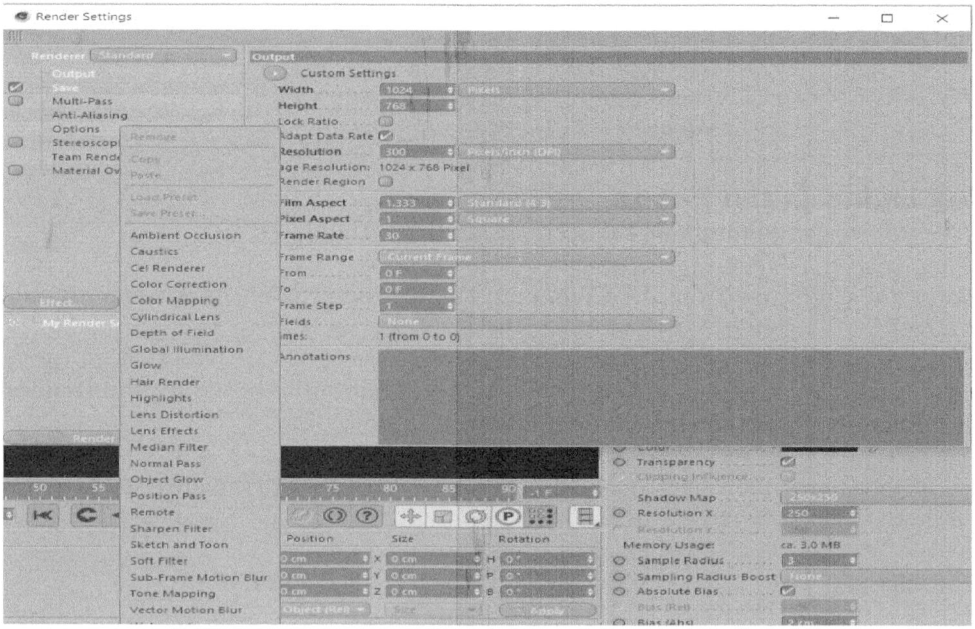

*Figure 11-4 The flyout displayed on choosing the **Effect** button*

The options available in the flyout displayed on choosing the **Effect** button are used to add effects such as Global Illumination, Glow, and so on while rendering a scene in CINEMA 4D.

2. In this flyout, choose **Global Illumination**; the **Global Illumination** area is displayed. In the **General** area, set the options, as shown in Figure 11-5.

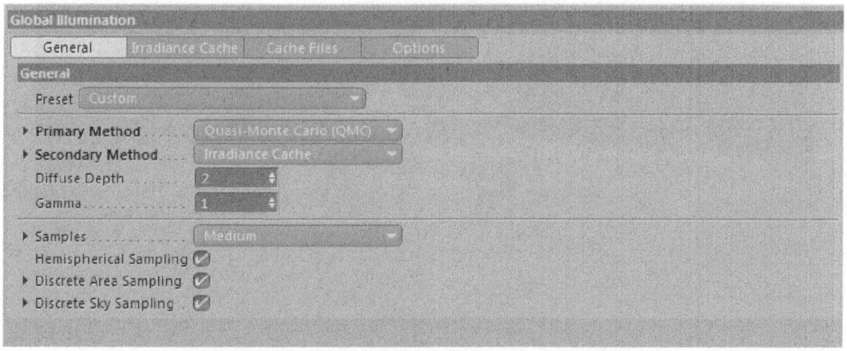

***Figure 11-5** The **Global Illumination** area*

3. In the **Global Illumination** area, choose the **Irradiance Cache** button; the **Irradiance Cache** area is displayed. In this area, enter **60** in the **Smoothing** spinner. Next, minimize the **Render Settings** window.

4. Press CTRL+R; the rendered clock is displayed in the viewport, as shown in Figure 11-6. Notice that the render now looks better.

***Figure 11-6** The rendered clock*

5. Maximize the **Render Settings** window. In this window, choose the **Effect** button; a flyout is displayed. In this flyout, choose **Ambient Occlusion**; the **Ambient Occlusion** area is displayed. Next, minimize the **Render Settings** window.

6. Press CTRL+R; the rendered clock is displayed in the viewport, as shown in Figure 11-7. You will notice that contact shadows are now prominent in the render.

Creating Render Passes

The Multi-pass rendering in CINEMA 4D allows you to post-edit your renders in a compositing package such as Nuke or Fusion. In this section, you will create ambient occlusion, shadow, diffuse, reflection, refraction, global illumination, and illumination passes.

Figure 11-7 The rendered clock

1. Maximize the **Render Settings** window. In this window, choose the **Multi-Pass** button; a flyout is displayed, as shown in Figure 11-8.

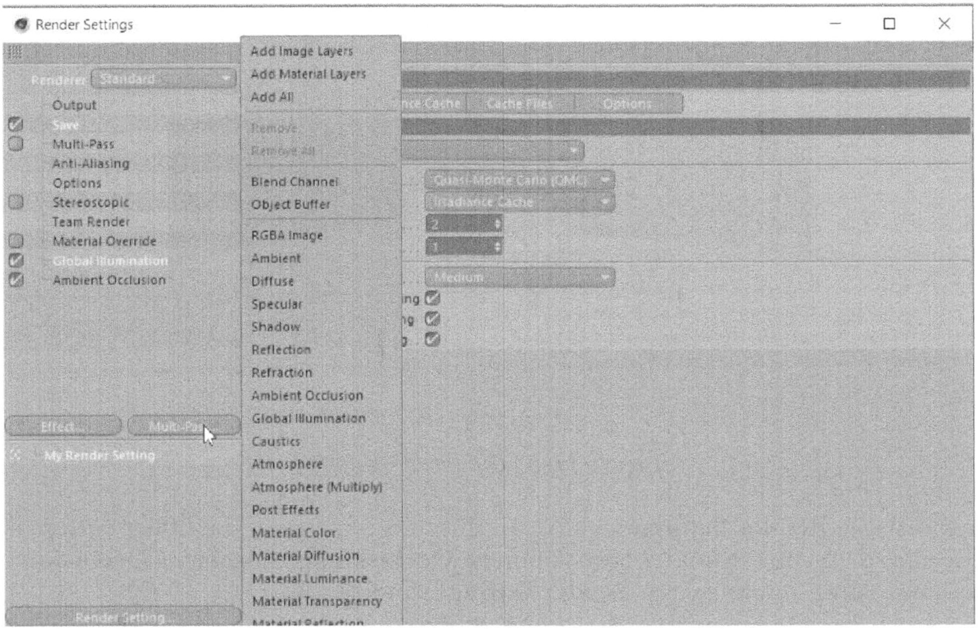

*Figure 11-8 The flyout displayed on choosing the **Multi-Pass** button*

The options in this flyout are used to create render passes such as shadow, reflection, specular, and so on.

2. In the flyout, choose **Ambient Occlusion**; the **Ambient Occlusion** pass is added to the **Render Settings** window.

The **Ambient Occlusion** pass shows how the regions of the image illuminated by the ambient light are affected by the Environment object. This pass simulates the soft shadows that appear in the crevices of the objects when lit by indirect light.

3. Choose the **Multi-Pass** button; a flyout is displayed. In this flyout, choose **Reflection**; the **Reflection** pass is added to the **Render Settings** window.

   The **Reflection** pass is used to display the reflective surfaces of an image.

4. Similarly, choose **Refraction**, **Shadow**, **Diffuse**, **Global Illumination**, and **Illumination** from the flyout; the chosen passes are added to the **Render Settings** window.

   The **Refraction** pass is used to display the refractive surface of the image. The **Shadow** pass is used to display the shaded areas of the image. The **Diffuse** pass is used to render diffuse lighting of the scene.

   In the world of computer graphics, Global Illumination is the process of interchanging the lights between different objects of a scene. Although it increases the rendering time, but it illuminates the entire scene uniformly.

5. Select the **Multi-Pass** check box in the **Render Settings** window.

6. Choose the **Save** option from the list displayed on the left in the **Render Settings** window; the **Regular Image** area is displayed. In this area, select the **Alpha Channel** check box, as shown in Figure 11-9.

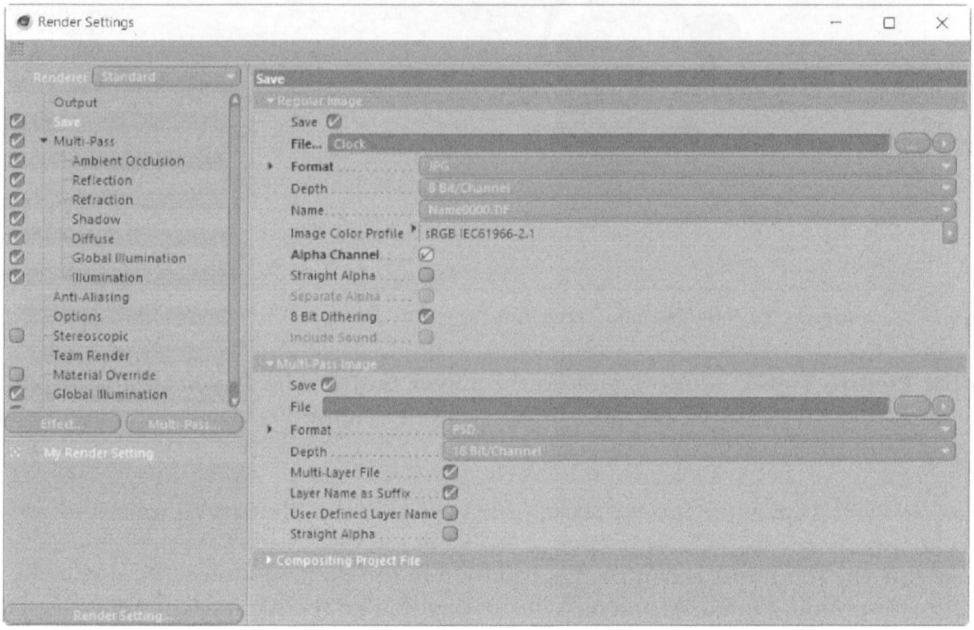

*Figure 11-9 Selecting the **Alpha Channel** check box in the **Render Settings** window*

The **Alpha Channel** check box is used to calculate a pre-multiplied alpha channel on rendering. The pixels in the alpha channel are either black or white. The black pixels indicate that there is no object present in the scene, whereas the white pixels indicate the presence of objects in the scene.

7. In the **Render Settings** window, choose the **Output** option; the **Output** area is displayed. In this area, set the parameters as follows:

   Width: **1920** Height: **1200**

   Now, close the **Render Settings** window.

   The **Width** and **Height** spinners are used to set the width and height of the rendered image, respectively.

8. Choose the **Render to Picture Viewer** tool from the Command Palette; the rendering begins in the **Picture Viewer** window, refer to Figure 11-10. You can adjust the zoom level of the rendered image by using the middle mouse button.

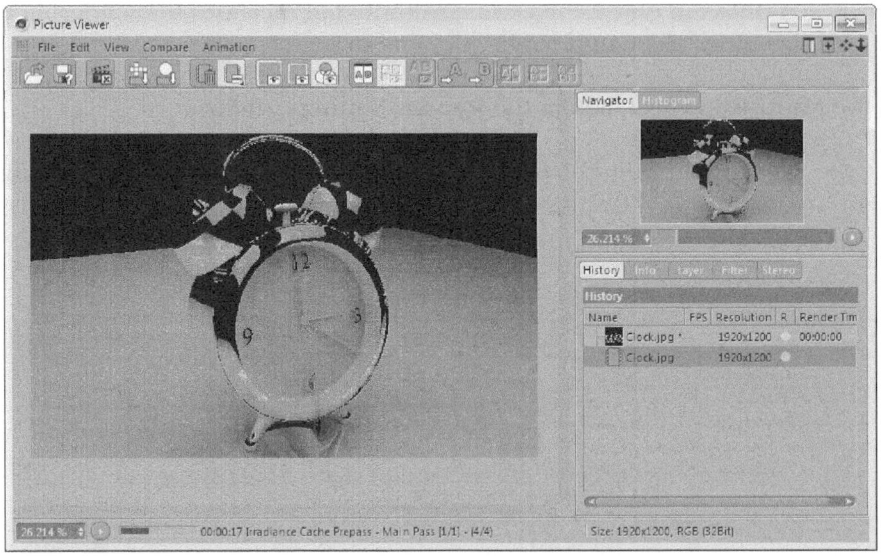

Figure 11-10 *The rendering process in the* ***Picture Viewer*** *window*

9. In the **Picture Viewer** window, choose the **Layer** button; the **Layer** area is displayed. In this area, select the **Multi-Pass** radio button, refer to Figure 11-11; all the render passes are displayed in the **Layer** area.

   Next, you will display the render passes one by one in the **Picture Viewer** window.

10. Make sure the rendering is completed and then in the **Picture Viewer** window, click on the icon corresponding to the **Alpha** pass in the **Layer** area; the **Alpha** channel is displayed, as shown in Figure 11-12.

11. Click on the eye icons of all the passes one by one excluding that of the **Ambient Occlusion** pass; the **Ambient Occlusion** pass is displayed, as shown in Figure 11-13.

*Figure 11-11 The render passes displayed in the **Picture Viewer** window*

*Figure 11-12 Displaying the **Alpha** pass in the **Picture Viewer** window*

*Figure 11-13 The **Ambient Occlusion** pass displayed in the **Picture Viewer** window*

12. Similarly, you can view all the desired passes by clicking on the display tags of the undesired passes in the **Picture Viewer** window. Figures 11-14 through 11-17 display different render passes.

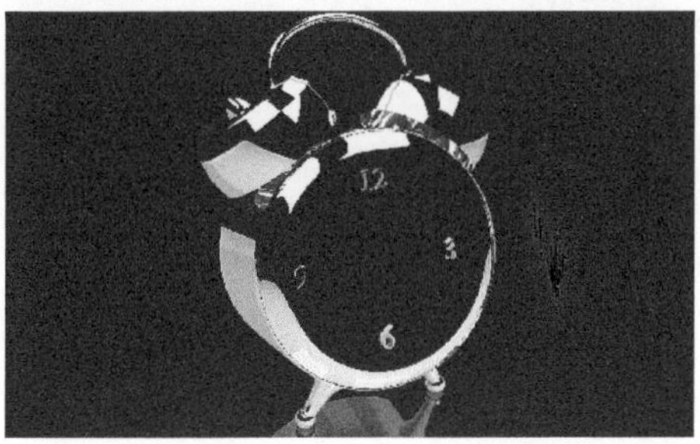

*Figure 11-14 The **Reflection** pass displayed in the **Picture Viewer** window*

*Figure 11-15 The **Global Illumination** pass displayed in the **Picture Viewer** window*

*Figure 11-16 The **Shadow** pass displayed in the **Picture Viewer** window*

*Figure 11-17 The **Diffuse** pass displayed in the **Picture Viewer** window*

Saving and Rendering the Scene

In this section, you will save and render the scene. You can also view the final render of the composition by downloading the file *c11_cinema4d_r20_rndr.zip* from *www.cadcim.com*. The path of the file is mentioned at the beginning of the chapter.

1. Choose **File > Save** from the main menu; the **Save File** dialog box is displayed. In this dialog box, browse to the location *\Documents\c4dr20\c11*.

2. Enter **c11tut1** in the **File name** text box and then choose the **Save** button.

3. In the Perspective viewport, set the camera angle using the Viewport Navigation Tools located on the top right of the Perspective viewport. Next, you need to render the scene. For rendering, refer to Tutorial 1 of Chapter 2.

   Figure 11-1 displays the final output.

Tutorial 2

In this tutorial, you will create caustics and render the beer mug, as shown in Figure 11-18.

(Expected time: 15 min)

The following steps are required to complete this tutorial:

a. Open the file.
b. Apply textures to the beer mug and floor.
c. Add lights to the scene.
d. Set caustics attributes.
e. Save and render the scene.

Opening the File

In this section, you will open the file.

1. Choose **File > Open** from the main menu; the **Open File** dialog box is displayed.

***Figure 11-18** The render of the beer mug*

2. In the **Open File** dialog box, browse to *\Documents\c4dr20\c11\c11_tut2_start* and then choose the **Open** button; the *c11_tut2_start.c4d* file is opened, as shown in Figure 11-19.

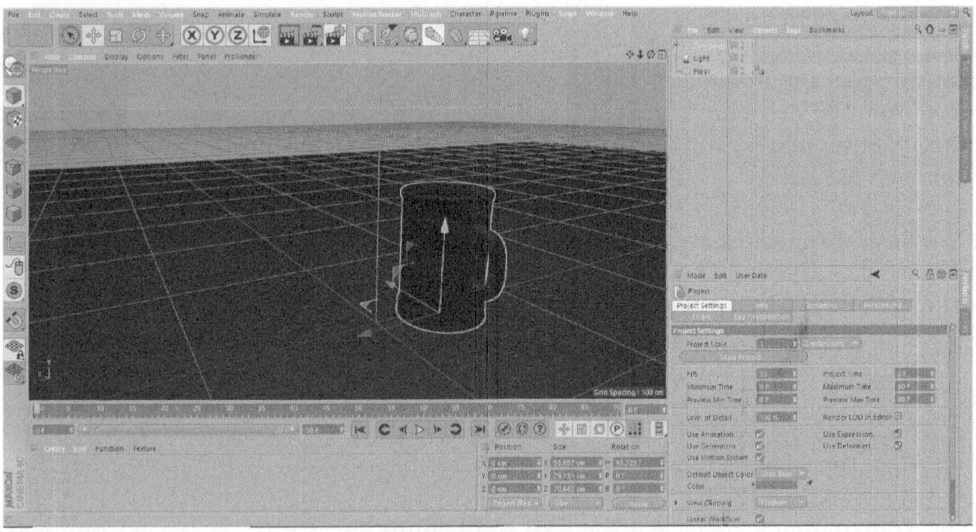

***Figure 11-19** The c11_tut2_start.c4d file*

Applying Textures to the Beer Mug, Beer, and Floor

In this section, you will add texture to the beer mug, beer, and floor.

1. Expand the *Beer Mug* group in the Object Manager. Double-click in the empty area in the Material Manager; a new material is created in the Material Manager.

2. Make sure that the new material is selected in the Material Manager and choose the **Basic** button from the Attribute Manager; the **Basic Properties** area is displayed in the Attribute Manager. Enter **matBeerMug** in the **Name** text box in the **Basic Properties** area; the new material is renamed as *matBeerMug*.

3. In the **Basic Properties** area, select the **Transparency** check box.

4. In the Attribute Manager, choose the **Transparency** button; the **Transparency** area is displayed. In this area, set the parameters as follows:

   Refraction: **1.5** Absorption Distance: **50**

   In the **Transparency** area, clear the **Exit Reflections** check box and then click on the triangle located on the right of **Absorption Color** to expand the parameter if not already expanded. Choose the **RGB** button and then enter the following values:

   R: **212** G: **216** B: **215**

5. Press and hold the left mouse button on the *matBeerMug* material in the Material Manager and drag the cursor to *BeerMug* in the Object Manager; the *matBeerMug* material is applied to the beer mug in the Perspective viewport.

   Next, you will create texture for *Beer*.

6. Double-click in the empty area in the Material Manager; a new material is created in the Material Manager.

7. Make sure that the new material is selected in the Material Manager and choose the **Basic** button from the Attribute Manager; the **Basic Properties** area is displayed in the Attribute Manager. Enter **matBeer** in the **Name** text box in the **Basic Properties** area; the new material is renamed as *matBeer*.

8. In the **Basic Properties** area, select the **Transparency** check box.

9. In the Attribute Manager, choose the **Transparency** button; the **Transparency** area is displayed. In this area, choose the **RGB** button and then set the parameters as follows:

   G: **239** B: **177** Refraction: **1.25**

   Enter **45** in the **Absorption Distance** spinner.

10. In the **Transparency** area, clear the **Exit Reflections** check box. Next, click on the triangle located on the right of **Absorption Color** to expand the parameter if not already expanded and then choose the **RGB** button, if not already chosen. Set the values in the RGB spinners corresponding to **Absorption Color** as follows:

    R: **235** G: **213** B: **54**

11. Press and hold the left mouse button on the *matBeer* material in the Material Manager and drag the cursor on *Beer* in the Object Manager; the *matBeer* material is applied to *Beer* in the Perspective viewport.

Next, you will create texture for *Floor*.

12. Double-click in the empty area in the Material Manager; a new material is created in the Material Manager.

13. Make sure that the new material is selected in the Material Manager and choose the **Basic** button; the **Basic Properties** area is displayed in the Attribute Manager. Enter **matFloor** in the **Name** text box in the **Basic Properties** area; the new material is renamed as *matFloor*.

14. In the Attribute Manager, choose the **Color** button; the **Color** area is displayed. In the **Color** area, choose the browse button located next to the **Texture** parameter; the **Open File** dialog box is displayed.

15. In this dialog box, browse to *\Documents\c4dr20\c11\Floor.jpg*. Next, choose the **Open** button; the texture is displayed on the Material slot in the Material Manager.

16. Press and hold the left mouse button on the *matFloor* material in the Material Manager and drag the cursor on *Floor* in the Object Manager; the *Floor* material is applied to the floor in the Perspective viewport, as shown in Figure 11-20. Next, press CTRL+R to preview the render.

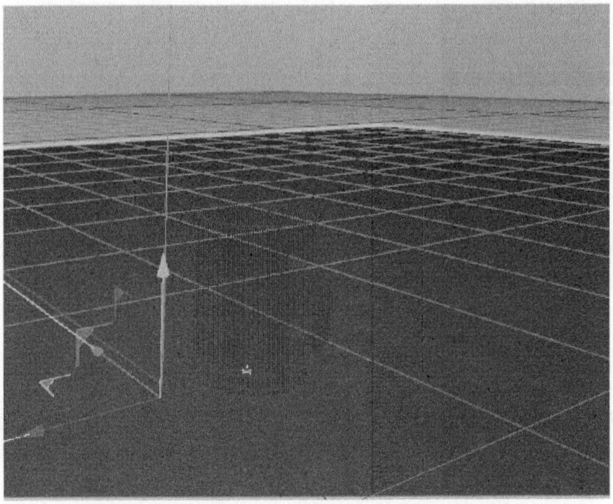

Figure 11-20 *The floor texture applied*

Adding Lights to the Scene

In this section, you will add lights to the scene.

1. Press and hold the left mouse button on the **Light** tool in the Command Palette; a flyout with various tools is displayed. Choose the **Spot Light** tool from it; the *Light.1* object is added to the Object Manager. Rename it as *Caustic Light*.

2. Make sure that the *Caustic Light* object is selected in the Object Manager. In the Attribute Manager, choose the **General** button; the **General** area is displayed. In this area, choose the **RGB** button and then set the **Color** parameter as follows:

   R: **205** G: **135** B: **11**

3. In the **General** area, select **Shadow Maps (Soft)** from the **Shadow** drop-down list. Next, select the **Volumetric** option from the **Visible Light** drop-down list.

4. In the Attribute Manager, choose the **Coord** button; the **Coordinates** area is displayed. In this area, set the parameters as follows:

   P . Y: **204** P . Z: **-350** ` R . P: **-30**

5. Choose the **Details** button; the **Details** area is displayed. In this area, make sure that the **Use Inner** check box is selected. Next, set the parameters as follows:

   Inner Angle: **30** Outer Angle: **43**

6. Choose the **Visibility** button; the **Visibility** area is displayed. In this area, enter **120** in the **Brightness** spinner. Next, press CTRL+R to preview the render.

Setting Caustics Attributes

In this section, you will set caustic attributes in the scene.

1. Make sure that the *Caustic Light* object is selected in the Object Manager.

2. In the Attribute Manager, choose the **Caustics** button; the **Caustics** area is displayed. In this area, select the **Surface Caustics** check box and set the parameters as follows:

   Energy: **8** Photons: **60000**

   The caustics are used to display the realistic patterns of focused lights in an image. The **Surface Caustics** check box is used to add surface caustics to the scene.

   The **Energy** spinner is used to control the brightness of the caustic effect by calculating the total start energy of the photons. The **Photons** spinner is used to determine the number of photons emitted from a light source in a scene. The number of photons directly affect the intensity of the caustic effect.

3. Choose the **Edit Render Settings** tool from the Command Palette; the **Render Settings** window is displayed. In this window, choose the **Effect** button; a flyout is displayed.

4. In this flyout, choose **Caustics**; the **Caustics** area is displayed, refer to Figure 11-21. In the **Caustics** area, make sure that the **Surface Caustics** check box is selected and enter **150** in the **Strength** spinner. Next, close the **Render Settings** window.

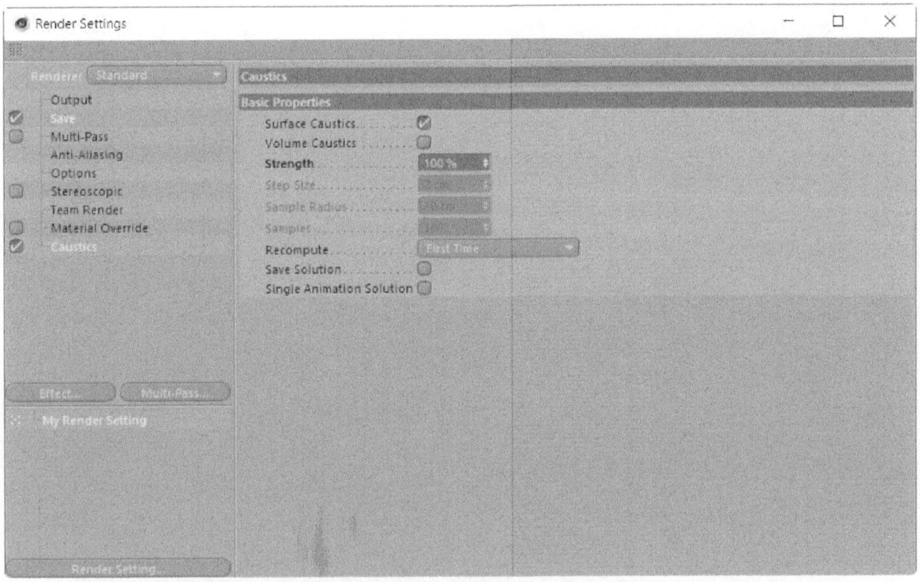

Figure 11-21 The ***Caustics*** *area in the* ***Render Settings*** *window*

5. Double-click on the *matBeerMug* material in the Material Manager; the **Material Editor** window is displayed.

6. In the **Material Editor** window, select the **Illumination** option; the **Illumination** area is displayed, refer to Figure 11-22. In this area, clear the **Receive Caustics** check box and enter **200** in the **Strength** spinner located next to the **Generate Caustics** check box, refer to Figure 11-22. Next, close the **Material Editor** window.

   The **Receive Caustics** option is used to enable or disable the receiving of the caustics on the surface.

7. Double-click on the *matBeer* material in the Material Manager; the **Material Editor** window is displayed.

8. In the **Material Editor** window, select the **Illumination** option, if not already selected; the **Illumination** area is displayed. In this area, clear the **Receive Caustics** check box. Next, enter **200** in the **Strength** spinner located next to the **Generate Caustics** check box. Close the **Material Editor** window. Next, press CTRL+R to preview the render.

Saving and Rendering the Scene

In this section, you will save the scene. You can also view the final rendered scene by downloading the file *c11_cinema4d_r20_rndr.zip* from *www.cadcim.com*. The path of the file is mentioned at the beginning of the chapter.

1. Choose **File > Save As** from the main menu; the **Save File** dialog box is displayed. In this dialog box, browse to the location *\Documents\c4dr20\c11*.

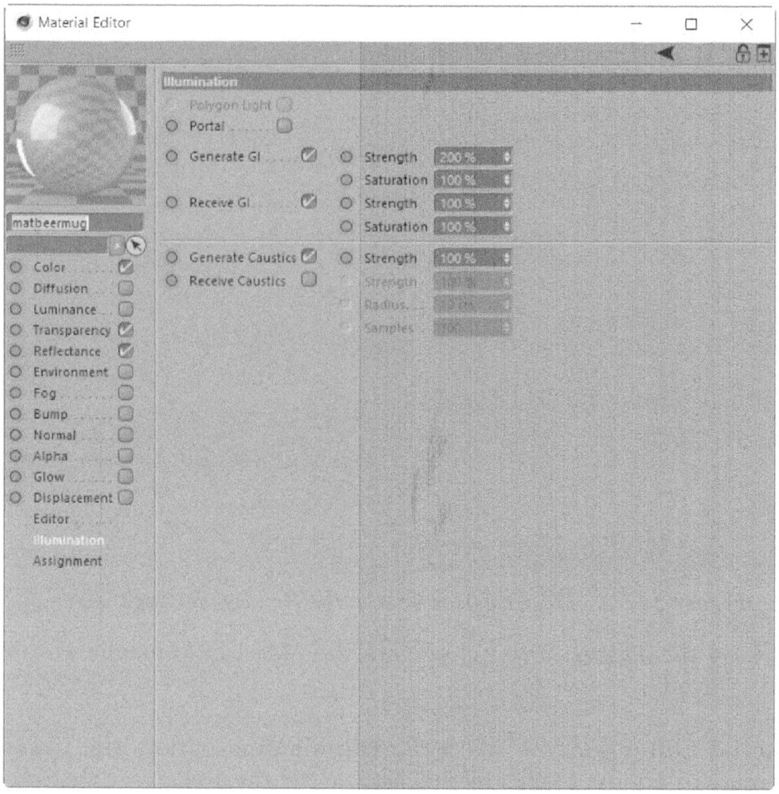

*Figure 11-22 The **Illumination** area displayed in the **Material Editor** window*

2. Enter **c11tut2** in the **File name** text box and then choose the **Save** button.

3. In the Perspective viewport, set the camera angle using the Viewport Navigation Tools located on the top right of the Perspective viewport. Next, you need to render the scene. For rendering, refer to Tutorial 1 of Chapter 2.

   Figure 11-18 displays the final output.

Self-Evaluation Test

Answer the following questions and then compare them to those given at the end of this chapter:

1. Which of the following passes is used to display the refractive surface of the image?

   (a) **Refraction** (b) **Shadow**
   (c) **Diffuse** (d) None of these

2. Which of the following spinners is used to determine the number of photons emitted from a light source in a scene?

   (a) **Photons** (b) **Surface Caustics**
   (c) **Energy** (d) None of these

3. Which of the following shortcuts is used to render the current view?

   (a) CTRL+R (b) CTRL+LMB
   (c) CTRL+Click (d) SHIFT+Click

4. The process of __________ transforms the mathematically created scene into a finalized 2D image.

5. The __________ parameter in the **Global Illumination** area is used to define the number of times the light is reflected.

6. The __________ option is used to display the realistic patterns of focused lights in an image.

7. The __________ check box in the **Render Settings** window is used to calculate a pre-multiplied alpha channel on rendering.

8. The **Effects** option in the **Render Settings** window is used to add desired effects while rendering a scene in CINEMA 4D. (T/F)

Review Questions

Answer the following questions:

1. Which of the following passes is used to generate soft shadows in the crevices of the objects?

   (a) **Ambient Occlusion** (b) **Illumination**
   (c) **Global Illumination** (d) None of these

2. Which of the following options is used to add surface caustics in a scene?

   (a) **Caustics** (b) **Energy**
   (c) **Surface Caustics** (d) **Photon**

3. The __________ pass is used to display the reflecting surface of an image.

4. The __________ spinner is used to determine the number of photons emitted from a light source in a scene.

5. __________ combines all texturing and lighting of the scene together to create a single flat image.

EXERCISE

The rendered output of the model used in the exercise can be accessed by downloading the *c11_cinema4d_r20_exr.zip* file from *www.cadcim.com*. The path of the file is as follows: *Textbooks > Animation and Visual Effects > MAXON CINEMA 4D > MAXON CINEMA 4D R20 Studio: A Tutorial Approach*

Exercise 1

Open the model that you textured in Tutorial 2 of Chapter 5. Next, render it with Global Illumination and Ambient Occlusion effects, as shown in Figure 11-23.

(Expected time: 25 min)

Figure 11-23 *Scene after rendering*

Answers to Self-Evaluation Test

1. a, **2.** a, **3.** a, **4.** rendering, **5. Diffuse Depth**, **6. Caustics**, **7. Alpha Channel**, **8.** T

Chapter 12

MoGraph

Learning Objectives

After completing this chapter, you will be able to:

- *Create clones*
- *Add MoGraph effectors*
- *Create the shatter effect using PolyFX*
- *Work with the MoSpline object*

INTRODUCTION

MoGraph is a huge advancement in the field of motion graphics. It is a toolset in CINEMA 4D which helps you to create spectacular visual effects, logos, and text.

MoGraph is a collection of objects, shaders, and scripts that can be combined to create models and animations. In this chapter, you will learn about some of the tools and effectors available in MoGraph toolset of CINEMA 4D.

TUTORIALS

Before you start with the tutorials of this chapter, you need to download the *c12_cinema4d_r20_tut.zip* file from *www.cadcim.com*. The path of the file is as follows: *Textbooks > Animation and Visual Effects > MAXON CINEMA 4D > MAXON CINEMA 4D R20 Studio: A Tutorial Approach*

Next, you need to browse to *\Documents\c4dr20* and create a new folder in it with the name *c12*. Next, extract the contents of the zip file in this folder.

Tutorial 1

In this tutorial, you will create an abstract model, shown in Figure 12-1 by using the MoGraph toolset. **(Expected time: 20 min)**

Figure 12-1 *The abstract model to be created*

The following steps are required to complete this tutorial:

a. Create the objects.
b. Create the clones of the object.
c. Change the background color of the scene.
d. Save and render the scene.

Creating the Objects

In this section, you will create a sphere and a cube object.

1. Choose **Create > Object** from the main menu; a cascading menu is displayed. Now, choose **Sphere** from it; a sphere is created in the Perspective Viewport and *Sphere* is added to the Object Manager.

2. Make sure *Sphere* is selected in the Object Manager. In the Attribute Manager, make sure the **Object** button is chosen; the **Object Properties** area is displayed. In this area, enter **300** in the **Radius** spinner.

3. Choose **Create > Object** from the main menu; a cascading menu is displayed. Now, choose **Cube** from it; a cube is created in the Perspective Viewport and *Cube* is added to the Object Manager.

4. Make sure *Cube* is selected in the Object Manager. In the Attribute Manager, make sure the **Object** button is chosen; the **Object Properties** area is displayed. In this area, set the parameters as follows:

   Size . Y: **60** Size . Z: **191**

   Select the **Fillet** check box and enter **10** in the **Fillet Radius** spinner.

5. In the Attribute Manager, choose the **Coord** button; the **Coordinates** area is displayed. In this area, set the parameters as follows:

   P . X: **-182.39** P . Y: **239.04**

   Figure 12-2 displays *Cube* positioned in the Perspective viewport.

Creating the Clones of the Object

In this section, you will create clones of the object using the **Cloner** object.

1. Choose **MoGraph > Cloner** from the main menu; the **Cloner** object is added to the Object Manager.

   The **Cloner** tool is a commonly used tool in MoGraph. It is used to create duplicates of the objects.

2. In the Object Manager, select *Cube* and then drag it to *Cloner*; the *Cube* is connected to *Cloner*.

3. Select *Cloner* in the Object Manager. In the Attribute Manager, make sure the **Object** button is chosen; the **Object Properties** area is displayed. In this area, set the parameters as follows:

   Count: **33** P . X: **-9** P . Y: **32**
   P . Z: **5** S . X: **97** S . Z: **97**
   Step Rotation . H: **5**

   Figure 12-3 displays *Cloner* in the Perspective viewport. Next, you will create copies of the *Cloner* object.

4. Choose **MoGraph > Cloner** from the main menu; the *Cloner.1* is added to the Object Manager.

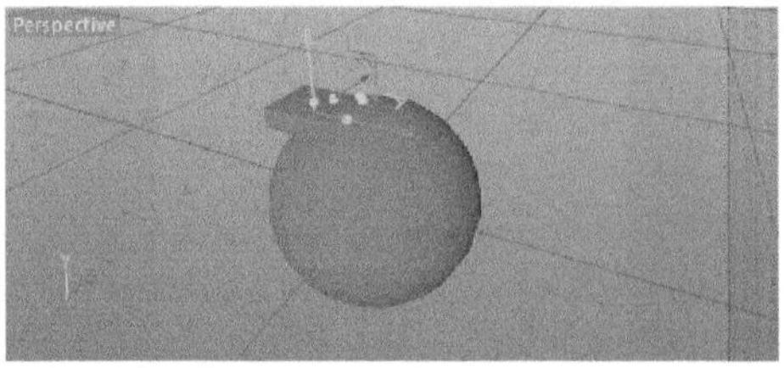

Figure 12-2 *Cube positioned in the Perspective viewport*

Figure 12-3 *Cloner displayed in the Perspective viewport*

5. In the Object Manager, select *Cloner* and then drag it to *Cloner.1*; the *Cloner* is connected to *Cloner.1*. Also, clones of *Cloner* are created in the Perspective viewport.

6. Select *Cloner.1* in the Object Manager. In the Attribute Manager, make sure the **Object** button is chosen; the **Object Properties** area is displayed. In this area, select **Radial** from the **Mode** drop-down list. Next, enter **15** in the **Count** spinner. Figure 12-4 displays *Cloner.1* in the Perspective viewport.

Figure 12-4 *Cloner.1 displayed in the Perspective viewport*

Changing the Background Color of the Scene

To change the background color of the scene to white in the final output, follow the steps given in Tutorial 1 of Chapter 2.

Saving and Rendering the Scene

In this section, you will save and render the model. You can also view the final render of the scene by downloading the file *c12_cinema4d_r20_rndr.zip* from *www.cadcim.com*. The path of the file is mentioned at the beginning of the chapter.

1. Choose **File > Save** from the main menu; the **Save File** dialog box is displayed. In this dialog box, browse to the location *\Documents\c4dr20\c12*.

2. Enter **c12tut1** in the **File name** text box and then choose the **Save** button.

3. In the Perspective viewport, set the camera angle using the Viewport Navigation Tools located at the top right of the Perspective viewport. Next, you need to render the scene.

For rendering, refer to Tutorial 1 of Chapter 2. The final output of the model is shown in Figure 12-1.

Tutorial 2

In this tutorial, you will create disco light effect shown in Figure 12-5 using the MoGraph toolset. **(Expected time: 30 min)**

Figure 12-5 *The disco light effect at frame 60*

The following steps are required to complete this tutorial:

a. Open the file.
b. Create clones.
c. Add effectors to the scene.
d. Set render attributes.
e. Save and render the scene.

Opening the File

In this section, you will open the file.

1. Choose **File > Open** from the main menu; the **Open File** dialog box is displayed.

2. In the **Open File** dialog box, browse to *\Documents\c4dr20\c12\c12_tut2_start* and then choose the **Open** button; the *c12_tut2_start.c4d* file is opened, as shown in Figure 12-6.

Creating Clones

In this section, you will create a light and then create its clone using the **Cloner** object.

1. Choose **Create > Light** from the main menu; a cascading menu is displayed. Next, choose **Light** from it; a light is created in the Perspective viewport and *Light* is added to the Object Manager.

2. Choose **MoGraph > Cloner** from the main menu; the *Cloner* object is added to the Object Manager.

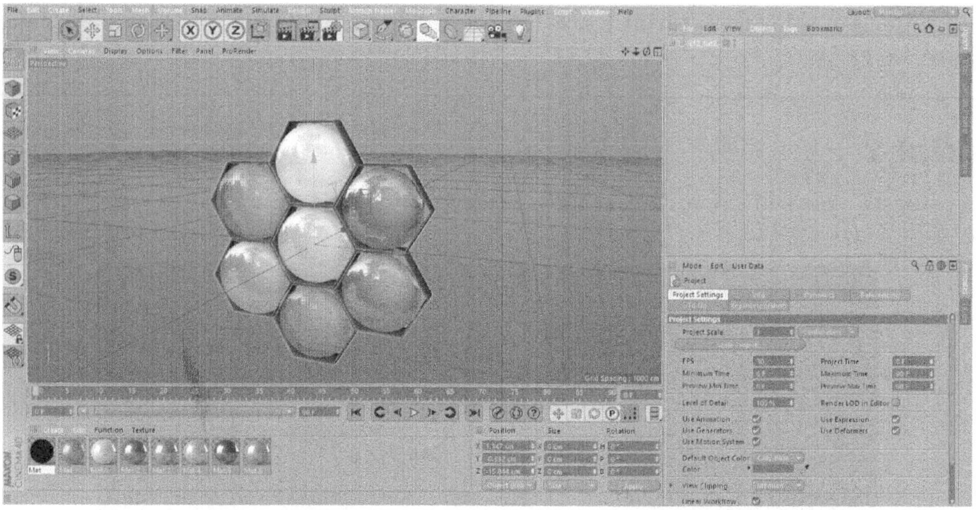

Figure 12-6 The c12_tut2_start.c4d file

3. Make sure *Cloner* is selected in the Object Manager. In the Attribute Manager, make sure the **Object** button is chosen; the **Object Properties** area is displayed. In this area, select **Radial** from the **Mode** drop-down list, as shown in Figure 12-7.

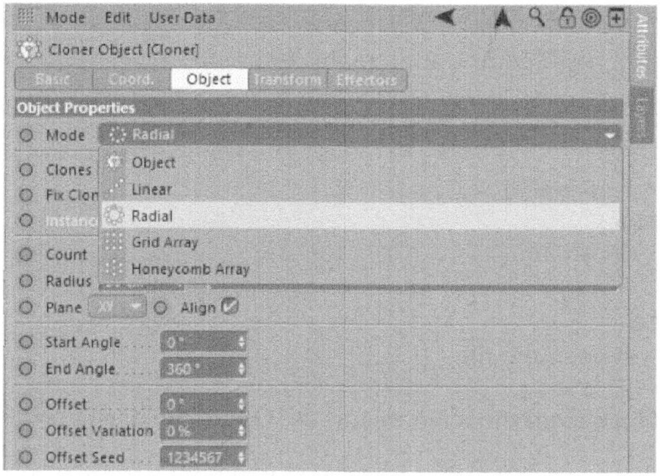

***Figure 12-7** Selecting **Radial** from the **Mode** drop-down list*

The **Radial** mode in the **Mode** drop-down list is used to create clones arranged in a circular shape around the center of cloner.

4. In the Object Manager, select *Light* and drag it to *Cloner*; the *Light* is connected to *Cloner*.

5. Select *Cloner* in the Object Manager. In the **Object Properties** area, select **Random** from the **Clones** drop-down list, as shown in Figure 12-8. Next, set the parameters as follows:

Count: **6** Radius: **482** Start Angle: **364**
End Angle: **-2**

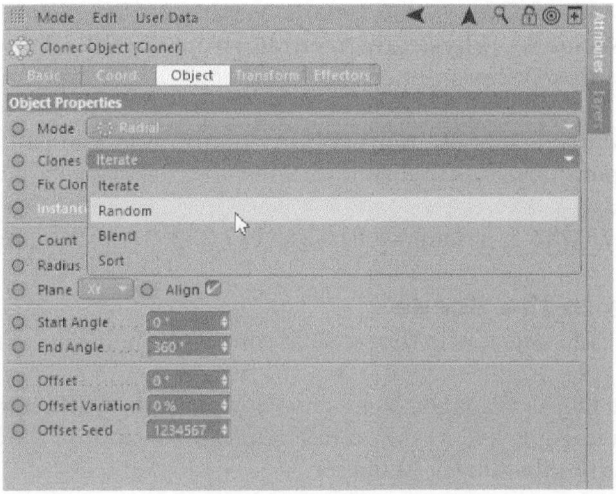

Figure 12-8 Selecting ***Random*** *from the* ***Clones*** *drop-down list*

The **Random** option is used to arrange the clones in a random manner. The **Count** spinner is used to define the number of clones to be arranged. The **Radius** spinner is used to define the radius of the cloner.

6. Make sure the *Cloner* object is selected in the Object Manager. In the Attribute Manager, choose the **Coord** button; the **Coordinates** area is displayed. In this area, set the parameters as follows:

P . X: **-7.772**	P . Y: **4.852**	P . Z: **-198.5**
S . X: **0.9**	S . Y: **0.86**	R . B: **-4**

Figure 12-9 displays clones of *Light* in the Perspective viewport.

Figure 12-9 *The clones of Light displayed in the Perspective viewport*

Next, you will set the properties of *Light*.

7. Select the *Light* object in the Object Manager. In the Attribute Manager, choose the **General** button; the **General** area is displayed. In this area, select **Shadow Maps (Soft)** from the **Shadow** drop-down list. Next, select **Visible** from the **Visible Light** drop-down list.

8. In the Attribute Manager, choose the **Details** button; the **Details** area is displayed. In this area, select **Inverse Square (Physically Accurate)** from the **Falloff** drop-down list and enter **177.258** in the **Radius/Decay** spinner.

9. In the Attribute Manager, choose the **Visibility** button; the **Visibility** area is displayed. In this area, set the parameters as follows:

   Inner Distance: **175.352** Outer Distance: **177.258** Sample Distance: **23.825**

Adding Effectors to the Scene

In this section, you will add effectors in the scene to control the behavior of the lights in the scene.

1. Select *Cloner* in the Object Manager. Next, choose **MoGraph > Effector** from the main menu; a cascading menu is displayed, as shown in Figure 12-10. Choose the **Random** option from it; *Random* is added to the Object Manager.

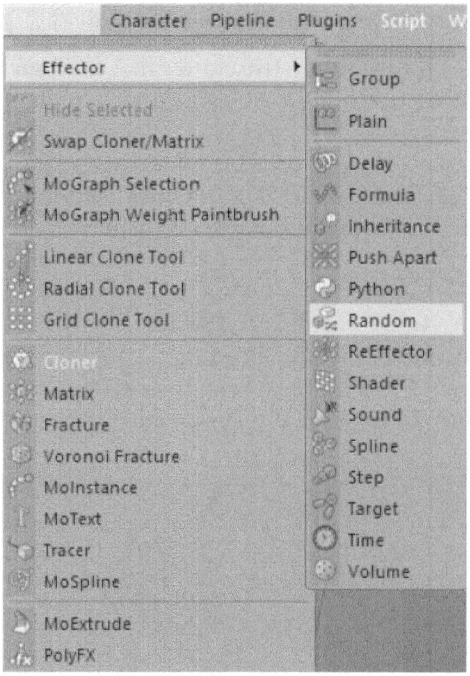

Figure 12-10 *Choosing **Random** from the cascading menu*

The **Random** effector is used to randomize the value of the clones. It is used to modify the position, rotation, size, color, and weight of the clones.

Note

*When you add the **Random** effector to the Object Manager, it is also added to the **Effectors** area of the **Cloner** object. To verify this, select the **Cloner** in the Object Manager and then choose the **Effectors** button; the **Effectors** area is displayed. In this area, you will notice that the **Random** effector is added.*

2. Make sure **Random** is selected in the Object Manager. In the Attribute Manager, choose the **Parameter** button; the **Parameter** area is displayed. In this area, expand the **Transform** area if it is not already expanded and make sure the **Position** check box is selected. Also, select the **Rotation** check box in the **Transform** area.

   The **Position** check box is used to define whether the **Random** effector will affect the position of the cloners. The **Rotation** check box is used to define whether the **Random** effector will affect the rotation of cloners.

3. In the **Color** area, select **Custom Color** from the **Color Mode** drop-down list, as shown in Figure 12-11.

   The **Custom Color** option in the **Color Mode** drop-down list is used to set the color of clones manually.

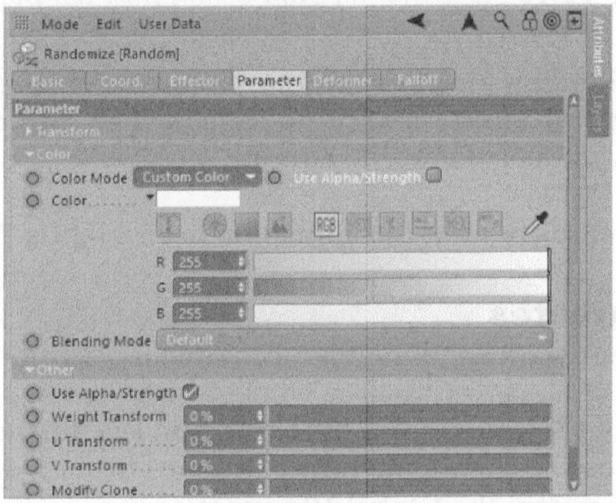

*Figure 12-11 The **Custom Color** option from the **Color Mode** drop-down list*

4. In the **Color** area, choose the **RGB** button and then enter **170** in the **G** spinner and **20** in the **B** spinner; the color of the **Random** effector changes in the Perspective viewport.

   Next, you will add the **Formula** effector to the scene. The **Formula** effector is used to create complex formulae.

5. Select *Cloner* in the Object Manager. Next, choose **MoGraph > Effector** from the main menu; a cascading menu is displayed. Choose **Formula** from it; *Formula* is added to the Object Manager.

6. Make sure *Formula* is selected in the Object Manager. In the Attribute Manager, make sure the **Parameter** button is chosen; the **Parameter** area is displayed. In the **Parameter** area, expand **Transform** if not already expanded and then clear the **Position** and **Scale** check boxes.

7. Expand the **Color** area, if not already expanded and select the **Effector Color** option from the **Color Mode** drop-down list. Next, select the **Add** option from the **Blending Mode** drop-down list, as shown in Figure 12-12.

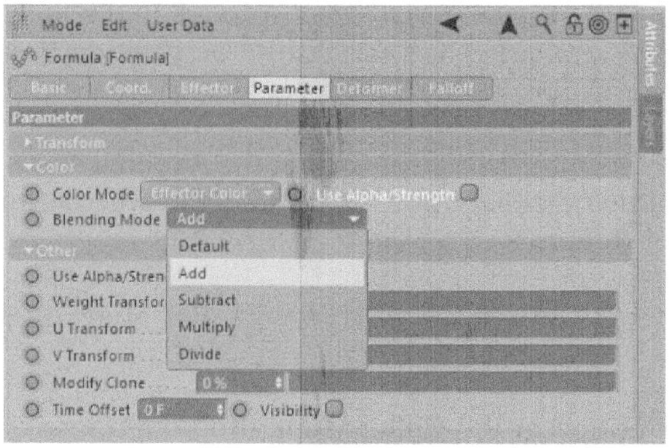

*Figure 12-12 Selecting the **Add** option from the **Blending Mode** drop-down list*

The options in the **Blending Mode** drop-down list are used to specify different modes for blending the colors of the effectors with the cloners. The **Add** option is used to add the colors of the cloner with the color of the effector.

8. Choose the **Play Forwards** button; the animation begins in the Perspective viewport.

Setting Render Attributes

In this section, you will set the global illumination, ambient occlusion, and glow attributes.

1. Choose the **Edit Render Settings** tool in the Command Palette; the **Render Settings** window is displayed. In this window, choose the **Effect** button; a flyout is displayed. From this flyout, choose **Global Illumination**; the **Global Illumination** area is displayed.

2. Choose the **Effect** button again; a flyout is displayed. From this flyout, choose **Ambient Occlusion**.

3. Choose the **Effect** button again; a flyout is displayed. From this flyout, choose **Glow**; the **Glow** area is displayed. In this area, select the **Use** check box. Next, enter **10** in the **Size** spinner and **13** in the **Intensity** spinner. Next, close the **Render Settings** window.

   After entering these values, press CTRL+R; the rendered output of the current frame is displayed in the Perspective viewport, as shown in Figure 12-13.

Saving and Rendering the Scene

In this section, you will save and render the animation. You can also view the final rendered sequence by downloading the file *c12_cinema4d_r20_rndr.zip* from *www.cadcim.com*. The path of the file is mentioned at the beginning of the chapter.

1. Choose the **Edit Render Settings** tool from the Command Palette; the **Render Settings** window is displayed. In this window, select the **Output** option; the **Output** area is displayed. In this area, enter **90** in the **To** spinner.

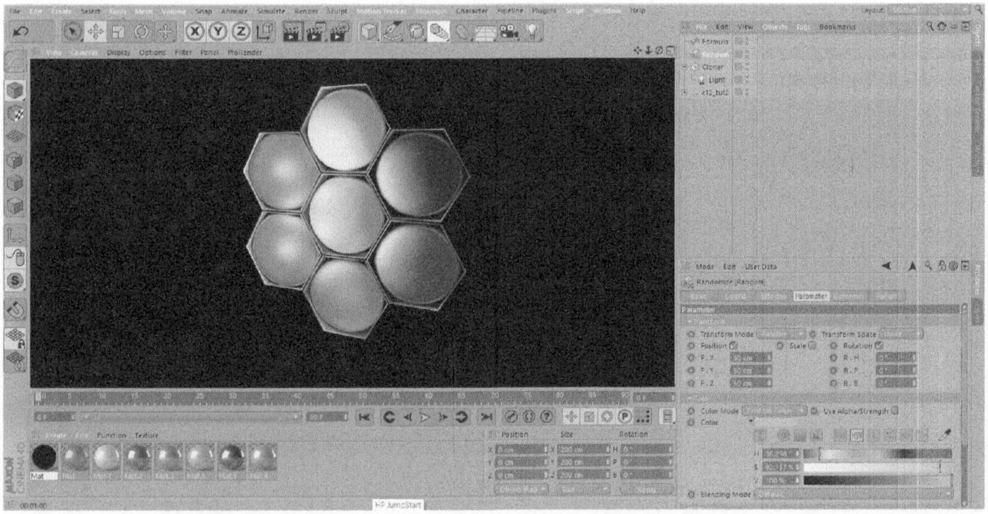

***Figure 12-13** The rendered view at the current frame*

2. Select the **Save** option from the list displayed at the left side in the **Render Settings** window; the **Regular Image** area is displayed. In this area, make sure that the **Save** check box is selected. Next, choose the browse button located next to the **File** text box; the **Save File** dialog box is displayed.

3. In the **Save File** dialog box, browse to *\Documents\c4dr20\c12* and enter **c12tut2** in the **File name** text box. Next, choose the **Save** button.

4. Select the **QuickTime Movie** option from the **Format** drop-down list. Next, close the **Render Settings** window.

5. Choose the **Render to Picture Viewer** tool from the Command Palette; the **Picture Viewer** window is displayed. Also, the rendering begins and final output is automatically saved at the specified location.

Tutorial 3

In this tutorial, you will apply the shattering effect using MoGraph toolset. Figure 12-14 displays the shattering effect at frame 81. **(Expected time: 15 min)**

The following steps are required to complete this tutorial:

a. Open the file.
b. Add effectors to the Kettle object.
c. Create camera.
d. Set render attributes.
e. Save and render the scene.

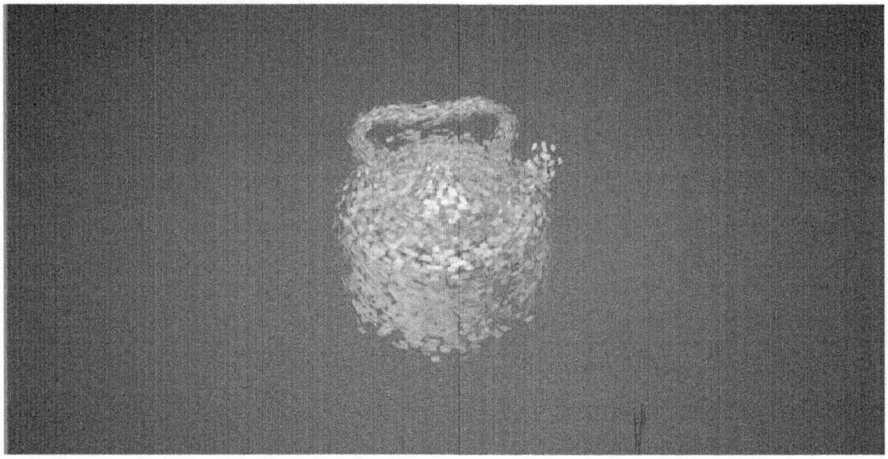

Figure 12-14 The shattering effect at frame 81

Opening the File

In this section, you will open the file.

1. Choose **File > Open** from the main menu; the **Open File** dialog box is displayed.
2. In the **Open File** dialog box, browse to *\Documents\c4dr20\c12\c12_tut3_start* and then choose the **Open** button; the *c12_tut3_start.c4d* file is opened, as shown in Figure 12-15.

Adding Effector to the Kettle Object

In this section, you will add effector to the *Kettle* object.

1. Make sure *Kettle* is selected in the Object Manager. Next, choose **MoGraph > PolyFX** from the main menu, as shown in Figure 12-16; *PolyFX* object is added to the Object Manager.

Figure 12-15 The c12_tut3_start.c4d file

The **PolyFX** object is used to create fragments of a polygon object in an irregular manner.

2. In the Object Manager, drag *PolyFX* to *Kettle*; the *PolyFX* is connected to *Kettle*.

3. In the Object Manager, make sure the *PolyFX* object is selected. Next, choose **MoGraph > Effector > Random** from the main menu; *Random* is added to the Object Manager and *Kettle* is fragmented in the Perspective viewport, as shown in Figure 12-17.

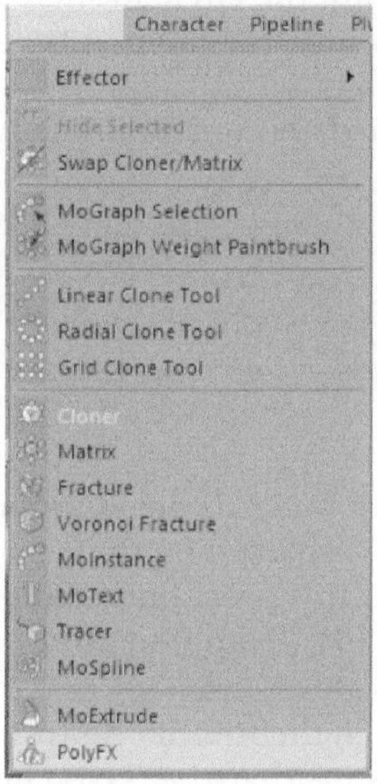

Figure 12-16 *Choosing* ***PolyFX*** *from the main menu*

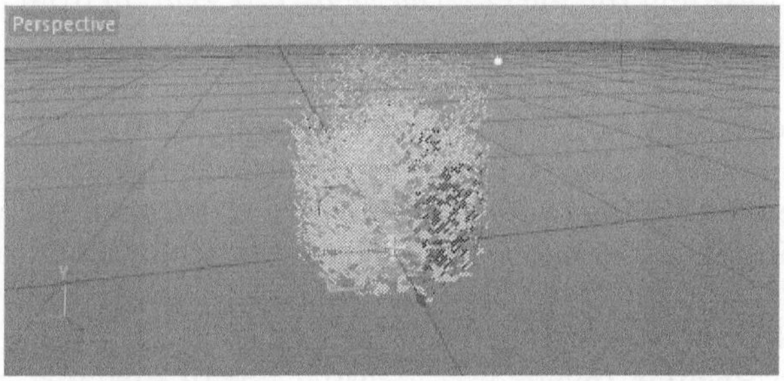

Figure 12-17 *The fragmented Kettle in the Perspective viewport*

Note

When you add the ***Random*** *effector to the Object Manager, it will be added to the* ***Effector*** *area of the PolyFX object. To verify this, select the PolyFX object in the Object Manager and then choose the* ***Effector*** *button; the* ***Effectors*** *area is displayed. In this area, you will notice that the Random effector is added.*

4. In the Animation toolbar, move the timeslider to frame 0. Alternatively, enter **0** in the **Current Time** spinner; the timeslider is set to frame 0.

5. Make sure that *Random* is selected in the Object Manager. Also, make sure the **Effector** button is chosen in the Attribute Manager. Next, enter **0** in the **Strength** spinner.

6. Right-click on the circle located on the left of the **Strength** spinner; a shortcut menu is displayed. Choose **Animation > Add Keyframe** from the shortcut menu; the circle located on the left of the **Strength** spinner turns red and a keyframe is added at frame 0.

7. Move the timeslider to frame 200 and enter **100** in the **Strength** spinner in the **Effector** area of the Attribute Manager. Right-click on the circle located on the left of the **Strength** spinner; a shortcut menu is displayed. Choose **Animation > Add Keyframe** from the shortcut menu; the circle located on the left of the **Strength** spinner turns red and a keyframe is added at frame 200.

8. In the Animation toolbar, move the timeslider to frame 100. Alternatively, enter **100** in the **Current Time** spinner; the timeslider is set to frame 100.

9. In the Attribute Manager, choose the **Parameter** button; the **Transform** area is displayed. Enter **280**, **320**, and **400** in the **P . X**, **P . Y**, and **P . Z** spinners, respectively.

10. Right-click on the circle located on the left of the **P . X** spinner; a shortcut menu is displayed. Choose **Animation > Add Keyframe** from the shortcut menu; the circle located on the left of the **P . X**, **P . Y**, and **P . Z** spinners turns red and a keyframe is created at frame 100.

11. Move the timeslider to frame 0 and choose the **Play Forwards** button from the Animation toolbar to view the animation of *Kettle*.

Saving and Rendering the Scene

In this section, you will save and render the scene. You can also view the final rendered sequence by downloading the file *c12_cinema4d_r20_rndr.zip* from *www.cadcim.com*. The path of the file is mentioned at the beginning of the chapter.

1. Choose the **Edit Render Settings** tool from the Command Palette; the **Render Settings** window is displayed. Select the **Output** option from the list displayed on the left side in the **Render Settings** window; the **Output** area is displayed. In this area, enter **200** in the **To** spinner; the **Frames** option gets updated automatically to **201 (from 0 to 200)**.

2. Select the **Save** option from the list displayed on the left side in the **Render Settings** window; the **Regular Image** area is displayed. In this area, make sure that the **Save** check box is selected. Next, choose the browse button located next to the **File** spinner; the **Save File** dialog box is displayed.

3. In the **Save File** dialog box, browse to *\Documents\c4dr20\c12* and enter **c12tut3** in the **File name** text box. Next, choose the **Save** button.

4. Select the **QuickTime Movie** option from the **Format** drop-down list. Next, close the **Render Settings** window.

5. Choose the **Render to Picture Viewer** tool from the Command Palette; the **Picture Viewer** window is displayed; the rendering begins and is automatically saved at the specified location.

Tutorial 4

In this tutorial, you will create an abstract animation using the MoSpline object. Figure 12-18 displays the animation at frame 0. **(Expected time: 20 min)**

The following steps are required to complete this tutorial:

a. Create a MoSpline object.
b. Create clones.
c. Apply material to the object.
d. Save and render the scene.

Figure 12-18 The abstract animation at frame 0

Creating a MoSpline Object

In this section, you will create an abstract shape using the **MoSpline** object.

1. Choose **File > New** from the main menu to open a new scene.

2. Choose **Create > Spline** from the main menu; a cascading menu is displayed. Choose **Circle** from the menu; the **Circle** object is added to the Object Manager.

3. Choose **MoGraph > MoSpline** from the main menu; the *MoSpline* object is added to the Object Manager.

4. Make sure *MoSpline* is selected in the Object Manager. In the Attribute Manager, make sure the **Object** button is chosen; the **Object Properties** area is displayed. In the **Object Properties** area, enter **85.1** in the **Start** spinner and **-12.5** in the **Offset** spinner.

   The **Offset** parameter is used to move the MoSpline segment. The output of this parameter is affected by the **Start** and **End** parameters. A positive value moves the segment forward whereas a negative value moves it backward.

5. In the Attribute Manager, choose the **Simple** button; the **Simple** area is displayed. In the **Simple** area, set the parameters as follows:

   Length: **5831** Segments: **56** Angle H: **176**
   Angle P: **271** Angle B: **360** Curve: **-143**
   Bend: **-87** Twist: **360** Width: **1.5**

   After entering these values, *MoSpline* is displayed in the Perspective viewport, as shown in Figure 12-19.

   The **Length** spinner is used to control the length of MoSpline or its segments. The **Segments** spinner is used to define the number of spline segments. The **Angle H** spinner controls the angle between the segment at the origin of the MoSpline and the last segment of the spline curve created. The **Angle P** spinner controls the angle around the last segment of the curve originating from the origin of the MoSpline. The **Angle B** spinner controls the angle between the first and last segment originating from the MoSpline. The **Curve** spinner controls the angle between the tangent of the first and the last segment point. The **Bend** spinner is used to bend a single spline along its length. The **Twist** spinner is used to twist a single spline along its length. The **Width** spinner controls the width of the sweep object.

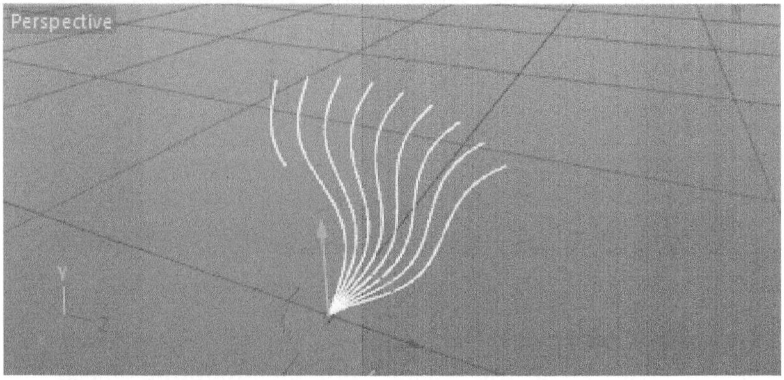

Figure 12-19 *The MoSpline displayed in the Perspective viewport*

6. Choose **Create > Generators** from the main menu; a cascading menu is displayed. Now, choose **Sweep** from it; the *Sweep* object is added to the Object Manager.

7. Make sure that *MoSpline* is selected in the Object Manager. Press and hold the left mouse button on *MoSpline* and drag the cursor to *Sweep* in the Object Manager; the *MoSpline* is connected to *Sweep* in the Object Manager. Similarly, drag *Circle* to *Sweep* in the Object Manager; *Circle* is connected to *Sweep* in the Object Manager.

Creating Clones

In this section, you will create clones of *MoSpline* using the **Cloner** object.

1. Choose **MoGraph > Cloner** from the main menu; the *Cloner* object is added to the Object Manager.

2. Select *Sweep* in the Object Manager. Press and hold the left mouse button on *Sweep* and drag the cursor to *Cloner* in the Object Manager; *Sweep* is connected to *Cloner* in the Object Manager.

3. Make sure that *Cloner* is selected in the Object Manager. In the Attribute Manager, select **Radial** from the **Mode** drop-down list and set the parameters as follows:

   Count: **11** Radius: **2**

4. In the Attribute Manager, choose the **Coord** button; the **Coordinates** area is displayed. In this area, set the parameters as follows:

   P . X: **121** R . P: **-90**

   After entering these values, clones are displayed in the Perspective viewport, as shown in Figure 12-20.

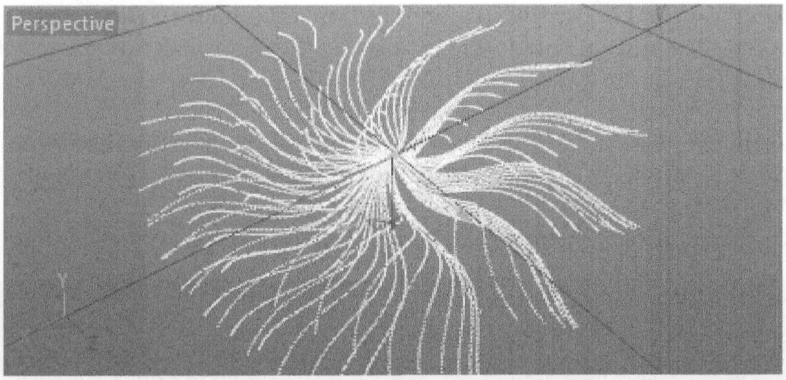

Figure 12-20 *The clones displayed in the Perspective viewport*

5. Make sure that *Cloner* is selected in the Object Manager. Next, choose **MoGraph > Effector > Formula** from the main menu. Make sure *Formula* is selected in the Object Manager. In the Object Manager, choose the **Parameter** button; the **Parameter** area is displayed. In this area, make sure the **Position**, **Scale**, and **Rotation** check boxes are selected.

6. In the **Parameter** area, set the rest of the parameters as follows:

   P . Z: **-34** Scale: **-26.4** R . H: **108**
   R . P: **151** R . B: **-190**

   After entering these values, clones are displayed in the viewport, as shown in Figure 12-21.

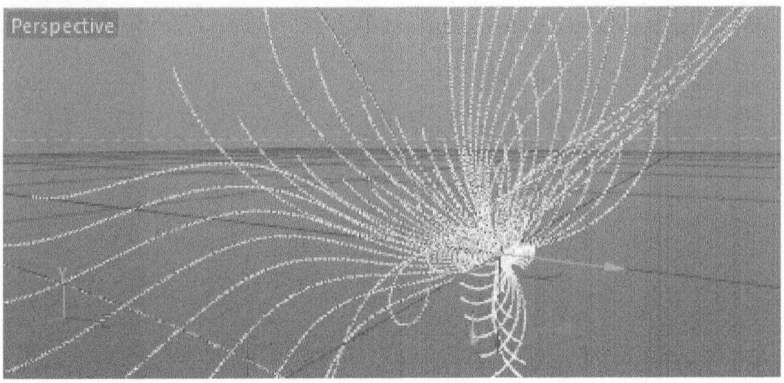

Figure 12-21 *The clones displayed in the viewport*

Applying Material to the Object

In this section, you will create material for the clones.

1. Double-click in the Material Manager; a new material with the name *Mat* is created. Double-click on *Mat*; the **Material Editor** dialog box is displayed.

2. In the **Color** area of the **Material Editor**, choose the arrow button corresponding to **Texture**; a flyout is displayed. Choose **Gradient** from the flyout.

3. In the **Material Editor**, choose the **Gradient** button; the **Shader Properties** area is displayed. In this area, set the colors of the gradient by using the following two shades of the green for the gradient: RGB (2, 83, 2) and RGB (29, 255, 0). Next, close the **Material Editor**.

4. Drag *Mat* from the Material Manager to *Cloner* in the Object Manager to apply material to the clones.

5. Press CTRL+R to preview the abstract shape. Figure 12-22 displays the render at frame 48.

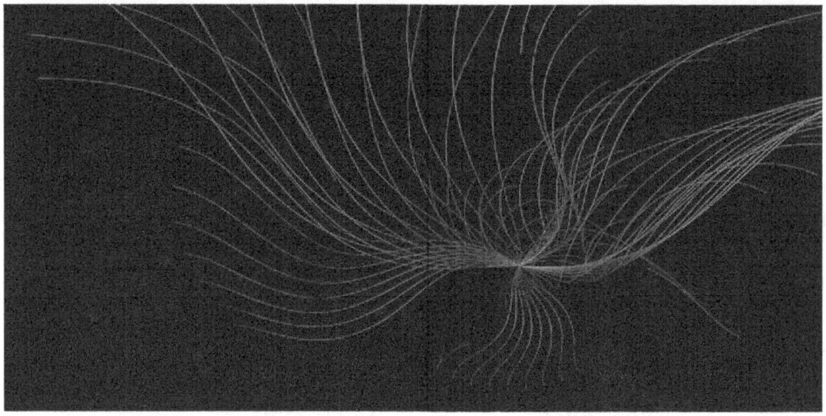

Figure 12-22 *The rendered image at frame 48*

Figure 12-23 displays the hierarchy of the objects in the Object Manager.

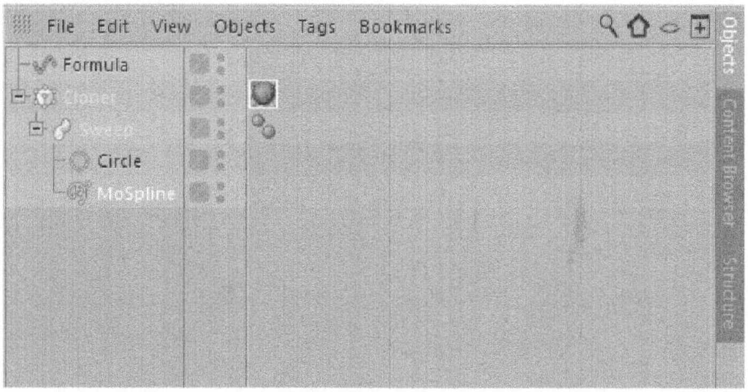

Figure 12-23 *The objects in the Object Manager*

Saving and Rendering the Scene

In this section, you will save and render the scene. You can also view the final rendered sequence by downloading the file *c12_cinema4d_r20_rndr.zip* from *www.cadcim.com*. The path of the file is mentioned at the beginning of the chapter.

1. Choose the **Edit Render Settings** tool from the Command Palette; the **Render Settings** window is displayed. Select the **Output** option from the list displayed on the left side in the **Render Settings** window; the **Output** area is displayed. In this area, enter **200** in the **To** spinner; the **Frames** option gets updated automatically to 201 (from 0 to 200).

2. Select the **Save** option from the list displayed on the left side in the **Render Settings window**; the **Regular Image** area is displayed. In this area, make sure that the **Save** check box is selected. Next, choose the browse button located next to the **File** spinner; the **Save File** dialog box is displayed.

3. In the **Save File** dialog box, browse to *\Documents\c4dr20\c12* and enter **c12tut4** in the **File name** text box. Next, choose the **Save** button.

4. Select the **QuickTime Movie** option from the **Format** drop-down list. Next, close the **Render Settings** window.

5. Choose the **Render to Picture Viewer** tool from the Command Palette; the **Picture Viewer** window is displayed. The rendering begins and is automatically saved at the specified location.

Self-Evaluation Test

Answer the following questions and then compare them to those given at the end of this chapter:

1. Which of the following tools in the MoGraph toolset is used to create copies of the objects?

   (a) **Object Cloner** (b) **Cloner**
   (c) **Linear Clone Tool** (d) None of these

2. Which of the following spinners in the **Object Properties** area of the **Cloner** object is used to define the number of clones?

   (a) **Count** (b) **Offset**
   (c) **Mode** (d) None of these

3. The __________ mode in the **Mode** drop-down list of the **Cloner** object is used to create clones in the shape of other selected objects.

4. The __________ check box in the **Parameter** area of the **Random** effector is used to define whether the rotation of cloners will be affected.

5. The __________ option in the **Color Mode** drop-down list in the **Color** area of the **Random** effector is used to manually set the color of the clones.

Review Questions

Answer the following questions:

1. Which of the following effectors in MoGraph toolset is used to create fragments of a polygon object in an irregular manner?

   (a) **Random** (b) **Shader**
   (c) **PolyFX** (d) None of these

2. The options in the __________ drop-down list available in the **Parameter** area of the effector is used to specify modes for blending the colors of the effector with the cloners.

3. The __________ effector is used to create complex formulae.

4. The __________ button in the **Render Settings** window is used to add desired effects while rendering a scene in Cinema 4D.

5. The __________ mode in the **Mode** drop-down list is used to create clones of circular shape around the center of the cloner.

EXERCISE

The rendered output of the model used in the exercise can be accessed by downloading the *c12_cinema4d_r20_exr.zip* file from *www.cadcim.com*. The path of the file is as follows: *Textbooks > Animation and Visual Effects > MAXON CINEMA 4D > MAXON CINEMA 4D R20 Studio: A Tutorial Approach*

Exercise 1

Create an abstract model, shown in Figure 12-24 by using the MoGraph toolset.

(Expected time: 15 min)

Figure 12-24 *The abstract model*

Answers to Self-Evaluation Test

1. b, **2.** a, **3. Object**, **4. Rotation**, **5. User Defined**

Chapter 13

Working with XPresso

Learning Objectives

After completing this chapter, you will be able to:

- *Work with the XPresso Editor*
- *Create and connect nodes*
- *Modify settings of nodes*

INTRODUCTION

XPresso is a node based system in MAXON CINEMA 4D that is used to build automated object interactions. These nodes are created and linked in the **XPresso Editor** by drawing lines from one port of a node to another port of the other node. These lines are also referred to as wires. In this chapter, you will learn to use the **XPresso Editor**.

TUTORIALS

Before you start the tutorials of this chapter, you need to download the *c13_cinema4d_r20_tut.zip* file from *www.cadcim.com*. The path of the file is as follows: *Textbooks > Animation and Visual Effects > MAXON CINEMA 4D > MAXON CINEMA 4D R20 Studio: A Tutorial Approach*

Next, you need to browse to *\Documents\c4dr20* and create a new folder in it with the name *c13*. Next, extract the contents of the zip file in this folder.

Tutorial 1

In this tutorial, you will control the lights of a traffic signal using the **XPresso Editor**, refer to Figure 13-1. **(Expected time: 45 min)**

Figure 13-1 *The traffic signal with the red light on*

The following steps are required to complete this tutorial:

a. Open the file.
b. Create an expression.
c. Connect the nodes.
d. Animate the traffic lights.
e. Save and render the scene.

Opening the File

In this section, you will open the file.

1. Choose **File > Open** from the main menu; the **Open File** dialog box is displayed.

2. In the **Open File** dialog box, browse to *\Documents\c4dr20\c13\c13_tut1_start* and then choose the **Open** button; the *c13_tut1_start* file is opened, as shown in Figure 13-2.

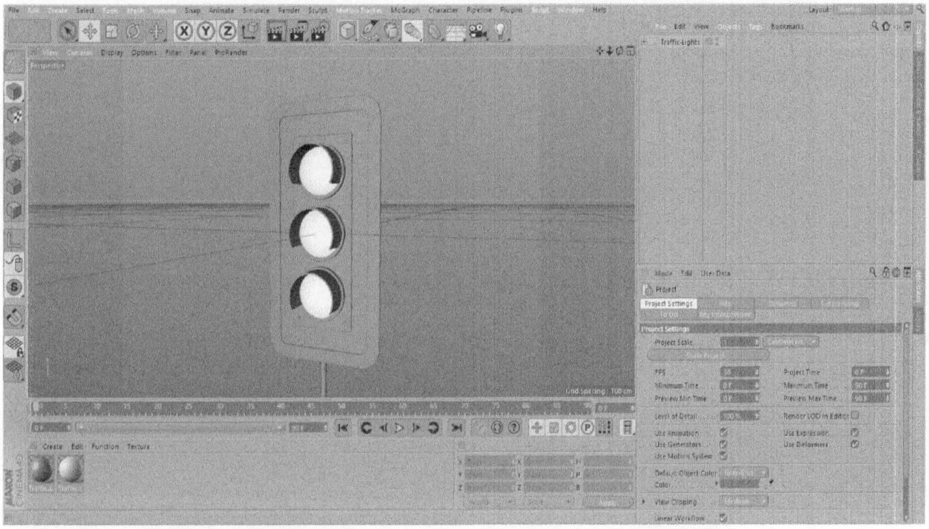

Figure 13-2 *The c13_tut1_start.c4d file*

Creating an Expression

In this section, you will create an expression in the **XPresso Editor**. Next, you will create custom parameters using the **Add User Data** option.

1. Select *Traffic-Lights* in the Object Manager. Choose **User Data > Add User Data** from the Attribute Manager menu, as shown in Figure 13-3; the **Manage User Data** dialog box is displayed, as shown in Figure 13-4.

   The options in the **Manage User Data** dialog box are used to add custom parameters to the attributes of the selected objects. It can be added to every object whose parameters are displayed in the Attribute Manager.

2. In the **Manage User Data** dialog box, make sure that **Data** is selected in the **User Data (Default)** node in the left pane of the dialog box and the **Properties** button is chosen in the right pane. In the **Properties** area, enter **Red** in the **Name** text box and select **Float Slider** from the **Interface** drop-down list, as shown in Figure 13-5. Next, choose the **OK** button in the **Manage User Data** dialog box; the **Red** spinner along with the slider is added to the **User Data** area in the Attribute Manager, as shown in Figure 13-6.

   The **Float Slider** option in the **Interface** drop-down list is used to add a slider and a spinner so that you can enter a value for specifying the user data parameter. It is the most commonly used user data parameter.

Next, you will add the Yellow spinner.

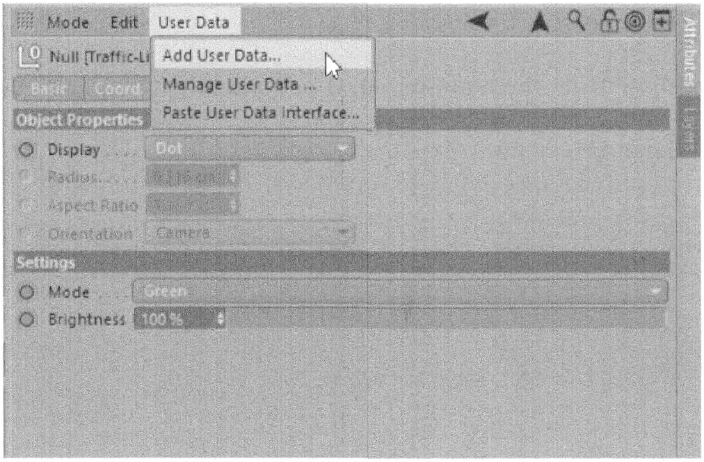

Figure 13-3 *Choosing* ***Add User Data*** *from the menu in the Attribute Manager*

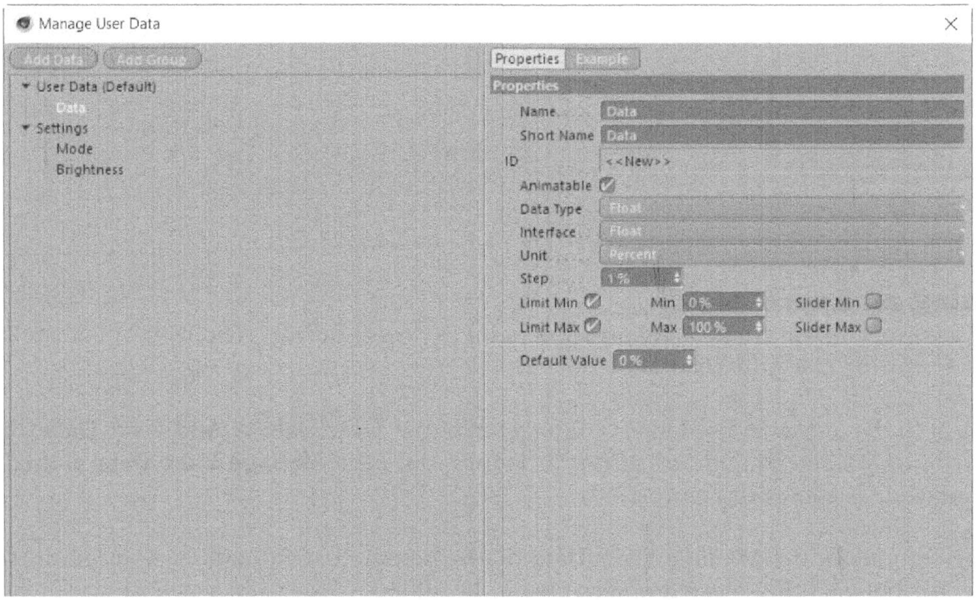

Figure 13-4 *The* ***Manage User Data*** *dialog box*

3. Make sure that *Traffic-Lights* is selected in the Object Manager. Choose **User Data > Add User Data** from the menu in the Attribute Manager, refer to Figure 13-3; the **Manage User Data** dialog box is displayed, refer to Figure 13-4.

4. In the **Manage User Data** dialog box, make sure that the **Properties** button is chosen. In the **Properties** area, enter **Yellow** in the **Name** text box and select **Float Slider** from the **Interface** drop-down list, refer to Figure 13-5. Next, choose the **OK** button in the **Manage User Data** dialog box; the **Yellow** spinner is added to the **User Data** area in the Attribute Manager, as shown in Figure 13-7.

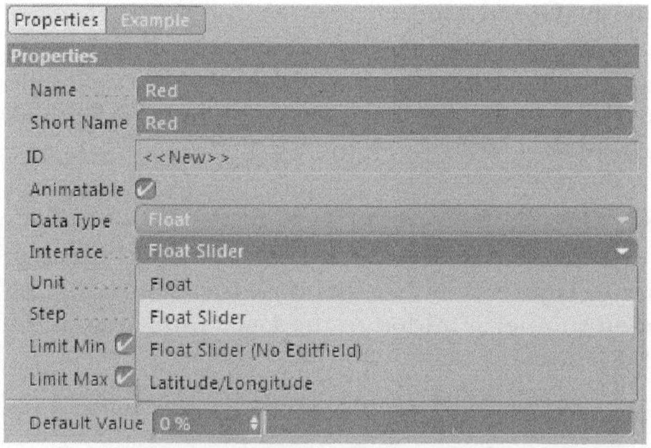

***Figure 13-5** Selecting **Float Slider** from the **Interface** drop-down list*

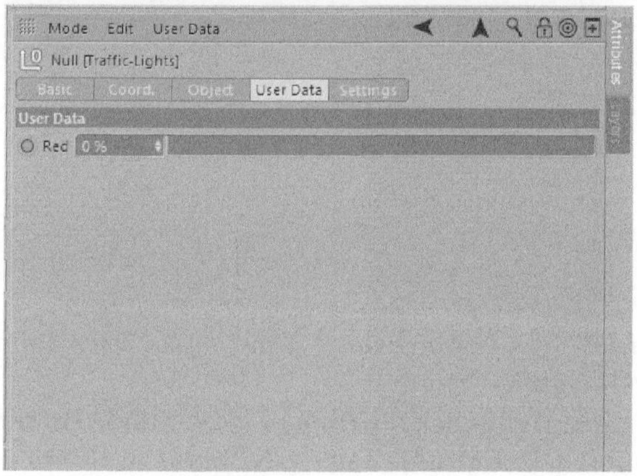

***Figure 13-6** The **Red** spinner added to the **User Data** area in the Attribute Manager*

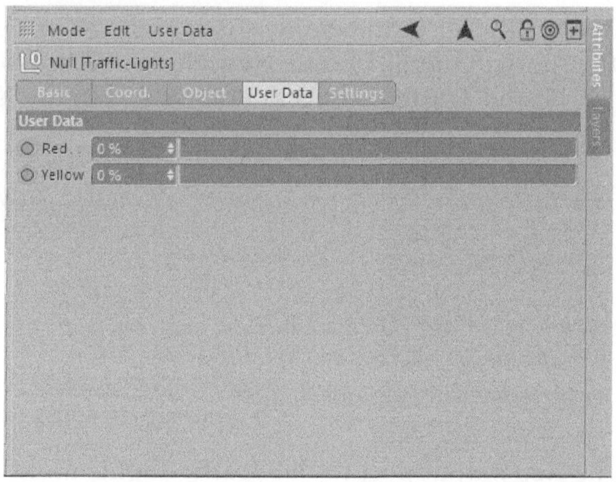

***Figure 13-7** The **Yellow** spinner added to the **User Data** area in the Attribute Manager*

Next, you will create the **Green** spinner.

5. Make sure that *Traffic-Lights* is selected in the Object Manager. Choose **User Data > Add User Data** from the menu in the Attribute Manager, refer to Figure 13-3; the **Manage User Data** dialog box is displayed, refer to Figure 13-4.

6. In the **Manage User Data** dialog box, make sure the **Properties** button is chosen. In the **Properties** area, enter **Green** in the **Name** text box and select **Float Slider** from the **Interface** drop-down list, refer to Figure 13-5. Next, choose the **OK** button in the **Manage User Data** dialog box; the **Green** spinner is added to the **User Data** area in the Attribute Manager, as shown in Figure 13-8.

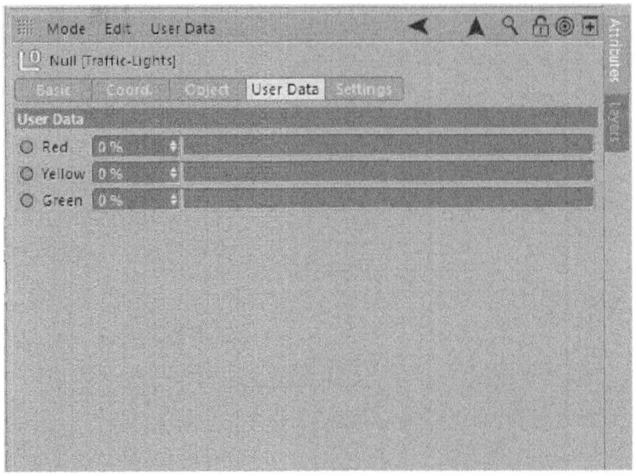

*Figure 13-8 The **Green** spinner added to the **User Data** area in the Attribute Manager*

7. In the Object Manager, right-click on *Traffic-Lights*; a shortcut menu is displayed. From the shortcut menu, choose **CINEMA 4D Tags > XPresso**, as shown in Figure 13-9; the **XPresso Expression** tag is added to *Traffic-Lights* in the Object Manager and the **XPresso Editor** is displayed, as shown in Figure 13-10.

8. In the **XPresso Editor**, right-click in the empty space in the **XGroup** area; a shortcut menu is displayed. From the shortcut menu, choose **New Node > XPresso > General > Object**, as shown in Figure 13-11; the **Traffic-Lights** node is added to the **XPresso Editor**.

Note
*The name of the object selected in the Object Manager is assigned to the added **Object** node.*

Tip
*If you have accidently closed the **XPresso Editor**, you can reopen it by double-clicking on the **XPresso** tag in the Object Manager. The **Object** node is used to represent a CINEMA 4D object, tag, or material.*

Next, you will add the **Red** output port to the **Traffic-Lights** node.

9. In the **XPresso Editor**, click on the output port (red square) of the **Traffic-Lights** node; a flyout is displayed. Choose **User Data > Red** from the flyout, as shown in Figure 13-12; the **Red** output port is added to the **Traffic-Lights** node.

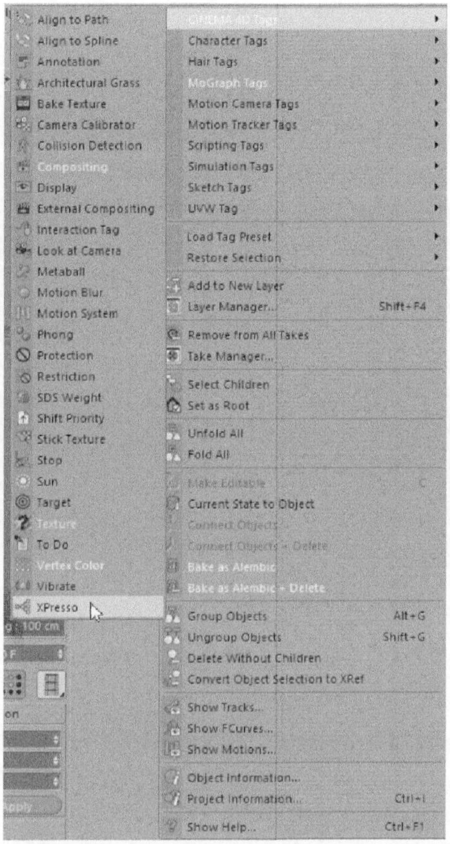

***Figure 13-9** Choosing **XPresso** from the shortcut menu*

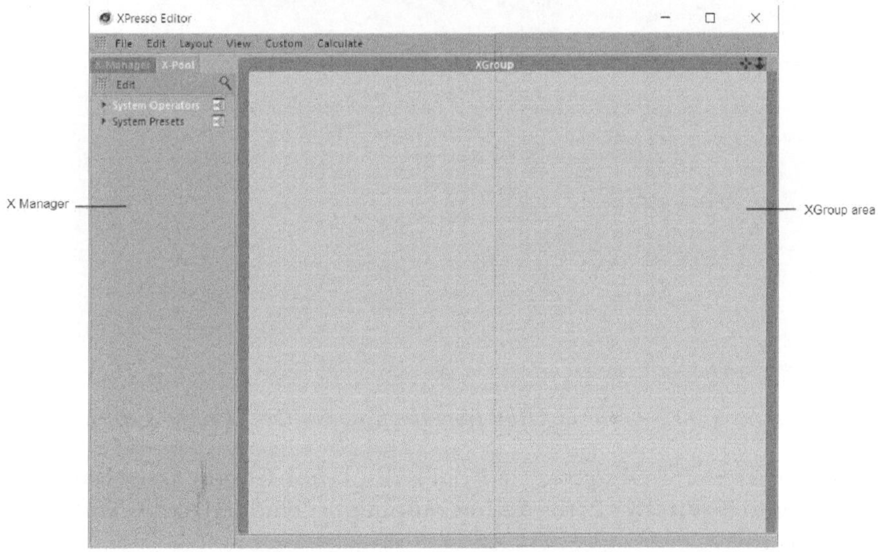

Figure 13-10** The **XPresso Editor

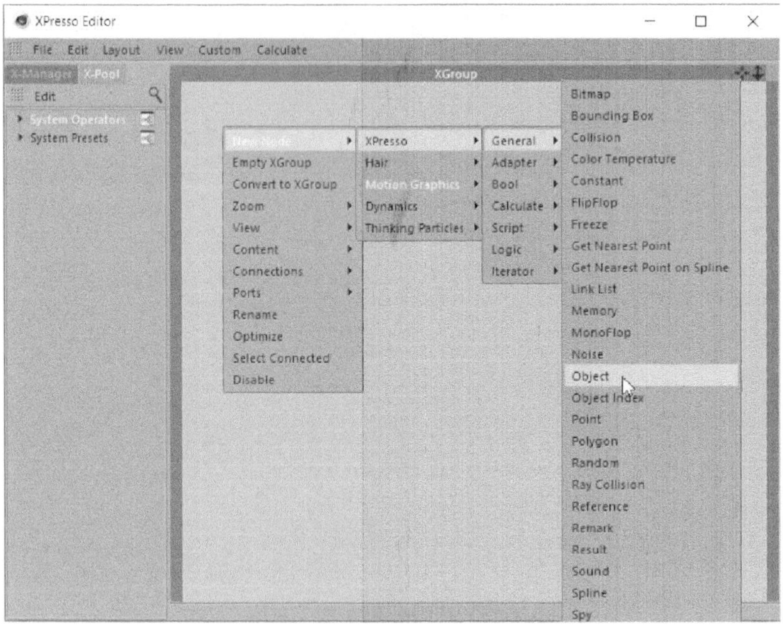

*Figure 13-11 Choosing **Object** from the shortcut menu*

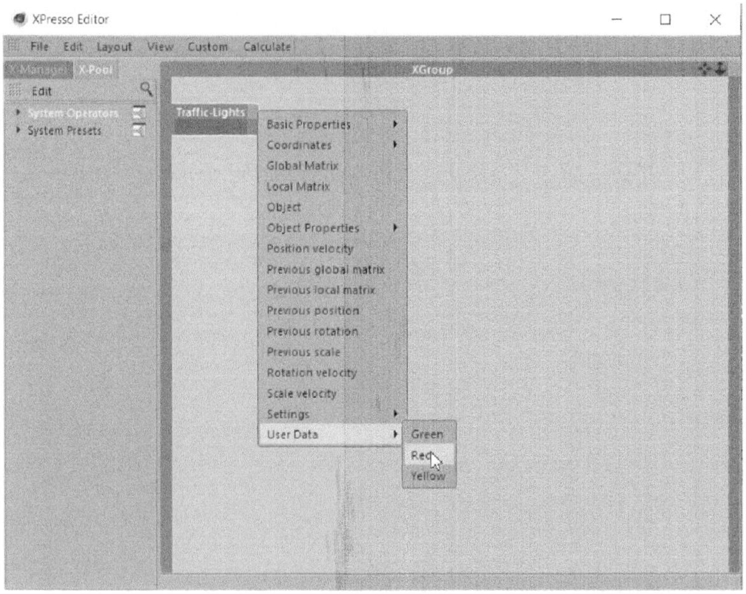

*Figure 13-12 Choosing **Red** from the flyout in the **XPresso Editor***

10. Click on the output port (red square); a flyout is displayed. Choose **User Data > Yellow** from the flyout, refer to Figure 13-12; the **Yellow** output port is added to the **Traffic-Lights** node, refer to Figure 13-13.

If the ports are not properly visible on the **Traffic-Lights** node, press and hold CTRL and then double-click on the node's title bar.

11. Similarly, add the **Green** output port to the **Traffic-Lights** node. Figure 13-13 displays the **Red**, **Yellow**, and **Green** output ports in the **Traffic-Lights** node.

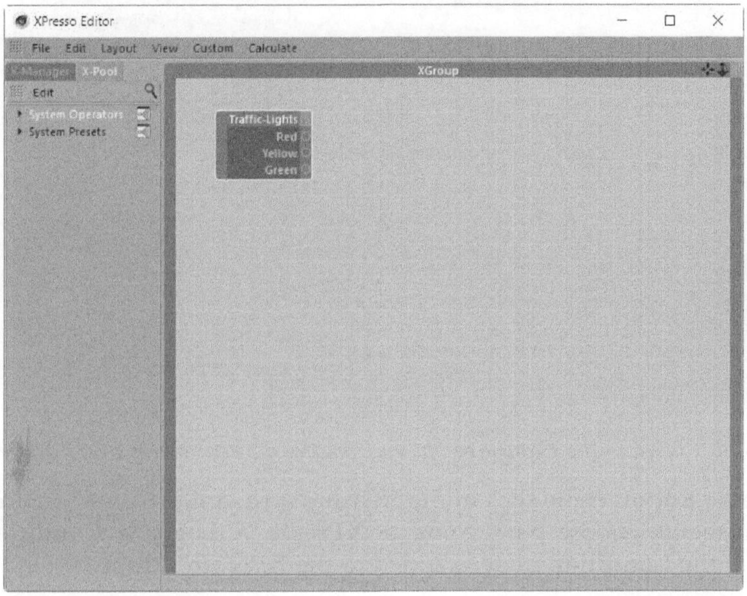

***Figure 13-13** The **Red, Yellow,** and **Green** output ports added to the **Traffic-Lights** node*

Next, you will add the **Compare** node to the **XPresso Editor**.

12. In the **XPresso Editor**, right-click in the **XGroup** area; a shortcut menu is displayed. From the shortcut menu, choose **New Node > XPresso > Logic > Compare**, as shown in Figure 13-14; the **Compare** node is added to the **XPresso Editor**.

13. In the **XPresso Editor**, make sure that the **Compare** node is selected. In the Attribute Manager, choose the **Basic** button; the **Basic Properties** area is displayed. In this area, enter **Compare 1** in the **Name** text box; the **Compare** node is renamed as **Compare 1** in the **XPresso Editor**.

The **Compare** node is used to compare two or more values to get a result.

14. Repeat step 12 to add two more **Compare** nodes to the **XPresso Editor**. Next, rename these nodes as **Compare 2** and **Compare 3** respectively, as done in the previous step.

Tip
You can also create the copies of a node by first pressing CTRL+C and then CTRL+V.

Next, you will add the **Condition** node to the **XPresso Editor**.

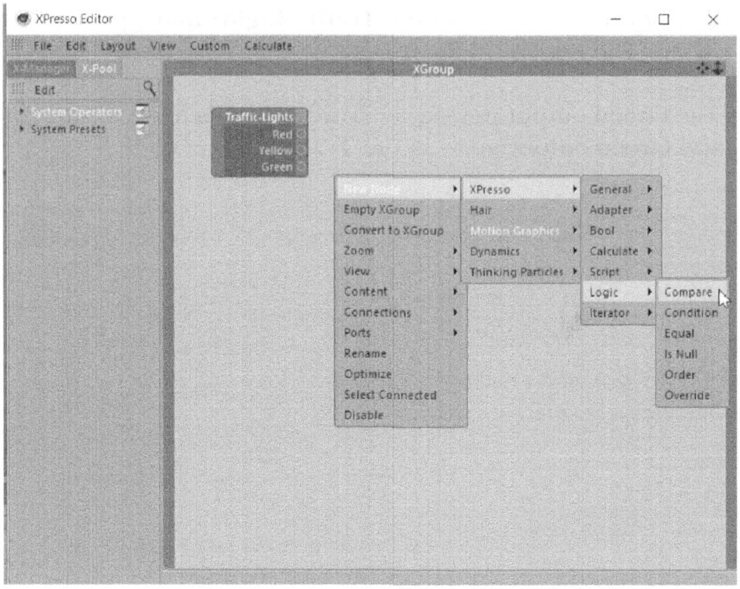

Figure 13-14 Choosing the ***Compare*** *option from the shortcut menu in the* ***XPresso Editor***

15. In the **XPresso Editor**, right-click in the **XGroup** area; a shortcut menu is displayed. From the shortcut menu, choose **New Node > XPresso > Logic > Condition**, as shown in Figure 13-15; the **Condition** node is added to the **XPresso Editor**.

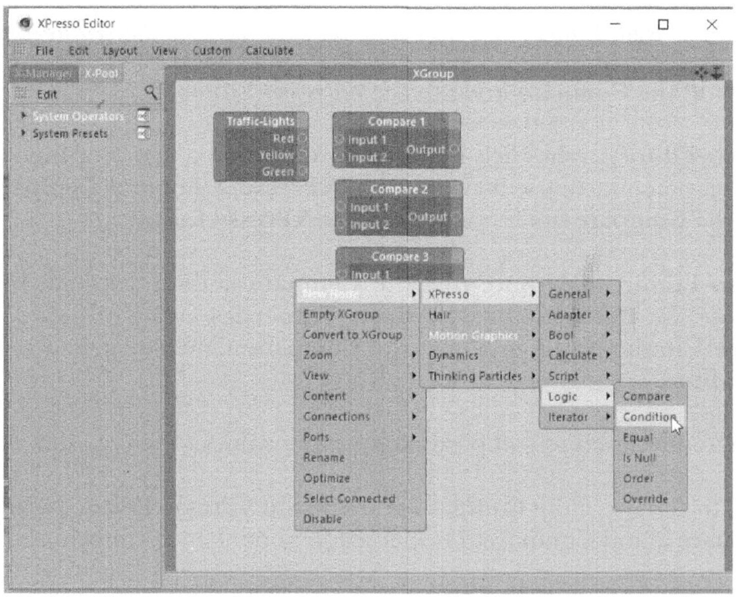

Figure 13-15 Choosing the ***Condition*** *option from the shortcut menu in the* ***XPresso Editor***

The **Condition** node acts like a switch which has two or more states.

16. Select the **Condition** node in the **XGroup** area, if not already selected. In the Attribute Manager, make sure the **Basic** button is chosen; the **Basic Properties** area is displayed. In this area, enter **Condition 1** in the **Name** text box; the **Condition** node is renamed as **Condition 1** in the **XPresso Editor**.

17. In the **XPresso Editor**, select the **Condition 1** node in the **XGroup** area. In the Attribute Manager, choose the **Node** button; the **Node Properties** area is displayed. In this area, select the **Color** option from the **Data Type** drop-down list, as shown in Figure 13-16.

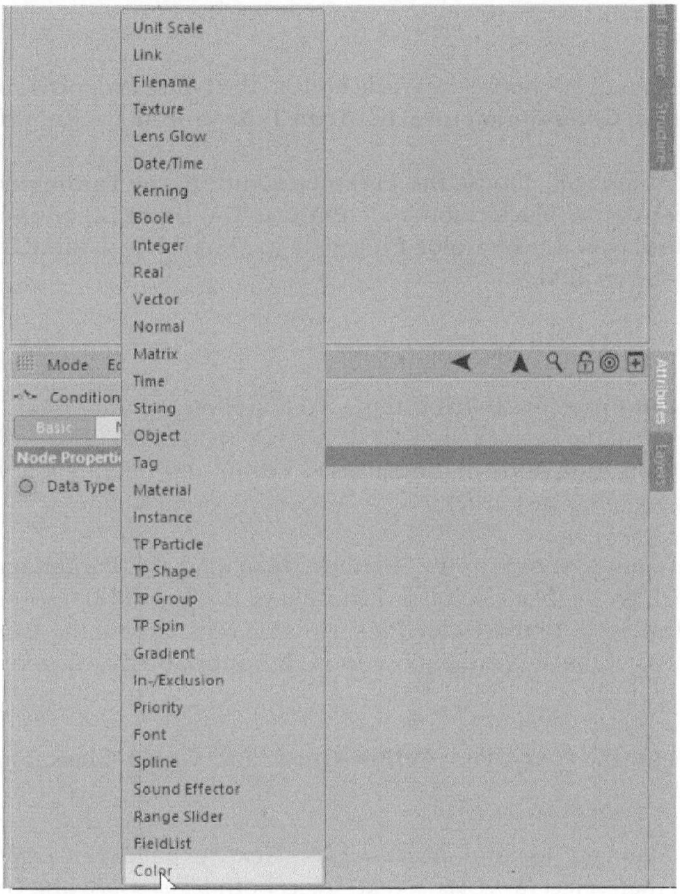

*Figure 13-16 Selecting **Color** from the **Data Type** drop-down list in the **Node Properties** area*

The options in the **Data Type** drop-down list are used to change the data type of the output node in the **XPresso Editor**.

18. In the Attribute Manager, choose the **Parameter** button; the **Parameter** area is displayed. In this area, click on the black color swatch next to the **Input [2]** attribute; the **Color Picker** dialog box is displayed. In the **Color Picker** dialog box, choose the **RGB** button and then

enter **255** in the **R** spinner; the red color is displayed in the color swatch and the black color swatch is replaced by red color.

19. In the **XPresso Editor**, right-click in the empty space of the **XGroup** area; a shortcut menu is displayed. From the shortcut menu, choose **New Node > XPresso > Logic > Condition**, refer to Figure 13-15; the **Condition** node is added to the **XGroup** area.

20. In the Attribute Manager, choose the **Basic** button; the **Basic Properties** area is displayed. In this area, enter **Condition 2** in the **Name** text box; the **Condition** node is renamed as **Condition 2**.

21. In the Attribute Manager, choose the **Node** button; the **Node Properties** area is displayed. In this area, select the **Color** option from the **Data Type** drop-down list, refer to Figure 13-16.

22. In the Attribute Manager, choose the **Parameter** button; the **Parameter** area is displayed. In this area, click on the black color swatch next to the **Input [2]** option; the **Color Picker** dialog box is displayed. In the **Color Picker** dialog box, choose the **RGB** button and then set the parameters as follows:

    R: **255** G: **255**

    The black color in the color swatch is replaced by yellow color.

23. Create a third **Condition** node in the **XPresso Editor** and rename it as **Condition 3** in the Attribute Manager, as done earlier.

24. Choose the **Parameter** button in the Attribute Manager; the **Parameter** area is displayed. In this area, click on the black color swatch next to the **Input [2]** option; the **Color Picker** dialog box is displayed. In the **Color Picker** dialog box, choose the **RGB** button and then enter **255** in the **G** spinner. Next, choose the **OK** button; the black color swatch is replaced by green color.

    Next, you will add the **Red-Glass**, **Yellow-Glass**, and **Green-Glass** nodes to the **XPresso Editor** window.

25. In the Object Manager, expand *Traffic-Lights*. Next, expand *Red-Light*, *Yellow-Light*, and *Green-Light* and then select *Red-Glass*. Next, select both *Yellow-Glass* and *Green-Glass* using the CTRL key. Now, press and hold the left mouse button and drag the cursor to the **XPresso Editor**; the **Red-Glass**, **Yellow-Glass**, and **Green-Glass** nodes are added to the **XPresso Editor**, as shown in Figure 13-17.

Connecting the Nodes

In this section, you will connect the nodes in the **XPresso Editor**.

1. In the **XGroup** area of the **XPresso Editor**, press and hold the left mouse button on the **Red** output port of the **Traffic-Lights** node and drag the cursor to the **Input 1** input port of the **Compare 1** node; a connection is established between the **Compare 1** and **Traffic-Lights** nodes, as shown in Figure 13-18.

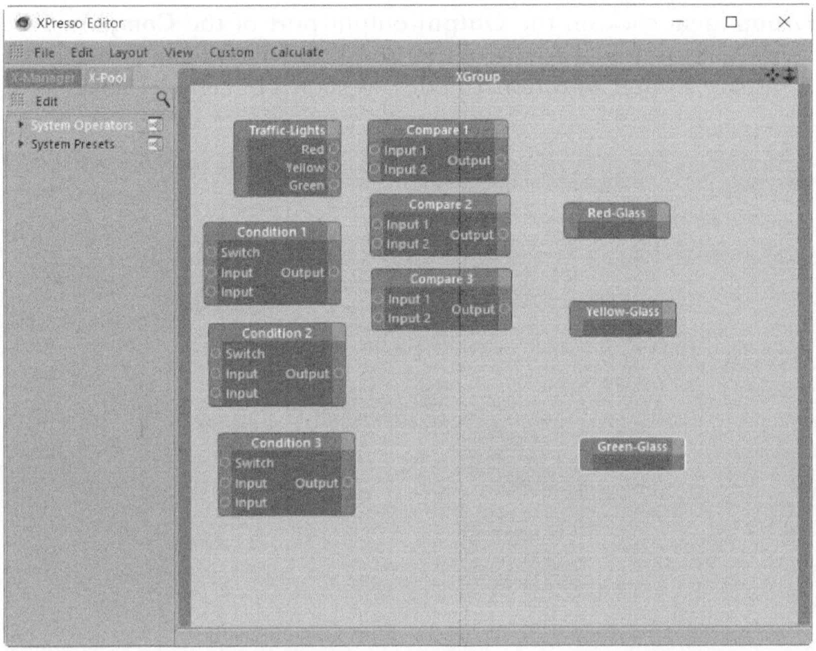

*Figure 13-17 The **Red-Glass**, **Yellow-Glass**, and **Green-Glass** nodes added in the **XPresso Editor***

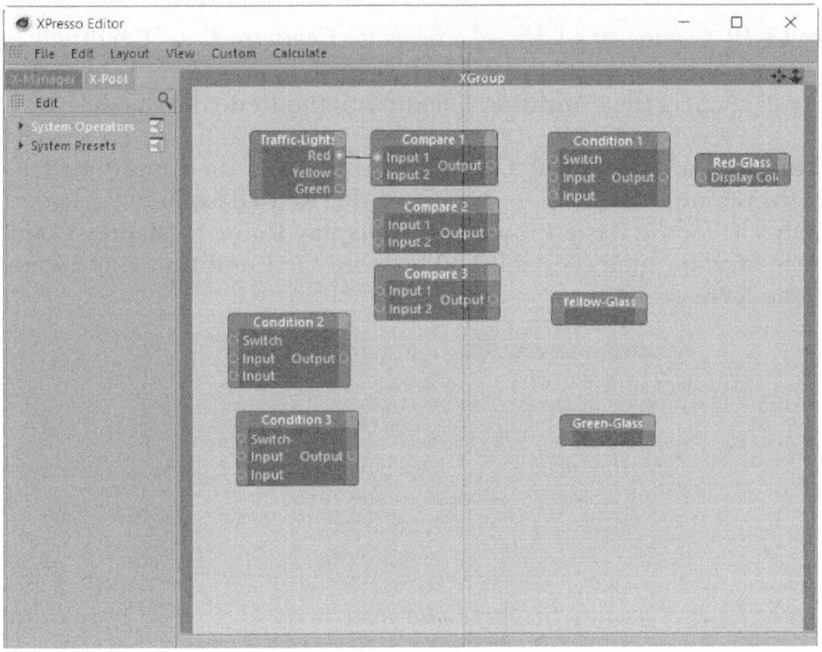

*Figure 13-18 Connection established between the **Red** output port of the **Traffic-Lights** and **Compare 1** nodes*

2. In the **XGroup** area, click on the **Output** output port of the **Compare 1** node and drag the cursor to the **Switch** input port of the **Condition 1** node; a connection is established between **Compare 1** and **Condition 1** nodes, as shown in Figure 13-19.

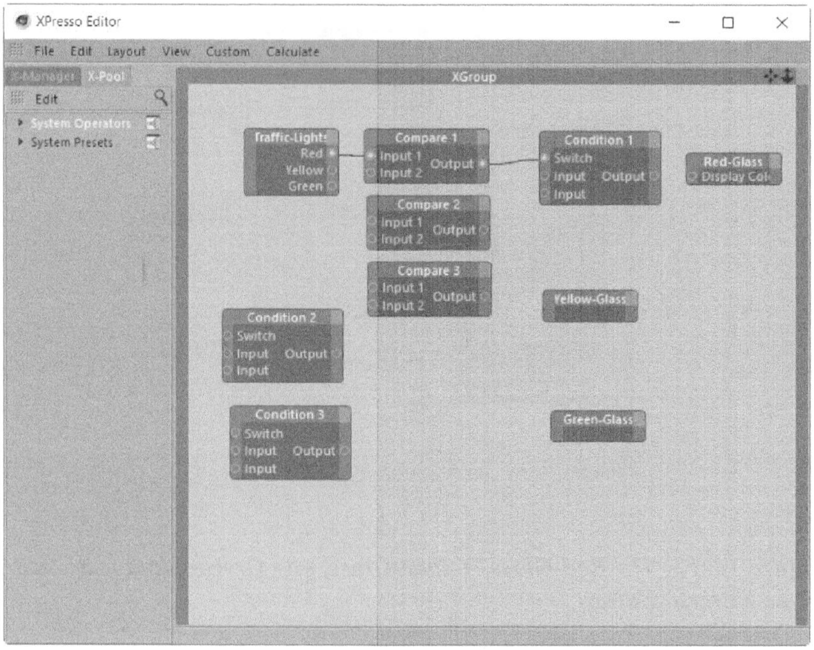

Figure 13-19 *Connection established between the **Compare 1** and **Condition 1** nodes*

Next, you will connect the **Condition 1** node with the **Red-Glass** node.

3. In the **XGroup** area, click on the **Output** output port of the **Condition 1** node and drag the cursor to the input port (blue square) of the **Red-Glass** node; a flyout is displayed. From this flyout, choose **Basic Properties > Display Color > Display Color**, as shown in Figure 13-20; a connection is established between the **Condition 1** and **Red-Glass** nodes. Minimize the **XPresso Editor**.

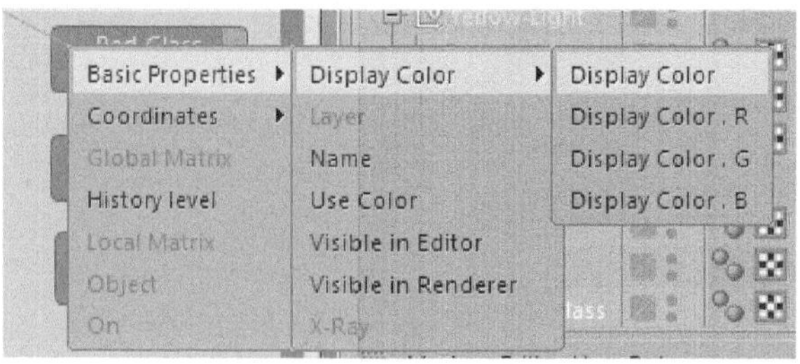

Figure 13-20 *Choosing **Display Color** from the flyout in the **XPresso Editor***

4. Select *Traffic-Lights* in the Object Manager. In the Attribute Manager, choose the **User Data** button; the **User Data** area is displayed. In this area, specify any value greater than 0 for the **Red** spinner; the red light is activated in the Perspective viewport, as shown in Figure 13-21. To deactivate the red color, enter **0** in the **Red** spinner.

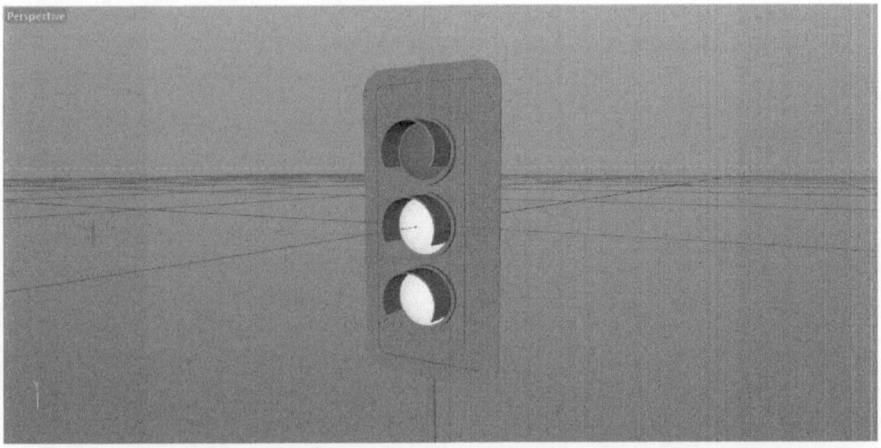

Figure 13-21 The red light activated in the Perspective viewport

The **Red** port of the **Traffic-Lights** node feeds data to the **Input 1** port of the **Compare 1** node. By default, the **Red** port passes down the value 0 to the **Input 1** node. Note that by default the **Input 2** option is set to 0 in the attributes of the **Compare 1** node in the **Parameter** area of the Attribute Manager. In the **Node Properties** area of the Attribute Manager, the **Function** option is set to **==** (equality operator). The **Condition 1** node will compare the value passed down by the **Red** port of the **Traffic-Lights** node and the value specified for the **Input 2** option in the **Parameter** area of the **Compare 1** node. The **Compare 1** node will output true (value 1) if the two values are same otherwise it will output false (value 0). When the value of output by the Red port is equal to the value specified for the Input 2 option, the **Compare 1** node will pass down a value of 1 down the tree.

The **Output** port of the **Compare 1** node is connected to the **Switch** port of the **Condition 1** node. Two states (colors) have been specified for the **Condition 1** node. The red color is specified for the **Input [2]** option and black color is specified for the **Input [3]** option in the **Parameter** area of the **Compare 1** node. The **Switch** attribute controls the state the **Condition** node will output. If the value 0 is specified for the **Switch** attribute, the **Condition 1** node will output the first state (red color). Likewise, if the value 1 is specified for the **Switch** attribute, the **Condition 1** node will output the second state (black color). When you specify a value greater than 0 for the **Red** attribute, the **Compare 1** node outputs a value 0 for the **Switch** port and the **Condition 1** node outputs the first state (red color).

Next, you will activate the yellow light of the signal.

5. Maximize the **XPresso Editor**. In the **XPresso Editor**, click on the **Yellow** output port of the **Traffic-Lights** node and drag the cursor to the **Input 1** input port of the **Compare 2** node; a connection is established between the **Compare 2** and **Traffic-Lights** nodes, as shown in Figure 13-22.

6. In the **XPresso Editor**, click on the **Output** output port of the **Compare 2** node and drag the cursor to the **Switch** input port of the **Condition 2** node; a connection is established between the **Compare 2** and **Condition 2** nodes, as shown in Figure 13-23.

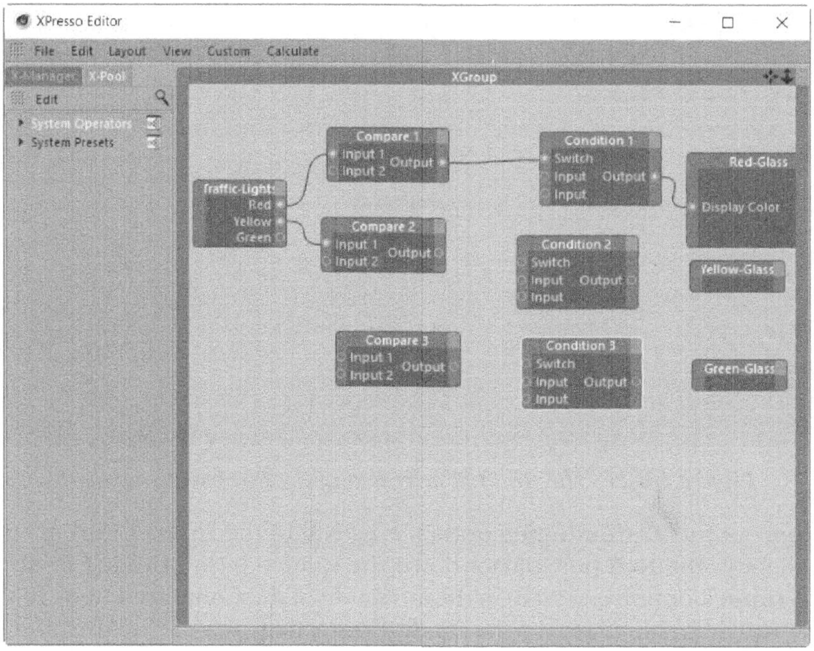

***Figure 13-22** Connection established between the **Yellow** output port of the **Traffic -Lights** and **Compare 2** nodes*

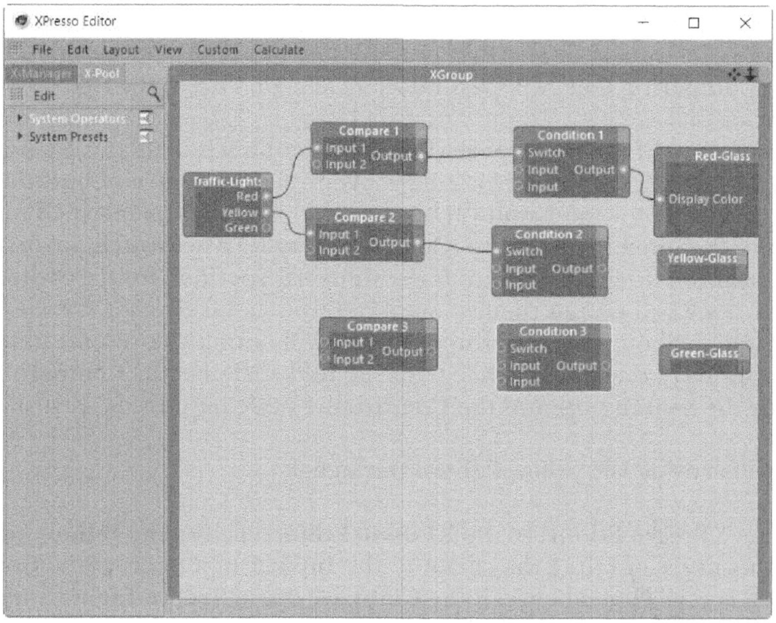

***Figure 13-23** Connection established between the **Compare 2** and **Condition 2** nodes*

7. In the **XGroup** area, click on the **Output** output port of the **Condition 2** node and drag the cursor to the input port (blue square) of the **Yellow-Glass** node; a flyout is displayed. From this flyout, choose **Basic Properties > Display Color > Display Color**, as shown in

Figure 13-24; a connection is established between the **Condition 2** and **Yellow-Glass** nodes. Minimize the **XPresso Editor**.

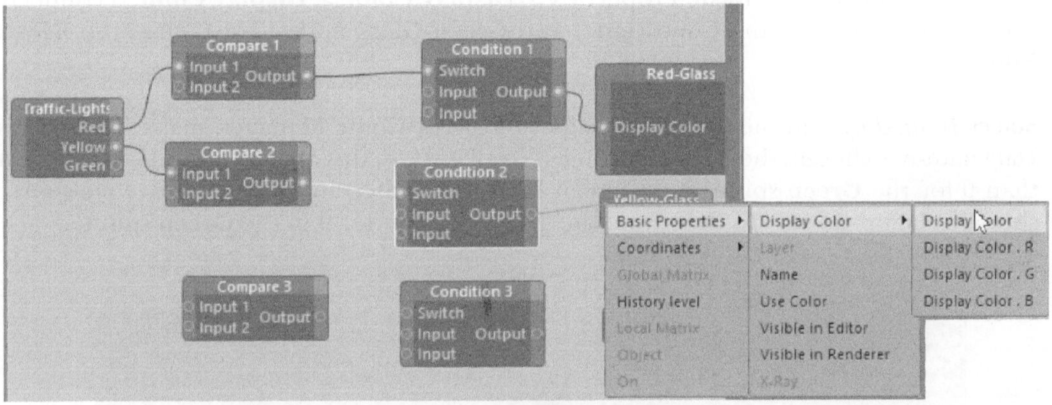

Figure 13-24** Choosing **Display Color** from the flyout in the **XPresso Editor

8. Select *Traffic-Lights* in the Object Manager. In the Attribute Manager, make sure the **User Data** button is chosen; the **User Data** area is displayed. In this area, specify any value greater than 0 for the **Yellow** spinner; the yellow light is activated in the Perspective viewport, as shown in Figure 13-25. To deactivate the yellow color, enter **0** in the **Yellow** spinner.

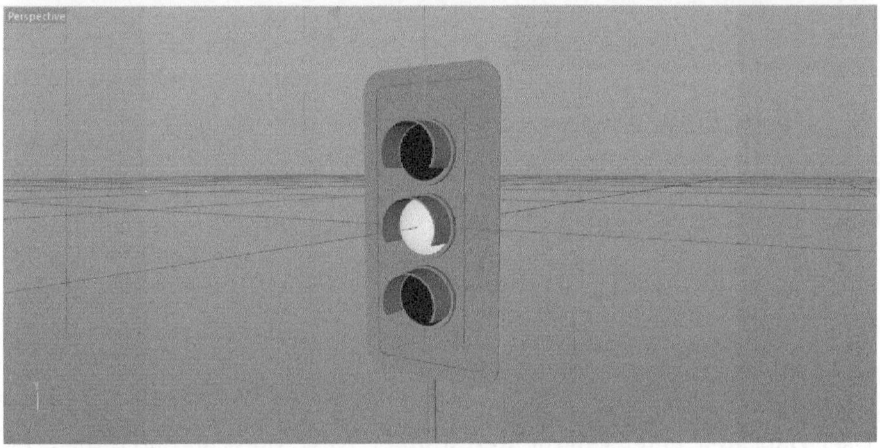

***Figure 13-25** The yellow light activated in the Perspective viewport*

Next, you will activate the green light of the traffic signal.

9. Maximize the **XPresso Editor**. In the **XGroup** area, click on the **Green** output port of the **Traffic-Lights** node and drag the cursor to the **Input 1** input port of the **Compare 3** node; a connection is established between the **Compare 3** and **Traffic-Lights** nodes.

10. In the **XGroup** area, click on the **Output** output port of the **Compare 3** node and drag the cursor to the **Switch** input port of the **Condition 3** node; a connection is established between the **Compare 3** and **Condition 3** nodes.

11. In the **XGroup** area, click on the **Output** output port of the **Condition 3** node and drag the cursor to the input port (blue square) of the **Green-Glass** node; a flyout is displayed. From this flyout, choose **Basic Properties > Display Color > Display Color**; a connection is established between the **Condition 3** and **Green-Glass** nodes. Next, close the **XPresso Editor**.

12. Select *Traffic-Lights* in the Object Manager. In the Attribute Manager, make sure the **User Data** button is chosen; the **User Data** area is displayed. In this area, specify any value greater than 0 for the **Green** spinner; the green light is activated in the Perspective viewport, as shown in Figure 13-26. To deactivate the green color, enter **0** in the **Green** spinner.

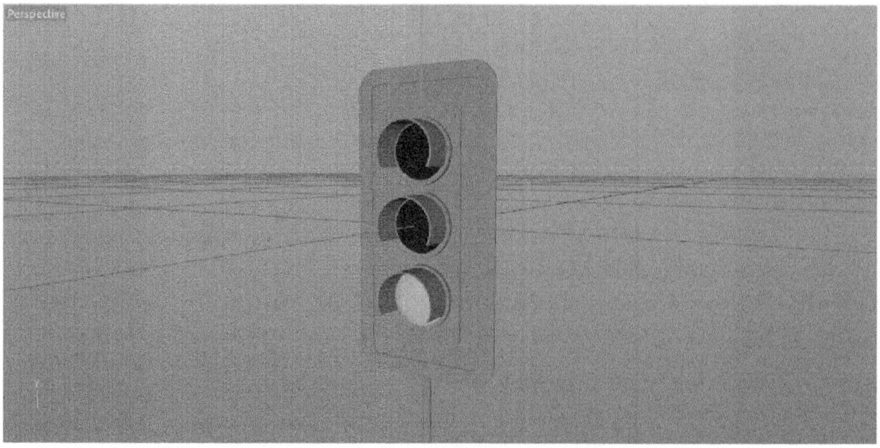

Figure 13-26 *The green light activated in the Perspective viewport*

Animating the Traffic Lights

In this section, you will animate the traffic lights using keyframes.

1. Make sure that the timeslider is set to frame 0. Select *Traffic-Lights* in the Object Manager.

2. In the Attribute Manager, make sure the **User Data** button is chosen and the **User Data** area is displayed.

3. In the **User Data** area, enter **1** in the **Red** spinner. Next, press and hold the CTRL key and then click on the name of the **Red** spinner to select it. Similarly, add the **Yellow** and **Green** spinners to the selection; the color of the labels changes.

4. Right-click on the selected labels in the **User Data** area; a shortcut menu is displayed. From this menu, choose **Animation > Add Keyframe**, refer to Figure 13-27; a keyframe is added at frame 0.

5. Move the timeslider to frame 25 and add a keyframe by repeating the process mentioned in step 4.

6. Move the timeslider to frame 26 and then enter **0** and **1** in the **Red** and **Yellow** spinners, respectively, in the **User Data** area of the Attribute Manager. Next, add a keyframe.

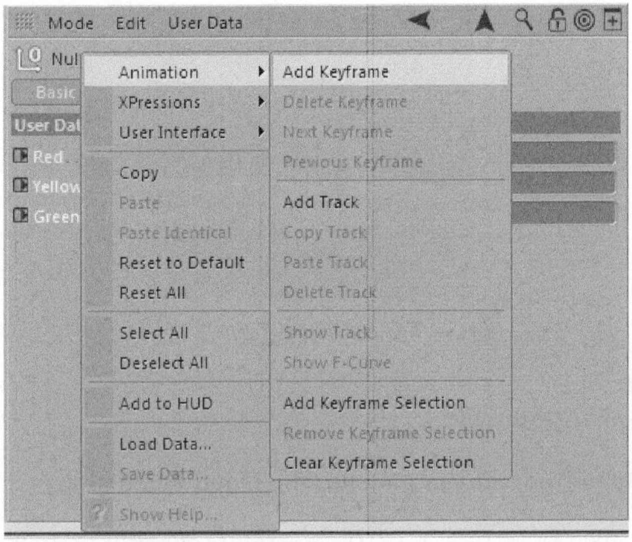

***Figure 13-27** The shortcut menu displayed on right-clicking in the **User Data** area*

7. Move the timeslider to frame 50 and add a keyframe by repeating the process mentioned in step 4.

8. Move the timeslider to frame 51 and then enter **0** and **1** in the **Yellow** and **Green** spinners, respectively, in the **User Data** area of the Attribute Manager. Next, add a keyframe.

9. Choose the **Play Forwards** button from the Animation toolbar to preview the animation.

Saving and Rendering the Scene

After completing the tutorial, you will save the file using the steps given next.

1. Choose **File > Save As** from the main menu; the **Save File** dialog box is displayed. In this dialog box, browse to the location *\Documents\c4dr20\c13*.

2. Enter **c13tut1** in the **File name** text box and then choose the **Save** button.

3. For rendering, refer to Tutorial 1 of Chapter 8.

Tutorial 2

In this tutorial, you will create custom parameters which will help you to deform an object, as shown in Figure 13-28.

The following steps are required to complete this tutorial:

a. Open the file.
b. Create an expression.
c. Connect the nodes.
d. Save and render the scene.

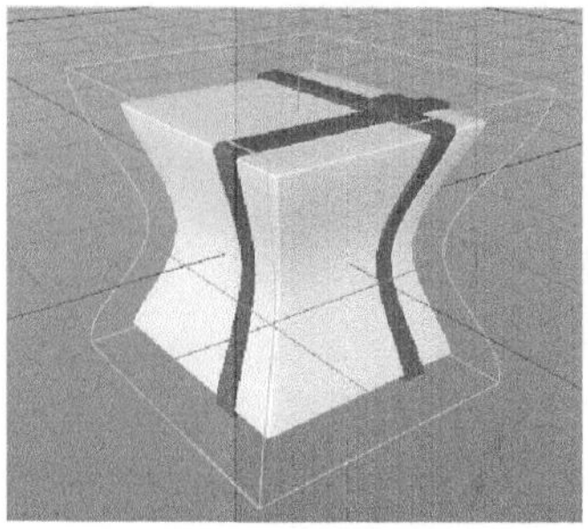

Figure 13-28 The deformed object

Opening the File

In this section, you will open the file.

1. Choose **File > Open** from the main menu; the **Open File** dialog box is displayed.
2. In the **Open File** dialog box, browse to *\Documents\c4dr20\c13\c13_tut2_start* and then choose the **Open** button; the *c13_tut2_start.c4d* file is opened, as shown in Figure 13-29.

Figure 13-29 The c13_tut2_start.c4d file

Creating an Expression

In this section, you will create an expression using the **XPresso Editor**.

1. In the Object Manager, right-click on *Gift*; a shortcut menu is displayed. In this shortcut menu, choose **CINEMA 4D Tags > XPresso**; the **XPresso Editor** is displayed.
2. Press and hold the left mouse button on *Gift* in the Object Manager and drag the cursor to the **XGroup** area of the **XPresso Editor**; the **Gift** node is added to the **XPresso Editor**, as shown in Figure 13-30. Next, close the **XPresso Editor**.

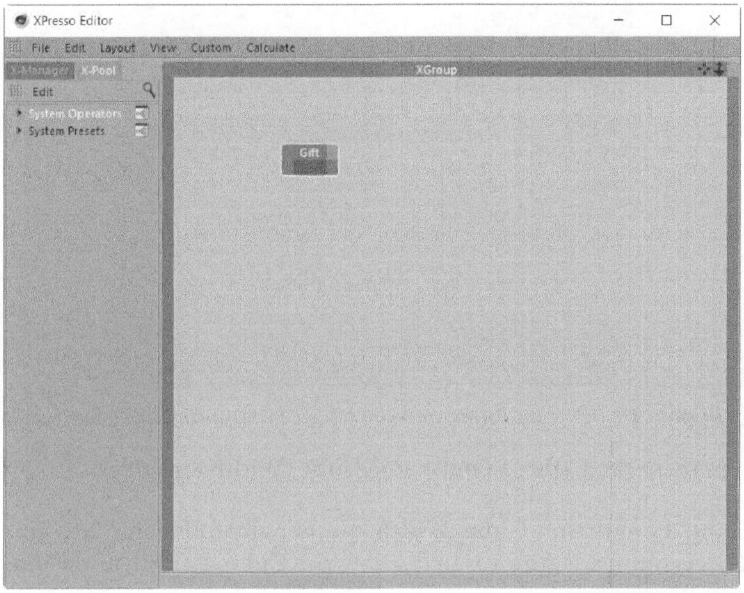

Figure 13-30 *The **Gift** node added in the **XPresso Editor***

Next, you will create user data.

3. Make sure *Gift* is selected in the Object Manager. Choose **User Data > Add User Data** from the menu in the Attribute Manager; the **Manage User Data** dialog box is displayed.

4. In the **Manage User Data** dialog box, make sure that the **Properties** button is chosen. In the **Properties** area, enter **Expand** in the **Name** text box and select **Float Slider** from the **Interface** drop-down list. Next, choose the **OK** button in the **Manage User Data** dialog box; the **Expand** spinner is added to the **User Data** area in the Attribute Manager, as shown in Figure 13-31.

Figure 13-31 *The **Expand** spinner in the Attribute Manager*

5. Make sure that *Gift* is selected in the Object Manager. Next, choose **User Data > Add User Data** from the menu in the Attribute Manager; the **Manage User Data** dialog box is displayed.

6. In the **Manage User Data** dialog box, make sure that the **Properties** button is chosen. In the **Properties** area, enter **Fillet** in the **Name** text box and select **Float Slider** from the **Interface** drop-down list. Next, choose the **OK** button in the **Manage User Data** dialog box; the **Fillet** spinner is added to the **User Data** area in the Attribute Manager, refer to Figure 13-32.

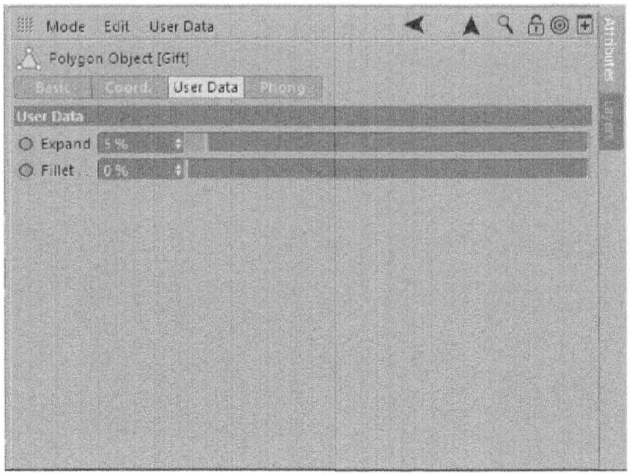

***Figure 13-32** The **Fillet** spinner added to the Attribute Manager*

Next, you will create the **Cube_Length** and **Cube_Width** spinners.

7. Create the **Cube_Length** and **Cube_Width** spinners by following the same steps when you created the **Fillet** spinner. Figure 13-33 displays the **Cube_Length** and **Cube_Width** spinners in the Attribute Manager.

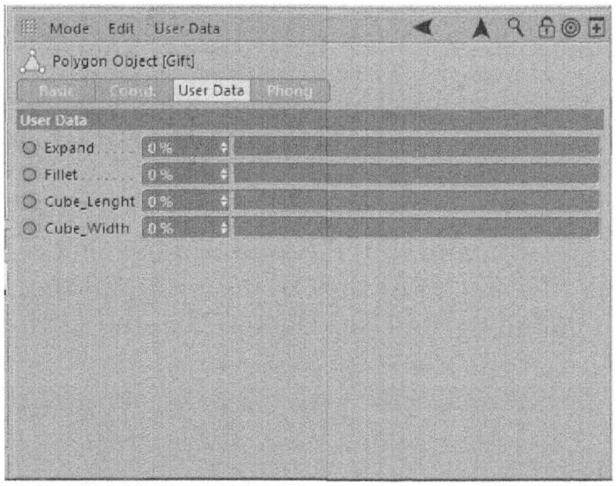

***Figure 13-33** The **Cube_Length** and **Cube_Width** spinners added to the Attribute Manager*

8. Open the **XPresso Editor**. In the **XGroup** area of the **XPresso Editor**, select the **Gift** node and click on its output port (red square); a flyout is displayed. Choose **User Data > Expand** from the flyout, as shown in Figure 13-34; the **Expand** output port is added to the **Gift** node.

9. Click on the output port (red square) of the **Gift** node; a flyout is displayed. Choose **User Data > Fillet** from the flyout; the **Fillet** output port is added to the **Gift** node, as shown in Figure 13-35.

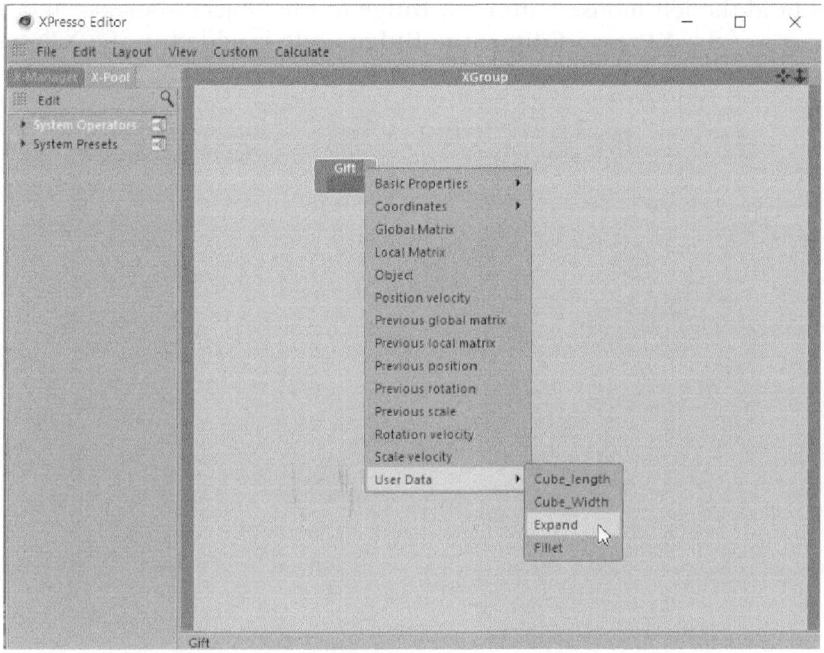

Figure 13-34 *Choosing* ***Expand*** *from the flyout in the* ***XGroup*** *area*

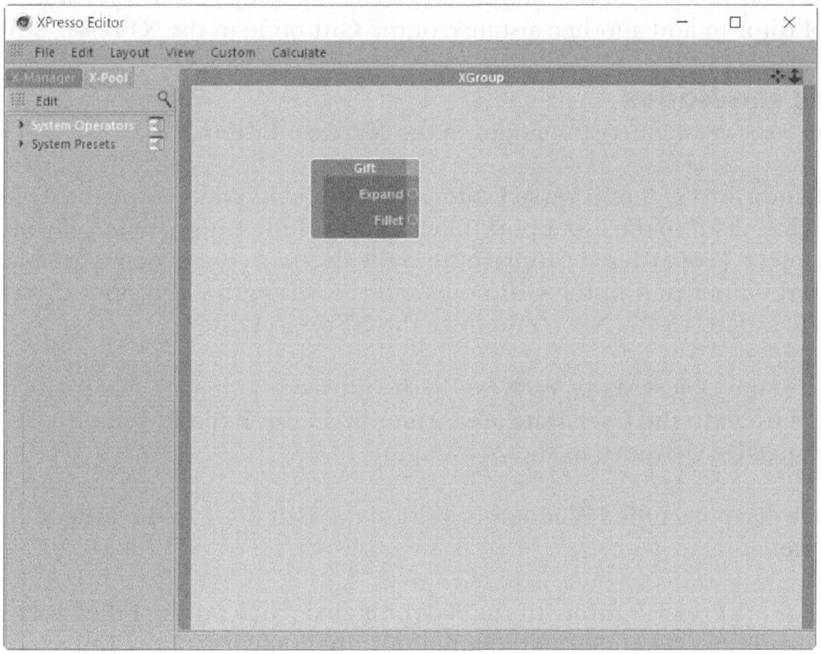

Figure 13-35 *The* ***Fillet*** *output port added to the* ***Gift*** *node*

10. Similarly, add the **Cube_Length** and **Cube_Width** output ports to the **Gift** node.

11. Press and hold the left mouse button on **Bulge** in the Object Manager and drag it to the **XGroup** area of the **XPresso Editor**; the **Bulge** node is added to the **XPresso Editor**, as shown in Figure 13-36.

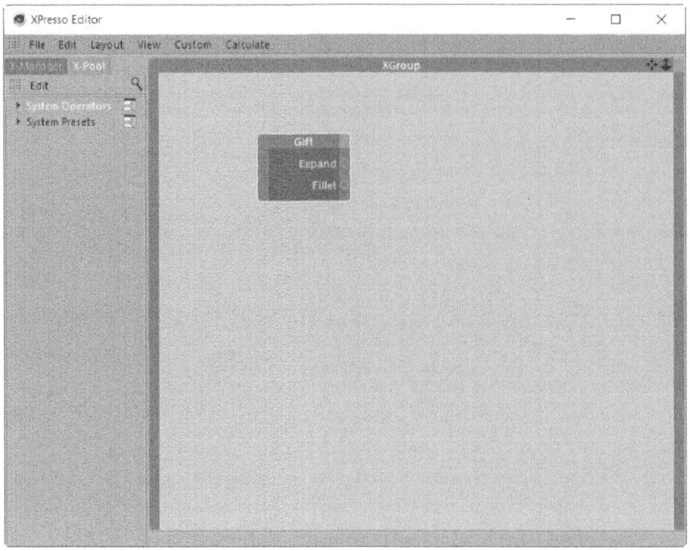

Figure 13-36 *The **Bulge** node in the **XGroup** area*

12. Press and hold the left mouse button on *Gift* in the Object Manager and drag it to the **XPresso Editor** to add another instance of the **Gift** node to the **XPresso Editor**.

Connecting the Nodes

In this section, you will connect the nodes in the **XPresso Editor**.

1. In the **XGroup** area of the **XPresso Editor**, click on the **Expand** output port of the **Gift** node and drag the cursor to the input port (blue square) of the **Bulge** node; a flyout is displayed. Choose **Object Properties > Strength** from the flyout; a connection is established between the **Expand** output port of the **Gift** node and the **Strength** input port of the **Bulge** node, as shown in Figure 13-37. Next, minimize the **XPresso Editor**.

2. Select *Gift* in the Object Manager. Next, in the Attribute Manager, make sure the **User Data** button is chosen. In the **User Data** area, enter **62** in the **Expand** spinner; *Gift* is expanded in the Perspective viewport, as shown in Figure 13-38.

   Next, you will connect the **Fillet** output port of the **Gift** node to the **Fillet** input port of the **Bulge** node.

3. Maximize the **XPresso Editor**. In the **XGroup** area, click on the **Fillet** output port of the **Gift** node and drag the cursor to the input port (blue square) of the **Bulge** node; a flyout is displayed. Choose **Object Properties > Fillet** from the flyout; a connection is established between the **Fillet** output port of the **Gift** node and the **Fillet** input port of the **Bulge** node. Next, minimize the **XPresso Editor**.

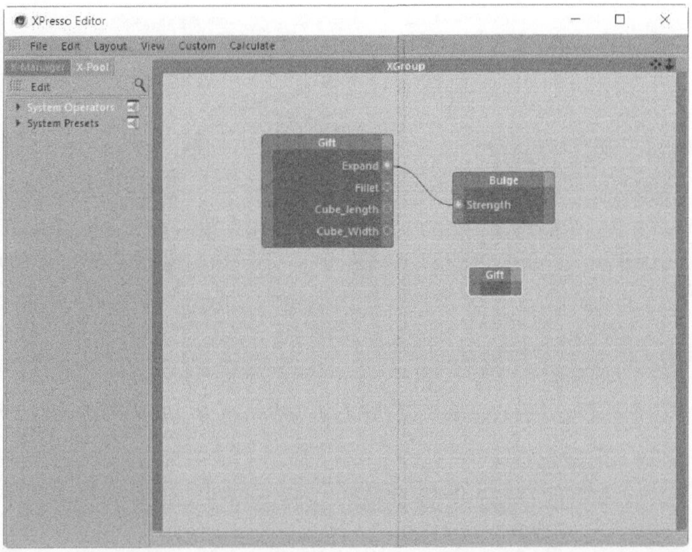

Figure 13-37 *Connection established between the **Gift** and **Bulge** nodes*

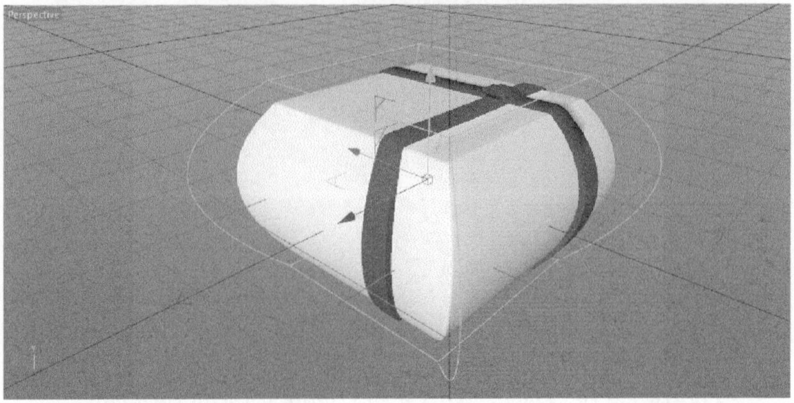

Figure 13-38 *Gift expanded in the Perspective viewport*

4. Make sure **Gift** is chosen in the Object Manager. In the **User Data** area, enter **19** in the **Fillet** spinner; the *Gift* deformation is softened in the Perspective viewport, as shown in Figure 13-39.

5. Maximize the **XPresso Editor**. In the **XGroup** area of the **XPresso Editor**, click on the **Cube_Length** output port of the first **Gift** node and drag the cursor to the input port (blue square) of the second **Gift** node; a flyout is displayed.

6. Choose **Coordinates > Scale > Scale . X** from the flyout; a connection is established between the **Cube_Length** output port of the first **Gift** node and the **Scale . X** port of the second **Gift** node, as shown in Figure 13-40.

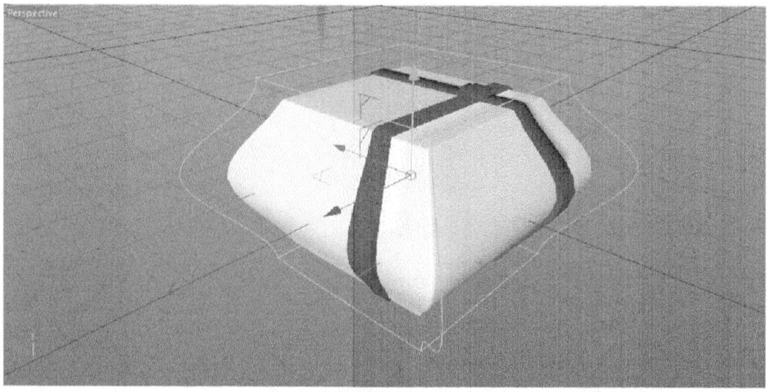

Figure 13-39 *The deformation of the Gift softened in the Perspective viewport*

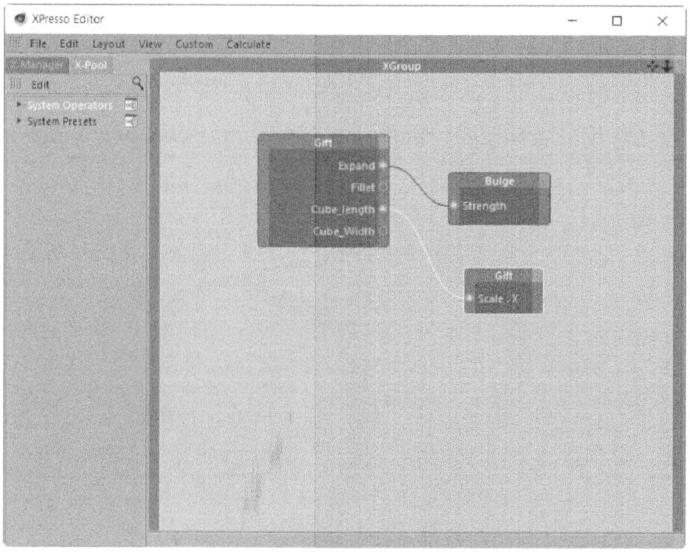

Figure 13-40 *The two **Gift** nodes connected with each other*

7. Similarly, connect the **Cube_width** port of the first **Gift** node to the **Scale . Y** port of the second **Gift** node. Next, close the **XPresso Editor**.

8. Select **Gift** in the Object Manager. In the Attribute Manager, choose the **User Data** button; the **User Data** area is displayed.

9. In the **User Data** area, enter values in the **Cube_Length** and **Cube_Width** spinners; the *Gift* is scaled along the X and Y axes in the Perspective viewport, refer to Figure 13-41.

Saving and Rendering the Scene

After completing the tutorial, you will save and render the file using the steps given next.

1. Choose **File > Save As** from the main menu; the **Save File** dialog box is displayed. In this dialog box, browse to the location *\Documents\c4dr20\c13*.

2. Enter **c13tut2** in the **File name** text box and then choose the **Save** button.

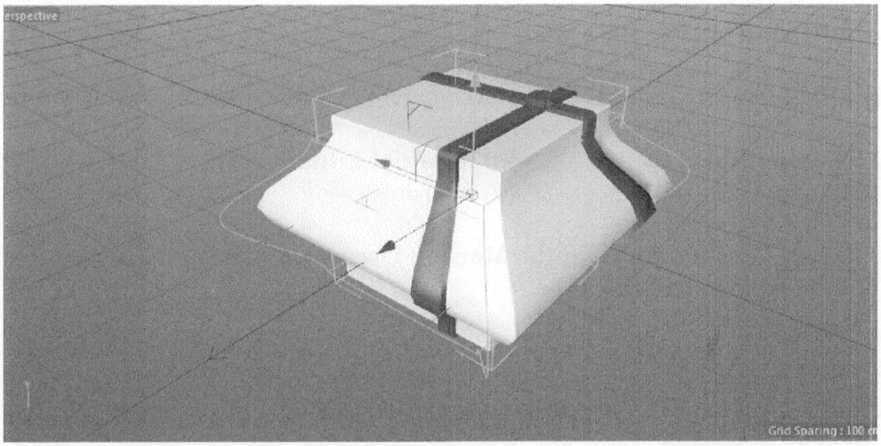

Figure 13-41 *The Gift scaled in the Perspective viewport*

3. For rendering, refer to Tutorial 1 of Chapter 8.

Self-Evaluation Test

Answer the following questions and then compare them to those given at the end of this chapter:

1. Which of the following nodes is used to compare two values using the comparison operators?

   (a) **Compare** (b) **Object**
   (c) **Range Mapper** (d) **Condition**

2. Which of the following nodes is used to represent a CINEMA 4D object, tag, or material?

   (a) **Object** (b) **Condition**
   (c) **XPresso** (d) **Compare**

3. The __________ option in the **Interface** drop-down list is the most commonly used user data parameter.

4. You can add any number of states to a __________ node by adding a port for each state from the inputs menu.

5. The __________ parameters are used to control the scene objects through the XPresso expressions.

Review Questions

Answer the following questions:

1. Which of the following options is used to create or build expressions by using nodes?

   (a) **XPresso Editor** (b) **Material Editor**
   (c) **Manage User Data** (d) **XGroup**

2. The ________ drop-down list in the **Manage User Data** dialog box is used to change the output of the data type of the node.

3. The ________ can be assigned to any object and can be saved in the scene.

4. The ________ node in the **XPresso Editor** acts like a switch.

5. The ________ dialog box is used to create, edit, and delete user data.

EXERCISE

The rendered output of the model used in the exercise can be accessed by downloading the *c13_cinema4d_r20_exr.zip* file from *www.cadcim.com*. The path of the file is as follows: *Textbooks > Animation and Visual Effects > MAXON CINEMA 4D > MAXON CINEMA 4D R20 Studio: A Tutorial Approach*

Exercise 1

Using the **User data** parameters and the **XPresso Editor**, animate the logo shown in Figure 13-42. **(Expected time: 35 min)**

Figure 13-42 *The logo at frame 49*

Answers to Self-Evaluation Test

1. a, **2.** a, **3. Float Slider**, **4. Condition**, **5. User Data**

Project 1

Creating an Indoor Scene

PROJECT DESCRIPTION

In this project, you will create an indoor scene and merge 3D objects into it. The final output of this project is shown in Figure P1-1.

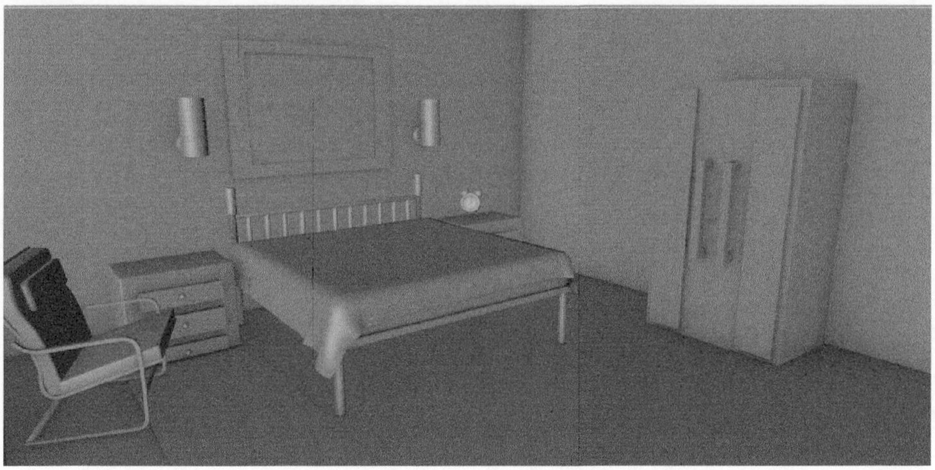

Figure P1-1 *The final output*

Creating the Room

In this section, you will create the room.

1. Choose **Create > Object** from the main menu; a cascading menu is displayed. Next, choose **Cube** from it; a cube is created in the Perspective viewport and *Cube* is added to the Object Manager. Rename *Cube* as *Room* in the Object Manager.

2. In the Attribute Manager, choose the **Object** button; the **Object Properties** area is displayed. In this area, set the parameters as follows:

   Size . X: **500** Size . Y: **300** Size . Z: **500**
   Segments X: **5** Segments Z: **5**

3. Choose the **Make Editable** tool from the Modes Palette; *Room* is converted into a polygonal object.

4. Choose the **Polygons** tool from the Modes Palette; *Room* is displayed in the polygon mode.

5. Invoke the **Live Selection** tool from the Command Palette. In the Attribute Manager, make sure the **Options** button is chosen. In the **Options** area, make sure the **Only Select Visible Elements** check box is selected.

6. Using the **Live Selection** tool, select the polygons of *Room*, as shown in Figure P1-2. Next, delete the selected polygons by pressing DELETE.

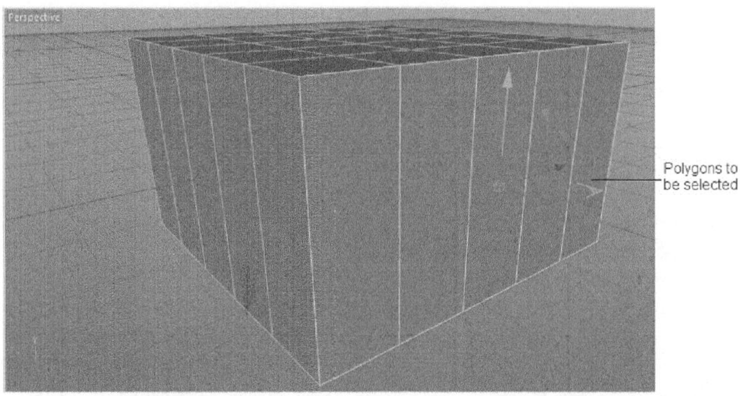

Figure P1-2 *The selected polygons displayed*

Creating the Bed

In this section, you will create the bed.

1. Choose **Create > Object** from the main menu; a cascading menu is displayed. Next, choose **Cube** from it; a cube is created in the Perspective viewport and *Cube* is added to the Object Manager. Rename *Cube* as *Base* in the Object Manager. Choose the **Model** tool from the Modes Palette; *Base* is selected in the Perspective viewport.

2. Press SHIFT+V; the **Viewport [Perspective]** area is displayed in the Attribute Manager. Clear the **Outlines** check box, if not already cleared from the **Active Object** area. Next, make sure that the **Sel.: Bounding Box** check box is selected.

3. Select *Base* in the Object Manager. In the Attribute Manager, make sure the **Object** button is chosen. Set the parameters in the **Object Properties** area as follows:

   Size . X: **203** Size . Y: **5** Size . Z: **198**

   Select the **Fillet** check box and enter **1** in the **Fillet Radius** spinner.

4. In the Attribute Manager, choose the **Coord** button; the **Coordinates** area is displayed. In this area, set the parameters as follows:

   P . X: **-120.5** P . Y: **-105**

   Press F5; all viewports are displayed. Figure P1-3 displays *Base* aligned in all viewports.

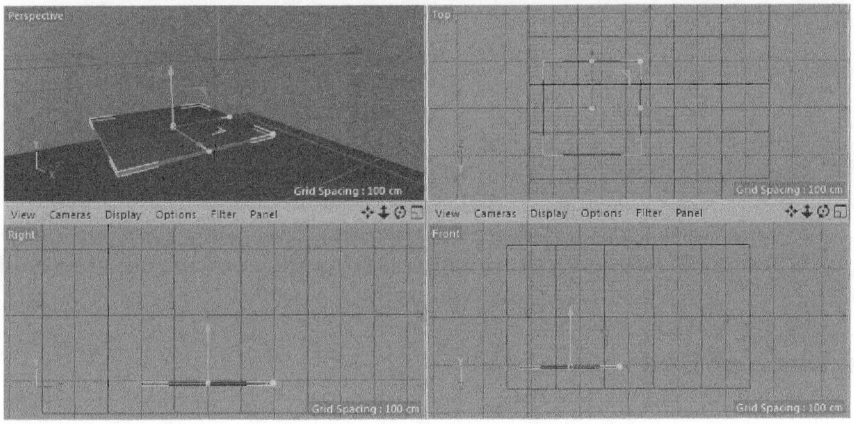

Figure P1-3 *The Base displayed in all viewports*

Creating the Mattress

In this section, you will create the mattress.

1. Choose **Create > Object** from the main menu; a cascading menu is displayed. Next, choose **Cube** from it; a cube is created in the Perspective viewport and *Cube* is added to the Object Manager. Rename *Cube* as *Mattress* in the Object Manager.

2. In the Attribute Manager, choose the **Object** button. In the **Object Properties** area, set the parameters as follows:

   Size . X: **190** Size . Y: **26** Size . Z: **190**

   Select the **Fillet** check box and enter **6** in the **Fillet Radius** spinner.

3. In the Attribute Manager, choose the **Coord** button; the **Coordinates** area is displayed. In this area, set the parameters as follows:

   P . X: **-115.039** P . Y: **-91.61** P . Z: **0.418**

   Figure P1-4 displays *Mattress* aligned in all viewports.

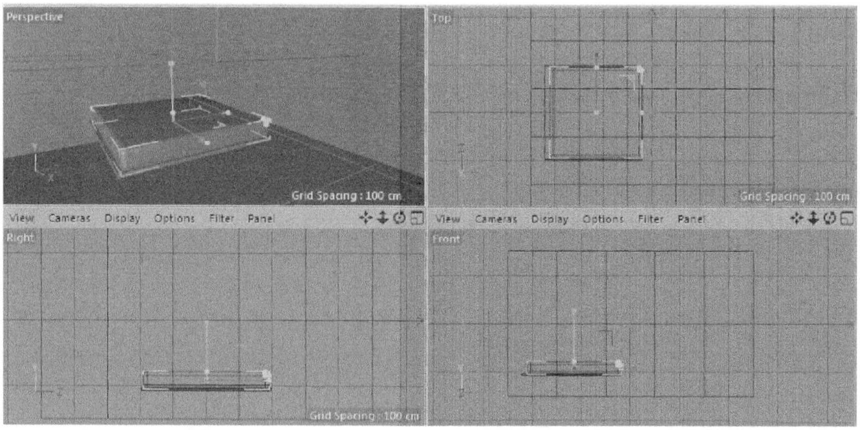

Figure P1-4 *Mattress aligned in all viewports*

Next, you will group *Mattress* and *Base*.

4. In the Object Manager, select *Mattress* and *Base* using the SHIFT key and then right-click; a shortcut menu is displayed. Choose **Group Objects** from the shortcut menu; a **Null** group is created in the Object Manager. Rename *Null* as *Bed*.

Creating the Legs of Bed

In this section, you will create the legs of bed.

1. Press F2; the Top viewport is maximized. Choose **Create > Object** from the main menu; a cascading menu is displayed. Next, choose **Cylinder** from it; a cylinder is created in the Front viewport and *Cylinder* is added to the Object Manager. Rename *Cylinder* as *Leg1*.

2. In the Attribute Manager, choose the **Object** button; the **Object Properties** area is displayed. In this area, set the parameters as follows:

   Radius: **3** Height: **46**

3. Choose the **Caps** button; the **Caps** area is displayed. In this area, select the **Fillet** check box and enter **0.5** in the **Radius** spinner.

4. In the Attribute Manager, choose the **Coord** button; the **Coordinates** area is displayed. In this area, set the parameters as follows:

   P . X: **-26.07** P . Y: **-127.059** P . Z: **-91.69**

Press F1; the Perspective viewport is maximized. Figure P1-5 displays *Leg1* in the Perspective viewport.

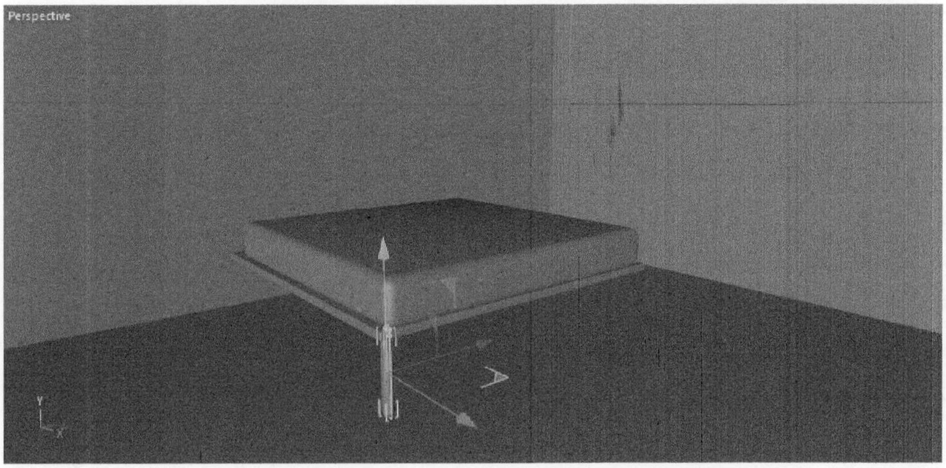

Figure P1-5 *The Leg1 displayed in the Perspective viewport*

5. Create a copy of *Leg1* in the Object Manager using the CTRL key; *Leg1.1* is added to the Object Manager. Next, in the Attribute Manager, make sure the **Coord** button is chosen. In the **Coordinates** area, enter **92.55** in the **P . Z** spinner. Figure P1-6 displays two legs in the Perspective viewport.

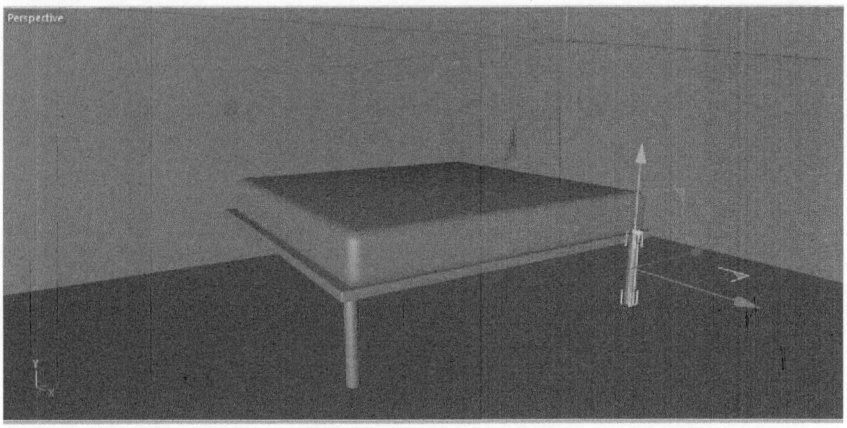

Figure P1-6 *Two legs displayed in the Perspective viewport*

6. In the Object Manager, create a copy of *Leg1.1* using the CTRL key; *Leg1.2* is added to the Object Manager. Make sure *Leg1.2* is selected in the Object Manager and choose the **Make Editable** tool from the Modes Palette; the *Leg1.2* is converted into a polygonal object. In the Attribute Manager, make sure the **Coord** button is chosen. Set the parameters as follows:

P . X: **-216.162** P . Y: **-93.045** P . Z: **-88.545**
S . Y: **2.46**

Figure P1-7 displays *Leg1.2* positioned in the Perspective viewport.

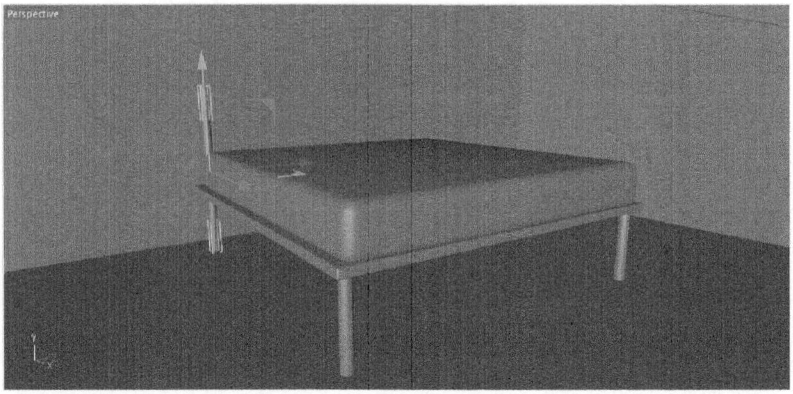

Figure P1-7 *The Leg1.2 displayed in the Perspective viewport*

7. Choose the **Edges** tool from the Modes Palette; the *Leg1.2* is displayed in the edges mode. Next, right-click in the Perspective viewport; a shortcut menu is displayed. Choose **Loop/ Path Cut** from the shortcut menu; the **Loop/Path Cut** tool settings are displayed in the Attribute Manager.

8. Click on *Leg1.2* in the Perspective viewport, as shown in Figure P1-8; a new edge loop is created. Now, press SPACEBAR to exit the tool.

Figure P1-8 *Clicking on an edge*

9. Choose the **Polygons** tool from the Modes Palette; *Leg1.2* is displayed in the polygon mode. Invoke the **Rectangle Selection** tool from the Command Palette. Make sure that the **Only Select Visible Elements** check box is cleared. Select the polygons of *Leg1.2* in the Perspective viewport, as shown in Figure P1-9.

10. Right-click on the selected polygons; a shortcut menu is displayed. Choose **Bevel** from the shortcut menu; the **Bevel** tool settings are displayed in the Attribute Manager.

11. In the **Tool Option** area, enter **1** in the **Offset** spinner and **5** in the **Subdivision** spinner. In the **Polygon Extrusion** area, enter **1** in the **Extrusion** spinner and then press ENTER; the selected polygons are bevelled, as shown in Figure P1-10. Choose the **Model** tool from the Modes Palette; the *Leg1.2* is displayed in the object mode.

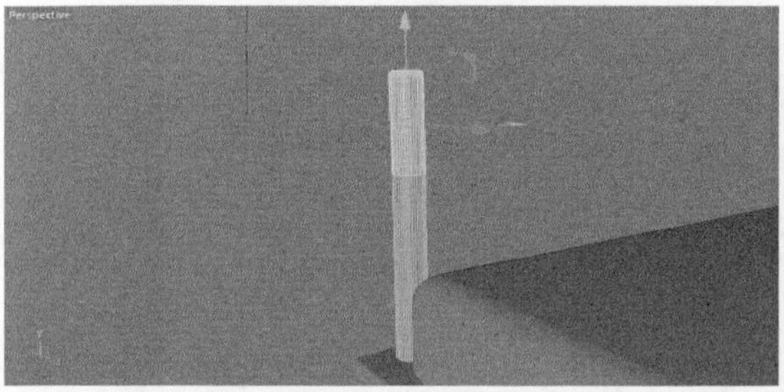

Figure P1-9 *The selected polygons*

Figure P1-10 *The selected polygons bevelled*

12. Select *Leg1.2* and create a copy of it; the *Leg1.3* is added to the Object Manager. In the Attribute Manager, make sure the **Coord** button is chosen. Next, enter **86.748** in the **P . Z** spinner. Press F5; all viewports are displayed. Figure P1-11 displays *Leg1.3* positioned in all viewports.

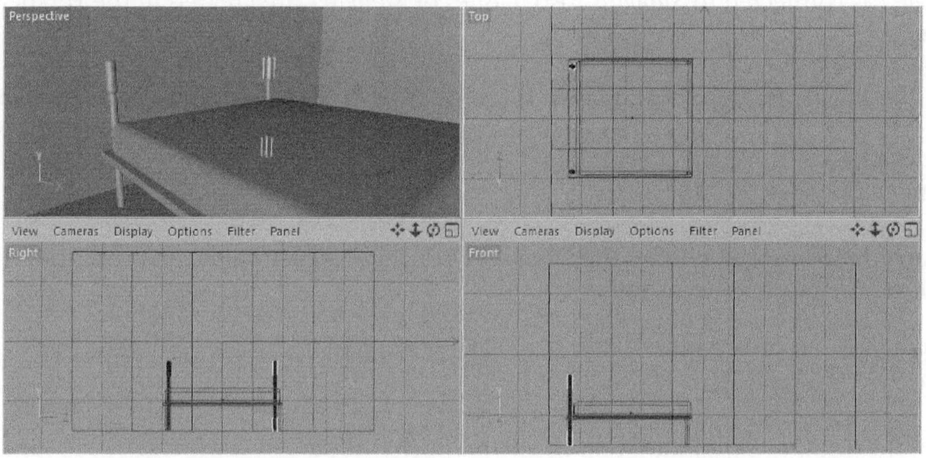

Figure P1-11 *The Leg1.3 aligned in all viewports*

Creating the Back Supports

In this section, you will create the back supports for the bed.

1. Press F1; the Perspective viewport is displayed. Choose **Create > Object** from the main menu; a cascading menu is displayed. Next, choose **Cylinder** from it; a cylinder is created in the Perspective viewport and *Cylinder* is added to the Object Manager. Rename the *Cylinder* as *Support1* in the Object Manager.

2. In the Attribute Manager, choose the **Object** button; the **Object Properties** area is displayed. In this area, set the parameters as follows:

Radius: **2** Height: **46**

3. Press F5; all viewports are displayed. Figure P1-12 displays *Support1* in all viewports.

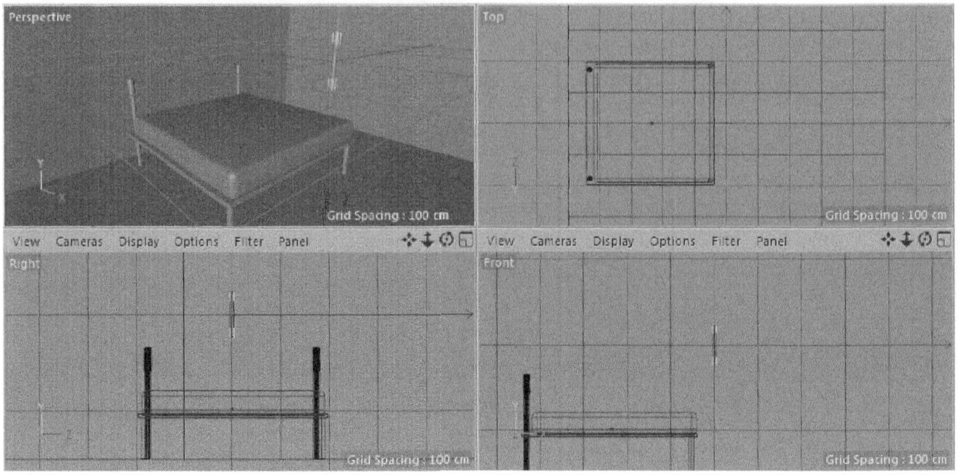

Figure P1-12 *The Support1 aligned in all viewports*

4. Choose **MoGraph > Cloner** from the main menu; *Cloner* is added to the Object Manager. Rename *Cloner* as *Support*. In the Object Manager, select *Support1* and then drag it to *Support*; the *Support1* is connected to *Support*. Also, clones of *Support1* are created in the Perspective viewport.

5. Choose *Support* in the Object Manager. In the Attribute Manager, make sure the **Object** button is chosen. In the **Object Properties** area, set the parameters as follows:

   Count: **11** P . X: **15** P . Y: **0**

6. In the Attribute Manager, choose the **Coord** button; the **Coordinates** area is displayed. In this area, set the parameters as follows:

   P . X: **-215.746** P . Y: **-80.4** P . Z: **-76.056**
   R . H: **90**

   Figure P1-13 displays *Support* aligned in all viewports.

7. Choose **Create > Object** from the main menu; a cascading menu is displayed. Next, choose **Cylinder** from it; a cylinder is created in all viewports and *Cylinder* is added to the Object Manager. Rename it as *Rod*.

8. In the Attribute Manager, choose the **Object** button; the **Object Properties** area is displayed. In this area, set the parameters as follows:

   Radius: **2** Height: **173**

   Select **+Z** in the **Orientation** drop-down list.

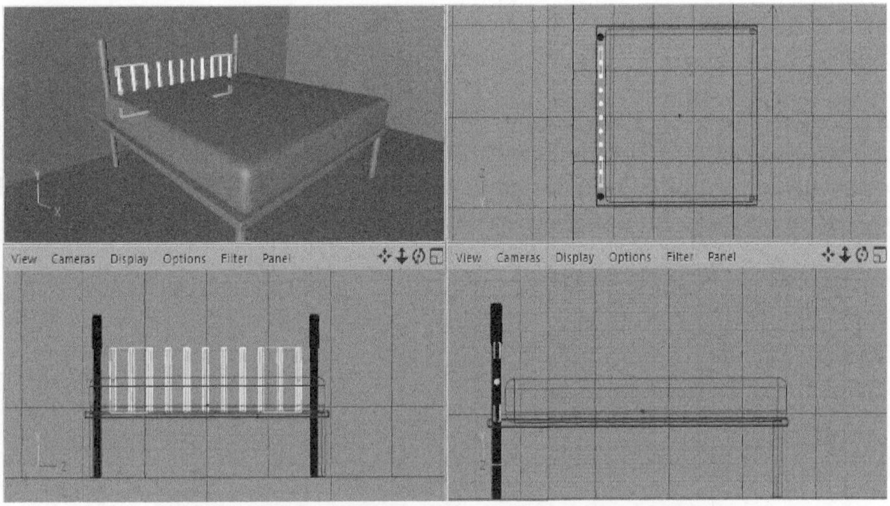

Figure P1-13 The Support aligned in all viewports

9. Choose the **Caps** button; the **Caps** area is displayed. In this area, select the **Fillet** check box and set the parameters as follows:

   Segments: **2** Radius: **0.6**

10. In the Attribute Manager, choose the **Coord** button; the **Coordinates** area is displayed. In this area, set the parameters as follows:

    P . X: **-215.417** P . Y: **-57.935**

Figure P1-14 displays *Rod* aligned in all viewports.

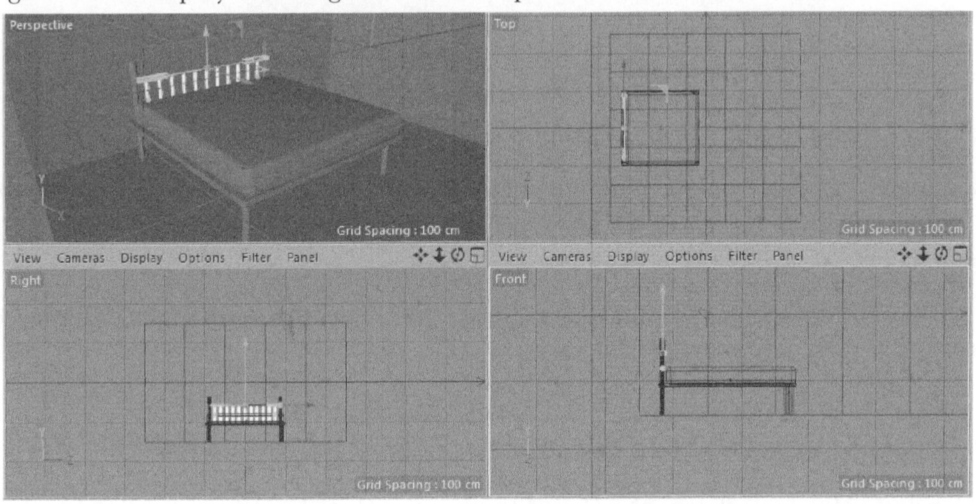

Figure P1-14 The Rod aligned in all viewports

Creating the Bedsheet

In this section, you will create the bedsheet for bed.

1. Make *Mattress* and *Base* editable by first selecting them and then pressing C. In the Object Manager, right-click on *Mattress*; a shortcut menu is displayed. Choose **Simulation Tags > Cloth Collider** from the shortcut menu, as shown in Figure P1-15; the **Cloth Collider** tag is added to the Object Manager.

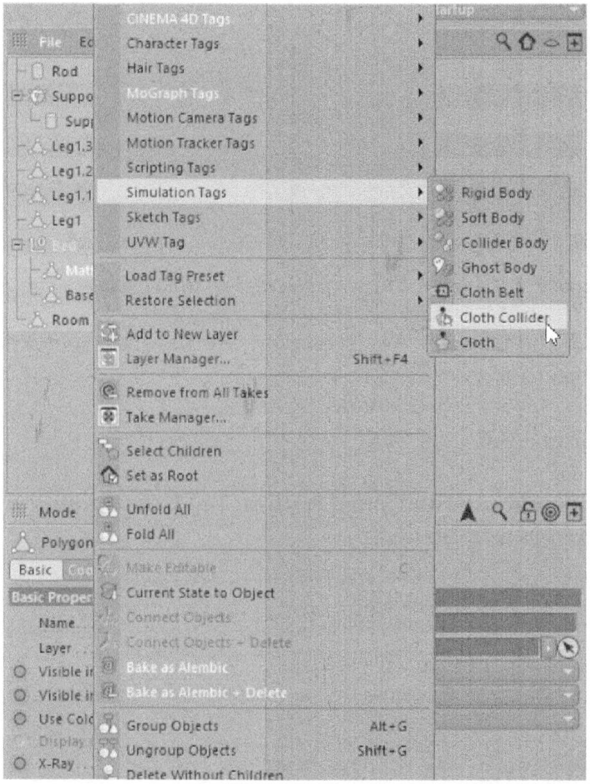

Figure P1-15 *Choosing* ***Cloth Collider*** *from the shortcut menu*

2. Choose **Create > Object** from the main menu; a cascading menu is displayed. Next, choose **Plane** from it; a plane is created in the Perspective viewport and *Plane* is added to the Object Manager. Rename it as *Bedsheet*.

3. In the Attribute Manager, choose the **Object** button; the **Object Properties** area is displayed. In this area, set the parameters as follows:

   Width: **198** Height: **232** Width Segments: **45**
   Height Segments: **45**

4. In the Attribute Manager, choose the **Coord** button; the **Coordinates** area is displayed. In this area, enter **-107.119** in the **P . X** spinner. Figure P1-16 displays *Bedsheet* positioned in all viewports.

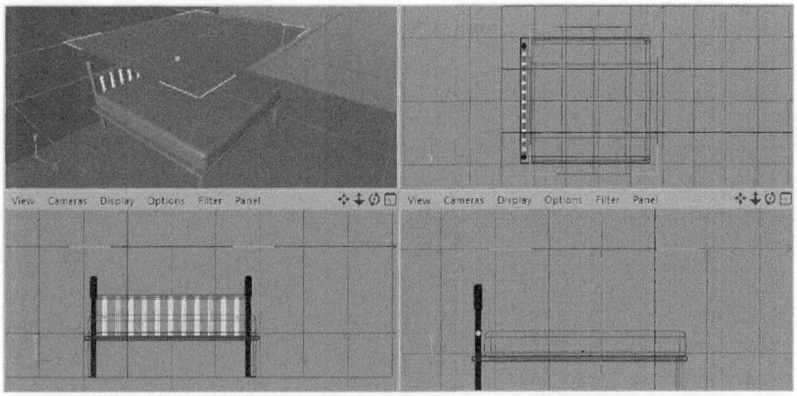

Figure P1-16 Bedsheet aligned in all viewports

5. Make sure *Bedsheet* is selected in the Object Manager and choose the **Make Editable** tool from the Modes Palette; *Bedsheet* is converted into a polygonal object.

6. In the Object Manager, right-click on *Bedsheet*; a shortcut menu is displayed. Choose **Simulation Tags > Cloth** from the shortcut menu; the **Cloth Expression [Cloth]** tag is added to the Object Manager, as shown in Figure P1-17.

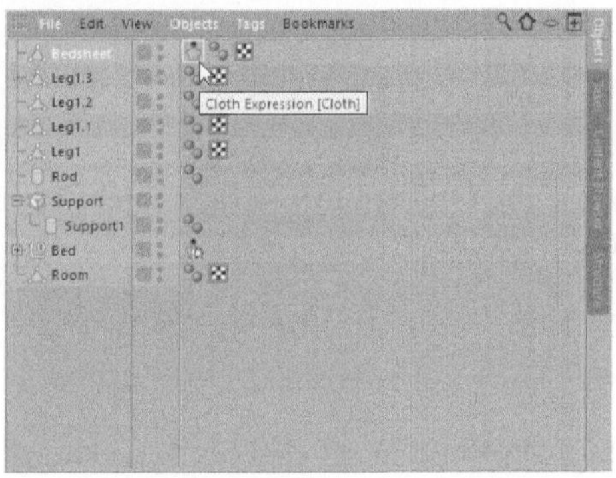

Figure P1-17 *The* ***Cloth Expression [Cloth]*** *tag added to the Object Manager*

7. Make sure the **Cloth Expression [Cloth]** tag is selected in the Object Manager. In the Attribute Manager, choose the **Dresser** button; the **Dresser** area is displayed. In this area, enter **20** in the **Steps** spinner next to the **Relax** button and then choose the **Relax** button; the draping simulation begins and the bedsheet spreads on *Mattress*, refer to Figure P1-18.

8. Select and delete the **Cloth Expression [Cloth]** tag from the Object Manager.

9. In the Object Manager, select *Leg1, Leg1.1, Leg1.2, Leg1.3, Bedsheet, Rod,* and *Support* using the CTRL key and then drag them to *Bed*; all objects are connected to *Bed.*

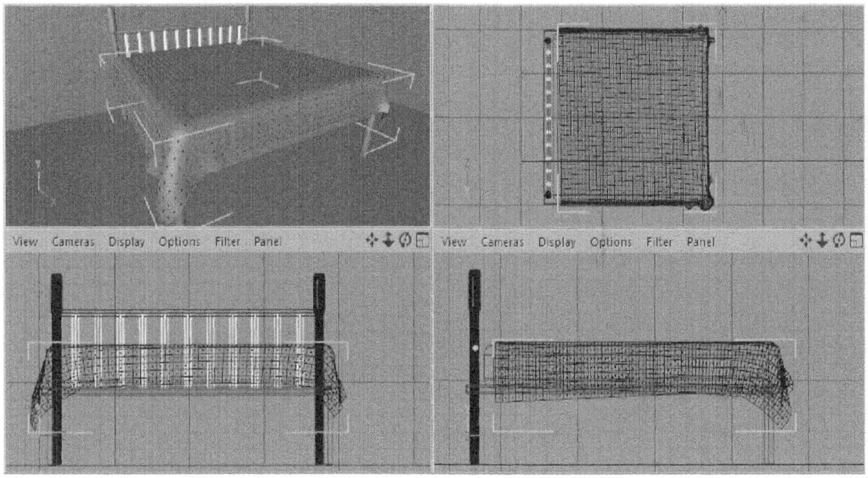

Figure P1-18 The bedsheet aligned on Mattress

Creating the Wardrobe

In this section, you will create the wardrobe.

1. Choose **Create > Object** from the main menu; a cascading menu is displayed. Next, choose **Cube** from it; a cube is created in all viewports and *Cube* is added to the Object Manager. Rename it as *Wardrobe*.

2. In the Attribute Manager, choose the **Object** button; the **Object Properties** area is displayed. In this area, set the parameters as follows:

   Size . X: **112** Size . Y: **198** Size . Z: **69**
   Segments X: **3**

3. Invoke the **Move** tool and align *Wardrobe* in all viewports, as shown in Figure P1-19.

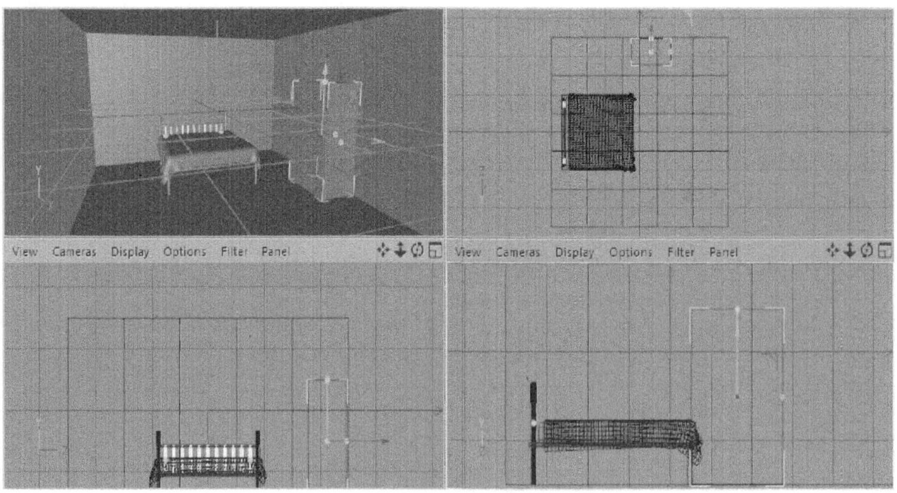

Figure P1-19 The Wardrobe aligned in all viewports

4. Make sure *Wardrobe* is selected in the Object Manager and choose the **Make Editable** tool from the Modes Palette; *Wardrobe* is converted into a polygonal object.

5. Press F1; the Perspective viewport is displayed. Choose the **Polygons** tool from the Modes Palette; *Wardrobe* is displayed in the polygon mode. Invoke the **Live Selection** tool. In the Attribute Manager, make sure that the **Only Select Visible Elements** check box is selected. Using the SHIFT key, select the front polygons of *Wardrobe* in the Perspective viewport, as shown in Figure P1-20.

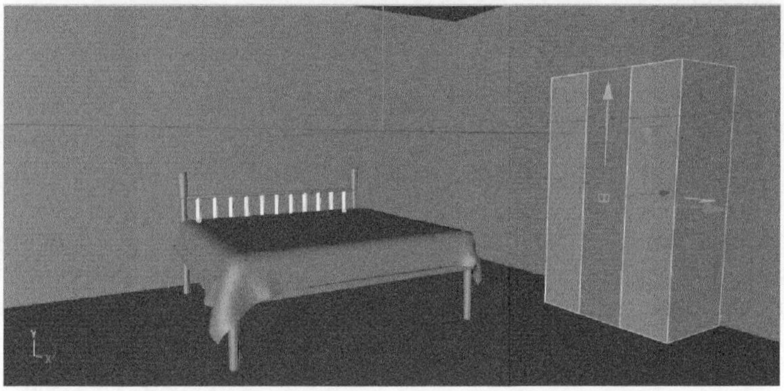

Figure P1-20 *The selected polygons displayed*

6. In the Perspective viewport, right-click on the selected polygons of *Wardrobe*; a shortcut menu is displayed. Choose **Extrude Inner** from the shortcut menu; the **Extrude Inner** tool settings are displayed in the Attribute Manager. Next, make sure the **Options** button is chosen in the Attribute Manager. In the **Options** area, make sure that the **Offset** spinner is set to **5**. Choose the **Tool** button; the **Tool** area is displayed. In this area, choose the **Apply** button; the selected polygons are extruded. Press SPACEBAR to exit the tool.

7. Make sure the polygons of *Wardrobe* are selected in the Perspective viewport. Right-click on the selected polygons of *Wardrobe*; a shortcut menu is displayed. Choose **Extrude** from the shortcut menu; the **Extrude** tool settings are displayed in the Attribute Manager.

8. In the Attribute Manager, choose the **Options** button; the **Options** area is displayed. In this area, enter **3** in the **Offset** spinner. Next, press ENTER; the selected faces of *Wardrobe* are extruded, as shown in Figure P1-21.

   Next, you will model the handles of *Wardrobe*.

9. Choose **Create > Object** from the main menu; a cascading menu is displayed. Next, choose **Cube** from it; a cube is created in the Perspective viewport and *Cube* is added to the Object Manager. Rename it as *Handle*.

10. In the Attribute Manager, make sure the **Object** button is chosen. In the **Object Properties** area, set the parameters as follows:

    Size . X: **6** Size . Y: **74** Size . Z: **6**

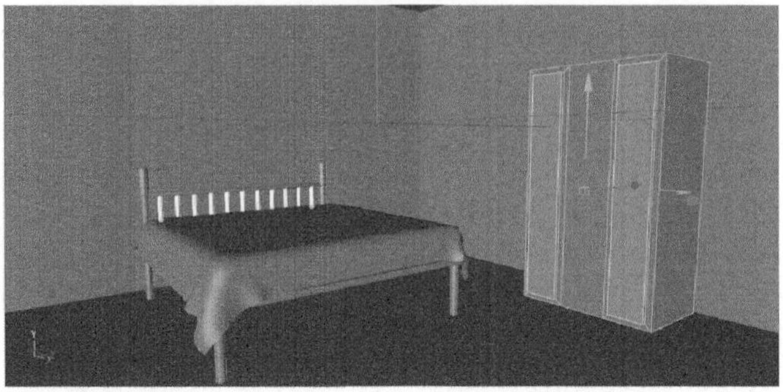

Figure P1-21 *The selected polygons extruded*

11. Make sure *Handle* is selected in the Object Manager and choose the **Make Editable** tool from the Modes Palette; the *Handle* is converted into a polygonal object.

12. Choose the **Edges** tool from the Modes Palette; *Handle* is displayed in the edge mode. In the Perspective viewport, right-click on the edges of *Handle*; a shortcut menu is displayed. Choose **Loop/Path Cut** from the shortcut menu; the **Loop/Path Cut** tool settings are displayed in the Attribute Manager.

13. Click on *Handle* in the Perspective viewport and add two new horizontal edges, as shown in Figure P1-22. Press SPACEBAR to exit the tool.

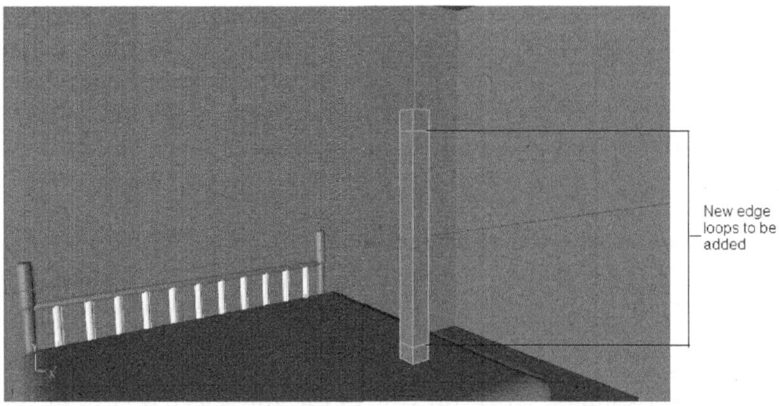

Figure P1-22 *The newly added edges displayed*

14. Choose the **Polygons** tool from the Modes Palette; the *Handle* is displayed in the polygon mode. Invoke the **Live Selection** tool and select two polygons of *Handle,* as shown in Figure P1-23.

15. In the Perspective viewport, right-click on the selected polygons of *Handle*; a shortcut menu is displayed. Choose **Extrude** from the shortcut menu; the **Extrude** tool settings are displayed in the Attribute Manager. Make sure the **Options** button is chosen. In the **Options** area, enter **5** in the **Offset** spinner and press ENTER; the selected polygons are extruded. Press SPACEBAR to exit the tool. Choose the **Model** tool from the Modes Palette to invoke the Object mode.

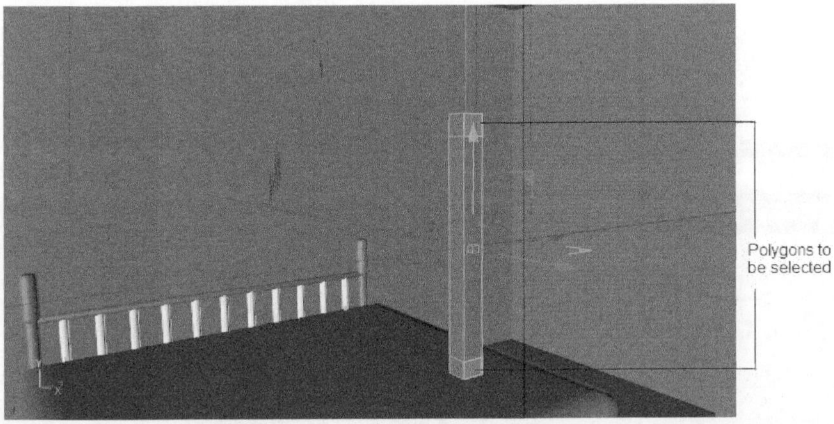

Figure P1-23 The selected polygons

16. Press F5; all viewports are displayed. Invoke the **Rotate** tool and rotate *Handle*. Next, invoke the **Move** tool and align *Handle*, as shown in Figure P1-24.

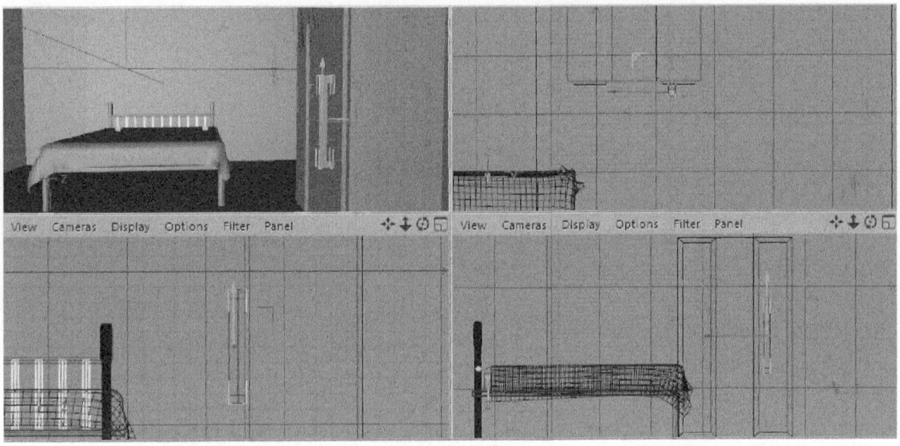

Figure P1-24 The Handle aligned in all viewports

17. Create a copy of *Handle* in the Object Manager; *Handle.1* is added to the Object Manager. Invoke the **Move** tool and align *Handle.1*, as shown in Figure P1-25.

18. In the Object Manager, select *Wardrobe*, *Handle*, *Handle.1* and then right-click; a shortcut menu is displayed. Next, choose the **Group Objects** from the menu; a **Null** group is created in the Object Manager. Rename *Null* to *Cupboard*.

Creating the Drawers

In this section, you will create the drawers.

1. Choose **Create > Object** from the main menu; a cascading menu is displayed. Choose **Cube** from the menu; a cube is created in the Perspective viewport and *Cube* is added to the Object Manager. Rename *Cube* as *Drawer 1*.

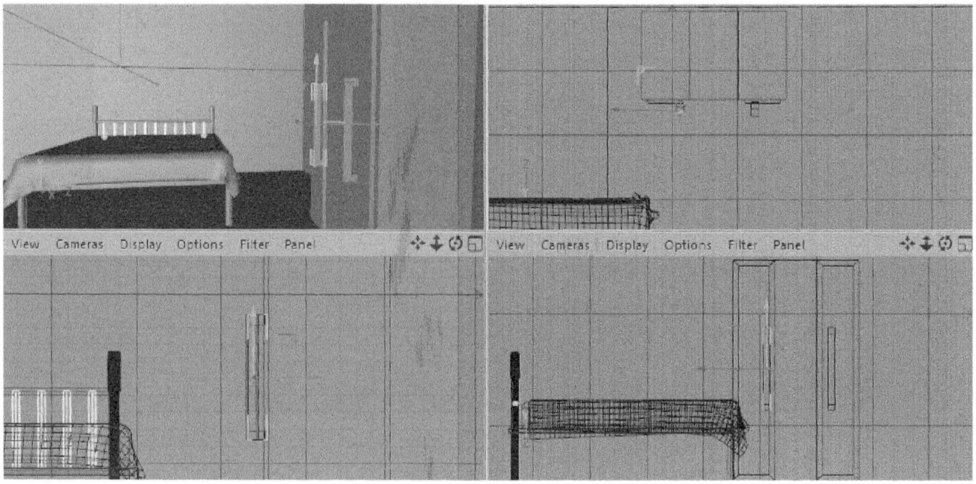

Figure P1-25 *The Handle.1 aligned in all viewports*

2. In the Attribute Manager, choose the **Object** button; the **Object Properties** area is displayed. In this area, set the parameters as follows:

   Size X: **50** Size Y: **66** Size Z: **75**

   Select the **Fillet** check box and enter **1** in the **Fillet Radius** spinner.

3. Make sure *Drawer 1* is selected in the Object Manager and choose the **Make Editable** tool from the Modes Palette; *Drawer 1* is converted into a polygonal object.

4. Press F3; the Right viewport is maximized. Choose the **Edges** tool from the Modes Palette; *Drawer 1* is displayed in the edge mode.

5. Right-click on *Drawer 1*; a shortcut menu is displayed. Choose **Loop/Path Cut** from the shortcut menu; the **Loop/Path Cut** tool settings are displayed in the Attribute Manager. Next, add two vertical edge loops, as shown in Figure P1-26. Now, add six horizontal edge loops, as shown in Figure P1-27. Press SPACEBAR to exit the tool.

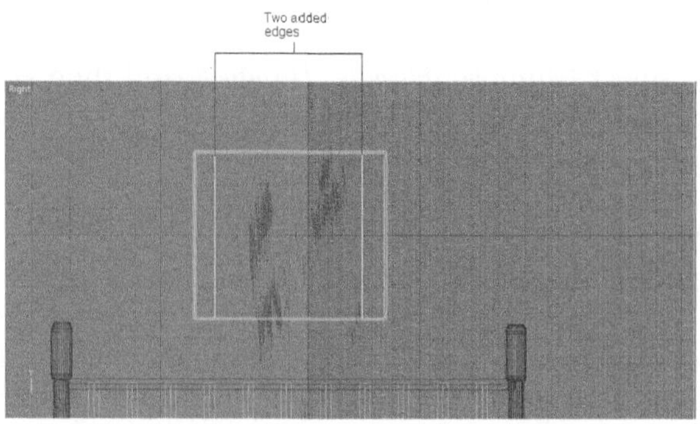

Figure P1-26 *Two vertical edge loops added*

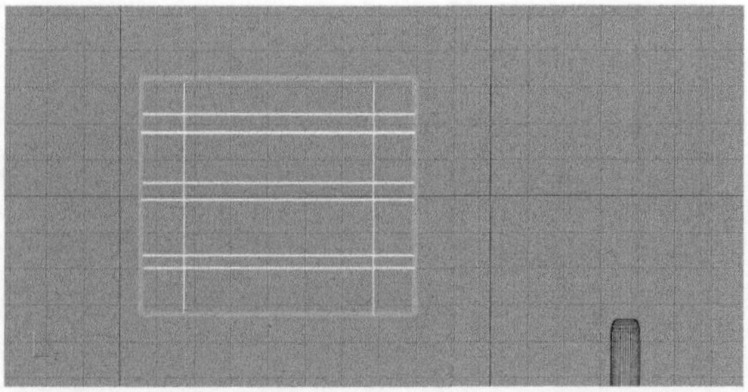

Figure P1-27 Six horizontal edge loops added

6. Choose the **Polygons** tool from the Modes Palette; the *Drawer 1* is displayed in the polygon mode. Invoke the **Live Selection** tool and select the three polygons of *Drawer 1* in the Right viewport, as shown in Figure P1-28.

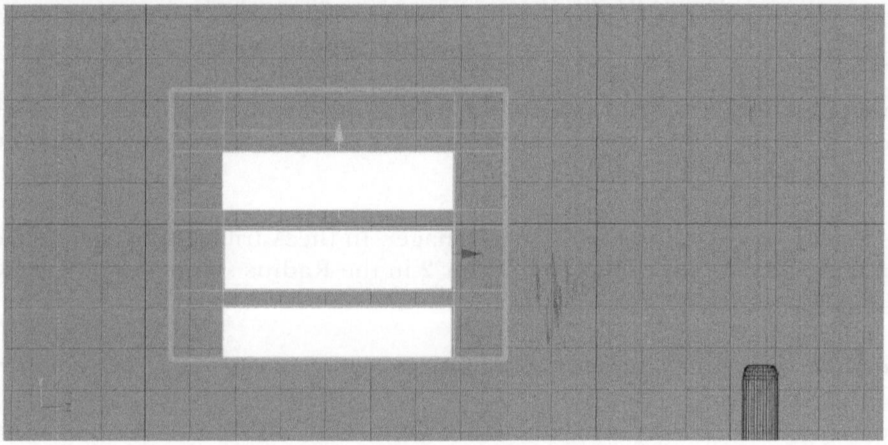

Figure P1-28 The selected polygons

7. Right-click on the selected polygons of *Drawer 1*; a shortcut menu is displayed. Choose **Extrude Inner** from the shortcut menu; the **Extrude Inner** tool settings area is displayed in the Attribute Manager. Next, make sure the **Options** button is chosen in the Attribute Manager. In the **Options** area, enter **1** in the **Offset** spinner. Next, press ENTER; the selected polygons are extruded.

8. Make sure the polygons of *Drawer 1* are selected in the Right viewport. Right-click on the selected polygons of *Drawer 1*; a shortcut menu is displayed. Choose **Extrude** from the shortcut menu; the **Extrude** tool settings are displayed in the Attribute Manager.

9. Press F5; all viewports are displayed. In the **Extrude** area, choose the **Tool** button; the **Tool** area is displayed. In the **Tool** area, choose the **Apply** button; the selected polygons of *Drawer 1* are extruded. Press SPACEBAR to exit the tool. Choose the **Model** tool from the Mode palette; the *Drawer 1* is displayed in the Object mode. Now, align the *Drawer 1* in all viewports, as shown in Figure P1-29.

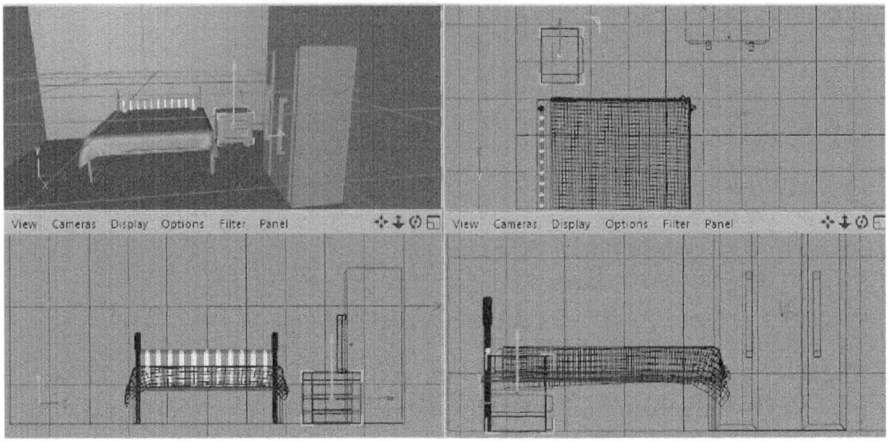

Figure P1-29 *Drawer 1 aligned in all viewports*

Next, you will create the knobs of *Drawer 1* using the **Sphere** tool.

10. Choose **Create > Object** from the main menu; a cascading menu is displayed. Next, choose **Sphere** from it; a sphere is created in the Perspective viewport and *Sphere* is added to the Object Manager. Rename it as *Knob 1*.

11. Make sure *Knob 1* is selected in the Object Manager. In the Attribute Manager, make sure the **Object** button is chosen. In this area, enter **2** in the **Radius** spinner and place *Knob 1* on *Drawer 1*.

12. Invoke the **Move** tool and align *Knob 1*, as shown in Figure P1-30.

13. Create two copies of *Knob 1* by using the CTRL key. Next, invoke the **Move** tool and the position *Knob 1.1* and *Knob 1.2*. Figure P1-31 displays *Knob 1*, *Knob 1.1,* and *Knob 1.2* in all viewports.

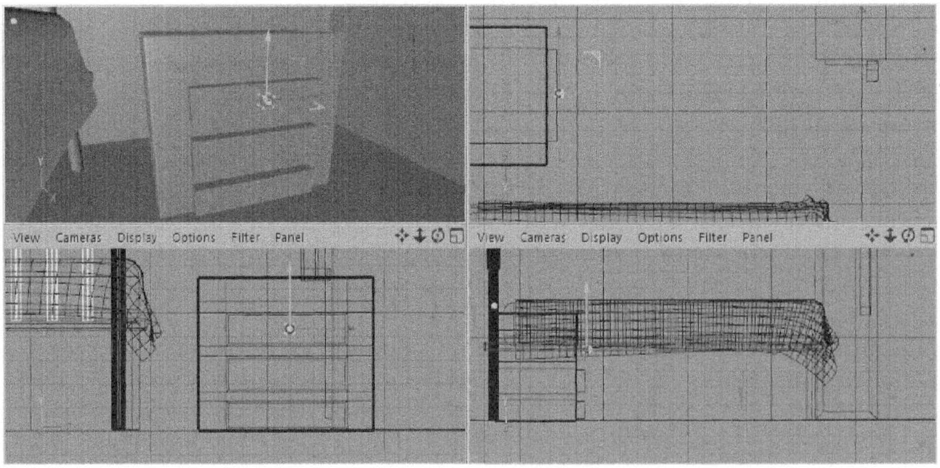

Figure P1-30 *Knob 1 positioned in all viewports*

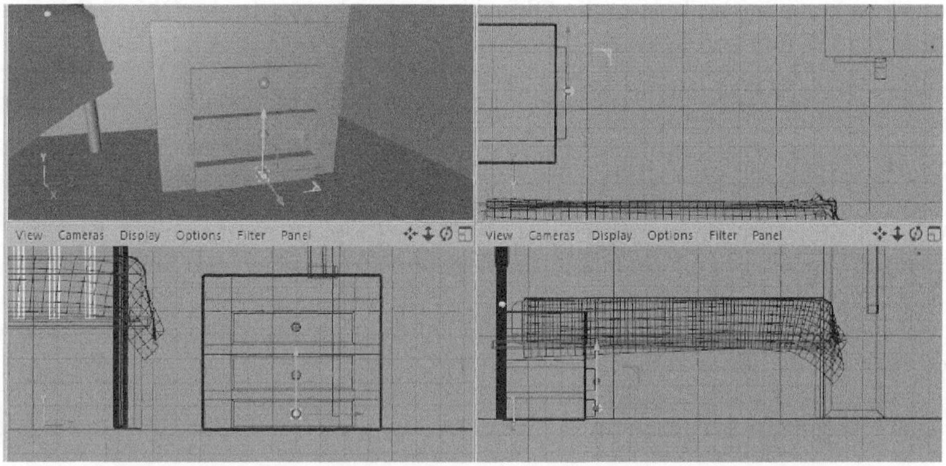

Figure P1-31 The Knob 1, Knob 1.1, and Knob 1.2 displayed

14. In the Object Manager, select *Drawer 1*, *Knob 1*, *Knob1.1*, and *Knob1.2* using the CTRL key. Next, right-click on the selected object; a shortcut menu is displayed. Next, choose **Group Objects** from the menu; the selected objects are grouped with the **Null** object in the Object Manager. Rename the *Null* to *Drawers*.

15. Create a copy of *Drawers* in all viewports; *Drawers.1* is added to the Object Manager. Invoke the **Move** tool and align *Drawers.1* in all viewports, as shown in Figure P1-32.

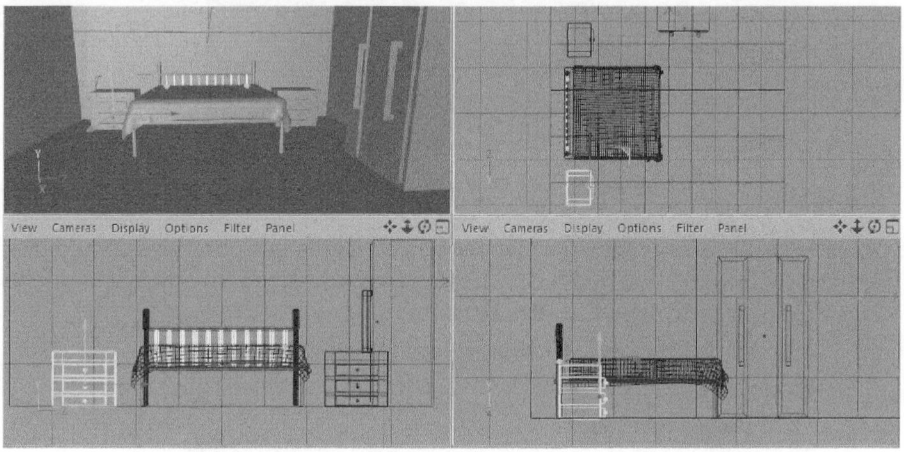

Figure P1-32 The Drawers.1 aligned in all viewports

Creating the Lights

In this section, you will create the lights.

1. Press F1; the Perspective viewport is displayed. Choose **Create > Object** from the main menu; a cascading menu is displayed. Next, choose **Cylinder** from it; a cylinder is created in the Perspective viewport and *Cylinder* is added to the Object Manager. Rename it as *Light1*.

2. In the Attribute Manager, make sure the **Object** button is chosen. In the **Object Properties** area, set the parameters as follows:

   Radius: **10** Height: **5**

   Select **-X** from the **Orientation** drop-down list.

3. In the Attribute Manager, choose the **Caps** button; the **Caps** area is displayed. In this area, select the **Fillet** check box and enter **2** in the **Segments** spinner located below it.

4. Make sure *Light1* is selected in the Object Manager and choose the **Make Editable** tool from the Modes Palette; the *Light1* is converted into a polygonal object.

5. Choose the **Polygons** tool from the Modes Palette; the *Light1* is displayed in the polygon mode.

6. Right-click on *Light1* in the Perspective viewport; a shortcut menu is displayed. Choose **Loop/Path Cut** from the shortcut menu; the **Loop/Path Cut** tool settings are displayed in the Attribute Manager. Next, add an edge loop, as shown in Figure P1-33. Press SPACEBAR to exit the tool.

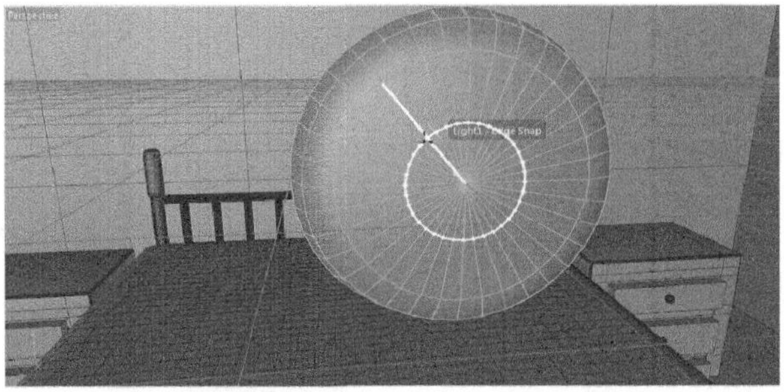

Figure P1-33 *The added edges displayed*

7. Select the polygons of *Light1*, as shown in Figure P1-34. Right-click on the selected polygons of *Light1*; a shortcut menu is displayed. Choose **Extrude** from the shortcut menu; the **Extrude** tool settings are displayed in the Attribute Manager.

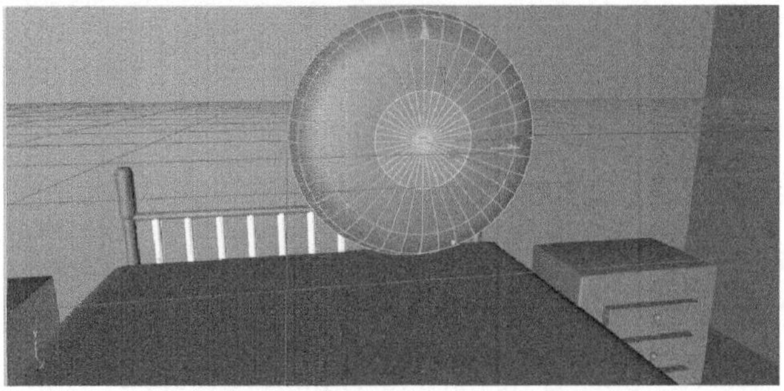

Figure P1-34 *The polygons selected*

8. In the Attribute Manager, choose the **Options** button; the **Options** area is displayed. In this area, enter **6** in the **Offset** spinner. Press ENTER; the selected polygons of *Light1* are extruded, as shown in Figure P1-35. Next, choose the **Model** tool from the Modes Palette; *Light1* is displayed in the object mode.

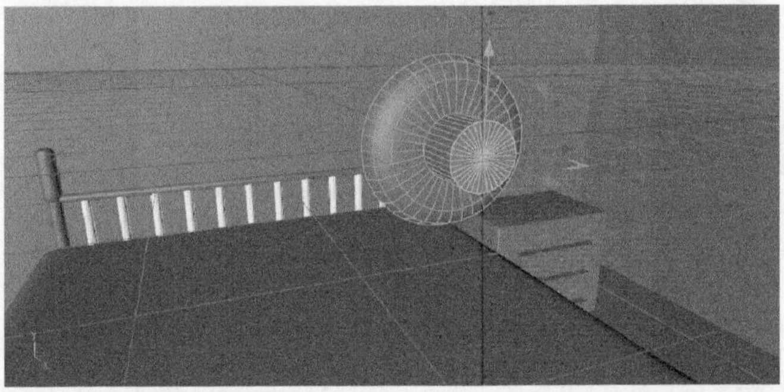

Figure P1-35 *The selected polygons extruded*

Next, you will model a cover for *Light1*.

9. Choose **Create > Object** from the main menu; a cascading menu is displayed. Next, choose **Cylinder** from it; a cylinder is created in the Perspective viewport and *Cylinder* is added to the Object Manager. Rename it as *Cover1*.

10. In the Attribute Manager, choose the **Object** button; the **Object Properties** area is displayed. In this area, set the parameters as follows:

    Radius: **10** Height: **45**

11. In the Attribute Manager, choose the **Caps** button; the **Caps** area is displayed. In this area, clear the **Caps** check box. Invoke the **Move** tool and align *Cover1* with *Light1* in the Perspective viewport. Figure P1-36 displays *Cover1* placed in the Perspective viewport.

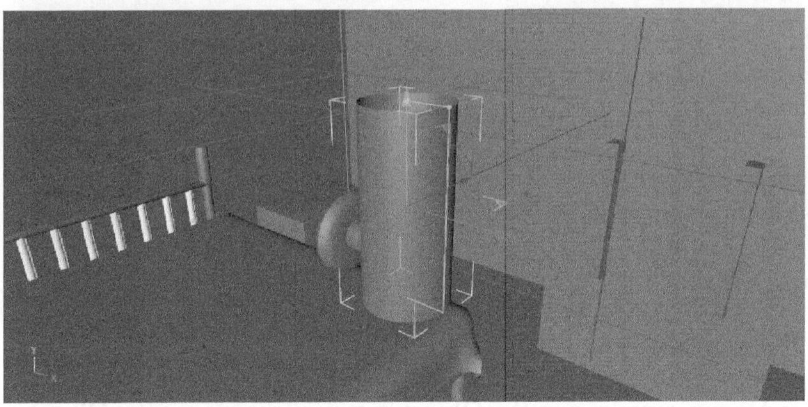

Figure P1-36 *Cover1 displayed in the Perspective viewport*

12. Press F5; all viewports are displayed. In the Object Manager, select *Light1* and *Cover1* using the CTRL key and then right-click; a shortcut menu is displayed. Next, choose **Group Objects**

from the menu; the selected objects are grouped with the **Null** object in the Object Manager. Rename the *Null* as *Lights*. Now, align *Lights* in all viewports, as shown in Figure P1-37.

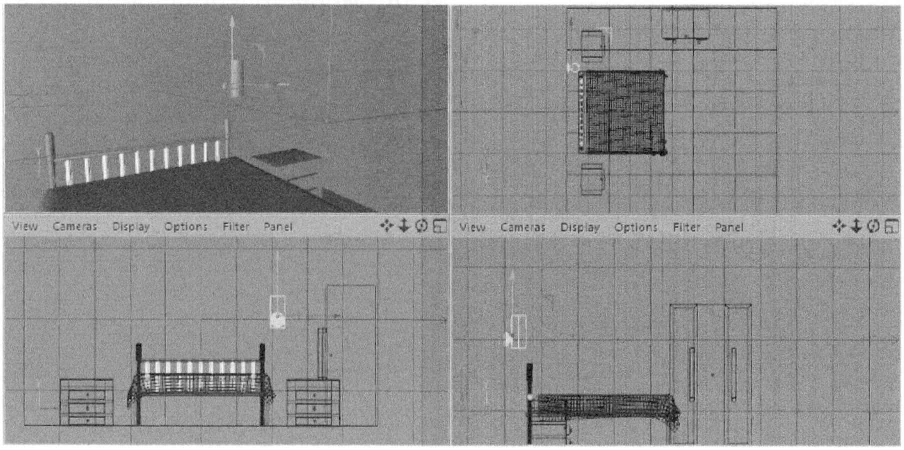

Figure P1-37 *The Lights displayed in all viewports*

13. Create a copy of *Lights* in the Object Manager; *Lights.1* is added to the Object Manager. Invoke the **Move** tool and place *Lights.1*. Figure P1-38 displays *Lights.1* aligned in all viewports.

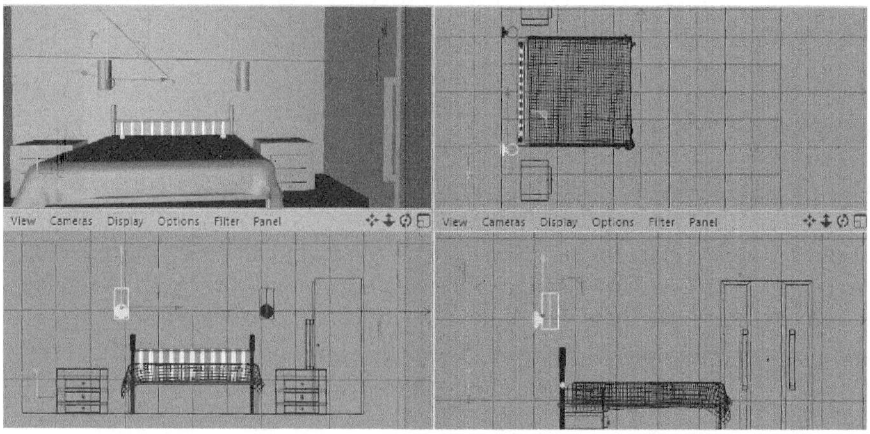

Figure P1-38 *The Lights.1 aligned in all viewports*

Creating the Mat

In this section, you will create the mat.

1. Choose **Create > Object** from the main menu; a cascading menu is displayed. Next, choose **Cube** from it; a cube is created in all viewports and *Cube* is added to the Object Manager. Rename it as *Mat* in the Attribute Manager.

2. In the Attribute Manager, make sure the **Object** button is chosen. In the **Object properties** area, set the parameters as follows:

   Size . Y: **1** Size . Z: **82.5**

3. Invoke the **Move** tool and align *Mat* with floor, as shown in Figure P1-39.

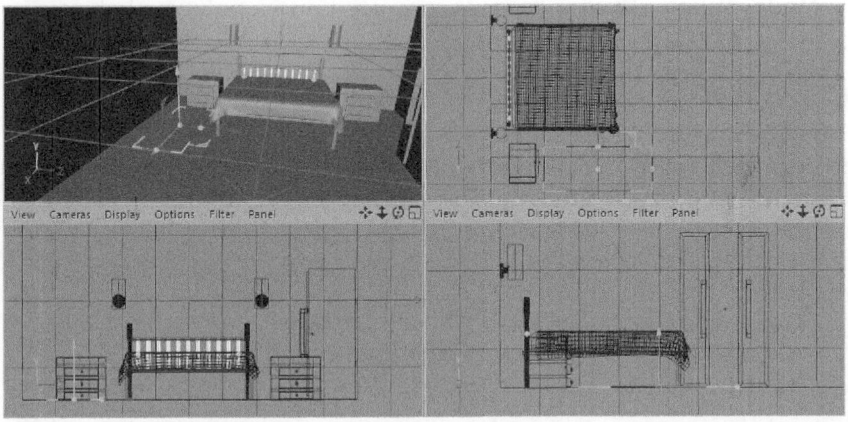

Figure P1-39 *The Mat aligned in all viewports*

Creating a Wooden Frame in the Scene

In this section, you will create a wooden frame in the scene.

1. Choose **Create > Object** from the main menu; a cascading menu is displayed. Next, choose **Cube** from it; a cube is created in the Perspective viewport and *Cube* is added to the Object Manager. Rename it as *Wooden Frame* in the Attribute Manager.

2. In the Attribute Manager, make sure the **Object** button is chosen. In the **Object Properties** area, set the parameters as follows:

   Size . X: **3** Size . Y: **114** Size . Z: **152**

3. Invoke the **Move** tool and align *Wooden Frame*, as shown in Figure P1-40.

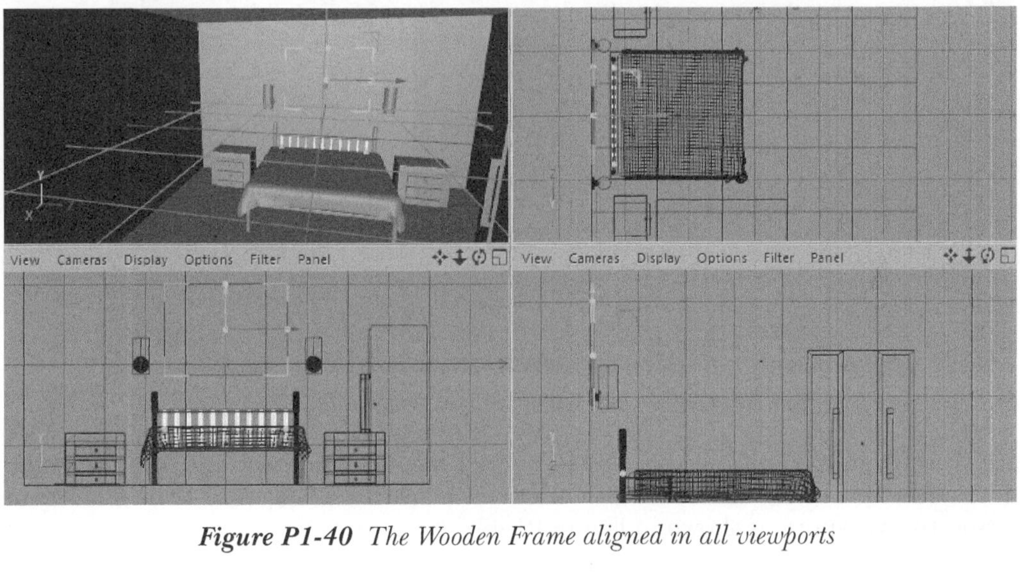

Figure P1-40 *The Wooden Frame aligned in all viewports*

4. Make sure *Wooden Frame* is selected in the Object Manager and choose the **Make Editable** tool from the Modes Palette; *Wooden Frame* is converted into a polygonal object.

5. Choose the **Edges** tool from the Modes Palette; the *Wooden Frame* is displayed in the edge mode.

6. Press F1; the Perspective viewport is displayed. Right-click on *Wooden Frame*; a shortcut menu is displayed. Choose **Loop/Path Cut** from the shortcut menu and then create two cuts, as shown in Figure P1-41.

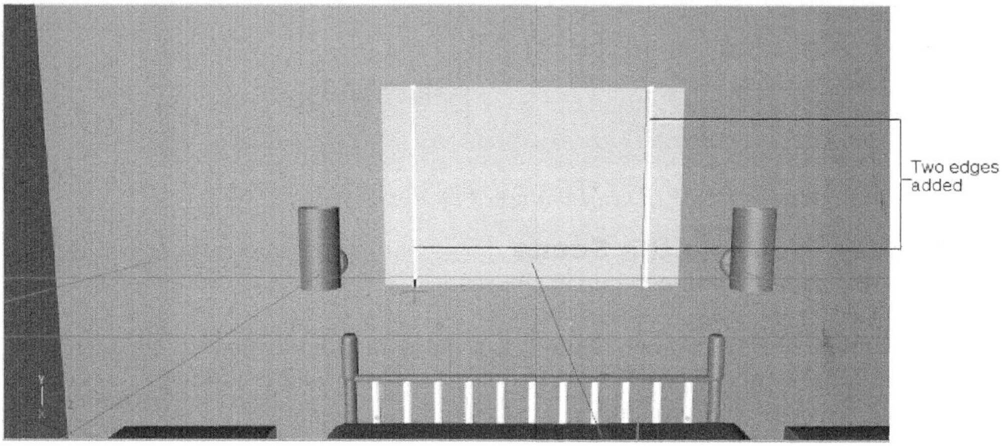

Figure P1-41 *The added vertical edges displayed*

7. Similar, add two more horizontal edges to *Wooden Frame* in the Perspective viewport, as shown in Figure P1-42. Press SPACEBAR to exit the tool.

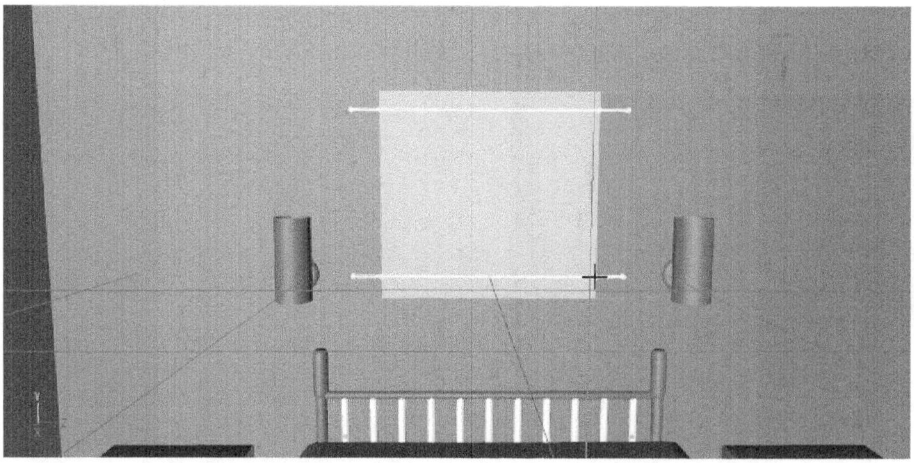

Figure P1-42 *The horizontal added edges displayed*

8. Choose the **Polygons** tool from the Modes Palette; the *Wooden Frame* is displayed in the polygon mode. Invoke the **Live Selection** tool and select the polygon of *Wooden Frame* in the Perspective viewport, as shown in Figure P1-43.

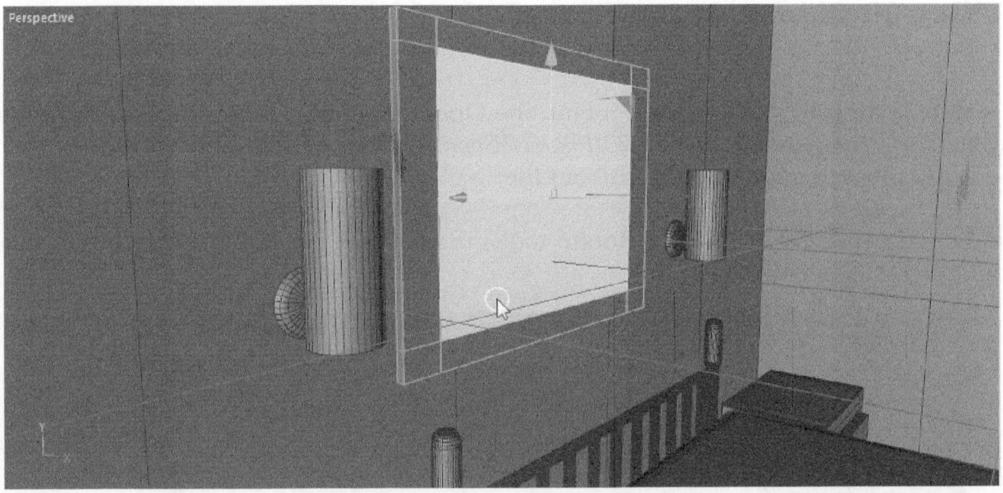

Figure P1-43 The polygon selected

9. Right-click on the selected polygon of *Wooden Frame*; a shortcut menu is displayed. Choose **Extrude Inner** from the shortcut menu; the **Extrude Inner** tool settings are displayed in the Attribute Manager.

10. In the Attribute Manager, make sure the **Options** button is chosen. In the **Options** area, enter **2** in the **Offset** spinner. Next, press ENTER; the *Wooden Frame* is extruded.

11. Make sure the polygon of *Wooden Frame* is selected in the Perspective viewport. Right-click on the selected polygons; a shortcut menu is displayed. Choose **Extrude** from the shortcut menu; the **Extrude Tool** settings are displayed in the Attribute Manager.

12. In the Attribute Manager, choose the **Options** button; the **Options** area is displayed. In this area, enter **-2** in the **Offset** spinner. Next, press ENTER; the *Wooden Frame* is extruded, as shown in Figure P1-44. Press SPACEBAR to exit the tool.

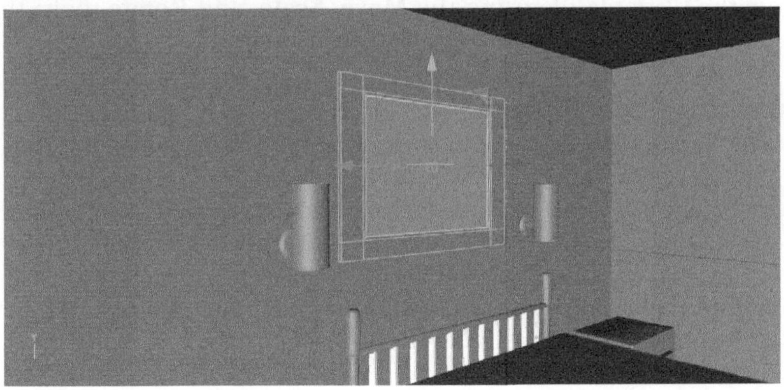

Figure P1-44 *The Wooden Frame extruded in the Perspective viewport*

Compositing 3D Objects in the Scene

In this section, you will composite 3D objects in the scene.

1. Choose **File > Merge** from the main menu; the **Open File** dialog box is displayed. In this dialog box, browse to *\Documents\c4dr20\Project1\Chair.c4d* and then choose the **Open** button; the *Chair.c4d* file is merged into the current file.

2. Position *Chair* using the **Move** and **Rotate** tools; the *Chair* is displayed in the Perspective viewport, as shown in Figure P1-45.

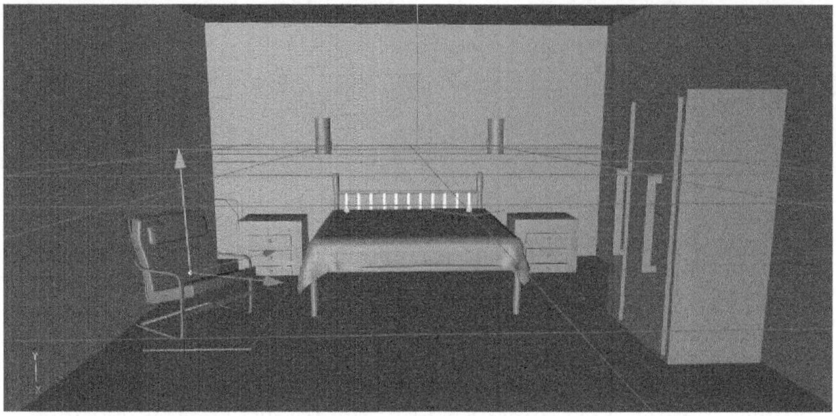

Figure P1-45 *Displaying the Chair positioned in the Perspective viewport*

Next, you will merge a *Clock* object in the scene.

3. Choose **File > Merge** from the main menu; the **Open File** dialog box is displayed. In this dialog box, browse to *\Documents\c4dr20\Project1\Clock.c4d* and then choose the **Open** button; the *Clock.c4d* file is merged in the current file.

4. Position and scale the *Clock.c4d* file using the **Move**, **Scale**, and **Rotate** tools; the *Clock.c4d* file is displayed in all viewports, as shown in Figure P1-46.

Setting the Camera in the Scene

In this section, you will set the camera in the scene.

1. Choose **Create > Camera > Camera** from the main menu; *Camera* is added to the Object Manager.

2. In the Attribute Manager, make sure the **Object** button is chosen. In the **Object Properties** area, set the parameters as follows:

   Focal Length: **32** Sensor Size (Film Gate): **37.2**
   Film Offset X: **8**

   Click on the **Camera Object [Camera]** tag in the Object Manager. Adjust the camera angle using the navigational tools.

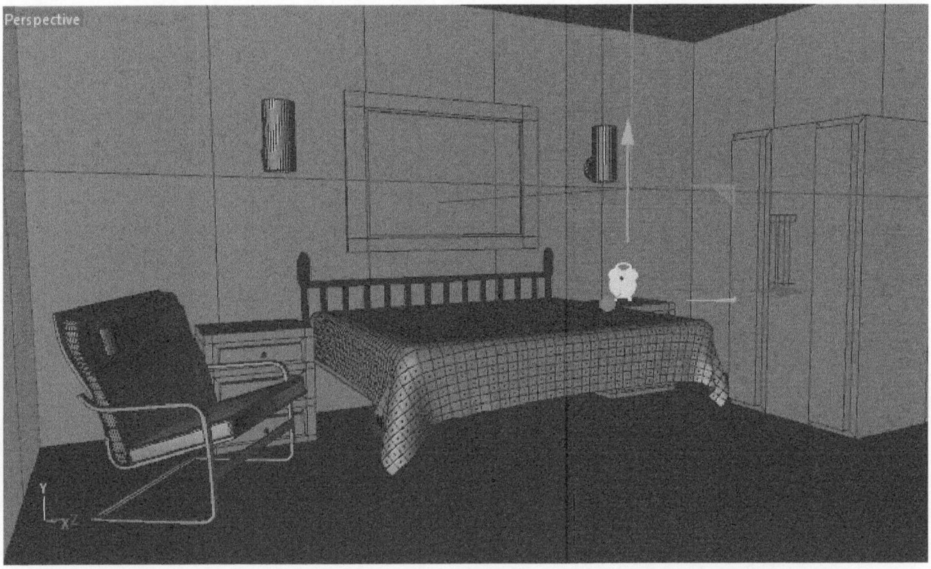

Figure P1-46 The Clock positioned in the Perspective viewport

Saving and Rendering the Scene

In this section, you will save and render the scene. You can also view the final render of the project by downloading the file *prj1_c4dr20_rndr.zip* from *www.cadcim.com*. The path of the file is mentioned at the beginning of the chapter.

1. Choose **File > Save** from the main menu; the **Save File** dialog box is displayed. In this dialog box, browse to the location *\Documents\c4dr20\Project1*.

2. Enter **prj1** in the **File name** text box and then choose the **Save** button.

3. Choose the **Render to Picture Viewer** tool from the Command Palette. Alternatively, press SHIFT+R; the **Picture Viewer** window is displayed.

4. In the **Picture Viewer** window, choose **File > Save as**; the **Save** dialog box is displayed.

5. In the **Save** dialog box, choose the **OK** button; the **Save Dialog** dialog box is displayed. Next, browse to the *\Documents\c4dr20\Project1*. In the **File Name** text box, type **prj1_rndr**. Next, choose the **Save** button; the file is saved at the desired location.

   Figure P1-1 displays the final output.

Project 2

Texturing an Indoor Scene

PROJECT DESCRIPTION

In this project, you will apply texture and light to the scene that you have created in Project 1. You will also render the scene. The final output of this project is shown in Figure P2-1.

Figure P2-1 *The final output*

Downloading the File

Before you start the project, you need to download the *prj2_c4d_r20.zip* file from *www.cadcim.com*. The path of the file is as follows: *Textbooks > Animation and Visual Effects > MAXON CINEMA 4D > MAXON CINEMA 4D R20 Studio: A Tutorial Approach*. Next, you need to navigate to the *\Documents\c4dr20* and create a new folder with the name *Project2*. Next, extract the contents of the zip file in this folder.

Opening the File

In this section, you will open the file.

1. Choose **File > Open** from the main menu; the **Open File** dialog box is displayed.

2. In the **Open File** dialog box, browse to *\Documents\c4dr20\Project2\Project2_start.c4d* and then choose the **Open** button; the *Project2_start.c4d* file is opened, as shown in Figure P2-2.

Figure P2-2 *The Project2_start.c4d file*

Applying Textures to the Room

In this section, you will apply texture to the room.

1. Select *Room* in the Object Manager. Next, choose the **Polygons** tool from the Modes Palette; *Room* is displayed in the polygon mode. Next, select the bottom polygons of *Room* using the **Live Selection** tool in the Perspective viewport, refer to Figure P2-3.

2. Double-click on the empty area in the Material Manager; a new material with the name **Mat** is created in the Material Manager. Next, rename it as **Floor**.

3. Make sure *Floor* material is selected in the Material Manager. In the Attribute Manager, make sure the **Color** button is chosen. In the **Color** area, choose the browse button located next to the **Texture** parameter; the **Open File** dialog box is displayed.

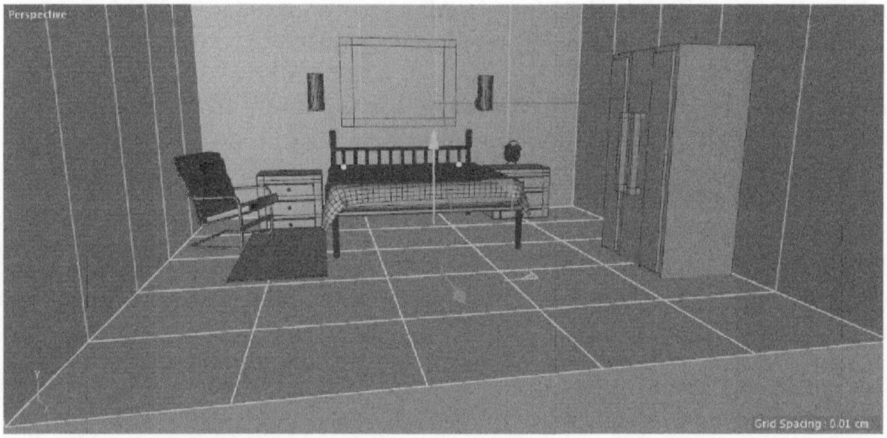

Figure P2-3 The bottom polygons of Room selected

4. In this dialog box, browse to *\Documents\c4dr20\Project2\floor.jpg*. Next, choose the **Open** button; the texture is displayed on the material slot.

5. Select the *Floor* material in the Material Manager and drag it on the selected polygons in the Perspective viewport; the *Floor* material is applied to the selected polygons of *Room*.

6. Make sure the **Texture Tag "Floor"** is selected in the Object Manager. In the Attribute Manager, make sure that the **Tag** button is chosen.

7. In the **Tag Properties** area, select **Cubic** from the **Projection** drop-down list and set the parameters as follows:

   Length U: **50** Length V: **50**

8. Make sure *Room* is displayed in the polygon mode. Next, select the polygons of the walls and roof in the Perspective viewport using the **Live Selection** tool, refer to Figure P2-4. You can also invert the polygon selection by pressing UI.

Figure P2-4 The polygons of the walls and roof selected

9. Double-click on the empty area in the Material Manager; a new material with the name **Mat** is created in the Material Manager. Next, rename it as **Wall**.

10. In the Attribute Manager, make sure the **Color** button is chosen. In the **Color** area, choose the **RGB** button and then set the parameters as follows:

    R: **255** G: **255** B: **255**

11. Select the *Wall* material in the Material Manager and drag it on the selected polygons in the Perspective viewport; the *Wall* material is applied to the selected polygons of *Room*, as shown in Figure P2-5.

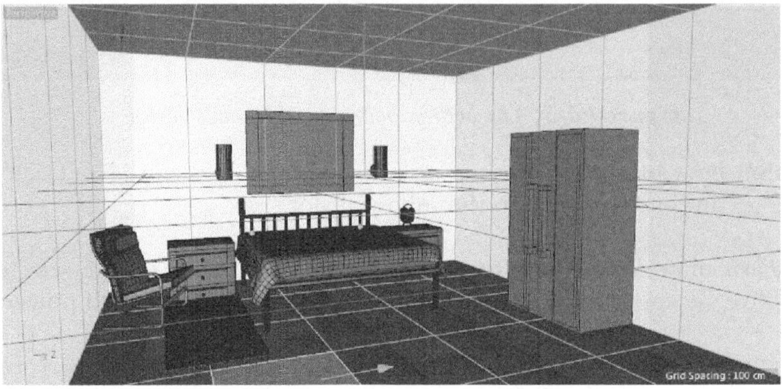

Figure P2-5 *The Wall material assigned to walls of the Room*

Applying Texture to the Mattress

In this section, you will apply texture to the mattress.

1. Double-click on the empty area in the Material Manager; a new material is created in the Material Manager. Next, rename it as **Mattress**.

2. In the Attribute Manager, make sure the **Color** button is chosen. In the **Color** area, choose the arrow button located next to **Texture**; a flyout is displayed. Choose **Surfaces > Tiles** from the flyout, as shown in Figure P2-6.

3. Choose the **Tiles** button located next to **Texture**; the **Tile Shader [Tiles]** settings are displayed. In this area, make sure the **Shader** button is chosen. In the **Shader Properties** area, choose the **Tiles Color 1** color swatch; the **Color Picker** dialog box is displayed. In this dialog box, choose the **RGB** button and then set the parameters as follows:

    R: **255** G: **255** B: **255**

    Next, choose the **OK** button; the **Tiles Color 1** is set to white color.

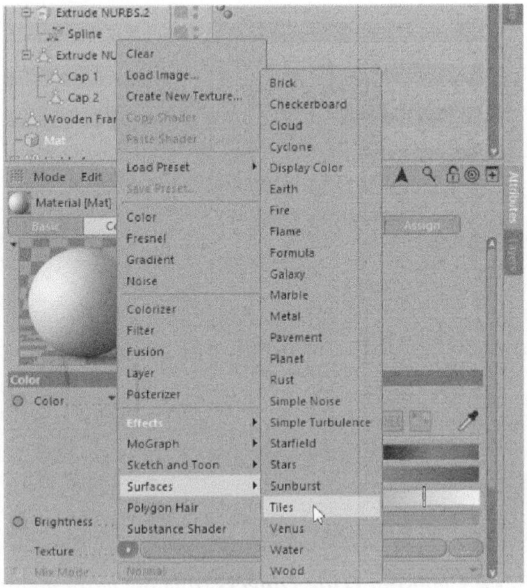

*Figure P2-6 Choosing **Surfaces > Tiles** from the flyout*

4. In the **Shader Properties** area, choose the **Tiles Color 3** color swatch; the **Color Picker** dialog box is displayed. In this dialog box, choose the **RGB** button and then set the parameters as follows:

   R: **0** G: **0** B: **0**

   Next, choose the **OK** button; the **Tiles Color 3** is set to white color.

5. In the **Shader Properties** area, select **Triangles 3** from the **Pattern** drop-down list. Next, enter **85** in the **Global Scale**, **U Scale**, and **V Scale** spinners.

6. Expand the *Bed* group in the Object Manager. Select the *Mattress* material in the Material Manager and drag the cursor to *Mattress* in the Object Manager; the *Mattress* material is applied to mattress in the scene.

7. In the Object Manager, select *Bedsheet* from the *Bed* group. Next, choose **Objects > Hide Objects** from the main menu in the Object Manager, as shown in Figure P2-7; *Bedsheet* gets hidden in the scene.

8. Make sure the **Texture Tag "Mattress"** tag is chosen in the Object Manager. In the Attribute Manager, make sure the **Tag** button is chosen. In the **Tag Properties** area, select **Cubic** from the **Projection** drop-down list and set the parameters as follows:

   Length U: **20** Length V: **20**

   Next, select the **Seamless** check box.

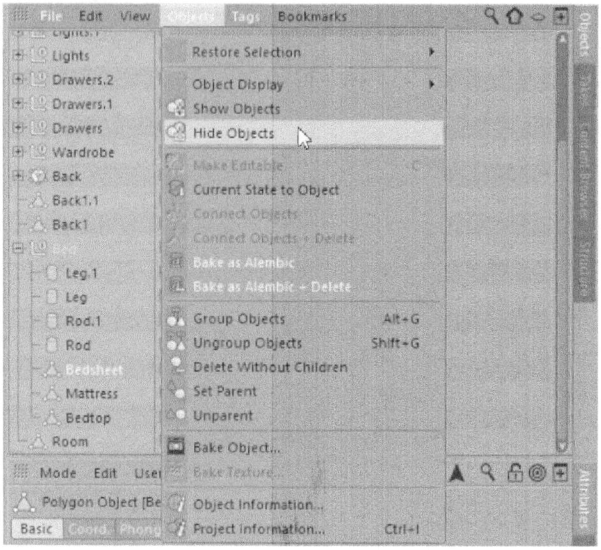

Figure P2-7 Choosing ***Hide Objects*** *from the main menu in the Object Manager*

On entering these values, the *Mattress* material is displayed in the Perspective viewport, as shown in Figure P2-8.

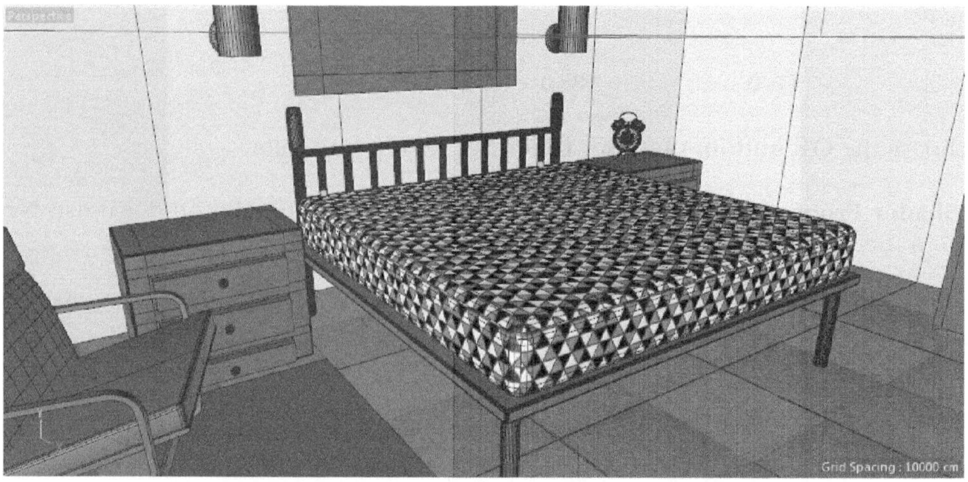

Figure P2-8 The Mattress material displayed

9. Make sure *Bedsheet* is selected in the Object Manager. Next, choose **Objects > Show Objects** from the main menu in the Object Manager; *Bedsheet* is displayed in the Perspective viewport.

Applying Texture to the Bedsheet

In this section, you will apply texture to the bedsheet.

1. Double-click on the empty area in the Material Manager; a new material is created in the Material Manager. Next, rename it as *Bedsheet*.

2. In the Attribute Manager, choose the **Color** button. Next, choose the arrow button located next to **Texture** in the **Color** area; a flyout is displayed. Choose **Surfaces > Tiles** from the flyout; the **Tiles** texture is displayed in the Attribute Manager.

3. Choose the **Tiles** button; the **Tile Shader [Tiles]** settings are displayed. Make sure the **Shader** button is chosen. In the **Shader Properties** area, choose the **Grout Color** color swatch; the **Color Picker** dialog box is displayed. In this dialog box, choose the **RGB** button and then set the parameters as follows:

   R: **215** G: **151** B: **13**

   Next, choose the **OK** button; the **Grout Color** is set to yellow color.

4. Choose the **Tiles Color 1** color swatch; the **Color Picker** dialog box is displayed. In this dialog box, choose the **RGB** button and then set the parameters as follows:

   R: **127** G: **48** B: **0**

   Next, choose the **OK** button; the **Tiles Color 1** is set to brown color.

5. Choose the **Tiles Color 2** color swatch; the **Color Picker** dialog box is displayed. In this dialog box, choose the **RGB** button and then set the parameters as follows:

   R: **111** G: **2** B: **2**

   Next, choose the **OK** button; the **Tiles Color 2** is set to red color.

6. In the **Shader Properties** area, select **Circles 1** from the **Pattern** drop-down list. Figure P2-9 displays the *Bedsheet* texture parameters in the **Shader Properties** area.

7. Select the *Bedsheet* material in the Material Manager and drag it on the *Bedsheet* in the Object Manager; the *Bedsheet* material is applied to the bedsheet in the Perspective viewport.

8. Make sure the **Texture Tag "Bedsheet"** tag is chosen in the Object Manager. In the Attribute Manager, make sure the **Tag** button is chosen. In the **Tag Properties** area, set the parameters as follows:

   Length U: **22** Length V: **12**

   On entering these values, the *Bedsheet* material is displayed in the Perspective viewport, as shown in Figure P2-10.

Applying Textures to the Supports and Legs of Bed

In this section, you will apply texture to the supports and legs of bed.

1. Double-click on the empty area in the Material Manager; a new material is created in the Material Manager. Next, rename it as **Wrought Iron**.

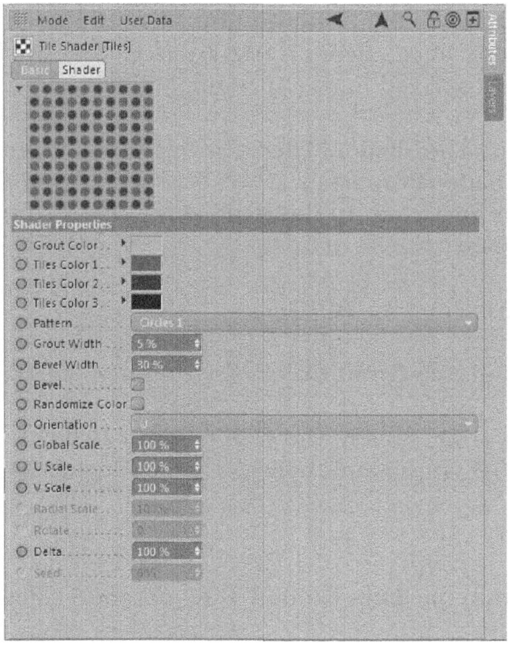

*Figure P2-9 The Bedsheet texture created in the **Shader Properties** area*

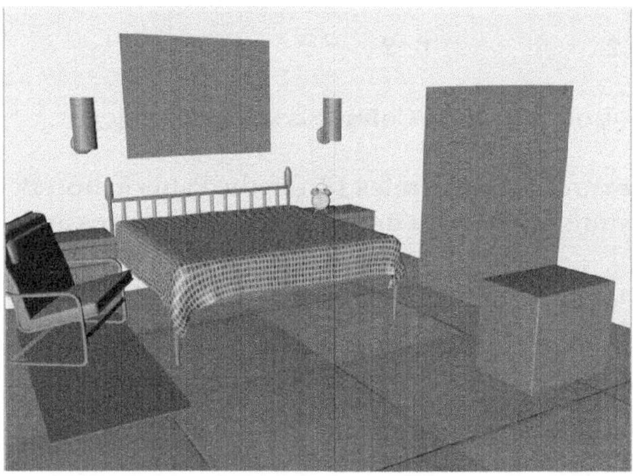

Figure P2-10 The Bedsheet material displayed

2. In the Attribute Manager, make sure the **Color** button is chosen. In the **Color** area, set the parameters as follows:

   R: **85** G: **85** B: **85**

3. In the Attribute Manager, choose the **Basic** button; the **Basic Properties** area is displayed. In this area, select the **Bump** check box. Next, choose the **Bump** button; the **Bump** area is displayed.

4. In this area, choose the arrow button located next to **Texture**; a flyout is displayed. Choose **Surfaces > Simple Noise** from the flyout; the **Simple Noise** texture settings are applied to the material. In the **Bump** area, enter **5** in the **Strength** spinner.

5. Choose the **Simple Noise** button next to **Texture**; the **Noise Shader [Simple Noise]** settings are displayed. In the **Noise Shader [Simple Noise]** settings area, make sure the **Shader** button is chosen. In the **Shader Properties** area, set the parameters as follows:

   U Frequency: **10**   V Frequency: **10**

6. Choose the left arrow button located on the right hand side of the Attribute Manager menu and then choose the **Reflectance** button; the **Reflectance** area is displayed. Next, enter **57** in the **Global Reflection Brightness** spinner. Now, select the *Wrought Iron* material in the Material Manager and drag the cursor on the *Support*, *Rod*, *Leg1*, *Leg1.1*, *Leg1.2,* and *Leg1.3* in the Object Manager; the *Wrought Iron* material is applied to the supports and legs of the bed. 

Applying Textures to the Drawers

In this section, you will apply texture to the drawers.

1. Double-click on the empty area in the Material Manager; a new material is created in the Material Manager. Next, rename it as **Drawers mat**.

2. In the Attribute Manager, choose the **Color** button. In the **Color** area, set the parameters as follows:

   R: **46**   G: **24**   B: **4**

3. In this area, choose the browse button located next to the **Texture** parameter; the **Open File** dialog box is displayed. In this dialog box, browse to *\Documents\c4dr20\Project2\ Drawers.jpg*. Next, choose the **Open** button; the texture is displayed on the material slot.

4. In the Attribute Manager, choose the **Reflectance** button; the **Reflectance** area is displayed. In this area, enter **38** in the **Global Reflection Brightness** spinner.

5. Select the *Drawers mat* material in the Material Manager and drag the cursor on *Drawers 1* in the *Drawers* groups in the Object Manager; the *Drawers mat* material is applied to *Drawers 1*. Similarly, apply the *Drawers mat* material to *Drawer 1* in the *Drawer.1* group in the Object Manager.

   Figure P2-11 displays the *Drawer mat* material applied to drawers.

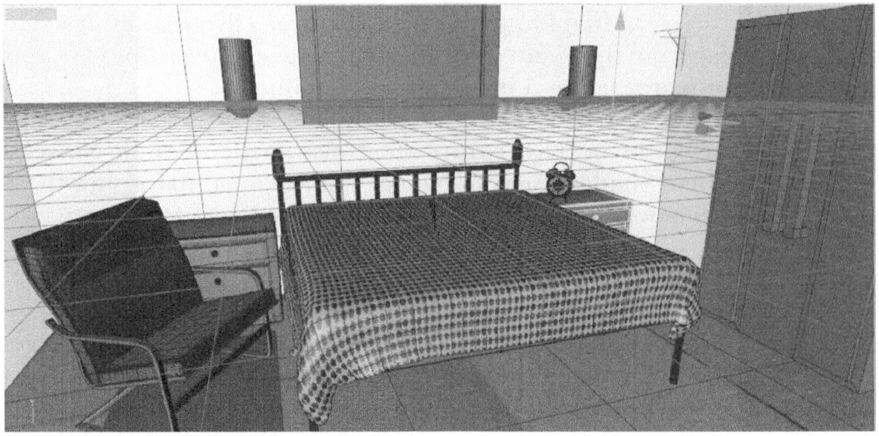

Figure P2-11 The Drawer mat material applied to drawers

Next, you will assign texture to the cupboard.

6. In the Object Manager, expand *Cupboard* group and select *Wardrobe* from it. Make sure the **Polygons** tool is chosen in the Modes Palette. Next, select the two polygons of *Wardrobe* in the Perspective viewport using the SHIFT key, refer to Figure P2-12.

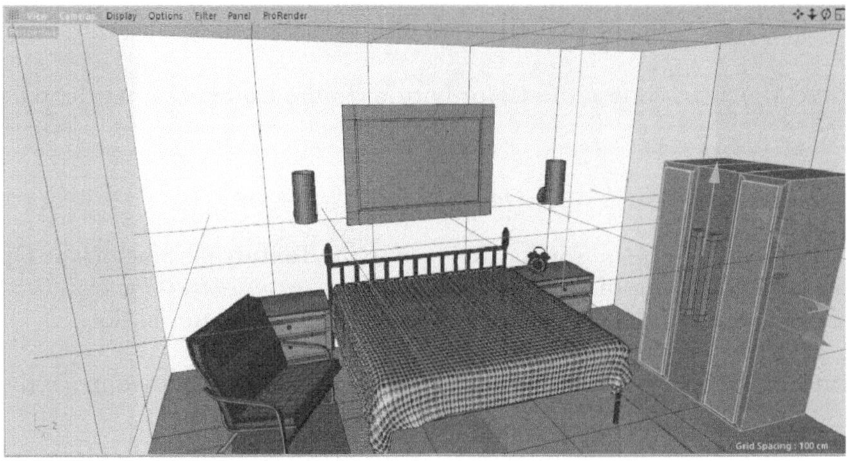

Figure P2-12 The selected polygons of Wardrobe

7. Double-click on an empty area in the Material Manager; a new material is created in the Material Manager. Next, rename it as **Mirror**.

8. In the Attribute Manager, make sure the **Color** button is chosen. In the **Color** area, set the parameters as follows:

   R: **0** G: **0** B: **0**

9. In the Attribute Manager, choose the **Reflectance** button; the **Reflectance** area is displayed. In the **Reflectance** area, make sure the **Default Specular** button is chosen. In the **Default Specular** area, select the **Phong** option from the **Type** drop-down list and **Maximum** from the **Attenuation** drop-down list. In **Default Specular** area, set the parameters as follows:

   Roughness: **0** Reflection Strength: **100** Specular Strength: **0**
   Bump Strength: **0**

10. Make sure the *Mirror* material is selected in the Material Manager and drag the cursor on the selected polygons of *Wardrobe* in the Perspective viewport; the *Mirror* material is applied to the selected polygons of *Wardrobe*.

11. Make sure the polygons of the *Wardrobe* are selected in the Object Manager. Next, choose **Select > Invert** from the main menu; the rest of the polygons of *Wardrobe* are selected, as shown in Figure P2-13.

Figure P2-13 *Selecting the rest of the polygons*

12. Double-click on the empty area in the Material Manager; a new material is created in the Material Manager. Next, rename it as **Almirah**.

13. In the Attribute Manager, choose the **Color** button. In the **Color** area, choose the browse button located next to the **Texture** parameter; the **Open File** dialog box is displayed. In this dialog box, browse to *\Documents\c4dr20\Project2\Almirah.jpg*. Next, choose the **Open** button; the texture is displayed on the Material slot.

14. Select the *Almirah* material in the Material Manager and drag the cursor on the selected polygons in the Perspective viewport; the *Almirah* material is applied to the selected polygons of *Wardrobe*. Now, press CTRL+R to render the scene. Notice that the *Mirror* and *Almirah* materials are applied to *Wardrobe* in the rendered scene, as shown in Figure P2-14.

    Next, you will assign texture to *Handle* of the *Wardrobe*.

15. Choose **Create > Node Materials > Metal** from the Material Manager menu; the **Metal** material is added to the Material Manager. Rename the material as *Steel*.

16. Make sure the *Steel* material is selected in the Material Manager. In the Attribute Manager, choose the **Metal** button. Next, select **Chrome** from the **Type** drop-down list. Also, select **Polished** from the **Finish** drop-down list.

17. Choose the **Base** button from the Attribute Manager. Choose the **RGB** button and enter **255** in the **R**, **G**, and **B** spinners. Next, enter **8** in the **Roughness** spinner.

18. Select the *Steel* material in the Material Manager and drag the cursor on *Handle* and *Handle.1* in the *Wardrobe* group of the Object Manager; the *Steel* is applied to *Handle* and *Handle1* in the Object Manager.

19. Similarly, assign the *Steel* material to the knobs of *Drawers* and *Drawers.1* in the Object Manager.

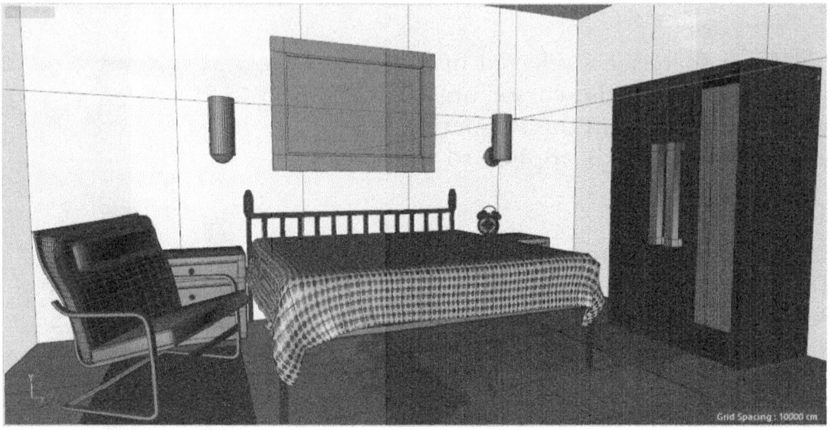

Figure P2-14 *The Almirah and Mirror materials applied to Wardrobe in the rendered scene*

Applying Textures to the Chair and Clock

In this section, you will apply texture to the chair and clock.

1. Double-click on the empty area in the Material Manager; a new material is created in the Material Manager. Next, rename it as **Chair mat**.

2. In the Attribute Manager, choose the **Basic** button; the **Basic Properties** area is displayed. In this area, clear the **Reflectance** check box.

3. In the Attribute Manager, choose the **Color** button; the **Color** area is displayed. In this area, set the parameters as follows:

   R: **208**　　G: **73**　　B: **30**

4. Choose the arrow button located next to **Texture**; a flyout is displayed. Choose **Fresnel** from the flyout. Next, enter **13** in the **Mix Strength** spinner.

5. Make sure the *Chair* group is expanded in the Object Manager. Make sure the *Chair mat* material is selected in the Material Manager and drag the cursor on *Chair > Cube.1*, *Chair > Subdivision Surface > Cube*, and *Chair > Subdivision Surface > Cube.1* in the *Chair* group; the *Chair mat* material is applied to them, as shown in Figure P2-15.

6. Select the *Steel* material from the Material Manager and drag the cursor on the *Extrude NURBS*, *Extrude NURBS.1*, *Extrude NURBS.2*, and *Cube.2* of the *Chair* group.

7. Make sure that the *Steel* material is selected in the Material Manager and drag the cursor on *Clock* in the Object Manager; the texture is applied to *Clock*.

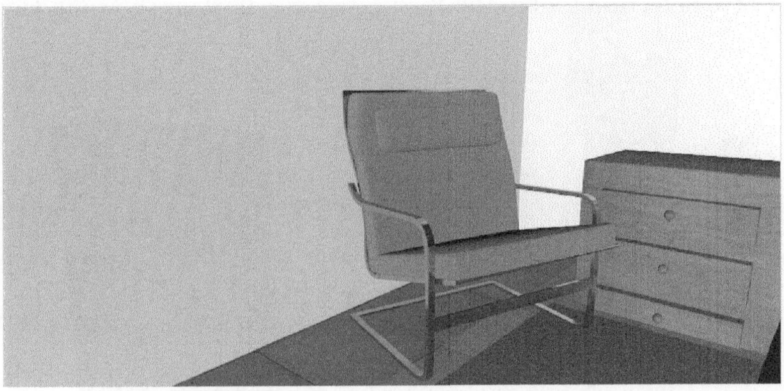

Figure P2-15 *The Chair mat material applied*

Applying Texture to the Lights

In this section, you will apply texture to the lights.

1. In the Material Manager, choose **Create > Load Material Preset > Visualize > Materials > Metal > Chrome** from the main menu in the Material Manager menu; the **Chrome** material is added to the Material Manager.

2. In the Object Manager, expand the *Lights.1* and *Lights* groups. Next, select the *Chrome* material in the Material Manager and drag the cursor to *Light1* in the *Lights.1* group. Similarly, assign the *Chrome* materials to *Light* in *Lights* group of the Object Manager.

3. Double-click on the empty area in the Material Manager; a new material is created in the Material Manager. Next, rename it as **Cover**.

4. Make sure the **Color** button is chosen in the Attribute Manager. In the **Color** area, set the parameters as follows:

   R: **236** G: **192** B: **17**

5. Make sure that the *Cover* material is selected in the Material Manager. Drag the cursor on *Cover1* in the *Lights.1* group; the texture is applied to *Cover1*. Similarly, assign the *Cover* material to *Cover1* in the *Lights* group of the Object Manager. Now, press CTRL+R; the rendered scene is displayed. Notice that the materials are applied to the *Lights* and *Light.1* groups and are displayed in the rendered scene, as shown in Figure P2-16.

Applying Textures to the Wooden Frame and Mat

In this section, you will apply texture to the wooden frame and mat.

1. Select *Wooden Frame* in the Object Manager. Choose the **Polygons** tool from the Modes Palette; *Wooden Frame* is displayed in the polygon mode. Next, select the polygons of *Wooden Frame* using the **Live Selection** tool in the Perspective viewport, as shown in Figure P2-17.

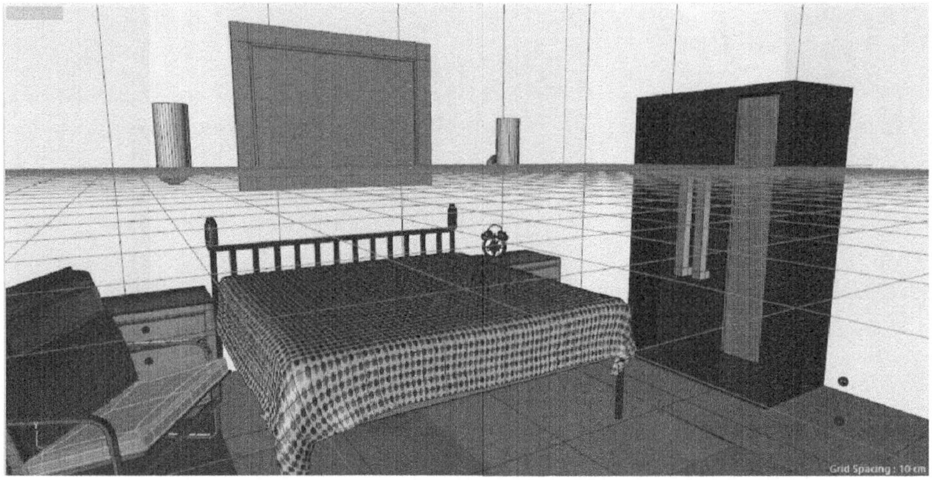

Figure P2-16 *The materials applied to Lights and Light.1 groups*

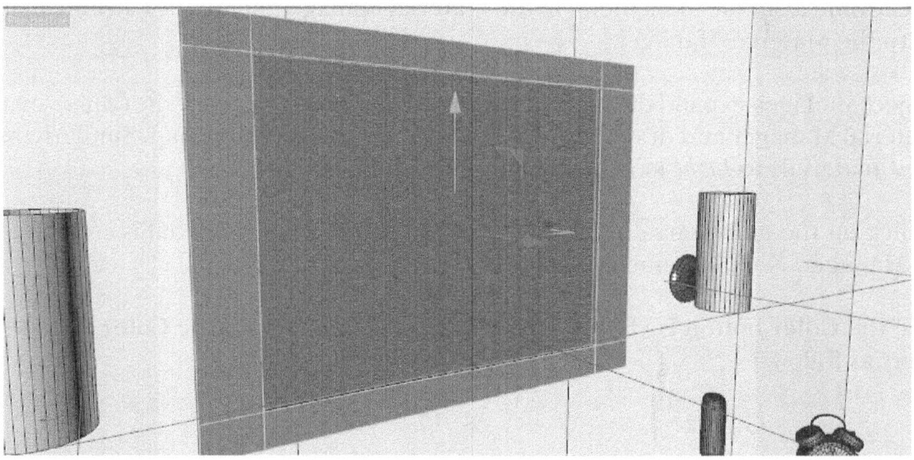

Figure P2-17 *The selected polygons of Wooden Frame*

2. Select the *Drawers* material in the Material Manager and drag the cursor on the selected polygons of *Wooden Frame*; the material is applied to the selected polygons in the Perspective viewport. Deselect the polygons of *Wooden Frame*.

3. Again, select the center polygon of *Wooden Frame* in the Perspective viewport, as shown in Figure P2-18.

4. Double-click on the empty area in the Material Manager; a new material with the name **Mat** is created in the Material Manager. Next, rename it as **Painting**.

5. In the Attribute Manager, choose the **Color** button; the **Color** area is displayed. In this area, choose the browse button located next to the **Texture** parameter; the **Open File** dialog box is displayed.

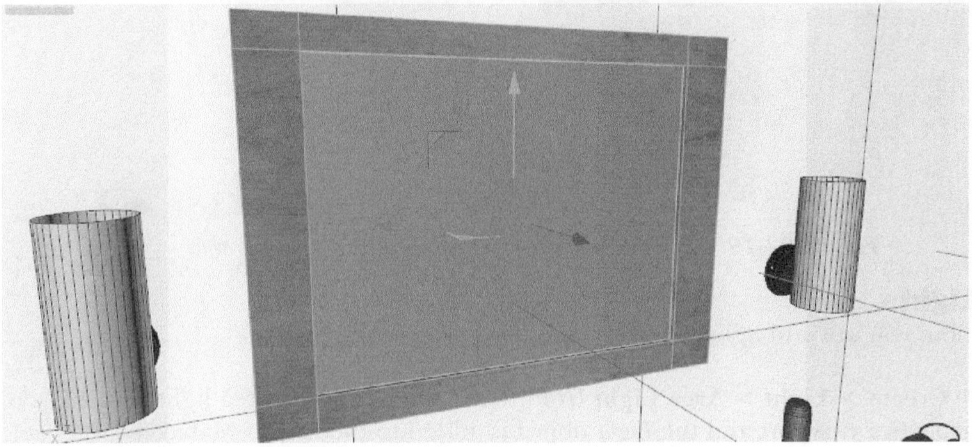

Figure P2-18 *The selected polygon of Wooden Frame*

6. In this dialog box, browse to *\Documents\c4dr20\Project2\Painting.jpg*. Next, choose the **Open** button; the texture is displayed on the Material slot.

7. Select the *Painting* material in the Material Manager and drag the cursor on the selected polygon of *Wooden Frame*; the material is applied to the selected polygon in the Perspective viewport.

8. Make sure the **Texture Tag "Painting"** tag is chosen in the Object Manager. In the Attribute Manager, make sure the **Tag** button is chosen. In the **Tag Properties** area, set the parameters as follows:

   Offset U: **-20** Offset V: **-7**

   After entering these values, the *Painting* material is mapped to the selected polygon of *Wooden Frame* in the Perspective viewport, as shown in Figure P2-19.

   Next, you will apply texture to the mat.

9. In the Material Manager, choose **Create > Load Material Preset > Visualize > Materials > Fabric > Carpet - Red** from main menu; the *Carpet Red* material is added to the Material Manager.

10. Select *Carpet Red* in the Material Manager and drag the cursor on *Mat* in the Object Manager; the *Carpet Red* material is applied to *Mat* in the scene.

Figure P2-19 The Painting material mapped to Wooden Frame

Adding Lights

In this section, you will add lights to the scene.

1. Choose **Create > Light > Area Light** from the main menu; the area light is displayed in the Perspective viewport and the *Light* object is added to the Object Manager.

2. In the Attribute Manager, make sure the **General** button is chosen. In the **General** area, enter **90** in the **Intensity** spinner. Select **Shadow Maps (Soft)** in the **Shadow** drop-down list.

3. Choose the **Coord** button; the **Coordinates** area is displayed. In this area, set the parameters as follows:

   P . X: **99.377** P . Y: **119.782** P . Z: **145.871**
   R . H: **-91.346** R . P: **44.324** R . B: **92.714**

4. Choose **Create > Light > Area Light** from the main menu; the area light is displayed in the Perspective viewport and *Light.1* object is added to the Object Manager.

5. In the Attribute Manager, choose the **General** button; the **General** area gets displayed. In this area, enter **50** in the **Intensity** spinner.

6. Choose the **Coord** button; the **Coordinates** area is displayed. In this area, set the parameters as follows:

   P . X: **-195.649** P . Y: **101.072** P . Z: **-153.428**
   R . H: **-76.552** R . P: **-67.519** R . B: **-49.898**

   Next, you will set the **Global Illumination** attributes in the **Render Settings** area.

7. Choose the **Edit Render Settings** tool from the Command palette; the **Render Settings** window is displayed. In this window, choose the **Effect** button; a flyout is displayed. Choose **Ambient Occlusion** from the flyout; the ambient occlusion attributes are applied to the scene.

8. In the **Render Settings** window, choose the **Effect** button; a flyout is displayed. Choose **Global Illumination** from the flyout; the global Illumination attributes are applied to the scene. Now, close the **Render Settings** window. Press CTRL+R to render the scene. Figure P2-20 displays the final rendered scene.

Figure P2-20 *The final rendered scene*

Saving and Rendering the Scene

In this section, you will save and render the scene. You can also view the final render of the project by downloading the file *prj2_c4dr20_rndr.zip* from *www.cadcim.com*. The path of the file is mentioned at the beginning of the chapter.

1. Choose **File > Save** from the main menu; the **Save File** dialog box is displayed. In this dialog box, browse to the location *\Documents\c4dr20\Project2*.

2. Enter **prj2** in the **File name** text box and then choose the **Save** button. Next, you need to render the scene. For rendering, refer to Tutorial 1 of Chapter 2.

3. In the Perspective viewport, set the camera angle using the Viewport Navigation Tools located at the extreme top right of the Perspective viewport. Next, choose the **Render to Picture Viewer** tool from the Command Palette. Alternatively, press SHIFT+R; the **Picture Viewer** window is displayed.

4. In the **Picture Viewer** window, choose **File > Save as**; the **Save** dialog box is displayed.

5. In the **Save** dialog box, choose the **OK** button; the **Save Dialog** dialog box is displayed. Next, browse to the *\Documents\c4dr20\Project2*. In the **File Name** text box, type **prj2_rndr**. Next, choose the **Save** button; the file is saved at the desired location.

   Figure P2-1 displays the final output.

Index

T

U

V

W

X

Y

Z

Other Titles of Interest- BPB/TICKOO SERIES

Publication by BPB/TICKOO SERIES

The following is the list of some of the publications by BPB/TICKOO series:

CINEMA 4D Textbooks

- MAXON CINEMA 4D R20 Studio Workbook
- MAXON CINEMA 4D R19 Studio: A Tutorial Approach, 6th Edition
- MAXON CINEMA 4D R18 Studio: A Tutorial Approach, 5th Edition

3ds Max Textbooks

- Autodesk 3ds Max 2019: A Comprehensive Guide, 19th Edition
- Autodesk 3ds Max 2018: A Comprehensive Guide, 18th Edition

Autodesk Maya Textbooks

- Autodesk Maya 2019 for 3D Artists
- Autodesk Maya 2019 Workbook
- Autodesk Maya 2018: A Comprehensive Guide, 10th Edition

ZBrush Textbooks

- Pixologic ZBrush 2018 for Digital Artists
- Pixologic ZBrush 4R8: A Comprehensive Guide, 4th Edition

Computer Programming Textbooks

- Introducing PHP/MySQL
- Introduction to C++ Programming, 2nd Edition
- Learning Oracle 12c: A PL/SQL Approach, 2nd Edition
- Introduction to Java Programming, 2nd Edition

AutoCAD Textbooks

- AutoCAD 2020 for Engineers and Designers - Basic and Intermediate
- AutoCAD 2020 Workbook
- AutoCAD 2019: A Problem-Solving Approach, Basic and Intermediate, 25th Edition

Autodesk Inventor Textbooks

- Autodesk Inventor Professional 2020 for Engineers and Designers
- Inventor 2020 Workbook
- Autodesk Inventor Professional 2019 for Designers, 19th Edition

AutoCAD MEP Textbooks

- AutoCAD MEP 2020 for Engineers and Designers
- AutoCAD MEP 2018 for Designers, 4th Edition

AutoCAD Plant 3D Textbook
- AutoCAD Plant 3D 2018 for Designers, 4th Edition

NX Textbooks
- Siemens NX 2019 for Engineers and Designers
- Siemens NX 2019 Workbook
- Siemens NX 12.0 for Designers, 11th Edition

NX Mold Textbook
- Mold Design Using NX 11.0: A Tutorial Approach

AutoCAD LT Textbooks
- AutoCAD LT 2020 for Engineers and Designers
- AutoCAD LT 2017 for Designers, 12th Edition

Solid Edge Textbooks
- Solid Edge 2019 for Engineers and Designers
- Solid Edge ST 10 for Designers, 15th Edition

SolidWorks Textbooks
- SOLIDWORKS 2019 for Engineers and Designers
- SOLIDWORKS 2018 for Designers, 16th Edition

SolidWorks Simulation Textbooks
- SOLIDWORKS Simulation 2018: A Tutorial Approach
- SOLIDWORKS Simulation 2016: A Tutorial Approach

Creo Parametric Textbooks
- Creo Parametric 6.0 for Engineers and Designers
- Creo Parametric 6.0 Workbook
- Creo Parametric 5.0 for Designers, 5th Edition

CATIA Textbook
- CATIA V5-6R2018 for Engineers and Designers

AutoCAD Electrical Textbooks
- AutoCAD Electrical 2019 for Engineers and Designers
- AutoCAD Electrical 2018 for Electrical Control Designers, 9th Edition

Autodesk Revit Architecture Textbooks
- Exploring Autodesk Revit 2020 for Architects and Building Designers
- Revit Architecture 2020 Workbook
- Exploring Autodesk Revit 2019 for Architecture, 15th Edition

Autodesk Revit Structure Textbooks
- Exploring Autodesk Revit 2019 for Structure, 9th Edition
- Exploring Autodesk Revit 2018 for Structure, 8th Edition

Autodesk Revit MEP Textbooks
- Exploring Autodesk Revit 2019 for MEP, 6th Edition
- Exploring Autodesk Revit 2018 for MEP, 5th Edition

RISA-3D Textbook
- Exploring RISA-3D 14.0

Bentley STAAD.Pro Textbooks
- Exploring Bentley STAAD.Pro (CONNECT Edition), 3rd Edition
- Exploring Bentley STAAD.Pro V8i (SELECT series 6)

AutoCAD Civil 3D Textbooks
- Exploring AutoCAD Civil 3D 2019 for Engineers and Designers
- Exploring AutoCAD Civil 3D 2018, 8th Edition

AutoCAD Map 3D Textbooks
- Exploring AutoCAD Map 3D 2018, 8th Edition
- Exploring AutoCAD Map 3D 2017, 7th Edition

Autodesk Navisworks Textbooks
- Exploring Autodesk Navisworks 2019 for BIM
- Exploring Autodesk Navisworks 2017, 4th Edition

Oracle Primavera Textbooks
- Exploring Oracle Primavera P6 Professional 18 for Planners and Engineers
- Exploring Oracle Primavera P6 R8.4

AutoCAD Raster Design Textbook
- Exploring AutoCAD Raster Design 2017

CAD/CAM/CIM/GIS/ANIMATION/CIVIL BOOKS

by **Prof. Sham Tickoo** (Purdue University, USA and Autodesk Authorised Author)

NX Nastran 9
For Designers
ISBN 978-93-8655-122-1
Price: ₹ 899/-

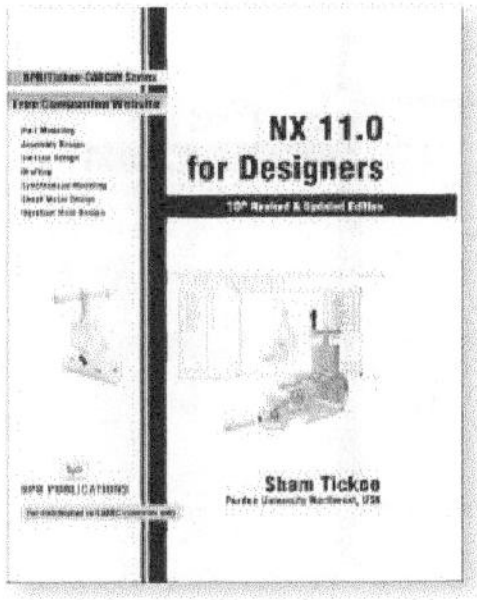

NX 11
for Designers
ISBN 978-93-8655-124-5
Price: ₹ 1099/-

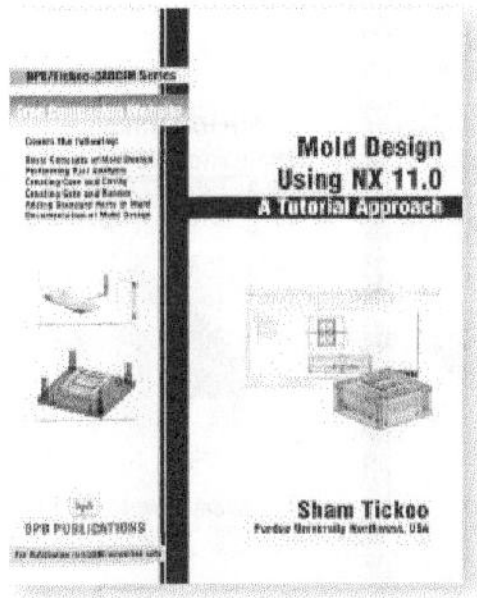

Mold Design
Using NX 11
ISBN 978-93-8728-406-7
Price: ₹ 599/-

Siemens NX 12.0
for Designers
ISBN 978-93-8728-407-4
Price: ₹ 1099/-

Autodesk Inventor Professional 2019
For Designers
ISBN 978-93-8817-629-3
Price: ₹ 1299/-

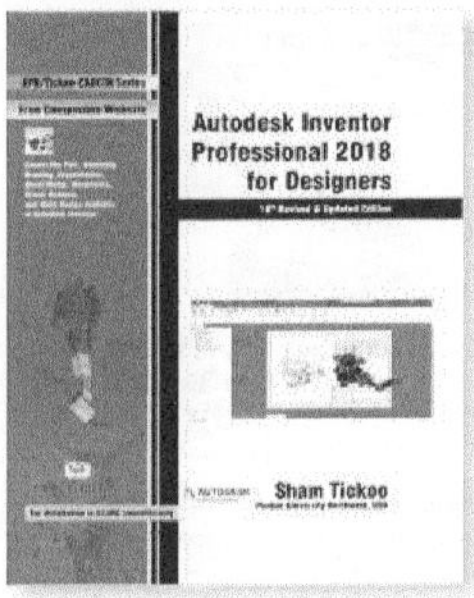

Autodesk Inventor Professional 2018
For Designers
ISBN 978-93-8655-164-1
Price: ₹ 1199/-

Autodesk Inventor Professional 2017
For Designers
ISBN 978-93-8655-126-9
Price: ₹ 1299/-

Autodesk FUSION 360
A Tutorial Approach
ISBN 978-93-8728-441-8
Price: ₹ 599/-

Solid Edge ST 10
For Designers
ISBN 978-93-8728-410-4
Price: ₹ 1099/-

Solid Edge ST 9
For Designers
ISBN 978-93-8655-120-7
Price: ₹ 1099/-

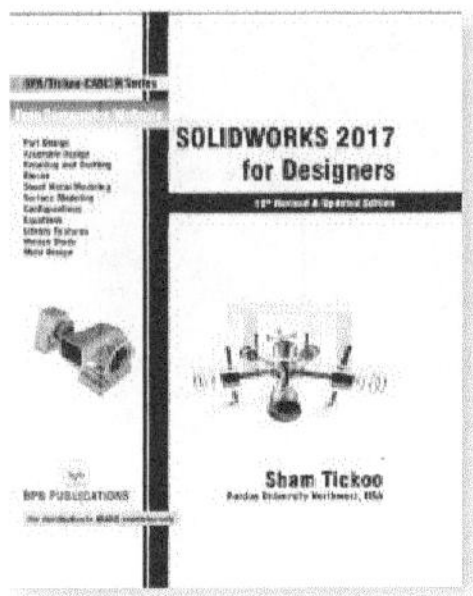

Solid Works 2017
For Designers
ISBN 978-93-8655-121-4
Price: ₹ 1299/-

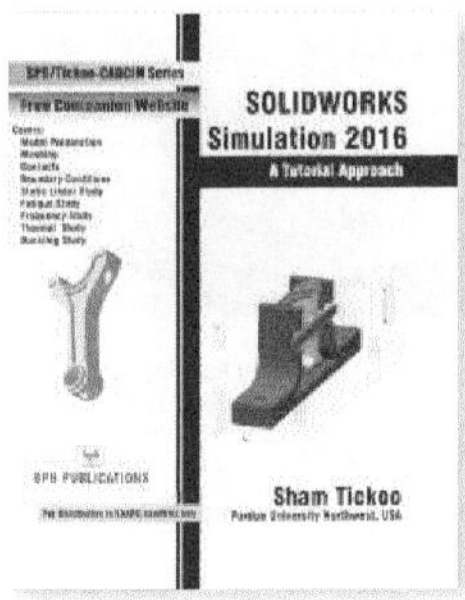

Solid Works Simulation 2016
A Tutorial Approach
ISBN 978-93-8655-175-7
Price: ₹ 499/-

Available on **www.bpbonline.com** and all leading book stores.

bpb PUBLICATIONS | #1 Publisher of Computer Books | 62 Years of Excellence | OVER 90 Million Books Sold Worldwide

CAD/CAM/CIM/GIS/ANIMATION/CIVIL BOOKS

by **Prof. Sham Tickoo** (Purdue University, USA and Autodesk Authorised Author)

Solid Works 2018
For Designers
ISBN 978-93-8728-409-8
Price: ₹ 1299/-

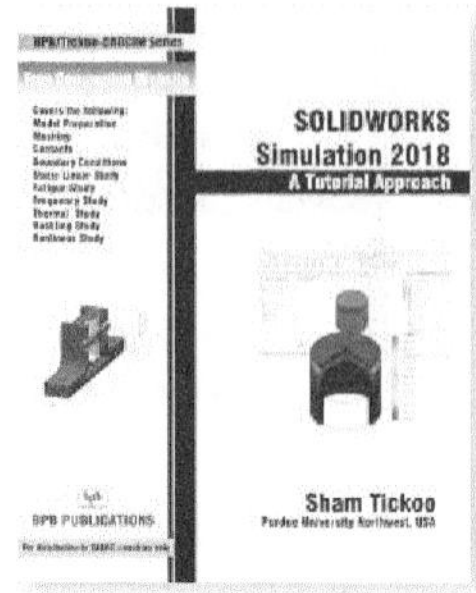

Solid Works Simulation 2018
For Designers
ISBN 978-93-8728-411-1
Price: ₹ 599/-

Solid Works 2018
A Tutorial Approach
ISBN 978-93-8817-631-6
Price: ₹ 799/-

Learning Solid Works 2018
A Project Based Approach
ISBN 978-93-8817-632-3
Price: ₹ 699/-

Exploring AutoCAD Civil 3D 2017
ISBN 978-93-8655-102-3
Price: ₹ 999/-

Exploring AutoCAD Civil 3D 2018
ISBN 978-93-8728-413-5
Price: ₹ 999/-

Exploring AutoCAD Map 3D 2017
ISBN 978-93-8655-103-0
Price: ₹ 875/-

Exploring AutoCAD Map 3D 2018
ISBN 978-93-8655-166-5
Price: ₹ 799/-

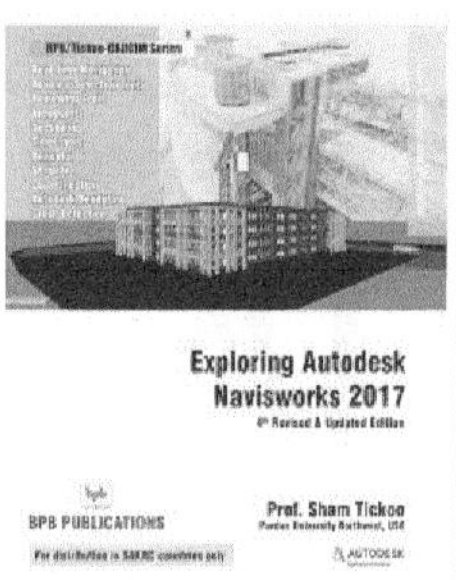

Exploring Autodesk
Navisworks 2017
ISBN 978-93-8655-104-7
Price: ₹ 699/-

Exploring Oracle
Primavera P6 R8.4
ISBN 978-93-8655-105-4
Price: ₹ 599/-

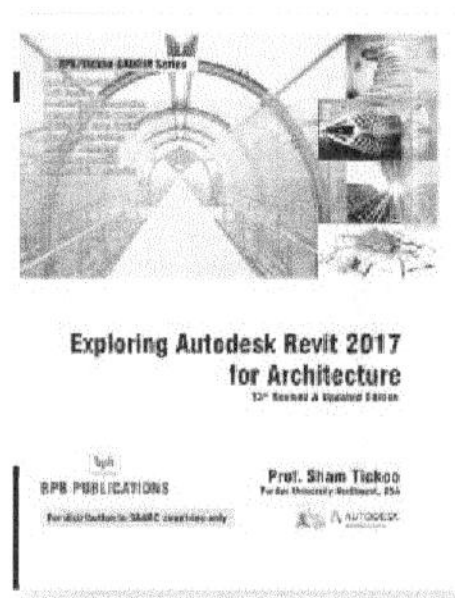

Exploring Autodesk
Revit 2017
For Architecture
ISBN 978-93-8655-106-1
Price: ₹ 999/-

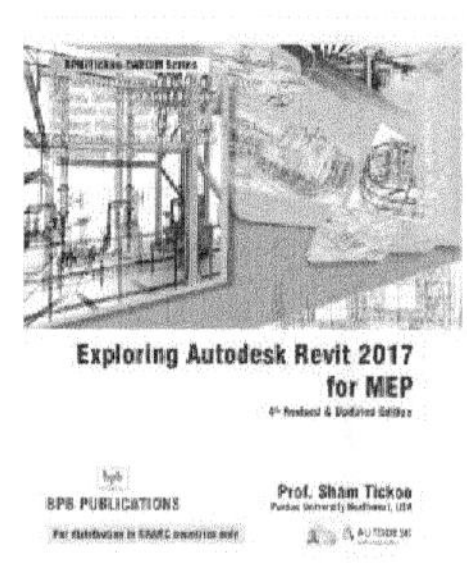

Exploring Autodesk
Revit 2017
For MEP
ISBN 978-93-8655-107-8
Price: ₹ 799/-

Available on **www.bpbonline.com** and all leading book stores.

PUBLICATIONS | #1 Publisher of Computer Books | 62 Years of Excellence | OVER 90 Million Books Sold Worldwide

CAD/CAM/CIM/GIS/ANIMATION/CIVIL BOOKS

by **Prof. Sham Tickoo** (Purdue University, USA and Autodesk Authorised Author)

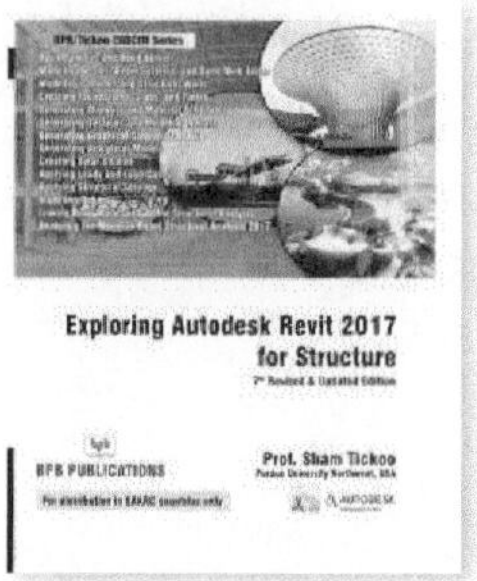

Exploring Autodesk
Revit 2017
For Structure
ISBN 978-81-8333-506-5
Price: ₹ 899/-

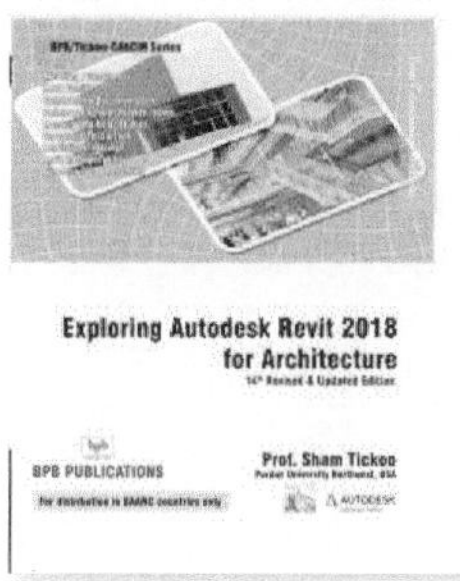

Exploring Autodesk
Revit 2018
For Architecture
ISBN 978-93-8655-172-6
Price: ₹ 999/-

Exploring Autodesk
Revit 2018
For MEP
ISBN 978-93-8655-173-3
Price: ₹ 799/-

Exploring Autodesk
Revit 2018
For Structure
ISBN 978-93-8655-174-0
Price: ₹ 799/-

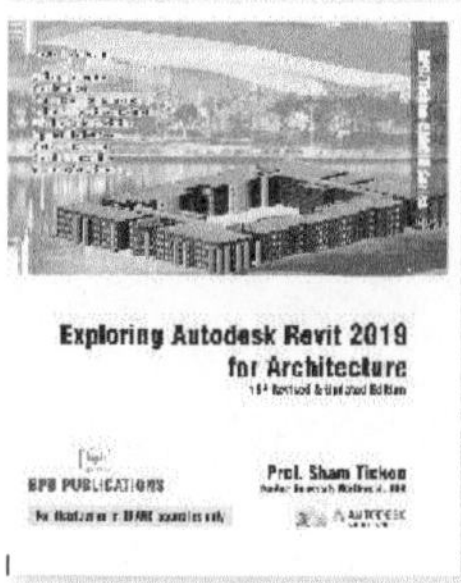

Exploring Autodesk
Revit 2019
For Architecture
ISBN 978-93-8817-633-0
Price: ₹ 1199/-

Exploring Autodesk
Revit 2019
For MEP
ISBN 978-93-8817-635-4
Price: ₹ 899/-

Exploring Autodesk
Revit 2019
For Structure
ISBN 978-93-8817-634-7
Price: ₹ 899/-

Exploring
RISA-3D 14.0
ISBN 978-93-8655-108-5
Price: ₹ 499/-

Exploring AutoCAD Raster Design 2017
ISBN 978-93-8655-109-2
Price: ₹ 499/-

Exploring Bentley STAAD.Pro (Select Series 6)
ISBN 978-93-8655-110-8
Price: ₹ 599/-

Exploring Bentley STAAD.Pro (Connect Edition)
ISBN 978-93-8728-414-2
Price: ₹ 499/-

Introduction to C++ Programming
ISBN 978-93-8655-116-0
Price: ₹ 699/-

Available on **www.bpbonline.com** and all leading book stores.

bpb PUBLICATIONS | #1 Publisher of Computer Books | 62 Years of Excellence | OVER 90 Million Books Sold Worldwide